K

K

A HISTORY OF BASEBALL
IN TEN PITCHES

TYLER KEPNER

DOUBLEDAY  NEW YORK

Copyright © 2019 by Tyler Kepner

All rights reserved. Published in the United States by Doubleday,
a division of Penguin Random House LLC, New York, and
distributed in Canada by Random House of Canada, a division
of Penguin Random House Canada Limited, Toronto.

www.doubleday.com

DOUBLEDAY and the portrayal of an anchor with a dolphin are
registered trademarks of Penguin Random House LLC.

Book design by Michael Collica
Jacket images: Topps® trading cards used courtesy of The Topps Company, Inc.
Jacket design by John Fontana

Library of Congress Cataloging-in-Publication Data
Names: Kepner, Tyler (Baseball writer), author.
Title: K : a history of baseball in ten pitches / Tyler Kepner.
Description: First edition. | New York : Doubleday, [2018] |
Includes bibliographical references and index.
Identifiers: LCCN 2018016158 | ISBN 9780385541015 (hardcover) |
ISBN 9780385541022 (ebook)
Subjects: LCSH: Pitching (Baseball) | Pitchers (Baseball) |
Baseball—United States—History.
Classification: LCC GV871 .K46 2018 | DDC 796.357/22—dc23
LC record available at https://lccn.loc.gov/2018016158

MANUFACTURED IN THE UNITED STATES OF AMERICA

3 5 7 9 10 8 6 4 2

First Edition

For Jen

"We're not leaving in the seventh-inning stretch, are we?"

Contents

Introduction

The kid hung in there as a rookie for the Mets: 11 wins, five losses, a 4.04 earned run average, and 170 strikeouts. But the next year he struggled, and then he got hurt, and soon he was traded to the A's and the Twins. Finally he landed with his hometown team, the Phillies, where he stayed for many years, except for one season with the Indians.

He retired with a record of 350–182, for a .658 winning percentage. He won five Cy Young Awards, made eight All-Star teams, and struck out 4,819. He was clearly one of the greatest pitchers in baseball history.

————

This was my life plan in 1986. I was eleven, the oldest a kid can be before reality invades his dreams. I can still throw strikes reliably for the New York media team in our annual games against Boston, and I can spin a loopy little curveball. My arm is never sore, because I don't throw hard and never have.

Before my lack of speed mattered, though, I believed in that handwritten stat sheet. I found it in a notebook a few years ago, in a box at my parents' house. By then I was deep into this project, exploring the history and stories behind every pitch, from Christy Mathewson's fadeaway to Clayton Kershaw's slider. Seeing my scribbles through the prism of actual history, it struck me that, for some pitchers, real life surpassed my wildest ambitions.

In my childhood baseball fantasy, where I could do anything I wanted, I still won fewer games than Greg Maddux. I had fewer strikeouts than Nolan Ryan, a lower winning percentage than Roy Halladay, fewer All-Star selections than Randy Johnson, fewer Cy Young Awards than Roger Clemens. I spoke with all of them, and hundreds more, for this book. I wanted to know how the masters did what they did, how they learned and applied their best pitches.

Stardom is at their fingertips, literally. That's the mystery and the madness of the craft. Even the slightest adjustment of a pitcher's fingers can turn an ordinary pitch into a major league weapon. If your body and brain can withstand all the failure, you'd be foolish to ever quit the job.

The pitcher is the planner, the initiator of action. The hitter can only react. If the pitcher, any pitcher, finds a way to disrupt that reaction, he can win. You need a little luck and relentless curiosity.

By watching baseball up close for so long, and getting to know the men who play it, I can see that I was never like them. My fingers move better on a laptop than they do on a baseball, and I'm lucky I found a skill that allows me to move within their world. But I still wish that my younger self had recognized the baseball for the amazing plaything it is, diving and darting and sailing and sinking, with no instruction manual.

In a different Pennsylvania town in the 1980s, another right-hander got it. Mike Mussina grew up in Montoursville, high in the mountains near Williamsport. On cold days he would throw against a cinder-block wall in his basement from about 30 feet away, under a dropped ceiling about six feet, eight inches high. He liked to experiment, and while he couldn't come up with much, he knew what he was missing and how he could find it.

"Listen, I didn't leave high school with a fastball, curveball, slider, change, sinker—I had a fastball and a lazy curveball, that was it," Mussina told me in the summer of 2016, over lunch at Johnson's Café in Montoursville, where he still lives. "I came from small-town America. I didn't see anybody else that did anything that I wanted to be able to do. But when I got to college and got to pro ball, now there's other guys out there—*Man, that's a pretty good slider, I wonder how he does that? That's a pretty good curveball, I'd love to be able to do that.* And so you're looking at other people, you're stealing ideas and seeing if you can do it."

The Orioles drafted Mussina in the twentieth round out of high school, in 1987, but he wanted to learn more, on and off the mound. He hates to travel but chose Stanford University and graduated in three years. The Orioles chose him again in 1990, this time in the first round, and the next year he was in the majors. He stayed for 18 seasons by constantly evolving.

Mussina doubts that many pitchers will last as long as he did, because there's less incentive to innovate. Pitchers throw harder, but they're not trained or expected to work deep into games. If they were, he believes, they'd have to develop more pitches to keep the same hitters guessing. Then, as their best stuff fades with age, they'd have other pitches to use.

If a starting pitcher does his job, Mussina believes, he should win half his starts. That was his logic long before he finished with 270 victories in 536 starts. But there's a catch: the quality of a pitcher's stuff will vary from game to game. In a few starts it will be crisp; in a few others it will be flat. Most of the time, he'll have just enough to compete.

What made Mussina great, his peers believed, is that he always had so many options, so many different pitches to grind his way through a start when he wasn't at his best. This is how he described his thought process:

"Boy, there's so many variables involved in the equation that you can't even discuss it, almost," he said, then does so at length. "It's not like there's nobody on base every time—there's guys in scoring position, nobody out, crowd's going crazy. You think, 'OK, I screwed up, we can't go with A. What's B, what's C, what's D?'

"Who's hitting? Is he hot or cold? Where are the base runners? What's the situation? Where are we in the game? Are we on the road? Are we at home? Is it nighttime? Is it daytime? What has he done the other two at-bats? Let's say it's the seventh inning. Where he's at in the box? How'd he look taking that pitch, or how'd he look fouling that pitch off?

"There's all these things going on in your head. And then you take in all this outside input and you say to yourself, 'Yeah—but I don't feel good with that pitch.' Because your brain tells you, 'Look, you should throw this,' but I haven't thrown one of those for a strike in four innings. Eventually you just have to have enough balls to say, 'Screw it, I've got to do it the way I should do it, and whatever happens, happens.' I can't just throw fastballs because he knows I don't have a good enough changeup today, or he knows I don't feel good with my slider today. He doesn't *really* know that. All he knows is that I have these five pitches I can throw. He doesn't really know that I don't feel good about this one. He may know that I don't *look like* I have great command because I have three walks already and I usually don't walk anybody, but he doesn't know that I don't feel good with my changeup—so let's throw it anyway.

"That's the kind of stuff you think about, and it's not planned. It's just experience. You just have to do it. But there's so many variables. We could talk for months about variables when you're trying to figure out what to throw."

————————

Those variables consumed me for three years. Wherever I went, in my travels as the national baseball writer for *The New York Times,* I sought people who could help me tell the story of every pitch. How did the great ones learn? How did their pitches move? When and why did they use them? What made them work?

I settled on 10: the slider, the fastball, the curveball, the knuckleball, the splitter, the screwball, the sinker, the changeup, the spitball, and the cutter. Mussina, who taught me more about pitching than anyone else I covered in 12 years as a beat writer, isn't sure there are only 10.

"There might be 10 defined, different things," he says. "But every guy that throws it is different. My sinker and Kevin Brown's sinker aren't the same. Not the same pitch. When it's going through the strike zone and the hitter's trying to hit it, my sinker and his sinker are not doing the same sinking. My curveball and somebody else's curveball? They're not the same. They may be technically the same, but when it's going through the hitting zone and somebody's trying to hit it—to the guy in the box, it's not the same. Mo's cutter and my cutter aren't the same thing. I call it that and he calls it that, but it doesn't do the same thing. So is there really a limit, a number, to how many pitches there are? Like I said, I was out there trying to invent stuff."

There is, indeed, no limit to the kinds of options available to a pitcher, or how he can use them. Lance McCullers Jr., who called Mussina one of his favorite pitchers to watch, threw 24 curveballs in a row to close out the American League Championship Series for Houston in 2017. He knows the spin rates of all his pitches, and studies their movement on an X-Y axis after every start. But by reading his stuff in the moment, he pumped curve after curve with a pennant on the line. There was no rule against it, only convention.

"No one would be like, 'Oh my gosh, he threw 24 *fastballs* in a row,'" McCullers told me later, clutching a champagne bottle in the clubhouse. "No one would say that. But this game continues to evolve. A couple of years from now, it may not be so crazy to think about."

The pitches are the DNA of baseball, the fundamental coding of the game. Joe Maddon, the Cubs' manager, says the sport could easily be called "pitching," because the pitcher controls everything. He is the most influential player on the field, by far, but he can't play every day. That factor, more than any other, makes baseball so interesting.

A major league pitcher is part boxer and part magician; if he's not punching you in the face, he's swiping a quarter from behind your ear. If you ever square him up, you'd better savor it. Even in batting practice, the world's best hitters tap harmless grounders and punch lazy fly balls. In the heat of competition, every hit is an exquisite anomaly.

Playing baseball—as a pitcher or a hitter—eventually just got too hard for me. I played through high school, but by then I was well into this career. In seventh grade, I started jotting down my thoughts and opinions about the game, copying the pages and stapling them into a magazine. From early 1988 through early 1995, I published 11 issues a year, every month except January, so I could study for exams. I conducted my first interview—with Pat Combs, a Phillies pitcher— the day after my fifteenth birthday.

The press box was the ultimate learning lab. Instead of asking pitchers how I should grip a slider, I asked writers how they crafted their stories, how they asked the right questions, how they found their ideas. Sometimes, they reported on me. One winter day in 1990, the ABC affiliate in town, WPVI, sent its human-interest correspondent to meet me at school and drive me home for a feature story. His name was Tug McGraw.

"Is that Joe in front of us?" he asked on our drive.

"Joe?"

"Joe Mama!"

Tug was a scamp, an affable rascal who named his pitches and wrote a children's book, *Lumpy,* from the perspective of a baseball. In second grade, when the teacher told us to write a letter to a famous person, I wrote to Tug and invited him to my birthday party. He didn't come, alas, but he did send back an autographed photo with the inscription, "Best of luck in school and sports, pal." He also returned the letter and signed that, too. Always with a smiley face.

Digging through files at the Hall of Fame library in Cooperstown, New York, I found a column on McGraw from 1977 by Bill Lyon, an elegant writer for *The Philadelphia Inquirer* who inspired and mentored me. He spoke with McGraw about the art of pitching, and McGraw held a baseball as they talked. His passion all but singed the yellowed newsprint.

"You know, if somebody called me at four in the morning and said, 'Hey, let's go out and play some catch,' I'd do it," McGraw said. "I love this little thing."

If there's anything in life more endearing than enthusiasm, I've never found it. I've seen a lot in baseball, and I'm proud to say I'm not jaded. Neither are the hundreds of folks who gave me their time and insights for this book. We all love this little thing, this miracle: baseball.

Tyler Kepner
Wilton, Connecticut

K

THE
SLIDER

A Little Bitty Dot

I can pinpoint the single happiest moment of my childhood. On October 8, 1983, when I was eight years old, the Philadelphia Phillies beat the Los Angeles Dodgers to win the National League pennant at Veterans Stadium. Everyone in the stands chanted "Beat L.A.! Beat L.A.!" On our way home, my dad let me honk the horn of his Chevette, like the other revelers on Broad Street. It was the best traffic jam ever.

Steve Carlton won the game, just as he had won the World Series clincher three years earlier, when I was too young to notice. In between he claimed his fourth Cy Young Award, a record at the time, leading the majors in wins and strikeouts and mesmerizing me completely. When I had tickets on his day to pitch, I would scramble to the front row near the first base dugout to watch him get loose, staring up in awe. He would bring his hands together, dip them down by his belt, and then raise them up near his head. He'd drop them lower as he turned, hiking his right knee up around his chest. For a moment, he'd curl the ball in his left hand, down behind his left thigh, before whipping it up and around for the pitch. Power and grace, personified.

I would imitate this windup at home, in the mirror, where I could be left-handed, too. I pitched like Carlton in Little League, right down to his facial twitches. I collected every baseball card that ever featured him, scoring his rookie card for $75 from a cash-strapped friend who had just gotten his driver's license. Thirty-two has always been my favorite number. I named the family dog Lefty.

I met Carlton in 1989, his first year of retirement, at a charity sign-ing at the Vet. I had just finished my middle school baseball career, and he signed my jersey, right above the 32 on the back. I didn't tell him that I wanted to be a sportswriter.

For most of his career, Carlton didn't talk to the media at all. To a young fan, that only added to his mystique. He loosened up later in his career, but not much. When I started this project, I wanted to talk to Carlton more than anyone else. We connected by phone, and this is the first thing he said: "So you're writing a book. Don't you know people don't read anymore?"

If that was a brushback pitch, I ducked.

"Well," I replied, "my first goal in life was to be you, and that didn't work out. So I'm going with my strengths."

He laughed and then talked for a while about the slider, the pitch he threw better than anyone else.

"I always had a little bitty dot on the ball," Carlton said. "If it was big as a quarter or half a dollar, that was a ring, or a circle, and hitters could see that. When I threw it, I wanted the spin real tight on it, so the ball is blurry like a fastball and you can't see the dot. The intent is to fool the hitter as long as you can, so he has to commit to a fastball, so he has to come out and try to get it, because he can't sit back on a fastball and hit it. You have to commit to the fastball—and that's where you want him."

The slider is faster than the curveball and easier to control, with a tighter break, shaped not like a loop but like a slash, moving down and away toward the pitcher's glove side. The trick, as Carlton said, is in the disguise, making a hitter swing over a pitch he thinks is a fastball. A dot—formed by the side-spinning rotation of the seams—would seem to telegraph the pitch. But some hitters call it a myth.

"I never saw it," says Matt Williams, who had 7,000 at-bats in the major leagues. "Guys have said, 'Well, all you have to do is look for the red dot and you'll know that it's a slider.' You've got a fifth of a second, right? I couldn't do it."

He is hardly alone. Batters hit just .233 in at-bats ending with sliders in 2017, their worst average against any pitch. The Pirates' Chris Archer, who has one of baseball's best sliders, gave a simple reason why: "Of all the true breaking balls—slurve, curve, slider—it looks the most like a fastball for the longest."

The origins of the slider, as we know it now, are murky. In 1987, hundreds of former players responded to surveys for a book called *Players' Choice.* They answered many questions, including the best slider of their day. Pete Donohue, a three-time 20-game winner for the Reds in the 1920s, could not give a name: "We didn't have one when I pitched," he replied.

Hmm—but what is this pitch, if not a slider? "It was a narrow curve that broke away from the batter and went in just like a fastball," said the great Cy Young, describing a pitch he threw in a career that ended in 1911.

Contemporaries of Young, like Chief Bender, an ace of the early Philadelphia A's, probably threw it, too. Bender's name virtually demanded he not throw straight, and he was, you might say, the chief bender of pitches in his era. Listing his repertoire for *Baseball Magazine* in 1911, Bender first mentioned his "fast curves," which would seem pretty close to what we now call a slider. George Blaeholder and George Uhle, whose careers ended in 1936, were early pioneers. Blaeholder, who pitched mostly for the Browns, had sweeping action on his fastball that was said to baffle Jimmie Foxx. Uhle, a 200-game winner, developed the slider late in his career, after his prime with the 1920s Indians. It startled Harry Heilmann, a Detroit teammate who was hitting off Uhle in batting practice.

"What kind of curve is that?" Heilmann asked.

"Hey, that's not a curve," Uhle replied. "That ball was sliding."

Waite Hoyt, an admiring teammate and the ace of the fabled 1927 Yankees, compared its action to a car skidding on ice. He added the pitch himself and credited Uhle for inventing it. Uhle told author Walter Langford that, as far as he knew, he threw it first.

"At least I happened to come up with it while I was in Detroit," he said. "And I gave it its name because it just slides across. It's just a fastball you turn loose in a different way. When I first started throwing it, the batters thought I was putting some kind of stuff on the ball to make it act that way."

Red Ruffing used a slider in his Hall of Fame career, which included four 20-win seasons in a row for the Yankees from 1936 through 1939. In that final season, the National League MVP was the Reds' Bucky Walters, a former third baseman who had learned a slider a few years earlier from Bender, a fellow Philadelphian. Walters led his league in all the major categories in 1939, and the next year lifted the Reds to their only World Series title between the Black Sox and the Big Red Machine—a span of 55 seasons.

In 1943, another MVP threw the slider: the Yankees' Spud Chandler, who shut out the Cardinals to clinch that fall's World Series. Chandler had learned the pitch from Ruffing, whose influence Rob Neyer and Bill James cited as a reason the slider soon made a breakthrough. The other factors, they said, were Walters's success and the fact that the pitch now had a name; it was not just another breaking ball. After three years at war, Ted Williams noticed the trend:

> We began to see sliders in the league around 1946 or 1947, and by 1948 all the good pitchers had one. Before that there were pitchers whose curves acted like sliders. Hank Borowy threw his curve hard and it sank and didn't break too much, so it acted like a slider. Johnny Allen's was the same way. Claude Passeau's fastball acted like a slider.

Williams called the slider "the greatest pitch in baseball," easy for a pitcher to learn and control. He worried about grounding the slider into the infield shift, reasoning that the only way he could put it in the air was by looking for it. Most hitters are late on the fastball if they sit on the slider, but Williams was not like most hitters. He batted .419 off the Browns' Ned Garver and .377 off the Tigers' Jim Bunning, who otherwise thrived with sliders.

"The big thing the slider did was give the pitcher a third pitch right away," Williams wrote in his book, *My Turn at Bat*. "With two pitches you might guess right half the time. With three, your guessing goes down proportionately."

Williams believed the popularity of the slider helped drive averages down. Bob Feller, the best pitcher Williams said he ever saw, had fiddled with the slider in 1941, and perfected it by the time he returned from the war. Mixing a slider with his devastating fastball and curve in 1946, Feller struck out 348—then considered an American League record. He described the pitch like this:

> It can be especially effective for a fast ball pitcher because it comes up to the plate looking like a fast ball. It has less speed, but not enough for the hitter to detect the slightly reduced speed early in the pitch.
>
> The slider darts sharply just before it reaches the plate, away from a right-handed hitter when thrown by a right-handed pitcher. It doesn't break much—four to six inches—but because it breaks so late, the hitter has trouble catching up to it.
>
> I didn't invent the slider—I merely popularized it. The pitch has been around since Christy Mathewson's time.

The slider's transformative power showed up in Feller's statistics, and in his clubhouse. Phil Rizzuto said that in his rookie season, 1941, the only pitcher he faced who threw sliders regularly was Al Milnar of the Indians. Feller was on that team, and so was Mel Harder, who taught the slider a few years later to Bob Lemon, who went on to the Hall of Fame. The logic behind the pitch was so easy to understand, and the pitch itself so simple to learn—generally, but not always: off-center grip, pressure applied to the middle finger, and possibly a late, subtle wrist snap—yet there remained an odd kind of backlash against it into the 1950s.

Pitchers threw fastballs and curveballs, sometimes a trick pitch like a knuckleball, and a spitball if they could conceal it. The conventional wisdom was that learning a slider would harm a pitcher's curveball. A curveball demands a different arm action—wrapping the wrist and pulling hard, straight down, to generate furious topspin. Throw too many sliders and you might lose the feel for staying on top of the curve.

"If you have a good curve, it's foolish to add the slider," said Sal Maglie, a curveball master who was turned away from using a slider by Uhle for that reason. "But all the young pitchers today are lazy. They all look for the easy way out, and the slider gives 'em that pitch."

Maglie said this in 1962, in an *Esquire* article that included his assertion that Roger Maris had feasted off sliders while blasting 61 homers the year before. To Maglie, expansion and "all the second-line pitchers in the league throwing sliders" had added at least 10 homers to Maris's total. The pitch was widely derided as a "nickel curve"—a breaking ball, yes, but a cheap knockoff of the real thing. That term is long gone, but "cement mixer," which describes a lazy and obvious slider, persists today.

The critics of the slider were blind to its impact. In his book *Head Game,* Roger Kahn asserted that the slider "saved major league baseball from becoming extended batting practice" after the offensive boom of the 1930s. That era had its masters—Lefty Grove, Dizzy Dean, Carl Hubbell—but few others were much better than ordinary. The slider gave pitchers a weapon they could learn and control with relative ease, a pitch that looked like a fastball much longer than the curveball did.

"I could always tell a curveball from a fastball in the first 30 feet of flight," Stan Musial told Kahn. "I picked up the speed of the ball and I knew who was pitching and I put the two of them together and I'd know just what the ball was going to do. Break or hop. The slider was tougher. I got my share of hits off sliders. But during the years I played for the Cardinals, the slider changed the game."

Musial played from 1941 through 1963. By then, a contemporary from his playing days, Johnny Sain, was an avid teacher of the pitch, winning pennants and building 20-game winners with startling regularity.

———————

Sain did not invent the slider in his long career as a pitcher and a coach, or use it very much as a pitcher. But he probably studied and imparted the principles of spin better than any coach ever has. Forever curious, Sain was the leading pitching mind of his era. He had seen the slider's rise, understood its impact, and spread its gospel like nobody before him.

"He was a genius in his field," says Roland Hemond, who hired Sain to instruct his White Sox pitchers in the 1970s. "Johnny Sain was a master."

Sain is remembered best for a rhyme—*Spahn and Sain and pray for rain,* a shorthand version of a poem by Gerry Hern, the sports editor of *The Boston Post* in 1948. Sain and Warren Spahn were the aces of the Braves' staff and carried the team to the pennant, the culmination of a three-year run in which Sain completed 62 of his 65 victories. He began the 1948 World Series by shutting out Feller and the Indians, the highlight of an unlikely 11-year playing career.

"I spent four years in the lowest minor leagues, the D leagues, and I never had overpowering speed," Sain told *The New York Times* in 1968. "So I kept practicing my breaking stuff, big curves and short ones. I started in 1936, and by the time I came up to the big leagues with Boston in 1942, I was throwing sliders."

Sain pitched mostly in relief that season, without distinction. He left for three years as a Navy pilot in World War II, spending the downtime building up his arm and experimenting with angles and pitches. He came back throwing breaking balls almost exclusively—90 percent of the time, he once guessed—and his creativity served him well when he moved into coaching, a fitting profession for the son of an auto mechanic. An open mind and skilled hands compelled Sain to innovate.

As a Yankees coach in 1961, he created a spinning device, first by impaling an apple with a television antenna. Sain could hold the antenna in one hand and twirl the apple with the other, tilting it this way or that to see the spin from various angles. He liked the idea so much that he transferred it to a baseball, drilling a wooden handle into the center and calling it The Spinner. Sain spent thousands of dollars developing his invention and sent it to the United States Patent Office. A Yankees pitcher, Luis Arroyo, called it the best tool he had ever seen.

"I'm most concerned about movement on the ball," Sain once said. "What makes it fool the hitter? Why does it do what it does?"

The Spinner showed pitchers how. Just by flicking their fingers on the ball as they held and moved the handle, they could see the way it spun. The more they toyed with it, the more knowledge they gained of their craft. Aspiring pitchers could purchase a Spinner by writing to Sain at PO Box 487 in Walnut Ridge, Arkansas. His pupils on major league teams could use them whenever they pleased, and if a pitcher got released, Sain often gave him a Spinner to take with him. Chances are Sain would soon follow him out the door.

As a coach, he bounced from the Yankees to the Twins to the Tigers to the White Sox, succeeding everywhere but doing so with independence that irritated the established order. He traveled with dozens of books and motivational audiotapes for his pitchers. He was their advocate, not the manager's friend, upending the logic of the day by emphasizing throwing—and experimenting with spin, even at moderate effort levels—over the rote running exercises that most pitchers hated.

"His big deal was turn and pull," says Jim Kaat, who thrived under Sain in Minnesota and Chicago. "So we would practice from 45 feet, straight backspin. Then he'd say 'turn and pull, turn and pull,' and it'd be like Mariano Rivera's cutter, and then we'd turn it a little more. He'd show us with the device. Every day we would throw.

"We'd play games—'OK, throw this as slow as you can and make it break as big as you can,' almost like Steve Hamilton's 'Folly Floater' [a version of Rip Sewell's Eephus pitch from the 1940s]. Then he'd say, 'OK, now let's put a little more velocity to it, let's see how short we can make it break and how hard we can throw it, without trying to muscle it.' He taught us how to make the ball do things. Velocity was never an issue."

The weapon most pitchers learned from Sain was not shaped like the arcing curveball, and certainly thrown much harder than the blooper Hamilton used for the Yankees in the 1960s. It had a two-plane break—over and down—which distinguished it from the cutter Rivera would perfect, which veered more than it broke. Yet it was not thrown as hard as the vicious sliders that Bob Gibson and Carlton were beginning to unleash on the majors.

Call it a short curve, or maybe a slurve, but basically it acted like a slider, and Sain's pupils used it to dominate the 1960s and early 1970s. All of these pitchers won 20 games under his guidance: Kaat, Whitey Ford, Mudcat Grant, Denny McLain, Jim Bouton, Al Downing, Jim Perry, Wilbur Wood, Stan Bahnsen. Later, as a minor league instructor with the Braves, Sain would mentor Leo Mazzone, who coached the celebrated Atlanta staffs of the 1990s. Tom Glavine always remembered Sain's advice on breaking balls: impart spin but think fastball, to protect your elbow through the delivery.

Too often, pitchers try to generate break with their elbows and forearms. The safer, more effective way is to do it with the wrist and hand. The former pitcher Jerry Dipoto, who would go on to be a general manager, remembers a daily drill that emphasized this. For 15 minutes every day, he and his Cleveland teammates had to throw all their pitches with a four-seam fastball grip. They would shape their pitches and create different breaks with their wrist, hand, and finger pressure.

"Creating break and spin is just about creating a fast hand," Dipoto says. "If you have a fast hand, you're gonna create movement. And the easiest way to work on training a fast hand is just by using it."

When the pitchers finally applied their grips, they would amaze themselves with the action they could impart. They would also know why they did it—and when a pitcher understands the way his pitch spins, Dipoto says, *it's on.* The pitchers had a name for this daily exercise in the art of the spinning baseball. They called it the Johnny Sain Game.

———

Bob Gibson decided to become a professional athlete at age 11, in 1947, the year Jackie Robinson joined the Brooklyn Dodgers. Gibson had lost his father before he was born, and his brother, Josh, who was 15 years older, helped raise him. Josh built a pitching mound at Bob's elementary school, and while he knew sports, he did not know a slider. Bob, therefore, did not know it either. He just threw it better than anyone ever had.

"I thought it was a curveball, because I didn't really understand the dynamics of all those pitches," Gibson says. "Since day one, I had always thrown a slider, and as I got bigger and stronger, I threw it harder. But I always threw it the same way."

His Triple-A manager for the Cardinals, Johnny Keane, told Gibson that the pitch he called a curveball was actually a slider. To be a curveball, he would have to start with his hand on top of the ball, and deliver it with a rolling wrist. Gibson could do that, but, he says, "it was slow and just kind of a flopper."

That was not his pitch. His pitch was a sharp, darting missile at 92 miles an hour, held with his index and middle fingers together between the seams, at their narrowest point, and his thumb on the seam below.

"It didn't really break that big, it was just really hard," Gibson says. "And I thought the harder I threw it the better it'd be, and that was true."

In popular lore, Gibson's heat and competitiveness are often mistaken for head-hunting. Yet he played 17 years and never led the league in hit batters. His slider was a big reason for the 102 he did hit, and the many close calls.

"Guys used to laugh at me all the time when I said they hit themselves," Gibson says. "They go, 'Yeah, right.' But no, they would. Because when you go guessing for a ball outside and you go out there to get it, especially with that slider out there a lot to right-handers, they would start out there to get that ball. Well, if I threw a fastball inside, especially a two-seamer, it's gonna hit them. And I wouldn't acknowledge, 'Oh, I'm sorry.' I would never acknowledge that. I just said, 'Gimme another ball, let's go,' so they thought I was throwing at everybody. And that was OK."

The Hall of Famer Billy Williams, who hit left-handed, handled Gibson fairly well. He liked the ball down and explained that Gibson's slider would sometimes drop squarely into his bat path. If he could extend his arms, Williams had a chance. That's how he hit 10 homers off Gibson, the most by any opposing hitter.

"But *here*," Williams adds, placing his hand a few inches from his belt, "you've got to get out in front. He'd throw a fastball to get you out in front, and you're way out here."

That pitch, the one that tied up lefties, was Gibson's stiff-wrist slider, which acted like a cutter and shattered many bats. He would break his wrist for a more sweeping slash away from righties, holding them to a .204 average, with a .287 slugging percentage, across 17 seasons.

Gibson's masterpiece was 1968, when he resolved to use the slider more, especially to left-handers, with catcher Tim McCarver's encouragement. Gibson authored one of the greatest seasons a pitcher has ever had, going 22–9 with a 1.12 earned run average, the lowest ever. He completed 28 of his 34 starts and was never removed from a game in the middle of an inning. He set a World Series strikeout record in Game 1 against Detroit, with 17, and overall went 7–2 with a 1.89 ERA in the World Series, twice winning MVP.

Baseball lowered the mound after the 1968 season, from 15 inches to

10, but Gibson kept on winning, adding another Cy Young Award in 1970. The change in the mound did not affect him much, because he threw from a three-quarters angle and could easily adjust the angle of his slider. Over-the-top pitchers with curveballs were more vulnerable.

There was a cost to Gibson's signature pitch: constant pain. Gibson does not believe he was tougher than modern pitchers, but he pitched with discomfort that would not be tolerated today, when injuries are more definable. On game days when his elbow really ached, Gibson would take Butazolidin after his warm-ups. Butazolidin, commonly used on horses, has since been banned by the FDA.

"My elbow was sore all the time, and it was sore basically from that stiff-wrist slider, because that's really hard on your elbow," Gibson says. "The one where you break your wrist and the break is a little bit bigger, that's not nearly as hard on your elbow as that stiff-wrist. It's like holding your fingers on top, with your thumb on the bottom, and rotating it like you're going to turn the doorknob, just with those three fingers. And if you do that, you can feel tension on your elbow—and you can imagine, throwing that 91, 92 miles an hour, what your elbow's going to feel like afterwards.

"And I threw a lot of 'em."

———

A young pitcher on those Cardinal teams noticed the slider's toll on Gibson. He decided he wanted no part of it. Steve Carlton never hurt his elbow throwing a baseball, and he remains very proud of that. Even as a boy, he refused to accept the idea that pitching had to be painful.

"Kids are invariably thinking if they're gonna make the ball spin a particular way, they have to force the ball to spin," Carlton says. "So they're gonna be twisting their hand and doing crazy things to it to get it to spin, to break. That just goes along with being a kid, because they don't know, so they think they have to do it this way.

"Even when I was a kid, I held my curveball and threw it. I didn't twist it. I never twisted it. Even on the curveball, it was just hold it and throw it. And that's why I had a good one: I never hurt my arm. Never had elbow problems."

That curveball was good enough—with a fastball, naturally—to get Carlton to the majors at age 20. He was so proud of his curve that before he had even made the majors, after a spring training game, Carlton challenged McCarver to call more breaking balls when behind in the count. They were shaving at the time, towels around their waists, and McCarver—already a five-year veteran—admonished the kid, loudly. But Carlton was probably right.

(McCarver would find, over decades of close friendship, that Carlton had an unusual but accurate sense of things. In the mid-1970s, as they prepared for a long drive on a hunting trip, McCarver noticed that Carlton had packed a caulking gun in the trunk. McCarver teased him about it, but Carlton didn't care. Somewhere near Mitchell, South Dakota, in 20-degree weather with snow falling, a pheasant flew into the radiator of Carlton's Chevy Blazer. The car was leaking antifreeze. Carlton stopped, removed the bird, found the caulking gun, and used it to plug the leak. Years later, he sold the Blazer with the caulking still in the radiator. "Lefty," McCarver told him, "I'll never question anything you do again.")

For all of his intuition, though, Carlton was not above asking questions. He pitched with Gibson on two pennant-winning Cardinal teams, watching and learning what to do and what to avoid. McCarver had encouraged Carlton to develop a pitch that moved laterally, because his fastball was straight and his curveball dropped straight down, as if from 12 to 6 on a clock. Carlton asked Gibson how he threw his slider.

"He said he kind of got it out there and turned it at a particular time; it was a timing element," Carlton says. "And he had a great slider—but his elbow always bothered him. I thought, 'I don't want to do that.' I didn't want to turn my hand, like turning-a-doorknob kind of thing. That puts a lot of pressure on the ulnar region of the elbow."

Carlton started experimenting with a cutter, offsetting his fingers on the fastball to get side-to-side action. What he really wanted, though, was two-plane movement: *"cut, cut, cut—and then drop,"* as Willie Stargell would one day describe it to him. All through the 1968 season, Carlton toyed with the shape of the pitch and his angles of release. As Gibson fashioned a performance for the ages, Carlton went 13–11. He was an afterthought in the World Series, mopping up twice in blowouts.

That off-season, the Cardinals played an exhibition series in Japan. They would face Sadaharu Oh, the left-handed slugger who stood at the plate like a flamingo and smashed 868 career home runs. They did not understand that Oh and the Japanese would take the exhibitions seriously.

"We thought everybody was gonna just play pat-a-cake, have some fun and have a beer," Carlton says. "It wasn't like that. They came out swinging. They're trying to kick our ass. So we had a clubhouse meeting without the coaches and the managers: 'We gotta step it up a little bit.'"

Oh hit a home run off Carlton; maybe two. Desperation was his inspiration.

"I told Timmy, 'I gotta break this out against Oh because I can't move him off the plate,'" Carlton says. "He picked that leg up and he was pretty tough at the plate. My first throw I threw it at his ribs and it kind of unsettled him. He kind of flew back. After he got that leg up, he just kind of jumped out of the way and it came over for a nice strike. That was a pretty good test right there, the first one I ever threw."

At spring training the next season, Carlton told the pitching coach, Billy Muffett, that he planned to use the slider quite a bit. Muffett was unsure; some teams, like the Dodgers, did not want their pitchers throwing sliders at all, for fear of elbow trouble. But as the season progressed, Carlton used it more and became a star: he struck out 19 Mets in a game that September and nearly won the league's ERA title, at 2.17.

He loved the pitch, sometimes too much. The next August, after McCarver had been traded, Carlton was 6–18 when he took the mound at Dodger Stadium. Joe Torre asked to catch him that night, with a plan to call only fastballs. Carlton obliged, shaking off Torre just once, for a slider that turned into a homer by Andy Kosco. It was the only run he allowed in a 2–1, complete game victory.

Carlton abandoned the pitch in 1971—"Steve Ditches 'Made in Japan' Slider," a *Sporting News* headline said—and while he won 20 games, he was not much better than he had been the year before. Unwilling to meet his demands for a $10,000 raise the next spring, the Cardinals traded Carlton to the Phillies for Rick Wise. By the time the Cardinals reached the postseason again, in 1982, Carlton had finished four Cy Young Award–winning seasons.

For the first, in 1972, he was reunited with McCarver, his personal catcher for much of the decade. The two were an unlikely pair— Carlton silent with the press, McCarver loquacious—but McCarver earned Carlton's respect with his tactics at bridge, the card game. McCarver's knack for remembering cards impressed Carlton, who figured he could apply the same skill to remembering pitches.

The 1972 season was Carlton's answer to Gibson's 1968. Only once before had a pitcher won at least 27 games with 30 complete games, 300 strikeouts, and an ERA under 2.00—Walter Johnson, in 1912, when his Washington Senators won 91 games. The 1972 Phillies won just 59.

Carlton never threw a no-hitter, but the best of his six career one-hitters came that April at Candlestick Park, in his third start for the Phillies. He allowed a leadoff single to Chris Speier and no other hits, facing just 28 batters, whiffing 14, walking one and needing only 103 pitches. He threw 20 sliders, 17 for strikes.

"It was freezing that night," McCarver says. "Worst playing conditions imaginable, but it didn't bother Steve. Nothing bothered him. Nothing. Impervious to outside pressures."

The slider was back, forever. All along, Carlton was determined never to hurt his elbow. He made every start for the Phillies for 13 years, and McCarver said he never met anyone stronger from the forearm to the hand. Dick Ruthven, a teammate, would ask Carlton how he threw the slider.

"I hold it like this," Carlton would say, "and I throw the shit out of it."

Carlton laughed as he told the story; it was a joke, but basically true. He would hook his wrist to set the pitch, holding his index and middle fingers less than a quarter-inch apart, angled diagonally across the stamp on the sweet spot. He wanted to feel as if he were holding the outer third of the ball and applying pressure equally with the two fingers. His thumb provided more pressure on the bottom seam, and he released the ball off the inside of his index finger.

"The slider's tough because the hitter has to come out and get it, because it looks like a fastball," Carlton says. "So he has to start swinging, and then it starts breaking. So that's where you get the check swings. Then you throw your fastball behind that, and then he's behind it, because he's coming out. He's waiting for another rhythm to it."

When Carlton pitched, McCarver said, the two most important people on the field were third baseman Mike Schmidt and the first base umpire—Schmidt to field the ground balls pulled by right-handers, and the umpire to call strikes on their check swings. The pitch was his ultimate finisher.

Carlton would do this well past his thirty-fifth birthday. His four best strikeout rates (8.5 or more per nine innings) came from 1980 to 1983, his age 35–38 seasons. It was the payoff from his punishing daily workouts with Gus Hoefling, a strength coach who came to Philadelphia when the Eagles traded for quarterback Roman Gabriel, his star pupil, from the Rams in 1973. Carlton was already a black belt in Shotokan karate and found, in Hoefling, a martial arts guru who could help him ward off the dangers he had seen in St. Louis. Carlton would churn his elbow in buckets of rice or ball-bearings. He did pushups with his fingertips. Gibson had told him, "If you throw, it's gonna hurt." Carlton wanted to be indestructible, with Hoefling's help.

"We gained strength in areas that most people didn't know how to exploit as trainers," Carlton says. "We went after weak tissue all the time, which would be the ulnar regions. We made that stronger, more able to take the stress. That was the whole idea."

Walter Johnson had held the career strikeout record at the end of every season from 1921 through 1982. But in 1983, the year of that pennant-clinching victory over the Dodgers, Carlton was the all-time king. Nolan Ryan took over for good the next season, but right to the end, at age 43 in 1988, Carlton's elbow withstood all those sliders. He finished with 329 victories and 4,136 strikeouts, and his 709 starts are the most among left-handers in the history of baseball.

———

For much of Carlton's prime, American Leaguers had their own version of a merciless left-handed slider: Ron Guidry's. Even when hitters knew he would throw it, Guidry could still frustrate the hell out of them.

"What drove me nuts was his slider would start in the strike zone, and by the time I would swing at it, it almost hit my back foot—*and I knew it was coming*," says Paul Molitor, who had 3,319 career hits. "I'd see Graig Nettles take two steps toward the third base line. He got the sign from the shortstop and I'd look and see him move over. So I knew it was a slider, I knew where it was going, and I still swung."

Molitor faced 14 pitchers more often than he faced Guidry. Yet Guidry struck him out more than anyone—20 times in just 74 plate appearances. Molitor is in the Hall of Fame and Guidry is not. But for Guidry's first 10 full seasons in the majors, no pitcher won more games.

From 1977 to 1986, Guidry earned 163 wins for the Yankees. He was third in that span in strikeouts, just behind two Hall of Famers (Nolan Ryan and Carlton) and just above two others (Phil Niekro and Bert Blyleven). Guidry, in his time, was in the pantheon of greats, Carlton in different-colored pinstripes.

"Their sliders would come with such late break and with such force," says Ken Singleton, who faced both in their primes and hit .180 against them. "Other guys would throw sliders and they would hang, you could see them, you could hit them. I was a good breaking-ball hitter, too, but theirs had such velocity, such late break, that by the time you committed, it wasn't where it was supposed to be."

Their careers unfolded differently. Carlton had 57 victories by his twenty-sixth birthday; Guidry had none. He had pitched college ball in his beloved home state of Louisiana and then struggled to assert himself in the majors. After a bad Guidry relief outing in August 1976, a raging George Steinbrenner offered this morale-booster: "You will never be able to pitch in this league."

The remark infuriated Guidry, because Steinbrenner said it in front of the Yankees' general manager, Gabe Paul. But it would have been accurate had Steinbrenner added "unless you develop a slider." Until he did, Guidry really was going nowhere. He knew he had to find a second pitch, and quickly.

"All I knew was, 'OK, look, I'm here, this is where I want to be, I can't waste time,'" Guidry says. "I had to learn everything I needed to in a short time."

Guidry's flat breaking ball fooled no one, and he had abandoned his high school curveball because it did not work with his mechanics. Guidry's left arm looked like a catapult as he delivered a pitch, and he could not throw a curve from that slot.

But frustration with a bullpen role turned into opportunity. Guidry learned pitching philosophy from one Yankee reliever, Dick Tidrow—"pitch 'em low, bust 'em high"—and learned his slider from another, Sparky Lyle, who threw with the same over-the-top technique.

Lyle had come to the majors with the Red Sox. As a farmhand, he became intrigued by the slider when Ted Williams, then a spring training coach, told him it was the best pitch in baseball. Williams told Lyle how a slider spins, but said the rest was up to him.

Lyle would lie in bed with a ball in his hand, wondering how to do it. He was in Double-A, living in a converted garage, and awoke at three one morning with the answer. Like Paul McCartney dreaming the melody for "Yesterday" and bolting to a piano to preserve it, Lyle dashed outside and tried his new slider against the wall of the garage. It was such an easy game to play.

Lyle introduced the pitch in a bullpen session the next day, drilled his catcher in the foot, and knew he had a keeper. The next season was his first of five for the Red Sox until 1972, when they traded him to the Yankees for a utility man named Danny Cater. A half century after the Babe Ruth sale, the Red Sox still hadn't learned. Lyle went on to win a Cy Young Award for the Yankees and teach Guidry his best pitch.

"Don't let it fly at the end," Lyle told him. "Pull it down."

By using the same arm action, Guidry could mimic Lyle while throwing the pitch harder than his mentor. Guidry was just 5 foot 11, 161 pounds—a whippet, Singleton called him—and could not relate to the pain that bigger men like Gibson endured from the slider.

"Nothing happens to the elbow," Guidry says. "I mean, it's almost the same as throwing your fastball. It's all thrown with your wrist; it was not done with your elbow. If you find any pictures, you'll see my elbow and Sparky's elbow, they're basically in a straight movement. Our arms are not bent to be able to throw it."

Guidry would need surgery to remove a bone chip from his elbow in 1989, and he never pitched again. But by then, he had done enough to one day have his number 49 retired by the Yankees. He made four

All-Star teams, set the team's single-game strikeout record (18), and followed Lyle as the AL Cy Young Award winner in 1978.

Guidry went 25–3 that season, beating the Red Sox at Fenway Park in a one-game playoff for the division title. Danny Cater had long since retired.

————

U.S. Route 167 passes through Lafayette, Louisiana, Guidry's hometown, and winds north through the state past Ruston, the hometown of another All-Star pitcher born in 1950: J. R. Richard. His first target was not a catcher's glove.

"How I got started, I used to kill birds and rabbits with rocks," Richard says. "My thing was just to throw, throw, throw every day. I would get a pocket of rocks and just go out to the woods throwing."

Sometimes Richard would tape rags together, or throw tennis balls. But mostly he threw those rocks. He did not play organized baseball until he was 15 years old. He threw four pitches, he said: fast, faster, fastest—and a slider he learned from a pitching manual he found along the side of U.S. 167.

"In the country, sitting on the porch every day, twiddling your thumbs, sometimes you just take off and go for a walk," he says. "Basically just something to do to keep you busy, if you weren't working in the fields. There was divine intervention."

Richard picked up the manual and took it home. He was not much of a reader then, and would travel many more roads before devoting his life to the Bible. At 15, that pitching book was his scripture, its descriptions and illustrations his guiding lights. The slider had been a completely unfamiliar pitch until he found the book. He absorbed its lessons and improvised on his own.

"We had a rock in the country called a coal rock, which was a round rock, and I used to practice a lot with that and see the movement of the rock, see what it was doing," Richard says. "A lot of stuff I learned on my own. The fastball came naturally."

Richard's high school slider had a wider, slower break than the one he featured in the majors. But it still left an indelible impression on those who saw him at Lincoln High in Ruston, where he never lost a game. The Astros made him the second overall pick of the 1969 draft.

"If you ask me who had the best slider I ever saw, it would probably be J. R. Richard," says Pat Gillick, the Hall of Fame executive who scouted for the Astros in the 1960s. "I was down there when we signed him and I thought he had the hardest slider, and the hardest slider to pick up, that I can ever remember."

In 1971 Richard tied a record for strikeouts in a major league debut, with 15 in a complete game victory in San Francisco. Willie Mays struck out three times. It was an early glimmer of overpowering talent, and the start of an exhilarating and tragic career.

Richard took years to gain footing in the majors, then broke through with a run of extraordinary seasons before it all ended, abruptly, at age 30. All of this was true for Sandy Koufax, too, and while everything else was different—their stuff, their throwing hand, their race, their teams' visibility and levels of success—people speak of Richard with the same kind of reverence they do of Koufax.

"Nobody struck me out," says Dusty Baker, but Richard did—24 times, more than any other pitcher Baker faced in his 19 seasons. "They had him and Nolan, both of them were nasty. But J.R. was the nastiest. He was 6 foot 8, big old hands; the ball looked like a golf ball in his hands. He had a big Afro and he pulled his hat way down, so you couldn't see his eyes, and he was kind of wild. Boy, he was nas-*tee!* And the nastiest part about him is you know it's 60 feet, 6 inches from the mound, right? He was throwing from about 50 feet. You had no time to pick up the ball."

For the entirety of his career, Richard was the tallest pitcher in the major leagues. He could hold eight baseballs in one hand, as he demonstrated for a 1979 *Sporting News* story that called his slider "the best 'out pitch' any man possesses today." Richard threw it nearly as hard as his 98-mile-an-hour fastball, often with better control.

By 1980 he was coming off consecutive seasons of 300 strikeouts, a feat that had been achieved by just three others: Rube Waddell in the 1900s, Koufax in the 1960s, and Nolan Ryan, his new Astros teammate, in the 1970s.

Ryan had just become baseball's first $1 million–per–year player, yet it was Richard who started the All-Star Game for the National

League at Dodger Stadium. He did not allow a homer through the season's first three months. He was holding hitters to a .168 average. And he would be bathed in the California sunlight, with hitters in shadows, when the game began at prime time in the East.

In the top of the first inning, Richard faced Reggie Jackson with a runner on third and two outs. He had just brushed Jackson back with a high fastball, running the count to 3–1. Working from the windup, Richard rocked back and lifted his left knee almost to his chin, turning and whipping his right arm through the air. Jackson swung hard, and the slider fooled him so badly that he lost his balance, his body whirling completely around, his back foot becoming his front.

On the ABC telecast, Keith Jackson said the slider measured 94 miles an hour. "If it was," said Don Drysdale, the Hall of Fame pitcher in the booth, "it was one of the quickest sliders known to mankind."

Jackson bit on another slider, this one in the dirt, striking out to end the inning—and that was as good as it would ever get for J. R. Richard. He would pitch in the majors only one more time.

Richard had complained of a stiff, dead arm in the first half, but his performance showed no decline. On July 14, back in Houston, he struggled to read the catcher's signs, and moved slowly. He left in the fourth inning and was placed on the disabled list.

This was the summer of "Who Shot J.R.?," the cliffhanger from the TV show *Dallas*. The comparison was irresistible—and misguided. Houston's J.R. mystery was not some manufactured drama. Richard's complaints were real. In late July he was diagnosed with a clot in the artery leading to his right arm. Doctors told him it was stable, and cleared him for supervised workouts.

At the Astrodome on July 30, with the team on the road, Richard began to sweat profusely, yet his arm had gone cold. He made a few throws and collapsed to the turf onto his left side. His ears rang. He lost feeling on the left side of his face. A blood clot in his neck had begun to cut off circulation to his brain.

Richard suffered a series of three strokes, underwent surgery, and never made it back to the majors. He battled depression, lost his fortune, and was homeless by the mid-1990s, often sleeping under a bridge at Fifty-ninth and Beechnut Streets in Houston.

"I had some people I knew when I was playing ball and I would go to their house and wash my clothes and eat, maybe spend a night or two, but some of those people had families and I did not feel right just coming in," he says. "So I would go under the bridge, and that's it. Everything became a point of survival. You're trying to survive; you have no transportation, no food, no finances. You ask yourself a lot of times: Where do I go from here? You don't have an answer."

Richard would connect with a local pastor, find work with an asphalt company, and receive help from the Baseball Assistance Team. The details are a bit hazy—Richard says that he lost brain cells because of his stroke, which still affects his reflexes on his left side and, sometimes, his speech. But he walks a lot, loves to fish, and is skilled at cooking baby back ribs. He says life is good.

And he can still remember his days of dominance.

"It was grand, to be in control," Richard says. "I felt like I was the baddest lion in the valley."

————

There was no magic moment in the development of Randy Johnson's slider. He knows that he was seven years old when he started playing baseball, in 1971, the same year Vida Blue rose to stardom for Johnson's hometown Oakland A's. Blue was also left-handed, so maybe he inspired Johnson, but he is not really sure. It was all so long ago, Johnson said in 2015, just before his induction to the Hall of Fame—and anyway, Blue did not throw a slider then.

Johnson could flip knuckle-curves as an amateur, but mostly he needed only a fastball. More important, though, was his ability to consistently harness the power of his 6-foot-10 frame. J. R. Richard led his league in walks three times by his age-28 season, and so did Johnson.

His first season in professional baseball was 1985. Johnson made eight starts for the Jamestown (New York) Expos, going 0–3 with a 5.93 ERA and more walks than strikeouts. He did not have his slider then because he was simply trying to survive, mechanically. Two years later, at Class AA Jacksonville, he pitched 140 innings—with 128 walks and 163 strikeouts. Jim Fanning, a former Expos manager, came to watch him.

"He wanted to know, 'What's wrong, is everything OK?'" Johnson says. "I go, 'Yeah, why?' He said, 'Randy, you could strike out 12 in six innings, but you could walk seven in three.' That's what I was dealing with, the inconsistency. I didn't need to be able to strike out 12, I just needed to be able to throw strikes. I couldn't repeat that, and as a professional athlete, it's frustrating when you know that you can do it, but you can't do it *today*—and you can't figure out why."

Around that time, Johnson learned his slider; he does not know precisely how or when. It was all a blur in the early years, a long slog with the Expos and the Mariners to unlock his potential. With his fastball and slider, Johnson had two luxury sports cars—but what good were they if he kept running them off the side of the road?

By 1992, Johnson had made an All-Star team, thrown a no-hitter, and averaged a strikeout per inning over two full seasons with Seattle. He was also coming off a season of 152 walks, a figure unequaled for more than a decade before, and more than a quarter century since. In his zest to overpower hitters, Johnson would speed up his delivery and overthrow his fastball. Calling for sliders, catcher Scott Bradley found, tended to calm things down. Johnson was a different beast to corral, and it gnawed at him.

"It bothered Randy that every other pitcher would go over scouting reports, and for some reason, because he was big and had control problems, they'd pretty much say, 'OK, Randy, just throw strikes, just get the ball over,'" says Bradley, who caught Johnson in his first three years with Seattle. "I think he was kind of self-conscious. If everybody else was going over scouting reports, he wanted to be a pitcher just like everybody else."

Sometime during the 1992 season, Johnson was scheduled to throw a bullpen session before a game against the Rangers at the Kingdome. The Mariners' bullpen was then located down the right field line, beyond the visitors' dugout, which Johnson passed on his walk there. Rangers pitching coach Tom House had gone to USC, like Johnson, and asked if he wanted to watch Tex throw in the Rangers' bullpen. Tex was Nolan Ryan. Johnson said yes, and it changed the course of his career.

"We've seen some things that you've been doing," House told Johnson, who demonstrated his mechanical flaw for me, many years later, in a boardroom at Chase Field in Phoenix. He rose from a table and faced a wall.

"I was landing *on the heel* of my foot, so I'd be spinning and I would lose my arm angle," he said, unfolding his frame toward another wall on his right. "Now look where that's going—all my momentum's kind of going off to the side, and my arm angle's dropping. You need to be consistent with your arm angle in order to throw a strike.

"But if you land *on the ball* of your foot, now all your momentum's landing on the ball and you'll go straight."

Johnson would demonstrate this lesson dramatically later that season, against Ryan and the Rangers in Arlington, when he struck out 18 in eight innings (and 160 pitches). But the off-season brought despair when Johnson's father, Bud, a police officer, died on Christmas. The change in mechanics, and the clarity of purpose he gained from the death of his father, set Johnson on a new career path.

"I got help mechanically, didn't have to struggle as much, and it was a little bit more fun," Johnson said. "And because it was fun throwing strikes, I was able to dig down deeper and pitch with a chip on my shoulder because of my dad dying. So I used my emotions and pitched with anger."

Everyone feared him. Johnson's physical presence was intimidating enough—the pterodactyl wingspan, the low-three-quarters delivery, the mullet and the mustache and the scowl. Add in a focused rage, and his fastball/slider combination was all but impossible to solve.

"He was gonna bully right-handers in with the fastball and slider, and bully left-handers away with the fastball and slider," says Mark Grace, who was 1-for-10 off Johnson until becoming his teammate in Arizona. "He didn't really need to pitch in. His weapons were so ridiculously good that he didn't really need to change his location. You knew where he was going with it and you still couldn't hit it."

Tony La Russa, who managed many games against Johnson, said there was no better pitch in his era than Johnson's slider, which Tim Raines nicknamed "Mr. Snappy." Gary Sheffield, the most dangerous right-handed pull hitter of his time, could not solve it.

"He throws it out like a slingshot, and it comes down on your back leg," says Sheffield, who hit .209 off Johnson. "By the time the ball gets to the plate, you think it's a strike, but it's bearing down on you.

Because he's so tall, you can't judge if the ball's close to you or not. And once you go forward on a cutting slider, it's hard to hold up."

Johnson won four Cy Young Awards for the Diamondbacks, part of a five-year stretch in which he averaged almost 350 strikeouts per season and beat the Yankees three times in the 2001 World Series, a year in which he struck out a mind-bending 419 hitters, postseason included. He reached 300 victories with the Giants in 2009 and made his final start two months before his forty-sixth birthday. Johnson— a right-handed hitter—lunged at a curveball in the dirt from the Astros' Roy Oswalt. His bat went flying and Johnson grabbed his left shoulder, seized by immense pressure. He struggled to get the ball to the plate in his warm-ups for the top of the fourth, allowing two home runs and a single before fielding a bunt by Oswalt. Johnson threw wildly to first and winced: he had torn his rotator cuff.

Surgery would have ended his season and career. It was not an option.

"I didn't want to go out that way," he says, so he came back, 10 weeks later, as a reliever. His arm was shot but his spirit still burned. "You tell players: 'You don't know when your last game is. You're a superstar now, you're in the limelight, but you don't know what's gonna happen today—and it may not even happen on the field. It could happen on the way to the ballpark, anything. Play the game.'

"It took me forever just to get to the major leagues and feel like I could compete. So when I could, I relished the moment."

———————

John Smoltz, who entered the Hall of Fame with Johnson in 2015, also had a wipeout slider. Two, actually: one before his 2000 Tommy John surgery, and one after. The first he learned from Leo Mazzone, who passed on the principles he learned from Johnny Sain in the Braves' farm system: think four-seam fastball, then turn and pull. When Smoltz's rebuilt elbow made turning the ball too painful, he changed its position in his hand—"I call it, like, putting the ball on a 45-degree angle," he says, "so when you throw it, it's already coming out cut."

After shoulder surgery in 2008, that slider was about all Smoltz had left. Released by the Red Sox the next summer, he got his final job because the Cardinals believed in his slider. Smoltz pitched well for a few starts and made his final appearance as a reliever in the playoffs. His fastball did not have its old extension, those explosive last few feet. But at 42, he could have kept pitching. He trusted his slider that much.

"I could have been that guy that just pitched with sliders," he says. "I could have been the Larry Andersen if I wanted to. That's just not who I am. I did not want to be hanging around if I didn't feel like I had the arsenal. I didn't want to be a specialist."

Smoltz did not need the work. He'd had a Cooperstown career as an elite starter and closer, and that was enough. For pitchers like Andersen, Jeff Nelson, and so many others, life as a slider specialist was a necessity, and a fine way to make a living. Together, Andersen and Nelson pitched for 32 years, almost entirely as setup relievers, and combined to hold right-handers to a .214 average.

They both improved their sliders by closely observing Hall of Famers at work. Andersen was already in his ninth season when he joined the Astros in 1986 and saw the power of Nolan Ryan's high leg kick. Andersen found that the higher he lifted his leg, the harder he threw his pitches. Nelson, who came up with the Mariners, admired Dennis Eckersley, the closer for the division-rival A's. He wore 43 in Eckersley's honor and tried to mimic his arm angle.

"He always threw three-quarters," Nelson says. "Once I started doing it, my fastball moved a lot more, my velocity stayed the same—but my breaking ball was huge."

Nelson also threw hard and had no fear of pitching inside. It was all to set up his sweeping slider, down and away from right-handers, taught to him in the minors by coach Pat Dobson—who had learned his on the 1968 Tigers from Johnny Sain. Nelson used his slider to humble some of his era's Hall of Fame right-handed hitters: Ivan Rodriguez hit .121 off Nelson, Frank Thomas .161, Paul Molitor .188, and Cal Ripken .200.

When Andersen talks to young pitchers, he tells them, "Don't make it break, let it break." He said he kept a loose wrist, put his fingers together, held a four-seam grip off-center, and pulled down on the side—a simple-sounding trick and a good cover for a wily craftsman.

Andersen was a master of disguise off the field, so mischievous that the Phillies once gave away plastic masks of his face for a summer Halloween promotion. His longevity—17 seasons—was all about deception and guile. Hitters knew he threw sliders, but which one?

"I was a three-pitch pitcher with three sliders," Andersen says. By altering the pressure of his fingertips or the position of the ball in his hand, he could spin out a cutter, a slider, or a slower slider. And when those pitches abandoned him at the biggest moment of his Phillies career—two outs, bottom of the tenth, one-run lead, Game 5 of the 1993 NLCS in Atlanta, Ron Gant at the plate—he improvised.

"He has thrown him three straight sliders," said McCarver, in the CBS booth, "and if there was ever a time to make sure that if a hitter beats you, he's gonna beat you with your best pitch, this is it."

Catcher Darren Daulton did not want to be beaten with anything, and another slider, he was sure, would fly a long way off Gant's bat. Daulton had a different idea: a changeup with a split-finger grip, the emergency lifeline Andersen had never come close to perfecting.

"He called that and my jaw hit the ground on the mound," Andersen says. "But why not? I threw it, it started off the plate away and came down to the outside corner, and Jerry Crawford rung him up."

It was the fiftieth and final save of Andersen's career.

———

The Phillies would win the pennant but lose the World Series to Toronto. By 2008, their city's streak without a major sports title had stretched to 25 years. It ended, at last, with a slider from a different right-handed reliever.

Brad Lidge had converted every save opportunity for the Phillies in 2008. He had done so largely with his slider, a pitch he had never even tried to throw until well into his professional career. The pitch had not always worked: three Octobers before, needing one out to send the Astros to the World Series, Lidge had thrown a flat slider that the Cardinals' Albert Pujols obliterated into the Texas night.

But it had been the right pitch, Lidge was sure. The first time he had ever faced Pujols, he ended the game by striking him out on a slider, on the front end of a strike-him-out/throw-him-out double play. It was the very first save of Lidge's career.

Earlier in the playoff at-bat, he had fooled Pujols with a slider, and his plan was to throw an even better one the next time, reasoning that a pitcher's stuff should get nastier the longer an at-bat lasts. But the added pressure undid Lidge: he wanted to make Pujols "swing and miss even worse," and so his legs uncoiled too quickly, his arm lagged behind a bit too long, and the slider hung in the strike zone, begging to be crushed. Pujols obliged.

Now, in Game 5 of the World Series, before another home crowd ready to explode, Lidge faced a similar challenge in Eric Hinske of the Tampa Bay Rays. Hinske was no Pujols, but his best skill was enough to ruin everything: Hinske could demolish a fastball. He had shown this the game before, with a homer to straightaway center off Joe Blanton. The blast was inconsequential—the Phillies won easily, to take a three-games-to-one lead in the series—but Lidge noticed the type of pitch Hinske had hit.

That bit of intelligence underscored what Lidge knew from his own history with Hinske. It was brief—just four pitches in June 2005—but memorable. The first time Lidge had faced Hinske, who then played for Toronto, he struck him out on a slider to end a game, just as he had done with Pujols. But the next night, Hinske, a left-handed hitter, scorched Lidge's first-pitch fastball off the right field wall.

Lidge processed all this as Hinske came up as a pinch hitter. The tying run stood at second base. Lidge did not think about Pujols, but the circumstances were the same: failing to clinch in Game 5 would send the series, and the momentum, back to the other team's park. The Phillies' pitching coach, Rich Dubee, and catcher, Carlos Ruiz, met Lidge on the mound. The infielders also huddled there, with second baseman Chase Utley stationed just behind Lidge's left ear. Utley was in perfect position to shout at Lidge if he chose the wrong strategy.

"If we would have said fastball," Lidge says, "he probably would have been like, 'Wait, wait, wait! Let's think about this.'"

Utley said nothing; Lidge's plan was to not throw another fastball until 2009.

"The last time I threw this guy a fastball, he crushed it off the wall," Lidge told Dubee. "We're going all sliders here."

If Ruiz gave him a sign, Lidge does not remember it. Maybe Ruiz patted the ground—signaling location, not the type of pitch—but

Lidge was committed to the pitch that had made him a star. If Lidge had never learned the slider, and had stuck with the curveball as his off-speed pitch—well, his elbow would probably have blown apart. But even if he had managed to stay healthy while throwing a curve, the best he could have been was a setup reliever, a middle man. Without the slider—without a true swing-and-miss weapon—Lidge never would have found himself on the mound at the end of a World Series.

As a boy in Colorado, he rarely found himself on the mound at all. Lidge did not pitch until his sophomore year at Cherry Creek High School, and then just occasionally, because he had shown a strong arm on throws from the outfield. As a senior, he lost his starting outfield spot to a sophomore, Darnell McDonald, who would go on to play in the majors. Lidge's only chance to play varsity was to pitch.

He took to it instantly, his velocity rising from about 83 miles an hour to 91 with a few weeks of instruction. Lidge also spun a curveball, just to have something slower to drop into the strike zone. But in Colorado, a poorly located curveball can hang in the thin air and be hit a long way. The rush of the fastball made pitching fun.

"Something just felt right with rearing back and throwing the ball as hard as I could," Lidge says. "That felt even better than hitting a home run for me."

Drafted by San Francisco in the 42nd round—teams now stop at 40—Lidge instead chose the University of Notre Dame, down at sea level, where his curveball had a much sharper break. Still, he had only a rudimentary understanding of the pitch, and it was not what got him drafted again. A fastball, by then touching 97, enticed the Astros to choose him in the first round in 1998.

The problem in pro ball was that Lidge needed something else. He was a starting pitcher then, and because starters face more hitters than relievers do, they need more options—at least three, generally. Lidge tried a changeup but never mastered it, and the more he used his curveball, the more his elbow swelled. He threw 74 innings, total, in his first three minor league seasons.

Somehow Lidge had never tried the slider. He had heard it could be more effective than the curveball, because it was thrown harder, but he feared that tinkering with a new pitch would distract him from perfecting his curve. He did not attempt a slider until his third spring training, in Kissimmee, Florida, in 2001, when an Astros coach, Dewey Robinson, altered his arm angle to alleviate the pain.

Lidge was a bit of a short-armer, releasing his pitches closer to his head than most pitchers do. With his hand further away from his head, Lidge's arm felt better but his curveball suffered. He trusted Robinson, whose analytical approach appealed to Lidge and whose status, as the pitching coordinator for the farm system, made him familiar to Lidge and important to his future.

Throwing the slider as if making a comma with his index and middle fingers, Lidge found that the pitch had too much horizontal spin, staying on the same plane as the hitter's bat. He wanted something to make hitters miss, and Robinson encouraged him to stay on top of the ball for a deep, almost vertical break that Lidge could control by altering his finger pressure and the angle of the ball. They played catch for a week before trying the slider on a mound. Lidge spiked the first two in the dirt, but on the third try, *like that,* his muscle memory kicked in. Everything felt right.

"It was, I guess for lack of a better word, miraculous," said Robinson, a former White Sox reliever, in 2010. "I've never, ever had somebody pick it up so quickly and so devastating. It had this huge break, it was an instant swing-and-miss pitch, and it was thrown harder than anybody I've ever taught before or since."

In about 14 months, Lidge was a major leaguer, and on that chilly night in Philadelphia, at the apex of his career, he reached for the pitch Robinson taught him. Hinske dribbled the first slider up the first base line, a weak foul. He checked his swing on the second slider for strike two.

Lidge could make his slider dive away from a left-handed hitter. "A little bit of inside-out," he calls it, and sometimes his frustrated victims would tell Lidge his pitch was not a slider at all, because sliders from righties do not break that way. Further, they would say, the seams on Lidge's slider did not form a red dot. That was because he threw them with topspin—top-to-bottom rotation, not sideways—yet still threw them hard, about 84 miles an hour in 2008.

Lidge stared at Ruiz's target and held the final slider of the season in his right hand. He gripped it as he always did but tilted it a bit to the right, and made sure that his index finger would be the last to leave the ball.

"On the very last one, it was one of those deals where I gripped the ball and I could feel, like, the grip was just right when I came set," Lidge says. "There were two strikes and I was like, 'OK, this is the one.' I could really feel it the second I gripped it in my glove that everything was just where it needed to be, and that last slider was going to be a good one."

Hinske had no chance. The pitch dive-bombed into Ruiz's black Wilson catcher's mitt, far below Hinske's swing. Lidge leaped in the air, his arms outstretched, then fell to his knees and cried: "Oh my God, we just won the World Series!" A teammate, Jayson Werth, would tease him about that reaction, telling Lidge he seemed to be speaking in tongues. Lidge did not mind. His slider was the snapshot of triumph for a generation of Philadelphia sports fans.

For all of these slider masters, though, there is still something missing about the pitch—respect, perhaps, or maybe widespread recognition. The curveball or the slider? When it comes to pitching, this is the Ginger or Mary Ann question.

"The curveball's so sexy, it's such a great pitch," says A. J. Ellis, a veteran catcher. "Broadcasters can recognize it and they really spice it up and describe it well. The whole stadium oohs and aahs. There's nothing better than seeing that guy jelly-legged, like he's drowning, as that curveball finishes its last 10 feet. It's a slow, slow, painful death."

Curvy, glitzy, and glamorous, the pitch is so perfectly Ginger that Tina Louise, the actress who played the stranded starlet on *Gilligan's Island*, actually dated Bo Belinsky, a playboy Angel of the 1960s who threw, yes, a curveball. The one described by Ellis belongs to the Dodgers' Clayton Kershaw, the ace of his era. Yet Kershaw's best pitch is actually the slider, his Mary Ann: alluring in its simplicity, comfortable and familiar but a knockout at the end.

Kershaw did not throw a slider at Highland Park High School in

Dallas. The summer after eleventh grade, he was the No. 4 starter on a junior national team behind future major leaguers Tyson Ross, Brett Anderson, and Shawn Tolleson. As a senior, he was the best high school pitcher in the country: undefeated with a 0.77 ERA and 139 strikeouts in 64 innings. The dominance foretold his success in the majors, after he had added the slider.

"His curveball *looks* the best, because everybody sees it on a GIF or on TV, that big break, guys turn the other way," says Anderson, his Dodger teammate in 2015, when Kershaw became the first pitcher in 13 years to strike out 300 hitters in a season. "But as far as hitter in, hitter out, the slider's his best pitch, because it looks so much like his fastball and he can throw it for strikes or he can get them to chase. The curveball is so big and there's so much break and it's so nasty that guys just take it automatically. It's tough to throw that pitch for a strike because there's so much movement."

That was Kershaw's problem in his last high school start before the 2006 draft. Without command of his curveball, he walked four hitters and gave up a home run. His failure was the Dodgers' gain, though, because six teams passed on Kershaw before the Dodgers grabbed him. Within two years, at age 20, he was pitching at Dodger Stadium. He struck out three in his first inning and started Game 1 of the NLCS the next fall.

Yet Kershaw's ascent was not as direct, or as easy, as those facts make it seem. Without the slider, it would not have happened.

"You adapt to survive, and that's basically what I was doing," Kershaw says. "I was kind of just putting along being mediocre, so I wanted to try to figure something out."

Kershaw? Mediocre?

"Yeah, I was," he insists. "Check the numbers. Check '08. Check the first half of '09."

In 22 games in 2008, Kershaw's ERA was 4.26. It was 4.34 by the end of May 2009, when the Dodgers played a four-game series at Wrigley Field. Four times already, Kershaw had lasted just five innings and thrown at least 97 pitches. Two other starts were headed that way before he was pulled in the fifth.

Kershaw was surviving, barely, but not adapting. He would snap off that picturesque curveball, hitters would stare at it for a ball, and Kershaw would fall behind.

"Eventually it got to the point where he was a one-pitch pitcher," Ellis says. "He was throwing a lot of heaters. Even though his fastball was elite, as it is today, guys are still able to hit a major league fastball, especially when they know it's all you can throw for a strike. And even if they weren't able to put it in play and hit it hard, they were able to foul it off because there were no speed changes, nothing that was throwing their timing off. They were on time for the fastball, so his pitch counts were getting out of control. It got to the point where a demotion to go work on some things—probably a changeup—was really strongly considered."

The slider saved him. Mike Borzello, a Dodgers coach in 2009, suggested Kershaw throw it while playing catch. Pitching coach Rick Honeycutt showed Kershaw a grip. Ellis, up for the weekend as an emergency third catcher, squatted behind the plate as Kershaw tried it out in the bullpen.

Ellis had caught Kershaw in the minors, and tried to nurse him through an awkward experiment with a changeup. This was different. The slider hurtled toward the plate on the same plane as the fastball for 58 feet—and then it bottomed out, below the hands, below the barrel. This is *usable*, Ellis thought, finally something besides a fastball that Kershaw could throw when behind in the count.

Kershaw had never tried the pitch before. He had never needed to. But just like that, he had it down.

"It's really tough to explain, because it's such a feel," he says. "You know when you throw it right. It's the same with any pitch. When it comes off your fingers the right way, you know it's the way it's supposed to. And when it doesn't, it feels that way instantly. With the slider, I kind of felt that right away. I felt when I did it right, and I felt when I didn't.

"Like the changeup, I still don't have that feel. It's still hard for me to figure that out, and I think it's just because it's such a feel pitch. The slider, it's more grip it and rip it."

Kershaw gripped it and ripped it and by 2011 had begun streaks unprecedented in major league history: four seasons in a row as the major leagues' ERA leader, and five in the top 3 in Cy Young voting.

He took home three of those awards, plus an MVP trophy. He earned a $215 million contract and built an orphanage in Zambia.

None of it would have been possible without the best pitch of baseball's best pitcher, the difference-maker for Gibson and Carlton and so many more, the spinner that changed the game.

THE
FASTBALL

Velo Is King

Every pitch is a decision. That is the beauty and the burden of the pitcher. Think there's downtime in baseball? Tell it to the man on the mound, all alone on that dirt bull's-eye. The catcher thinks along with him, back behind the plate, but the pitcher rules the game. Nothing happens until he answers these questions: Which pitch should I throw, where should I throw it, and why? It is an awesome responsibility.

"It's about being in control—who's in control of the game?" says Jamie Moyer, one of the nicest people you'll ever meet, whose competitive fire kept him pitching until the year he turned 50. "I don't want to sound brash or rude, but if they came to me at 3:00 and said, 'OK, tonight we're starting at 7:06,' I'd say, 'We'll start it when I'm ready to throw the first pitch.'"

With each pitch thereafter, the calibration changes—sometimes slightly, like the position of the sun, and sometimes seismically, like an earthquake. But it always comes down to the pitcher's internal computer, and his default setting is the four-seam fastball, thrown with the index and middle fingers separated slightly across the widest gap between the seams. As the backspinning ball hurtles through the air, four seams cycle through each revolution. It is the easiest pitch to steer, and gives the hitter the least time to react. Every pitcher, no matter what else he throws, understands this rule:

The best pitch in baseball is a well-located fastball.

"For sure it is, because if you can't do that then you can't use your other stuff, because you use that other stuff based on your fastballs," Madison Bumgarner says. "I don't throw a two-seamer. I feel like my curveball and slider/cutter—whatever you want to call it—are pretty close; some days one's better than the other. But the fastball's always got to be number one."

That is where Bumgarner turned in Game 7 of the 2014 World Series, when faced with a decision few others had ever confronted. Just six pitchers before and one since—the Cubs' Mike Montgomery, in 2016—had been in position for a Golden Pitch, a term used by the Society for American Baseball Research for a pitch that could win or lose the championship for either team. By definition, this spot arises only in Game 7 of the World Series, in the bottom of the ninth inning or later, with the visitors leading and at least one runner on base. Those precious pitches, loaded with cork, yarn, and possibility, can make the ballpark go silent or crazy.

For Bumgarner, the steely left-handed ace of the San Francisco Giants, there was no doubting his weapon of choice. There never is. His mind-set, and a deceptive delivery that offers hitters no basis for comparison, gives Bumgarner an extraordinary edge.

"The thing that's different about him compared to a lot of guys is there's conviction behind every fastball he throws," says A. J. Ellis, who faced Bumgarner more than any other pitcher across his first 10 years in the majors. "It might not go to the area he wants it to go all the time, but it comes with aggression, and it comes with conviction."

Bumgarner entered Game 7 in Kansas City in the fifth inning with a 3–2 lead. He had shut out the Royals in Game 5 and also beaten them in the opener, when he worked seven innings in a blowout and gave up just a solo home run. Here, Bumgarner retired 14 in a row after a leadoff single. Then the earth shook.

With two outs in the ninth, Alex Gordon looped a sinking liner to center field. It fell for a single, skipped past one outfielder, and squirted away from another. Gordon huffed his way around second, but left fielder Juan Perez, a former high school pitcher, fired a strong one-hop throw to shortstop Brandon Crawford. The third base coach, Mike Jirschele, wisely held Gordon at third, 90 feet from tying Game 7. The next hitter could win it with one swing.

It was Salvador Perez. It had to be. Bumgarner had pitched shutout ball in the 2010 World Series against the Texas Rangers, and again two years later against the Detroit Tigers. In his three games against the Royals, he had allowed only that solo homer—to Perez. If he struck again, Perez would ruin everything.

Fifty-two years before, in another Game 7 involving the Giants, Ralph Terry had faced this precise problem. For Terry, a Yankees right-hander, the predicament was even more acute. Just two years earlier, in 1960, he had become the first pitcher ever to allow a home run to end the World Series, by the Pirates' Bill Mazeroski in Game 7. Terry had warmed up five times that day on a steep bullpen mound down the left field line at Forbes Field. He was worn out when he finally got into the game, and could not adjust to the flatter mound on the field. His foot came down early, everything was up, and Mazeroski smashed a high, cutting fastball over the left field wall.

In 1962, though, Terry had seized Game 7 from the start. Like Bumgarner, he had thrown nine innings to win Game 5, but his team had lost Game 6 to force a decisive finale. Because of rainouts, Terry started on five days' rest for Game 7, and carried a 1–0 lead into the bottom of the ninth at Candlestick Park. After a leadoff single and two strikeouts, Willie Mays doubled to right.

Like Juan Perez, Roger Maris hit the cutoff man to keep the tying run at third. And like Salvador Perez, the next batter had already homered in the World Series off the pitcher he would face with Game 7 in the balance. It was Willie McCovey, and even with a base open, Terry told manager Ralph Houk that he wanted to pitch to him.

An intentional walk to McCovey would have loaded the bases for Orlando Cepeda, another future Hall of Famer Terry feared even more. He also knew that this strategy had backfired for the Dodgers in the playoff to decide the NL pennant; after an intentional walk had loaded the bases in the ninth inning, Stan Williams walked in the go-ahead run. With an NL umpire behind the plate for Game 7, Terry guessed, he would have little margin for error against Cepeda.

With so many factors to consider, Terry says his mind did not flash back to 1960, and the possibility that he might—*again!*—give up a homer to end Game 7. He had house and car payments back in New York, with a wife, one child, and a baby on the way. That was pressure enough.

"I thought about the money difference," Terry says. "The winners got $12,000 and the losers got $8,000. I was making about $40,000. We needed the money in those days."

Terry did think about the homer McCovey had pulled off him at Candlestick in Game 2. He had thrown a cut fastball, inside but low enough for McCovey to extend his long arms. Terry resolved to avoid that spot this time.

"I wanted it high, in here," Terry says, shaking his hand near the chest of his pinstriped jersey on Old-Timers' Day at Yankee Stadium in 2016. Terry noticed his second baseman, Bobby Richardson, shading McCovey to his left—too far, Terry thought, but he knew better than to challenge his infielders' instincts. "They know how your ball's coming out."

McCovey hit a line drive, right to the spot Richardson was standing.

"I saw some film later on, from behind," Terry says. "I came in, he leaned back and got on it with his hands and put a lot of topspin on it—*whack!* He really hit it hard, but I thought, 'I got a man over there somewhere,' and boy, it was right at him. It wasn't like he made a sensational play.

"It was a fastball—crowded him," Terry says, smiling. "And I said, 'Thanks, Abner Doubleday, for inventing the game with a second baseman.'"

––––––––––

The San Francisco Giants never did win a World Series until Bumgarner came around. By 2014, they stood to capture their third in five seasons, if only he could solve Salvador Perez. Bumgarner, too, remembered the homer from earlier in the World Series, but he did not change his plan of attack: fastballs with conviction.

While backing up the plate on Gordon's hit, Bumgarner and catcher Buster Posey talked briefly about Perez. He is naturally aggressive, a tendency that would only be heightened with a chance to hit a walk-off homer in Game 7 of the World Series. They could use that impulse against him.

"Perez is a good fastball hitter, but Bum is so good at elevating the ball when he wants to," Posey says. "We both felt confident that in that situation, we were going to try to play off of Perez's anxiousness. That's somewhat instinctual, to know the type of hitter and say we probably can expand here. Could he have still got a hit? Sure. But we felt like that was the best way to attack him. The fastball's a high-percentage pitch, probably the lowest risk, because you figure his command is gonna be the best as well."

Thirty regular starters threw harder in 2014 than Bumgarner, whose average fastball was 92.1 miles an hour. But his superior confidence in the pitch was deeply ingrained; he threw nothing else at South Caldwell High School in Hudson, North Carolina, but was still drafted tenth overall by the Giants, at age 17. With Gordon on third in Game 7, no other pitch made sense.

"It's a little bit of a pride thing," Bumgarner explains. "I'm not like all these young guys that come up here throwing 100, but I like my fastball and I like to throw it. So a little bit of that, and we knew he was going to be aggressive and chase. So if I could throw it up there, we had a good feeling about it.

"We could have thrown a curveball and bounced it in front of the plate, and I think we might've gotten him on that, too, but then you're putting a little bit more on Buster. I trust Buster, he blocks almost all of them for me, but you never know. What if it hits the corner of the plate and bounces over his head or something stupid like that? That's not the way that you want to blow the lead right there.

"Could have thrown him the cutter or whatever, but you're taking a chance on leaving something over the plate and hanging it, and then bouncing it again. So it was the easy decision for us."

Bumgarner's first pitch sailed up and away, letter-high at 92 mph, and Perez swung through it for a strike. For the second pitch, Bumgarner tried an even higher fastball, over the plate but even with Perez's neck. Perez didn't bite on that, but Bumgarner went up again with his third pitch, about shoulder-high. Perez took the bait for another swinging strike.

One more strike could end it now, and Bumgarner poked his left index finger to his left nostril, blowing a snot rocket to the ground. This seemed almost too easy. Would Perez be so antsy that he'd go for a pitch over the plate, but up by his helmet? No. He did swing at the fifth pitch, armpit-high, and fouled it back.

Two balls, two strikes, five fastballs in a row, all at 92 mph. The plate umpire, Jeff Nelson, pointed at Bumgarner. Posey balled his right hand into a fist between his legs, then pounded his glove and bent the top of the pocket. He sprang into a half-crouch as Bumgarner delivered his 291st pitch of the World Series, spreading his arms wide and stepping toward first in his smooth, unmistakable style. Posey held his target up around Perez's chest—and Bumgarner missed his spot.

The pitch split the plate, above the belt but not as high as Bumgarner had wanted it. The pitch Perez had hit for a homer, in Game 1, was low enough to be a called strike, Bumgarner thought. This pitch, he says, was just high enough to be a ball. "It wasn't a whole lot different," he conceded, but that little bit meant everything.

Bumgarner found one extra mile per hour for this pitch, at 93 mph, but Perez was still too eager. He popped it up, in foul ground, to third baseman Pablo Sandoval. Posey flung his glove and mask to the sky and embraced Bumgarner as teammates swarmed from all directions. Champions, again.

"I think I got too excited," Perez said the next spring. "That's why I swing at a lot of pitches up. But now I got experience. I know what happened."

A year later, Perez would follow Bumgarner as the World Series MVP, hitting .364 in the Royals' triumph over the Mets. By then, he had also had his rematch with Bumgarner, again with Posey catching, at the 2015 All-Star Game in Cincinnati. This time Bumgarner used all his pitches and struck out Perez on a curveball. Funny thing, though—the third strike skipped past Posey, and Perez reached first base safely.

Had that happened in the World Series, Gordon would have scored to tie the game. Instead, when it had mattered most, when the stakes were the highest they could possibly be, Bumgarner had chosen the fastball. He had chosen wisely.

Pitching has always been a delicate balance of velocity and command. More of one can mean less of the other. In the early days, the pitcher was merely a tool for initiating action, a delivery device to place the ball in a specific spot. Throwing too hard would impede that goal if pitchers were wild, overpowering, or both.

An 1864 article in the *New York Clipper*—cited by Peter Morris in *A Game of Inches,* a treasure of research from 2006—reminds umpires that the pitcher cannot lift his foot until the ball leaves his hand. The desired result, the story said, was less speed, greater accuracy, "and the transfer of the interest of a match from the pitchers to the batsmen and outerfielders."

Pitching then looked almost nothing like pitching now. In 1884, the National League finally allowed overhand pitching, from a six-foot-by-six-foot square, 50 feet from the plate. Try to imagine Randy Johnson pitching like that. He can't.

"You think you know something, and you go to the Hall of Fame and you see how the game started off," Johnson said, after a Cooperstown tour in 2015. "There was no pitcher's mound there. There was a box— *there was a box!*—and you could move from one side of the box to the other side of the box. I don't remember how big, but you could run in this box. Not that you're gonna run far, because it's a small box."

That is the origin of the term "back through the box," to describe a hitter lashing a ball straight over the pitcher's mound. Tony Mullane, a big winner for the Reds in the nineteenth century, was known as "The Apollo of the Box." The king of the box, in those days, was Old Hoss Radbourn, who was 59–12 with a 1.38 ERA in 1884. He logged nearly 700 of the 1,000 or so innings pitched by his Providence Grays.

"Radbourn was said to stand in the right-hand rear corner, turn his back on the batter similar to the way Luis Tiant did it in the 1970s, and then take a hop, skip and deliver his pitch from the left side of the box," wrote Craig R. Wright and Tom House in *The Diamond Appraised.* "His motion was much like a modern shot-putter's turn."

A Giants pitcher of the 1890s, Amos Rusie of Mooresville, Indiana, threw so hard that they changed the game to account for him. Rusie—known as the Hoosier Thunderbolt—led the league in strikeouts and walks by such a wide margin that a pitcher's rubber, located 60 feet, 6 inches from the plate, replaced the box for good in 1893. Strikeouts fell by 44 percent that season.

By then, a new pitching star had just begun to emerge: Denton True Young, known as Cy for a wheeling, cyclone-like delivery in which he hid the ball from the hitter. Big for his time—6 foot 2, 210 pounds—he set nearly every longevity record with a disciplined lifestyle forged on a farm in Ohio as a boy. As he wrote in *Sporting Life,* in 1908: "A man who is not willing to work from dewy morn until weary eve should not think about becoming a pitcher."

That quote is not inscribed on his annual award for pitching excellence, but maybe it should be. In any case, while Young did not specialize in strikeouts—he ranks first in innings pitched but twenty-first in strikeouts—he understood which pitch was most important.

"My favorite pitch," he said, "was a whistler right under the chin."

Young led the AL in strikeouts in 1901, the league's first season. Then Rube Waddell took over, joining the A's the next June. For the rest of the decade, no one came close to Waddell in strikeouts, or eccentricities. He was known for leaving the dugout during games to chase fire trucks passing by the ballpark. Sam Crawford, a hitting star of the time, told Lawrence Ritter in *The Glory of Their Times* that Waddell threw so hard, he would have to pour ice water over his arm before games. "I've got so much speed, I'll burn up the catcher's glove if I don't let up a bit," Waddell would say.

Fastballs inspire that kind of colorful imagery. As he built his legend in the Negro Leagues, in the 1920s and '30s, Satchel Paige mesmerized hitters with his "trouble ball," a general term for his two fastballs—a "bee ball" that stayed on a level plane and a "jump ball" he said rose as much as six inches. Paige was such a control artist, he was said to warm up with a stick of chewing gum for a plate; he practiced hitting the corners of the wrapper. It wasn't the only home plate substitute he could find at a drugstore.

In 1971, when Paige was elected to the Hall of Fame, he recalled his tryout for Bill Veeck with the Indians in 1948: "He asked me to throw at a cigarette as a plate, and I threw four out of five over it."

Other Negro League stars, like Smokey Joe Williams and Bullet Joe Rogan, had fastballs baked into their nicknames. (Williams inflicted so much soreness on his poor catchers' palms that he needed two catchers per game.) In scouting reports for the Hall of Fame, Buck O'Neil compared Williams to Walter Johnson and Rogan to Bob Feller. Johnson was known as the Big Train, and Feller as Rapid Robert.

From 1902 to 1948, Waddell, Johnson, Lefty Grove, and Feller took turns as the AL strikeout king, combining for 32 strikeout titles. (Dazzy Vance won seven in a row in the NL, for Brooklyn in the 1920s.) Grove did it in each of his first seven seasons with the A's, starting in 1925, and collected nine league ERA crowns. He built his speed by throwing rocks as a boy in Maryland, and a humorist of the time, Arthur "Bugs" Baer, said Grove could throw a lamb chop past a wolf.

"Did you ever see speed like that in a human arm?" marveled Connie Mack, owner and manager of the A's, in spring training of 1930. "Why, it gives you a sore arm to watch him, doesn't it?"

We'll never really know who was fastest, because it took until 1974 for radar guns to reliably measure velocity; Danny Litwhiler, a former major league outfielder, popularized their use while coaching at Michigan State. Before then, the best pitchers could do was engage in primitive speed contests; Feller threw fastballs alongside a moving motorcycle and tested himself on photoelectric Army devices. He claimed Johnson was fastest, anyway.

"Johnson was so great," Feller wrote in his memoir, "that he almost belongs in his own Hall of Fame."

———

Let's face it: you'll never be Walter Johnson, but you do have a fastball. Pick up a baseball, throw it, and there it is. It is probably very slow, relative to major leaguers' fastballs, but whatever else you throw, this pitch will be your fastest and straightest. Typically, the catcher signals for it with the index finger, the ol' number one. If it's especially fast, it's a heater, but with apologies to Bruce Springsteen, it's never a "speedball"—and a hitter who swings and misses it doesn't really look like a fool, boy. When a hitter guesses wrong and swings hard at a puttering off-speed pitch, *then* he looks like a fool. If he can't catch up to a fastball, he's simply lost the game's most primitive one-on-one battle.

"George Brett hit some of the shots heard 'round the world off me," Goose Gossage says. "But, man, that was the greatest part of what I did, challenging those great hitters when they *know* it's gonna be the fuckin' fastball!"

Gossage remains as brash as his old fastball, slinging opinions with such unsparing force that the Yankees, in 2018, stopped inviting him to spring training. Win enough macho duels, though, and you also might develop a personality to match.

"There's no better feeling as a pitcher than to just tell the guy what's coming—'Here, fastball, get in the box, let's go,' and they still couldn't hit it," says Frank Tanana, the major league strikeout leader in 1975. "You can be loud when you have that kind of stuff, and have the immaturity to go with it."

By the end of his career, when he teased hitters with curveballs and changeups, Tanana was a changed man, a devout Christian with a gentle nature off the mound. (He would sign autographs with the inscription "Jesus Loves You!") But Tanana was tough enough to grind out 616 career starts, most without great stuff. Only 17 pitchers have ever started more games, mostly Hall of Famers but also a few like him: Tommy John, Jim Kaat, and Jamie Moyer.

No pitcher has ever allowed more homers than Moyer, and John once gave up 287 hits in a season while striking out only 65 (think about that). Kaat led his league in hits allowed three seasons in a row, but he also won 60 games in that stretch, including one in the World Series. All three pitched past their forty-fourth birthdays, sacrificing a few miles per hour for a lot of durability.

"Sometimes a dad'll come up to me and say, 'Hey, my son's a junior in high school and they've got him clocked at 91!'" Kaat says. "And I'll say, 'Really? Teach him how to pitch at 86.'"

Kaat wishes teams would take their hard-throwing prospects and tell them to work three innings without topping 90 miles an hour. (Think of the movie *Speed,* but on a mound.) Then, he believes, they would understand the art of their craft and learn to keep their best fastballs in reserve for critical moments, giving hitters a new and startling look. But times have changed.

"Somebody asked me, 'How many times in your career do you think you threw the ball as hard as you could throw it?' And I said zero," Kaat says, explaining that a showoff might get hurt and lose his spot on the staff. "We wanted to throw for rhythm and control and condition our arm that way."

There have always been exceptions, of course, pitchers who threw their hardest at all times. Nolan Ryan, the career leader in strikeouts and walks, exerted himself like a short reliever yet somehow threw more innings than anyone born after 1887 except Phil Niekro, a knuckleballer.

"I never had the ability to back off my fastball," Ryan says. "I always pitched maximum effort."

Ryan had a paper route as a teenager, rolling *The Houston Post* by hand every morning, which helped build his shoulder muscles. Then again, he flung the papers from the car window with his left arm, and we've never seen an outbreak of paperboys becoming strikeout kings. Ryan knew he was an outlier, crediting his ability to throw hard to God, and a perfect alignment of genetics and will. He actually expected Steve Carlton to wind up with the career strikeout record, guessing that Carlton would pitch longer because he was left-handed and famous for conditioning.

Before the 1980 season, when he left the Angels for Houston as a free agent, Ryan said he asked for only a three-year contract, to take him through age 35. He actually got a four-year, $4.5 million deal, making him the first player ever paid $1 million per season. But he had no idea he would keep pumping fastballs for well more than a decade.

"Power pitchers faded away once they got in their early thirties," he says, "and I had no reason to think I was going to be any different."

Ryan's elbow finally gave out at the Seattle Kingdome on September 22, 1993. Pitching for the Rangers, he served up a grand slam to Dann Howitt (the last of the five homers in Howitt's short career), and then departed before he could finish his last batter, Dave Magadan.

"I was like, 'Something's not right,'" Magadan says. "He was barely getting the ball to the plate. Howitt hit the grand slam, then I came up and it went ball 1, ball 2. He threw a strike, and I think at that point he walked off the mound. The trainer didn't even go out there. I was like, 'Oh, we might not ever see him again.' It was sad."

It was sad because there may never be another pitcher like Ryan, though today's all-out, all-the-time generation will try. More common, and more effective, was the artistic approach of Greg Maddux. In the rare times Maddux fell behind in the count, hitters knew they might get a fastball. But it was not the same fastball every time.

"It may be only a B.P. fastball," Tony Gwynn once wrote in a scouting report for ESPN.com. "He will take something off the pitch, make the hitter get out in front and force him to hit the ball weakly."

While this was not especially effective against Gwynn, who hit .415 off Maddux, it highlights the value in changing speeds and giving up power for command. In the 1960s and '70s, Catfish Hunter was a master of this for the A's and Yankees. Early in games, Hunter would nip around the edges of the plate to establish the umpire's strike zone. Then he would work the corners with precision, changing speeds on the fastball to bait hitters into weak contact. Hunter did not throw hard, but few have ever used a fastball better.

"He did not have any exceptional pitch," says Dave Duncan, who caught him with the A's. "He was exceptional because he could hit a gnat in the ass."

To Duncan, the pitcher most like Hunter was Tom Seaver, whom he coached near the end of Seaver's career with the Chicago White Sox. Jim Evans, an AL umpire then, tells a story that illustrates the way Seaver thought.

"I was working the plate in Detroit in 1985," Evans says. "We stayed at the Hyatt Regency in Dearborn; we generally didn't stay where the clubs stayed, but for some reason the White Sox were there. So I was sitting at the bar after the game, and Seaver tapped me on the shoulder: 'Hey, nice job back there tonight, thank you. I just think you missed one pitch.'"

It was a 1–1 fastball to Kirk Gibson in the middle innings, Seaver explained, and Evans had called it a strike. Nothing remarkable, Evans thought. So why, hours later, was it on Seaver's mind?

"I don't want you to call that pitch a strike," Seaver said, as Evans recalls it. "That was a mistake. I got it up too high, like a ball or two above the waist, and I don't want any batter to get used to swinging at that pitch. My fastball is still my best pitch, my bread-and-butter, but if I keep throwing that one up there, they're gonna kill me. I can't get away with that pitch, and if the umpire's calling it a strike, they're gonna start swinging at it and I'll get in trouble."

Command is not everything, but it matters more than sheer speed. The longtime pitching coach Don Cooper, who helped guide the White Sox to the 2005 title, ranks his priorities in this order: location, movement, velocity. A star pupil, Mark Buehrle, made more than 30 starts for 15 years in a row by following those principles. His fastball averaged about 86 mph.

"We're trying to turn guys into professional glove-hitters, because no matter what style you are, you still have to do that," Cooper says. "If you can do that with 95 or 96, even better. But the common denominator is hitting the glove."

The pitcher who tries too hard to reach back for more velocity often works against his interests. The veteran starter Dan Straily says he throws some of his best fastballs to pitchers, who pose such little threat that he simplifies his mechanics and hits his spot easily. When a power hitter comes up, though, pitchers often try to overdo it. With the Marlins in 2017, Straily said, he saw too many pitchers foolishly try to blow heat past Giancarlo Stanton.

"We faced a guy the other day: 90, 91, 90, 91, all on the corners," Straily said that summer. "Giancarlo steps in the box and it's 95, 96—but everything's right down the middle."

It is possible to be Picasso with a machine gun, as reliever Dan Plesac colorfully described Curt Schilling's fastball command to writer Jayson Stark. But such artistry and power form a rare combination indeed; nobody born between 1857 and 1985 can top Schilling's career strikeout-to-walk ratio of 4.38-to-1.

———

The Kansas City Royals visited Yankee Stadium in early May 2016. The last time they had been to New York, the previous November, they celebrated a championship at Citi Field. Chris Young had beaten the Mets in relief in the World Series opener, and pitched well in his Game 4 start in Queens. He was almost 37, but the Royals eagerly re-signed him for two years and about $12 million.

Young was something of an anomaly. A former Princeton center, he stands 6 foot 10 but threw his fastball below 90 miles an hour. Yet Young was still hard to hit, with a fastball that stayed true through the strike zone much longer than most pitchers' did. In the lingo of the game, Young had a sneaky fastball, good finish. His pitches had *life*—that final, forceful burst that both fools and overwhelms a hitter.

"Life, to me, is almost a mystical concept," says Alan Jaeger, a highly regarded pitching trainer in Southern California, speaking unironically. "Some people seem to have more life than others and they might be throwing the same velocity."

This night, though, Young's pitches were dead on arrival. The Yankees battered him for five home runs, and he was gone by the third inning. Young had not lost his ability to throw at his peak velocity. But his ERA was 6.68, and nothing was working. He didn't know it then, but Young would not win another start for the rest of his career.

"Last year I could throw an 86-mile-an-hour fastball with life and miss my spot, and the guy would swing and miss or foul it off," he said that night. "Now I throw it 89 without life, and they hit it in the stands. That's the difference. It's always been more about life than velocity. You can see it in their swings."

Life has long been used to differentiate fastballs—a tiebreaker, of sorts, for some of the greats. Luke Sewell, a catcher from 1921 to 1942, used it to distinguish Bob Feller from Lefty Grove.

"Grove's fast one actually was past the batter and into the catcher's mitt quicker than Bobby's," he said. "Feller's fast one, though, had more life to it."

Every hitter in the majors can handle velocity. Pitchers always have the advantage, on a pitch-by-pitch basis, because batters get three strikes and nobody hits .500. But give a hitter enough looks at a straight fastball, and he'll drive it somewhere hard. Gary Sheffield speaks for his brethren when he says, "If you ask any hitter, they would rather face a guy throwing 98 than a guy throwing 92 with filth."

Filth means anything deceptive—not just breaking balls, but

fastballs that move differently than most. With modern analytics, we know which pitchers are more likely to survive with high fastballs. We know that while J. A. Happ and Koji Uehara do not throw hard, their fastballs spin so much that they don't drop at the same rate as most pitchers' fastballs.

To hitters who see thousands and thousands of fastballs fall a certain way, a pitch with an unexpected trajectory can be baffling. You might yell at your TV when your favorite hitter swings through a high, slow fastball. But there's more in play than it seems.

"When they say 'He's got that good, riding fastball,' I just think it doesn't fall off," Jason Giambi says. "With most guys, gravity will kind of take hold of it. Some guys just get those extra rotations, whether it stays on their fingers a little bit longer, or they've got a release point so they get that true plane—it's what you want. I mean, no pitcher wants that ball to fall into the strike zone. If you can keep it riding high, kind of above that belt area, you're gonna get a lot of strikeouts."

You'll also get plenty of balls a hitter just misses. When a pitch lacks life, Mike Mussina says, it seems to just barely make it to the catcher, no matter how fast it might be. But when it's lively, it seems capable of carrying straight through the catcher, the umpire, and the backstop. Hitters can't do much with it, even when they connect.

"Something caused that guy to miss that ball by a sixteenth of an inch," Mussina says, "so it's a fly ball to center instead of a ball off the wall or a homer."

Don Sutton—the Mussina of his era—threw a level-plane fastball that Tim McCarver found impossible to hit squarely; he faced him 70 times, with two extra-base hits and countless pop outs. Jim Palmer, a contemporary, conceded that while fastballs might not rise, some simply do not sink. He adds, assuredly, "I could make the ball go up. Backspin."

For most of baseball history, the rising fastball was taken as fact. Bob Shaw, who pitched 11 years in the majors and beat Sandy Koufax in the 1959 World Series, wrote a pitching manual in 1972 that described how to throw a four-seam fastball. The pitch is easier to control, he writes, and the seams blend together visually, to make the ball look smaller.

"If you can apply enough spin and velocity while gripping the ball across the seams, you can overcome the downward force of gravity and make the ball rise," Shaw asserts. He adds, with no equivocation, that "throwing across the seams produces vertical or upward movement."

This is a fairly consistent theme for fastball pitchers, especially of Shaw's generation and earlier. Don't tell Bob Gibson a fastball can't rise.

"Ah, those are scientists," he says. "They also used to say it didn't break, too. Oh yeah, it goes up. They never had a bat."

In *Fastball*, an enchanting 2016 documentary directed by Jonathan Hock, Hank Aaron, Ernie Banks, and Eddie Murray insist the fastball can rise. In Jane Leavy's definitive Sandy Koufax biography, from 2002, Jim Bunning sneers at the theory that the rise on Koufax's fastball was an optical illusion: "Physics is full of shit," he says. Leavy also quotes Frank Robinson's advice for his Baltimore teammates before facing Koufax in the 1966 World Series: "If it starts at the belt, take it because it's going to choke you."

Pat Gillick, the Hall of Fame executive, swears that a fastball can rise. As a minor league pitcher for the Orioles in the early 1960s, he was teammates with Steve Dalkowski, the almost mythical left-hander who fanned 1,324 hitters (and walked nearly as many) in 970 minor league innings. Dalkowski never reached the majors, but Gillick—who became one of most astute scouting minds in baseball history—can still picture his hopping fastball. He says only one catcher, Cal Ripken Sr., could handle it.

"What was funny about him, he wasn't wild in and out, he was wild up and down," Gillick says. "You could tell Steve, 'Look, I want you to throw a pitch 58 feet,' and he would attempt to throw a pitch 58 feet and it would be over the catcher's head. The ball rose so much between the pitcher's mound and home plate."

It literally rose?

"Oh yeah, absolutely," Gillick insists. "Absolutely. Well, you know, when you hit a home run, you put backspin on the ball and the ball carries out of the ballpark. And he had so much spin on it, so much rotation on the ball, the ball just kept carrying and kept rising."

Don't take Gillick's word for it? How about the man who threw more innings and won more games than any lefty in history? In *The Head Game*, Warren Spahn tells Roger Kahn, "If you throw enough and put enough backspin on the pitch, you get a fastball that goes against gravity." Spahn compared a fastball's flight to an airplane lifting off. "If a physicist wants to argue," he concludes, "let's just say backspin levels off the baseball."

An actual physicist, Robert K. Adair, addressed the topic in his book, *The Physics of Baseball*, taking the wise approach of respecting the perspective of the men on the field while explaining what they actually see. Like the curveball, he explains, the hopping fastball makes a smooth arc—but gets half of its hop in the final 15 feet of its journey. By then, the hitter has begun his swing and cannot adjust.

"Such a hopping fastball, thrown with a lot of backspin, does not 'rise' in the sense that it increases its height above the ground as it passes the batter, but it does rise with respect to the trajectory it would have without the spin. . . . If the batter bases his swing on the trajectory of the ball with the lesser spin but the pitcher has put extra spin on the ball, he will complain that the ball 'hopped' right over his bat—and I would agree."

Adair would get no argument from Eddie Perez, a Braves catcher who pinch hit against Randy Johnson with two outs in the bottom of the ninth inning on May 18, 2004. Johnson had retired 26 in a row, but Perez was a nemesis who had several career hits off his fastball. With two strikes, Perez expected a slider.

The catcher, Robby Hammock, set his target thigh-high, on the inside corner. Johnson fired a laser above the belt, outside, close to 100 miles an hour. Perez swung hard in futility. Perfect game.

"Even if I was looking for that fastball, I wouldn't have hit it anyway," he says. "You see it as a strike and all of a sudden . . ."

Perez makes an upward slash with his right hand, like a stage actor taking a bow. You know, I remind him, scientists say that kind of movement is impossible.

"No, it goes that way, too," Perez says, and who am I to argue? I believe in science, but I'd like to believe in baseball mythology, too.

––––––––––

History remembers 1968 as the year of the pitcher. Denny McLain won 31 games, Bob Gibson had a 1.12 earned run average, Don Drysdale threw 58⅔ consecutive scoreless innings, and only one American League batter, Carl Yastrzemski, hit .300.

The season's strikeout leader is less celebrated: the Indians' Sam McDowell, with 283. He finished his first inning of the year by fanning the Angels' Don Mincher with a 3–2 slider. When Mincher came up in the third inning, McDowell ran the count full again. Mincher expected a slider, but McDowell, a tall lefty with the best fastball of his era, had other plans.

"I wanted a fastball up and in because the left-hander can't hit a ball up and in," McDowell says. "So I reared back and I was gonna throw as hard as I could, and it got away from me and hit him in the cheek. He immediately went to the hospital. I went and visited him and I was scared half to death. I never had that feeling in my life, and never want it again. It was total fear."

McDowell pitched 15 years in the majors, but by the end he had descended into alcoholism. He found sobriety in retirement and became a counselor, dedicating his life to helping the afflicted. He drew from that experience when I asked how it feels to unleash a fastball that crushes another man's face.

"You don't really focus on the injury as much, once everything quiets down and gets back to the game, because now you've gotta focus on what you're doing," he says. "But after the game's over with, I mean, it's just scary as hell. It's like—well, I won't say it's exactly like it, but one of the areas I work in is suicide prevention. And with each individual that's attempting suicide, while you're stabilizing him and getting him to come down so you can get him professional help, you're trained to be focused on what to say, how to say it, what your reaction should be to his reaction. But I know that in every case I've ever had, when it's all over with, and the individual is in the EMS or the ambulance, I just shake like you can't believe, from the fear."

Fastballs have the power to kill. It happened to Ray Chapman, a Cleveland shortstop, on August 16, 1920, when facing the Yankees' Carl Mays at the Polo Grounds. Chapman was a renowned bunter; he still holds the single-season record for sacrifice hits, with 67 in 1917. As he led off the top of the fifth, under overcast skies after light showers at game time, Chapman moved his back foot, perhaps preparing to bunt down the first base line.

Mays, a right-hander with a submarine delivery, noticed. He aimed his fastball up and in. Chapman, a right-handed batter, was not wearing a helmet—those would not come to baseball for three decades—and the ball struck his left temple. It caromed back to Mays, who thought for a moment that it had hit part of the bat. Mays tossed the ball to first baseman Wally Pipp, but in an instant, he knew what had really happened. Chapman slumped to the ground, blood pouring from his left ear. He staggered up, began walking to the center field clubhouse, flanked by teammates, then slumped as he neared second base.

As Mike Sowell recounts with gripping detail in *The Pitch That Killed*, Mays, in the immediate aftermath, pointed to a rough spot on the surface of the ball. The umpire, Tommy Connolly, examined it and tossed it out of play, unaware that he was, effectively, trashing the murder weapon. After the game, Mays would say the ball had been wet.

An ambulance took Chapman to nearby St. Lawrence Hospital, where doctors determined that Chapman had sustained a fracture extending 3½ inches to the base of his skull on the left side. A piece of bone, 1½ inches square, had pressed against his brain, which was shoved against the right side of his skull from the force of the impact with the ball. Blood clots had formed. Doctors operated for an hour and 15 minutes, but they could not save him.

Jack Graney, an Indians outfielder and Chapman's roommate, would go to his grave believing Mays had thrown at his friend on purpose. At the hospital, he had decried the danger of Mays's pitch.

"A batter has a chance to dodge the fastball thrown by an ordinary pitcher, but Mays has a freak delivery and his fastball has a sudden dip to it that never gives a batter a chance to dodge."

Mays learned of Chapman's death the next morning, when a Yankees secretary came to his apartment to tell him the news. Later that day, he gave a statement to John F. Joyce, the assistant district attorney:

It was a straight fast ball and not a curved one. When Chapman came to bat, I got the signal for a straight fast ball, which I delivered. It was a little too close, and I saw Chapman duck his head in an effort to get out of the path of the ball. He was too late, however, and a second later he fell to the grounds. It was the

most regrettable incident of my career, and I would give anything
if I could undo what has happened.

Joyce ruled the death accidental, closing the investigation and releasing Mays from custody. He interviewed no witnesses, and the ball itself
was gone, "mixed in with the other baseballs removed from play that
day," as Sowell writes. That in itself was somewhat rare in those days,
and while lights were still years away, Chapman's death changed the
game by showing the consequences of using dark or defaced balls. In
1924, the NL used about 54,000 baseballs. In 1919, the year before
Chapman's beaning, it had used about 22,000.

Players today may know little, or nothing, of Mays and Chapman,
but they don't need to. The threat of a fastball to the head, and what
could happen, is understood as a workplace hazard. Giambi compares
the rare fastball to the head to the every-play brutality of the NFL.

"You end up getting smoked and you're kind of out of it," he says.
"Everybody hears the stories about guys getting their careers ruined,
but I don't know—it's just one of those things you don't think about,
I guess, like being a race-car driver and going fast. It's just part of the
game."

If hitters cannot manage that fear, they cannot play. But pitchers
must also find a way to cope with their power to inflict damage. Walter
Johnson always understood that his pitches could be lethal, ever since
his semipro days as a teenager out West. This is how a breathless fan
described Johnson to the Senators in 1907:

"The boy throws so fast you can't see 'em . . . and he knows where he
is throwing the ball, because if he didn't, there would be dead bodies
strewn all over Idaho."

Johnson was in the majors by the end of that season, on his way to
perhaps the greatest career any pitcher has ever had: 417 wins, a 2.17
ERA, 3,509 strikeouts, and a record 110 shutouts. If he had a weakness,
Ty Cobb explained late in life, it was a fear of himself.

"I know Johnson was afraid he would hit and kill a batter," Cobb
said in a 1958 *Sporting News* story. "When he saw me crowding the
plate, he would steer his pitches a little bit wide. I got some hits off
him only because I knew he pitched wide to anybody who crowded
the plate off him."

As Johnson told writer F. C. Lane in 1925: "The bean ball is one of the meanest things on earth and no decent fellow would use it. . . . The bean ball pitcher is a potential murderer."

Johnson was plenty dominant and proved himself to his manager right away. So did Feller, another phenom, who said in his memoir that it would have been "outrageously criminal or immoral" to deliberately bean a hitter.

"If a manager had ordered me to stick a ball in a batter's ear," Feller wrote, "I would have told him to stick it in his own ear."

Yet for much of baseball history, pitchers often had to pass a manager's toughness test. Spahn starred in the Boston Braves' farm system in 1942, but the major league manager, Casey Stengel, ignored him because Spahn refused an order to throw at a hitter.

"Warren wouldn't knock a guy down like Casey said," Spahn's teammate Lew Burdette told the former commissioner Fay Vincent in *We Would Have Played for Nothing,* an engrossing oral history of the era. "He said, 'You're gutless,' and sent Warren back down to the minors."

Spahn pitched just four games for a bad Braves team that season, then left for three years in the military. He went on to win 363 games and help the Braves beat Stengel's Yankees in the 1957 World Series. Years later, Stengel finally apologized for the slight.

As the fastest pitch and the easiest to control, the fastball offered the perfect vessel for a primitive show of guts. As a rookie for the A's in 1967, Rick Monday took a fastball to the face from Gary Peters of the White Sox. Fifty years later, Monday could press his index finger on the point of impact, an inch or so to the right of his nose, and still feel pain. Just before he blacked out, Monday said, he could hear Chicago's manager, Eddie Stanky, screaming from the dugout.

"The next time I faced Peters was in Chicago again, and Stanky was yelling again: 'Knock him down!'" Monday says. "The first pitch was right here [close to his head] and I took it. Next pitch, I ducked—it was over my head and broke the bat."

After Monday swung at the next pitch, he says, he flung his bat at Peters to show he would not back down.

"Because they wanted to see, as a young player, how long it took you to get up, *if* you got up, and if you'd ever bother them again," Monday says. "It was a game about intimidation, and you'd get away with it."

Being mean was just part of a pitcher's job. Most did not want to cause injury, but these were hardened competitors with little to no financial security, fighting for their careers. A high and tight fastball had a clear purpose, with no apologies.

"I wasn't really throwing at them, but I didn't care whether I hit them or not," Bob Gibson says, distilling the intimidator's mind-set. "Today they dare you to come inside, and if you do, the umpire kicks you out of the ballgame: 'Oh, you're throwing at somebody!' No, I'm not throwing at him. If I threw at him, I would hit him."

Doug Griffin, a Red Sox infielder, took a Nolan Ryan fastball to his helmet in April 1974. Griffin would one day tell the *Herald News* of Fall River, Massachusetts, that it felt "like a train going through my head, a loud whistle," a sensation that lasted two weeks. He missed two months but singled twice off Ryan the next time they met.

To Ryan, inside pitching just isn't what it used to be.

"Well, I think it's been taken out of the game *a lot*," he says. "What we considered pitching inside versus what they think pitching inside is today is totally different. And it seems to me like a lot of pitching inside nowadays is cutters. So it's just changed; the game goes in phases like that."

Ryan cited the aluminum bat as a critical factor in the way pitchers learn to use their fastball. Ryan, who was born in 1947, never once faced a hitter with an aluminum bat. In the mid-1990s, when he served as a volunteer coach for TCU, Ryan was startled by its impact.

"I had trouble getting my pitchers to pitch inside," he says. "You could pitch inside and a guy can still hit the ball off the handle and be very successful, so a lot of pitchers didn't want to pitch inside."

Gossage sings lead in the chorus of former players lamenting what the game has become. But his crass language shouldn't obscure his points. The best lesson he ever received, he said, came from the man he called the greatest player he ever saw: Dick Allen, the AL Most Valuable Player for the White Sox in 1972, when Gossage was a 20-year-old rookie teammate. Throwing hard came naturally to Gossage; as a boy in Colorado Springs, he would kill rabbits and birds with rocks, just like J. R. Richard. But Allen taught him how to intimidate a hitter.

"He said the best thing you can do is knock one of those fuckers on their ass," Gossage says. "The rest of that bench over there is watching. They don't want any part of you. They know you're going to establish in.

"Dick taught me to pitch in, right here," Gossage continues, meaning the hitter's lead elbow, just above the inside edge of the plate. "He said, 'As hitters, we see this pitch and we panic, because it looks as big as a basketball, and we've got to get the barrel there and God can't hit it. We identify this ball away from us and we may be able to get a bat on it, foul it off, or hit a ball down the right field line. But this ball in here, we gear up, we see it, and we can't hold up.'

"The last thing these kids think about today is the first thing hitters used to think about: 'I might get knocked on my ass.' These guys would get killed today, because they don't even know how to get out of the way of a ball. They have no clue. And then they take exception to it and they stare out at the pitcher. Back in the day they would have gotten drilled."

Gossage says he hit only three batters on purpose: Andres Galarraga, whom he just didn't want to face; Ron Gant, who had admired a long foul ball; and Al Bumbry, who had taken out two teammates with hard slides. But when he beaned Ron Cey in the helmet in the 1981 World Series, leaving the concussed Cey in a heap at the plate, it jolted Gossage severely.

Like McDowell with Mincher, Gossage stayed in the moment; he was working, too busy to consider the consequences. But it took him a month or two into the next season, he said, to feel comfortable letting loose with his fastball.

"When he was laying in the batter's box, I thought he was dead," Gossage says, before pivoting to an essential truth that can never be legislated out of the game. "There are inherent risks in baseball."

One inherent risk is simply the act of throwing a baseball, repeatedly, at high speeds.

"It's definitely an unnatural motion—overhead, throwing like that, putting that kind of stress on your shoulder and elbow," Justin Verlander says. "I mean, the natural motion is softball, underhand. Those girls or guys throw every day, they throw 200 pitches a day, they practice as long as they want. We can't do that, because we get really sore."

Likewise, Mike Mussina is convinced that pitching overhand is unnatural.

"We don't walk around with our arms over our head," he says, drawing the same softball comparison as Verlander. "There's no unnatural stress throwing a ball underhand, but there's unbelievable unnatural stress throwing a ball overhand, and that's just how it is. So every pitch you throw is stress on your body that it really wasn't born to have."

In a 2015 study, doctors at Henry Ford Hospital in Detroit found that while high velocity does not, by itself, endanger the ulnar collateral ligament, throwing too many high-velocity pitches does. The study put the threshold at 48 percent; if you throw a greater percentage of fastballs than that, you're adding significant risk to your UCL.

A 2013 article in *Nature,* the weekly science journal, explained that while chimpanzees sometimes throw objects, only humans do so with high speed and accuracy. This ability helped early hunters survive—but the species of baseball pitcher was eons away.

"Paleolithic hunters almost certainly threw less frequently than modern athletes, who often deliver more than 100 high-speed throws over the course of a few hours," the study says. "Unfortunately, the ligaments and tendons in the human shoulder and elbow are not well adapted to withstanding such repeated stretching from the high torques generated by throwing, and frequently suffer from laxity and tearing."

Precisely, says Dr. Glenn Fleisig, the research director at the American Sports Medicine Institute. The motion itself is not the issue.

"Throwing overhand is natural; windmill pitching is not," he says. "You know what my proof is? Do you remember when your son was two and you rolled the ball to him, and he picked up the ball and kind of pushed it with his shoulder toward you? Did he do windmill pitching? No. Humans, especially males, we like to pick up things and throw them. If you and I went to the lake and were gonna throw a rock, I wouldn't do a windmill throw. I would do an overhand throw. And my friend who doesn't do any sports, if I gave him a rock, he'd still throw overhand. So, basically, throwing overhand has been around as long as people have, and throwing overhand is natural. Throwing balls and rocks and things, that's natural. But throwing 100 throws as hard as you can every fifth day is not natural. When there's too much of that, that's when the injuries happen."

Baseball America once ran a cover of Steve Avery—who starred for the Braves in the early 1990s before injuries hit—with his left arm painted gold. Some young pitchers are like that, born with the precious gift to fire thunderbolts, the separator between ordinary and special. The ordinary arm will never dispense thousands of pitches, and probably never get hurt. But a special arm is vulnerable, pointing its owner to glory, despair, or both.

Sometimes a pitcher does not even know what he possesses. That is how it was for Jarrod Parker the first time he threw a baseball 98 miles an hour. It was a rainy day, the first start of his senior year of high school in Indiana. Parker was already a pro prospect, and when he left the game, he looked at his father for a signal of how hard he had thrown on the scouts' radar guns. His father held up eight fingers.

"And I'm like: 'Eighty-eight? Well, it's cold, whatever, it's early,'" Parker said in 2014, in the Oakland Athletics' clubhouse. "And he was like, 'No—98.' It never feels that much different between throwing a pitch at 88 or 98. You can't see it."

Soon Parker was a top 10 pick in the nation, but his arm just could not withstand its own heat. He had Tommy John surgery in the minors to repair a torn ulnar collateral ligament. After two strong seasons for the A's, including a club-record 19 starts in a row without a loss, Parker tore his UCL again. As he tried to recover, he fractured his elbow. Twice.

How many kids dream of the chance to match up against Verlander in the playoffs, as Parker did twice? Without question, he made it. Yet his career also embodies the sad paradox facing developing pitchers: you've got to throw hard to get signed, but throwing too hard, too often, too young is a recipe for breakdown. As UCL injuries interrupt or end more and more professional careers, the majority of Tommy John surgeries—56.8 percent, according to a 2015 study cited in *The Arm*, Jeff Passan's brilliant exploration of the epidemic—are now performed on teenagers.

In the early 2000s, after the Red Sox fired him as general manager, Dan Duquette ran a youth sports academy in Massachusetts. While children of a previous generation typically played multiple sports, Duquette noticed that they now tended to play just one, because of pressure to make their high school team.

"As these kids specialize, they're trying to throw harder before they're mature enough to throw hard, before their bodies can withstand the stress of it," he says. "And they're throwing on a year-round basis. So the one thing that is clear is that you need a rest and recovery time after the season's over, and if you want to condition your arm for a long season, you should do a long-toss program before getting on the mound when the season starts."

Alan Jaeger, the pitching trainer who advocates long-toss programs, draws a direct correlation between that exercise and velocity. If someone can throw a ball 300 feet, Jaeger says, he can pitch at 86 to 92 miles per hour. At 350 feet, he insists, the corresponding velocity is 93 to 97.

"Think about everybody's arm as a treasure chest, and there's treasure in there based on their size and weight and DNA," Jaeger says. "We don't know what kind of treasure's in there, but we'd like to find out."

For most of baseball history, it was assumed that the foundation of that treasure—the fastball—could not be taught. To a large degree, that is true. How else to explain cases like Matt Bush, who was chosen first overall by San Diego in the 2004 draft, one spot before Verlander?

Bush threw 96 mph in high school, but the Padres took him as a shortstop—and Bush couldn't hit. He floated to the Rays' system and showed promise as a pitcher, but was sent to prison for more than three years after driving under the influence and nearly killing a motorcyclist at spring training in 2012. Three years later, at a work-release program in Jacksonville, he would pitch in the parking lot of a Golden Corral restaurant, using a concrete parking block to push off with his back leg. The ball exploded from his arm, with accuracy. The next year he was a vital member of the Rangers' bullpen, armed with one of the hardest fastballs in the majors.

"Velocity doesn't come from a program," says Roy Silver, a former minor leaguer who worked with Bush in that parking lot and signed him for Texas. "If you're an atheist, it comes from your ancestors; if you're not an atheist, it's God-given. This guy just spent four years in jail and he's throwing 100 in a big league game? Are you serious? These are freaks of nature."

One of the game's most dominant closers, Billy Wagner, threw 100 mph with the wrong hand. Wagner was always small, and when he was five years old, he was roughhousing with a bigger kid named Chip, tossing around a hat like a football. ("We didn't have a football," he explains. "We had a hat.") Chip fell on Wagner and broke his right elbow. Wagner threw left-handed while wearing a cast, then got the cast off and broke his right elbow again when he fell off the monkey bars. He kept throwing as a lefty. Things worked out.

"I can't do anything left-handed other than throw," Wagner says. "I can't hold a pencil. I almost poke myself in my eye with my left hand if I'm trying to eat. It's crazy. For God to bless me and say, 'Hey, you're gonna throw 100 miles an hour left-handed'—it's just not something that happens every day."

The majors' fastest pitcher, Aroldis Chapman, started on his path without even trying. As a boy in Cuba, he did not burn to throw fastballs for a living.

"I wasn't into baseball, it wasn't a big deal for me," he says, through an interpreter. "I was a first baseman, just kind of messing around a little bit. This coach decided to put me on the mound. They're all looking for pitchers, and one day he goes, 'Hey, Chapman, give it a try!' I wasn't really feeling it, but I was out there and I started throwing hard.

"The rest is history. No more first baseman."

In 2010, as a 22-year-old rookie for the Reds, Chapman threw a pitch 105 miles per hour, the highest ever recorded. He would soon have a tattoo of a flaming baseball with the digits "105" inked on the inside of his left wrist. In 2016, a month after recovering from a blown save to win Game 7 of the World Series for the Cubs, Chapman signed with the Yankees for five years and $86 million. He is, in the truest sense of the word, a trailblazer.

"One hundred miles per hour is the new benchmark," says Tom House, the former pitcher and coach who founded the National Pitching Association. "I think in the next five to eight years, most pitchers, to sign a pro contract, are going to have to show 97, 98, and touch 101, 102. That's where the research is going."

Research is the buzzword around Driveline's modest headquarters at an industrial park near Sea-Tac Airport. Hundreds of pitchers flock there every year, striding with purpose around the parking lots, holding kettlebell weights over their heads, or wiggling long sticks—called shoulder tubes, for warm-up and recovery—in front of their chests. Kyle Boddy founded Driveline in 2008, and takes the title of research and development director. He pitched in high school, but his arm always hurt and no one could tell him why. He worked as a software developer at Microsoft but was fascinated by the science of pitching, and probing the secrets to arm health and potential.

By now he has several units at his complex, including one to store Driveline's inventory of brightly colored PlyoCare balls, weighing 3.5 ounces to 4.4 pounds. (Standard baseballs are 5 to 5.25 ounces.) In another unit, while one pitcher works in a screened-in bullpen, others fire the weighted balls, from close range, at padded walls. Still another unit acts as a laboratory, with 12 high-speed cameras surrounding a mound, capturing biomechanical data while a cluster of computers tracks every movement in intimate detail.

Boddy's data points a clear direction for the game.

"We're reaching a point where the maximum velocity is around that 110 mile per hour mark, like 107," he says. "I just don't think people are going to throw much harder than that. But what you're going to see, and what we are seeing evidence of, is that there's this curve that gets shifted to the right where everybody throws 95 now. There's a stabilization. It creates a profile of a pitcher, like: 'This is what we want.' Front offices are so advanced, they know what will succeed at the big-league level."

Major league hitters are so advanced that they can handle a steady stream of fastballs. In fact, as pitchers throw harder, they also throw fewer total fastballs—a better fastball makes for better off-speed stuff, because the hitter must start his swing sooner and therefore has less time to react. But with an ever-growing pool of hard-throwing amateurs, the soft-tosser with guile is being naturally selected out of the game. Picture pro baseball as a carnival attraction with a sign at the entrance: YOU MUST THROW THIS HARD TO RIDE THIS RIDE.

"How many prospects do you see coming up that throw 88, 90?" says Trevor Bauer, the Indians right-hander and the first established major leaguer to train at Driveline. "Watch the Futures Game—there's not a single guy throwing under 94, and most guys are sitting 96 to 98. Sure, it's the Futures Game and you have one inning and all that adrenaline, but watch All-Star Games from the last five or 10 years in the big leagues. It's ridiculous. Average velo rises every single year. Doesn't seem to have any sort of limit on it right now."

Bauer threw 78 miles an hour as a freshman in high school in Southern California. He quickly grew tired of seeing harder throwers, with worse results, get more opportunities. Before his sophomore year, at the urging of a pitching coach, Jim Wagner, Bauer visited Ron Wolforth, who runs the Texas Baseball Ranch in Montgomery, Texas, and learned how to train to throw hard. Bauer went on to dominate college hitters at UCLA and was drafted third overall by Arizona in 2011. His journey to the majors made him a realist about breaking through the pro gates.

"It took a long time for people to realize that velo is king, at least in the draft process, amateur ball, and up into minor league ball," Bauer says. "Once you get to the big leagues and you're here, getting outs is king. But up until the big leagues, velo is king, and in the minor leagues, guys that have poor results but throw really hard get a lot more opportunities than guys that have really good results but throw 86, 88.

"A lot's changed in five or 10 years. You get to college and college coaches say, 'Hey, locate this, throw a changeup, let's get people out,' and you're like, 'OK, that's what it takes to be successful at this level'—but you didn't realize, because the information wasn't sitting there telling you, 'Hey, you're not going to get drafted unless you do *this*.'"

Throw hard, he means.

"So it's just taken a while for the research to be done, and for methods to be developed to train velocity reliably, and then for that information to be spread through enough high-level people that people start trusting it."

Now, some of the more progressive college programs, like Vanderbilt and Oregon State, use Driveline training techniques for their pitchers—weighted balls, long toss, and so on. More than 10 MLB teams have visited Boddy's complex in Washington, and major leaguers regularly consult with him, Wolforth, and others to rebuild their fastballs and learn to train with less soreness.

The coaches are learning, too, as the game rapidly evolves. Wolforth started his business in 1993, and a decade ago, he said, teams viewed him as a pariah. He could help pupils throw hard enough to get signed, but mainly built pitchers who could win teddy bears at carnivals, not actual games. In that case, he thought, what was the point?

"There was real criticism: you get a Wolforth guy in 2008, he's going to throw the ball through a car wash and not get it wet, but I'm not sure he could throw it over the white thing," Wolforth says. "And now, when we send a guy up, not only can they throw it over the white thing and throw it hard, but they can also recover, and their pitchability goes very high. We have shifted our emphasis and broadened it."

Today, Wolforth says, he spends more time teaching mechanics, secondary pitches, and command than teaching velocity. He consults with about half of the major league teams and has helped rejuvenate the careers of several wayward pitchers, including at least two former Cy Young Award winners.

When pitchers suddenly throw harder, Wolforth says, they must also learn the right way to decelerate in their follow-through; using Volkswagen Beetle brakes on a Maserati, he said, invites disaster. Wolforth believes that with a comprehensive, individualized program, all pitchers can find their maximum velocity. But that is only part of what they need.

"The radar gun doesn't tell us if they can pitch or not," Wolforth says. "It's a very simple, snap way to tell something, and sometimes it's not the best way, but people like it because it immediately gives you feedback and it's comparable."

With so many hard throwers, Tom House believes, the traditional starting pitcher, as we have long known the role, will soon cease to exist. Future staffs, he predicted, will be made up of 12 pitchers throwing three times a week, with nobody working more than 45 pitches per game or going more than once through the lineup.

To some extent, this is already happening. Only 15 pitchers worked 200 innings in 2017, matching the previous year for the fewest ever in a nonstrike season. The World Series teams got there without asking much of any individual pitcher—the Astros' innings leader (Mike Fiers, with 153⅓) did not even meet the minimum standard to qualify for the ERA title, and the Dodgers had just 12 games all season in which their starter threw 100 pitches, the fewest in the majors.

In 1976—in a 24-team league—47 pitchers reached 215 innings. By 2017, that number had fallen to zero across the game's 30 teams. With such an inventory of pitchers who can throw hard for short bursts, teams now build five- or six-inning starters and let relievers handle the rest.

"When I first got called up, the pitchers they were going with were guys that were 88 to 92, with sink and cut—veteran guys that could spot it up," says Brian McCann, the longtime catcher. "Over time, we've realized that the prospect in Triple-A that throws hard is a way more uncomfortable at-bat than the other guy."

The Reds' Joey Votto, who combines slugging and patience better than any modern hitter, says the velocity spike has led to more swings and misses, but also to more mistakes cruising down the middle, begging to be crushed for home runs. Max Scherzer, a dominant right-hander for the Nationals, says hitters know they can't string together singles against such overpowering stuff, so they tailor their swings to hit fly balls. They drive more misplaced fastballs into the seats and accept more strikeouts as a trade-off.

In 2002, the average fastball was 89 miles an hour. In 2017, it was 92.8 mph. With velocity, home runs, and strikeouts rising, pitchers' workloads are falling. It is not a healthy trend.

"These guys only know one thing, because organizations are telling them one thing: give me everything you have and we'll take care of the rest," John Smoltz says. "It's taking, on average, 25 pitchers per year per club, and no one's paying attention to it because their theory is, 'There's just so many arms, we don't need to.'

"I'm not stuck in the old school, but I'm saying, 'Whoa, let's slow the roll a little bit.' I maintain that in three to five years, this game will crash. If I'm right, the pitching cannot keep up, and/or fans are gonna go, 'Uncle, I can't take it, it's 10 pitchers a game, I can't take the pitching changes, I can't take the length of the games.' They're trying everything they can to speed up the game, but we're not gaining any speed-up time."

In 2017, batters struck out nearly 3,000 more times, while hitting roughly 2,000 more homers, than they had in 2014, the year that ended with Madison Bumgarner's flurry of fastballs to Salvador Perez. That means a lot fewer balls in play, and a lot more standing around. The average time of a nine-inning game reached three hours, five minutes in 2017, an all-time high—and the average fastball velocity rose for the seventh year in a row.

Those two trends are joined tightly together, another paradox in a sport full of them: when the fastball speeds up, the game slows down.

THE
CURVEBALL

A Karate Chop with a Ball

Mike Montgomery's throwing program for the 2016 season began just before New Year's on Via Saludo in Valencia, California. He had no reason to believe that his work would stretch until November, to Ontario Street in Cleveland, where he would throw the most anticipated pitch in the history of the Chicago Cubs.

It was Montgomery's ninth professional season. He had reached the majors only a few months earlier, in June 2015 with the Seattle Mariners. He threw two shutouts for them but was otherwise ordinary. When his agent floated the idea of leaving for a $2 million contract in Japan, the Mariners seemed content to let him go. Their nonchalance bothered and inspired Montgomery. He would show them he was better than they thought.

First, though, Montgomery needed a catcher. He asked his mom, Jeannette, a former third baseman for the softball team at Cal Poly Pomona. She strapped on catcher's gear, caught her son's best fastball, and barked, "Is that all you got?" Montgomery, unnerved, tried other stuff, too.

"I would throw her my curveball and she would catch it," he said. "And I'm like, 'Man, maybe this pitch ain't that good then, if my mom can catch it.'"

As a boy, Montgomery had been drawn more to basketball than baseball. But his father, David, rooted for the Atlanta Braves, and he watched their games on TBS at the family's home in California. Montgomery liked the Braves' aces, Greg Maddux, Tom Glavine, and

John Smoltz. He was tall and lanky and left-handed—the only lefty in the family—and when spring came around, coaches told him to pitch. As a sophomore at Hart High School, he made the varsity with a fastball, a changeup, and a palmball that acted as a curveball; Montgomery used the high seams like training wheels, the ball rolling off his fingers for a slow, loopy break.

The Kansas City Royals signed Montgomery as the thirty-sixth pick in the 2008 draft, and his palmball/curve did not come with him. The pro balls were stitched tighter, the seams lower, and the old breaking ball barely moved. In time Montgomery would understand that pro balls—including the even harder version in the majors—were better for breaking balls, because they were not as loose and could thus spin more. With the Royals, though, his curveball was hopeless. The fastball/change combination got Montgomery to Triple-A, but his attempts at a curveball were laughable. Once, in Omaha, it bounced on the grass and ricocheted off the hitter's elbow.

Without a reliable third pitch, Montgomery lost his status as a top prospect. But when the Royals traded him to Tampa Bay before the 2013 season, Montgomery had a few things that would help him: a gregarious personality, an inquisitive mind, and no fear of throwing a lot. In 2014 he befriended a teammate, Nate Karns, and played catch with him every day. Karns showed Montgomery his grip for a spike curveball, in which the index finger is raised and curled, with the tip resting lightly on the leather; the middle finger and thumb do all the work. Montgomery modified Karns's grip, removing the index finger completely when he let the curveball go, and worked on the pitch relentlessly. A coach, Neil Allen, let Montgomery throw 40 or so curveballs in a row in the bullpen, just to get the feel.

With the curveball, feel is big. The fastball, like nearly every other pitch, is thrown with backspin. The curveball is thrown with topspin, the seams whooshing downward as the pitch tumbles to Earth. Only certain pitchers have the loose, easy wrist action to make a ball act that way.

"Being able to spin the ball, either you can or you can't," says Nolan Ryan, who may have thrown the most devastating curve of all. "If they don't really have that ability—yeah, you can teach them a curveball, but will it be an exceptional pitch? I don't think so. I think people either have that ability or they don't."

A quick wrist is critical to disguising the pitch. Since a curveball is thrown so differently on release—with the pitcher's hand facing his head, not facing the batter—it's easy to telegraph. If a hitter sees that hand position, he knows he'll get a curveball. He also knows it's coming if the ball pops up before plummeting down. The curveballs that go *out* and then tumble down, after an imperceptible wrist turn, work best.

"The way many of us were taught to throw the curveball was to mentally think fastball out of the hand," said Bryan Price, the longtime pitching coach and manager. "Even as you get up into what we call your power position, as your hand comes forward, it's in fastball position first, and then accelerates into curveball position. That gives you hand speed through the pitch and gives you a tighter spin, tighter break, and more deception."

Montgomery often struggled to control his curveball, but he always had the hand to impart spin. Andrew Friedman, who traded for Montgomery with the Rays, noticed the exceptional spin rate, and suggested he use it more. Montgomery was still not sure; he knew the curve was a separator—when he pitched well, that was usually the reason—but he could not trust it.

The Rays gave up on Montgomery before the 2015 season, his fifth at Class AAA. He would make 99 starts at that level, more than the combined total of Jon Lester, John Lackey, and Kyle Hendricks, three of the starters on the 2016 Cubs. But Montgomery used his apprenticeship wisely, as a laboratory for new grips and angles of release, trying to unlock the mystery of the pitch he knew he needed.

By the start of the 2016 season, he was ready, and his curveball was the difference. But he still needed more convincing.

"Monty, you have a swing-and-miss breaking ball," said Mel Stottlemyre Jr., the Mariners' pitching coach, after a side session in spring training. Montgomery insisted that his changeup was better and his curve was too erratic. "No, no, no," Stottlemyre continued. "Believe me, I've been around this game a long time—I'm telling you, your breaking ball is that good."

Montgomery was emboldened. On opening day in Texas, in relief of Felix Hernandez, he struck out the first batter he faced, Delino DeShields, on a wicked curveball. DeShields stared back at the mound, puzzled by a pitch he had not seen from Montgomery before. After another strikeout, Montgomery faced Prince Fielder, the dangerous left-handed slugger. He was nervous but confident. He aimed the curveball at Fielder's front shoulder and it dropped over the middle for a called third strike.

On the bench after the inning, teammates bombarded Montgomery with praise. He stopped doubting his curveball after that.

"Man, my curveball is good," he thought, "and I don't know if I even understand that it can get better."

The Cubs understood. They traded for Montgomery in July, encouraged by the curveball. All his years of tinkering were paying off: the data showed that Montgomery's curveball was spinning about 100 rpm more than it had the year before. Chris Bosio, the Cubs' pitching coach, echoed Friedman and Stottlemyre: that's your best pitch, so use it more. Montgomery would double his curveball usage, from 12 percent in 2015 to 24 percent in 2016. By the end of that regular season, opponents had a .103 average off Montgomery's curve in his career.

As the summer went on, Montgomery kept buying in. The statistics guided him. After every game, on his phone or in the Cubs' video room, Montgomery logged on to BrooksBaseball.net to learn how many inches, vertically and horizontally, his curve had moved, comparing his results to those of other lefties. He remembered how certain pitches had felt coming off his hand, and matched them up with the data. The numbers comforted Montgomery. They told him never to worry, even when his best pitch deserted him as he prepared for the biggest moment of his life.

Montgomery was not part of the plan for Game 7 of the World Series against the Indians. Joe Maddon, the Cubs' manager, wanted to use three pitchers—Hendricks, Lester, and Aroldis Chapman—to secure the team's first championship in 108 years. He tried, but all of them wobbled. Montgomery warmed up in the third inning, then again in the fifth, the ninth, and the eleventh. He had already pitched four games in the World Series, and he did not have much left. Not only was he tired—much like Ralph Terry in 1960—he was bouncing his curveball everywhere. He did not throw a single strike with it in warm-ups.

In the bottom of the tenth, after the Cubs had taken a two-run lead in the top of the inning, Maddon called for the right-handed Carl Edwards Jr. to close it out. With two outs and no base runners, Edwards allowed a walk to Brandon Guyer and a run-scoring single to Rajai Davis.

The Indians had come to the eighth spot in their order, where Coco Crisp had started and gotten two hits. But with one out in the top of the ninth inning of Game 7, the Cubs' Jason Heyward had stolen second and taken third on a throwing error by the catcher. Fearing a sacrifice fly, Indians manager Terry Francona removed Crisp from right field and replaced him with Michael Martinez, who had a much stronger throwing arm.

The threat passed. But with the Indians down to their last out of the season, it was Martinez coming to bat, with no position players behind him on the bench. Martinez had a .197 average and just six home runs in almost 600 career trips to the plate. Of all the position players in the last quarter century with as many plate appearances as Martinez, none had a lower OPS—on-base plus slugging percentage— than his .507.

Martinez was a major league hitter in name only, having gone almost seven weeks since his last hit. And his last hit *off a curveball*? That had come more than a year earlier, on September 6, 2015. In 11 at-bats since that had ended with a curveball, Martinez had struck out nine times.

Maddon did not know this specific information, offhand, as Martinez came to bat in the tenth. But he did know that Martinez would have no chance to hit a Mike Montgomery curveball. For Montgomery, the Cubs had distilled their scouting reports on the Indians' hitters this way: Can he, or can he not, hit your curveball? Martinez most certainly could not. Maddon knew that pitch could win the World Series.

"I love Montgomery's curveball in that moment," Maddon said later, and Montgomery loved it, too.

Yes, he had lost the pitch in the bullpen. But the positive

reinforcement that had washed over him all season, on the field and the computer screen, calmed any nerves he might have felt. He did not stop to imagine the scene back in Chicago, outside Wrigley Field, where throngs of revelers anxiously awaited that blessed "F" on the score strip of the famous red marquee. The final score would stay 8–7, Montgomery believed, if he simply threw that curveball, the fully formed version of the pitch he had thrown to his mom back home.

She was in the stands now, with Miguel Montero catching. Montero came to the mound and Montgomery asked, "What's the plan?" They both knew the answer, but Montero said, "Let me think about it," and trotted back to the plate. Later, Montero would tell his pitcher that of course he had no doubt: curveballs all the way. He just didn't want Montgomery to dwell on it.

But Montgomery already was, in a good way.

"I wasn't thinking about the World Series, really," he says. "I was just thinking about me being able to throw a strike in that moment. That's all I cared about. I knew all I had to do was throw strikes and just take my chances that that was gonna work. Obviously, I'm not gonna walk the guy; that's not gonna help us. If he hits a homer? I didn't even think about it. I just said: 'I'll just throw a strike and take my chances.' I have confidence as long as I throw it, especially to that batter, to Michael Martinez, that was the game plan: to throw a curveball in the zone for a strike. And sure enough I throw a perfect first-pitch curveball right in there. He took it for a strike, and at that point I knew it was over, because that was the biggest hurdle, throwing that first one for a strike in that situation. And from there on I was in control."

Only seven other pitchers had thrown a pitch that could win or lose the World Series for either team. Now Montgomery's first had been perfect. He had the right matchup, and he had the right weapon.

For the final curveball, the one that slayed the Billy Goat and brought a catharsis to millions, Montgomery set his sights on the middle of the batter's box on the first base side. Nearly seven months before, Prince Fielder had stood there in Texas and watched the pitch buckle into the zone for strike three. This one was not as sharp, a little lazier, but still low and tight enough that a hitter like Martinez could do nothing with it. He tapped it softly to third, where Kris Bryant scrambled in to scoop it. Bryant lost his footing but still fired across the infield to Anthony Rizzo, who made the catch and raised his arms in triumph. Rizzo stuffed the ball in his back left pocket and romped toward Bryant. Montgomery flung his glove in the air and embraced them. He got the glove back but never touched the ball again.

"When we had our parade, a couple of us went up to [Rizzo] and said, 'You know, that's supposed to be my ball, that was my first-ever save,'" Montgomery said. "But he had it because he presented it to Ricketts at that time. I'm OK with that."

Tom Ricketts owns the Cubs, so he got the curse-breaking curveball. Montgomery got a ring, a memory, and the certainty that his job is the best there is.

"I enjoy, obviously, being competitive—but I also enjoy just the creativity you can have being a pitcher, because you're the one in control," Montgomery said. "You're the one with the paintbrush. Everyone else is reacting to what you do."

The reaction to Montgomery's curveball was overwhelming joy, bottled up since 1908. By then the pitch had been around just 45 years, from its beginnings on a craggy beach in Brooklyn. Or so the legend goes.

———

If you had to group pitches into two categories, you would choose "fastball" and "other." The "other" makes pitching interesting. If the ball went straight every time, pitchers would essentially be functionaries, existing merely to serve the hitters. Long ago, that is just what they were, as the name implies. Think of pitching horseshoes: you're making an underhand toss to a specific area. That was pitching for much of the 1800s. For 20 years—1867 through 1886—batters could specify whether they wanted the pitch high or low. The poor pitcher was forced to comply.

Baseball might have continued as a test of hitting, running, and fielding skills had pitchers not discovered their potential for overwhelming influence. What if they could make the pitch behave differently? Long before cameras and websites could classify every pitch into a type, many of the offerings intended to deceive a hitter—in-shoots and out-shoots, in-curves and out-curves and drops, in the old parlance—were largely known as curveballs. The "other" was, simply, everything that wasn't a fastball.

In researching the history of curveballs at the Hall of Fame Library in Cooperstown, I was struck by how many people claimed to be the inventor. In 1937 *The New York Times* published an obituary of a man named Billy Dee of Chester, New Jersey, who was said to have invented the curveball in 1881. Dee threw a baseball with frayed seams and, intrigued by its movement, said he practiced and practiced until "I soon was able to loop the old apple without the benefit of the damaged seam." Sounds impressive—but what's this? A 1948 *Times* obituary of one George McConnell of Los Angeles, "an old-time Indian fighter" who "decided that the 'English' being put on billiard balls could be used with a baseball." That was in 1878.

There are many more such stories in the files and the history books at Cooperstown. Fred Goldsmith has a case, like James Creighton and Phonie Martin and Alvah Hovey and more. There's even a hoary old Ivy League debate from the 1870s: Did Charles Avery of Yale curve first, or Joseph Mann of Princeton?

Peter Morris untangles it all in *A Game of Inches,* quoting a letter from Mann to the *Times* in 1900 that sums it up neatly: "As long as baseball has been played and baseballs have had seams with which to catch the air, curve balls have been thrown."

Mann goes on to assert that, in spite of this, no one thought to use those curving balls for pitching until he did so in 1874. Then again, Mann admits he was inspired by watching Candy Cummings one day at Princeton. Mann said Cummings's catcher told him he could make the ball curve, though it did not do so that day.

Confused yet? The plaque in the Hall of Fame gallery for W. A. "Candy" Cummings boldly settles things in seven gilded words: "Pitched first curve ball in baseball history." The plaque dates this discovery to 1867, when Cummings was the amateur ace of the Brooklyn Stars. History should always be so easy.

The Cummings backstory is so indelible, so rich in imagery, that if it's not true . . . well, it should be. It has never been debunked and would be impossible to do so. Cummings is practically a charter member of the Hall, going in with the fourth class of inductees in 1939. His story links the discovery of the curveball to the curiosity of a 14-year-old boy on a beach in Brooklyn. What could be more American than that?

Here is how Cummings described it for *Baseball Magazine* in 1908:

> In the summer of 1863 a number of boys and myself were amusing ourselves by throwing clam shells (the hard shell variety) and watching them sail along through the air, turning now to the right, and now to the left. We became interested in the mechanics of it and experimented for an hour or more. All of a sudden it came to me that it would be a good joke on the boys if I could make a baseball curve the same way.

Cummings was born in 1848 in Ware, Massachusetts, and various accounts say that he played the old Massachusetts game before moving to Brooklyn. Cummings himself did not mention this in his retelling of the curveball's origin story, but to Morris, it was a significant detail. In the 1850s, pitchers in Massachusetts were permitted to throw overhand, which made curveballs easier to throw.

"He had probably seen rudimentary curves thrown as a youngster in Massachusetts, and when he moved to Brooklyn and began playing the 'New York game,' the delivery restrictions made the pitch seem impossible," Morris wrote. "Yet the example of throwing clamshells made him think that it might be possible, and his arm strength and relentless practice enabled him to realize his ambition."

Cummings emphasized two points: his solitary persistence in perfecting the pitch despite ridicule from his friends, and the physical toll imposed by the delivery restrictions of the day. Pitchers then worked in a four-by-six-foot box, and could not lift either foot off the ground until the ball was released.

"The arm also had to be kept near the side and the delivery was made with a perpendicular swing," Cummings said, in an undated interview published after his career. "By following these instructions it was a hard strain, as the wrist and the second finger had to do all the work. I snapped the ball away from me like a whip and this caused my wrist bone to get out of place quite often. I was compelled to wear a supporter on my wrist all one season on account of this strain."

Cummings left Brooklyn for a boarding school in Fulton, New York, in 1864. He tinkered with his curveball there—"My boy friends began to laugh at me, and to throw jokes at my theory of making a ball go sideways"—and joined the Star Juniors, an amateur team in Brooklyn. From there he was recruited to the Excelsior Club as a junior member, in both age and size: he would grow to be 5 foot 9, but his weight topped out at 120 pounds.

In the curveball, though, Cummings found an equalizer. He showed that pitchers of all sizes could rely on movement and deception—not simply on power—to succeed. Soon, the notion would be ingrained as baseball fact that a pitcher with dominant stuff could humble even the brawniest hitter. Cummings began to prove this in 1867, with the Excelsiors in a game at Harvard.

"A surge of joy flooded over me that I shall never forget," he wrote in the *Baseball Magazine* piece. "I felt like shouting out that I had made a ball curve; I wanted to tell everybody; it was too good to keep to myself. But I said not a word, and saw many a batter at that game throw down his stick in disgust. Every time I was successful I could scarcely keep from dancing from pure joy. The secret was mine."

The movement could be very erratic, Cummings conceded, but in time he learned to control it, and to manipulate the umpires. When the ball started at a hitter's body, and caused him to jump before bending into the strike zone, the umpire called it a ball. Cummings adjusted by starting the pitch in the middle so he could get strikes, even though the movement carried it away.

"When it got to the batter it was too far out," he said. "Then there would be a clash between the umpire and the batter."

By age 23 Cummings was a pitcher for the New York Mutuals of the National Association. The pitching was done from 45 feet away, in that box, with a sidearm motion—and the numbers were similarly unrecognizable today. Cummings started 55 of the Mutuals' 56 games, working 497 innings and giving up 604 hits, with a 33–20 record and a 3.01 earned run average. When the National League began in 1876, Cummings pitched for the Hartford Dark Blues and went 16–8. He went 5–14 for the Cincinnati Reds in 1877, his final season.

A curious contemporary, Bobby Mathews, would go on to have more success. Mathews was even shorter than Cummings—just

5 foot 5—and as their careers overlapped in the National Association, Mathews was one of the few who could mimic Cummings's sidearm curve. Generations of pitchers would follow Mathews's example: see something interesting, study it, and make it their own.

"He watched Cummings' hands carefully, noting how he held the ball and how he let it go, and after a few weeks' careful practice in the same way could see the curve in his own delivery," explained an 1883 article from *The Philadelphia Press,* unearthed by Morris. "Then he began to use it in matches, striking men out in a way that no one but Cummings had ever done before, and in a short time he was known as one of the most effective pitchers in the field."

That was the first of three consecutive 30-win seasons by Mathews for the Philadelphia Athletics of the American Association. He did not make the Hall of Fame, but he followed Cummings as the curveball's most prominent practitioner, carrying the pitch through the sidearm era and helping to establish it as fundamental to the game.

Assuming that you believed in it at all.

———————

For decades after Cummings's last pitch, many people doubted the very notion that a ball could curve. It was a staple of baseball debate that the curveball just might be an optical illusion. A favorite exercise for skeptics was to challenge a pitcher to prove his powers by bending a ball around a series of poles. This happened a lot.

"The majority of college professors really believe that the curve ball was as impossible as the transmutation of gold from potato skins," said a man named Ben Dodson, in the *Syracuse Herald* in 1910.

Dodson said he witnessed a demonstration at Harvard by Charles "Old Hoss" Radbourn, probably in the 1880s. Radbourn—whose "pitching deity; dapper gent" persona would one day make him a Twitter sensation—was an early hero of the National League. In 1884, for the Providence Grays, he was 59–12 with a 1.38 ERA and 73 complete games. The professors, safe to say, had a lot of misplaced confidence when they arranged their poles and dared Radbourn to throw curves to his catcher, Barney Gilligan.

"Radbourn, standing to the right of the pole arcade, started what appeared to be a perfectly straight delivery," Dodson said. "It turned with a beautiful inward bend and passed behind the pole just in front of Gilligan—an inshoot, and a corker. He repeated this several times. Then, standing inside the upper part of the pole-zone, he threw out-shoots that went forty feet dead on a line, and swung out of the arcade."

Dodson went on to describe Radbourn's "drop balls," though not all of these pitches were curves, as we think of them today. Radbourn threw a wide array of pitches that would now be classified as curveballs, changeups, sinkers, screwballs, and so on. That day at Harvard, his charge was to prove that something besides a fastball really did exist, and Dodson, for one, considered the matter closed.

"It was a wonderful demonstration and settled the argument about curve pitching forever," he said. "And yet—because they never thought about publicity in those days—not a reporter was at hand, and the story lives only in the memories of those who saw it done."

What a pity. For some, the matter was still debatable midway into the next century, as Carl Erskine recalls. As a minor leaguer, Erskine had gotten a tip from a rival manager, Jack Onslow, who told him he was telegraphing his curveball by the way he tucked it into his hand. In Cuba before the 1948 season, Erskine taught himself a new grip and trusted it one day to preserve a shutout after a leadoff triple in the ninth. The circumstances mattered, because the team had a standing bonus of $25 for a shutout.

"My inclination was, 'Oh boy, I gotta go back to my old curve, I gotta get this shutout,'" Erskine says. "So I had a little meeting on the mound with myself, tossed the rosin bag: 'You made a commitment that you weren't gonna go back to the old curve; stick to it'—and I got the side out without that run scoring. From then on, I had good confidence in that, and the rest is history."

Erskine's history included five pennants with the Dodgers and one narrowly missed brush with infamy. On October 3, 1951, he was warming up in the bottom of the ninth inning at the Polo Grounds alongside Ralph Branca, with the pennant at stake against the Giants. Manager Charlie Dressen called to the bullpen and asked a coach, Clyde Sukeforth, which pitcher looked better.

Dressen liked the curveball; he would say of the slider, disdainfully:

"They slide in and slide out of the ballpark." But when Sukeforth reported that Erskine was bouncing his curve, Dressen chose Branca.

"People say, 'Carl, what was your best pitch in your 12 major league seasons?'" Erskine says with a laugh. "I say it was a curveball I bounced in the bullpen at the Polo Grounds. It could have been me."

Instead it was Branca who threw the fateful fastball that Bobby Thomson lashed into the left field seats—the celebrated "Shot Heard 'Round the World" that gave the Giants the pennant. We'll never know how Thomson might have handled Erskine's curve, but the Giants were stealing signs, so he might have hit that, too.

In any case, it was around this time that Erskine's pitch all but buried the tired debate about its veracity.

"TV came in around the late '40s and there was a show early on, Burgess Meredith was the emcee, called *Omnibus*," Erskine explains. "They sent a crew to Ebbets Field one day and they asked for me and Preacher Roe, who was a left-hander who threw an overhand curve, to come out early. The purpose was to film us throwing a curveball, and to prove or disprove whether a ball actually curved.

"So we got ready to go out there, and I took a new baseball and scuffed it up a little bit in order to make sure I had good bite on it. So I warmed up and the director of this film stood behind me and said, 'I'm not a baseball guy, so I don't know what I'm looking for here. Could you throw me a couple of curveballs so I could see what it is I'm trying to film?' So with this scuffed-up baseball I threw an overhand curveball and it broke big. And this director says, 'My God, is there any doubt?' So he was a novice at seeing pitches, but the first one he saw: 'Holy cow! There's no question!'

"So they put that show on, Preacher threw from the left side and I threw of course from the right side, and then they used this dotted line that was superimposed somehow on the film. And you could basically say, well, there is no doubt: yes, a rotating pitch can break out of a straight line and be a curveball."

As Erskine described the mechanics of the curveball, he spoke of using the middle finger to apply pressure to the ball, lead the wrist, and help generate tight rotation. The index finger is almost in the way, he said, which reminded him of a character he met in the "3-I" League (Iowa, Indiana, Illinois), where he played in 1946 and '47.

"One of the greatest all-time pitchers that I met when I was in the minor leagues was Mordecai Brown," Erskine says. "He lived in the Terre Haute House—that was the Phillies' affiliate—and he would come down and talk to us in the lobby, show us his hand, where he had this farm accident and it took away not only his first finger of his right hand, it even took the knuckle. So he had a hand that had three fingers—naturally, his nickname was 'Three Finger' Brown—and it gave him the ultimate best use of that second finger for the curveball, because the first finger was out of the way completely.

"He was a real gentleman, always dressed in a shirt and tie. Naturally, an old gentleman by that time, and we were just kids in the minors. But we were fascinated to talk to him, and he was anxious to show us his hand, tell us how he learned to pitch without the first finger, or even the first knuckle. It gave him the ultimate advantage if you want to throw that curveball with lots of tight rotation. The second finger became his first finger. So he must have had a wicked curveball."

Indeed he did, and his story captivated fans. Mordecai was five years old, helping his brother cut food for horses at their uncle's farm in Nyesville, Indiana, when his right hand slipped into the feed chopper. The accident mangled every finger, and a doctor amputated the index finger below the second joint. A few weeks later, his hand still in a splint, Mordecai and his sister were playing with a pet rabbit, trying to make it swim in a tub. Mordecai lost his balance and smashed his hand on the bottom of the tub, breaking six bones.

It was a brutally painful, almost slapstick way to form the perfectly gnarled curveball hand. Nobody could mimic Brown's curveball.

"When Brown holds the ball in that chicken's foot of a hand and throws it out over that stump, the sphere is given a peculiar twist," wrote the Chicago *Inter Ocean* in 1910, at the height of Brown's fame with the Cubs. "It behaves something like a spitter. It goes singing up to the plate, straight as a drawn string, then just as the batter strikes at it, it darts down like a snake to its hole."

On his way to the Hall of Fame, Brown went 49–15 with a 1.44 ERA across the 1907 and 1908 seasons. He won all three of his World Series games in those years, allowing no earned runs over 20 innings to lead the Cubs to consecutive championships. He died in 1948, shortly after he would have met the young Carl Erskine. In 2003, Bill James and

Rob Neyer ranked Brown's curveball as the second best in the history of the game. The best, they said, belonged to Sandy Koufax.

———

In January 2014, I was chairman of the New York chapter of the Baseball Writers' Association of America. In this role, I emceed and helped plan our annual awards dinner. Clayton Kershaw and Max Scherzer would be receiving their Cy Young Awards, and I sat them on the dais on either side of Koufax, who was there to present for Kershaw. I thought all three would enjoy one another's company. Sitting just to Kershaw's right, by the lectern, I noticed throughout the evening how engaged the young pitchers were with Koufax, how easily they chatted. For Scherzer, it was a master class on the curveball.

"My God, could you imagine a better person in life to ever talk to about throwing a curveball?" Scherzer told me a year later, at spring training with the Nationals in Viera, Florida. "I literally sat there on my iPhone just writing down notes: 'How are you doing this, what do you do on that?' There's definitely some principles I still think about from that conversation, what you want to do with the shape, how you want to spin the ball, the mental approach to it. Those were really good conversations."

Scherzer had learned the curveball midway through the 2012 season with the Detroit Tigers. His pitching coach, Jeff Jones, drilled Scherzer on throwing his signature slider slower and slower and slower until it morphed into a curve, which is just what Scherzer needed against left-handers. His power slider broke toward them, dropping into their "nitro zone," he said, with speed too close to his fastball. A slower option, with more of a vertical drop, could be effective against hitters from both sides.

This is a big reason many organizations implore their prospects to master the curve before the slider. It is a pitch that no hitter—even perhaps the greatest ever—wants to see.

"Ted Williams used to call once a month and we would chat about the team," said Dan Duquette, the former Red Sox general manager. "So the day after I traded Aaron Sele, Ted calls me up. He goes, 'OK, hot shot, why in the hell are you trading the best curveballer in the

American League?' I said, 'Well, he didn't want to pitch in Boston.' He goes, 'I don't give a damn, he's got a good curveball! Let me tell you something: that curveball can get out a left-hand hitter just as well as it can get out a right-hand hitter! Now don't be trading those guys when you get 'em!'"

Williams spent his whole career with the Red Sox and never faced Koufax, a career Dodger. Their primes did not overlap, anyway. In 1960, when Williams retired, Koufax went 8–13 with a 3.91 ERA and 100 walks. It was his sixth season of mediocrity. The next six would be some of the greatest in the history of baseball.

In those six seasons, Koufax went 129–47 with a 2.19 ERA. He won five ERA titles, four strikeout titles, three Cy Young Awards, and two World Series MVP awards. He was unquestionably aided by the tall mound at Dodger Stadium, where his career ERA was 1.37, two runs better than it was everywhere else. He reigned from that perch till his very last strikeout in the 1966 World Series.

"I go up there and Koufax throws me the first high fastball: *shooo*," the hitter, Hall of Fame pitcher Jim Palmer, says now. "Then he throws me the curveball and it looks the same—*the same!*—and John Roseboro catches it on the ground. And I'm going, *this* is Sandy Koufax."

Palmer's at-bat happened right after the second fly ball in a row that center fielder Willie Davis lost in the sun. Those errors cost Koufax the game and he never pitched again, retiring at age 30 with an arthritic left arm, a decade before medical advancements could have saved his career. The memory of his curveball is seared in the minds of his helpless foes.

"It sounded like a little tornado, *bzzzzz*," Orlando Cepeda told Jane Leavy, Koufax's biographer. "So fast and noisy, it scared you."

Koufax has giant hands, and when he opened his glove wide from the stretch, savvy hitters knew he was gripping his curveball. Usually, it didn't even matter. Koufax understood biomechanics decades before the industry, and knew how to propel his body to the plate with maximum efficiency and force. The curveball, he told a rookie teammate in his final season, is not very complicated.

"He said it's an elbow pitch, and you come up over the top and pull down hard on the front of the ball, like you would on a fastball, where you pull down hard on the back of the ball," Don Sutton says. "On the curveball you're doing the same thing but you're just pulling down hard on the front of the ball."

Koufax's wisdom on the curveball echoed the words of Henry Roper, an old minor leaguer who was Sutton's sixth-grade teacher in Molino, Florida. Sutton had started Little League just the year before, as a shortstop, but decided to be a pitcher because they seemed to have the most fun. He brought his glove to school every day and played catch with Mr. Roper. He never once took a mound without a curveball, and the pitch never bothered his arm.

"I think it's one of the worst-taught pitches in baseball, because we're teaching people to get out front and pull the window shade and turn the doorknob," Sutton says. "Those are all great phrases, but you're doing it with an empty hand. The simplest way I was taught was the curveball is a karate chop with a ball in your hand. So load up at a 90-degree angle with your upper arm and your lower arm and throw the karate chop, and the ball will come out spinning."

Sutton would go on to pitch for 23 seasons, finishing with 324 victories, including a club-record 233 for the Dodgers. He is in the Hall of Fame, like Bert Blyleven, who learned the curve, indirectly, from Koufax. Born in Holland, Blyleven moved to California as a boy, and his father took him to a Dodger game to see Koufax face Juan Marichal. Even from the upper deck, Blyleven could see the vicious drop on the Koufax curve. It captivated him, and he would listen with his father to Vin Scully calling games on radio.

"I used to keep score just when Koufax and Drysdale pitched, because I liked writing down the strikeouts," Blyleven says.

He liked collecting them, too. Blyleven practiced his curveball against a wall, visualizing it breaking the way Scully described, making sure his thumb was on top of the ball on release, to impart that last bit of hellacious spin. At 19 he was in the majors with the Twins, and when he retired at 41, he had 3,701 strikeouts, trailing only Nolan Ryan and Steve Carlton. The career leader in strikeouts by a hitter, Reggie Jackson, fanned 49 times against Blyleven, by far his most frequent tormentor.

"You didn't hit it," Jackson says of the Blyleven curve. "He had to hang it to hit it. The quickness of the break, the speed of the pitch, the velocity, whatever the term—the break was big and it was hard. It was electric."

There is no shame in saying this for Jackson. Even the best hitters, with the biggest egos, can be helpless to handle a pitch from the gods. Just ask Mike Schmidt, the best third baseman in major league history, about Ryan's curveball.

"Well, I could hit Nolan's fastball," Schmidt says. "I couldn't hit his curveball in a million years for a base hit. And over the years, in probably 40 or 50 at-bats from him, I probably saw 100 curveballs—hanging, snapping off the table for strikes, in the dirt—*whoom, whoom,* they're everywhere, and I don't think I ever swung at one, because it was starting behind your head, you know."

Schmidt rose from his seat in the lobby of the Phillies' training complex in Clearwater, Florida. He assumed his familiar right-handed stance, and flinched at the imaginary Ryan curve.

"I was always doing this," he says, then adds he was still astonished at breaking up a Ryan no-hitter in the ninth inning by actually hitting that dastardly curve. "I don't know why it happened or how it happened, but: curveball, hit it up the middle. Maybe one of the few curveballs I hit up the middle my whole life. So his curveball to me was the most intimidating pitch to have to deal with *at all.* From a right-hander's standpoint, it was ridiculous. *Ridiculous.*"

Ryan developed a changeup near the end of his career. But for much of his first 20 seasons, he threw only the fastball and curve. Like Koufax with the wide glove, Ryan telegraphed his curveball by grunting when he threw a fastball. If he didn't grunt, the curve was coming. Hitters had no time to react, anyway.

Ryan found stardom after his December 1971 trade from the Mets to the Angels. The biggest reason was the Angels' pitching coach, Tom Morgan, who smoothed his mechanics, allowing him to stay on top with his curveball.

"In my delivery I was a rusher, because when I got in trouble I tried to throw harder," Ryan says. "So what you do is you just develop a pattern of rushing your delivery and not allowing your arm to catch up with your body. That's not how you throw harder or a sharper curveball. So understanding what I had to do from a mechanical standpoint, and then being able to implement that consistently, my curveball got better as my delivery improved."

For an extraordinarily hard thrower, like Koufax, Ryan, or Dwight Gooden, the curveball can be the ideal complement. Alan Ashby, who caught Ryan in Houston and struggled to hit Gooden, said it was almost impossible to be ready for two vastly different pitches that started from the same spot.

"They had that curveball that came out of the same, almost eye-high location all the time," Ashby said. "It's always that in-between that kills us mediocre hitters. You couldn't hit the fastball because they had that curveball, and you couldn't hit the curveball because they had that fastball."

Roy Halladay reached the majors with a knuckle-curve, and nearly threw a no-hitter with it in his second career start, in 1998. Back in the minors after that, he learned a more traditional curveball from Chris Carpenter, and found he could control it better: throw it softer for a strike, or pull it harder to finish in the dirt.

"I could throw a fastball for a strike in any count, whether I was cutting it or sinking it, and then I was able to throw a curveball in any count, whether it be 3–2, 3–0, 3–1," he said. "If I could throw it in any count knowing it was gonna be for a strike, that played so much into a hitter's head, knowing they can't sit on any pitch, ever, 100 percent convinced it's gonna be a fastball."

Al Leiter, a power lefty known for hard fastballs and cutters, decided he had to apply this principle to have a chance in Game 7 of the 1997 World Series for the Marlins. He watched video of David Wells and Andy Pettitte, other lefties who had attacked the powerful Indians lineup. Leiter determined that his very first pitch would have to be a curveball, reasoning that he would disrupt the Indians' timing by startling them with something soft.

He got the pitch over, and Omar Vizquel took it for a strike. Leiter pitched well, the Marlins won, and two years later, with the Mets in a tiebreaker for the National League Wild Card at Cincinnati, he did it again with a shutout.

"You have all these guys speeding up, looking for 90 to 93 inside, and here I'm throwing a 78-mile-an-hour slow curveball that wraps around the back side of the plate, getting called strike one," Leiter says.

"And now it's like, 'Oh shit, you've got 78 that wraps around the back door, outer half, and I still gotta look inside because you're gonna bust me in and break my bat?' When I had that combination, those are the games I was nailing it."

———————

No pitch elicits more colorful comparisons for the way it is thrown than the curveball. There is the karate chop, as Don Sutton says. "Like a gun," says A. J. Burnett, who learned his knuckle-curve—he always called it his hook—from his grandpa. A pitching coach, Gil Patterson, compares the motion to arm wrestling. When Barry Zito threw his curve, Patterson says, "If the catcher didn't catch it, you felt like it would boomerang and come back to you." Adam Wainwright, the curveball master for the St. Louis Cardinals, uses a nickname for the pitch, Uncle Charlie, in his Twitter handle.

"It's like you're hammering—or fishing, casting a line," Mike Mussina says. "That's what you're doing."

Bob Tewksbury, a control artist of the 1990s, would practice as a boy with a tennis ball can, flipping it end-over-end so the rotation mimicked a 12-6 curveball. Drew Storen, the former closer for the Nationals, used a hockey puck for the same purpose. Tom Gordon's father taught his son the curveball by placing a bucket six to eight feet behind a seven-foot fence. Gordon would stand about six feet from the fence, make a backwards C with his fingers, rotate his thumb upward, and dump curves into the bucket, over and over. He practiced so much he killed the tree he used as a rubber.

"I had to plant another one," Gordon says.

With the Royals in 1989, Gordon finished second in AL Rookie of the Year voting to Gregg Olson, another right-handed curveball master. Olson, a closer for the Orioles, would work on his form by spinning a paper cup—smoothly, longways, not end-over-end. If it didn't wobble, it had the right spin.

Olson played for the Dodgers at the end of his career, long after his All-Star prime, when he rendered helpless some of the game's best left-handed hitters (Ken Griffey Jr., Don Mattingly, and Rafael Palmeiro combined to go 3-for-33 off him). Olson would set his grip by locking his fingertip around a seam. Koufax, he said, showed him a better way.

"His hands were enormous compared to mine," Olson says. "He would take his middle finger and slide it down along the seam that he wanted. And then he would shove the finger against that seam so the side of the finger is now flush up against the seam. If you grab a baseball and do that, the baseball is just dying to spin out of your hand. So I did that my last couple of years—that's what I teach kids now—and it's an amazing difference if you just grab that baseball. I wish I would have had that early on. That would have been hours of amusement."

When Floyd Bannister pitched for the Rangers, his son, Brian, liked to stand behind the pitchers while they threw in the bullpen, to see the movement from their point of view. Brian Bannister grew up to pitch for the Mets and the Royals, and later joined the Red Sox as a pitching consultant and coach, equally versed in the science of the craft and the mind-set of the craftsmen. To Bannister, the curveball is unlike anything else in pitching.

"The curveball is unique," he says. "It's its own special pitch, because the break comes from the spin. With the slider, the changeup, the splitter—the break comes from gravity. You're dealing with a unique pitch with the curveball, because the rate of topspin is what makes it go down, and go down faster than gravity."

The slider, he explains, is a game between how hard a pitcher can throw it while also maximizing the pull of gravity. The curveball is all spin, right through to the pitcher's finish.

"On the curveball, you're actually trying to tuck the arm and decrease the radius of the arc, which increases the spin—whereas on the slider, you maintain a full arm length and a full follow-through and all the spin is created by the wrist and fingertips," Bannister says. "Two totally different approaches, which is why some guys throw sliders better and some guys throw curveballs better and why most guys struggle to throw both. Somebody like Clayton Kershaw is very rare, to throw elite versions of both."

The curveball can start as something else before finding its true identity. Mike Mussina taught himself a curveball that Olson, his future Baltimore teammate, said nobody else could ever throw.

"When I was a kid, I couldn't throw a curveball," Mussina says. "I mean, everybody's teaching you how to throw curveballs, get ahold of it like this and whatever, and I'd throw it and it just wouldn't do anything. It was like: 'That can't be what I see on television. That's crap.'

"So I started messing around, and I'm throwing knuckleballs—and I could throw a knuckleball, but the ball would spin too much. And so I figured: 'Wait a minute, what if I can do that on purpose? Can I fire my fingers out hard enough that I can make the ball do that on purpose—like, fast?' And I just kept working at it, working at it, working at it, working at it, and that's how I held a curveball for most of college—flick my fingers out and the ball would come out with topspin. Now, it wasn't biting and nasty, but it was good."

It was good enough to take to the majors, with the Orioles in 1991, but it was not the curveball Mussina used for most of his career. That was one he learned at Stanford from a teammate, Lee Plemel, who tucked his curveball into his palm and held his index finger up, resting it lightly on top—the spike curveball. That grip felt comfortable instantly, and Mussina could vary its speed and shape much more than he could with his old one. It worked from different arm angles, too.

"It's like any technological advancement," Mussina says, pointing to his smartphone. "Why would I talk on a rotary phone when I could talk on this now? It's the same thing, my own evolution. I found something better."

Mussina, at various times, could find any kind of pitch. He faced Wade Boggs so many times that he once flipped him a knuckleball, just to mix things up. Midway through another game, Mussina called catcher John Flaherty to the mound and told him what to signal for the splitter. Flaherty reminded Mussina he didn't have a splitter; "Today I do," Mussina replied.

Mussina won 20 games in 2008, bringing his career total to 270. If he had gotten much closer to 300 wins, he reasoned, he would have had to go for it. As a 40-year-old father of three, he didn't want to pitch three more seasons—but he could have, because his will matched his talent. Mussina was capable of invention, and hungry enough to constantly pursue it.

"I don't know if I was completely lucky, but it's just not that easy to do that kind of stuff, apparently," he says. "And it took me a little while to figure that out, but once I did, that's how I was able to play. It wasn't because I threw 96. It was because I could keep learning, I could keep adjusting, and I had a large—not large—but a pretty good selection of ways to pitch. I didn't just have to be throwing as hard as I could, plus a curveball. I could be a thumber, I could sink the ball, I could throw 75 percent sinkers instead of 75 percent four-seamers."

A thumber?

"A thumber's just like a guy who throws a lot of junk, that you might as well throw with your thumb, as hard as you're throwing it," he says, smiling. "Instead of throwing it, you're just kind of flipping it, junking it. That's what a thumber is—a junkball pitcher."

Every junkballer has a curve. When the fastball goes, a slow, looping curveball, with impeccable command, sound mechanics, and a durable body, can keep a pitcher going for a long time.

"I saved my best fastball for 20 percent of the time and the other 80 was just nibbling and changing speeds," says Frank Tanana, describing how he survived after injuries zapped his heat. "So when I threw my 80 or 85, it seemed like 95, because the other stuff was so crappy—or so slow, I should say. It's just an art, and I was very blessed."

Steve Stone could describe himself the same way, for different reasons. Stone was 33 years old in 1980, when he went 25–7 for the Orioles. He wears a custom-made ring with "Cy Young" surrounding a diamond on the face, commemorating his award for the achievement. Stone won largely by throwing as many curveballs as he could—seven out of 10 pitches, most days. His trick was to vary his curves at three speeds, depending on where he held the ball and how he applied finger pressure. Maybe all those curveballs hurt his longevity, he says; he lasted just one more season, a casualty of elbow pain.

But the recognition from his big year led directly to a long and successful career as a broadcaster. And maybe the curveball didn't ruin his arm at all.

"I had also completed my twelfth year of pro ball," Stone says. "And this might have eluded you, but I'm not the size of C. C. Sabathia. So I think being a relatively smaller pitcher at 5'9"—or 5'9" and a quarter; I swelled up during the season—my arm only had so many pitches in it."

———

Gregg Olson also blew out, and when he describes his best curveballs as coming from "a violent turn of the elbow," injuries sound inevitable. Actually, Olson says, a mechanical change was responsible; his drop-and-drive, hip-twisting motion looked peculiar but worked for him, and his arm reacted badly when the Orioles forced him to learn a slide step. His favorite pitch is blameless.

"When you come through and your hand's facing your face and you're pulling down in front, I believe that is fine for your arm," Olson says. "My curveball was thrown correctly and it was protected with my body."

Adam Wainwright's most famous curveball was the called third strike to the Mets' Carlos Beltran that ended Game 7 of the 2006 NLCS. (He would also end that fall's World Series with a strikeout, against Detroit's Brandon Inge, but that was on a slider.) Looking back, Wainwright says, the Beltran pitch was a product of youthful swagger; ahead in the count, 0–2, it was crazy to throw a strike to such a dangerous hitter.

But the pitch was just that good, and would remain so for many years. In 2013, two years after Tommy John surgery, Wainwright threw a staggering 276⅔ innings, including the postseason. A year later, he won 20 games. Wainwright's brother, Trey, who is seven years older, showed him a curveball grip at age 10. The pitch felt perfectly natural. "Back then there was no talk of age limits to throw curveballs, which I believe plays into people hurting their arms by not throwing it till later in life," Wainwright says. "Everybody's parents think it's bad for them to throw curveballs, but we have a higher rate of Tommy John [surgeries] than ever, and everybody's throwing harder than ever. So people are building arm strength, building arm strength, building arm strength, and then they say, 'All right, you're in high school now, you're throwing 90, now we can work on a curveball.' So what you're doing is you're taking an arm that's fully developed and strong and throwing bullets, and then all of a sudden you're entering a totally new movement at max speed rather than bringing along a properly thrown curveball. A curveball's much less strain on your arm than a slider is. A slider is a variation of the fastball, and you kind of have a wrist twinge. It's just not as good on your elbow."

Curveball enthusiasts say this all the time: the slider is more dangerous, and the curveball, *when taught properly,* is just fine. Teaching it, though, is the problem. There are far more young pitchers than there are coaches qualified to teach a safe curveball.

"I tell kids and I tell parents: throwing a curveball will not hurt your arm if you throw it properly, but the problem is that most people don't throw it properly," Nolan Ryan says. "So they have to learn to throw it properly. If you do that, it won't hurt your arm any more than a fastball. Everything's the same, it's just your hand position on the ball. So with kids, it's a touchy thing to get 'em to understand what they have to do and what they shouldn't do. It's not something you learn overnight, either."

What do kids do when they throw the curveball improperly?

"They try to put spin on the ball by putting pressure on the elbow, which is not where you get it," Ryan continues. "You get the spin on the ball, it's in your hand and your wrist."

Jon Lester, the veteran left-hander who won titles with the Red Sox and Cubs, says the curveball itself is not a problem. The danger, he says, is that kids often struggle to repeat the proper mechanics.

"People always ask, 'How old can I be when I start throwing curveballs?'" Lester says, shrugging his shoulders. "Throw 'em when you're two years old. That's not the problem. The problem is your mechanics. The problem is you have a 12-year-old, he can't repeat his arm slot. That's the torque on the elbow. That's the problem with throwing a curveball when you're younger: you can't repeat. You're not strong enough."

When a pitcher throws a curveball properly, the arm protects itself by tucking itself in, toward the glove-side rib cage, as it follows through. A slider puts more pressure on the elbow because it requires full extension. Blyleven dismisses the notion that curveballs cause injury—"A myth," he says. "A slider will hurt your arm more"—and Mussina echoes him. Mussina never had arm surgery and says that whenever something felt off, the fastball caused him more discomfort than the curve.

"Anytime that I had a sore elbow or anything like that, I never, ever, ever felt like it was my curveball that did it," he says. "Never. It was never really in a place that seemed like my curveball would be the reason."

Mussina lives in the shadow of Williamsport, Pennsylvania, home of the Little League World Series, and has served on the Little League International board of directors. Every August, there's a mild outcry when folks watch 12-year-olds spinning curveballs in Williamsport on ESPN. Yet Mussina doesn't rail against the dangers of the pitch, and neither does Dr. Glenn Fleisig, who studied the issue with his colleagues by tracking the progress of 481 youth pitchers for a decade. Their report, issued in 2011, found no relationship between throwing curveballs before age 13 and serious arm injury after.

"What was a strong indicator was pitching too much," Fleisig says. "So the kids who pitched year-round baseball in high school and these travel teams, they get hurt whether or not they're the ones who throw the curveballs."

For pitchers of all ages, Fleisig says, the fastball and curveball exert similar amounts of stress on elbows and shoulders; the curveball, in fact, was found to have 5 to 10 percent less stress on the shoulder, though that was deemed statistically insignificant. (The study did find "significantly less elbow and shoulder torque and force" from the changeup.)

If kids who throw curveballs get hurt more often, Fleisig says, don't blame the pitch.

"The kids who threw curveballs at the younger age were also the ones with the pushy parents," he says, "and also the ones who played year-round."

Need more testimony? Here's Tom House, the former reliever and pitching coach: "The curveball, which everybody thought was the worst pitch on the arm, is actually the easiest pitch on the arm, because if it's thrown properly, it's the strength position, and it's the slowest velocity. When you're karate-chopping a brick, you're not doing it with your palm, you're doing it with the side of your hand, just like you throw a curveball. If you twist when you do it, that's where all the issues in the elbow come in."

Curveball hysteria is misguided. There is just no evidence that, *with proper technique,* curveballs are bad for developing arms. And it's not just recent science. Here's Bob Shaw, a longtime pitcher and coach, in his 1972 pitching manual:

"At what age should a youngster start throwing a curve ball?" Shaw wrote. "In my experience, most of the good curve-ball pitchers have started young. You can injure your arm at any age if you do not throw the curve correctly. Age is not a factor."

––––––––––

You see it all the time in the clubhouse, or if you watch the relievers while they're sitting in the bullpen. They'll flip balls to themselves, like a lifeguard lazily whirling her whistle around her fingers while staring out at the water, just to pass the time. In this case, though, there's a purpose: spin. It's not the same kind of spin, exactly, but the more idle time you spend flicking that ball, exercising the wrist and fingers on the muscle memory of a curveball, the better.

"You've got free time, you're just sitting around during a game," Mike Montgomery says. "Why not grab a ball, grip it how you would, and just spin it?"

Hitters would rather you didn't. One of the best, Mike Piazza, learned this at a young age as a bat boy for the Dodgers. Someone asked Bill Madlock, the veteran third baseman, how to hit a curveball. "Don't miss the fastball!" Madlock replied. By then he had won four batting titles.

"It's just harder to hit," says Mark Teixeira, who slugged 409 home runs. "Drop a ball from a 20-foot ladder and have me try to hit it, going straight down. Even for the best hitters in the world, that's gonna be tough to do. Now, give me a 100-mph fastball—straight, in the zone—I'll hit it every time. I may not get a hit, but I'm gonna hit it. But if you do it the other way, that's what a curveball does. A good curveball with a lot of break, it's not necessarily that I don't recognize it, but it's moving so much that it's tougher to square up."

A few decades ago, some worried that the slider would all but wipe out the curveball, because it is easier to throw and easier to get called in the strike zone. Candy Cummings found a way to work around that problem; a century later, it persisted.

"The strike zone was bigger in my day," says Carl Erskine, who pitched from 1948 to 1959. "Just under the letters used to be a called strike; now if it's above the belt, it's a ball. So the strike zone has been compressed, and that's caused pitchers to adapt more to breaking pitches that are smaller. It's hard to get the big curveball a called strike sometimes, because it starts above the strike zone and breaks down into it. Sometimes the umpire sees it too high."

Al Jackson, a stalwart lefty of the early Mets, later became a coach with the Red Sox. In 1977, he lamented to *The Boston Globe*'s Bob Ryan: "Pitchers have become so slider crazy that the curve is fast becoming a dying art."

Yet the slider never came close to eliminating the curveball. Ryan and Blyleven overlapped with Mussina and Olson, who overlapped with Zito and Wainwright, and so on. Now, as pitchers dominate with high, hard stuff as never before, it is more and more critical to have the contrast of a tumbling curveball.

"Guys are throwing so hard, if they can throw a slower pitch, it's too big a speed variance to cover," Wainwright says. "If you're throwing fastball/slider, everything's hard, so a hitter can gear up for basically one tempo, one speed. Whereas if you've gotta worry about hard/slow, it's very tough."

John Smoltz, a power version of Mussina, loved the curveball. When Smoltz had his hard stuff going, as he usually did, the curve would give him a free strike. Hitters prepared for a fastball or slider, and when Smoltz tossed a curveball instead, they'd be so surprised at the different shape and speed that they'd lock up and watch it drop in the zone. Smoltz calls the curveball a forgotten art and is glad to see it coming back through stars like Kershaw and Madison Bumgarner. There's really no excuse for a curveball—at least the kind to steal a strike—to be missing from a pitcher's tool belt.

"When I was first coming up, you'd see the big 12-6 curveball, with Matt Morris and Darryl Kile for the Cardinals," says David Ross, who caught in the majors for 15 seasons, through 2016. "I think that's starting to come back. It's just evolution. When guys are throwing so hard now, you have to commit a little bit sooner as a hitter, and you're way out in front. It's one of those things where the fastball's so hard, so the 12-6 starts at your head and drops in for a strike, or it starts where the fastball does and it's more of a chase pitch."

Ross ended his career riding off the field in Cleveland on the shoulders of his Cubs teammates, after Montgomery's final curveball won Game 7 of the World Series. That concluded a season in which major league pitchers threw 7,732 more curveballs than they had in 2015, according to Statcast data from MLB.com. The average curveball was also spinning more, at 2,462 rpm, up from 2,302. In 2017, pitchers threw curveballs with 10.6 percent of all pitches, a 15-season high.

There are get-me-over curveballs to dump in the zone for called strikes, and curveballs in the dirt to bait a free swinger. But more and more, Montgomery is convinced, pitchers are throwing true curveballs: pitches in the zone, meant to induce swinging strikes. It is simple evolution, with the information flowing from the front office to the field. The data tells decision makers what to seek, so now they seek curveballs with high spin rates.

Mussina rolls his eyes at all this. He practically spits out the term: "Spin rate. That's the dumbest thing I've ever heard." What he means is that spin rate for a curveball matters only as much as the radar gun reading for a fastball. It doesn't mean the pitch is any good; not even close, actually. A great pitch that cannot be commanded is not, in fact, a great pitch. As hitters say about a bad curveball: "You hang it, we bang it."

Yet as the curveball's essential raw ingredient, spin rate is important to know. Organizations use those figures to tell them, empirically, which of their prospects might have a major league pitch. A nondescript pitcher with a high spin rate now gets chances once reserved only for those with a mid-90s fastball: *Hey, there just might be something here.*

Collin McHugh had made it through high school, college, and four years of pro ball without ever hearing of spin rate. A former eighteenth-round draft choice, he was 24 years old and pitching in the Arizona Fall League in 2011 when a coach circulated a thick packet of detailed statistics. McHugh found his name near the top of the list for rpm on his curveball.

"It was right up there with Verlander and Kershaw and Felix, some of these guys with really good curveballs," McHugh says. "To see myself in that echelon with any one thing that I did, it gave me confidence. It gave me at least some kind of reference to say, 'I'm not just some other Double-A guy somewhere. There's something that I do exceptionally well, and I want to try to capitalize on it.'"

The next year McHugh was in the majors. He bounced from the

Mets to the Rockies, and while his statistics were bad, the fast-spinning curveball still made him a prospect. The Astros signed him off waivers, and in 2015 he went 19–7 to help them reach the playoffs.

The Mets lost McHugh, but they held on to Seth Lugo, a thirty-fourth-round draft pick with a curve he had first honed, as a boy, with the tennis-ball-can drill. Lugo's first minor league manager, Frank Fultz, took one look at the pitch and told him it would someday lift him to the majors. Five years later, with injuries ravaging the Mets' rotation, Lugo earned a promotion and sparkled down the stretch. His curveball had the best spin rate in the league.

That August 30, in the sixth inning of a win over Miami, Lugo let loose a curve at 3,498 rpm, the highest recorded in the first two years of Statcast. Lugo was ahead in the count to Xavier Scruggs, 1–2, and wanted the pitch below the zone. Scruggs, who swung over the ball as it plunged hard and late, knew right away he had seen something extraordinary.

"Guys will swing and miss all the time, but you know when it's a different swing and miss," Scruggs says. "That ball didn't go anywhere near where I thought it was going."

Eleven days later, the Dodgers' Rich Hill toyed with the Marlins for seven perfect innings. Hill threw curveballs with 57 percent of his pitches, the crowning example of the freedom he felt the year before, when the Red Sox signed him from the independent Long Island Ducks. Working with Bannister, Hill learned different ways to shape his curveball, and trusted Bannister's advice to throw it much more often than any other pitcher in the game. Hill pitched well for Boston, then signed a 2016 contract with Oakland for $6 million.

Traded to the Dodgers, Hill sliced curveballs through the National League, ending with six shutout innings against the Cubs in the play-offs. That December, the Dodgers brought him back with a three-year, $48 million contract—a jackpot, at last, after 15 pro seasons, a deal that would soon lead Hill to the World Series. He wept at the news conference announcing it.

"I think that's life, right?" Hill said, reflecting on the rocky path brought to riches by perseverance and a killer curve. "You're going to be thrown a lot of different curveballs."

THE
KNUCKLEBALL

Grabbing the Wing of a Butterfly

The old knuckleballer grips his favorite pitch with three fingernails. Most pitchers use two, but for him that makes the pitch wobbly, impossible to control. Jim Bouton uses his ring finger, too. This is the grip he displayed for the nation four decades ago on the set of *The Tonight Show,* and the grip he showed me in his backyard a couple of years ago, high up in the Berkshires near Great Barrington, Massachusetts.

Bouton was 78 then, yet he was still throwing a couple of times a week. He built a cinder-block backstop in a sunlit corner of the yard, and hit the strike zone most of the time. His hat did not fall off anymore, as it did for the Yankees, back when he threw hard and beat St. Louis twice in the 1964 World Series. We played catch for 15 minutes, and his knuckler hit my glove every time. Mine hit his, too; the three-finger grip was the closest I'd ever come to controlling this most peculiar pitch.

If we were really on our games, though, we'd have let loose a few wild pitches. The best knuckleballs often zig and zag away from the mitt, sending their catchers scrambling. But if Bouton's knuckler can't quite dance like it did for the Seattle Pilots, it remains his pitch—slower now, but authentically his.

It was good for Jim to have company, said his wife, Paula Kurman, who has a doctorate in interpersonal communications from Columbia. They have been married since 1982 and have lived in the Berkshires for more than 20 years, among the foxes and black bears, surrounded by pine trees. A cloud might roll by, straight through the screened-in porch, and there are no other homes in sight. Their children are grown and live elsewhere.

Bouton had a stroke on August 15, 2012. They know the date because it was the fifteenth anniversary of the death of Bouton's daughter, Laurie, in a car accident. Bouton's body was largely unaffected. But his mind, the one whose pointed and poignant observations produced the classic *Ball Four* in 1970, will never be the same. He has a brain disease: cerebral amyloid angiopathy, a form of dementia. He struggles with numerical concepts. Processing questions can be frustrating. Writing is too complicated to organize and enjoy. Life is filled with unforeseen gaps in understanding.

"Sometimes we'll have conversations and it's like it's 10 years ago," Kurman said. "Things are flowing along. And then you step in this pothole and you didn't know it was there."

He still remembers a lot of old baseball stories, many in precise detail from years of retelling. He is gentle and funny and kind, as ever. And when I mention that I always keep my baseball glove in the trunk of my car, he eagerly scurries to find his own: a brown, well-worn Louisville Slugger marked with his old number, 56, in thick black pen. Let's play catch.

There are no potholes in the yard, only green grass and pine trees and sunshine. It remains for Jim Bouton as he once wrote: he can still grip a baseball, and baseball still grips him. The knuckleball endures.

————

Baseball people like to say that your worst day at the ballpark is better than your best day at the office. It reminds them that the baseball life is really not too bad. Yes, it's stressful, with relentless travel and meager pay in the minors. But somebody wins every day, you're outdoors a lot, and deep down you recognize that, of all the industries out there, you're lucky to work in the baseball one.

Maybe for that reason, I've found that most people in baseball tend to be . . . pretty nice. And of all the subsets of folks in the game, knuckleball pitchers might be the nicest. They are also part of the smallest group, which helps explain it. Almost all knuckleballers were rejected by the game before they could last very long. They earned their living by grabbing the wing of a butterfly and then, somehow, steering it close enough to the strike zone, again and again, to baffle the best hitters in the world.

"Most of our careers were headed in a different direction, and out of desperation, we all found the knuckleball," says Tim Wakefield, who won 200 games with it. "So I think the knuckleball itself has humbled most of us to a point where we're grateful that we still have a job and we're still able to compete."

"Compete" is the word Charlie Hough uses to explain his reason for throwing it. Hough was a decent pitcher in Class A for the Dodgers, but after six months in the Army reserves, his shoulder hurt when he tried to pitch again. With average stuff to begin with, Hough guessed that his future would be working at the Hialeah Race Track, two blocks from his home in Florida.

Then a scout named Goldie Holt showed him how to throw a knuckleball. Hough gave it a try.

"If you want to compete, you compete," he says. "You find something."

That something, for Hough and just a few dozen others in baseball's long history, is a pitch as quirky as its name. Pitchers once threw it with their knuckles actually pressed against the ball, and the knuckles are still prominent in the visual presentation. But the pitch is really thrown with the fingertips—"positioned between the thumb, index and middle fingers," as Wakefield wrote in his book with Tony Massarotti, "as if it were a credit card being held up for display."

The whole concept of the knuckleball is to be fundamentally different from every other pitch. With almost everything else, pitchers want to increase spin for greater velocity or a more deceptive break. They manipulate the ball to serve their will, to send it to a specific spot. If executed properly, the pitch will obey.

Because knuckleballers want no spin at all, they don't engage the same muscles as conventional pitchers. If a robot could pitch, it would throw like a knuckleballer, like one mechanical piece instead of a flexible acrobat stressing multiple leverage points to impart spin. The physical dangers of repeated throws at maximum effort do not apply for these craftsmen. Theirs is the safest pitch of all, but the trade-off is severe: it is also the hardest to master, and to trust.

Simply put, the trick is to use the seams to deflect the air and move the ball erratically, like an airplane flying into turbulence. A University of Iowa study, cited by the author Martin Quigley, described the aerodynamics like this: "When the ball leaves the pitcher's hand, it runs head on into a 'wall' of air. This air pushes at the front of the ball and pulls at the back. The air also tends to 'pile up' on the seams and rough surfaces. The forces holding the ball back build up so fast that the ball slows down suddenly and drops unusually fast . . . usually a short distance in front of the plate, and causes the batter to swing 'where it was, not where it is.'"

This results from what is known, in science, as the Bernoulli Effect, which states that the pressure within a flowing fluid (including a gas, such as air) is less than the pressure surrounding it. An object that is not spinning—or just barely spinning—will move toward an area of less pressure. As Robert K. Adair, PhD, wrote in *The Physics of Baseball,* the seams on a ball create chaos: "If the ball is thrown with very little rotation, asymmetric stitch configurations can be generated that lead to large imbalances of forces and extraordinary excursions in trajectory."

Then we have the unofficial explanation, from the batter's box, by the longtime outfielder Bobby Murcer. Trying to hit Phil Niekro, Murcer memorably said, was "like trying to eat Jell-O with chopsticks."

A good knuckleball will leave you laughing and stupefied, like a comedian who also does magic tricks; Satchel Paige called his the "bat-dodger." The pitch has a deep and rich history in the game, yet remains so uncommon that it is often an object of ridicule.

Sometimes the teasing is playful: in Wakefield's heyday with the Boston Red Sox, catcher Mike Macfarlane would cry "Freak show!" in the clubhouse before games. Sometimes, it is not so much teasing as a deep dislike, for practical reasons. Joe McCarthy, the Hall of Fame Yankees manager, groused that when a knuckleball breaks, the catcher misses it, and when it doesn't, the batter crushes it. He had little use for pitchers who did not throw hard.

"Any time you've got a soft ball pitcher," McCarthy would say, "then you've got a .500 pitcher."

Hough was .500 personified, with a career record of 216–216. Nobody else with that many victories has precisely the same number of losses. Then again, nobody else has made 400 appearances as both a starter and reliever, and few others have spent a quarter century on major league mounds.

Hough is a very nice guy, too. Bobby Valentine, who was teammates with Hough in Los Angeles, managed him in Texas, and hired him as a coach in New York, called him one of the best baseball men in the world. But Hough was not simply happy to be there. Nice does not mean pushover. Floating knuckleballs for a living takes a special kind of athletic bravery.

"I think you need a *huge* ego," Hough says. "You need to believe that you're the best pitcher in the world when you're in there. When they put down '1' for Nolan Ryan, he threw it 100 miles an hour. When they put down '1' for me, I threw what I felt like was a pitch they couldn't hit."

Adrenaline is the enemy. If you overthrow a knuckleball, it spins— and if it spins, you're in trouble. Trusting it defies logic, but doing so is essential. The pitchers who throw it do not frustrate easily. They need to stay calm so their pitch will behave. Low-key, happy-go-lucky people—with the guts to bring Silly String to a battlefield—just might have a chance.

The knuckleball is, at once, the most frustrating and fascinating pitch in baseball. It is also relatable, much more than any other pitch, to the fan in the stands. No one sees a turbocharged fastball or jack-knife curve and thinks: "Yep, I could do that." Yet anyone can look at a dancing knuckleball and say, "You know what? Maybe."

Bouton's knuckleball was like a character of its own in *Ball Four*, his famous diary of the 1969 season. Like Bouton, the pitch was a nonconformist struggling for respect in the game. It had intrigued Bouton as a boy, when he rooted for Hoyt Wilhelm and the New York Giants. He learned the grip from a cereal box that told the story of a knuckleballer named Dutch Leonard.

"It was like a magic thing," Bouton told me, several years ago. "You didn't need to be big. You didn't need to be strong. The idea was to throw a ball with perfection, really. And once you've thrown a success-ful knuckleball, you become entranced by it. If you've hit somebody in the chest with a knuckleball, you'll never forget it."

When something leaves us awestruck, we usually can't do it or wouldn't want to try—a mural on a church ceiling, a rousing guitar solo at a concert, a chainsaw-juggling act at a circus. Yet a fluttering knuckleball at a ballgame seems to be within our grasp. That is part of its appeal, and a reason it stands out as one of the more colorful patches on the baseball quilt.

But the premise that anyone can become a knuckleballer? Well . . . it's dead wrong. There are many reasons the pitch always flirts with extinction, but the most fundamental is this: it's really, really hard to throw. Fastball pitchers are born; knuckleballer pitchers are painstakingly self-made.

"People watch us throw and they say, 'Oh that's easy,'" Wakefield says. "Throwing it 65 or 70 miles an hour, anybody could do that. But in reality, it's really hard. And to be able to throw it for strikes consistently, that's the big thing. I mean, every middle infielder had a good knuckleball—but can they get on the mound and throw it to a hitter with a game on the line?"

Indeed, plenty of position players fool around with knuckleballs while playing catch—Mickey Mantle and Cal Ripken Jr. were well known for it, and R. A. Dickey, who won the 2012 National League Cy Young Award, says a different teammate would find him every year to show off his version.

But pitching from the slope of a mound makes it harder to keep the palm behind the ball, and changes everything. And even if a pitcher has the patience and the temperament for it, the knuckleball still requires the same kind of extraordinary athleticism as any other pitch—that is, the ability to repeat sound mechanics. This delivery is just engineered differently, for a much different kind of result.

"From your shoulder down you're all stiffed up, everything's locked in, there's no flip of your wrist," says Phil Niekro, the greatest knuckler of all. "In baseball—curveball, slider—it's all what you do with your wrist and the movement of the ball, the spin of the ball. Here, you want to throw something that's not gonna do anything at all, and you figure: 'What the hell, it's not doing nothing, but it'll do more than any other pitch you throw up there.'"

By doing nothing, the pitch with no spin can do anything.

————

Could it be that the first pitcher famous for the knuckleball, the last-chance weapon of the friendly warrior, was a notorious scoundrel? History knows Eddie Cicotte best as one of the eight Chicago White Sox banned for life for conspiring with gamblers to throw the 1919 World Series. Cicotte sent the signal by hitting the Cincinnati leadoff man in the back in the opener.

By then, Cicotte was well known as a master of the knuckleball, which he threw about 75 percent of the time. His nickname, after all, was Knuckles, and he threw the pitch—at first—by resting his knuckles on top of the ball. Cicotte had played with Nap Rucker (another early knuckleballer) in the minors in 1905, but would cite a 1906 minor league teammate, Ed Summers, with developing the pitch in its modern form.

Lew Moren, who pitched a few years for the Pirates and Phillies, would unveil his knuckler in the National League at roughly the same time as Cicotte and Summers in the American League. The knuckleball showed up in their 1908 stats: Cicotte led the league in wild pitches, Summers in hit batters. That July, Summers explained the difference in their grips to *Baseball Magazine:*

"I watched Eddie Cicotte, who first used it, and followed him. He rested the ball on his knuckles, but I couldn't see the value of that, because I couldn't control it, and one can put but little speed on it. . . . I found by holding the ball with my finger tips and steadying it with my thumb alone, I could get a peculiar break to it and send it to the batters with considerable speed and good control."

Summers said the pitch was not a knuckleball, and he was right, in the literal sense. But the pitch he threw is the one that would carry that name through the ages. In 1908, *Sporting Life* used the term "finger nail curve" to describe a pitch by Ralph Savidge of the Reds. The ball made no revolutions and moved erratically, but actually, Savidge would say, he did not really use his nails to throw it.

"I never know what's going to happen after the ball leaves my hand," he told the same publication in 1909. "Sometimes it breaks upward and sometimes it drops and it is just as liable to break to either the right or left."

Savidge would make just five appearances in the majors, and while the knuckleball appeared sporadically—a Phillies pitcher, Tom Seaton, won 27 games with it in 1913—it faced the first of many death scares with the banishment of Cicotte after the 1920 season. Fortunately for the knuckleball's survival, something else was banned after that season: the spitball.

When Eddie Rommel reached the majors with the A's in 1920, he brought a knuckler taught to him by a semipro first baseman, Cutter Drury, who had suggested it as a spitball alternative. In time, Rommel noticed that the softer he threw it, the more it would move. He led the majors in victories in 1922, with 27, and even flummoxed the Browns' George Sisler, who hit .420 that season.

"If it made a one-way hop, the batter would be able to set himself and familiarize himself with the break," Sisler said, as quoted by Rob Neyer. "But that's just where Rommel's success comes in. It goes down one time and the next will take an upward break. I believe I hit more infield flies against Rommel than any other pitcher in the league."

Rommel went 171–119 in all, but his ending was proof that even knuckleballers have physical limits, and arms that can be destroyed by abuse. As Neyer described, Sunday baseball was illegal in Philadelphia in 1932. So that July 10, in the middle of a 10-game home stand, the A's made a one-day trip to Cleveland. Times were good for the A's, who had won the last three AL pennants, but owner-manager Connie Mack still tried to save on train fare by bringing along only two pitchers. Lew Krausse worked the first inning, and Rommel—who had also worked the prior two days—*pitched the next seventeen.* He gave up 14 runs, a major-league-record 29 hits, and never won another game. Finished at 35, he would fashion a second act as an umpire for 24 years.

With Rommel's success, a pattern was setting in—one prominent knuckleballer gives way to another, with a few more flitting on and off the scene. Jesse Haines and Freddie Fitzsimmons overlapped Rommel, with better careers, but they threw the pitch off the knuckles, not the fingertips, and Haines (a Hall of Famer) sometimes used it just a dozen times a game. The 1945 Washington Senators had four knuckleballers in their rotation and nearly snagged a pennant, but just one—Dutch Leonard—had a winning career record. The others had little success outside the war years.

Gene Bearden, a 22-year-old minor leaguer who had already bounced through three organizations, found himself aboard the USS

Helena in the South Pacific in July 1943. Bearden was in the engine room when a Japanese destroyer struck his ship with a torpedo. As Bearden climbed a ladder to escape, another torpedo strike sent him crashing to the floor, unconscious, with a mangled knee and a severe gash to his head.

"Somebody pulled me out," Bearden would tell the Cleveland *Plain Dealer*. "They told me later it was an officer. I don't know how he did it. The ship went down in about 17 minutes. All I know is that I came to in the water some time later."

About 200 men died in the attack, but Bearden was rescued by an American destroyer after two days on a raft. At a Navy hospital in Florida, he had an aluminum plate inserted in his head and an aluminum cap and screw in his crushed kneecap. He took seven months to walk again and spent all of 1944 in the hospital.

Doctors told him to forget baseball, but Bearden returned anyway. He could not raise his right leg very high off the ground, and could not use a full windup. But he had no limp, and he won—15 games for the Yankees at Class A in 1945, then 15 more the next season in the Pacific Coast League for Casey Stengel.

Stengel had managed Leonard with the Dodgers, and noticed Bearden working on a self-taught knuckleball in spring training. He encouraged Bearden to use it, and a catcher, Bill Raimondi, called it often and handled it well. Traded to Cleveland before the 1947 season, Bearden was a rookie sensation in 1948, going 20–7 and clinching the pennant in a playoff at Fenway Park.

Most pitchers feared throwing inside at Fenway, where Red Sox hitters could pull pitches for homers down the short foul lines. Yet Bearden, with the moxie that runs so strong in the knuckleball family, worked inside anyway, surprising the Red Sox and going the distance in a five-hitter. A week later—after shutting out the Braves in Game 3 of the World Series—Bearden was back on a different mound in Boston, closing out the Indians' last championship in Game 6.

Bearden headed for Hollywood and appeared in two movies—*And Baby Makes Three* and *The Monty Stratton Story*—but his stardom quickly faded. He pinched a sciatic nerve in his leg the next spring, and his control, shaky in the best of times, deserted him. Batters hunted fastballs, and as Ed McAuley wrote in the *Cleveland News*, "Gene's fastball never was more than an invitation to an extra-base hit." After stints with four more teams, Bearden was out of the game just five years after his World Series triumph.

————

Only two pitchers have gotten to the Hall of Fame with fingertip knuckleballs—not counting Wade Boggs, a third baseman who knuckled through a scoreless inning for the Yankees in 1997 and reprised the act for Tampa Bay two years later, just before retiring.

Cooperstown's first true fingertip knuckleballer was Hoyt Wilhelm, who made his major league debut the year he turned 30 and pitched until the month he turned 50. Voters needed eight ballots before electing Wilhelm in 1985. The next inductee was Phil Niekro, who earned a staggering 208 victories *after turning 35*. He made it on his fifth try, in 1997.

For both men, persistence was everything.

"My first year in professional baseball, in 1959, I was pitching in Kearney, Nebraska, and I remember meeting Phil Niekro," Bouton once told me. "I was sitting in the bleachers before a game and I see this skinny, crew-cut kid in the outfield, and he's throwing the knuckleball. I could see, even from a distance, that ball was moving. So I walked over and introduced myself and told him I throw a knuckleball, too. I said, 'What do you throw besides the knuckleball?' And he said, 'Nothing, just the knuckleball.'

"We had a nice chat and I thought to myself, 'Phil Niekro, that poor son of a bitch. He's never gonna make it because he's only got one pitch—and I, Jim Bouton, I'm on my way to the big leagues because I have all these pitches.' And then when I was in the big leagues, after my 20-win season, I remembered him and thought, 'Oh that poor kid, he's still in the minor leagues and I don't know how he hangs on because I'm on my way to the Hall of Fame.' Well, guess what? That poor kid, limited to one pitch—he's in the Hall of Fame now. It's a good reminder for me of the tortoise and the hare."

Niekro would make 716 career starts, fifth on the career list, yet 102 of his first 103 appearances came from the bullpen. In the 1950s and most of the '60s, that was usually where knuckleballers went—and Wilhelm was the model.

In Wilhelm's teen years in North Carolina, Leonard was rising to stardom in Washington. Wilhelm, who did not throw hard, noticed a photograph of Leonard's knuckleball grip in the Charlotte newspaper. He practiced with a tennis ball and found that the feel came naturally.

That experience convinced Wilhelm that the knuckleball could not be taught. Though he would spend many post-playing years as a coach, he believed that if you did not throw the pitch as a kid, you could never pick it up as a man. Though countless examples contradict this, Wilhelm was firm: you either have it or you don't.

"Nobody has ever asked me to teach them, but even if they did, I wouldn't," Wilhelm told *The Atlanta Journal* in 1973. "It's an unortho-dox pitch. You have to have a knack to throw it to start with."

Wilhelm favored a fastball/slider/changeup mix for young pitchers, but if he happened to see his old pitch, he loved it. Coaching the Yankees' rookie leaguers in 1991, he insisted that a promising lefty from Texas keep throwing his knuckler, even though the other instructors wanted him to stop.

"He was just a crusty old dude," Andy Pettitte would say, many years later. "I loved him to death. I'd come back and say, 'Hoyt, dad-gum it, why did I do this?' or, 'Why didn't I do that?' And he'd say, 'Pettitte, just keep turning 'em to the right,' meaning when they get to first base, turn them to the right, back to their dugout. That's all he would say: 'Pettitte, just keep turning 'em to the right.'"

The other coaches persuaded Pettitte to scrap his knuckleball, but late in his career he would joke that he just might revive it as a last resort. He stayed strong to the end and never did, and besides, Pettitte said, the pitch would have gone stale by then. The knuckleball needs constant nurturing, as his old coach believed and proved.

Wilhelm was the first pitcher to appear in 1,000 games. He twice led his league in earned run average and no-hit the Yankees for Baltimore in 1958—incredibly, through 2017, it remained the last complete game no-hitter against them. Ted Williams ranked Wilhelm with Bob Feller, Bob Lemon, Eddie Lopat, and Whitey Ford among the five toughest pitchers he faced.

"Wilhelm had a sure-strike knuckler, then a real good knuckler, then with two strikes, a real bastard of a knuckler, dancing in your face," Williams wrote in his autobiography. "The closest thing to an unhittable ball I ever saw."

You might think teams would hold on to a pitcher with that kind of weapon, especially in the era before free agency. By any measure, Wilhelm was an elite and versatile performer, and his pitch made him almost ageless. Yet teams never seemed to trust him very long. Over 21 years, Wilhelm spent time with nine teams—not counting the Royals, who took him in the expansion draft and traded him—but never stayed more than six years in one place.

Even if he chafed at teaching his signature pitch, Wilhelm helped its spread by encouraging Wilbur Wood, a journeyman left-hander who had bounced between the minors and majors for seven seasons before joining the White Sox in 1967. As a boy, Wood had learned to throw a pitch off the fingertips that imparted no rotation. His father taught it to him and called it a palmball, which typically means changeup. Wood did not think much about terminology; he just liked having a pitch to stifle the big kids on the sandlots of Boston.

Wood reached the majors at 19 but struggled to stick. His fastball, he says, in a thick and endearing accent, was "a few yahds too short," so batters could wait for his curveball and crush it. With Chicago, Wood decided to revive his father's pitch, and Wilhelm, his new teammate, eagerly approved.

"That's when I just said, 'What the hell, I gotta make a change,' and that's when I made the change, really, to go 100 percent with the knuckleball," Wood says. "His biggest thing was: 'If you're going to do it, you've got to stay with it and you've got to throw it. It's great to throw a curveball, fastball, slider, whatever else it may be, but you're either gonna make or break with the knuckleball.' Hearing those words, it's a pretty easy decision, isn't it?"

For the next several years—until a line drive shattered his kneecap—Wood was a sensation. He led the league in appearances three years in a row. Then he became a starter and ripped off four straight seasons with at least 20 victories and 300 innings pitched. Just two others—Fergie Jenkins and Robin Roberts—had done that since the 1930s, and no one has done it since. Across a five-year period, Wood made

199 of 224 starts on fewer than four days' rest. His 1972 workload (376⅔ innings) is the most by any pitcher since 1919. Staggering facts, all, and only one part of Wood's legend is typically overstated: he did start both games of a doubleheader, in 1973, but it was a disaster. He got 13 outs, gave up 13 runs, and lost twice.

In any case, Wilhelm had proven in his own career that trusting the knuckleball meant everything. In 1969, when he saved the NL West division clincher for the Braves, Wilhelm was 47 and his catcher, Bob Didier, was 20. Facing a dangerous hitter, Alex Johnson, Wilhelm fell behind, 3–0, and Didier twice flashed the fastball sign. Both times, Wilhelm shook him off. Didier trotted to the mound.

"Wilhelm says, 'What the fuck are you doing? The only thing you know about pitching is it's hard to hit! Get your ass behind the plate right now!'" Didier recalls. "So I turned around, 3–0 knuckleball, 3–1 knuckleball, 3–2 ground ball to short, we're Western Division champions. After the game [sportswriter] Furman Bisher came up to me and said, 'Bob, you really showed me something the way you settled Wilhelm down in that big situation.' Yeah, I really settled him down all right; he was chewing my ass out!"

The winner that day was Niekro, completing his first 20-win season. He was 30 by then, but the skinny, one-pitch kid who had earned Jim Bouton's pity was well on his way. He had never doubted his knuckleball because he had never thrown anything else. It was his father, Phil Sr., who used the pitch in desperation.

Phil Niekro Sr. worked in the coal mines and pitched as a teenager; somewhere, Phil says, he has news clippings of his father striking out 17 or 18 in a game with his fastball. One cold spring day, Phil Sr. was called in to pitch without having warmed up. He blew out his arm and turned to the knuckleball, taught to him by an old minor league catcher named Nick McKay. Phil Sr. passed the pitch on to his daughter, Phyllis, and then to his son, Phil; Phyllis, her brother would say later, handled his knuckler better than some major league catchers.

Joe Niekro, younger than Phil by five years, struggled to learn it as quickly; his hands were too small. Joe had enough other pitches to fashion a decent major league career, then found stardom for the Astros when he came home to the knuckler in his mid-30s. But Phil never strayed.

"Me and my buddy John Havlicek"—the NBA Hall of Famer—"would get the bat and choose sides and that's when I would throw it, to get all the girls and boys out in that little town of Lansing, Ohio," Phil Niekro recalls. "So I was throwing it all the time. I didn't know there were knuckleball pitchers in the big leagues. I didn't even know what a knuckleball was. It was just something I had fun with, playing catch with my dad."

Phil used the knuckler to make the Bridgeport High School varsity team as a freshman, and he signed with the Milwaukee Braves at age 19. He would spend two decades perfecting the pitch for the franchise, from 1964 through 1983. By the time he finished, with a one-game cameo for the Braves in 1987, he had thrown 5,404 innings; only Cy Young, Pud Galvin, and Walter Johnson threw more. Niekro never apologized for his pitch.

"He has as much confidence in the knuckleball's effectiveness as Aroldis Chapman does throwing 106," R. A. Dickey says. "It blows you away, the mentality he must have possessed as a competitor."

For his 300th victory, as a Yankee on the final day of the regular season in 1985, Phil tried something new. He waited until the final out to throw a knuckleball.

He had failed in four attempts at 300. On the fourth try, on September 30 in New York, he carried in his back pocket a note from Phil Sr. that said: "Win—I'll Be Happy." Phil Sr. wrote it because he could not talk; Phil and Joe, by then a Yankee teammate, had visited him in the hospital the day before, in Wheeling, West Virginia. Phil Sr. was on a breathing tube, his health failing.

Phil's last chance came on October 6 in Toronto. His hard stuff, such as it was, seemed strong in the bullpen, and he figured that fastballs might confuse the tired Blue Jays, who had won their first division title the day before. Knucklers had not worked lately, anyway, and Niekro liked the idea of proving he could win without them. It worked in the first inning, and he kept on going through eight.

Joe came out to warm up Phil before the ninth. With two outs, a runner on second, and Phil's old Braves teammate, Jeff Burroughs, coming to bat, manager Billy Martin sent Joe to the mound for a conference. The brothers agreed that Phil should throw a knuckler, at last, for their dad. George Steinbrenner had arranged for the Yankees' TV feed to be played through the phone to the hospital, so their mother, Henrietta, could give play-by-play to Phil Sr. The final knuckleball dipped down and away, and Burroughs swung over it to end the game. The brothers took the ball to the hospital the next day.

"He had a smile on his face," Phil says. "I walked up and gave him that ball and said, 'This is yours as much as mine,' and put my Yankee hat on him. The doc came in and said, 'He's been up all night waiting for you guys to get here.' So we stayed the next few days, and in a couple of weeks he was home. I got to pitch another couple of years, Joe got traded to Minnesota and got to the World Series, and I think that's what he wanted to see in his lifetime: both his boys, one got to the World Series, the other won 300 games and then 18 more. Because he was struggling for about two years there, and then after Joe and I both retired, he passed. But that's why he was hanging on."

———

When knuckleballers meet, they bond instantly. They are all Jedi knights, possessors of a shadowy power few can understand or believe. The old recognize it in the young.

"I grew up a Dodger fan in Northern California," Tom Candiotti says. "I can't remember the exact year, but my older brother takes me to a Giants game, and the Dodgers are coming out before BP, stretching. Charlie Hough comes out to left field and I'm down the line there at Candlestick with my glove. And he goes, 'Here!'—and he throws me a knuckleball. So I throw one back to him like that, and he goes, 'Hey, kid, that's not bad!' He throws me another one, I throw it back. So we played catch for about five minutes with me in the stands, just throwing a knuckleball, and I go, 'That was cool, I played catch with that number 49 guy out there!'"

Candiotti would grow up to wear 49, too, like Hough and Wakefield, a tribute to the retirement age of the great Wilhelm. His was a typically wild backstory—an undrafted college pitcher with a nothing fastball, Candiotti tagged along on a summer trip with a buddy who was trying out for the independent Victoria (British Columbia) Mussels. Candiotti brought his fishing pole, not his baseball glove, but a scout recognized him, told him to hop on a mound, and signed him for

$400 Canadian a month. The money did not go far. "I'm probably still wanted for dining and dashing up there," Candiotti says.

The Royals soon signed Candiotti, lost him in the minor league draft, and before long, without ever having pitched in major league spring training, Candiotti was on a big league mound for the Brewers. He told his catcher, Ted Simmons, that he threw an occasional knuckler, and tried one as a goof for his last warm-up pitch. Simmons startled Candiotti by calling it for his very first pitch in the majors. It sailed for ball one of a four-pitch walk.

The knuckleball was Candiotti's destiny, but he didn't see it. The Brewers implored him to work on his knuckleball, but Candiotti resisted. The knuckleball was just for fun, a gimmick he had learned from his dad, and he was proud of his fastball and curve, even if they screamed Triple-A. Then he signed with Cleveland as a minor league free agent and a new teammate, soon to be 47, changed everything.

Phil Niekro, back for more after that 300th win, played catch with Candiotti every day, comparing knuckleballs. Candiotti threw his as hard as he could, imagining a dastardly knuckler that would fool the hitter and the catcher and peg the umpire in the chest. Niekro told him to settle down, throw it softer, in the zone. You want them to hit it, he said.

Oh, and one more thing: you shouldn't throw anything else.

"I said I still had a curveball!" Candiotti says. "He goes, 'Trust me, this is what's gonna keep you in the big leagues for a long time. Keep working on it and developing it.' He was my own pitching coach. He'd sit next to me on the bench when I started. The other pitching coaches, they don't know what to say to you."

Coaches can try. The good ones will study a knuckleballer's mechanics and learn the proper checkpoints in his delivery. But unless you have thrown it, knuckleballers say, you just cannot relate. They tell each other to be their own coach, to know their pitch intimately. That is why they enjoy talking about it—with each other, with conventional pitchers, with writers. They have to immerse themselves in the culture of the knuckleball to even have a chance. R. A. Dickey would take a ball around with him in his car, steering with his left hand, practicing grips with his right.

Rare is the knuckleballer who has not talked shop with the others

Steve Carlton warms up near the first base dugout at Veterans Stadium. His peerless slider helped make him the first pitcher to win four Cy Young Awards—and the last to work 300 innings in a season, in 1980.

Bob Gibson started nine World Series games, completing eight and going 7–2 with a 1.89 ERA. He set a single-game strikeout record in the 1968 opener, with 17.

A perfect game flipped Randy Johnson's famous scowl into a smile in 2004. Eddie Perez, who struck out to end it, insists the final fastball rose.

That's eight—*count 'em, eight!*—baseballs in the mighty right hand of J. R. Richard, whose overpowering fastball and slider still inspire awe in those who faced him.

Brad Lidge, whose topspinning slider baffled hitters because it never had a telltale red dot, strikes out Eric Hinske to win the 2008 World Series for the Phillies.

"My favorite pitch," Cy Young said, "was a whistler right under the chin."

Carl Mays closed out the World Series for the Red Sox in 1918. Two years later, with the Yankees, his errant fastball killed the Indians' Ray Chapman.

Walter Johnson, greeting President Calvin Coolidge at Griffith Stadium in Washington, D.C., "was so great that he almost belongs in his own Hall of Fame," said Bob Feller.

Two of baseball's greatest power pitchers, Bob Feller (left) and Satchel Paige, were teammates on the Indians' 1948 championship team.

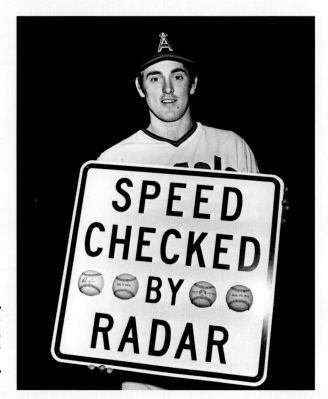

With the Angels in 1973, Nolan Ryan set the single-season strikeout record (383) while going 21–16 with a 2.87 ERA and 26 complete games, including two no-hitters.

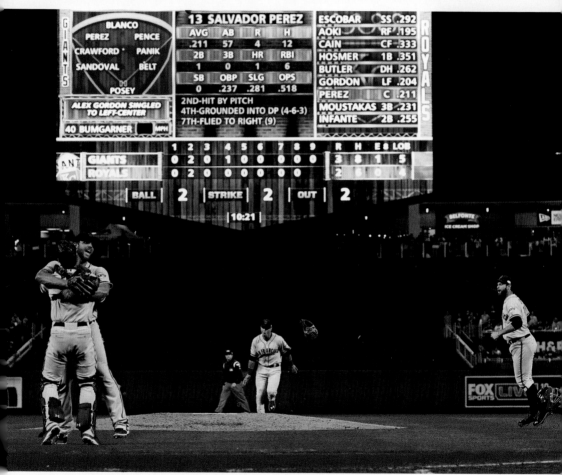

Madison Bumgarner embraces Buster Posey after baiting Salvador Perez with a high fastball for the final out of the 2014 World Series in Kansas City.

Many claimed to have invented the curveball, but only Candy Cummings gets credit on a Cooperstown plaque: "Pitched first curve ball in baseball history," it reads.

Sandy Koufax (left) and Jim Palmer shake hands before Game 2 of the 1966 World Series. Palmer, age twenty, threw a shutout. Koufax, age thirty, never pitched again.

Mike Mussina—shown as a Yankee at Camden Yards, his old home with the Orioles—earned 270 victories with an ever-evolving array of weapons.

The Cardinals' Adam Wainwright learned his signature curveball from his older brother at age ten.

The Cubs' Mike Montgomery charges across the mound in joy after his curveball won Game 7 of the 2016 World Series in Cleveland. Yes, he got his glove back.

in their small fraternity. Phil and Joe Niekro helped Wakefield. Hough helped Dickey. Candiotti helped Steven Wright. They all have a piece of each other's success.

"I always thought if each organization gave up two of their good athletes that aren't gonna make it and see if they can make knuckleball pitchers out of them, me and Charlie Hough and Tim Wakefield can open a knuckleball school," Phil says. "We'll send these guys to it, evaluate them, work with them for a couple of months and report back to the organization: hey, he has a shot or he doesn't have a shot."

It can be done. When the Brewers decided that a prospect named Steve Sparks had no future as a conventional pitcher, they told him to learn a knuckleball. Sparks had never tried it before, and as his first resource he scoured his childhood baseball cards, purchased with the money from his *Tulsa World* paper route as a teen. Sparks studied the grips of Hough and the Niekros, learning to minimize drag on the ball by making sure no fingers touched the seams. Before reporting to winter ball in 1992, Sparks met with Candiotti at the Astrodome, where Candiotti's Dodgers were finishing the season. He peppered him with six pages of questions, and learned to lock his wrist by turning it inward slightly, keeping it from rolling over and imparting spin.

Sparks would pitch nine seasons in the majors, weathering the American League in the steroid era. He was not Tim Wakefield, but he was a reasonable facsimile. As his career wound down, in 2004, Sparks put the knuckleball brotherhood above another payday.

"My agent told me the Yankees wanted me to throw to them, to prepare for their playoffs with [Wakefield's] Red Sox," Sparks says. "He told me they said, 'Name your price.' I'd probably get a nice hotel and $10,000 if I wanted, I didn't even know. But I just told them I'd rather not. Tim was a friend and it just didn't feel right."

The benefits of having a knuckleballer are clear enough: at worst he can absorb innings in blowouts, save the other relievers, and make a spot start now and then. But opportunities are scarce, and most teams are too timid to try. The Red Sox invested eight seasons in the development of Charlie Zink—a knuckleballer from the baseball powerhouse Savannah College of Arts and Design—but gave him just one big league start, in 2008. Zink allowed eight runs.

In 2016, the Rays hoped to take advantage of the humidity of their climate-controlled dome by cultivating low-cost knuckleballers. Their pitching coordinator, Charlie Haeger, had thrown the knuckler briefly in the majors, and they gathered a few prospects, including former position players, to try the pitch. In the end, they gave seven September relief outings to Eddie Gamboa.

"A lot of organizations will shy from it because they don't have anybody to instruct or they're not familiar with it," Haeger says. "It's that uniqueness that people are maybe a little scared of at times."

In 2013, MLB Network hired Wakefield to coach five former college quarterbacks in a reality show called *The Next Knuckler*. Most of the contestants, Wakefield says, had no feel for the pitch, no chance at all. Josh Booty, who had played briefly in the majors as an infielder, won the contest, signed with the Diamondbacks, and never made it out of spring training.

"I've probably worked with 12 guys," Dickey says. "I've seen one that might have a chance. *Might*. It takes a complete surrender to doing what is necessary to cultivate the pitch, and a lot of guys don't have that. Most guys have some entitlement, like: 'I shouldn't have to go on the back field at the minor league complex and grind it out against Gulf Coast Leaguers.' It's hard, because most guys come to this pitch when they're older, and they've had somewhat of a career as something else. It's a real struggle, having to start all over again from the ground up."

The success stories are the exception. The miracle is that anyone at all can throw the pitch consistently. Most pitchers like it when the wind blows in, to reduce the chances of home runs. Knuckleballers hate it, because more wind behind the pitch can cause it to whoosh away from the catcher or dive into the dirt. Most pitchers, unless they're scuffing the ball, have no reason to fret about the length of their fingernails. Knuckleballers depend on it.

Joe Niekro got a 10-game suspension in 1987 when, during a game in Anaheim, he emptied his pockets for umpires and an emery board and sandpaper flew out. He tried to explain that of course he had those products—he needs to groom his nails on the bench between innings. Did they really think he could dig them out of his pocket and deface baseballs in the middle of the field?

"Put yourself out there on the mound with 30,000 people, six TV cameras, and four umpires around you, and you've got an emery board in your back pocket," Phil Niekro says, still bothered by his brother's punishment decades later.

"Explain to me how you're gonna take that emery board out of your back pocket and doctor the ball up, when everybody's watching. You can't do it. As soon as he threw the emery board out of his back pocket, the umpire threw him out of the game. If I was out there, they would've had to handcuff me. Until you show me something on camera that I'm using an emery board in my back pocket to take it out on the mound and scuff up the ball, you've got nothing, because you can't do it. And if you did they would sure as hell see it."

The grip on a knuckleball is naturally unstable. The fingers and the nails must be strong enough to lock the ball in place as the pitcher whips his arm through the air. Use of the seams can vary from pitcher to pitcher, but the general rule is to leave them alone. Engaging the seams leads to friction, which leads to tumbling, which leads to trouble.

The knuckleballer should have a short stride, the better to stay behind the ball and send it on its wobbly path. He should follow through down the center of his body, almost as if hitting himself in the protective cup, because finishing over either leg could cause that dreaded spin. (A benefit of this is that knuckleballers tend to finish in a strong fielding position; Niekro won five Gold Gloves and Dickey won one.)

Hough urged Dickey to keep his mechanics compact by imagining he was pitching through a doorframe. Once he's through it, Dickey says, he visualizes a vertical shoebox at the top of the zone and tries to put the pitch there. When he was at his best, in 2012, Dickey led the league in strikeouts by throwing a flat knuckler that stayed high; hitters expected it to fall and swung under it. He remained an effective starter thereafter, but that same strikeout pitch largely abandoned him. It bothered Dickey because he wanted to be trustworthy, to fight the notion that his pitch was not.

"A conventional pitcher gives up 10 runs in a game? 'Ah, it was one of those days,'" Dickey says. "If I give up 10 runs in a game? 'I told you so.' That's the difference. And that's across the board with guys in those offices, all across baseball."

One reason for the lack of trust, though, is that no other starter takes the mound with just one option. If another starter is struggling with one pitch, he tends to have at least two others. And while pitchers from the 1930s and '40s may have incorporated the knuckleball into a wider repertoire, today's knucklers don't.

It is all or nothing—the Niekro doctrine—and it is not all up to the pitcher, either.

––––––––

The best advice for catching a knuckleball might have come from Mike Sandlock, who played for the Braves and the Dodgers from 1942 to 1946. He slipped back to the minors after that, and might have stayed there if not for his success with Johnny Lindell, a converted outfielder whose knuckler earned them both a promotion to the Pittsburgh Pirates in 1953. It did not go well: Lindell led the league in walks and wild pitches, and Sandlock in passed balls. Neither ever played in the majors again.

"A knuckleball is like a dame," Sandlock once said. "If you reach for it, you're licked. You've got to wait until it reaches for you."

John Flaherty played 14 years in the majors and was used to weird events; in his debut, for Boston in 1992, he caught an eight-inning, no-hit loss by Matt Young. Back with the Red Sox in spring training of 2006, Flaherty was asked to replace Doug Mirabelli, who had been traded after serving as Wakefield's personal catcher. Flaherty got a knuckleball glove from Wilson, caught some soft deliveries from Wakefield in the bullpen, and didn't think much of it.

Then Wakefield took the mound for batting practice and told Flaherty he would mix in some hard knucklers, too.

"That kind of threw me off, because when he's throwing them soft, you can kind of wait and let the ball catch you, so to speak, instead of you trying to catch the ball," Flaherty said. "But when he started throwing them harder, then it's like, 'Oh shit, I don't know where this is going.' It was almost like it could be a hard slider, it could be a hard split going down, it could be a screwball. It kind of got in my head a little bit.

"And then when we got into a game, he walked the first batter, Luis Castillo, who could run. And I said, 'Wait, I haven't even thought about throwing a runner out.' So that was a whole other level. I turned to

Tim Timmons, the home plate umpire, and I said, 'You're working the last game I'm ever gonna catch.' In the first inning. He said, 'No, no, you're gonna get it.' I said, 'I don't want to get it. That's the problem. I don't want to do this.' And I caught him for another inning, it went pretty well, caught three more innings and then said all the right things to the media, how I'm gonna get it, I'm gonna work at it, it's gonna be fine.

"Then I walked into [manager Terry] Francona's office the next morning: 'Gone, time to go.' Best decision I ever made."

In truth, Flaherty said, he was already wavering on how much he still wanted to play. But the knuckleball confirmed his feeling. He tried to imagine himself in the cauldron of Yankee Stadium, with a runner on third and a knuckleball darting somewhere near his regular catcher's mitt (the oversized pillow, he said, had been uncomfortable). The effort it would take to roll with that knuckleball, and endure the embarrassment, was just not worth it.

With Flaherty gone, the Red Sox turned to Josh Bard—and watched in horror as he committed 10 passed balls in April, seemingly well on his way to the modern record of 35 by the Rangers' Geno Petralli, when he caught Hough in 1987. In hindsight, Bard says, he was the wrong man for the job. He was long-levered, big for a catcher at 6 foot 3, and liked to extend his glove to reach for pitches. The concept of letting the ball travel went against Bard's instincts, and he constantly felt he was letting down the team.

"It was the only thing in my life that the harder I tried at it, the worse I got," Bard says. "You felt a ton of tension, and the only way to deal with it was to almost not care about it. That's not really in my DNA." He smiled: "I was more of a chaser than I was a catcher."

With nowhere else to turn, and Wakefield set to face the Yankees on May 1, the Red Sox panicked, trading Bard and a young pitcher to San Diego to reacquire Mirabelli. They whisked him from the airport to Fenway Park, Mirabelli changing into his uniform in the back of a police cruiser careening through the tight city streets. The Red Sox stalled, delaying the first pitch by eight minutes, and Mirabelli left his protective cup behind in the car. But he made it in time to guide Wakefield through seven strong innings of a Red Sox victory.

A decade later, another Boston knuckleballer, Steven Wright, would emerge as an All-Star. His primary catcher in the first half, Ryan Hanigan, sat across the locker room from Wright one day, the skin on his bruised lower legs the color of old bananas. Nothing felt natural about catching a knuckleball, Hanigan said. A catcher wants to snag other breaking balls—except for the high curveball—before they dart out of the zone. Letting the knuckler get deep was testing him, and Hanigan was only barely passing. Wright had given him a choice of six or seven gloves, none of them a good fit. The job wiped him out mentally, too.

"There's so many innings in a year, you've got to relax as a catcher," Hanigan said. "But there's no relaxing. You have to catch it in an action stance. You have to be up on your legs, engaging your muscles, not what you'd call sitting back. He's a lot more taxing for me than anybody else, by far."

Even a two-strike count can bring a well-founded sense of dread for a catcher. Consider the plight of the Rangers' Orlando Mercado, working with Hough on June 16, 1986. Hough took a no-hit shutout into the bottom of the ninth inning in Anaheim, but lost it on an error and a single. That happens. Later that inning, though, Hough lost the game on a *strikeout*. A third-strike knuckler bounced away from Mercado for a passed ball, and Hough was too stunned to cover the plate. Wally Joyner, who had reached second on another passed ball, dashed home from there to end the game.

In the archives of Baseball-Reference.com, this was the first game ever to end on a strikeout–passed ball—and the knuckleball just had to be the culprit. Robert K. Adair, the physicist, concluded that hitting the knuckleball squarely is essentially an accident, and suggested a strategy of striking out and hoping for a passed ball. Bob Didier agrees.

"When I managed in the minor leagues, I told my team the best way to hit a knuckleball pitcher is get two strikes, swing, and start running," Didier says. "Because the catcher probably ain't gonna catch it."

Didier had never played above Class A when he reported to spring training with Atlanta in 1969. That March the Braves traded their starting catcher, Joe Torre, and another catcher got hurt. Didier was young, but he had a few hits—and somehow, despite no prior experience with the knuckleball, he could handle Phil Niekro. He made the team.

"You know how you block a ball in the dirt and you put your body in front of the ball? I did that with the ball in the air," Didier says. "I tried to center my body behind my glove and if I missed it with my glove, it caught my body and it would kind of stay in front of me. I would have 10 or 12 balls a game when Niekro was pitching that missed my glove and hit my chest at 60 or 65 miles an hour. Keep your body behind your glove and hopefully behind the ball, and use whatever you could—legs, stomach, chest, shoulder—to just keep it in front."

That first season, Didier led the majors in passed balls, with 27. The toughest pitches, he said, were the ones from Niekro that would swoop over his left shoulder. Then the Braves traded for Wilhelm, and Didier battled the corkscrew action of his softer knuckleballs.

"After a game, I felt like I'd caught a doubleheader or a 15-inning game or something," Didier says. "I was just worn out, fighting that. I can't think of another word, other than *fighting* a knuckleball."

Pitchers can help in that fight. Sparks created a prototype for a knuckleball catcher's glove—the Pro Sparks model, by Rawlings—with reduced weight in the padded area and special attention to the curved webbing, to keep balls from escaping on tag plays. And with so little margin for error in the running game, knuckleballers tend to work especially hard on their pickoff moves.

But the pitch still makes for a different kind of day for everyone. A game of incredible speed is suddenly played in slow motion. Some hitters would rather avoid it altogether. Their typical theory on trying to hit it? See it low, let it go; see it high, let it fly.

"You have to wait as long as possible—and then explode," said Jesse Barfield, who had four homers off Hough but was 3-for-25 against the Niekros. "If you've played Slo-Pitch Softball, you know what I'm talking about. So you treat it almost like that. Wait, wait, wait—and then explode."

You look like a fool if you miss, but the explosions can live forever. Reggie Jackson's third home run in Game 6 of the 1977 World Series came off a knuckler from Hough. Barry Bonds's record seventy-third homer in 2001 came off a Dennis Springer knuckleball. Aaron Boone, who had been 1-for-10 off Wakefield, belted his knuckler for the pennant-winning homer in Game 7 of the 2003 AL Championship Series.

A year later, though, facing elimination in Game 5 of the ALCS, Wakefield tiptoed through shutout innings in the twelfth, thirteenth, and fourteenth, surviving two passed balls and beating the Yankees. He would start the opener of the World Series when the Red Sox won their first title since 1918.

"The challenge is that you need to know going in there's gonna be walks, there's gonna be stolen bases, and there's gonna be passed balls," Francona says. "As a manager, if you can't handle that, you have a chance to miss out on a really good pitcher. So I kind of learned early: take your hands, put them under your butt and sit on them, and stay out of the way. And you'd look up and Wake would be pitching into the seventh or eighth inning."

Most managers cannot afford to do that; few pitchers can throw a knuckleball like Tim Wakefield or will ever come close. College and high school coaches want to win, not give away games as an aspiring knuckleballer learns his quirky craft. A low minor league setting is the best laboratory, but even there, teams tend to see more potential in the waves of hard-throwing prospects they draft every year.

But the pitch will survive, because the aggravation is worth it—and deep down, baseball people like it. When Sparks pitched, umpires routinely tossed him knucklers when they gave him a new ball. (John Shulock and Greg Kosc had especially good ones.) Conventional pitchers might not need the knuckleball, but they envy it just the same. Says Chuck Finley, the longtime Angels lefty, "Every starting pitcher would love to go out there for just one game and throw nothing but knuckleballs."

And for all its unpredictability, throwing the knuckleball takes the kind of toughness widely admired by the smartest people in the game.

"I've got a lot of respect for Wake because he goes out on the mound and fights," Pedro Martinez said in Wakefield's book. "If he doesn't have a good knuckleball, he ain't got shit. But he fights."

When all else fails a pitcher—when the gun runs out of bullets and the blade on the sword turns dull—he can always try a slingshot.

Why not? There's really nothing to lose. It probably won't work, and he probably won't understand it, anyway.

"You could throw two knuckleballs that look the same, have no spin coming out, but they do two different things," Steven Wright says. "One might move all over the place and one might not do anything. Like, how does that happen?"

Wright laughed. He was riding the knuckleball to an All-Star season, and even he was completely baffled.

"That's the beauty of it, man," he says. "When it's working, it's fun as hell. When it's not working, you just chuck and duck."

THE
SPLITTER

Through the Trapdoor

I was 12 years old the first time I visited the Hall of Fame. I remember noticing the tag on the inside of George Brett's hat: 7¼. This astonished me. I wore fitted hats all the time back then, and my head size was 7⅜. I had a bigger head than George Brett.

This had no practical application, of course. All it really meant was that, if George Brett and I ever found ourselves at one of those hat stores in the mall, and we both wanted to buy the same hat, we would never have to fight for the last one—an unlikely scenario, for sure, but at 12 it sort of mattered. My head was already bigger than the head of a grown-up baseball superstar. How about *that*!

This feeling came to me again, almost 30 years later, when talking with Dennis Eckersley about the split-finger fastball. Eckersley's Hall of Fame career spanned the era of the split-finger craze: from the mid-1970s, when the pitch was still evolving from its forkball roots, through the late 1990s, when injury fears dimmed its popularity. Eckersley had thrived with precision command of a fastball and slider, but never mastered a changeup. A right-hander, Eckersley yearned for a pitch that would dive straight down, or down and away from left-handers. He just did not have the fingers for it.

"You know how some guys carry around softballs so they can split their fingers?" he said. "I actually had the doctor make a cast for me. I strapped it on, and I'd have my two fingers in there for a while. I'd drive around with that cast on in the off-season. That's how sick I was!"

Sometimes, Eckersley said, the pitch would work for him in the bullpen. But it was never consistent enough to use in the ninth inning, when there's no room for error, and remains a fanciful wish, a superpower beyond his reach. If only he could have split his fingers like ... *me?*

In the course of our talk, I held my index and middle fingers in front of me, like a flat peace sign, the way a pitcher would before straddling the commissioner's signature on either side of a baseball's seams. Eckersley howled.

"That's a major split!" he cried. "I can't do that!" Brian Anderson, Eckersley's broadcast partner that day and the brother of a former major league pitcher, stood nearby. He split his fingers, too. "This is as far as I can go," Anderson said. His spread was much narrower than mine. "You don't want to hurt something there," Eckersley told me, admiringly. But it didn't hurt at all.

I felt a little like George Costanza on *Seinfeld*, when he learns he would be a perfect hand model. Really, these hands? Was the great Dennis Eckersley—an A+ source on this kind of thing—actually telling me my fingers were better equipped to throw the split-finger fastball than his?

Well, yes and no. Eckersley is enthusiastic about a lot of topics. I've also shaken hands with enough major leaguers to know that my fingers—while apparently quite flexible—are pretty stubby next to theirs. And nearly everyone I've talked to about the splitter says long fingers are essential, locking the pitch in place to keep it from flying away.

Functionally, then, my better-than-Eckersley finger spread is useless. Just as my big head would not help me hit .390 like George Brett, my freakish fingers would not help me harness the magic of Bullet Joe Bush, Shigeru Sugishita, Elroy Face, or Bruce Sutter.

When it comes to that final name, especially, I am not alone. Of the millions of people who have ever thrown a baseball, Sutter stands alone as the master of the split-finger. Few pitches in the game's history are as synonymous with one man as the splitter is with Sutter. Like Mariano Rivera would do with the cut fastball, Sutter took an existing pitch, modified it, and inspired a generation of imitators.

But while others could at least mimic Rivera's method of throwing the cutter, Sutter was almost a singular phenomenon in the history of his pitch.

"Nobody could throw it the way he threw it," says Roger Craig, the coach most synonymous with the splitter. "I could never learn to throw that, or teach that. Bruce Sutter's really the one."

————————

History assigns a prominent place to Craig for the sudden rise—and sharp demise—of the split-finger fastball in its modern form. He deserves the acclaim, but context is important. Before Roger Craig, there was Fred Martin. He taught the pitch to Sutter, and the two of them showed it to Craig. Without Martin, the splitter would never have taken off the way it did.

Because of Martin, there is a plaque in Cooperstown for Sutter, with the split-finger fastball mentioned in the very first line. Because of Martin, there is a dream home for Sutter on Red Top Mountain in Georgia, with a Cy Young Award displayed in the man cave. One day in 2016, Sutter was repairing a broken drawer and found a black-and-white photo of Martin, some four decades old, holding up a baseball with his right hand. Wearing a Cubs uniform as the sun splashes his craggy face, Martin looks not at the camera but at his creation: the grip he taught Sutter, with the index and middle fingers stretching to hold the ball on either side of the seams, like prongs supporting the diamond of an engagement ring.

For Sutter, the pitch was just as precious and far more valuable. Without it, he never would have pitched above Class A. Sutter learned it in 1973, when his future was bleak. His manager that season, Walt Dixon, wrote this in a report to his bosses: "Bruce Sutter will make the major leagues when a communist regime is ready to take over this country."

Martin was not the kind of guy who dealt in sarcasm. And Sutter was not the kind of pitcher who gave up easily—on baseball, anyway. He had dropped out of Old Dominion because he wanted more time to play ball. He went back home to Pennsylvania and worked at a printing shop in Lancaster, where a local meatpacker sponsored a semipro team called Hippey's Raiders. The draft was over, but a Cubs scout, Ralph DiLullo, noticed Sutter's enormous hands. He gave the kid the last $500 from his annual bonus budget.

"When I saw those hands," DiLullo told writer Gerry Fraley years later, "I said to myself, 'Wow, that kid can do something with those hands.'"

Back then, nobody linked long fingers with the splitter, because Sutter hadn't thrown it yet. Martin had, as a kind of changeup, but nobody really noticed. As a 31-year-old Cardinals rookie in 1946, Martin jumped to the Mexican League and thrived for parts of two seasons. But he was barred for a year upon his return and spent almost all of the 1950s in the minors. He managed for a year in the Cubs' chain and then became a coach—in the majors for a while, but mostly in the minors, where he met Sutter.

Sutter had tried to learn a slider in 1972, but it hurt his elbow after just two pro games. Back home that winter, he paid a doctor to reroute a pinched nerve in his elbow; knowing he was expendable, Sutter planned not to tell the Cubs. He confessed the next spring, when the Cubs nearly cut him, and his gumption saved his job. The Cubs kept Sutter more for his will than his talent, and assigned him to play for Dixon in Quincy, Illinois, where he was the mop-up man in blowouts. "You might as well have a D on your hat," Dixon told him one day, "because you're in for the duration."

Like most organizations then, the Cubs had one pitching coach for the entire minor league system. Theirs was Martin. He would visit the affiliates every month and show the pitchers several ways to throw each pitch. They would work on the pitches until his next visit, experimenting with grips in hopes of unlocking something worthy of the majors.

"He showed us all how to throw the split-finger," says Sutter, who quickly realized he had an edge. All his life, Sutter had thrown breaking pitches by applying pressure with his index finger instead of his middle finger. It was counterintuitive, and it wasn't much help on the curve or the slider, but it felt right. With the splitter, Sutter found a pitch that was meant to be thrown like a fastball, but required a dominant index finger to generate its straight-down—or down-and-away-from-a-lefty—movement. Sutter did not split his fingers very far apart or wedge the ball too deep between them, as he would have if throwing the slower forkball. With his thumb positioned to the side, Sutter squirted the ball through, imparting it with a devastating tumble. Sutter said he made one small adjustment the first day Martin showed him, moving his index finger just a bit off the left seam, and never changed it again.

"I'd like to tell you I had to work at it," Sutter says, "but it broke right away."

It did take Sutter time to control the pitch, to learn when to make it do what. His overall performance at Quincy was ordinary—10 hits per nine innings and a 4.13 ERA—and fellow farmhands wondered if he would have a roster spot in 1974. Luckily, he had an advocate.

"He wouldn't have made it out of spring training had it not been for Fred Martin," says Mike Krukow, a teammate who would also go on to a long career. "He said, 'Give this guy a chance.' But then Bruce broke camp, and they were only gonna give him until June when the new draft came in. If he didn't show anything by then . . . well, he tore it up. It was amazing."

As he got to know Sutter, Krukow was not surprised. Whatever Sutter did—shooting baskets, playing pool, throwing darts—his fine motor skills were incredible. He was perfectly suited for this quirky new pitch, the only man Krukow ever saw who could manipulate it with such precision, commanding the pitch to the left or the right, into or out of the strike zone, depending on the pressure he applied to his index finger.

"He brought that pitch into baseball in such an impactful way that if you didn't try it, you were an idiot," Krukow says.

Sutter was in the majors for good by 1976, and Martin was his confidant, building a bond with positive reinforcement and a trust forged over dinners at his Phoenix home in spring training. As his wife cooked, Martin would open scrapbooks and spin stories, with the toughness of a coal miner's son but the softness of a favorite uncle. He spoke often of his years in Mexico, and being blackballed, and shared the nuances of the craft: how to deal with rain, or a hot hitter, or a bad umpire. He promised his pitchers they would never allow three homers in a row—because after two, they should drill the third guy.

"He was from Oklahoma, and he was always real suntanned, looked like his skin was dried out," Sutter says. "Looked like one of those Old

West cowboys, always had the cigarette hanging out of his mouth. It was just different times."

In the Hall of Fame, Sutter represents the Cardinals. He played four seasons in St. Louis, led the league in saves three times there, and closed down Game 7 of the 1982 World Series by striking out Milwaukee's Gorman Thomas—with a high fastball, actually. But his greatest years were really his five with the Cubs. Sutter had more saves, a better ERA, and a better strikeout rate with Chicago, where he won his Cy Young Award in 1979.

His pitch was a revelation. Sutter was the closer—or fireman, as the job was known then—by the end of his rookie season. Joe Coleman, a veteran forkballer, set up for Sutter and was amazed by how different their seemingly similar pitches behaved. Coleman's forkball hardly spun at all, dropping almost like a knuckleball. But Sutter's splitter, Coleman said, spun like a helicopter. Pete Rose said flatly that the pitch was impossible to hit.

"I had never seen a pitch like that, ever—nor had anybody, because his was thrown with incredible vertical variance," says Ted Simmons, who faced and caught Sutter. "So visually it's starting at your forehead and you say it's high and then *vvoomp,* right in the middle. Then he throws it right in the middle and, *bang,* you go after it like a fastball and when you start to swing it dives vertically, and the ball's in the dirt."

When Sutter threw his best splitters, he never even saw them drop; his head would bob precisely as the pitch fell through the trapdoor. If he kept his head up to watch it, it meant he was not finishing his delivery and getting the proper whip at the end. When he struggled in those early years, he would ask the Cubs to fly in Martin for a few days. Sutter needed the reassurance of a calm mentor, and trusted him implicitly.

"You're gonna get a lot of help when you're struggling, and if you don't have someone you trust, you're gonna get confused and change something else," he says. "That's what you always have to worry about. With Fred's personality, he knew what to say around me to get me relaxed. He knew hollering at me is not gonna work. Bullshitting me is not gonna work. You had to tell me something that I believe that'd work. He had that knack."

One of Martin's visits was in San Diego, on a Cubs road trip. As

Sutter got loose in the bullpen for an early mound session, Roger Craig, then managing the Padres, asked Martin about the split. They went to the bullpen and Sutter showed Craig the grip. Sutter's pressure points made that precise pitch unique to him, Craig thought. But the up-close look greatly intrigued him: *this was a fast forkball that tumbled.*

Martin would not live long enough to see where Craig would take the pitch. As Sutter embarked on his Cy Young season, Martin, 63, was dying of cancer. The Cubs played only day games at Wrigley Field then, and Sutter and some teammates would visit Martin in the hospital after they played. Sutter was there when Martin died on June 11, 1979.

"We were kids; we just thought he was sick," Sutter says, softly. "We didn't think he was going to die."

"In a way, it hurts you more than when you lost an actual relative, because of what he meant to us," Krukow says. "I mean, he was our guy. You had that feeling of emptiness and loneliness."

Sutter would find another mentor in Mike Roarke, a different Cubs minor league instructor who would later coach him in St. Louis. Sutter would leave the Cardinals for a six-year contract with the Braves in 1985, but by 1988 he was finished. He had a pinched nerve in his shoulder, and when he came back too soon from arthroscopic surgery, he tore his rotator cuff. His special pitch went with it, forever.

"I never threw it again, really, where I could throw it right," Sutter says. "No, I couldn't. You had to get your arm in position. You had to get your arm up quick, and I couldn't do that anymore. I lost those muscles in my back, part of the rotator cuff, those muscles were pinched off by that nerve again at the end, so I never could get my arm in position to throw it the right way."

Does he miss it?

"It's one of those things—you don't miss the pain," Sutter says. "I mean, I was in a lot of pain when I left. In fact, I started keeping balls, I think, when I was at 290 saves. I didn't know which one was gonna be my last one, because, man, I was hurt. But I got through it, I got to 300 and that was the last pitch I ever threw."

His last pitch was a fastball, alas, for a swinging third strike past Roberto Alomar. Sutter joined Rollie Fingers and Goose Gossage as the only pitchers with 300 saves, and made it to Cooperstown in 2006.

In his speech, he said he would never have reached the majors without learning Fred Martin's pitch. The pitch did not change how the game was played, Sutter told the crowd, but it represented a new way to get hitters out. Everyone who uses it, he said, owes Martin a measure of thanks, because he taught it first.

"I know he has a crowd around him right now," Sutter said, "and he's showing someone how to hold the split-finger."

———————

The splitter, as taught by Martin, applied by Sutter, and imitated by pitchers ever since, stands on its own as a pitch. But it sprang from a diverse lineage, with traces of the changeup, the knuckleball, and the sinker running through its yarn. Buck O'Neil, the Negro Leagues legend and the first black coach in the majors, thought the splitter was a myth—it moved so viciously, he said in Joe Posnanski's *The Soul of Baseball*, it must have been a *spitter.*

The splitter is sometimes referred to as a forkball, because a pitcher splits his index and middle fingers into a V to throw both pitches. But if there's open space at the bottom of the V, it's the faster-moving splitter. If the bottom of the V is flush against the ball—that is, tucked farther back in the hand—it's the slower-moving, nearly spin-less forkball.

"Fred knew it was different than the forkball," Sutter says. "Actually when I first got called up and I went to Pittsburgh, I met Elroy Face, and Elroy showed me how he held his. He said it was more like a knuckleball. His was slower and it didn't spin a lot, where mine had a lot of spin. Mine had a backup spin, like a backup slider. It had a dot, but it was going in the opposite way. The slider's breaking right to left. My ball would break left to right most of the time."

After that final out in 1982, Keith Hernandez was the first to embrace Sutter and catcher Darrell Porter, rushing over from first base to start the celebration. Mostly, though, Hernandez and Sutter were rivals—and Hernandez owned him, going 15-for-35 with seven walks. He said he tried to think of Sutter as just another sinkerballer.

The pitch does sink, and the differences can be subtle. In 2015, closer Jeurys Familia helped the Mets to the World Series with an arsenal of sinkers and splitters to go with a slider. Familia said he simply threw the splitter like the sinker, but spread his fingers a bit more. Just as the sinker would, the splitter helped Familia against lefties in particular.

"His splitter's like 96 and it sinks a foot," catcher Travis d'Arnaud explains. "His two-seamer's like 99 and it sinks half a foot."

Familia's velocity was extreme—"He's a freak," says Oakland reliever Blake Treinen, whose own freakish 100-mile-an-hour sinker once made him an answer on *Jeopardy!*—but d'Arnaud's sketch holds up: a splitter is indeed slower than a sinker, and drops more. It is not as slow as a changeup, but like a changeup, it is slower than a fastball and tends to drop away from the opposite-hand hitter . . . unless it doesn't.

"The split was somewhat unpredictable at first," says Chuck Finley, a 200-game winner, mostly for the Angels in the 1990s. "Sometimes it worked as a cutter, and then as a screwball. I don't believe, at the time, a lot of lefties were even throwing one."

Finley is indeed one of the few left-handers associated with the splitter, an oddity that makes it a little like the knuckleball, which is also thrown almost exclusively by right-handers. Because lefties are harder to find, they tend to get more chances to stick, and rarely must resort to a last-chance trick like the knuckler or splitter. Lefty relievers invariably need a breaking ball that moves away from a lefty hitter; once they have that to go with a fastball, there's usually little need for a third pitch.

If they do try one, it's usually a changeup. If that doesn't work, the splitter can be another option.

"The only reason I throw it is because I can't throw a changeup," says Chasen Shreve, a left-handed Yankees reliever. "I tried for years and I couldn't do it, so my college pitching coach said, 'Try this'—and the first one I threw was just ridiculously good."

Finley, too, learned the splitter only after exhausting all attempts at a changeup. He was suited for it because he threw from a high angle, which a pitcher must do with the splitter so his fingers get on top and yank it down. (Mark McGwire faced Finley more than any other pitcher, and hated it. "He was *nasty*," says McGwire, who hit .188 against him. "He was 6-6 and straight over the top, so he was actually even taller. Nasty.")

Many masters of the split-finger turned to the pitch for the same reason as Finley and Shreve. Ron Darling's hands were too big for the changeup. John Smoltz threw his changeup too hard. Dan Haren could never turn over his wrist comfortably, and begged the Cardinals to let him throw his old high school splitter in the minors.

"They said as long as you don't abuse it, you can throw it," Haren said. "I started throwing it quite a bit—low-A, high-A—and I got to the big leagues quick."

Haren stayed for 13 seasons and made three All-Star teams. By the end, in 2015, he guessed that there were so few pitchers who threw the split-finger, he could probably name them all. Even fewer threw the forkball, which is harder to control because of the way it almost knuckles as it drops. It also requires even longer fingers, which can be a problem. As a young catcher in St. Louis, Todd Zeile would call for forkballs from Jose DeLeon, who threw them in a way that made his thumb bleed when he scratched it after release.

"The fingernail on the index finger of his throwing hand was always a little bit longer and sharper because his hands were so big, and he tried to dig into the side of the ball to get a little extra traction," Zeile says. "And then when he'd follow through—if you think of following through like holding a peace sign—he'd snap his wrist, and his index finger would snap down and cut the side of his thumb.

"After three or four innings, it was almost inevitable. They put New-Skin and stuff over it, but they could never put a bandage on it because it wasn't allowed. So if he lasted long enough and if his forkball was effective, he'd be bleeding at some point past the fifth. What you used to be able to see, when he was having effective games, is he'd dab his thumb on the right side of his pant leg and have a blood spot. People thought it was coming from his leg, but it was coming from the cut on his thumb."

Finger strength is central to the forkball's best-known origin story. The first pitcher known to throw it was Bert Hall, for a Class B team in Tacoma on September 18, 1908. The local paper, the *Daily Tribune*, referred to it as a "fork ball," and *The Seattle Times* described its motion as wiggling, writing that it "beats all the spit-ball and knuckle ball combinations to death." Hall apparently learned the pitch from the team's player-manager, Mike Lynch, who had experimented with it but found that it tired his fingers. Hall, who had worked as a plumber and had a strong wrist, was more effective with it and briefly reached the majors, with the Phillies in 1911. He pitched in just seven games, returned to Tacoma, and took his funky new pitch back with him.

The forkball needed a more successful pitcher than Hall to market it, and Bullet Joe Bush could have been the guy. After winning championships with the 1913 A's and the 1918 Red Sox, Bush hurt his arm and could no longer throw curveballs. With a diminished fastball in 1920, he needed a new pitch to survive. A furious Ty Cobb insisted it was a spitball, but umpires found no wet spot. Bush—who would star for the Yankees' first championship team, in 1923—had actually found a forkball, but would not divulge his secret until years later.

"It was while I was experimenting on different deliveries that I placed the ball between my index and middle fingers, resting the bottom of the sphere on my thumb, and threw it," Bush told *The Saturday Evening Post* in 1929, as quoted by Rob Neyer and Bill James. "I discovered that the ball took a funny hop. I tried it again, moving my thumb to the inside of the ball. It took another peculiar hop as it passed over the plate. I repeated the same thing a number of times, moving my thumb in different positions under the ball and noticed that it broke over the pan in all sorts of strange ways."

Bush said he worked on the pitch so much that his fingers and thumb would get sore—even though his hand was large. "A pitcher with a small hand would have great difficulty controlling this pitch," said Bush, who claimed to be the pitch's inventor and the first to call it the forkball.

Yet Bush proved to be an unwilling publicity agent. By keeping quiet about his pitch until retirement, Bush kept a competitive advantage but prevented its spread. It was not until the 1940s that another pitcher would be widely known for the forkball: Tiny Bonham, who used it to help the Yankees win two World Series. His time in the Bronx overlapped with Joe Page, a lefty reliever who closed out the championships of 1947 and 1949.

That was just about it for Page, who struggled the next season but made it back for a few games with the Pirates in 1954. That spring he met a right-hander named Elroy Face, who had been hit hard as a rookie the year before, when he threw only a fastball and curve.

Branch Rickey, the legendary executive, told Face he was sending him to a minor league team in New Orleans, with instructions to learn an off-speed pitch. Face noticed that the forkball seemed to be working for Page, so he tried it.

"It took half the season to stretch the fingers to get the ball back in there," Face says. "At night my fingers used to ache a little bit from trying to throw it, trying to get it spread out."

Once he did, Face says, he never lost the feel. Like so many practitioners, Face had big hands, which he used in his post-baseball job as a carpenter at Mayview State Hospital in Pennsylvania. Retired at 88, he said in 2016 that he could still comfortably grip his pitch the way he did as a premier reliever. His highlight was an 18–1 season in 1959, followed by a World Series title with Pittsburgh the next year. He holds the Pirates' record for games pitched, with 802.

Page appeared just seven times for the Pirates, and not very effectively. His pitch, it turned out, was not the same one Face had admired in the spring of '54. When the men compared grips years later, Face noticed that while his fingers touched only leather, one of Page's always touched a seam.

In practice, Face says, his forkball served the same purpose as a changeup. He aimed for the middle of the plate, down, and let the ball sink whichever direction it wanted. Deception was everything.

"It worked as a good changeup with the same motion," Face says. "If they were looking for that, I could throw the fastball by 'em. And if they were looking for the fastball, they were out in front."

Face would teach his changeup/forkball to a contemporary, Lindy McDaniel, who would last 21 seasons in the majors. But the pitch, he remembers, was not in the arsenal of another National Leaguer of the era: Roger Craig, a righty who won big with the Dodgers (two championships), lost big with the Mets (46 defeats in two years), and became the most vocal acolyte and influential teacher the pitch has ever known.

"He got all the credit for the pitch," Face says. "But I don't think he ever threw the forkball."

———

Roger Craig didn't teach the forkball, either. He has always, *always* emphasized that the split-finger fastball is a different pitch, and still makes sure to include the word *fastball* in its name; if pitchers think fastball while throwing it, they will do so with fastball arm speed and deceive the hitter. But, yes—Craig threw many pitches, and the forkball was not among them.

"I had a pretty good fastball, a good curveball and slider, and I threw kind of a straight change, palmball type pitch," Craig says. Then he tore his rotator cuff—in the final game ever played by the Brooklyn Dodgers, on the road in Philadelphia in 1957—and everything changed. Unable to rely on pure stuff, Craig lasted nine more seasons, mainly by commanding a sinker. His experiences would serve him well.

Craig was the first pitching coach for the Padres, in 1969, before a stint with the Astros in the mid-1970s. It was there, he said, that he first began experimenting with the pitch that would become the splitter. Craig's meeting with Martin and Sutter came when he returned to San Diego later in the decade, around the time he was also running a baseball school.

"I'd have kids 17, 18 years old, starting to put some pop on the ball, and they were looking for a changeup pitch," Craig says. "Actually, they were not looking for it. When you see you can throw hard enough, that's all you want to throw."

Yet sooner or later, Craig knew, those kids would *need* to learn an off-speed pitch. And if they tried on their own, he feared, they would hurt themselves. Craig wanted to show them something safe, and the split-finger fastball required no manipulation of the wrist. It was just a fastball with a wider grip.

Craig became pitching coach for the Tigers in 1980 and taught the pitch to Milt Wilcox the next season. Wilcox was throwing it in the bullpen one day in Oakland in 1982, with Jack Morris watching. Morris was a star by then, but his slider had started to flatten and he needed an out pitch. In his previous start, in Anaheim, he had been torched for six runs without a strikeout. Wilcox showed Morris his grip.

"So I'm getting loose and I throw about 20, and *nothing*," Morris says. "I was about ready to quit and he goes, 'Put your thumb on the side this time, make sure you get your hand out in front, pull through out here.' So I threw about three more and the fourth one was just—*whomp,* straight down. And immediately I go, 'Holy shit, this is like cheating. If I get this down, there ain't nobody alive gonna hit it.' And two starts later I was throwing it in games."

Morris would go on to win more games than any other pitcher in the 1980s, and reach the Hall of Fame in 2018. Robin Yount, who rarely struck out, whiffed more times off Morris than any other pitcher, and said the splitter made Morris a star.

"That pitch alone took him to greatness," Yount says. "It was one of those pitches I never could recognize, because it always looked like a fastball to me. I swung at plenty of bouncing split-fingers from that guy. Most good hitters can recognize pitches early; you see the ball leave the pitcher's hand and can realize what the pitch is by the rotation. And a split-finger just didn't have the look of anything else.

"Now, in saying that, a lot of guys tried to throw them, but only a handful could really throw them well."

Many in that handful learned under Craig. The 1984 Tigers rolled to a championship, going 7–1 in the postseason with all of their starters—Morris, Wilcox, and Dan Petry—throwing the split-finger fastball. The pitch itself became a star.

"Most people believe Babe Ruth was the greatest baseball player ever—I wonder if he could have hit the split-finger fastball." Morris said after beating the Padres in Game 4 of the World Series, for his second complete game victory. "Ty Cobb? I've seen his swing. I know he couldn't hit it!"

Craig temporarily retired after the World Series, but his pitch had helped win a championship, and everyone wants to imitate a winner. A year before Buddy Ryan's "46" defense made him a celebrity coach with the Chicago Bears, the split-finger gave Craig the same status. He was not shy about explaining it, and even wrote a book chronicling the 1984 season.

In it, Craig explains that Wilcox threw the pitch on his fingertips, while Morris—who refers to it today as a forkball, not a split-finger fastball—tucked it back in his palm. He instructs readers not to grip the ball too deeply.

"The important thing is to assume a grip which feels comfortable and allows you to throw strikes," Craig wrote. "You can concentrate on the thumb once you feel comfortable gripping the ball with your middle and index fingers. Try to manipulate the thumb by imparting a little pressure upon release of the ball. This will give the pitch a tumbling effect. You also can curl the fingertips of your middle and index fingers, especially the index finger. That friction will give the pitch even more of a tumbling effect."

The tumble was essential, and so baffling that perhaps only a five-time batting champion with 20-12 vision could make it seem easy to hit. Wade Boggs had more at-bats off Morris and Dave Stewart than any other pitchers in his Hall of Fame career. He hit .363 off them.

"I could see the tumble, and if it started out up, it was gonna be a strike, but if they threw it down in the zone it was gonna tumble out of the zone," Boggs said. "So that was the thing. But when my eyes started to go bad, I couldn't see the tumble anymore."

That made Boggs like most hitters, who struggled to identify just what they were seeing. Was it a fastball, or maybe a changeup, and where did that drop come from? The effect was so devastating, and so well-chronicled, that at one point George Steinbrenner offered Craig and his wife an all-expenses-paid trip to Hawaii if Craig would tutor the Yankees' pitching coach. Craig declined.

In September 1985, on their way to the only 100-loss season in franchise history, the Giants hired Craig as manager. Attendance at his first game was 2,668. The important stuff happened beforehand, anyway.

"The first day I took all our pitchers down to the bullpen and I told them I'm not gonna push this on anybody, I'm gonna show everybody how to throw it and if you can learn to throw it, good, it could help the ball club," Craig says. "Anyway, I asked one pitcher who said he'd never thrown it before and it was Mark Davis. I said, 'OK, I'm gonna use you as my example.' So I got him on the mound and instead of having him throw a fastball with the seams, the two-seamer, I opened his fingers about an eighth of an inch. I said, 'Throw another fastball,' and I kept opening his fingers on every pitch until he had it out about, oh, three-quarters of an inch or something, and from then on he couldn't throw the ball as hard, but it would go down a little bit."

Two years later, with San Diego, Davis made the All-Star team. The next year he won the NL Cy Young Award. By then the Giants had become a winner, with a division title in 1987 and a pennant in 1989. And the splitter, as they would say years later, had gone viral.

Even at the time, it stood out as a quintessential '80s fad. In *The New Yorker,* Roger Angell likened the splitter to the Rubik's Cube. In *Sports Illustrated,* Ron Fimrite compared Craig's faith in the pitch to "the way Cap Weinberger believes in Star Wars—as the ultimate defense weapon." Hands across America—big hands, anyway—were letting those splitters fly. Heck, even the era's best *hitter,* Tony Gwynn, showed off his splitter grip for his 1986 Topps baseball card.

"I think it is the pitch of the future," Angels closer Donnie Moore told the *Los Angeles Times* in April 1986. "I think it's going to be a pitch like the slider was. Now almost everybody throws a little slider. I think in years to come, it's going to be *the* pitch."

Moore, once a Cubs farmhand, had learned the splitter from Fred Martin. His pitching coach in the Braves' system, the great Johnny Sain, encouraged him to trust it. Yet while the pitch made Moore an All-Star, he hung it at the worst moment, to Boston's Dave Henderson when the Angels were one strike away from the 1986 World Series. Henderson golfed it over the left field fence for a homer and the Red Sox soon claimed the pennant. Moore questioned his pitch selection after the game: "Maybe if I had tried to blow it past him, we'd be drinking champagne right now," he said.

(Moore's life unraveled in the years to follow. In 1989 he shot his wife, who survived, and then shot himself to death—an act of madness that almost certainly had much more to do with a history of domestic violence than with an errant split-finger fastball.)

Usually, the splitter was responsible for moments of glory. Red Sox lefty Bruce Hurst learned it from Craig before a game in 1984, and used it to beat the Mets twice in the 1986 World Series. The Blue Jays made the playoffs four times, and won their first World Series, with Tom Henke and his splitter locking down the ninth. Stewart's forkball helped him to four consecutive 20-win seasons and the MVP award in the 1989 World Series for Oakland—against Craig's team.

The Giants could not blame Craig for teaching Stewart the pitch. Stewart learned his forkball by modifying a splitter grip Sandy Koufax had shown him with the Dodgers at spring training in 1982.

"Sandy had really helped me with my mechanics when I was younger, and he told me, 'Hey, look, I want you to split your fingers a little bit and that should give you more downward movement on the ball,'" Stewart says. "I started experimenting a little more, and the split-finger that Sandy had pretty much taught me to throw, I changed it into a fork."

But it took a while. Traded the next year to Texas, Stewart shelved the pitch at the insistence of manager Doug Rader. His career sputtered and he drifted to the Phillies, who released him in May 1986. Signed by his hometown A's two weeks later, Stewart finally unleashed the forkball in Tony La Russa's first game as their manager, on ABC's *Monday Night Baseball* in Boston that July. Roger Clemens was 14–1 at the time, but Stewart beat him—the first of his eight victories over Clemens, without a loss, after joining the A's.

Oakland's championship rotation included two other starters, Mike Moore and Bob Welch, who threw Stewart's pitch. That was how it spread, from one master to others, alluring to both failing and thriving pitchers.

Mike Scott was failing: through the 1984 season he was 29–44 with a 4.45 ERA for the Mets and the Astros. With Craig temporarily retired, the Houston general manager, Al Rosen, asked him to tutor Scott for a few days. Scott entered Craig's San Diego baseball school as a washout, and left as an ace.

"The first couple, three days, he says, 'I just can't,'" Craig says. "He didn't have a good breaking ball but he had that good, live fastball and he said, 'I can't get it.' I said, 'You're getting it, you're getting it, just give it a couple more days.' He came up with one of the best in baseball."

Scott quickly became Craig's most celebrated protégé, and he thanked him with a division-clinching no-hitter in 1986—against the Giants. Historically Scott belongs more to the family of (alleged) scuffballers, but his influence on the splitter could be felt long after his last game in 1991.

Scott taught the splitter to Clemens at a golf event after the 1986 season, when both pitchers won the Cy Young Award. Clemens did not use it for a while; he was winning big with a slider as the main complement to his fastball. But by the late 1980s and early '90s

Clemens had turned to the pitch he called "Mr. Splitty"—and won five of his record seven Cy Young Awards after doing so.

"It's a devastating pitch to have," Clemens says. "It's game-changing. It's a huge out pitch if you need it. I consider it to be a violent pitch, even though it's not violent on your arm the way I throw it. I don't hook a seam."

In a game of 110 pitches, Clemens guessed, he would throw 20 or 30 splits. But hitters always thought he threw more, he said, because that was the third-strike pitch they would see on the highlights. To Clemens, the key to the pitch's deception was its presentation out of the hand.

"They see your fat wrist," he says. "When you throw breaking balls, you've got a thin wrist. But you see fat wrist on heater and split."

Naturally, learning a splitter did not work for everyone. Of all his pupils, Craig said the one with the best split was a right-hander named Randy O'Neal, who spent seven undistinguished seasons with five teams and lacked a respectable fastball to go with it. Other pitchers simply didn't have the hand for it. When Steve Carlton joined the Giants in 1986, Craig could not impart his new trick.

"Steve Carlton had real small hands for a big guy, and he just could not get his fingers spread apart," Craig said. "He used to sit during the game and have the trainers tape his fingers apart on a baseball and keep it in there the whole game trying to stretch it out. But he never really could get it. You have to have a little bit better than average-sized hand to throw a good one."

Mostly, though, the enduring memory of the Giants' staff under Craig is a procession of pitchers with dive-bombing splitters. When Craig arrived, the Giants' best reliever was a right-hander named Scott Garrelts, who had actually learned the splitter the year before, in winter ball. In Craig, he had a mentor who could refine it and the license to use it as often as he wanted.

Garrelts wanted to use it a lot. In 1984 he had a 5.65 ERA, but armed with the splitter in '85, the same hitters who owned him seemed helpless. He made the All-Star team and threw the split at 90 miles an hour. Tony Gwynn called Garrelts's splitter the best he ever saw; when Garrelts was at his sharpest, from 1985 to 1987, he held Gwynn to one hit in 18 at-bats.

"The thing with how Roger taught it is, obviously, split the fingers—but then it was more, you'd snap your wrist out, more like a fastball," Garrelts says. "The way I was throwing it, it was good and bad. I was really pronating—like, *really* hard. And the good thing was I had a lot of movement, a lot of downward movement, a lot of movement away also. The bad thing was: it's not so good on your arm. But there's that risk-reward. Those '85, '86, '87 seasons, especially being in the bullpen, I could throw really, really hard but I could definitely tell it was hard on my elbow."

Garrelts also threw his slurvy breaking ball in a way that stressed his elbow, which would eventually require Tommy John surgery. When he recovered from that, his shoulder gave out. Garrelts never threw a major league pitch in his 30s, but by then he had won an ERA title, started twice in the World Series, and spent parts of 10 years in the majors. He did what he had to do.

"If you need that pitch, you'd better throw it, because you don't want to look back 15 years from now and think, 'Maybe I should have thrown it,'" Garrelts says. "That's the decision everybody's got to make."

———

Bobby Valentine managed in Japan in 1995. At the end of the next season, he began a long stint managing the Mets. When Valentine returned to Japan as a manager in 2004, he recognized something that had largely disappeared from the American game: the splitter.

"It was a noticeable difference, because they just never discontinued the process," Valentine says. "We were similar in the '80s and early '90s, a similar amount of guys throwing it, I'll bet. And then we stopped, and they continued."

Major league teams overreacted, Valentine said, when split-finger maestros like Garrelts, Scott, and Sutter got hurt. The panic never spread overseas, Valentine says, partly because the mind-set behind the splitter was deeply embedded in Japanese baseball culture. It is the perfect substitute for the changeup.

"The reason the Japanese throw it as opposed to a straight changeup is because they don't think you should throw a slower pitch without movement," Valentine says. "It's just part of the pitching vernacular:

slower pitches move, faster pitches are straight; it's just the way the Japanese baseball brain works. They'll use a split, some form of a split, because they know it's a very similar arm stroke and the only thing that's different is the placement on the ball, which will propel the ball forward and also relieve the force behind the ball, so therefore you can't throw it as fast as your arm speed would dictate."

Hideki Matsui, who left Japan to join the Yankees in 2003, said his biggest adjustment as a hitter was facing so many changeups; the pitch was indeed rarely thrown in Japan, but nearly everyone threw a splitter. Japanese pitchers who preceded Matsui to the majors—Hideo Nomo, Shigetoshi Hasegwa, Kazuhiro Sasaki—brought the split with them. So did others who followed, like Hiroki Kuroda, Junichi Tazawa, and Koji Uehara.

"I used to only throw sliders and I wanted to expand my repertoire, and that's how I started throwing the pitch," says Uehara, the former Boston closer, whose splitter struck out St. Louis's Matt Carpenter for the final out of the 2013 World Series. Uehara's inspiration?

"With me it's Hideo Nomo," he says. "And with older generations there was a player called Shigeru Sugishita. I've only heard of him; I've never seen him throw. But he was supposed to have a really devastating splitter."

Sugishita threw his last pitch in 1961, long before Uehara was born. Known as the God of Forkballs, he was a three-time winner of the Sawamura Award as Japan's best pitcher. In 1954, for the Chunichi Dragons, he was also the Central League's MVP, going 32–12 with a 1.39 ERA across a staggering 395⅓ innings. Then he was MVP of the Japan Series. A god, indeed.

Sugishita turned 91 in 2016, when my friend Gaku Tashiro of Sankei Sports asked him a few questions for this book. Sugishita said that he learned the forkball at Meiji University in 1948, after first trying a knuckleball as an off-speed pitch. A coach noticed he had longer fingers than most pitchers and suggested the forkball, then thrown by only a few U.S. pitchers.

He took to the pitch instantly. The next year, Sugishita was pitching for the Dragons, and in 1950 he led his league in strikeouts. Nobody else, he said, was throwing the forkball.

"My advantage was that my two fingers are able to open widely," he told Tashiro, explaining that he got about three feet of vertical drop on the pitch. "It was helpful to grip the ball and to throw it with no spin. Sometimes the catcher could not catch my forkball because it was breaking too much."

Sugishita's forkball inspired the next generation of Japanese pitchers. By the mid-1970s, kids who had grown up in the 1950s were using the pitch in force. Helping their effort was that, for many years, the Japanese baseball was slightly smaller than the one used in MLB, making it a bit easier to throw for a split.

"Oh yeah, everybody threw it in Japan," says Clyde Wright, who pitched three years for the Yomiuri Giants after his major league career ended in 1975. "Young kids coming out of high school, all of 'em threw it. Everybody threw it. You get two strikes on you, you knew you were gonna get some kind of split-finger."

Ty Van Burkleo, a future major league hitting coach who played in Japan from 1988 to 1991, said: "It got to the point where, 3–1, I'm sitting forkball. If they threw me a fastball, I was like, 'Challenge me!'"

Tazawa, a future top setup man in the majors, was born in 1986 and said that in his youth, nearly every Japanese pitcher threw a split. Things changed, he said, after Nomo joined the Dodgers in 1995. Interest in Major League Baseball exploded, and with easier access to the American game, young pitchers started learning changeups, two-seamers, and so on.

American hitters, though, were confounded by the splitter, and have largely continued to flail away at it. While no Japanese pitcher has won a Cy Young Award, several have been dominant relievers or slotted comfortably into the front of winning rotations. Nomo started the All-Star Game as a rookie—he struck out Kenny Lofton and Edgar Martinez on splitters in the first inning—and went on to pitch two no-hitters.

The pitch's decline in popularity in the United States makes it less familiar to hitters.

"I don't think American and Latin kids see it anymore, because nobody teaches it," says Brian Bannister. "It's very, very rare, because of the perceived health risk, that a kid is willing to put his career on the line, not even knowing if it's true or not. And so it's not taught, therefore the hitters never see it; they don't get opportunity to practice against it. So in Japan, where it's taught more prevalently—it's taught like a changeup and everybody throws one—a lot of those pitchers have come over and had a ton of success because it's a lost pitch."

What is largely lost here is still ingrained in the Japanese game. Americans who sign there are generally told that they must learn the pitch. When Chris Leroux joined the Yakult Swallows in 2013, he could not throw the split without pain. He altered his arm angle and was bombed in five starts. But his teammate Tony Barnette, a career minor leaguer in the U.S., had a different experience.

"I had tinkered with it in junior college and even a couple of times in the minor leagues, but it was never really a pitch I took seriously," Barnette says. "Then I went over there and they kind of hammered it home. My pitching coaches said, 'Let's try the split, let's try the split.' They kept introducing it. Ended up being the right decision."

Barnette spent six years in Japan, finishing with 41 saves in 2015. At 32, with a sharp splitter but no major league experience, he signed a two-year, $3.5 million contract with the Texas Rangers. His ERA as a rookie was 2.09, and he appeared in every playoff game.

The splitter didn't hurt his arm, and even if it did, Barnette said, he would still throw it.

"Some people say the split causes Tommy John—now all of a sudden nobody's throwing splits, and guess what, they're still having Tommy Johns," Barnette says. "It's not a science. I don't think it has any more pressure than any other pitches I throw. It feels pretty comfortable, it feels pretty natural—and at this point in my career, what do I care? It's getting late in the game. I'm gonna use what I got, how much I've got, until I don't got it no more."

———————

To prove the point that the splitter must be dangerous, pitchers often suggest that you spread your index and middle fingers as wide as possible.

"You'll get this incredible tenseness in your forearm, just physically spreading your fingers," says Ron Darling, who still could not resist throwing a lot of splitters in his prime with the Mets. "I consider it, in the short run, an incredible pitch. In the long run, I think it thwarted the length of my career."

Mike Mussina is also suspicious of the splitter, because of how tightly the pitcher must grip the sides of the ball. Then again, Mussina said, his hand is not really big enough to throw the pitch, and he rarely did. When his Yankee teammate Andy Pettitte tried to throw splitters in early 2002, the pitch hurt his elbow and led Pettitte down a dark road: in his recovery, he has admitted, he briefly resorted to human growth hormone.

When John Burkett pitched in Triple-A for the Giants, his pitching coach suggested he use a splitter to get Craig's attention and earn a promotion. The plan worked, but in time the pitch caused a grinding sensation in his elbow; once, Burkett said, his hand actually throbbed on the mound from a forearm spasm. Ken Hill, later Burkett's teammate in Texas, also felt a strain from the pitch and was rarely effective after age 32. Hill could not say for sure that the splitter caused his trouble, but it sure sounds painful.

"I'd get to a certain pitch count, my arm would be on fire," Hill says. "Right in the elbow."

Then there are cases like Chuck Finley, who logged more than 3,000 innings and said his hand was so big that gripping the splitter did not stress his fingers at all. Finley's wrist and elbow stayed loose and the pitch never hurt his arm. Nor did it bother Curt Schilling, who lasted through age 40 and was at his best in October, still strong after long seasons. Schilling used the splitter to become the only pitcher ever with more than 3,000 strikeouts and fewer than 750 walks. Don't tell him the pitch is dangerous.

"I think it's one of the easiest pitches in the world on your arm, because you don't change anything," Schilling says. "You don't manipulate the ball with a split, you just split your fingers. It literally is what it sounds like—you throw your fastball and split your fingers. I don't have to curl my wrist, I don't have to spin the ball. My elbow doesn't do anything other than what I do on my fastball for the most part. It's the easiest pitch to learn, easiest pitch to teach, and in my mind one of the easiest pitches to throw."

Clemens, Morris, and Stewart also had long careers. Jack McDowell, the 1993 AL Cy Young Award winner for the White Sox, was done at 33, but he has cited a surgical error that caused nerve damage. Sutter's pinched nerve, he said, came from a birth defect. Scott, who was finished at 35, refused to blame the splitter.

"I know it's one of the theories out there, but I guarantee you that it didn't shorten my career," he told ESPN in 2003. "People were having arm problems with it, which I really have a hard time believing because it's basically a fastball with the fingers split on the baseball. It's no different from throwing a fastball."

Craig draws a distinction between the pitch he taught and the forkball that preceded it.

"I never had a guy go all the way down," Craig says, referring to a ball pushed back in the palm. "That's like the forkball, and how many forkball pitchers do you remember? Elroy Face, Lindy McDaniel—they put it so deep they put some pressure on your arm. But the split-finger, if you throw it right, the way I taught it, you might hurt your arm—but you might hurt your arm throwing a rock."

Dr. Glenn Fleisig said there was no scientific data to cast the splitter as inherently dangerous. Yes, it might cause pain for some pitchers, but that doesn't mean the risk is universal. Sometimes, a splitter might only seem to cause an injury.

"Maybe it was the amount of pitching, total," Fleisig says, "and it just showed up on the splitter."

The industry doesn't want to take a chance. In 2017 only three of the 58 pitchers who qualified for the ERA title threw a split even 10 percent of the time: Masahiro Tanaka, Kevin Gausman, and Ricky Nolasco. Of the other 55 starters, according to FanGraphs, only three tried a splitter even once.

Yankees pitching coach Larry Rothschild says coaches would rather emphasize a changeup than a splitter, since the pitches work similarly. Even so, he could not say for sure that the splitter was any riskier than a hard slider—and besides, he added, fastballs might cause the most arm tension, anyway. Late in 2016, one of Rothschild's starters, Nathan Eovaldi, was found to need a second Tommy John surgery. Eovaldi threw splitters with 23 percent of his pitches, but said he had no plans to stop doing so when he returned.

A generation earlier, Bryan Harvey said the same thing. A two-time

All-Star closer with a devastating splitter, Harvey would wrap his fingers around a softball in the clubhouse; he did not have big hands but was determined to make the most of what he had. In May 1994, before Harvey returned from an elbow injury with the Marlins, Gordon Edes asked him if the pitch caused the pain.

"All I know is that I'm going to keep throwing it," Harvey said. He was 30 years old and would pitch just five more games in his career.

In an industry forever trying to solve the riddle of pitching injuries, stories like that stand out. The split-finger fastball is like a breed of dog that bites a few famous people. Word gets around and people avoid the breed altogether. There are plenty of other dogs to choose from.

Garrelts, who coaches kids in Shreveport, Louisiana, says people tend to ask him the same two questions about his career: Did you throw a no-hitter, and did you pitch in the World Series? He laughs and says he lost a no-hitter with two outs in the ninth and lost two starts in the World Series.

What about the pitch that made him famous for a while, the unhittable pitch that swept through his generation?

"Nobody's asked anything about the splitter," Garrelts says. "Nobody."

THE
SCREWBALL

The Sasquatch of Baseball

The final line on Christy Mathewson's Hall of Fame plaque is the most concise, exquisite bit of prose in the museum: "MATTY WAS MASTER OF THEM ALL." It is presented as a quotation, though the source is lost to time, if there ever was one. Perhaps it was just accepted gospel about Mathewson, the only member of the Hall's first class in 1936 who never lived to see the building. Mathewson was exposed to poison gas as an Army captain in France during World War I and spent the last years of his life fighting tuberculosis. It was a sad ending to a towering life that needed no embellishment. Mathewson really was the master.

No pitcher in baseball history has as many wins as Mathewson (373) with an earned run average so low (2.13). Only one man with even 250 wins (Lefty Grove, with 300) had a better winning percentage than Mathewson's .665. He led his league in strikeout-to-walk ratio nine times and threw three shutouts for the Giants in the 1905 World Series. More than that, though, Mathewson had a *story:* at a time when many ballplayers were mostly hard-bitten, poorly educated ruffians, Mathewson was a dignified, Christian gentleman from Factoryville, Pennsylvania, where, as a boy, he honed his famous control by throwing a ball—three inches wide—through a four-inch hole in the door of his father's barn. Mathewson went on to Bucknell, where he played sports but also sang in the glee club and belonged to the campus literary society. He was a man of letters beyond his many Ks; at the height of his fame, in 1912, Mathewson wrote a book that gave a detailed look at what happens on the field and why.

He called it *Pitching in a Pinch*—and what he did in that spot was throw his famous fadeaway, the pitch now known as the screwball.

"Many persons have asked me why I do not use my 'fade-away' oftener when it is so effective, and the only answer is that every time I throw the 'fade-away,' it takes so much out of my arm," he wrote. "It is a very hard ball to deliver. Pitching it ten or twelve times in a game kills my arm, so I save it for the pinches."

Mathewson, a right-hander, continued: "Many fans do not know what this ball really is. It is a slow curve pitched with the motion of a fast ball. But most curve balls break away from a right-handed batter a little. The fade-away breaks toward him."

In two paragraphs Mathewson defined the pitch forever, describing its effect on the pitcher and the hitter. He also added just enough mystery to cloud exactly what this pitch really is. Using a fastball motion to disguise a slower pitch—one that moves into the same-hand hitter—is also fundamental to the changeup. But a changeup is not shaped like a curveball, and generally is not tough on the arm. So if the pitch is not a changeup or a curve, it's something else. In the decades after Mathewson, it would be called the screwball, an oddity now all but extinct.

For years, the pitch was considered to be Mathewson's alone. In 1934, a former teammate, Red Murray, told the *Brooklyn Eagle* that the fadeaway was so hard to learn, and put such strain on the pitcher's wrist, that Mathewson was "the only man ever to master" it. Murray said Mathewson's inspiration had come from umpiring freshman games at Bucknell and wondering if he could make a curveball spin in reverse. Maybe so, but Mathewson himself cited an early teammate, Dave Williams, with giving him the idea for the fadeaway in 1898. Williams could not control the pitch well—he would make just three appearances in the majors, for the team now known as the Red Sox in 1902—but he showed Mathewson how to throw it.

"I was trying to work my way through college by pitching for a team in a little Pennsylvania mountain town called Honesdale," Mathewson told the Chicago *Inter Ocean* in 1910. "One day I saw a left-handed amateur throwing the ball with that peculiar reverse twist. I thought it might help me, so I learned it, but I worked at it steadily for five years before I got it perfected."

Mathewson, who referred to Williams by name in other sources, went on to distinguish his pitch from that of Virgil "Ned" Garvin, a turn-of-the-century journeyman who pitched for six teams in seven seasons.

"All the sporting books credit old Virgil Garvin with being the inventor of the fade-away," he said. "Well, maybe he was, but [Williams] had never heard of Virgil Garvin in all his life. He simply stumbled onto it by chance just as I had stumbled onto him."

When Mathewson joined the Giants in 1900, at age 19, he showed off his pitches for George Davis, the shortstop and manager, in practice. Davis immediately rejected the roundhouse curve, a pitch Mathewson called his pride and joy. Mathewson tried a tighter curve—a drop ball—which impressed Davis, who asked if he had anything else.

"I've a sort of freak ball that I never use in a game," Mathewson said. It was his fadeaway, which he hadn't even named and could rarely control. But he broke off a beauty to Davis, who swung and missed by a foot. Eyes bulging, Davis asked for another, and missed that one, too.

"That's a *good* one!" Davis declared, as recalled by Mathewson for *St. Nicholas* magazine in 1912. "That's all right! It's a slow in-curve to a right-handed batter. A change of pace with a curve ball. A regular fallaway or fadeaway. That's a good ball!"

Other Giants were similarly amazed, and Davis told Mathewson to practice the pitch diligently so he could control it for the future. He would pitch just six times that season, with more walks than strikeouts, but soon began a captivating magic act on the mound: a no-hitter in 1901, a 30-win season in 1903, those record three World Series shutouts in 1905, and so on. All along, Mathewson eagerly shared the secrets of his fadeaway: turning over his hand, snapping his wrist away from his body—it was all there, in print or in person, waiting to be imitated.

"Many times I have tried to teach other pitchers in the Big League—even men on opposing clubs—how to throw this ball," he said. "But none have ever mastered it."

A richer origin story than the Dave Williams version involves Rube Foster, a Hall of Famer best known for organizing the Negro National League in 1920. Foster was a top pitcher before that, and John McGraw, as Giants manager, is said to have recruited him to help his pitchers. A legend persists that Foster then taught Mathewson the fadeaway, though the evidence clearly contradicts this. Even so, the fact that Foster also threw it, with great success, supports Rob Neyer's theory that nobody really knows who used it first. John Clarkson and Tim Keefe were well known for changing speeds in the 1880s, like another ace of that time, Mickey Welch, who said late in life that he recognized Mathewson's fadeaway as the same pitch he had used.

"Just about anybody could have invented it," Neyer wrote. "Once everybody realized that you could make a baseball curve *that* way by twisting your wrist *this* way, it wouldn't have taken a genius to realize that reversing the process should be possible, the result being what we might call—and what might actually have been called—a 'reverse curve.'"

"Reverse curve" is the most accurate shorthand for screwball, a baseball term that long ago crossed over into everyday life. In the 1930s, the prime of the great Giant lefty Carl Hubbell, "screwball" came to describe a specific genre of Hollywood comedies: battle of the sexes, often with a woman's madcap antics upending a stuffy man's world. In his book about Depression-era films, Andrew Bergman wrote that "screwball comedy," like Hubbell's famous pitch, was "unconventional, went in different directions and behaved in unexpected ways."

By that description, the knuckleball would fit better. But screwball just *sounds* right, as it does when describing a personality type: eccentric at best, deranged at worst. If someone is known as a screwball, he's not a reliable guy, and it's not a reliable pitch, either. The definition has become self-fulfilling: it's so bizarre and deemed such a health risk that pitchers use alternatives—the changeup, mostly—to achieve the same result. The pitch has all but vanished from the majors over the last three decades, so much so that the Hall of Fame slugger Jim Thome, who played 22 seasons, said he had *heard* of the pitch, but never *seen* it. The screwball, in that way, is the Sasquatch of baseball: believed to exist but with no credible evidence from many experts.

The record does show that Thome batted once against a Reds left-hander named Daniel Ray Herrera, grounding out in 2009. Herrera made 131 appearances from 2008 to 2011, and without the screwball, he would have made none. He used it because he could not throw a changeup, and it distinguished him just enough to give him his modest career.

Herrera's quirky profile fit the pitch: he is 5 foot 6, and at the time of his debut, no pitcher had been shorter in more than 50 years. He is also the only major leaguer ever to attend Permian High School in Odessa, Texas, best known as the featured football program in *Friday Night Lights*.

"When I was in high school, they actually tore down the outfield fence so they could have spring football practice," Herrera says. "So our center field and right field would be just dirt pits from the guys rustlin' around on the ground out there."

In college, at New Mexico, Herrera found that his changeup moved sideways, almost like a sinker, without the downward fade he needed. He tried pronating his wrist more deliberately, and found that the more he did it, the more over-the-top spin he imparted on the ball. Herrera snapped down with his wrist, just as he would for a curveball, but in the opposite direction. His command was shaky, but he knew a good weapon when he saw it: this new pitch had curveball spin but ran away from a right-hander. The oddity alone made it valuable.

"When I started throwing it, everyone kept calling it a changeup, a changeup," he says. "And in the back of my head I kept saying: 'A changeup doesn't move like this; a changeup doesn't spin like this.' I actually didn't classify it as a screwball when I started throwing it. I just knew it was something different, and hopefully I could work with it in the future."

It took 1,345 picks and 45 rounds in the 2006 draft, but Herrera was finally chosen by the Rangers. Within two years he was pitching in the majors for the Reds, relieving Aaron Harang—who is 13 inches taller—against a stacked Phillies lineup. In his first inning, he struck out a power-hitting lefty (Ryan Howard) and a power-hitting righty

(Pat Burrell). Jamie Moyer, the ageless Philadelphia left-hander, sought out Herrera before the next day's game.

"You have to show me how to throw that pitch," Moyer cried, before Herrera could even say hello. "I need to revive my career!"

Herrera was stunned. Here he was, with one game in the majors, and a veteran of two decades had noticed him, just because of the screwball. It would be a recurring theme in Herrera's brief career. Pitchers would regularly ask him for guidance, but none could repeat what he did. They usually weren't flexible enough to get their arm over their head, as Herrera did. And if they could, they couldn't throw anything else from that slot.

"Daniel really had to clear his head to get into that position," says Bryan Price, who coached Herrera with the Reds. "It's hard to throw other pitches of similar quality from such a dramatic position, because the head has to clear to get on top of the ball to such a degree. From what I've seen, from the guys I've had who've thrown screwballs, it would be very difficult to have quality secondary pitches—meaning fastball command or a breaking ball—off that pitch."

Some pitchers, like Mike Norris, are born to throw the screwball. Don't think so? Go grab a household item, like a ketchup bottle or a paper cup. Chances are you pick it up with your palm turned in, toward you. Norris says he always did this the opposite way, with his palm turned away from his body. His mother, Lulu, worried he would drop the milk when he lifted it from the kitchen table. Norris never did.

As an amateur, Norris was practicing one day at Balboa Park in San Francisco when he noticed an unmistakable figure off in the distance: Juan Marichal, the star Giants righty with the impossibly high leg kick and nasty screwball. Norris did not ask for an autograph, but for his screwball grip. Marichal obliged, and in 1980 Norris went 22–9 and nearly won the Cy Young Award. His trick was a screwball thrown at three speeds, with such deception that his manager, Billy Martin, called it a dry spitter.

"Mine was an optical illusion," Norris says. "So with the arm speed, it looked like a fastball, then the seams started turning over, going the other way, and it looked like it just stopped in midair. It moved about two feet, and I could throw it from one side of the plate to the other. So this is why they'd have difficulty hitting it, because they're throwing their hands at it and it's not there yet. Now it's starting to go down, and the velocity as it goes down is incredible. It's even harder going down than it is going away."

With Norris's screwball drifting and dropping away from them, left-handers hit just .185 off him in 1980. Yet Norris's description of the pitch, and the way he threw it—the further back in his palm, the slower it was—again evokes the changeup. The pitches are close cousins, often mistaken for twins. The Reds once had two lefties, Tom Browning and John Franco, who threw a pitch with the same action. But Franco's came from a circle-change grip, so his was called a changeup. Browning used a two-seam grip, pulling his thumb down to impart the slashing movement away from a righty. His was called a screwball but served the same purpose, and helped him pitch a perfect game in 1988.

"My fastball was probably major league average, if that, although some guys may say it was never that," Browning says. "But [my screwball] complemented it so much that it allowed my fastball to look better, look firmer, because they had to stay back a little bit in case I came with the changeup—or the screwball."

Warren Spahn, whose 363 wins are the most ever by a lefty, basically carved out a second prime—in his late 30s and early 40s—by perfecting an off-speed pitch that flummoxed right-handed hitters. The pitch was widely known as a screwball, and that's what Joe Torre, his catcher at the end, also calls it.

But here's Roger Angell describing Spahn teaching the pitch in spring training in 1987. Angell calls it a sinker-screwball, but it accurately describes a circle change: "His left thumb and forefinger were making a circle, with the three other fingers pointing up, exactly as if he were flashing the 'O.K.' sign to someone nearby. The ball was tucked comfortably up against the circle, without being held by it, and the other fingers stayed up and apart, keeping only a loose grip on the pill. Thrown that way, he said, the ball departed naturally off the inside, or little-finger side, of the middle finger, and would then sink and break to the left as it crossed the plate."

Spahn's late-career dominance was nearly unprecedented; he is the only pitcher in the last century with two 20-win seasons after turning 40. He missed three years to military service in his early 20s, saving

wear on his arm at a critical age. His father, Ed, a wallpaper salesman, emphasized momentum in his son's delivery, transferring weight
from back to front with an exaggerated leg kick that Spahn believed
protected his arm.

"Dad had a theory about pitching," Spahn told *The Washington Post*
in 1955. "He used to say if you learned to throw properly you could
pitch forever without hurting your arm. He was right, too."

If it was, indeed, a screwball that Spahn threw, it certainly didn't
hurt him. And while the screwball's most notorious victim is thought
to be Carl Hubbell, consider that Hubbell's arm trouble might have
been caused by piling up four seasons in a row with at least 300
innings—and besides, he did pitch past his fortieth birthday and go
down as an all-time great.

"I've heard about how he inverted his arm in a weird way, and when
I was younger I thought, 'Well, I'm gonna play for 10 or 15 years,
and then what if my arm does that?'" Herrera says. "I always kind of
looked at the angle of it, but nothing has ever changed. My arm hasn't
twisted inward like that. So maybe it is a legend, who knows? But I
think I'd make that sacrifice—and then just write upside down with
my left arm."

———————

Ah, the inverted arm of Carl Hubbell. You might think Hubbell's
staggering success would be a powerful selling point for the screwball.
For a decade (1929–38) he had 195 wins, a 2.81 ERA (best in the
majors), and two Most Valuable Player awards. He dominated the
Senators in the 1933 World Series, allowing no earned runs across
20 innings, and the next summer he used the screwball to strike out
five Hall of Famers in a row at the All-Star Game: Babe Ruth, Lou
Gehrig, Jimmie Foxx, Al Simmons, and Joe Cronin.

Alas, physical deformity trumps all that. Hubbell, nicknamed "Meal
Ticket" for the Depression-era Giants, blamed his own meal ticket for
the way his arm bent awkwardly at his side, turned out to the left as if
in perpetual follow-through on a screwball. Jim Murray—who once
wrote that Hubbell "looks as if he put it on in the dark"—shared this
anecdote in the *Los Angeles Times* after Hubbell's death in 1988:

The screwball was not really a pitch, it was an affliction. I met Hubbell only once. He was in his late 60s but still the gaunt, spare, Gary Cooperish character I remembered as a kid. I gave him a ride to the airport on his way to scout some phenom in Northern California for the Giants.

"Tell me," I asked him, "was that screwball that hard a pitch to throw? Hard on the arm?" Hubbell laughed. And rolled up his sleeve. He showed me a left arm you could have opened wine with. It should have had a cork on the end of it. I whistled. Why did he risk it? Hubbell laughed again. "In those Depression days, you would have let them twist your neck for a living. An arm was nothing."

The screwball gave Hubbell a career—and like Mathewson, he was inspired by another pitcher with just a sliver of time in the majors. Claude "Lefty" Thomas appeared in seven games for Washington in 1916, but otherwise spent 18 pro seasons in the minors. Near the end of his wandering, with the Des Moines Demons of the Class A Western League in 1925, he caught the attention of Hubbell, then with the Oklahoma City Indians and just starting his career.

In an interview in his clip file at the Hall of Fame, Hubbell mentions that Thomas made pitching seem so easy. Others could throw harder, but Thomas just flipped sinkers down and away to right-handers for harmless ground balls. Hubbell decided to pitch the same way.

"I must have had the right kind of instincts to pick him," Hubbell said. "It's like learning to walk: monkey see, monkey do. I picked the right monkey."

As he worked on the sinker, Hubbell found he could get more spin when he turned the pitch over with his wrist at the end. This was the screwball, christened as such by the Oklahoma City catcher Earl Wolgamot. As Hubbell told *The New York Times'* George Vecsey in 1984, Wolgamot caught the pitch in warm-ups one day and called it "the screwiest thing I ever saw."

Hubbell said he could tell right away the pitch was unnatural—"my elbow had to fly up just as I turned it loose"—and, apparently, so could the Tigers. At spring training with Detroit in 1925, coach George McBride forbade him from using it, insisting it would ruin his arm.

Ty Cobb, then Detroit's manager, may have ordered McBride to say this, though Hubbell said he never actually spoke to Cobb, who was gone when the Tigers released Hubbell in 1928, without ever letting him pitch in an exhibition game.

Hubbell moved on to the Beaumont Exporters of the Texas League. He decided the only way to distinguish himself was to use the screwball, whether it hurt him or not. That June Beaumont played in Houston, site of the Democratic convention, and a delegate named Dick Kinsella took in the game. Hubbell pitched a four-hitter, impressing Kinsella, a scout for the Giants and a friend of McGraw, who was still their manager.

According to author Frank Graham, Kinsella called McGraw and told him of his discovery. He warned McGraw that Cobb had rejected Hubbell because the screwball might damage his arm, but McGraw laughed it off. He had managed Mathewson, after all.

"That's a joke," McGraw said. "When Matty was pitching it, they called it a fadeaway and it never hurt his arm. If there isn't anything wrong with him, I'd like to know more about him."

Kinsella agreed to follow Hubbell around for a while, leaving the convention for a more promising prospect than the Democrats' nominee, Governor Alfred E. Smith of New York. Smith would lose in a landslide to Herbert Hoover that November, but Kinsella secured the contract of a pitcher who would win prodigiously, long after Hoover left office.

Hubbell was the National League's MVP in 1936, guiding the Giants to the World Series with a 26–6 record and a major-league-best 2.31 ERA. The screwball was a big part of his mystique.

"I've tried never to let pitching success turn my head; but it has twisted my arm," Hubbell wrote the next spring in a story for *This Week* magazine. "This left 'salary wing' of mine hangs from my shoulder strangely, with the palm facing out and backward. Because of this strange twist, I can throw a screwball with ease. The screwball, a reverse curve which breaks, in my case, away from a right-handed batter instead of toward him, as a southpaw's natural hook does, has ruined many pitchers' arms. However, although it has 'swiveled' my arm at the elbow, it never hurts."

Alas, by the next summer, just after his 200th career victory, Hubbell could no longer raise his arm to his shoulder without elbow pain. A doctor in Memphis removed bone chips and a calcium deposit on the joint, and Hubbell believed he knew the reason.

Before the 1940 season, he told an interviewer that the ban on spitballs—by then nearly two decades old—had forced pitchers to "invent freak deliveries" to do their jobs. The balls they were using, meanwhile, were slick and shiny, because umpires quickly discarded any ball that might be scuffed. Hubbell insisted it was murder on that salary wing:

"These unorthodox pitches result in a great strain on the arm. Take my screwball, for instance—the peculiar twist I must give it if I hope to fool anybody with it is the reason for those splintered bones I had in my elbow."

Hubbell remained a useful pitcher in his final four seasons, finishing 253–154 in a remarkable career that made him an inner-circle Hall of Famer. Even so, Hubbell was never interested in passing down the screwball; a teammate who tried it, Cliff Melton, was also bothered by elbow pain. The hazards to Hubbell were ever present in that mangled throwing arm, at once the best and worst advertisement the screwball ever had.

———

The screwball had its moments after Hubbell's dazzling prime. The Cardinals' Harry Brecheen beat the Red Sox three times in the 1946 World Series. Luis Tiant—the father of the future Boston ace— finished his career in Cuba, where he threw one of the best screwballs the island has ever seen. Verdell "Lefty" Mathis, a star in the Negro American League in the 1940s, used screwballs to thwart one of the game's great sluggers, Josh Gibson. Mathis loved facing lineups stacked with right-handed hitters—including Gibson, whose Cooperstown plaque says he hit nearly 800 homers.

"I always used the screwball on Gibson, low and away," Mathis told the author John Holway. "He never hit a home run off me."

In popular lore, though, the screwball still belonged to Hubbell. In

Players' Choice, the 1987 book that polled hundreds of ex-players on various topics, Hubbell got about four times as many votes for best screwball as any other pitcher. Still, there were prominent pitchers who featured it in their arsenal, including Juan Marichal, who was yet another Giants Hall of Famer.

Marichal had first been intrigued by the screwball at Class A in 1959, knowing that Ruben Gomez had thrived with it in the majors. He asked Andy Gilbert, his manager in Springfield, Massachusetts, how to throw it, learning that the pitcher must break his wrist the opposite way as he does for a curveball. For Marichal, though, there was a handicap: he could not throw the screwball sidearm, as he did for his other pitches. He had to throw it overhand.

That would be a challenge, but as a right-hander, Marichal believed he had to try it. Candlestick Park opened in 1960 and favored left-handed hitters, meaning he would need a pitch that broke away from them. He picked it up quickly, and in 1962 began a string of eight All-Star seasons in which he averaged more than 21 wins per year. Even those who hit him well, like Joe Torre, admired Marichal's wide repertoire.

"He would throw you a fastball, a curveball, a screwball; he had a big curveball and he threw a slider—and then he threw everything [sidearm] too, except the screwball," Torre says. "I tried not to look at his delivery because he had that big leg kick and he threw basically stiff-arm. But he was remarkable, because with the wild windup and the big leg kick, his control was better than anybody else's. He could throw the ball over a rosin bag, I guarantee it."

Marichal's most famous game was his marathon duel with Spahn at Candlestick in 1963. Marichal twirled 16 shutout innings and Spahn 15, until Willie Mays bashed a hanging screwball for a game-ending home run. Marichal would pitch 12 more seasons, finishing 101 games above .500, though a championship eluded him; he made just one appearance in the World Series.

That was in 1962, when Ralph Terry played the hero for the Yankees. Four years later, Terry was barely hanging on, trying to learn a knuckleball at the instructional league for the Mets. There he met a plucky young lefty named Frank Edwin "Tug" McGraw, who had lost 16 of his 20 major league decisions. Terry went golfing with McGraw, and

passed on a tip that would one day help two franchises win their first World Series.

McGraw had a clean, overhand delivery, and Terry thought the screwball would be a good fit. He had learned it from Spud Chandler, the 1943 AL Most Valuable Player for the Yankees, who had once coached Terry with the Kansas City A's. Terry remembered how Marlin Stuart, an otherwise ordinary righty in the 1950s, had humbled the great Ted Williams with screwballs. Williams generally owned Terry (career average: .455), but on June 20, 1958, Terry retired him three times in a row with screwballs.

"That's a good pitch," Williams told Terry after the game. "Don't use it all the time."

That was the screwball's reputation: a valuable weapon that must be conserved, for fear of injury. And while McGraw picked up the pitch from Terry in about 10 minutes—"Man, he *had* it, just like Warren Spahn, right over the top," Terry says—he met the same kind of resistance Hubbell had found decades earlier.

A Mets coach, Sheriff Robinson, would not let McGraw use it. Yet Terry's explanation made sense to McGraw, who used the pitch in the minors and felt no soreness. As McGraw wrote in his first autobiography:

> What Ralph Terry had taught me was to rotate my arm in such a way as to get opposite rotation from every other breaking pitch. When you throw the baseball over the top of your head or ear, it makes just as much sense to turn your wrist inside-out. If you put a clock in front of you, you twist the ball toward three o'clock. It turns your whole arm all the way back to your shoulder. By the time you release it you lose some velocity, but the ball breaks away from a right-handed hitter instead of toward him the way a curve does. The fastball will tail away from a right-handed hitter, and a curve will break into him. But this one broke away and destroyed his timing.

Sounds good, but the Mets were not convinced. They buried McGraw in the minors for all of 1968, then left him unprotected for three rounds of the expansion draft. He went unclaimed, and the next spring they finally relented and let him throw screwballs. McGraw instantly became an ace reliever, struck out Hank Aaron to help save a playoff game, and won a championship ring with a team forever known as the Miracle Mets.

McGraw also met Hubbell that season, at an Old-Timers' Game at Shea Stadium. They compared screwball grips and noticed they gripped the pitch differently to get the same action. McGraw held his parallel to the seams, Hubbell across them.

"We came to the conclusion that it's not so much how you hold it in your hand as how you release it," McGraw wrote. "You know, the way a guy holds the ball, against the seams or with them, is just a matter of comfort. But what counts is the thing that gives the ball its final rotation."

The screwball became integral to McGraw's persona. He was the epitome of the lovable screwball, thumping his glove on his thigh as he bounded off the mound between innings, leading an orchestra in a dramatic reading of "Casey at the Bat." In the 1970s he even authored a nationally syndicated comic strip about a team of misfit players. Appropriately, he called it *Scroogie.*

As McGraw's fastball waned, he called it his Peggy Lee—as in, "Is That All There Is?" There were variations to the fastball, and McGraw named them, too. The Bo Derek, he said, "had a nice little tail on it." The Cutty Sark sailed, the John Jameson went straight (like Irish whiskey), and the gopher ball was his Frank Sinatra pitch—as in, "Fly Me to the Moon."

The most important pitch McGraw ever threw came for the Phillies in the ninth inning of Game 6 of the 1980 World Series, with two out and the bases loaded. Police dogs circled the field at Veterans Stadium to keep the fans from rushing the turf. McGraw noticed the K-9 Corps and instantly made the connection: here he was in the ninth, needing a K.

Somehow, the silly thought relaxed McGraw. He ran the count full to the Royals' Willie Wilson, setting him up for a screwball. Wilson hesitated just long enough on his swing, flailing at the high fastball to end it.

McGraw exulted, whirling his left arm like a windmill and bouncing as he turned to third base and caught Mike Schmidt in his arms.

Seventy-five years after Mathewson's fadeaway had carried the Giants to a championship, the screwy pitch from a screwy lefty had delivered the Phillies the title.

———

McGraw's success highlighted the last peak era for the screwball. It had briefly made Mike Norris an ace in Oakland, and in 1984, Willie Hernandez would use it to win the AL Most Valuable Player award while leading Detroit all the way. Hernandez had learned the screwball two years earlier from Mike Cuellar, the former star lefty for the Orioles.

But the true locus for the screwball, in these years, was Dodger Stadium. In 1974, the Dodgers' Mike Marshall won the NL Cy Young Award with one of the most mind-bending seasons in major league history: a record 106 relief appearances, with more than 200 innings, while leading the Dodgers to the pennant. Seven years later, Fernando Valenzuela carried them to the championship, becoming the only pitcher ever to win the Rookie of the Year and Cy Young awards in the same season. Both men featured the screwball as their primary weapon, but had little else in common.

Marshall was a right-handed reliever from Michigan. He does not work in organized baseball and condemns its understanding of pitchers. Valenzuela was a left-handed starter from Mexico. He has broadcast the Dodgers in Spanish since 2003 and remains extraordinarily popular, at once familiar and larger than life.

The Dodgers share a spring training complex with the Chicago White Sox, whose former manager Robin Ventura said the one pitch he had always wanted to face was Valenzuela's screwball. Ventura, who grew up in California, was in junior high when Fernandomania swept through the game in 1981. He was playing in the majors a dozen years later, when Valenzuela pitched for the Orioles.

"That was the only time in my career that I went to the plate and thought, 'I'm just going to watch this—from, like, right here, I'm going to watch it, because I want to see it,'" Ventura says. "Not even a thought of hitting it. I was gonna purposely just sit and watch. He didn't throw that hard back then, but just that action of when he turned it over, it was still a good pitch."

Careers like Marshall's and Valenzuela's, marked by uniquely memorable peaks, tend to reinforce the screwball's reputation as an outlier kind of pitch. There is a reason Mathewson and Hubbell both used the word "freak" to describe it. Marshall's last manager in the majors, Joe Torre, describes him like this: "He was a freak of nature, because he threw every single day."

This is nonsense to Marshall, who has a PhD in exercise physiology from Michigan State and has devoted his life to kinesiology, the study of human movement. He threw a pitch that supposedly destroys the arm, yet endurance was his hallmark. As a rookie with Detroit in 1967, Marshall threw his slider the usual way—releasing it over the top of his index finger—and his elbow hurt so much he could not raise it to brush his teeth. His studies, supported by his use of high-speed film, showed him that the proper way to pitch—the *only* way to do so safely, he insists—was to pronate on everything. And pronation—that is, a counterclockwise turn—helps the screwball.

"When you throw the screwball, you start out with the hand facing away from you, which means you are already in a full pronated situation," Marshall says. "And you can't do anything but put spin on the ball. But the way that I throw, you come in and drive and my elbow pops up, and the powerful inward rotation gives me a very high spin velocity. I can start it over your head and it'll end up at your ankles— one of those pitches that will really bite the air molecules."

Like so many others, Marshall was initially told not to throw the screwball. His fifth organization, the Montreal Expos, finally let him throw it in 1970, and he went on to lead the majors in relief appearances for the decade. He calls the screwball "an absolute must" for any pitcher, and has spent many years as a college coach and private pitching instructor in Zephyrhills, Florida.

Yet for all the innovation in baseball lately, the sport has never turned to Marshall in any official way. His unwavering support of the screwball is just a small part of the revolution he believes he could unleash: 10 miles an hour added to everyone's fastball, and pronated breaking balls that never damage the elbow. Baseball teams are willing to innovate with their methods, but not to blow them all up.

"There's no major league team that seems to be interested in having a completely injury-free pitching motion," he says. "These traditional pitching coaches, they just get together and talk about this stupidity stuff, and nobody's interested in learning how to have the very best pitchers you could possibly get. Of course, this would change baseball. You're gonna have to move the mound back."

That's quite a thought, but it's also a fantasy—the pitching distance has been 60 feet, 6 inches since 1893, and it's not changing. Velocity is climbing, anyway, and for his part, Valenzuela laments the loss of nuance in the modern game.

"If scouts don't see 90-plus, I don't think they can sign pitchers," he says. "I can see a good pitcher in Mexico with good control, but if the velocity's not there, they say no. No velocity, no prospect for the big leagues."

Valenzuela threw a fastball and curveball when he signed with the Dodgers in 1979, at age 18. Mike Brito, the scout who signed him, visited Valenzuela that summer at Class A in Lodi, California, and decided he needed a third pitch. After the season he sent another pitcher he had signed, Dodgers reliever Bobby Castillo, to teach Valenzuela the screwball.

"We believed that his fastball was below average, so we needed a pitch to make his fastball better," Brito says. "That was the pitch that made him successful in the big leagues."

Valenzuela, it turned out, had just the right wrist for the screwball, and soon he would catapult to stardom, packing stadiums and connecting with Los Angeles fans in a way no other Dodger ever has. The Dodgers rode him hard, and in Valenzuela's first 10 seasons only one pitcher in the majors (Jack Morris) logged more innings.

That workload, not the screwball, is probably the main reason for Valenzuela's sharp decline in his 30s. Even so, his prime was so inspiring that you'd think some pitcher, with two weapons but not a third, might ask him how he threw his best pitch.

As he leaned on a fence in Arizona one spring day, signing autographs and watching the Dodgers practice, Valenzuela considered the question and shook his head.

"If somebody approached me, I'd try to help them out," he said. "Right now? Nobody."

Really? All those pitchers in camp, majors and minors, and nobody asks?

"Nobody," Valenzuela said.

———

We see this phenomenon with the splitter, too—a pitch proven to be a devastating weapon, but now mostly hidden behind layers of yellow police tape. At least some pitchers still throw splitters, though. Almost nobody throws a screwball on purpose anymore. Most pitchers still need something that moves away from the opposite-handed hitter. But there are more options today, and the screwball is a relic.

"What you see nowadays is a modern variation of it, and it comes in the form of a Felix Hernandez or Zack Greinke changeup," says Brian Bannister. "It's the modern, power, flat-spin-axis changeup. That's how it's evolved. Instead of in your mind trying to throw a backwards curveball, in a way it's, 'Let's throw a changeup with no vertical rise,' one where the bottom just falls out—like James Shields. The ball is spinning like a helicopter, therefore it has no backspin and no vertical rise and the bottom just falls out. That to me is the modern screwball."

Jim Mecir, a right-handed reliever for Oakland and four other teams from 1995 to 2005, was the last pitcher to have a long career throwing screwballs. Mecir learned it at Eckerd College from a coach, Rich Folkers, who played for several teams in the 1970s. Mecir threw it as a classic reverse curveball, turning his fingers away from his head and pulling down, never pronating, never hurting his elbow—and always keeping his catchers on alert.

"Just like a left-handed breaking ball," says A. J. Hinch, who caught him briefly for the A's. "You'd have to remind yourself to catch it with your thumb up, because it was going to go the wrong way."

Mecir's career was a testament to ingenuity. Born with a clubfoot, he could not generate much power with his legs as he pushed off the mound. His strength came from his upper body and he threw awkwardly, with an open delivery that kept him from having a good curveball or slider. The screwball was his remedy—but he wouldn't recommend it.

"I teach pitching lessons and I would never think about—especially with liability now—'Hey, do you want to throw a screwball?'" Mecir says. "Because I don't know, myself. I just know it works for me. My mechanics were a little different and it's what I had to do."

It is not a pitch anyone seems interested in teaching, from Hubbell on down. In 2016 Fox aired a drama series called *Pitch* about a woman, played by Kylie Bunbury, who makes the majors by throwing a screwball. But fantasy did not meet reality: her on-set coach, the former Oriole Gregg Olson, has never taught a screwball to a nonactor. Too hard on the shoulder, he says.

Even as a family heirloom, the pitch often stays on the basement shelf. Clyde Wright was 1–8 for the Angels in 1969, learned a screwball from Marv Grissom in winter ball, and immediately had a dream season: 22 wins, an All-Star appearance, a no-hitter. His son, Jaret, went on to pitch in the majors, too, but Clyde never thought to teach him a screwball.

"No, no, no, no, no," Wright says. "He had the circle change. When you can throw it 97, 98 and you can get it over with the breaking ball and the changeup, you really don't need it."

Jaret Wright's career began with great promise—he nearly pitched the Indians to victory in Game 7 of the 1997 World Series—but injuries ultimately held him back, even though he never used the screwball. Clyde is not convinced the pitch is dangerous. It never hurt his elbow, he said, yet pitchers today seem to be constantly in pain.

"If they're worried about it hurting arms, then somebody's a lot dumber than I am," Wright says. "How many guys go on the DL every year in the big leagues—and not one of them throws the screwball that I've heard about."

Yet Wright, too, knows the story of Carl Hubbell and his inverted pitching arm. That example is not the reason the screwball has gone away, but it symbolizes the pitch's notorious reputation. Few people threw the screwball to begin with, and now there's almost nobody to advocate for it, let alone teach it.

"There's just too much at stake now," Bannister says. "With the money in the game, it's not worthwhile for a coach to put his own career on the line to destroy a kid's arm. Whether he would or not isn't the issue, it's just that any form of risk in pitching, as far as health is concerned, is considered taboo."

"Teams in general are always in this limbo between performance and health. You have these massive investments in money and kids, and you don't want to blow them out because you only get so many draft picks, and they're expensive. But at the same time, there's this sacrifice in performance that a lot of older pitchers used to have, because they were willing to go places with the pitches and with their arm action that most teams won't approach nowadays."

Some pitchers, like Hector Santiago and Trevor Bauer, have periodically promoted the screwball in recent years, rooting for its return. They've never really stuck with it, or stood out enough for people to pay much attention, but as teams chase every little edge, they're more and more open to shattering old perceptions. Theoretically, this could help the screwball's chance of survival.

One day in 2016, around the batting cage in Houston, Astros pitching coach Brent Strom spoke about the splitter, how it was the rage of the 1980s. "I want the next rage," said general manager Jeff Luhnow, smiling. "But we're not gonna tell you what it is."

Could it be the screwball? Strom, a contemporary of Marshall, McGraw, Jim Brewer, and other screwball masters of the 1970s, wouldn't dismiss it.

"It's the easiest pitch to throw and nobody throws it," he said. Because the arm is already pronated on a screwball, Strom explained, it's in a better position to decelerate than it is for other pitches. Think of a car slowing down as it approaches the stop sign, instead of slamming on the brakes.

That is the analogy used by Brent Honeywell Jr., a top right-hander in the Tampa Bay farm system whose background and attitude make him the screwball's best hope. Honeywell's father, Brent Sr., is Mike Marshall's cousin. Marshall coached Brent Sr. at Saint Leo University in the 1980s, and taught him the screwball. Brent Sr., who pitched briefly in the minors, passed on the pitch to Brent Jr., telling him the screwball would take him to the majors.

Honeywell is not especially close with Marshall, who disagrees strongly with any teaching not precisely aligned with his own. Specifically, he worries that the Rays will ruin Honeywell by forcing him to throw a traditional breaking ball, not the pronating version Marshall favors.

But Honeywell did work with Marshall as a teenager, and he stays limber and flexible by training with a six-pound shot put, a Marshall technique. He also has a strain of iconoclasm in the way he talks about the family pitch: when it comes to the screwball, Honeywell is a true believer. Before the Rays could even think about taking the pitch away from him, Honeywell said, he told them to forget it.

"I think there's this false thing about it that it hurts people's arms," Honeywell says. "That just scares people away. It's actually better on your arm than another pitch, because it takes the stress off the elbow, is what it does. You pronate to maximum pronation, is what people call it. I just call it turning it over. When you turn it over as far as you can turn it over, you're getting full-on pronation and it takes the stress off your elbow. It's better for your arm. It's what Mike says and what is scientifically proven."

Honeywell succumbed to Tommy John surgery in spring training 2018, but insisted the procedure was inevitable and had nothing to do with his screwball, which had dazzled his U.S. teammates at the Futures Game in 2017. The Astros' Derek Fisher called it a "dinosaur pitch," and Lewis Brinson, now with the Marlins, was awestruck.

"I don't know what it is," Brinson said, "but it started in their dugout and ended up in the strike zone."

Jim Hickey, who spent 11 seasons as Tampa Bay's pitching coach before joining the Cubs in 2018, does not call the pitch a screwball. "Remember Daisuke Matsuzaka and the 'gyroball,' how it was gonna revolutionize the game—and it was a freaking changeup," Hickey said, referring to the Japanese sensation who never quite matched his hype for the Red Sox. "Brent's more inside the ball than you would be with a conventional change, but I'm not sure you'd call it a screwball."

Honeywell is used to skeptics; teammates joke with him that his precious pitch is nothing more than a glorified changeup. He laughs off the doubts. "It's gonna be the first time they've ever seen a changeup move like that," he says.

Fair enough. The screwball is its own pitch. But this is roughly what has happened, in simplest terms: the screwball gave way to the splitter and the splitter gave way to the changeup. And all three pitches, in most cases, are different means to the same end.

With his family connection, Honeywell has a natural tie to the screwball. For others, there's little reason to reach so far back through history to find it. Even Herrera doubts it will ever return.

"You're looking for a revival of something from the old times, and I just don't think it can," he says. "I don't think guys are really, actually willing to try and develop it. Most of the guys that I've tried to show, they'll throw it a couple of times and they'll either say, 'That will hurt my elbow' or 'It's just too weird.'"

The weird pitch that hurts the elbow. In the graveyard of baseball, those words could be etched on the tombstone of the screwball, a pitch that once brought glory to so many. The fadeaway, it turns out, was the right name all along.

THE
SINKER

The Furthest Strike from the Hitter's Eyes

The sinker used to be baseball's most sensible pitch. Its allure was efficiency, not force. Throw it low for ground balls, conserve pitches, last deeper in games.

"All you had to do was take it off the plane that the hitter was starting his swing at," says Steve Rogers, a five-time All-Star for the Montreal Expos. "Just take it off the plane *that much*, in the last 10 feet, and it's a soft ground ball."

A sinker is really just a fastball, usually thrown with the index and middle fingers aligned with the seams at their narrowest point, the hand slightly pronated at the finish. It is also called a two-seamer because, thrown this way, only two seams bite the air for each revolution.

Yet it is not really a fastball in the way we tend to think of that pitch. You would not test your arm strength at a carnival booth by throwing a sinking fastball. You'd slap your fingers across the seams and fire it as hard and as straight as you could. With that kind of fastball, four seams backspin each time through the air, defying gravity just a bit longer.

"If you throw it 96, 97 miles per hour, the ball gets to home plate before the spin has a chance to make it sink," Tommy John says. "But the metrics people don't want that. They want speed, speed, speed."

They might not be wrong. If we started the sport all over again, untethered to tradition, we might structure it the way many analysts now prefer: pitchers throw fastballs up and curveballs down (the north-south approach, as they say) for short bursts, then turn the game over to another pitcher, and another, and another, all throwing hard. With a deep supply of power arms today, why bother conserving pitches? And if you've trained all your life to throw hard, why sacrifice speed for sink?

"It's a harder sell, because there's a lot of glory in throwing the ball hard," says Dave Duncan, one of the most successful pitching coaches in history, mostly for the A's and the Cardinals. "If you throw 98, 100 miles an hour, you get a lot of attention. How are you gonna get signed as an amateur? You think they're out there signing 90-mile-an-hour guys? No, they're not signing them. You know why? Because scouts see a guy that throws 99, and he may not be able to throw it through a door, but that scout can say, 'Hey, this guy's got a great arm, he throws hard, all he needs is someone to tweak him a little.'

"It's safe. But that guy that throws 92, 93, sinking fastball, decent control and movement on the ball? That's the guy I love."

Duncan—who had been a power-hitting catcher in his 11 years as a player—loves the sinker for a very logical reason. The easiest way to score runs, he reasons, is with extra-base hits. Except for hard grounders right down the line, almost every extra-base hit is a ball in the air. Pitchers, therefore, should live at the bottom of the strike zone with a hard slider, hard curve, changeup—or, most reliable, a two-seam sinker.

Duncan built those pitchers in St. Louis, helping the Cardinals become consistent contenders and two-time champions in the early part of this century. He encouraged Chris Carpenter, a league-average pitcher in Toronto, to use more sinking fastballs, and Carpenter became a star, passing on the gospel to teammates like Adam Wainwright, who continued to spread the message.

In 2011, Duncan's final season as a full-time pitching coach, the Cardinals won the World Series. That season, according to Baseball Savant, major league pitchers threw more than 167,000 pitches that were classified as two-seam fastballs or sinkers. The Cardinals' staff ranked second in the majors in such pitches, throwing them more than 34 percent of the time.

Not all old coaches are as enthusiastic as Duncan. Bill Fischer started and relieved for four teams in the 1950s and '60s, distinguished by how often batters put his pitches in play. Fischer holds the record for most consecutive innings without a walk, with 84⅓ in 1962, and averaged just 3.4 strikeouts per nine innings. Coaches told him to throw two-seam fastballs, not four-seamers, and he followed orders. But he never liked the results, and when Fischer became a coach he vowed his pitchers would be different.

"I had Roger Clemens," Fischer said in 2017, at age 86, still in full uniform at the Royals' spring training camp, rambling through the back fields in Surprise, Arizona, on a golf cart with his name on it.

"The first year in Boston, he struggled, his arm was bothering him. I said, 'How do you hold your fastball?' He said, 'With the seams.' I said, 'Roger, you gotta turn that ball around in your hand and throw four-seamers.' He said, 'I pitched this way in college and I had success, I want to do it the same way.' He was a hardheaded son of a bitch.

"So we went to Sarasota to play an exhibition game and Tom Seaver was gonna pitch against him; Tom was with the White Sox. I said, 'Tom, I got a guy I'd like you to talk to,' so I took him over there. First thing Tom Seaver said is: 'I'm gonna talk to you, and I don't want you to open your mouth till I tell you. Kid, how do you hold your fastball?' He said, 'With the seams.' Tom said, 'Well, you might as well go home right now because you ain't gonna be worth a shit. You want to be good?'"

Fischer laughed: "Roger listened this time. After that I had no trouble with him anymore. He went all four-seam fastball, he got faster and faster and faster. Holy Christ!"

Seaver did understand the value of the sinker. In his book *The Art of Pitching* he explains that low pitches are effective because the batter cannot hit a ball squarely if he sees only its top half. He describes how he turns the ball on its side a little, applies pressure with the outside of his index fingertip, instead of from the middle finger, and lets the ball move down and in on a right-hander. But this "turned two-seam fastball," as Seaver called it, was not his preferred option. He saved it, he wrote, for "when the good riding fastball has deserted me."

The two-seamer is fine if it's all you've got, and it's handy for a double play. A few Hall of Famers were known more for sinkers than four-seamers, like Grover Cleveland Alexander, Bob Lemon, Don

Drysdale, and Greg Maddux, who mastered everything. Maddux didn't even call it a sinker or a two-seamer, and didn't think about diminished velocity.

"Whatever," Maddux says. "I called it a fastball—a two-seam fastball that runs in front a little bit. That was just my fastball. I threw as hard as I could."

Maddux envisioned an X on both edges of the plate, and tried to throw pitches that followed those lines: in and away on one side, in and away on the other side. With four possibilities—*both* directions on *both* sides—the hitter could never account for them all. His only hope would be to read the movement, yet with Maddux, the pitch would go right for the sweet spot and then veer away, as if magnetically repelled. Steve Stone, the Cy Young Award winner who broadcast Cubs games when Maddux reached the majors, said this action sent Maddux to Cooperstown.

"Late movement," Stone said. "If you have gradual movement, they're gonna knock the crap out of you. Late movement is the whole thing."

Maddux called the sinker "the furthest strike from the hitter's eyes—a little bit harder to see, a little bit harder to hit." His successor in baiting hitters with it would be Roy Halladay, a Cy Young Award winner for the Blue Jays and the Phillies. The pitchers had strikingly similar rate statistics: Maddux averaged 8.5 hits allowed per nine innings, 1.8 walks per nine, 6.1 strikeouts per nine; for Halladay, it was 8.7, 1.9, and 6.9.

Demoted to Class A in 2001, after 33 starts across three seasons in the majors, Halladay reinvented himself, dropping his arm angle to three-quarters, which made his fastball naturally scoot a few inches to the third base side. This was a relief to Halladay, because the straighter fastball unnerved him; he felt he had to be too perfect with it. The sinker—coupled with the cutter, which he perfected later in his career—helped free Halladay from anxiety.

"Before I felt like if I wasn't on the corners, I was in trouble," Halladay said in March 2017. "With the sinker I could basically start it middle of the plate and just let it run. And as a young pitcher not able to really throw the ball anywhere I wanted all the time, it allowed me to throw a sinker on that side that was running to their hands, and then a cutter that was either running away from a righty or into a lefty. Everything was running away from the plate.

"So it really just gave me so much—it gave me the ability to be aggressive, to go after guys and challenge them, knowing that the ball's moving. Even if I could get it to move three or four inches going either direction, I'm missing the barrel, and that was my only goal. I wanted them to swing at every pitch, I wanted them to put it in play, but I was trying to stay off the barrel."

Luke Scott, then of the Orioles, once demonstrated this for me by his locker at Camden Yards. I was covering the Yankees and a pitcher named Darrell Rasner had gotten off to a good start. Rasner was not overpowering, but for a while he was quite effective and I asked Scott why. He explained why pitches off the barrel are hit so weakly, which I knew but had never seen illustrated quite this way.

Scott held a brown bat in the air, perpendicular to the ground. In his other hand he held a pink bat, parallel to the ground. Holding the brown bat steady, he lightly tapped the pink bat against it, starting around the middle and proceeding down. For several inches, the brown bat barely moved.

Then, for only two or three inches just before the name on the barrel, it jumped, as if spring-loaded. It was like finding the jelly inside a doughnut—*this* part was different. *This* was the sweet spot. And then, for the last few inches, the bat seemed dead again.

Connecting squarely on the barrel can make the ball seem weightless. So when it runs off that sweet spot, and the hitter buries it into the ground, the ball can seem heavy, unable to be lifted, like an anchor plunging to the bottom of the sea.

Here's how catcher Mickey Owen described the sinker of Bill McGee, a sidearmer for the Cardinals in the 1930s and '40s, to *Baseball Magazine* in 1941: "He throws a ball that seems like a cannon ball when it comes into a catching mitt." Some three decades later, the Yankees' Thurman Munson said Mel Stottlemyre's sinker felt like it weighed 100 pounds.

Randy Jones, Brandon Webb, Dallas Keuchel, and Rick Porcello won Cy Young Awards by throwing heavy sinkers, and Chien-Ming Wang was a runner-up. Kevin Brown made six All-Star teams and earned baseball's first $100 million contract with a sinker that brimmed with rage.

"He looked vicious," said Torii Hunter, the former star outfielder. "I mean, he looked like a cowboy that wants to draw on you on the mound. He cut his sleeves, he was jacked. He had that sinker with teeth. It was coming at you like this"—Hunter chomped his teeth vigorously, like a rabid dog—"ready to bite your bat off."

If forced to choose, a sinkerballer wants movement over velocity. For some, the terminology is important. Brad Ziegler, a longtime reliever, makes a conscious effort not to think of his sinker as a fastball—because "fastball," to Ziegler, means "try to throw it hard." The harder he throws, the flatter his pitch becomes, and that means a line drive or worse.

Avoid the barrel, and the pitcher will usually win the encounter. An even better plan is to avoid the bat entirely, but that's not always possible against the world's best hitters, and seeking strikeouts is an easy way to run a high pitch count. Halladay—a seven-time league leader in complete games—couldn't fathom why so many pitchers throw balls with two strikes. He knew *why*—they want to entice a jumpy hitter to swing at something he can't touch—but he also knew that good hitters take those pitches.

"I felt like with two strikes—0–2, 1–2—if they didn't swing at it, it was gonna be strike three," Halladay said. "I wanted something that they either had to swing at and put in play, or it was gonna be a strike. It's changed a lot in the way people think about pitching: they want to stay just off the plate and avoid contact."

Orel Hershiser used a term that defines the sinker mentality: *bat stimulus*. Hershiser, a slightly built Dodgers righty, won 204 games but is best known for a glorious two-month stretch in 1988. He finished that regular season with a record 59 consecutive scoreless innings, then started the postseason with eight more. His breathtaking ledger from that September and October: an 8-0 record, 0.46 ERA, eight complete games and seven shutouts in 11 starts, plus a save. He was MVP of the NLCS and the World Series, lifted to the sky after vanquishing a powerful Oakland team to win the Dodgers' last title. Hershiser's mind-set, described decades later over lunch before a Dodger broadcast, is the perfect distillation of the sinkerballer's creed.

"Because I didn't really consider myself a strikeout pitcher, I thought, 'OK, then really it's about contact—but it's *really* about weak contact,'" Hershiser says. "And then it's also about pitch count and being able to complete games and get deep into games. So what you're looking for is early, weak contact, and the best way to get that is movement.

"But you also have to give the hitter something to start the bat. So for me it was about bat stimulus. I've got to give him something visually that he likes, and then I've got to make it move. Greg Maddux would say, 'Make strikes look like balls and make balls look like strikes.' That's pitching. And there's two ways to really get a hitter out, which is to convince him what's coming and throw the opposite, or convince him what's coming, throw it, and put it in a hard place to hit."

Moving down and tailing off the plate, the sinker is a model of expedience, producing quick outs or, at worst, a bunch of singles. To Rogers, the Expos' first great pitcher, down and in to a righty was the magic quadrant of the strike zone. He wanted his sinkers there, and his fingers pointed the way. Rogers's goal was to drive the ball down to that area, and by pointing there when he threw, he accentuated the pressure on the ball with his index finger.

One of Rogers's earliest coaches was Cal McLish, an old right-hander from Oklahoma who was part Choctaw, part Cherokee and had perhaps the most mellifluous full name in the annals of baseball: Calvin Coolidge Julius Caesar Tuskahoma McLish. His message to Rogers was simple: "All right, son, just get out in front and get whippy!"

Rogers did not know what that meant, and McLish never had much to add—but there was a lot of truth in it. McLish had thrown sinkers and knew the late life essential to the pitch came from a whippy sort of arm action at release, an almost imperceptible turning over of the wrist.

The one McLish lesson that did help Rogers was a primer on the slider. It was a pressure pitch, the coach explained; turn the fingers in and apply pressure on the middle finger, and you've got a slider, sweeping down and away from a right-hander. In that case, Rogers thought, shouldn't the reverse hold true for a sinker?

He already had calluses on his index finger, and the middle finger just seemed to be getting in the way when Rogers pronated his wrist as he let the ball go. What if he shifted his fingers slightly, so the index finger applied pressure on the outer side of the left seam, and the middle finger sat on the white, touching no seams, just along for the ride?

That adjustment sent Rogers on his way, and he became a preeminent ground ball specialist. Elbow surgery in 1978 helped refine his mechanics, and also caused just enough drop in velocity to give his sinker even more fade.

This was the pitch Rogers threw in the decisive fifth game of the 1981 NLCS, with the season on the line against the Dodgers. He had been a playoff star that fall, beating the Phillies twice, the Dodgers once, and collecting 80 of a possible 81 outs—though just 10 by strikeout, typical of a sinkerballer. Now he was on in relief, for the top of the ninth inning of a 1–1 game at frigid Olympic Stadium.

It was a Monday—Blue Monday, as it has forever been known in Montreal, describing four things at once: the mood of the fans, the day of the week, the winning team's color, and the hero of the game. Rogers faced four batters. Steve Garvey popped to second. Ron Cey flied out to deep left. Then came Rick Monday, with Pedro Guerrero on deck.

"I did not throw a single pitch mechanically correct until the three pitches to Guerrero, after the adrenaline was out of my system," Rogers said. "I was just overthrowing everything. I was a top-down pitcher. I had to be tall and then down, tall and then down. And I was losing the angle of the mound because I was so pumped up in the bullpen. I was throwing the ball hard, as hard as I could throw it, maybe 91."

Rogers said he was not bothered by pitching in relief. It was just his excitement, with a pennant at stake, that hurt him. He wishes he had faced Monday with a man on base.

"It probably would have been a great service to me if either Cey or Garvey had gotten a base hit, because what would it have done? You go in the stretch," Rogers said. "Then it takes the windup out of the picture, and that's what I was overdoing."

An overthrown sinker never has time to dive into that special quadrant, the one where Rogers imagined his finger pointing. Monday swung hard at the 3–1 pitch and smoked it high over center field. It cleared the blue wall as he rounded first, leaping and punching the icy air with his fist.

Guerrero struck out, but it didn't matter. The Dodgers got the final three outs to win the NL title, on their way to a World Series victory. The Expos never made the playoffs again. The sinker had sunk them.

———

Montreal could have used a closer like Zach Britton. In 2016, Britton converted all 47 save chances for the Orioles, plus another in the All-Star Game, which he finished by using his sinker for a double play grounder from slugger Nolan Arenado. Britton's 0.54 ERA that season was the lowest ever for a pitcher with at least 65 innings.

Britton honed his sinker by using a contraption first created by Branch Rickey, the visionary architect of the Brooklyn Dodgers. One of Rickey's most promising pitchers in the late 1940s was Rex Barney, a hard-throwing right-hander who fired a no-hitter in 1948 and twice started games in the World Series. He was also among the wildest pitchers in baseball history, and Rickey devised a system of strings for the bullpen mound in Vero Beach, Florida, to help his control.

"Creating a visible strike zone in the pitcher's mind, regardless of where the batter may be standing in the batter's box, helps a pitcher throw to the intended spot," Rickey wrote, in personal papers that were later published. "Pitching to the strings will accelerate the mastery of control, and pitchers, particularly the young ones, should be given ample opportunity to use them."

Rickey gave specific installation instructions: two six-foot poles driven 12 inches into the ground, with a system of strings to be moved up or down to pinpoint a particular zone. The Dodgers had just moved their spring operations to Vero Beach, and the Rex Barney strings became a fixture there, long after he was gone.

Barney never did find his control; he threw his last pitch in 1950 but stayed in the game for decades, serving as the Orioles' public address announcer until his death in 1997. Ten years after that, a young Britton was toiling in the Baltimore farm system when a coach, Calvin Maduro, tried to teach him a cutter. Maduro used an unconventional, curveball-like grip—but when Britton tried it, the pitch would not obey. It was supposed to move in on a righty, but instead darted down and away. Maduro was dumbfounded but told Britton to go with it.

"Pitching's so weird, because everyone's arm action is different," Britton says. "Even though it may look the same, it's different—their bodies are different, the way they put pressure on the ball is different. That grip is a good sinker for me. If I gripped it like a two-seamer, it probably wouldn't even move."

Britton's sinker got him to the majors, but he mostly struggled as a starter. He switched to the bullpen in spring training 2014, when the Orioles introduced a new pitching coach, Dave Wallace. Britton had worked with strings before; Rick Peterson, the Orioles' former minor league pitching guru, also believes in them. But in Wallace, Britton had a genuine Dodgers disciple to guide him.

Wallace had a brief major league career in the 1970s and established himself as a coach in the Dodgers' system. He used the strings—portable now, if still cumbersome—as a tool in other jobs, with the Mets and the Braves. In the spring of 2014, Wallace and Dom Chiti, the bullpen coach, encouraged Britton to use the strings for every bullpen session, and to throw only sinkers.

Britton had been too wild as a starter. He needed better command of his sinker, and Wallace moved the knots within the strings to an area about six inches square, low and away. That is the critical spot, to Wallace; get the ball down and away, consistently, and everything else will be easy by comparison. He has another name for his tiny zone: a quality major league strike.

"We usually give a guy 20 throws, and a lot of guys don't get 10," Wallace says. "But what you find out is if they get eight, there's another five or six that are real close, because of the level of concentration."

For Britton, it was a revelation. Visualization, he found, was everything. If he wanted to throw the sinker for a strike, he would aim it at the equipment logo on the catcher's chest protector, just below the neck, and the movement would take it to the zone. If he wanted to throw it for a ball, he would aim it at the catcher's shin guards, and the movement would carry it to the dirt, for a chase.

Soon enough, Britton was threading his sinker through the strings about seven out of 10 tries. He took the pitch into games, and familiar hitters, used to getting ahead of him, were suddenly behind in the count. That made them vulnerable to his sinker off the plate—and

Britton knew how to get it there, because he knew how his ball should behave.

"That drill really helped me understand what my pitch is actually doing," Britton says.

———

Orel Hershiser had worked with the strings as a young pitcher for the Dodgers, and his intellect helped him last 18 seasons in the majors. For much of that time he kept a copy of Robert K. Adair's book, *The Physics of Baseball*, in his travel bag. Yet he also grasped the benefits of a rudimentary teaching tool.

"The strings are amazing," he says. "They're stationary, and as a pitcher, your head's not always still. So you might think you just threw a good pitch, but you don't actually know. Or maybe you're being led to believe it was good by the catcher, the way he caught it—but you didn't necessarily see where the catcher's set up, or maybe the catcher's lazy. But with the strings, when the ball hits it right there on the corner, it rattles, and you know you just threw a ball and it hit the corner.

"Your vision can lie to you, and the strings helped you get your eyes lined up, that you're actually throwing a correct pitch. It's the combination of the visual, mental, and physical."

That is what Ferguson Jenkins had discovered, too, as a teenager in Chatham, Ontario, in the late 1950s. Every Tuesday and Thursday in the winter, Jenkins would throw to a strike zone of movable strings at a local gymnasium—not at full strength, just hard enough to study and internalize the way his ball should move.

Jenkins would become the greatest pitcher in Chicago Cubs history. With command of a sinker allowing him to last deep in games, Jenkins threw at least 289 innings in seven different seasons, mostly for the Cubs. Every time he did, he earned at least 20 wins.

"I used the top of the ball, where the printing's at, and my fingers were close together," Jenkins says. "A great pulling pitch. All you do is pull it backwards. Pull it hard, and you get that sink."

Jenkins was 284–226 with a 3.34 ERA and made the Hall of Fame. Tommy John was 288–231 with the same ERA, and has never come close. John is mostly known for the revolutionary 1974 elbow surgery that bears his name, but he also honed his pitching savvy with strings.

When John was a boy in Indiana, he scavenged for soda bottles and used the redemption money on a pitching book by Bob Feller. In it, Feller described how to set up a strike zone made of strings, like Rickey's contraption at Dodgertown. John's father built it for him in the backyard.

"The top string would be mid-thigh or just above mid-thigh; the bottom string would be about six inches below the knee; the inside string would be on the outside half of the plate and the outside string would be about six to eight inches off the plate," he says. "That was my strike zone, and that's what I threw to. I didn't want the high strike—I wanted to concentrate on throwing the ball low and away, low and away."

At 18 John signed with Cleveland, and at 20 he was pitching in the majors, throwing nothing but sinking fastballs and curves. He gripped both the same way and always pitched in a hurry: *get the ball and throw it,* no time to fiddle with grips. In his seventh full season, with the White Sox, John learned a slider from new pitching coach Johnny Sain. He practiced it so much that his fastball suffered, and John turned to Ray Berres, an old catcher who had been his first pitching coach in Chicago.

"I was hoping you would call," Berres barked. "Stick that fucking slider up your ass! Never add a pitch if it's gonna make your existing pitches worse!"

After Dr. Frank Jobe's famous operation in 1974—in which he used a tendon from John's forearm to replace his torn ulnar collateral ligament—John pitched for 14 more seasons. He was 46 when he made his 700th and final career start. Only one other lefty, Steve Carlton, has ever made more.

———————

To impart even more sink, while adding a dash of funk to make up for diminished velocity, some pitchers drop to a submarine angle. Usually, though, it's nobody's first choice.

Darren O'Day figured his baseball career was over when he failed to make the team as a freshman at the University of Florida. But a friend asked him to play for a men's league the next summer, and as O'Day played catch with his brother to get ready, he fooled around with a sidearm angle. Just like that, he had the kind of sinking action he never could get overhand. He went on to become an All-Star setup man for Baltimore.

"If you throw it right, you can get an element of topspin that you can't get overhand, and you're usually not throwing quite as hard, either, so the ball's going to sink more," O'Day says. "The big thing about it is hitters just aren't used to seeing it, so they can't pick up the spin as easily."

An unfamiliar motion can help a pitcher enormously; some recent aces, like Clayton Kershaw, Max Scherzer, Jake Arrieta, Madison Bumgarner, and Chris Sale, use deliveries so distinct that hitters have little basis for comparison. And just a split second of indecision further shifts the advantage to the pitcher.

Submariners are not as rare as knuckleballers, but they belong in a similar category. They do something different, hear predictable taunts from opposing fans—"This isn't softball" is a popular one, Brad Ziegler says—and frustrate hitters with a method most players use as a lark.

On a team flight with the Tigers in 1995, the Hall of Famer Al Kaline approached Mike Myers, a soft-throwing, overmatched rookie. Kaline noticed that Myers was around the strike zone a lot and thought he needed a different look to succeed. He asked Myers if he had ever dropped his arm angle. Of course, Myers replied.

"I always threw sidearm in the outfield anyway, just screwing around, for fun," Myers says. "Like how every second baseman throws a knuckleball."

Myers tried the low angle—not quite submarine, where the pitcher releases from so low that his knuckles almost scrape the dirt, but close enough—and it worked. He led the majors in appearances the next two seasons and would pitch almost 900 career games. Hitters would tell Myers that his 80-mile-an-hour sinker looked about 15 mph faster because he set it up with slow, Frisbee-like sliders.

The forefather of all modern sidearm slingers is Grover Cleveland Alexander, who went by Pete and was also called "Ol' Low & Away." Alexander—born in 1887, during the first of President Cleveland's nonconsecutive terms—earned 373 victories, tied with Christy Mathewson for third all-time. Alexander, who pitched mostly for the Phillies and the Cubs, had a reputation as one of the game's fastest workers. That was consistent with his pitch, the sinker bearing down and in on right-handers.

"What's the use of doin' in three pitches what you can do in one?" he said, as quoted by Martin Quigley in *The Crooked Pitch.* Indeed, Alexander was so efficient that he led his league in innings seven times and twice won both ends of a doubleheader, both times with two complete games. A teammate and opponent, Hans Lobert, described Alexander's best pitch this way to Lawrence Ritter in *The Glory of Their Times:*

"He had little short fingers and he threw a very heavy ball. Once, later on, when I'd moved over to the Giants, Alex hit me over the heart with a pitched ball and it bore in like a lump of lead hitting you. I couldn't get my breath for ten minutes afterward. Matty was just as fast, but he threw a much lighter ball."

(Ivan Rodriguez, the Hall of Fame catcher, described a similar sensation many years later. The fastest pitcher he ever caught, Rodriguez said, was the Tigers' Joel Zumaya, whose ball felt light. But when Rodriguez caught sinkers from a young Kevin Brown in Texas, the ball felt so heavy he worried it would shatter his thumb—inside his glove.)

Alexander surely threw harder than most of his era, but also understood the advantage of being unusual. As he said in *Baseball Magazine,* in an undated clip quoted by Rob Neyer, "I believe that the side arm motion is much more baffling to the batter than the overhand delivery. For that reason I have developed the side arm delivery and have cultivated it so that I have it down pretty well."

In 1926, at age 39, Alexander clinched the Cardinals' first World Series with a performance so heroic that Ronald Reagan would play him in a 1952 film, *The Winning Team,* chronicling Alexander's triumph over alcoholism and epilepsy. In the series, Alexander beat the Yankees in Games 2 and 6, then came into Game 7 from the bullpen and struck out Tony Lazzeri with the bases loaded. That's the end of the movie, but it was really just the end of the seventh inning; the game actually ended when Babe Ruth, of all people, was caught stealing second. Ruth's rationale was the ultimate compliment to Alexander: he needed to be in scoring position, he believed, because there was no way the Yankees could get two more singles to score him from first. And good luck hitting that sinker in the air for extra bases.

The Yankees recovered in grand style, sweeping Pittsburgh in the 1927 World Series to cement their status as the most fearsome team of all time. Their pitching star was another sidearming sinkerballer: Wilcy Moore, a 30-year-old rookie, who had turned to the style after breaking his arm two years earlier, closed out Game 1 and went the distance in the finale.

Moore was a hybrid, a spot starter who also finished games in relief. He led the AL in saves three times—before that statistic was created—and was an early forerunner of the sidearming late-inning stoppers who would follow decades later. Two, Kent Tekulve and Dan Quisenberry, are forever intertwined. Neither threw hard, but neither was defined that way, either.

"Watching Quisenberry as a kid, they didn't have radar guns on the TV," says Brad Ziegler, who grew up in Kansas City and would imitate Quisenberry with Wiffle balls. "It wasn't about that at the time. It was about getting outs. You get outs, you've got a shot to pitch."

Submarine pitchers generally work only in relief, so the manager can pick their spots (say, to get a double play) and take advantage of their durability—which comes mainly from not throwing very hard or throwing many pitches. Everyone in the ballpark knows the aim of a submariner: to sink the ball and get the batter to hit it on the ground. By inviting contact, though, a pitcher also invites chaos if those grounders find holes. Some teams would rather avoid the style altogether.

It should be no surprise, then, that Tekulve and Quisenberry were not drafted. Neither, for that matter, was O'Day. Ziegler was released and pitched for an independent team before the A's signed him and eventually changed his angle. Those four submariners overcame the collective rejection to pitch about 3,000 games in the majors.

Before he could pitch in his first, in 1974, Tekulve had to listen to an old scout over beers after a game in Double-A. Tekulve had thrown sidearm all his life and found immediate success in the minors with the Pirates. But the scout, George Detore, told him his sinker would never trick big league hitters unless it moved better in the strike zone.

More sophisticated hitters, Detore insisted, would take his good sinkers, which were off the plate, and hammer the flat ones in the middle.

"So I started experimenting with stuff,"Tekulve says. "The first thing you do is you go up to three-quarters, like a normal human being—but I went up there and it was a total disaster. If I was throwing it 82 miles per hour, it was a lot, and it was perfectly straight. Eighty-two miles per hour and perfectly straight is defined as batting practice. So that didn't work."

From three-quarters, Tekulve was missing his topspin, the furious rotating action that propelled the ball down and forced hitters to bury it into the dirt. Throwing in the outfield a bit later, he thought of Ted Abernathy, a longtime major leaguer who had pitched for Tekulve's hometown Reds. Tekulve swung his arm lower, almost to the ground— and unlocked the pitch that would make him the game's all-time leader in relief appearances when he retired in 1989.

"The very first one I threw, I knew—*this is it,*"Tekulve said. He was throwing it harder, and the ball was diving at precisely the right spot: three feet in front of the plate, after the hitter had committed himself to swing, a fat strike until its final tumble. "From that day forward, I knew what the sinker was and what it was gonna be—and it was gonna be good."

Tekulve was 27 by the time he made his debut. He soon became an expert on angles and grips and their effects on the movement of a baseball delivered from below. If he raised his fingers by 45 degrees— instead of pointing them straight down—Tekulve could produce a more dramatic tailing action into a right-hander. "The revolutions still matched up," he says, matter-of-factly, meaning that the moment of deception, the critical three-foot mark, would still be the same.

Tekulve would close out the 1970s, saving Game 7 of the World Series for the Pirates in his 101st appearance of the season. Tekulve's final sinker did not do much—he described its flight to me with a farting noise—but Baltimore's Pat Kelly could only lift a harmless fly ball to center. As the Orioles nursed their defeat, their first base coach, Jim Frey, could not shake the memory of Tekulve's quirky dominance. Named as the new manager of the Royals, Frey decided to find his own version. At an off-season banquet, he asked Tekulve for a favor.

The Royals' bullpen in 1979 had allowed more than five runs per nine innings. Its best performer, oddly, was a rookie with a funny name and a sidearm delivery. He had managed only 13 strikeouts in 40 innings, but his control and ability to generate grounders offered promise. Frey wondered if Tekulve could help Quisenberry with his mechanics in spring training.

Quisenberry had started throwing sidearm as a senior at the University of La Verne, in California, because his arm had grown tired from the workload of 194 innings. But the motion ran in his family: Quisenberry's older brother, Marty, had been a submarine pitcher who was scouted, though not signed, by the Royals.

When no team drafted Dan, either, his coach called the scout who had once shown interest in Marty. The Royals, it turned out, needed a pitcher for their Class A team in Waterloo, Iowa. Their bonus offer was a Royals bat, pen, and lapel button. Quisenberry accepted.

"I was really pretty excited," he told *Sports Illustrated,* "especially about the lapel button."

Quisenberry started and finished his first game for Waterloo in 1975. It was the only start of a career that lasted until 1990. Quisenberry became a star, as he would tell it, immediately following his tutorials with Tekulve—one in Fort Myers and another in Bradenton in that spring of 1980.

"We want this guy to be like you," Frey told Tekulve, as Quisenberry recounted it to Roger Angell. "He throws a little like you already, but basically he doesn't have shit."

Quisenberry went on to tell Angell all the ways Tekulve helped him: how to bend at the waist and extend his front leg, how to land with a hop to keep from falling over. He was wild and uncomfortable, he said, bouncing balls everywhere. But the coaches liked the extra movement on his sinker.

By the World Series, in which Quisenberry pitched in all six games of the Royals' loss to the Phillies, he had taken to calling the sinker his "Titanic pitch"—it sinks to the bottom—and crediting Tekulve with his transformation. Years later, Tekulve said Quisenberry was simply being kind.

"I did not change very much at all with Quisenberry," Tekulve says. "He was pretty much in the right place. He had the sink late. He didn't throw it as hard, but he didn't have as many revolutions, so therefore he still had it sinking at the right spot. There were only a couple of very minor things I suggested to him, and I think probably what benefited him more than anything else, as a young guy coming in, was having somebody who had just had success in the last World Series—somebody that did it—tell him, 'Hey, you're right.'"

Many years later, Tekulve would encourage Ziegler in a similar way, reminding him not to fear hitters, because they never like to face a submariner. That was clearly true for Quisenberry, who thanked Tekulve by sending a pair of plaid socks—the quintessential gift for Dad—to Three Rivers Stadium as a Father's Day gift in 1980.

That season began a stretch of six in which Quisenberry averaged more than 35 saves. He did his best to live up to the contract he made with his sinkers.

"Have I ever told you about my agreement with the ball?" Quisenberry asked Angell, who said no. "Well, our deal is that I'm not going to throw you very hard as long as you promise to move around when you get near the plate, *because I want you back*. So if you do your part, we'll get to play some more."

———————

The Cubs retired No. 31 in honor of two pitchers, Greg Maddux and Ferguson Jenkins, who both finished their careers with more than 3,000 strikeouts and fewer than 1,000 walks. Only two others in history—Curt Schilling and Pedro Martinez—have ever done this, and Jenkins was the first.

Jenkins joined the Cubs in a trade from the Phillies in April 1966, the same month Maddux was born. He was 23 and had made a few relief appearances, but no starts. That July the Cubs signed another former Phillie, Robin Roberts, for the final stop of his Hall of Fame career.

Roberts was 39, the oldest player in the National League, and he also helped coach the Cubs' pitchers. He preached the importance of the sinker to Jenkins, imparting two main lessons culled from more than 600 starts in the majors: the hitter wants a ball up over the plate, and doesn't really want to swing at the first pitch. With such impeccable control, Jenkins forced hitters to swing early, for fear of falling behind. He knew how he wanted them to hit.

"A sinker down over the plate, and down around the knees, was something that was gonna help me get guys to hit on top of the ball—not through the ball," Jenkins says. "And I had a good infield, guys with good gloves who knew what to do."

With Ron Santo at third, Don Kessinger at short, Glenn Beckert at second, and Ernie Banks at first, Jenkins had far better infielders and a smoother playing surface than he'd ever had in the minors. That eased his transition after his trade, and he won 20 games in 1967, his first full season as a starter. From that year through 1980, Jenkins would lead the majors in victories.

He did it, essentially, by becoming Roberts's clone. The sinker allowed them both to zip quickly through innings. Their control made them prone to home runs—only Jamie Moyer surrendered more than Roberts and Jenkins—but it tended to minimize damage. Jenkins also hated allowing walks because he much preferred to pitch from the windup.

Maddux did much of his bullpen work from the stretch, reasoning that his pitches with men on base would matter most. He joined the Cubs as a rookie in 1986, three years after Jenkins retired, and took his stylistic cues from Hershiser, another right-hander with a similar build and intuition about the craft. Asked in 2015 why he trusted his two-seamer and used it so often, Maddux replied: "Well, I saw Hershiser do it."

Maddux watched Hershiser whenever he could, delighting in the way he defied the traditional wisdom of coaches, who warned against pitching down and in to left-handers.

"I guess I was just stubborn enough not to believe them," Maddux says. "It was a pitch I was capable of throwing, and I saw Hershiser use it. As a young player I thought, 'Well, I'm going to do it, too.'"

Maddux's first role model was his older brother, Mike, who would have a long career as a major league reliever and coach. As teenagers in Las Vegas, they were tutored by a retired scout named Ralph Medar. He believed they would play professionally but knew that was not the main goal.

"In order to have success at a high level, you're going to rely more on movement than velocity," Maddux says, quoting Medar. "He taught me at a young age it was movement, location, the ability to change speeds—*and then* velocity, in that order, which I think still holds true today."

Medar switched Maddux from a four-seam fastball grip to a two-seam grip, and lowered his arm angle from high- to low-three-quarters. Maddux became entranced by the movement of his fastball, which would start at the hip of a left-hander and curl back to clip the inside corner for a strike. He would execute a pitch and ask Medar how it moved, not how fast it went.

Maddux was a senior in high school when Medar died of a heart attack. But the Cubs' scouting report on Maddux, before the 1984 draft, reflected the lessons Medar had imparted: "He throws 86–89 consistently with very good movement," wrote the scout, Doug Mapson. "His movement isn't a gradual tailing type but a quick, explosive, bat-breaking kink."

Mapson wrote that if Maddux (then just 5 foot 11, and almost done growing) were more physically imposing, he could have been the first overall pick. The Cubs passed on him anyway at No. 3, taking a strapping college left-hander, Drew Hall, who would win just nine games in his career. They grabbed Maddux in the second round (at pick number 31) and he would win 355—the most of anyone who started his career after Jackie Robinson integrated the majors in 1947.

"Maddux had the 100-mile-an-hour mind," says his agent, Scott Boras, who first saw Maddux in high school. "He had insights to the game that people with raw physical talents weren't even close to."

Pitching for the Braves in 1995, Maddux began the World Series by beating Hershiser and the Indians with surgical mastery: a complete game two-hitter on 95 pitches, with no walks or earned runs. He was at his best, soon to win his fourth consecutive Cy Young Award and, for the second season in a row, scoring at least 260 in ERA+, a metric that measures ERA against league average, adjusting for ballpark factors. Only one pitcher—Bob Gibson in 1968—had come close to that figure in the last 80 years. Close, but not better.

While some aces overpowered hitters with muscle (Roger Clemens, Randy Johnson), Maddux simply gripped his best pitch the usual way, along the narrow seams, "nothing different than a kid in Little League," he says. He was a virtuoso at calling his own game, knowing precisely how to read hitters' swings; on the bench, he would predict exactly where a batter would hit a ball. He set up hitters to get themselves out, and the sinker was his kill shot, best fired with two strikes.

"I usually threw it after a cutter," he says. "I had a cutter that I would start for a strike and end up as a ball, and I had a fastball that started in as a ball and ended up as a strike. I very rarely ever threw that two-seam fastball inside unless I threw a cutter or two before it. A hitter remembers the last pitch probably better than any pitch he's seen out of my hand."

Maddux started throwing the cutter in earnest in 1992. He was off to a very good start in his career, with the first four of his record 16 consecutive 15-win seasons, but he needed a complementary pitch to make his sinker more effective. He tried the cutter against the first batter he faced that year, the Phillies' Lenny Dykstra. It came in on Dykstra but did not dart back over the plate, as usual. Instead, it kept slicing.

"He checked his swing and it hit him on the wrist—and it broke his wrist," Maddux says. "Lenny said to me, 'Hey, when did you start throwing a cutter? I thought it was gonna move back over the plate!' That was when I recognized: 'OK, yeah, this is gonna work.'"

Maddux won that game, on his way to 20 victories in his first Cy Young season. He moved to the Braves in free agency and returned to the Cubs in 2004, when he earned his 300th victory. He remembers the precise moment, with the Dodgers at age 42, when he knew it was time to go.

"I threw this ball, it was absolutely perfect," Maddux says. "It came out of my hand just the way it's supposed to, down and away, painted the corner, and I took a peek up there at the radar gun and it said '82.' And I went, 'Whoa.' It was a strike. I mean, it was a meaningless 1–0 fastball. It wasn't like strike three. It was just, everything was absolutely perfect and I just—I lost too much speed.

"Do you have to throw hard to win? No. Do you need to throw hard enough to compete? Absolutely. And I think I just lost too much speed to be able to go out there and compete."

Maddux has never called velocity meaningless. It ranks fourth on Ralph Medar's list, but it is still on there. Maddux personified efficiency: six times, he threw a nine-inning shutout in fewer than 90 pitches, doubling the total of any other pitcher in the last 30 years. But he does rank tenth in career strikeouts, with 3,371, and he never wanted hitters to connect.

If they did, at least, Maddux's best pitch was the balm. It took the sting out of contact. On the day he was introduced as a Hall of Famer, in January 2014, Maddux summarized the essence of his success: "Have a good moving fastball that does something the last 10 feet, and be able to locate. That's what gave me an opportunity to win."

Maddux won more times than anyone alive, through precision, intuition, and unrelenting confidence in a pitch that exemplifies restraint. If a pitcher trusts brains over brawn, trusts his defense, and trusts the long game—even today—he will understand this succinct summary of the virtues of a sinking fastball.

"You throw strikes," Maddux says, "and they stay in front of the outfielders when they hit it."

———

At least, they used to. Pitchers from Maddux's generation—like Derek Lowe, the former Boston standout—have noticed the decline of their best pitch. They still praise its virtues but acknowledge that hitters have adjusted.

"The strike zone's changed, and the swing path of hitters has changed," Lowe says. "A lot of these hitters are taught to swing down-to-up, so [the sinker] goes right into the current swing path. The game today is velocity, so a lot of people say, 'If I could throw 95 with a four-seamer or 92 with a two-seamer, I'm gonna throw 95.' It is a dying art."

In 2017, major league pitchers threw almost 23,000 fewer two-seamers and sinkers than they had in 2011. Of the 10 playoff teams in 2017, only one ranked in the top third in percentage of two-seamers and sinkers: the Twins, who lost the AL Wild Card Game. Most teams, like the champion Astros (twenty-first), ranked in the bottom third of such pitches.

Charlie Morton collected the final out of that season on a grounder to second by the Dodgers' Corey Seager. That was fitting for Morton, a 33-year-old veteran whose sinkers had earned him the nickname Ground Chuck, but it was also misleading. Morton—the first pitcher ever to win two Game 7s in the same postseason—had a career year by throwing harder than ever before, elevating his fastball and using more curves. He had grown tired of relying on batted balls to succeed.

"I was a sinker guy, throwing 60, 70 percent sinkers, and they were hitting my sinker," Morton explained during the ALCS. "So the game plan has changed. The idea that I'm going to make these guys put the ball in play and try to induce soft contact, that's out the window. . . .

"Lefties, I'm not trying to do that. I'm not trying to let them hit the ball. At least, I'm not trying to encourage them to hit the ball. Before, the assumption [was that if] you have a good sinker, you can get the ball on the ground. That wasn't the case.

"Lots of four-seams, curveballs, and cutters."

Morton was only reacting to the adjustments many hitters made in the middle of the decade, when teams started aggressively shifting infielders to gobble up grounders, and the balls themselves suddenly turned livelier. Major League Baseball denied any changes to the ball, but the fundamental calculus of hitting had evolved. Batters finally seemed to understand the folly of hitting down on the ball, their popular philosophy echoing Dave Duncan: *there's no slug on the ground.*

"You see hitters trying to do damage more on certain pitches that, in the past, it was accepted they weren't gonna try to do damage on— like the sinker," the veteran Brandon McCarthy says. "More guys are capable of hitting that and elevating it. Not everyone's successful at it, but it's a different approach than we saw years ago. Historically, there were guys that were pure roll-over candidates down there. They were easy outs. Now they can elevate that ball, get under it, and drive it."

More than ever, it seems, teams want fastballs with a high spin rate, the kind that stay true through the zone, rather than sinkers. With coaches emphasizing a swing's launch angle and downplaying the risk of strikeouts, sinkers, as Lowe says, fall right into the barrel of the bat. Al Kaline says modern hitters know where to look for the ball, because the shoulders-to-knees strike zone of his day is long gone.

"Pitchers can't hit the corners all the time, and that's why there's so many home runs, because the hitters have a very small strike zone to look at right now," says Kaline, a 3,000-hit man for the Tigers. "That's why you see everybody uppercutting the ball, because they know everything's gonna be down low."

Hitters set a record with 6,105 home runs in 2017, and they continued their assault in the World Series with a record 25 in seven games. Yet pitchers who had made a living with sinkers still believed in the pitch. Can't today's hitter just dig it out of the dirt and golf it into the stands?

"No, not a good one," says Tommy John, who would still rather throw a sinking fastball at 86 mph than a straight one at 93. "I mean, I couldn't pitch to these guys today, because I'm 75 years old. But I would take my chances with 'em. They don't see pitchers like that anymore."

––––––––––

Most pitchers want the other fastball, at least at first. Curt Schilling stumbled through three organizations until 1992, when the Phillies' pitching coach, Johnny Podres, asked to see his fastball. Schilling used a two-seam grip, the only one he had ever known. Podres suggested a four-seamer, and Schilling, who craved power and precision, found the pitch he'd been missing.

Yet he also knew, from studying a rival, that velocity was not everything. A darting, well-placed sinker led a superior pitcher's portfolio.

"Early in my career I tried to figure out why Greg Maddux was so much better than me," says Schilling, who threw much harder. "He was good because he changed speeds, number one, and he made the ball move in both directions on both sides of the plate. You could not sit on a spot; you could not sit on a pitch. I knew I wasn't gonna throw a two-seamer at that point, so my game plan became: *find the hitter's hole and throw the ball there.* To do that, I needed to throw the four-seamer, because I needed to know where the ball was gonna be when it crossed the plate."

Schilling envied the Maddux two-seamer, but once he found the four-seam fastball, he never threw the old one again. He figured it was wiser to devote his attention to one kind of fastball, not divide it between two. The decision reinforces the image of the two-seamer as the little brother of fastballs, a weaker version of the same thing that still wants in on the action. He can't survive on brute strength, so he has to be cunning. He might have a chance to play, but given a choice, you wouldn't pick him first.

No coach would change a pitcher who can make the ball sink violently, down and away from the opposite-hand hitter, like a bowling ball spinning toward the gutter. But the general rule, now more than ever, is that pitchers sink the ball because they have to.

If you've got a big fastball, you'd better use it.

THE
CHANGEUP

A Dollar Bill Hooked on a Fishing Line

The changeup is an artistic pitch," Bobby Ojeda says, and not all pitchers are artists. Anyone would envy its results, those feeble, flailing hacks off the front foot from a hitter fooled by a pitcher's arm speed. But every changeup is the product of hard-won patience, and the maturity to accept a counterintuitive mind-set. The hitter brings a bat to the cage match. The pitcher brings a feather duster.

Ojeda pitched 15 seasons in the majors after learning the changeup from Johnny Podres, who used it to bring the Brooklyn Dodgers their only championship, in 1955. It was Ojeda's lone off-speed option, because the curveball shredded his elbow. For pitchers with other choices, the delicate brushstrokes of the changeup can be maddening to master.

"Most guys, if they're trying to learn something and it's not instant success, they just stick it in their back pocket," says Jamie Moyer, the everlasting lefty who learned his changeup at Saint Joseph's University from Kevin Quirk, an alum who was pitching in the minors. "I don't know how many times I threw the changeup over the guy I was playing catch with, either over his head or five feet in front of him, because the grip was so awkward for me. But you spend enough time with it, it becomes part of you. I play catch with my son in the driveway now, and I go right to it. It's not quite the same pitch, but that feel comes back."

Between innings, while warming up, pitchers signal for the changeup by opening their glove hand as if gripping a grapefruit. They might then pull the glove back an inch or two, as if pulling the string on a toy.

Think of a dollar bill hooked on a fishing line, resting on the ground. The pitcher is the guy who yanks it back, just out of reach of the sucker who thought he'd found easy money. That is the changeup.

Throwing it takes not just guile and artistry but courage. Consider your trusty, hardworking index finger. Now try throwing a baseball without using it very much. If that finger could talk, it would question your sanity: *You sure you don't need me for this?* The pitcher must block out that noise.

"I stood on the mound in instructional league and Johnny helped me with the grip," says Frank Viola, another 15-year lefty who learned from Podres. "We played around with it and he said, 'Throw it.' I kid you not: I don't think I got it halfway to home plate. It just went straight into the ground. And I'm like, 'You gotta be kidding me, Johnny, there's no way!' He just said, 'Trust me, it's gonna come together.'"

After several years of practice, it did come together for Viola, just as it has for so many others with the right combination of genetics, gumption, and guts. Cole Hamels, a star lefty for the Phillies and the Rangers, thinks of turning off his most important muscles to do it.

"It's like you dead-arm it," Hamels says. "That's what I try to tell people: fastballs are strong, changeups are dead. So if you can grasp that concept of how to control and deaden something in your body, then you're able to get the basic idea."

Arm speed sells the pitch. The hitter sees fastball from the motion of the arm and the spin of the ball, which sputters as it crosses the plate, fading away from a right-handed hitter when thrown by a lefty, and vice versa. It is typically 10 miles an hour slower than the same pitcher's fastball, a cousin of the screwball, splitter, and sinker that has grown in acceptance as pitchers use it more.

Throwing slowly to disrupt hitters is nothing new. Long before Bugs Bunny did it in a famous 1946 cartoon—the term "Bugs Bunny changeup" still evokes a helpless slugger swatting at air—Connie Mack made it the secret weapon for his Philadelphia A's.

Down the stretch in 1929, with the A's sure of winning the pennant, Mack called an aging pitcher, Howard Ehmke, into his office at Shibe Park. He sat Ehmke down and told him they would have to part. The crestfallen Ehmke, who was 35 and in his fourteenth major league season, replied that he had always wanted to pitch in the World Series.

"Mr. Mack," he declared, "there is one great game left in this old arm."

Mack was delighted to hear it, and shared his plan. What he meant, he told Ehmke, was that he wanted him to stay behind on the next A's road trip, to study the Chicago Cubs as they played the Phillies. The A's would be meeting the Cubs in the World Series, and Mack wanted Ehmke—not the great Lefty Grove—to start the opener.

As Red Smith related in a tribute to Ehmke, Cubs manager Joe McCarthy had a premonition of what Mack might do. As McCarthy told another writer, Ring Lardner, "We can hit speed. But they've got one guy over there I'm afraid of. He's what I call a junk pitcher."

It was Ehmke, and his array of slow-moving pitches baffled the powerful Cubs and their three future Hall of Fame hitters—Rogers Hornsby, Hack Wilson, and Kiki Cuyler. Ehmke set a then–World Series record with 13 strikeouts in a complete game, 3–1 victory. It was the last game Ehmke ever won, and the A's prevailed in five.

The changeup goes against a hitter's macho instinct. The fact that it is marketed as a fastball, but in fact is something else, was once seen, by some, as a sign of weakness by a pitcher afraid of a challenge. This is absurd, because it takes a special kind of nerve to throw slowly on purpose. But not too long ago, a pitcher who beat a hitter with a changeup could expect an insult in return.

On August 1, 1978, the Reds' Pete Rose came to the plate with two out in the top of the ninth inning at Atlanta–Fulton County Stadium. Rose had hit in 44 consecutive games, the longest streak since Joe DiMaggio's record of 56 in 1941. He was hitless in the game, a blowout loss to the Braves, and was facing Gene Garber, a sidearming closer with a peculiar habit of turning his body completely to the center fielder while delivering a pitch. This was not the quirk that bothered Rose, though. What bothered him is that, with two strikes, Garber threw him a changeup. Rose whiffed to end the streak.

"A 16–4 game and Garber's pitching me like it was the seventh game of the World Series," Rose fumed to reporters later. "In that situation, most guys try to throw hard, or get you with sliders. They won't try to jerk you around."

For Garber, it was clear what he would throw with the crowd on its feet and history in the balance. The changeup was his best pitch, as it would become for more and more pitchers in the coming years. As Mario Soto, a star for the Reds in the early 1980s, would say in 2015: "That is *the* pitch right now in baseball. Any pitcher in the major leagues right now that doesn't have a good changeup, he's gonna get in trouble."

Even the hard throwers envy it. Sometimes, the fruitless pursuit of a changeup becomes a joke; every spring training, the Yankees' Mariano Rivera would report that he was trying to learn a changeup, to laughs from the beat writers. The hot-tempered Kevin Brown even tried to pick it up from Moyer and Doug Jones, his cerebral changeup-throwing Orioles teammates, in 1995.

"We went to Boston for a four-game series and Kevin said, 'Show me how to throw a changeup, I think I could throw a good one,'" Jones says. "I told him, 'You'll need a year and a half to really be consistent, but I'll show you some really simple ways to throw it and we'll see what it looks like.' And for four days we'd play catch every day, and he would throw a good one and then two bad ones, and a good one and three bad ones, then a good one. And after four days, he said, 'I can't throw the changeup, I quit.' I said, 'Well, OK.' He really didn't want a changeup. But that's how we learn things."

Jones learned his changeup, or at least observed its grip for the first time, from a future fictional closer. Willie Mueller pitched briefly for the Brewers in 1978 and 1981 but is best known for a role in *Major League* as Duke Simpson, the menacing Yankees reliever. Bob Uecker, playing broadcaster Harry Doyle, noted that Duke was so mean, he threw at his own kid in a father-son game.

Like Mueller, Jones pitched for Milwaukee only briefly—four games in April 1982, just long enough to say that he had reached the majors, and to know he didn't belong. The Brewers let him go two years later, after a rough season spent mostly at Double-A. Jones was 27 and satisfied that he had at least worn a big league uniform. It was more than he could have expected in high school, when he threw so softly that his father—a sprint-car driver, no less—told him speed was overrated: "Remember, the harder you throw the ball, the less time you have to duck."

Jones never threw hard. He had carved out a professional career with a well-located sinker, but could not master the changeup. Mueller threw it to him one day while playing catch in the outfield, and Jones asked to see the grip. It was the first time he had seen a three-finger changeup, with the middle and ring fingers on top. It planted a seed.

In 1985 Jones found work with the Indians, driving a beat-up Camaro from Southern California to spring training in Tucson. He broke down in Blythe, talked his way into a parts store that had closed, bought a carburetor, and chugged in at two in the morning. Jones turned the car over to a friend of a friend who sold things on consignment. The extra cash helped.

He made a team: Double-A again, in Waterbury, Connecticut. One night in New Britain, Jones was told to pitch the last three innings of a game. He wore himself out firing fastballs—such as they were—in his first inning. How would he get through two more? He thought of the changeup, and it worked. Jones struck out five of the next six batters. He was on his way, even if the Indians didn't notice for a while.

A few weeks later, manager Jack Aker—an old fireman for the Kansas City A's—met with Jones in the bullpen. His bosses had told him to ask Jones if he wanted to coach the next season.

"I about fell off the bench," Jones says. "I didn't know whether to be flattered or insulted. I said, 'I think I've figured out something, and I'd like to run with it right now. But thanks for asking.'"

His persistence paid off. Jones returned to the majors in September 1986—more than four years after his previous game—and found so many ways to manipulate his changeup that he really had three variations, including one that would start at the hip of a left-handed hitter, then loop softly over the inside corner for a strike.

His deception helped him earn a spot on five All-Star teams, if not much respect. In 1988 Jones became the first pitcher ever to earn a save in 15 consecutive appearances. Topps commemorated the feat with a "Record Breaker" card that featured Chris Codiroli—a different Indians righty with a walrus mustache—on the front. In 2006, Jones received only two votes for the Hall of Fame and was dropped from the ballot. The same year, Bruce Sutter received 400 votes to gain induction. Their final career save totals: Jones 303, Sutter 300.

Jones is hardly the only changeup artist to be underestimated. Jamie Moyer, too, was urged to become a coach while pitching in the minors. He declined the offer and, at 49 years old in 2012, became the oldest pitcher in major league history to record a win. Moyer finished with 269 victories, one more than Jim Palmer. But like Jones, Moyer, too, slipped off the Hall of Fame ballot after just one year.

———

In the courtyard outside the Hall of Fame Library are statues 60 feet, 6 inches apart: Johnny Podres and Roy Campanella, the hallowed Brooklyn battery of 1955. Podres beat the Yankees twice in that World Series, on his twenty-third birthday in Game 3 and again in Game 7, with a 2–0 shutout in the Bronx.

The statues, linked by a stone pathway in the grass and sculpted by Stanley Bleifeld, symbolize the unity of pitcher and catcher. Yet before the cathartic final pitch of 1955, Podres and Campanella disagreed.

"Campy had called for a fast ball, but I'd shaken him off," Podres wrote that winter, in a piece for *The Saturday Evening Post.* "It was the only time I did that the entire Series."

Podres would spend decades as a coach proving the wisdom of his uncanny instincts. He chose wisely for the winning pitch—a changeup, dutifully beaten into the ground by Elston Howard. Pee Wee Reese scooped it at shortstop, fired to Gil Hodges at first base, and the Bums at last were kings. As the World Series MVP, Podres got a Corvette.

Four days later, he was back home in upstate Mineville, New York. It was there that his high school principal had once persuaded a friend who scouted for the Dodgers to come see the town's young phenom. Podres responded by throwing a no-hitter against Ticonderoga, enticing the Dodgers to offer him $6,000—more than his father's annual salary working in the mines. After the World Series, a hometown parade brought more gifts: a new shanty for ice fishing, and a 24-inch television set for Podres's mother. She put it in the room where Johnny was born.

Podres would help pitch the Dodgers to more championships in Los Angeles, and he worked for the organization when they won another in 1988. Owner Peter O'Malley was so elated then that he treated the organization to a vacation in Rome for a week. Podres quickly grew restless.

"We were going to Pompeii, my wife and I on the bus with Pods, and he said, 'Hey, Guy, let's go to the race track,'" says Guy Conti, another pitching coach in the Dodgers' system. "I said, 'Pods, my wife would kill me if I got off this bus and decided, in Pompeii, to go to the race track!' But that was him. He was just a down-to-earth man. He wasn't no big shot, he was just Johnny Podres."

Podres retired from playing after the 1969 season—when he pitched, naturally, for the Padres—but he could throw the changeup for decades, demonstrating it for his pupils with the Padres, Dodgers, Red Sox, Twins, and Phillies. Conti marveled at the way Podres could whip his left arm, as if throwing a fastball, and then spit out a pitch that seemed to suspend itself in midair. Logically, you knew it was impossible, but Podres's pitching could defy reason.

"He was convinced his changeup rose, and you didn't doubt him," Bobby Ojeda says. "It's against the laws of physics that any ball rises; they don't rise, it's impossible. But he was convinced he rotated the shit out of that changeup so much that it rose."

Ojeda did not know Podres's background when he first started working with him as a Red Sox farmhand in Elmira, New York, in 1978. But he could tell that this was a true baseball guy: a big gut, a cigarette, and a no-nonsense presence, gruff but encouraging, that commanded respect and awe. He's probably done a lot in this game, Ojeda thought, because he really knows his stuff.

Twenty years later, not much had changed. Ryan Madson was 17 years old, assigned to Martinsville, Virginia, for rookie ball with the Phillies. Madson already threw a changeup, taught to him by Fletch Jernigan, a coach he had met at age nine who learned the grip from a story he read in the *Orange County Register*. Madson would throw the pitch and Podres would make a big show, taking off his cap, stopping the bullpen session. "Did you see that!" he would say, as Madson beamed. He knew then that he had a real weapon—and Podres, most likely, had discovered something besides a major league changeup.

"He had a knack to be able to tell real early in a young pitcher's career, in the minor leagues, whether he'd be able to pitch in the big leagues or not," says Dave Wallace, who coached with Podres in the Dodgers' system. "He recognized character, makeup, competitiveness, balls—whatever you want to call it, he just knew."

Wallace turns his voice to a smoker's growl, imitating Podres:

"He would say to me: 'That guy's gonna pitch in the big leagues!'—or he would say, 'Wait till the lights come on and he's gonna melt!'" Wallace shook his head. "It might take a couple of weeks or a month, but he had an innate ability to recognize if you had 'it' or not. It was unbelievable."

If Podres believed in you, he would not give up. He understood that every pitcher—even those of identical height and weight—has a different physiology. But if a pitcher had "it," Podres would persist until he brought it out.

In time, the Podres changeup would have a profound impact on cities starved for championships, just as it had on Brooklyn in 1955. Viola would use it in 1987 to bring the Minnesota Twins their first World Series crown. Pedro Martinez—who learned it from Conti, who learned it from Podres—would use it to help the Boston Red Sox win the 2004 World Series, their first title in 86 years.

In 2005, a half century after his own precious moment, Podres shared his memories with Jim Salisbury of *The Philadelphia Inquirer*. His best pitch in Game 7 was the fastball, he said, "hard stuff all day" in the Bronx shadows until that final changeup to Howard. He was glad the ground ball went to Reese, the veteran captain, who had played for the Dodgers since Podres was in grade school.

"I know it meant a lot to a lot of people," said Podres, who would die in 2008, at age 75. "Sometimes when I'm home doing nothing, I put the video in. I get the feeling that I'm young again. What a time that was."

———

Stu Miller never closed out a World Series. In popular lore, he is best known for a balk in a 1961 All-Star Game at windswept Candlestick Park. Miller was not really blown off the mound—he swayed a bit—but the incident came to symbolize the notorious conditions then for baseball in San Francisco.

Jim Palmer, the Hall of Famer for the Orioles, has a more fitting memory of Miller from 1965. The Orioles called Miller "Bullet," mocking his low- to mid-80s fastball. But the pitch looked a lot harder because Miller paired it with his generation's best changeup.

"I'm 19, I'm in the bullpen, and we're at Dodger Stadium playing the Angels," Palmer says. "I'm standing at home plate, pretending I'm a hitter. He's throwing his changeup and I know it's coming. I'm striding—*and then he throws a fastball*, up and in, and I thought I was gonna have a heart attack. The difference between his fastball and changeup was unbelievable."

Palmer can still see the Yankees' Tom Tresh (2-for-22 against Miller) swinging wildly, and futilely, at Miller's changeups—while Mickey Mantle knelt in the on-deck circle, laughing. Mantle hit his 500th homer off Miller, but otherwise was 2-for-17. Harmon Killebrew, the mighty Twins slugger, was just as bad.

"I can't remember anybody else throwing like that," says the Yankees' Bobby Richardson, who also struggled with Miller. "He'd turn his neck and you'd be out in front of everything. John Blanchard would sit on the bench and say, 'I'm not going up there, he's gonna make me look foolish.'"

Miller bobbed his head as he delivered the pitch, adding an extra dash of hesitation and confusion. It was not on purpose, he would insist, but it helped the effectiveness of a pitch he learned in Class D with the Cardinals at the urging of manager Vedie Himsl.

"He said, 'You have to come up with a change-up. And the key is to make it look like a fastball,'" Miller told Dan Brown of the *San Jose Mercury News*. "That's all he said. And I thought, 'That sounds good.' I went out and threw one and he said, 'Oh, my gosh.' It came that naturally."

Miller pitched 16 seasons, mostly for the Giants and Orioles. He had 153 saves, won a league ERA title, and left an impression of invincibility on a pitcher bound for Cooperstown.

"Of all the guys that I've seen—Mariano, Jeff Reardon, Eckersley—you could load the bases up, and unless Tony Oliva was hitting, I'd take Stu Miller and his changeup over any of them," Palmer says. "Over any reliever I've ever seen. You could not time it. It was just incredible."

(Oliva, a three-time batting champion, hit .538 off Miller. In baseball there is always an exception.)

Miller pitched for the Orioles' first championship team in 1966. Their third World Series title—and last, to date—came in 1983. Catcher Rick Dempsey was the most valuable player and Scott McGregor pitched a shutout in the clincher. Both had come to Baltimore seven years earlier in a trade with the Yankees. It was not the Yankees' only contribution.

As a high school pitcher in El Segundo, California, McGregor learned a changeup from Tom Morgan, a Yankee reliever from the 1950s who scouted in Southern California. McGregor modified the grip to a palmball, a pitch thrown pretty much as it sounds: from deep in the palm, enveloped in fingers. It spun the same as his fastball, but nearly 15 mph slower.

As a Yankees farmhand, though, McGregor threw fastballs, curveballs, and occasional cutters. It got him to Triple-A, but his manager there, the future Hall of Famer Bobby Cox, stressed that he would not reach his potential unless he developed his changeup. McGregor knew how to throw the pitch but could not quite grasp the mind-set.

"The hard thing to do is go to the big leagues and say, 'OK, I'm gonna throw it a little slower,'" McGregor says. "You go, 'Really? I figure I gotta throw it harder.' But they don't care how hard you throw it. You've just got to learn how to get the change of speeds."

For McGregor that meant three distinct speeds—curveball, fastball, changeup—from the same arm motion. His was a fun windup to imitate: he would raise his hands over his head, swing them down over his right knee, and then spread them behind his back, like a bird taking flight, pausing there before whipping his left arm through. Earl Weaver, McGregor's first manager with the Orioles, had implored him to keep his curveball below 70 miles an hour, and the "funky-ass deceptive motion," as McGregor calls it, was the only way to do it.

With it, though, McGregor had his repertoire: a fastball in the 80s, a changeup in the 70s, and a curve in the 60s. Ken Singleton, the Orioles' right fielder, marveled at how all the pitches looked the same from his vantage point, and hitters were also confused. In McGregor's eight-year prime (1978–85), only Ron Guidry won more games in the AL.

McGregor starred in the 1979 postseason, but the Orioles blew a three-games-to-one lead in the World Series and lost to Pittsburgh. Four years later, they held the same lead before Game 5 at a different Pennsylvania ballpark, Veterans Stadium in Philadelphia. McGregor strode through the visiting dugout and told his teammates not to worry: "I got this," he said.

He threw only one curveball—to bait Joe Morgan, who had homered twice off curves in the series—and otherwise mixed changeups and fastballs in a 5–0 triumph. There were 67,064 fans at the Vet for the twilight start, the highest attendance for a World Series game in the last half century, yet few crowds could ever have been so quiet. I was there, and by the end, McGregor had so thoroughly humbled the Phillies that many fans had left. I scrambled to the front row behind first base for the final inning, and watched McGregor's oddly subdued reaction when Cal Ripken Jr. snagged Garry Maddox's soft liner to end it.

"They show the last out and the kids always tease me," says McGregor, now the Orioles' pitching rehab coordinator in Sarasota, Florida. "They go, 'Show us what you did, Mac!' Because I throw it, I put my glove under my arm and give a little fist pump. You're in such a mode where you can't think about it. I kept pushing it out of my brain the whole time. I couldn't think, 'If we win this thing, we're the world champs!'"

McGregor was just 29, but in five years he was finished. Arm speed comes from a sturdy shoulder, and by 1987 his was loose and sore, incapable of producing the speed variance that had made him a star. When he took the mound at the Metrodome on April 27, 1988, the Orioles were 0–19 for the season. As the Twins ravaged McGregor, Ripken came to the mound and asked if he was throwing the changeup.

"They're all the same speed anymore," McGregor told his shortstop. "Just back up a little bit. You might be a little safer."

There was a runner on base with two out in the fourth inning when manager Frank Robinson removed McGregor—just in time. Had the next batter homered off him, McGregor's ERA would have been stuck at 4.00 forever. Instead he finished at 3.99, with a career record 30 games above .500, a World Series ring, and the memory of overpowering hitters his way.

"I tell the guys, 'The changeup is a power pitch,' and they just look at me," McGregor says. "I go, 'You challenge them, balls-out throwing it, and you'd be surprised. You give it that effort and they go to hit it and it's not there? They got no chance.'"

Frank Viola did not face McGregor that final day at the Metrodome, but it was his home park, and he was at the top of his profession. Viola had just won the World Series MVP award for the Twins, beating the Cardinals in the first and seventh games the previous fall. He was on his way to winning the American League Cy Young Award, the first by a left-handed Minnesota changeup maestro, with two more to follow in the 2000s by Johan Santana.

The Twins had drafted Viola in the second round in 1981, just after his famous duel with Ron Darling in an NCAA tournament game at Yale Field. Darling fired 11 no-hit innings for Yale until allowing a bloop single in the twelfth. Viola twirled 11 shutout innings for St. John's to beat him, 1–0.

Viola did not throw a changeup then—"He didn't need it," Darling says—just a moving fastball, a curve, and an occasional slider. But the mix was enough to earn Viola an invitation to spring training in 1982. The Twins were terrible, and Viola had more polish than most of their pitchers. By June he was in the majors—nominally, anyway.

That season Viola had a 5.21 ERA. In 1983 he led the majors in earned runs allowed. He needed a put-away pitch, and before the next season Podres introduced the changeup. After those first few tentative tries, they spent more than a year playing with grips. Viola needed to believe in the pitch before he could find the nerve to use it. But because his results were improving, even without it, there seemed to be no urgency.

Then midway through the 1985 season, the Twins hired Ray Miller, the former Baltimore pitching coach, as their manager. By early September Podres was gone, grumbling that Miller did not like him because Podres knew more about pitching than he did.

Podres knew enough to deliver one vital message to Viola as he left the clubhouse: "Don't you ever give up on that changeup!" Viola did as instructed, and could not believe what he'd been missing. Sometimes he would call home and ask his father, in wonder, "How did I ever get here without this?"

Viola tried to throw his changeup 10 to 15 miles per hour slower than his fastball. He rested his middle and ring fingers on top of the ball and applied pressure with his pinkie, below the left seam. He formed the OK symbol—the "circle" in "circle change"—with his index

"He was just a crusty old dude," Andy Pettitte said of Hoyt Wilhelm, the Hall of Fame knuckleballer who later coached in the Yankees' farm system. "I loved him to death."

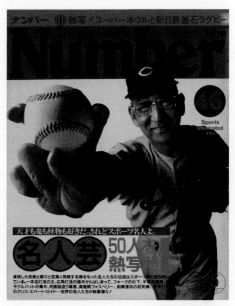

Shigeru Sugishita, known as the God of Forkballs, inspired generations of Japanese pitchers to use the splitter.

Phil Niekro, a 318-game winner, knuckled his way to a staggering 5,404 innings pitched, the most of anyone born after 1887.

For Bruce Sutter, 1979 was a bittersweet year: he won the NL Cy Young Award but lost his mentor, Fred Martin, who taught him the split-finger fastball.

BROWN vs. MATHEWSON
GREATEST TREAT of THE YEAR for BASEBALL FANS

CINCINNATI, OHIO, SEPT. 1, 1916.
"YOU CAN POSITIVELY
COUNT ON MY PITCHING
AGAINST BROWN ON
SEPT. 4th."

CHRISTY
MATHEWSON,
MANAGER
CINCINNATI REDS.

"THREE
FINGERED"
BROWN

BROWN'S
TWIRLING
HAND

CHRISTY
MATHEWSON

CHICAGO, ILL.
"MORDECAI BROWN
WILL BE READY
TO BATTLE
AGAINST
MATHEWSON
LABOR DAY."

JOE TINKER,
MANAGER CUBS.

—1916.—

First Game at 1:30 P.M. | DOUBLE HEADER LABOR DAY | First Game at 1:30 P.M.
STARS OF MANY YEARS TO PITCH FOR CHICAGO CUBS AND CINCINNATI REDS | WEEGHMAN PARK | THE DAILY NEWS BOYS BAND WILL RENDER MUSIC

NORTH CLARK AND ADDISON STREETS.
RESERVED SEATS AT A. G. SPALDING & BROS., 28 S WABASH AVE. TEL. CEN. 448.

Christy Mathewson's fadeaway and Three Finger Brown's curveball were early-century marvels. This was the final career game for both, with Mathewson beating Brown, 10–8.

Warren Spahn, throwing a ceremonial first pitch before the 1999 World Series in Atlanta, earned 363 victories, a record for a lefty, with a screwball that helped him thrive into his forties.

The screwball might have caused Carl Hubbell's notorious inverted pitching arm. It also earned him two MVP awards and a spot in Cooperstown.

The irrepressible Tug McGraw twists his throwing hand inward, just as he would on his screwball, for the cover of his children's book in 1981.

Fernando Valenzuela, whose screwball captivated baseball in 1981, presents Clayton Kershaw with the first of his three Cy Young Awards in April 2012.

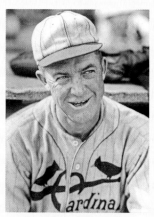

The sidearming Grover Cleveland Alexander won 373 games with a sinker that "bore in like a lump of lead," according to a rival.

Fergie Jenkins—the first pitcher ever to finish with more than 3,000 strikeouts and fewer than 1,000 walks—delivers the ceremonial first pitch before a 2008 playoff game at Wrigley Field.

Kent Tekulve, the yellow submariner, helped the Pirates win their last title in 1979. When he retired 10 years later, he had made more relief appearances than any other pitcher in history.

Among them, Tom Glavine, John Smoltz, and Greg Maddux earned 648 victories and six Cy Young Awards for the Braves.

Pitchers for the 1967 Tigers—including changeup master and future coach Johnny Podres (second from left, hand on hip)—get a spring training lesson from the great Johnny Sain.

Armed with a changeup he learned from Johnny Podres, the Twins' Frank Viola (right, with teammates Kirby Puckett and Juan Berenguer) lit up the Metrodome by winning twice in the 1987 World Series.

"His hands were just ridiculously long," Curt Schilling said of Pedro Martinez, his Red Sox teammate, shown here in the shadows at Angel Stadium in 2003.

Jamie Moyer tosses a changeup for the Rockies in 2012, the year he turned fifty.

Stephen Strasburg, with his dominant index finger on the side of the ball, delivers a changeup for the Nationals in 2012.

The last legal spitballer, Burleigh Grimes, won Game 7 of the 1931 World Series for the Cardinals after his father brought him his favorite slippery elm bark from Wisconsin.

Adjusting his cap—or loading up for a spitter? Gaylord Perry always kept hitters guessing.

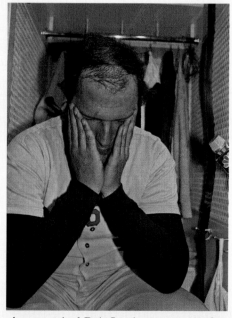

An anguished Bob Stanley, moments after his wild pitch helped doom the Red Sox in Game 6 of the 1986 World Series. He said it wasn't a spitter; the Mets still aren't sure.

	1	2	3	4	5	6	7	8	9	R	H	E
CIN	0	0	0	0	0	0	0	0		0	0	1
PHI	1	3	0	0	0	0	0			4	5	0

"All of a sudden it's over, and it's kind of like, 'Well, now what?,'" said Roy Halladay in 2017, recalling his emotions after his playoff no-hitter. "You want to keep going."

Mariano Rivera, whose cutter made him a legend, earned a record postseason 42 saves—matching his hallowed uniform number.

finger and thumb while hooking the right seam. To take still more speed off the pitch, he would tuck it further back in his palm. To Viola, the changeup allowed him to dominate, even if hitters felt differently.

"You wouldn't believe the feedback you'd get from hitters during a game," he says. "You might strike a guy out on a changeup and they're yelling at you from the dugout: 'Throw it like a man!'"

Viola could laugh off the taunting by pointing to his record. In his first seven seasons throwing the changeup, only one pitcher in the majors, Roger Clemens, won more games.

The changeup was so good that Viola could give it away and still win. When the Twins traded Viola to the Mets in 1989—several years before interleague play—Toronto pitcher Todd Stottlemyre gave some friendly advice to his father, Mel, the Mets' pitching coach. The Blue Jays' hitters, Todd reported, had noticed that Viola would lift his right index finger off his glove when he dug inside to grip his changeup. Yet even with this intelligence, the Blue Jays had lost twice to Viola that season.

Viola would make two All-Star teams for the Mets and retire in 1996. Fifteen years later, he embarked on a second career as a coach in their organization, building off lessons from Podres. One of his prospects at Triple-A in 2014 was Noah Syndergaard, a hulking right-hander with a monster fastball but little trust in his secondary pitches.

Viola told Syndergaard about a game he pitched for the Twins. Podres instructed the catcher not to move all day. Throw whatever he calls, Podres told Viola, and watch what happens. Viola listened, succeeded deep into the game, and came off the mound to see Podres smiling.

"Son, what'd you learn?" Podres asked him.

"I guess my stuff's pretty good."

"You've got to learn to trust it," Podres replied.

Syndergaard absorbed the lessons and made it through his first full season at the highest minor league level. The next spring he was in the majors, and Viola spoke with pride about his progress.

"Look at him now," he said. "It's nothing different. It's just confidence in knowing that he cannot be afraid to throw a 2–1 changeup if the catcher's calling it. If the catcher's got enough confidence in Noah to put it down, Noah's gotta say, 'Hey, if he's got confidence, I've gotta have confidence, too.' And that's what makes you the pitcher you're going to become."

Syndergaard would use more and more changeups as the season went on. His final victory of a standout rookie year came in the World Series.

————

Before he was known mostly as the older brother of a Hall of Famer, Ramon Martinez was a star for the Dodgers. He signed with them in 1984, at age 16, and soon developed a changeup. His long fingers made the pitch feel natural, and Martinez went on to win 135 games and toss 20 shutouts—three more than Pedro.

Martinez learned his changeup from Johnny Podres, recognizing it instantly. It was the primary weapon of his hero in the Dominican Republic.

"Mario Soto, he was my idol growing up, the guy that I watched, but I never got in touch with him," Ramon Martinez says. "It wasn't like I could see him and ask him, 'How do you throw the changeup?' Now it's easier; we can go and talk to the kids and teach them how to throw the changeup or breaking pitch. But at that time, to meet Mario Soto, it would be tougher."

Juan Marichal was the first Hall of Famer from the Dominican Republic. He was Soto's idol and the most prominent Dominican pitcher until Pedro Martinez. In between were World Series stars like Joaquin Andujar and Jose Rijo. Soto never got there, joining the Reds just after their titles in the 1970s. But his changeup endures.

"The best changeup I've ever seen in baseball, *the best*—and he threw 95, too—was Mario Soto," says Mike Brito, the famed scout in the white Panama hat who operated the radar gun behind home plate at Dodger Stadium for decades. "When he was on top of his pitches, nobody could hit him."

Soto was 23 years old and pitching irregularly out of the Reds' bullpen in 1979. That September, he was called into a one-run game in the fifth inning with the Braves' Dale Murphy at the plate.

"It was a 3–2 count and Johnny Bench keeps calling fastball, fastball, fastball, and then slider," Soto says. "I said, 'No,' and he got mad at me.

He said, 'What do you want to do?' I said, 'I want to throw a changeup.' He said, 'Changeup, you're crazy!' But I threw that then, and that ball just dropped straight down. It dropped so much and I struck him out. From there on I say: 'No more sliders.'"

Soto had learned the changeup from Scott Breeden, a Reds minor league coach. At his best, he could sink it to the right, cut it to the left, or make it drop. He honed the pitch meticulously at spring training in Tampa, reporting to the Reds' complex around 6 a.m. and dropping changeups into a target he had drawn on the back of the concrete center field wall.

Tom Seaver, the ace of the staff, noticed Soto's diligence and became his teacher. Seaver threw his changeup along the seams, somewhat like his sinker, while Soto threw his across the seams and applied pressure with his knuckles. Soto kept his own grip but embraced the finer points Seaver imparted.

"Do you try to throw strikes with every pitch?" Seaver once asked.

"Yeah," Soto said, to Seaver's dismay. "Why not?"

"Because you have pretty good control. You want to take advantage of that."

No one had ever explained to Soto the value in pairing stuff with command. Before that, he said, he had simply tried to throw a strike with every pitch; that is the definition of control. Yet simply finding the zone, he learned, was not the point. Putting your pitches where you wanted them to go—in *or* out of the strike zone, tricking hitters into swinging at stuff they could not handle—was the definition of command. That was an art.

———

That same realization hit Pedro Martinez at his first All-Star Game, with the Expos in 1996. On the bench in the right field bullpen in Philadelphia, he marveled at the warm-up of Tom Glavine, the Atlanta left-hander squarely in his prime as a master of the off-speed pitch. From close range, Martinez noticed Glavine directing his changeups and curves to precise locations, in and away. Martinez threw those same pitches, but never like that. The license to locate, as shown by a peer, was a revelation.

"To me, that was so important, because I normally would rely on the difference in speeds between the fastball and the changeup," Martinez says. "I was never worried about spotting the changeup or spotting the breaking ball. A lot of people tell me, 'Oh Pedro, you were so gifted.' I say, 'No, I was just a patch of a lot of players. I wasn't born with all this.'"

The next season, Martinez began one of the most remarkable stretches a pitcher has ever had. In a time of extreme slugging, Martinez led the majors in earned run average five times in seven years. His ERA from 1997 to 2003 was 2.20. The major league ERA for those seasons was 4.48. In simple terms, Martinez was twice as good as the average major league pitcher.

Curt Schilling was his teammate on the curse-breaking 2004 Red Sox, the second time Schilling rode shotgun to a World Series title with a winner of multiple Cy Youngs. In Arizona, he had seen Randy Johnson dominate with brute force: hard fastballs, hard sliders, endless ferocity. Martinez, Schilling said, was all feel. He was an intimidator, for sure, but succeeded by adjusting to what he saw and outwitting the hitter.

Extraordinary vision sharpened those powers of observation, and Martinez's body—deemed by the Dodgers to be too small for a starter—helped him execute his plans. Being shorter than Ramon gave him better balance, and while he was not quite double-jointed ("Almost," he says), Martinez could bend his fingers over the back of his hand for maximum flexibility.

"His hands were just ridiculously long," Schilling says. "That's one of the reasons why he had such a good changeup. Bigger fingers allow you more control over the baseball. It's the same as basketball, right? If you have big hands in basketball it's an enormous advantage. Now think about a ball one-tenth that size, how much more of an advantage you have with bigger hands. I think, to some guys, throwing a baseball is like throwing a golf ball, or a tennis ball.

"That's one of the things I implore people when they're drafting pitchers: look at their hands. Because a guy with small hands is what he is, and maybe he might have velocity, but his stuff is not gonna change that much. Whereas a guy with big hands, you could teach him anything you want."

You could, but it still might take a while to find something that works. Ramon Martinez's fingers were even longer than Pedro's, and he threw his changeup with his index, middle, and ring fingers on top of the ball. Pedro tried the same grip after signing with the Dodgers, with mediocre results.

He was 18 years old at extended spring training in 1990 when Guy Conti taught him the circle change he had learned from Podres. With his index finger hugging the left side of the ball and the fingertip tucked beside his thumb, Martinez wrapped his third and fourth fingers across the four seams. The pitch felt unnatural at first, but within two weeks it was behaving as Conti wanted. It would look like a strike to a lefty before slashing down and away, out of the zone. And it would look like a ball to a righty, who would give up on it, only to see the pitch veer back in to clip the outside corner.

Conti was entranced by Martinez from the first time he saw him in the Dominican Republic, in a group of other young and unfamiliar pitchers. Conti knew the Dodgers had signed Ramon Martinez's brother, but saw nobody with Ramon's 6-foot-4 build. He found Pedro, who is five inches shorter, by the sound of his fastball, the way his fingers snapped off the seams as he let it go. He figured the kid must be special.

Soon they formed a lifelong bond. Martinez calls Conti his white daddy. Conti calls Martinez a borderline genius. That intellect showed up in Martinez's understanding of the changeup and the subtleties of using his fingers to locate it.

"By taking that index finger off the ball, you take 50 percent of your velocity off," Conti explains. "Now, throw as hard as you can. You're only gonna throw it with 50 percent of your velocity. That middle finger is gonna be the only thing that really propels the ball.

"So what we did—which he could do, because his fingers were long like Ramon's—was we moved the ball even further. He was throwing that changeup *with the inside* of the middle finger and the fourth finger. Most pitchers couldn't get such a grip on it, but he could do that, and he could jerk that ball in there. It was really a funky grip, but he got it."

Pedro Martinez—like virtually every pitcher—emphasizes that a well-located fastball is the most important pitch in baseball. His changeup was used to accentuate the fastball, and it was only good because his fastball was good. Yet even after his sterling 1999 regular season, when he was 23–4 with a 2.07 ERA and 313 strikeouts, Martinez evolved.

He had strained a lat muscle against Cleveland in the first game of the playoffs that October. When the decisive fifth game began in a blizzard of offense at Jacobs Field—it was 8–8 in the middle of the fourth—Martinez arrived from the bullpen to spin six no-hit innings. His performance gave the Red Sox their first postseason series victory since 1986, and he did it without throwing a fastball. The Indians feared it, but it never came. Martinez unplugged a thunderous lineup with finesse.

"That's where I used everything I learned from Maddux, from Glavine, from my brother, from Roger Clemens, from Nolan Ryan, all the people I used to see pitch, that's when I came out to display everything," Martinez says. "Because up to that point, I was a power pitcher. I was someone that would rely on 80 percent fastballs and blow it by you. And that day I didn't have it, so I had to run to different sources. I had to run to the changeup, I had to run to the little cutter, I had to run to the curveball, I had to rely on location, and that's when everything came together. For me, pitching at 87 and pitching at 97 was pretty much the same, except that I knew how to do it on either side—power or just, you know, outsmarting you."

The 2000 season would be even better: a third Cy Young Award, a 1.74 ERA, and a WHIP (walks plus hits per inning pitched) of 0.737, the best in baseball history for a pitcher who qualified for the ERA title. It also included the game of which Martinez is most proud.

It was August 24, 2000, late in a stretch of 20 games in a row for the Red Sox without a break, in the heat of a pennant race with the Yankees. Boston's bullpen was exhausted and the team was beginning a road trip in Kansas City against the lowly Royals. For the only time he could remember, Martinez says, he was asked before a game to pitch at least eight innings.

Then he gave up five runs in the first.

Single, single, pop out. Single, single, double. Strikeout, double, ground out. The next inning, he gave up a homer. There was no way to explain it, Martinez says, and no advance warning of such a beating. But he persevered because his team needed him and he somehow got the game to the ninth, helping the Red Sox win. "That was as satisfying to me as probably winning a game in the World Series," Martinez says.

He would do that, finally, four years later in St. Louis. Martinez fired seven shutout innings in Game 3, bringing his team to the precipice of the title. He never pitched again for the Red Sox, but wears their cap in bronze on his plaque in Cooperstown.

Two plaques in the Hall credit pitchers specifically for their success with the "change of pace"—Tim Keefe, a 342-game winner in the 1800s, and Joe Williams, a Negro Leagues star from 1910 to 1932. But Martinez's was the first to include "change-up" in the text, and likely not the last. Someday, perhaps, there will be those inspired by Martinez, like Felix Hernandez, who had been in the majors four seasons before deciding to teach himself a changeup. Hernandez was already a star, but said Martinez and Freddy Garcia had shown what an effective weapon the pitch could be.

"I tried to throw it because I wanted to take it to the next level," Hernandez says. "I wanted to be the best I can be."

Hernandez holds the pitch like a two-seam fastball, with an extra finger (the middle one) on the white part of the ball between the narrow seams. Some hitters consider it a splitter or a sinker, because it dives down—and sometimes in—to a righty and tends to be only three or four miles an hour slower than his fastball.

"He doesn't throw strikes," says Evan Longoria, "but his stuff is so good that he gets guys to swing, just because you *think* it's a strike."

Longoria batted cleanup for the Rays on August 15, 2012, when Hernandez threw a perfect game at Safeco Field, finishing by freezing Sean Rodriguez on a sinking changeup—*at 92!*—for the final out. Hernandez had fallen behind 2–0, and then pulled even with sliders.

"I said, 'All right, now he's definitely coming back heater,'" Rodriguez says. "Nope. Off-speed. Tip your cap."

Martinez threw nine perfect innings once, in 1995, but the game was still scoreless and he gave up a double to lead off the tenth. He never threw an official no-hitter, but his two hitless innings to start the 1999 All-Star Game, in which he struck out five of six hitters at Fenway Park, was a touchstone moment for his fans back home.

"You remember that All-Star Game?" says Kelvin Herrera, the star reliever who was nine that summer. "Filthy!"

Herrera says his country came to a stop when Martinez pitched; it felt like a national holiday every five days. In time Herrera would come to throw changeups under pressure in October, and earn a World Series ring of his own with the Royals. But he understood that Martinez's pitch was a singular sensation.

"If you see Pedro's hand, it's like, so flexible," he says. "Pedro's changeup is unique. You cannot have that one."

––––––––––

The best pure hitter to make his debut after 1939—that is, after Ted Williams—was Tony Gwynn. Across two decades for the Padres, from 1982 to 2001, Gwynn hit .338 and won eight batting titles. He came to bat 323 times against Greg Maddux, Tom Glavine, John Smoltz, and Pedro Martinez, and struck out just three times.

Yet Glavine held Gwynn to a .303 average—outstanding for most hitters, but far below Gwynn's standards. Gwynn thought Glavine's changeup never seemed to reach the plate. When Glavine complimented Gwynn on his plate coverage, Gwynn responded this way:

"You make it tough on me because lefties aren't supposed to throw changeups to lefties, and you do."

Glavine, who won 305 games in his Hall of Fame career, was not alone in that strategy; it also worked well for Jamie Moyer, among others. But it defies convention for a left-hander to throw a slow pitch down and in to a lefty—the danger zone for pitchers, exactly where many left-handed hitters want it. Glavine said he still had not mastered that skill in 1991, when he won his first Cy Young Award.

The caricature of Glavine is that he lived on the outside corner and rode soft stuff to Cooperstown. His athleticism tends to be downplayed. As a high school senior in Billerica, Massachusetts, Glavine was chosen in two drafts: in the second round by the Braves and in the fourth, as a center, by the NHL's Los Angeles Kings. Five rounds later, the Kings took Luc Robitaille, a future Hall of Famer.

Glavine got to pro ball without a changeup. Two years later, in Double-A, he was using a forkball and winning. The Braves had signed a veteran catcher, Ned Yost, to guide their pitching prospects. Yost was unimpressed by Glavine's forkball, which bounced at the plate but fooled anxious, overmatched hitters. Their conversations went like this:

Yost: "Tommy, you gotta get a changeup."

Glavine: "Changeup? My split's awesome."

Yost: "Tommy, your split sucks. You get to Triple-A and the big leagues, those guys are gonna freakin' spit on that thing and it's gonna be worthless for you. You gotta get a changeup."

"Well, he didn't believe me," said Yost, whose plainspoken bluntness would one day help him as a manager. "He went to Triple-A and started getting his ass whupped, and I remember he lost 17 games his first or second year in the big leagues with that split. He started throwing that changeup and it took him to the Hall of Fame."

Glavine's first hint that Yost was right came from Bo Jackson, then a Memphis Chick, who launched a mammoth blast off Glavine's forkball in the summer of 1986. His 7–17 record for the Braves in '88 also signaled his need for a true out pitch—and it rolled right up to him the next spring in West Palm Beach, Florida. In the outfield during batting practice one day, Glavine picked up a ball that slipped in his hand as he went to toss it back. Gripping it with his middle and ring fingers—not his index finger—Glavine's toss faded down and to the left, just the way a lefty's changeup should.

He quickly deduced the happy accident: removing his index finger from the top of the ball was like stepping off the accelerator. With just the third and fourth fingers to guide the pitch, Glavine had a built-in change of speed. He no longer had to slow his arm down to produce it.

"I could throw that pitch as hard as I wanted to, and it just didn't come out the same," Glavine says. "That's the reason it was so deceptive, because my arm speed and everything was exactly the same as it was on my fastball. I didn't have to manipulate anything." By 1991 the pitch had become Glavine's safety valve: on days when his other stuff was lacking, the changeup was always there, giving him a chance to win. Yet he still did not consider himself a complete pitcher. As good as his changeup was, he obeyed the old taboo—and it frustrated him.

"I didn't handle lefties the way I handled righties, in large part because I didn't throw my changeup to lefties," Glavine says. "So I was eliminating my best pitch against left-handed hitters. I finally got fed up with it and said, 'Why can't I throw changeups to lefties? It's my best pitch.'"

Glavine started doing it, and the Braves kept winning. He sold himself on the idea for good in spring training in 1994, his first as a teammate of Fred McGriff, the left-handed slugger acquired the previous summer. Glavine asked McGriff, who had hit him well, what he thought about a lefty throwing changeups to a lefty.

"It seems like a good idea," McGriff said. "I don't know how I could keep it fair."

Glavine tried it in practice against McGriff, who unloaded on the pitch and crushed a long drive—but foul, over the first base seats. Just a loud strike.

"So that's kind of the mind-set that I had: if I can get it in there and throw it right, yeah they might kill it, but I just don't see how they can keep it fair, and it's one more thing for them to think about," Glavine says.

"It was the same with righties. I didn't pitch in all that much, but when I went in, it was always a fastball. Well, heck, if I can throw a changeup in to a right-hander and make him start thinking: *When it comes in here, I don't know if it's hard or soft,* just like they had to do when I was pitching away—man, that would open up a whole other can of worms for me.

"I remember one of the first times I threw it in to a right-hand hitter was Scott Rolen, when he was with the Phillies, and I saw him after the game and he's like, 'Are you kidding me? Now I gotta worry about *that* pitch inside? At least inside it was a matter of guessing, but I only had to guess hard. Now I gotta guess hard *or* soft? And I gotta guess *when* you're going in there?'

"So those are all the kinds of reactions I was looking for, and when I got them it was kind of like: 'OK, I'm onto something.'"

Glavine's continual evolution helped him pitch past his 42nd birthday. He even won another Cy Young Award, in 1998, when he narrowly edged another changeup master bound for Cooperstown.

———————

The 1998 season was Trevor Hoffman's best. He led baseball with 53 saves, part of a career collection of 601. He earned the first of seven All-Star selections and helped the Padres win the pennant. The lyrics to Hoffman's anthem, "Hell's Bells" by AC/DC, forecast doom for all who dared to face him: thunder, hurricane, lightning, death.

With Hoffman, though, the intimidator's ultimate weapon—the blazing fastball—was a memory by then. It left him forever on a beach in Del Mar, California, in August 1994, just after the players' strike began. Tossing a football with friends, Hoffman dove for a pass in the surf and felt a pang in his shoulder. Then, in a beach volleyball game, he dove for a ball in the sand, like an outfielder in full extension for a sinking line drive. Hoffman heard a distinct *pfffft* sound, he says, "like air coming out of a tire." He had torn his rotator cuff.

The mid-90s fastball that had catapulted Hoffman to the majors in 1993—less than three years after converting from shortstop with the Reds in Class A—would never return. The long off-season gave Hoffman time to strengthen his arm so he could pitch in 1995 and delay surgery. It also gave him time to think.

"It expedited the transition every power pitcher has to make—they have to learn how to pitch and develop other pitches," Hoffman says. "I still felt like I was going to throw as hard, I still gave it the same effort level, but the gun didn't read it. It kind of forced me into thinking, 'What are you gonna do now to get people out?'"

Hoffman never started a game in the majors, but he had started just enough in the minors to be forced to experiment with secondary pitches. A Reds scout, Larry Barton, had shown him a grip for a circle change, but the pitch was ordinary, like his curveball and slider, and Hoffman did not trust it. He always feared it would slip from his hand.

With the Padres in 1994, Hoffman's catch partner was Donnie Elliott. They were not too different, a pair of right-handed relievers for a last-place team who had already played for a few organizations. Hoffman asked how Elliott threw his changeup, and learned the basis for a grip that would make him a star.

Elliott, who would pitch only once in the majors after 1994, had invented a grip in which his index finger and thumb pinched a seam on the left side of the ball. For Hoffman, it felt like sliding his body from the wooden arm of a couch to the soft pillows in the middle. The ball was centered better in his hand with Elliott's grip, allowing Hoffman to engage his thumb, index finger, and middle finger—the most reliable steering digits.

Hoffman could spot his diminished fastball with impeccable command, and he deadened his changeup by shoving it deeper in his palm. He began to use this combination in earnest in 1995, throwing a fastball around 90 miles an hour and a changeup, at times, around 72.

"He had so much of his hand on it," says Robin Ventura, who was 0-for-5 with four strikeouts against Hoffman. "He threw it, you'd see it, and then it would disappear for a second—and then it would keep coming."

Hoffman converted 88.8 percent of his career saves, a figure almost identical to Mariano Rivera's 89.1. But postseason success eluded Hoffman, who made it to the playoffs just four times in 18 seasons. He pitched only one game in the World Series and blew the save. All that time as a closer and he never experienced the defining moment of the position: leaping into the catcher's arms to end the baseball season.

Yet Hoffman's attitude about it could serve as a model for dealing with disappointment, and goes a long way to understanding the ethos of an athlete. Everyone wants to win a title, but perhaps more important is earning the chance to compete for it. Hoffman did that in 1998, even without a championship ring as the prize.

"I've kind of gotten over wishing for it," he says. "I had my opportunity. I was in the '98 World Series. We had Game 3 with a chance to close it down, and I didn't. It's not really a wish for another opportunity, having been there. I just didn't seize the moment."

The Padres had lost the first two games in New York against the dynastic Yankees, who had gone 114–48 in the regular season. Back in San Diego, the Padres led by a run in the top of the eighth with a runner on first and no outs. With AC/DC's bells clanging and 64,667 fans roaring and waving towels, Hoffman trotted in from the bullpen. He got one out, then issued a walk.

Scott Brosius came to the plate, having homered in his previous at-bat. He checked his swing on a curve for strike one, then took two changeups in the dirt for balls. Hoffman never threw him another.

After the second changeup, the Padres' pitching coach, Dave Stewart, visited his pitcher on the mound. Brosius pulled a fastball foul down the third base line, then smashed another—89 miles an hour—over the center field fence for a three-run homer. The Padres never recovered. Hoffman had been beaten, but not with his changeup.

"The 2–2 fastball that I threw to Scott Brosius in the World Series— that's probably the optimal time that I should have thrown it, and I didn't," Hoffman says. When nudged, he added why. "You know what? Dave Stewart came out one time the whole year, and it was in that moment. He came out and said, 'We need to be aggressive here.' I threw a pitch that I probably shouldn't have.

"But that's the way it goes. At least it was a strike. If he missed it or swung through it or took it, it was gonna be a strike."

It was, and it went a long way. The single most important changeup of Trevor Hoffman's career is the one he never threw.

———

Stephen Strasburg remembers sitting in the left field seats as a teenager at Petco Park and peeking into the Padres bullpen to watch Hoffman warm up. He recognized the artistry of Hoffman's changeup but could not repeat it quite that way.

"He let it fall off the fingertips and almost, like, paintbrush it down," Strasburg says. "You have to have a tremendous feel of the baseball to be able to do that, and for me, I have to throw everything off of my fastball. I have to throw everything as hard as I can."

Strasburg learned his changeup at San Diego State from the Aztecs' pitching coach, Rusty Filter, but there was no reason to use it much in games. The point would be to keep hitters off his high-90s fastball, but they never proved they could hit that pitch, anyway. Strasburg blitzed through college with 375 strikeouts in 243 innings. He was picked first in the 2009 draft by the Nationals, who promoted him to Washington a year later.

That season, Ivan Rodriguez caught all but one of Strasburg's starts. Rodriguez, who would retire the next season with the record for games caught, thought Strasburg's changeup was even better than his celebrated curveball. Strasburg threw it about 90 miles an hour, which was still sometimes 10 mph slower than his fastball.

Most major leaguers could handle that pitch, on its own, but not when they had to respect a changeup, too. Rodriguez encouraged Strasburg to finally use the pitch he had never needed.

"I trusted whatever he called, absolutely," Strasburg says. "I would throw it down and they'd be so geared up for the fastball, they'd see that and it'd disappear. I'd get a lot of swings and misses that way."

Another San Diego boy needed the changeup simply to have a chance. Cole Hamels—a high school freshman in the fall of 1998—had also watched and admired Hoffman while growing up in San Diego. He recognized the way Hoffman tormented hitters with a pitch they knew was coming. If Hamels's peers also noticed, they were not trying to learn it.

"Guys were really trying to learn split-fingers and sliders, anything else besides the changeup," Hamels says. "They wanted to see instant results, and the changeup's not instant results. While you're learning it, you're spiking it into the ground or you're hanging it and guys are crushing it. With a slider or a curveball, you see right away how it's really affecting a hitter. So guys are more attracted to the instant success as opposed to the long-term success, and you start to see that some guys just don't like to work as efficiently or as diligently as it takes to be able to succeed at something."

Hamels was playing the long game. He threw only 81 or 82 miles an hour as a freshman at Rancho Bernardo High School, and did not make the varsity team. But the school's star at the time, a junior named Matt Wheatland, was thriving with the changeup. Wheatland would play for Team USA at a tournament in Taiwan on his way to becoming a first-round draft pick of the Tigers. Hamels, sufficiently impressed, learned Wheatland's changeup from his coach, Mark Furtak.

Hamels thought the pitch might compensate for his late-blooming velocity and give him a varsity spot as a sophomore. He was right, but had no idea just how effective his changeup would be.

"We had a ton of scouts at all of our games, big tournament games, all these potential first-round picks—and I was able to make guys swing and miss by a mile," Hamels says. "And that's where I'm like, 'Hmm, that's weird. Why are they missing so bad?' So I'm like, 'OK, I'm gonna do it again,' and they would miss by a mile again. They're not making the adjustment. I was *bouncing* them and guys were swinging. I'm like, 'Well, I guess this pitch is really deceptive.'"

Hamels injured his left arm that summer when he ran into a parked car playing touch football. When he tried to pitch that night, he fractured his humerus bone. A few years earlier, Furtak had been at the game in San Diego when Tom Browning, the stalwart Reds left-hander, suffered the same injury. Browning had 123 career victories at that moment and never won again. Hamels feared for his future.

"This is not a normal arm," Furtak told doctors at the hospital. "You need to do something special."

Doctors inserted two rods in the humerus. Hamels missed a year. But he grew two inches, to 6 foot 3, and when he returned as a senior, he could finally throw his fastball in the low 90s. He trusted in his changeup throughout his recovery.

"For that whole year, I still kind of knew that would be the easiest pitch, because it's not a lot of stress on the area," Hamels says. "You're not trying to muscle and engage and jack everything around. So mentally, I was like: at least I know I can always throw *this* pitch."

He has never stopped. Hamels went undefeated as a senior in 2002 and signed with the Phillies as a first-round pick. Six years later, he was MVP of the World Series. Seven years after that, he was traded to the Rangers and led another team into October.

The stuff he had in high school, Hamels guessed, would not make him a first-round pick anymore. There is too much emphasis on velocity, he said, too many travel-ball programs he worries will burn out top prospects, endanger their arms, or both.

"Every generation's gonna get better and better; you never know when it's gonna stop," Hamels concedes. "But every generation's gonna keep pushing the limit."

There may well be a limit to how fast a human being can throw a baseball. There will never be a limit to the joys of fooling the world's best hitters with something slow.

THE
SPITBALL

Hit the Dry Side

The Brooklyn Dodgers met an old friend on a trip to St. Louis early in the 1955 season. Preacher Roe, a sly and slender lefty who had just retired to West Plains, Missouri, entertained his former teammates at the Chase Hotel. He needed their advice.

"We sat around a big table, all talking to Preacher," recalls Carl Erskine, a top Dodgers starter then. "He said, 'Fellas, I want to ask you a question: *Sports Illustrated* has offered me $2,000 to tell them how I threw the spitter. You think I should do that or not? With that $2,000 I can blacktop my driveway and I can fix up my house. I could really use that $2,000. What do you think?'

"The guys all said, 'Yeah, go ahead, Preach, sure, why not?' I did not. I admired Preacher. He was a great study to watch pitch. He was very clever and won a lot of games; he was really a pitcher's pitcher. So I didn't say yes to that. As we were leaving the dining room, Preacher said, 'I didn't hear you speak up.' I said, 'No, I didn't, Preacher. You were such an outstanding pitcher without the spitter, I'd hate to see you taint your whole career by talking about throwing it.'

"So anyway, Preacher did the article, he got the $2,000, and sometime later when I talked to Preach he said, 'Carl, you know what? I just ruined my chances for the Hall of Fame by admitting I threw the spitter, and you're the only one that advised me not to do it.' And I said, 'Well, Preacher, I saw you pitch, you were a pitcher's pitcher. You could have won without the spitter.'"

Maybe, maybe not. While Erskine believed in Roe, the man himself didn't: in his confession, Roe said he turned to the pitch after slumping to 4–15 with the Pirates in 1947. Reviving the spitter, which he had practiced with Harry Brecheen as a Cardinals farmhand, was his last chance. He made the most of it, becoming a regular All-Star, though not quite a Cooperstown candidate, for the Dodgers. Cheating only made sense.

"Why shouldn't I have?" Roe told Dick Young in the story. "I was about through when I decided to get me the pitch. 'If I get caught,' I told myself, 'they'll kick me out. If I don't, I'm through anyway, so how can I lose?'"

He didn't lose very often. Roe won so much—a .715 winning percentage over seven years with Brooklyn—that he guessed the spitter earned him $100,000. On the bench between innings, Roe would pop a stick of Beech-Nut gum in his mouth and announce, "I'm gonna get me a new batch of curveballs." In the game, he'd spit on the meaty part of his thumb while pretending to wipe his brow. Then, while hitching his belt, he'd subtly wipe his index and middle fingers on the saliva. Two wet fingers on top, a dry thumb underneath, and Roe was ready. He compared it to squeezing a peach pit or watermelon seed with your fingertips.

"The idea is to get part of your grip wet, and the other dry," he said. "When the ball leaves your hand, it slips off your wet fingers and clings, just tiny-like, to the dry part of your thumb. The ball jumps on account of it. If it's a good 'un, it drops like a dead duck just when it crosses the plate."

Roe's confession only confirmed his reputation. As Stan Musial wrote decades later, "I'd always be first-pitch hitting against Roe, because when he had two strikes on you, he'd usually load up, and I hated to get a shower." Anticipation of the spitter helped Roe, and he knew how to destroy evidence. He was never caught in the act.

"Preacher was a psychologist—he would psyche guys out," Erskine says. "They thought the spitter was coming every pitch, practically, and half the game they'd be saying to the umpire, 'Look at the ball, look at the ball!' So the umpire would call for the ball, and Preacher would stomp around and look at his hand like, 'Uh-oh, you probably got me this time,' and then instead of tossing the ball in, he'd roll it to the umpire on the ground!"

Like steroid users decades later, Roe stayed ahead of the cops and thrived. But his pang of regret to Erskine—at least for going public and bursting his cloud of mystery—showed that he knew what he had done. The specter of the dark arts would indeed follow Roe to his grave; when he died in 2008, the word "Spitball" appeared in the headline of his *New York Times* obituary.

———

Spitballs and scuffed balls are something like the Wonder Twins of pitches. They don't really belong in the team picture, like Superman, Batman, and the rest. But they're two of a kind, they're constantly shifting shapes, and lots of folks would rather not admit to their existence.

They're also illegal, but they didn't start that way. After two chaotic decades or so, the spitball was banned for 1920, the same year the country went dry under Prohibition. The rule simply turned the mound into a speakeasy, with many pitchers going undercover to get the same slippery edge as their predecessors.

The physics behind the spitball is simple enough: when the ball slides off wet fingers, it loses backspin and therefore rotates less—something like a knuckleball, which should not rotate at all, or a forkball tumbling in its final plunge.

Defacing the surface of a ball produces the same kind of effect—added movement, to the opposite side of the scuff. This also dates to the game's early days. Imagine what the baseballs looked like in the early twentieth century:

"We'd play a whole game with one ball, if it stayed in the park," said Wahoo Sam Crawford, a Hall of Famer who played from 1899 to 1917, in *The Glory of Their Times*. "Lopsided, and black, and full of tobacco and licorice stains. The pitchers used to have it all their way back then."

Crawford hit often against Jack Chesbro, who won 41 games for the Highlanders (now the Yankees) in 1904 while throwing almost nothing but spitters. Four years later, Ed Walsh of the White Sox won 40 and worked 464 innings; in between, he dominated the 1906 World Series. The spitter helped Walsh to a 1.82 career ERA—the best in baseball history for pitchers with at least 1,000 innings.

"I think that ball disintegrated on the way to the plate and the catcher put it back together again," Crawford said. "I swear, when it went past the plate it was just the spit went by."

Nineteenth-century pitchers experimented with spitballs, too. Bobby Mathews, a curveball pioneer of the 1870s and 1880s, would spit on his palm and apply the saliva to a specific area. Umpire Hank O'Day, who had been a pitcher in Mathews's time, wrote of this in *Baseball Magazine* in 1908: "In the course of two or three innings, the ball would be perfectly black except in the spot where it was rubbed and there it would be perfectly white."

Mathews had a few big years, but apparently not enough for his pitch to spread. For that, it took a playful and perceptive minor leaguer, George Hildebrand, who wasn't even a pitcher. Hildebrand—who later served 22 years as an AL umpire—played briefly in the outfield for Brooklyn in 1902, the same year he was teammates in Providence with a young righty named Frank Corridon. Fooling around with a wet and soggy ball while warming up on a drizzly day, Corridon pegged his catcher in the shins. Hildebrand noticed and encouraged Corridon to "shoot 'em in faster." Hildebrand and Corridon both continued experimenting with the pitch, and when Hildebrand joined a team in Sacramento later that season, he shared the idea with another pitcher.

That pitcher, Elmer Stricklett, would be the Johnny Appleseed of the spitball. When a group of major leaguers visited for an exhibition series, Stricklett captivated them with his spitball, and he proudly spread the secret. In spring training of 1904, he passed it on to two future Hall of Famers who propelled the pitch to prominence.

Stricklett pitched in the White Sox' chain then, but was loaned to a New Orleans team for an exhibition with the Yankees. Chesbro took notice of the spitball, and Stricklett encouraged him to learn it. Mostly, though, he had made Walsh his project that spring in Marlin, Texas. Walsh didn't even know what the spitball was when Stricklett suggested it.

"He showed me what he meant and threw the spitball, and I saw something!" Walsh would tell the *Courant Magazine* in 1956. "It broke two ways, straight down and out."

Stricklett instructed Walsh to place his fingers on a wet spot between the seams and let the ball slip out. The two were not teammates long—Stricklett pitched only once for Chicago—but Walsh worked on his parting gift for two years before deciding to trust it in 1906. Sharp-eyed opponents could tell when Walsh was about to throw a spitter, because his cap would bob from the movement of his jaw when he wet his fingertips behind his glove. But it couldn't have been much of a problem: for a seven-year stretch, through 1912, no pitcher had more strikeouts than Walsh, and only Christy Mathewson had more wins.

The spitter was legal throughout Walsh's career. Just before his death in 1959, he railed against the injustice of its ban to the *Fort Lauderdale News:*

"Everything else in the game favors the hitter. Livelier baseballs, smaller ball parks. They've practically got the poor pitchers working in strait jackets. Those guys have the right to make a living, too."

Walsh said curveballs, not spitters, hurt arms, and that knuckleballs were more prone to hit batters. He said he admired his successors for breaking an unjust law.

"Some people call 'em cheaters," Walsh said. "They're not. They're just guys doing everything they can to win."

That's one way to think about it. Satchel Paige offered another: "I never threw an illegal pitch," he said. "The trouble is, once in a while I toss one that ain't never been seen by this generation."

The ethics of spitters and scuffed balls offer a window to a kind of logic that seems convoluted, yet makes perfect sense to many in the game. To Keith Hernandez, whose Mets were flummoxed in the 1986 playoffs by Houston's Mike Scott, the method of subterfuge is everything: do something illicit away from the field—corking a bat, injecting steroids—and that's cheating. Do something on the field, in front of everyone, and get away with it? As Hernandez wrote in his book, *Pure Baseball:* "More power to you."

Orel Hershiser nods and laughs at the distinction between cheating and its benign cousin, gamesmanship. "Oh, I understand," he says, "if you can be a magician." Hershiser doesn't quite buy it, and offers this definition:

"A pitcher is cheating when he puts a certain spin on the ball but the ball does something unnatural for that spin. That's cheating. Because a hitter hits off of spin and release and trajectory, so he's reading all of those things and hitting what he predicts the ball is going to do because of what you've told him from the spin and the release and the trajectory. So if I put Vaseline on the ball, which creates a completely different spin for the release and trajectory, and that makes the ball dive because of that—OK, then that's cheating. If I cut the ball and the ball has a certain spin but now it does double the movement it should for that amount of spin, that's cheating."

When Larry Andersen would be accused of scuffing the ball, he felt both flattered and offended. It happened to Andersen frequently, because he played for the 1986 Astros and had wicked movement on his pitches. But he swears he left the funny stuff on the side.

"I could go out to the bullpen right now and scuff it and make it do stuff," Andersen says. "But mentally and emotionally, it wasn't right. I played with a lot of guys who didn't always go by the rules, but for me, I just couldn't do it. I couldn't get it out of my head that I was cheating if I did it."

As manager of the Chiba Lotte Marines, Bobby Valentine was mystified by his pitchers' attitude toward using a doctored ball. In Japan, it is just not done.

"The code of honor that all Japanese pitchers pitch by concerning the ball is that it has to be a perfect sphere," Valentine says. "So they use balls right out of the box. We rub 'em up to make 'em dirty, but if the ball is ever dirty there, if it's ever scuffed, if it ever has a piece of pine tar from the bat on it, it's illegal to throw—and they don't do illegal."

Pushing the legal limit is a personal decision, and players generally stay out of each other's way on those matters. That code explains the silence that helped stoke the steroid era; if you suspected your rival of juicing, you kept it to yourself—partly because you wouldn't want anyone snooping around your clubhouse, either.

For all the stories of players howling from the dugout about scuffing or spitball suspects, most of the time they kept quiet for one simple reason:

"Because there was always somebody on your team that probably did something, too," Joe Torre says. "Guys used to come back and bitch about it and you'd say, 'Hit the dry side.' What are you gonna do?"

Now, as the chief baseball officer for MLB, Torre must punish pitchers who flout the rules. Few cases come up, though, partly because players allow subtle rule-bending. Most will accept some chicanery— like applying something tacky to the pitcher's fingers, to get a better grip—as long as it's done right.

"Just don't make it blatant," says A. J. Ellis, the veteran catcher. "Because when you make it blatant you're basically saying that we don't care, we're not afraid of you, we're not afraid you guys are gonna get upset about this. We don't respect you; we don't really think you guys are worthy of hiding anything."

———————

The movement to outlaw the spitter, and other forms of doctored baseballs, was rooted at least partly in business. In the 1919 regular season, Babe Ruth swatted 29 home runs in his final season with the Red Sox, stoking the public's appetite for offense. Taking away a pitcher's weapon could only help offense—which, in turn, would be popular with fans. And removing *that kind* of weapon, which was unsavory by nature, would signal that baseball was actively striving for a clean game. That, perhaps, could help the image of a sport still trying to appeal to a wealthier class of fan.

Mostly, though, the whole thing was just kind of gross.

"There is nothing very pleasant in the sight of a big fellow emptying the contents of his face upon a ball," wrote *Sporting Life* magazine. "There's something creepy and 'slimy' in the very suggestion of the spitball."

That piece—quoted by Dan Gutman in *It Ain't Cheatin' If You Don't Get Caught*—was written in 1908, and one of many columns pleading for an end to so-called freak deliveries. Pitchers were making a mockery of the game, as Rob Neyer has written, scrambling to top each other with new and creative ways to deface the ball. "Frankly," Neyer wrote, "it became a joke."

Barney Dreyfuss, the influential Pirates owner who helped create the first World Series, led the banishment brigade. Before the 1918 season, he warned pitcher Burleigh Grimes that the spitball would soon be banned, and told him to learn something new in the minors. When Grimes refused, Dreyfuss traded him to Brooklyn. Grimes would return to the Pirates after 10 years and 177 victories, and said decades later that pitchers basically ruined all the fun with their unrelenting hijinks.

"The real reason the spitter was barred," Grimes said, "was because pitchers were roughing the ball with pop bottle caps, sandpaper, emery and whatnot, ripping a stitch or two of the seam with razor blades and such, and discoloring the ball with tobacco, licorice, coffee and in other ways."

Sometimes, though, they made such discoveries by accident. Warming up under the stands on a rainy day in Atlanta in 1907, minor leaguer Russ Ford threw a pitch that struck a post behind his catcher, Ed Sweeney. When Sweeney returned the ball, Ford noticed a rough spot from where it had struck the post. When he pitched the ball again, it veered sharply, away from the scuffed side. Ford knew he was on to something, and worked on the pitch for two years, scuffing the ball with a jagged soda bottle and fooling his teammates in batting practice. Eventually Ford found safer ways to scuff; an umpire said he hid emery paper in a hole in his glove, and Ty Cobb believed he used an emery ring. Ford wanted hitters to think he was throwing the spitter. "He would deliberately show his finger to the batter," Cobb wrote in his memoirs, "and then wet it with salvia."

For a while, it worked. After a one-game cameo in 1909, Ford went 26–6 with a 1.65 ERA for the Highlanders in 1910—the only season ever by a Yankees pitcher with that many wins and such a low ERA. He managed to keep the pitch a secret until 1913, when Cy Falkenberg of Cleveland caught on. It spread from there, and after the Yankees' Ray Keating and the Cubs' Jimmy Lavender were found with emery paper on the mound in 1914, the pitch was banned. Ford and Falkenberg quickly faded from the scene.

A similar fate befell Hod Eller, who found a "shine ball" with the Reds in 1917. On a dark, damp day at the Polo Grounds, Eller noticed his pitch behaving strangely after he had vigorously rubbed off the dirt from one side. He quickly learned that by doing this and throwing hard, he could make the ball rise—three to four inches vertically, he said, somewhat dubiously, or five to six inches to the side.

"I used to reverse the break sometimes by holding the smooth spot on the under surface of the ball," Eller told *Baseball Magazine*. "You could get a terrific drop to the ball by holding it that way, somewhat like the break of a spit-ball and much more effective than the average curve."

The AL president Ban Johnson swiftly ordered an end to the shine ball, an edict as toothless as an 1897 rule forbidding players from defacing the ball. Life was grand for Eller, who went 19–9 in 1919 and beat the White Sox twice in the tainted World Series. Chicago's Eddie Cicotte also threw the shine ball—he rubbed it against colorless paraffin wax on his pants—but he conspired with gamblers to lose. So did Lefty Williams, whom Eller beat twice. Eller retired Shoeless Joe Jackson, another of the "Eight Men Out," on a grounder to end the farce in Game 8.

The Black Sox scandal would not explode until 1920, but the curious performances had at least stirred suspicion in the immediate aftermath. Coupled with the financial incentives in boosting offense, the atmosphere was ripe for a rule change. By spring training, this had become law:

At no time during the progress of the game shall the pitcher be allowed to: (1) Apply a foreign substance of any kind to the ball; (2) Expectorate either on the ball or his glove; (3) Rub the ball on his glove, person, or clothing; (4) Deface the ball in any manner; (5) or to deliver what is called the "shine" ball, "spit" ball, "mud" ball, or "emery" ball. For violation of any part of this rule the umpire shall at once order the pitcher from the game, and in addition he shall be automatically suspended for a period of 10 days, on notice from the president of the league.

Each team could designate up to two pitchers who would still be allowed to use the pitch in 1920. That year's World Series was a spitball extravaganza: Grimes tossed a shutout for Brooklyn and Stan Coveleski won three complete games to lead Cleveland to its first title. As the rule stood, though, Grimes, Coveleski, and the 15 other eligible spitballers would suddenly be forced to give up their best pitch forever.

In a letter to NL owners, Bill Doak, a 20-game winner for the Cardinals, argued that barring the pitch would "deprive all these pitchers of their greatest power," and Grimes made similar pleas through the press. They met a sympathetic audience: the NL voted 6–2 to allow the designated spitballers to use the pitch for the rest of their careers, and the AL soon agreed.

Three of the grandfathered spitballers—Coveleski, Grimes, and Red Faber, who used tobacco juice on the ball—wound up in the Hall of Fame. Grimes would be a World Series hero for the Cardinals in 1931, nearly spinning a no-hitter before President Hoover in Game 3 and then working into the ninth, despite severe abdominal pain, to win Game 7. Grimes's secret: original slippery elm bark imported by his father from his native Wisconsin. Grimes had run out of his supply, wrote his biographer, Joe Niese, and the drugstore-brand tablets in St. Louis made him nauseous.

Grimes outlasted all the other legal spitballers, retiring in 1934. Frank Shellenback, a marginal White Sox pitcher who was left off their list, flung legal spitters in the Pacific Coast League through 1938. That September, in Williamston, North Carolina, tenant farmers Evan and Ruby Perry welcomed a son named Gaylord into the world. He would master spitball skulduggery and ride its greasy path to Cooperstown.

"Ballplayers don't think a good spitballer is a criminal," Perry would write, many years later. "They think he's an artist."

The ban on doctored baseballs simply sent the practice deeper underground. As a catcher for the Milwaukee Braves in the early 1960s, a young Joe Torre called spitters for a veteran, Lew Burdette. But that was all Torre knew.

"You didn't know where it was coming from," he says. "I mean, Burdette threw a spitter and I caught him, but I couldn't tell you where he got it, because he wouldn't tell anybody. I knew what it was going to do, but I had no clue where he got it."

Perhaps he got it from Grimes, though both men denied it. After his playing career, Grimes coached in the Yankees' minor league system in the late 1940s, just as Burdette was coming through. In a book interview with former commissioner Fay Vincent, Burdette said he asked Grimes how to throw a spitball, but Grimes refused to say.

"But I'll tell you one thing: you can go through gyrations and all," Grimes told him. "If you can get hitters—who are egotistical so-and-sos, you know—if you can get one of the first three guys in the first inning to go back and complain, by the fifth inning the batboy will be yelling, 'Look at the ball!'"

Burdette would fluster hitters by holding his hand in front of his mouth, touching his forehead, fiddling with the ball in his glove, adjusting his cap and wetting his fingertips on his tongue. After Grimes watched Burdette on TV, he told him, "You got it down good." Richie Ashburn complained constantly to Burdette, never cursing but accusing him on the field of throwing a "crapping spitter." Finally, Burdette complied, digging the ball into the dirt on the mound to overload one side with mud. It zagged under Ashburn's bat for strike three.

"Now that's a crapping spitter!" Burdette told him.

"I'll never complain again, Lew," Ashburn replied. "I'll never complain again."

Burdette was the hero of the 1957 World Series for the Milwaukee Braves, completing all three of his victories over the Yankees, including a Game 5 shutout against Whitey Ford. Ford had beaten Warren Spahn in the opener, and the two matched up twice again the next fall. Ford and Burdette had been teammates—under Grimes's tutelage—in the Yankees' farm system, and Burdette taught Ford his trick.

"Did you ever notice how many times Whitey used to tie his shoe-lace during the game?" Spahn told Vincent. "Because Burdette taught him how to throw a mud ball. And he'd wet the ball and put it on the ground and it was a little heavier on one side than the other, and he'd make the ball move because of that."

Spahn said he toyed with Burdette's spitter in the bullpen, but used it just once in a game and allowed a home run.

"Then I talked to Burdette about it and he says, 'You got to have two wet fingers and a dry thumb,'" Spahn said. "I remember him saying that so much."

In *Slick,* his 1987 memoir with Phil Pepe, Ford said Burdette taught him the mud ball late in his career; he gave no exact date, but hinted that it may have been 1963, when he went 24–7. Ford explained that he "needed something to help me survive," and said he would simply wet the ball with saliva and touch it to the dirt while grabbing the rosin bag. He threw the pitch as hard as he could, with the dirt on top as he released it. The pitch behaved like a screwball, sinking away from a righty but rotating more than a pure spitter. If a hitter asked for the ball before he threw it, Ford said, he would lightly brush it against his pants leg, knocking off the dirt.

The mud ball emboldened Ford. Seeking a new challenge, he thought of a way to scuff the ball while rubbing it up. One current major league pitching coach can do this with his fingernails, but Ford had a friend pay a jeweler $55 for a ring with a rasp—a half-inch long and a quarter-inch wide—welded onto it.

"Why would anybody have any use for something like this?" the jeweler asked the friend, who told him just to shut up and make it. The handiwork delighted Ford.

"I would put the part of the ring with the rasp underneath my finger," he wrote. "On top, I covered the ring with flesh-colored Band-Aids, so you couldn't tell from a distance that I had anything on my finger. Now it was easy to just rub the baseball against the rasp and scratch it on one side. One little nick was all it took to get the baseball to sail and dip like crazy."

Opponents suspected Ford, but umpires tended not to push too hard. Bill Fischer, a journeyman reliever of the era, recalls sweating profusely with the bases loaded one day in Cleveland. From behind he heard a voice: "This'd be a good time to load one up, Fish." It was the second base umpire. Now imagine the deference shown to a pitcher like Ford.

"There was one time when Whitey was scuffing up the ball and the umpire came out, and he knew," teammate Jim Bouton said a few years ago. "I forget who it was, but he was one of those old-timer guys who's not gonna be a wise guy or a big shot—this is Whitey Ford, he's one of the greats. A certain amount of respect is due.

"So he went to the mound and the conversation went, 'Uh, Whitey, I see the ring there. I tell you what, what you need to do is call time out and go in and change your jock strap. And when you come back, don't have the ring on.' He was giving him a cover to do that.

"That was just part of the deal: if you could sneak it in there, it was considered to be clever. It isn't a criminal offense or anything like that. If you could get away with it, then do it. And everybody else, if they could have done it, would have done the same thing."

Ford had other ways of getting an edge, sometimes literally. His catcher, Elston Howard, might scrape the ball against a sharpened clasp on his shin guards; a contemporary of Ford's, the Hall of Famer Jim Bunning, had used a similar technique with his belt buckle. Ford also mixed baby oil, turpentine, and resin to form a sticky substance he could use to grip the ball in cold weather. To conceal it, he hid it in a bottle of roll-on deodorant he would keep in his warm-up jacket. Boys being boys, Mickey Mantle once swiped the bottle, put it in Yogi Berra's locker, and howled as Berra got his arms stuck to his sides.

The most notorious AL cheater of the time, though, was probably John Wyatt, a reliever who earned 20 saves for Boston's Impossible Dream pennant winners of 1967. Wyatt was so committed to subterfuge that he was said to smother Vaseline nearly everywhere—even in his mouth. He finally came clean nearly 20 years later, to the *Fort Lauderdale Sun-Sentinel,* with some sound logic.

"I cheated, but I faced some tough hitters," Wyatt said. "Had to do something against those cats. They could make a guy look real bad."

―――――――

In 1968, the year he threw 58⅔ consecutive scoreless innings, the Dodgers' Don Drysdale capitalized on his (accurate) reputation for throwing the occasional slippery pitch. In a commercial for Vitalis hair tonic, Drysdale looked in for the sign against a Giants hitter. When the hitter called time out, Drysdale casually removed his cap and ran his fingers through his hair.

"Greaseball! Greaseball!" cried Herman Franks, the Giants' manager, storming from his dugout. "See him rub his hair! He's gonna throw a greaseball, that's illegal!"

A disgusted Drysdale grimaced, tossed his glove on the grass, and retreated to the clubhouse. There, he found a bottle of Vitalis, returned to the mound and held the bottle high for all to see.

"Vitalis has no grease, and spreads easily through your hair," the announcer said. "If we all used Vitalis, we could help put an end to the greaseball."

Poor Gaylord Perry. He had the same idea as Drysdale, but his agent pitched it to the wrong company. Vaseline turned down Perry for an endorsement deal by sniffing: "We soothe babies' asses, not baseballs."

Ever resourceful, Perry found other ways to monetize his money pitch. In 1974, he published a confessional memoir, *Me and the Spitter*, with Bob Sudyk. If it hurt his Hall of Fame chances, the damage was minimal. When Perry retired in 1983, just two other pitchers, Walter Johnson and Steve Carlton, had 300 wins and 3,500 strikeouts. He made it to Cooperstown on his third try, in 1991.

As Grimes planted at least some seeds for Burdette's trickery, another legal spitballer helped Perry. After his long career in the Pacific Coast League, Frank Shellenback served as a supervisor and scout for the Giants. He taught the secrets of his illicit pitches to Bob Shaw—"I do *not* recommend their use," Shaw wrote in his pitching manual—and Shaw passed them on to Perry at Giants spring training in 1964. Watching Shaw throw his spitball, Perry wrote, "I knew how Tom Edison felt when he discovered the electric light."

"He wet his two fingers, placed them on top of the ball, wound and fired," Perry wrote. "And down it went."

In Shaw, a future pitching coach, Perry had found a seasoned and savvy mentor. By then Shaw had played seven seasons, won a World Series game, and saved an All-Star Game. He and Perry were inseparable.

"He was a good teammate," Perry said in 2018. "He told me how his career went, and I paid attention to him. He was an excellent setup pitcher. I learned a great deal by watching him set hitters up, good hitters that he got out very easily."

In the musty files of the library at the old *Sports Illustrated* offices in Manhattan, a sheet of notes for a 1973 article included a primer from Shaw on how pitchers load spitballs:

They apply whatever they use to the forehead, the back of the wrist, the forearm, the side of the pant leg, or the belt. The idea is to change the location, so when umpires look in one spot, it's not there. You can hit your glove and remove it from your wrist in one motion. You never load up with more than you can remove with one swipe. When you do apply it to the hand, you put it on the second and third fingers. That way, you can pick up the rosin bag with the thumb and index finger and not disturb your load.

Shaw detailed some of the loading agents: slippery-elm lozenges, saliva, Vaseline, or K-Y Jelly, the water-soluble lubricant. He said it was also essential to use plenty of mannerisms to bother the hitters. By 1973 Perry was expertly applying all these lessons, inspired by frank words from Shaw in the bullpen early in the 1964 season: "Gaylord, I don't think you've got enough right now to be a starting pitcher. There comes a time in a man's life when he must decide what's important. He must provide the best way he can for his family."

For Perry, a 25-year-old mop-up reliever, that meant putting the spitter into action. He had a 4.50 career ERA when he came in to pitch the bottom of the thirteenth in the second game of a doubleheader on May 31, 1964, against the Mets at Shea Stadium. Ten slippery, scoreless innings later, a baseball outlaw was born.

Perry would lick his fingers, legally, and pretend to dry them off with the rosin bag (a move he would practice with his daughter Amy's bean bag). When his mouth got dry, a teammate gave him a slippery-elm lozenge. When the first baseman, Orlando Cepeda, got a ball to end the inning, he rolled it on the grass to dry it off. When a fight broke out in the stands, diverting people's attention, Perry simply spit on the ball.

"Nice going, kid," Shaw told Perry. "You made it."

Perry called his spitter the super-sinker, and that is how it often behaved. It veered so hard, down and in on righties, that some refused to use their favorite bats for fear that Perry would break them. He learned to disrupt hitters with a series of six gyrations before the pitch, touching his hat, hair, ear, neck, wrist, and some part of his uniform.

Like any smooth criminal, he constantly searched for new strategies. At the 1966 All-Star Game, on a broiling day in St. Louis, Perry noticed Sandy Koufax with red-hot Capsolin rubbed on his pitching arm. Koufax needed the searing heat to distract him from his aching elbow; Perry needed it to sweat more.

"Capsolin is like putting on a blowtorch," says Dave Duncan, who caught Perry with Cleveland and later coached him with Seattle. "He'd lay on the training table and the trainer would smear his entire back with a coat of it. You couldn't even go in the room, it was so strong. Shoot, I don't know how he did it. I couldn't even put a drop of it on my shoulder without dying."

Perry was so furtive that, for a while, he strictly guarded his methods, even when another famous trickster begged him for his secrets at the 1970 All-Star Game. "Gaylord, tell me, where do you get it?" Richard Nixon asked, nudging Perry in the ribs with his elbow. "Mr. President," Perry replied, "there are some things you just can't tell the people for their own good."

Nixon erupted in laughter—Perry was, indeed, far better at concealing information than the president. When the book came out in 1974, Perry swore he was reformed, and Duncan says Perry indeed threw forkballs that season, not the spitters he had thrown the year before. But his spitball hiatus didn't last long.

Two years later, with the Rangers, Perry compared pitches with Bert Blyleven, a fellow future Hall of Famer. First Blyleven showed Perry his curveball.

"Then it was my turn to lube up in the bullpen, and it was like a new toy, like Christmas time," Blyleven says. "The ball's sinking, no seams, you know. The ball's slipping out of your hand, and all that slippage creates so much torque on your elbow, and the next day my elbow was barking. But Gaylord was a mule. He was a strong, strong son of a bitch."

Perry bounced to San Diego in 1978 and won his second Cy Young Award. He befriended a young setup man, John D'Acquisto, who encouraged Perry to run for exercise. Perry begged off. "I've got the magic pitch," he said, and D'Acquisto knew what made it work.

"You couldn't find it, because it was K-Y Jelly," D'Acquisto says. "K-Y Jelly dissipates, and he had it everywhere. There wasn't one spot, and it just looked like beads of sweat. Are you gonna throw a guy out for sweating? What Gaylord told me was, 'Johnny, you don't need much, just a little bit.' And I go, 'Yeah, but you've got it everywhere,' and he says, 'Well, that's so it doesn't look like you're getting it from one spot.'"

Three years later, D'Acquisto was trying to hang on with the Angels, who thought he was losing his velocity. He found a tube of K-Y Jelly in his locker, a flashing red light from the pitching coach, Tom Morgan. "You need to start using this," Morgan said, but D'Acquisto says he didn't have the right arm action to throw it. A year later, he had pitched his last game. If only he could have harnessed Perry's pitch.

"He was a beauty, man," D'Acquisto says. "He was a beauty."

———

Even in retirement, pitchers suspected of doctoring balls rarely like to talk about it. Don Sutton (who was sometimes called "Black & Decker," after the power tool company) once threatened to sue umpire Doug Harvey, who ejected him from a game for allegedly defacing a ball. Sutton was happy to talk about his curveball, but not about scuffing.

Phil Regan turned eighty in 2017 and was still coaching in the minors for the Mets. One morning that spring, I asked him about his well-known reputation for slick deliveries. This was a man who once dropped a Vaseline tube from his jacket pocket on the bases. Yet, at first, he demurred.

"Who told you that?" he barked, then dove into a story about a game at Wrigley Field on August 18, 1968. Pitching for the Cubs against Cincinnati, Regan was repeatedly cited for throwing illegal pitches. Twice, when the batter put the ball in play for an out, the plate umpire Chris Pelekoudas ordered him back to the plate to hit again. It was quite a scene, Regan said; his catcher was tossed from the game, but he kept pitching because the umpires found nothing on his cap or glove. The next day, league president Warren Giles flew to town for an emergency meeting and promptly undercut the umpires, holding a news conference and praising Regan as a "fine Christian gentleman." One little problem: the umpires were right about Regan.

"They said they called 14 illegal pitches," Regan said. "They missed three!"

Then he winked, smiled, and walked away.

Policing pitchers was a tedious and somewhat humiliating process for umpires, who could rarely catch pitchers in the act. Before that 1968 season, baseball had tried to strengthen the 1920 rule by decreeing that any pitcher going to his mouth before delivering a pitch would be ejected. The leagues hoped to eliminate fruitless mound searches and speed up the game, but by mid-March, after a rash of spring training ejections, the rule was amended again: the penalty would be a balk with runners on base, or a ball without, and a pitcher could still blow on his hand or lick his fingers, just not while standing on the dirt. Six years later, umpires were told they could issue a spitball warning without evidence, just by observing something strange in the flight of the ball.

Yet for all of that, few pitchers were actually caught in the act. One of the most notorious, and hapless, perpetrators ended up teaching pitching for a living: Rick Honeycutt, the future coach for the Dodgers. It was the last day of September in 1980, the end of an All-Star season gone awry. After starting 6–0, Honeycutt had gone 4–17 for the last-place Mariners. He was starting in Kansas City against the World Series–bound Royals. On his way to warm up in the bullpen, Honeycutt passed a bulletin board. Foolish inspiration struck.

"I saw a thumbtack and I was like, 'Well, I know that would scuff up a ball,'" Honeycutt says. "You hear about guys doing certain things, and you think, 'What the heck, why not?' It was just a stupid and idiotic move, really."

Honeycutt knew only the basics: when a ball is scuffed, you put the scuff on the opposite side of the way you want it to move. But he had never practiced it before, and had no plan for disguising the thumbtack. He tried to stick it through his glove, but when it wouldn't pierce the leather, he taped it on with a flesh-colored bandage.

For two innings, Honeycutt tried nothing. Then, with two out in the third, he scraped a ball and delivered it to Willie Wilson, who smacked it to right for a triple. On the next ball Honeycutt sliced, George Brett singled.

"Then Kunkel comes out," Honeycutt says. That would be Bill Kunkel, the very last umpire you'd want behind the plate if you were nervously trying to scuff a ball with no clue how to do it. Kunkel had pitched for the 1963 Yankees, with Whitey Ford.

"He said he'd loaded up a ball once in a while when he was pitching," says Jim Evans, a fellow AL umpire at the time. "We would chat and he would say, 'Here's a guy you gotta watch, this is what he does.'"

Honeycutt might not have been a suspect before, but these she-nanigans were just too obvious. Kunkel ejected him, and Honeycutt panicked. "They can't kick me out of the game forever, can they?" he asked a coach. Honeycutt was relieved to get a fine and the standard 10-day suspension, but he never pitched for the Mariners again. They traded the young lefty to Texas that winter and he went on to pitch 17 more seasons.

The opposite of Honeycutt, in every way, was Mike Scott. While Honeycutt was clumsy, ineffective, and easily caught, Scott was cunning, overpowering, and elusive. In four years as a Met, from 1979 to 1982, he was 14–27 with a 4.64 earned run average. He went to the Astros, won a Cy Young Award, nearly won another, notched 306 strikeouts in a season, threw a division-clinching no-hitter, and got his number retired.

Here is an alternate summary of Scott, from a former major league All-Star of the era who saw Scott's image on TV in the Fenway Park clubhouse in 2015: "Mike Scott, when he was with the Mets, he was the worst motherfucking pitcher in the league. As soon as he started scuffing, it all changed. He said 'split-finger.' Split-finger, my ass!"

The cranky ex-player was crudely accurate, in a way: in those first four seasons, among all major league pitchers with at least 350 innings, Scott was indeed dead last in the category ERA+—he performed nearly 25 percent worse than the average pitcher of the time. But Scott did learn a split-finger fastball, as described in that chapter. That was the pitch that dove into the dirt. The pitch that nearly vanquished the Mets in the 1986 NLCS was something different.

"It was like sandpaper, chicken scratch," Keith Hernandez says. "It was all right there, one side. It overloaded one side when he threw it, whichever side had the scratch, and he'd make it run this way, and he'd turn it over and make it run the other way. He was doing it on his fastball. It would move a foot and a half, trying to get you to chase. I never saw a guy whose fastball ran that much—and he threw 97, 98, and he knew exactly what he was doing with it, too."

In Game 1 of the NLCS, Scott shut out the Mets with 14 strikeouts. He threw another complete game four days later, allowing three hits and a run. The Mets collected every ball Scott pitched that came into their dugout, and claimed to have dozens scuffed in the same spot. Yet

Dutch Rennert, the plate umpire that night, said the Mets never asked him to check a ball that hadn't already hit the dirt. Rennert said he checked at least once an inning, and found nothing.

"I believe the pitches Mike Scott are throwing are legal, and I believe it with all my heart," Doug Harvey, who worked the plate for Game 1, told the writer George White. "During the season I must have checked 65 to 70 balls that Mike Scott threw, and not one showed any sign of scuff marks."

The Mets believed the umpires couldn't catch Scott because one of his fielders was scuffing the ball for him—and, Hernandez says, because Sutton's threatened lawsuit, in 1978, had essentially handcuffed baseball's cops. (Sutton withdrew it, having made his point when the league backed down without a fine or suspension.)

Only by winning Game 6 at the Astrodome, in 16 wild innings, did the Mets survive the series. Had they played a Game 7 and faced Scott—who was named Series MVP—they knew they had no chance.

"Mike Scott intimidated a ball club that did not get intimidated by anybody," said Bobby Ojeda, who won Game 2 of that series. "All he had to do was throw his glove on the mound and we'd go, 'OK, we don't want to play today.' But he was a master at making that thing work, which is kind of cheating, you know? But you've still gotta make it work. It's like Tom Brady with the deflated footballs. You've still gotta make the throw."

Alan Ashby, the Astros' catcher in that series, speaks in amazement about Scott's splitter, the way he didn't even have to spread his fingers very wide to get devastating action.

"But the splitter was a part of the arsenal," Ashby says. "It was a combination of stuff, and I'll leave it at that."

I suggested that maybe Scott does not get enough credit for how great he was, since he is so widely remembered for alleged scuffing. Ashby smiled, uncomfortably. He didn't know how to respond.

"Well, I don't know," Ashby replied. "He's got a Cy Young to enjoy. He's playing golf every day. Hard for me to answer and be real with you."

Scott has never admitted to scuffing, exactly, and rarely appears in public. The closest he came was in an MLB Network documentary about the 1986 postseason: "They can believe whatever they want to believe," Scott said. "Every ball that hits the ground has something on it. . . . I've thrown balls that were scuffed but I haven't scuffed every ball that I've thrown."

————

The Mets went on to stage another epic sixth game in the World Series against Boston. Facing elimination at Shea, they were down to their last strike when a wild pitch by Bob Stanley skipped under Mookie Wilson's legs and past catcher Rich Gedman, scoring the tying run just before Bill Buckner's infamous error. Ron Darling said he has always assumed, because of the way the ball moved and Stanley's well-known reputation for throwing a spitter, that Stanley had, indeed, loaded one up for the fateful wild pitch. That's sort of how it sounded when I asked Gedman about it, during his final season in the majors with the Cardinals in 1992.

I had been captivated by the 1986 World Series—who wasn't?—and was writing a piece about it for my homemade magazine. I remember Gedman speaking very quietly and thoughtfully.

"You're probably the first guy that's asked me that since about a week after it happened," he said. "It was just one of those pitches that did something it normally doesn't do. Bob Stanley's a sinkerball pitcher. I was waiting for a sinker and got what appeared to be a cutter or a slider. I don't know if it was the grip on the ball or what.

"I look back and I see the pitch in my mind and there's no business I had missing that ball. But the pitch itself did not—it's like getting crossed up in a way. I felt like Bob Stanley took a lot of heat for no reason at all. If I had to see that pitch on TV, I'd say that was a passed ball and not a wild pitch. But I also know what happened."

Stanley has coached for years in the Blue Jays organization, and I saw him a while back at spring training. He talked about his sinker, and said he threw it about 90 percent of the time because breaking balls were harder on his arm. When I asked if he ever threw a spitter, Stanley was surprisingly candid.

"Yeah, I cheated, sure," he said, explaining that he simply loaded sweat on his fingers by wiping his brow. "You just grip the ball without any seams, just flat."

He talked a bit about how times had changed, how a pitcher like Perry—"Oh my God, he had all kinds of shit in his mouth," he said—would have a tougher time today. For Stanley, who pitched from 1977 to 1989, it was fairly easy.

"When I threw it, they never saw me do it," he said. "When I wanted them to think a spitter was coming, I'd throw 'em a palmball instead. I'd get away with it because I had a good sinker. They could never catch me because it was sweat, it wasn't like Vaseline. If they checked [someone else's] ball, they could feel the Vaseline, but this was just sweat—'I don't know, it dripped off my fingers.'"

He said he would only throw it with two strikes, never on the first pitch. That was my signal to go for it, to ask about the pitch I'd always wondered about, from the moment it left his hand to Gedman's heartfelt recollection to Darling's assertion. Here goes:

"What about the wild pitch in Game 6?" I asked. "That was with two strikes—was that a spitter?"

"That was a fastball in," Stanley said. "They set up outside, it went in."

Oh. Just an ordinary fastball.

In my mind, I could hear the losing horn from *The Price Is Right,* the jingle they play when someone falls short of the big prize. If a guy with a two-strike spitter really did let one slip at the absolute worst moment in 1986, I guess we'll never know.

––––––––––

The next year was a strange one, marked by a curious single-season spike in home runs and a cluster of ball-doctoring incidents in August. First was the Joe Niekro episode in Anaheim, when Niekro, then with the Twins, emptied his pockets for umpires and flung an emery board and sandpaper to the grass. A week later in Philadelphia, umpires found sandpaper glued to the glove of the Phillies' Kevin Gross. Both were suspended 10 games.

Later that month, the Yankees visited the Angels, starting Tommy John against Sutton. A year before, Sutton had earned his 300th victory for the Angels, cheekily telling reporters, "I've been trying legally, and illegally, to get here for years." Given his reputation, and the hot topic in baseball at the time, it was no wonder the Yankees' telecast zoomed in on Sutton throughout the game, focusing on a small patch on the palm of his left hand. When he rubbed up a ball with both hands, was Sutton defacing it?

Jim Palmer, the Hall of Fame Orioles pitcher, had always believed as much. When he lost to Sutton on the final day of the 1982 season, giving Sutton's Brewers the AL East title, Palmer said he noticed scratches across the name of the league president on the balls Sutton threw. At some point in their careers, Palmer said, Sutton told him how he scuffed.

"I said, 'How do you scuff a ball?'" Palmer says. "He said, 'Well, you use 180 sandpaper, you superglue it on your hand and you rub the ball up.' I said, 'I don't rub the ball up.' He said, 'Well, if you want to scratch the ball, you just put it there and rub the ball on it and you've got your scuff.'"

Sutton has denied a version of that story, but that method was on George Steinbrenner's mind as he watched the broadcast. Steinbrenner angrily, and repeatedly, called the Yankees' dugout until reaching manager Lou Piniella. He demanded that Piniella tell the umpires to check Sutton, but Piniella would not. He didn't want the umps checking John, too.

John and Sutton had been teammates, and John was also a frequent target of suspicion. He said he told Piniella to do whatever he wanted that night, because he was clean. And John knew what Sutton was up to, anyway.

"Sutton had a Band-Aid, and the reason he did was because he wanted the Yankee people to respond to him," John says. "I know he did, because I did the same thing to Tony La Russa."

John explained that Piniella had once argued about an Oakland pitcher the night before John's scheduled start. John expected La Russa, the A's manager, to retaliate by asking the umps to check him. That morning, he visited a baseball card store in New Jersey and bought a card of La Russa.

"I had it in my hip pocket and I had a Sharpie," John says. "I wanted the umpires to come out and check me. I was gonna back away, go into my pocket, draw my hand up, and flip the card on the ground. When they picked it up, I was gonna go over to Tony with the pen and say, 'Tony, would you sign this for me please?' But he never checked me! He messed up my time for fame. I would have been on Johnny Carson."

Brian Moehler had no such plans when umpires checked him at Tropicana Field in 1999. Moehler, a Tigers right-hander, was pitching well against the Devil Rays, who thought his pitches were moving suspiciously. Umpires inspected Moehler and may—or may not—have found sandpaper taped to his right thumb. He was suspended 10 days and did not appeal.

So, what was really on his thumb? Moehler still isn't saying.

"Well, it depends who you ask," he says. "One of the umpires said he saw something and the next one said he didn't, and they said they had some balls that had some scuffs on 'em."

Pause.

"Does that stuff go on?" he continues. "Yeah, it does. Do I sit here and say I know how to do it? Yeah, if I had gotten a scuffed ball, I had a pretty good idea how to do it. It's not something that's taught, but as a pitcher you kind of fool around with it, like someone with a knuckleball, you joke around with it, you get a scuffed ball that hits the track or something, you learn where the scuff is and which way to make the ball move.

"So have I ever had a ball that's scuffed that was given to me? I remember I had an umpire one time, the game had gotten out of hand and the ball had hit the track. They always check the balls, obviously, and he brings the ball to me and he goes, 'Have fun!' I was like, 'OK!' Was I aware of how to do it? Oh yeah, I was aware of how to do it. I think a lot of guys are."

Actually, Moehler says, in the moment he was more concerned about his glove, which had metal eyelets around the holes for the laces. Those were once standard on gloves, but are illegal now because pitchers could easily use them to scuff. Moehler got his glove back, no questions asked, and he used it for the rest of his career.

In some ways, he says, his crime helped him. After that, some hitters would always ask the umpires to check the ball.

"I would walk halfway to home plate, flip the ball to the umpire, and then when he gave me another ball I'd stand there and act like I was scuffing it up and walk back to the rubber," Moehler says. "If a hitter went up there thinking I was scuffing the baseball, I had an advantage. Because the hardest thing in sports is hitting a baseball, and he's gotta worry about doing that—but now in the back of his mind, he thinks I'm scuffing it."

Moehler ended up leading the AL in losses in 1999, with 16, and he finished his career well under .500. But he tricked hitters long enough to last 14 seasons in the majors, through 2010, and now scouts amateur talent in Georgia for the Red Sox. Friends say he would make a great pitching coach.

———

The mental edge of a scuffball suspect is nothing new. These words come from Chet Brewer, a star for the Kansas City Monarchs of the Negro National League in the late 1920s, but they sound timeless:

"A cut ball? I got credit for that," he told John Holway in *Black Diamonds*. "If I picked up a rough one, I didn't throw it out of the game. I didn't exactly put the cuts on it myself, but I could pitch it."

Brewer, who died in 1990, said that when he barnstormed against Swede Risberg, one of the banned members of the 1919 White Sox, the balls Risberg brought came pre-scratched. Knowing how to use a scratch was a matter of survival.

"When I learned the screwball, they said, 'Heck, he's scratching the ball,' so I knew that I was getting on them," Brewer added. "I'd face the outfield and rub the ball up, turn around, throw a screwball: 'Oh, he cut it!' But it was more a psychological thing."

Scuffing charges never dogged Mike Mussina, but like any smart pitcher, he would never reject a ball that came to him with a mark. This was Mussina's order for every catcher: if a ball hits the ground, *never* volunteer it to the umpire. Any ball that touches dirt, around the plate or the infield, might be a bar of gold in the pitcher's hand.

"Say a guy hits a ground ball to short and they throw it back to me from first base—as soon as I grab the ball, I'm running my thumb over these," Mussina says. He is holding a ball and referring to the white area within the horseshoe. "Do I have a sinker out of this ball? And if I find one I think's pretty good, I flip it to the other side to see if it's scuffed up on the wrong side."

By that he means the opposite side; if both horseshoe areas are scuffed, they'll counteract each other, to no advantage. If there's a scuff where the seams narrow—the sweet spot—it creates a four-seam sinker, a pitch that spins like a straight fastball but veers away, in the direction opposite the scuff.

But watch out for those high seams.

"If the seams are really high, even if I'm scuffed up just a little bit, they're gonna cause too much resistance naturally," Mussina says. "It's not gonna have enough of an effect to do anything."

A common lament among retired pitchers is that too many balls are now thrown out of play. To them, it underscores a lack of craftsmanship on the mound.

"I've literally seen teammates, when there's a scuff on the ball, they get rid of it," Jamie Moyer says. "They'll say, 'Oh, it does funny stuff,' and you go, 'Wait a minute, that funny stuff can be a benefit to you!' But they don't know how to do it."

Maybe not, but they also rarely get the chance. Hitters are conditioned to ask umpires to discard any ball that skips. Umpires and catchers know this, so catchers tend to have an almost reflexive response: they'll spear a ball from the dirt, transfer it quickly to their throwing hand, and hold it up for the ump to keep or reject.

Some fielders still try: catchers may deliberately short-hop their throws before innings, and outfielders may do the same on routine throws to the infield. But times have changed.

"When I played, a ball hit the dirt, it was still in play," says Chili Davis, who played from 1981 to 1999. "Today's game, if a catcher throws a ball down to second on a short hop, or a ball gets blocked in the dirt, that ball's out of the game. It's just automatic now."

Pitchers also seek ways to look natural while applying moisture or tackiness to their fingers. One former player, now a broadcaster, reached into his team's ball bag for me and pulled out a canister of colorless Tuf-Skin, a spray that helps secure athletic tape. With one spritz of Tuf-Skin on my arm, I had an invisible island of instant tackiness for my fingers. That's also why pitchers like putting clear BullFrog Sunscreen on their arms: grab the rosin bag, aimlessly touch the BullFrog spot, and you'll have just enough stickiness to help guide your pitches. One catcher said he has seen pitchers leave the dugout between innings and wrap their fingers around a ball coated with pine tar, leaving just enough residue on their hands to get a better grip when they return to the mound.

Next time you go to a game, notice all the surfaces a pitcher touches with his hand. Pitchers are fidgety creatures, constantly tugging and swiping and scratching their caps, their sleeves, their skin, *something*. Take a look at Corey Kluber, the two-time Cy Young winner for Cleveland who generates extraordinary movement with his pitches. Kluber grabs his tongue on the mound before every pitch—which has been legal again for years—then wipes his hand on the side of his pants.

"The way they rub the balls up now, they rub them all up in advance," Kluber says. "They're not rubbed up all day, and they sit in the bucket with all the dust and stuff, and they get so slippery. Just get a little bit of moisture on your hand, at least. You've still gotta wipe it off, obviously, but you get a little bit of moisture on your hand so the ball's not as dry."

Kluber does this no matter the weather, but such tactics are especially handy in the cold and at high altitude, where it's harder to generate moisture.

"I tell you what," says one NL veteran, "if they could get a camera behind the dugout in Colorado, it would be like a mad scientist's laboratory down there, people doing anything they can to find a grip."

Most players, even hitters, tend to accept this practice. A pitch can be an instrument of destruction, after all, and hitters would rather the pitcher know where it's going than accidentally fire a cue ball at their head. It is a fine distinction, to be sure, but this is the logic: tackiness helps command and finish on a pitch, and that's OK. Sandpaper or K-Y Jelly help enhance movement, and that's not.

"In the cold weather in Minnesota, you had to have something to grip the curveball," says Jim Kaat, who starred for the Twins in the 1960s. "Pitchers for years have lobbied: if hitters can use pine tar to grip the bat better—it doesn't help 'em hit it any farther—we should be able to use pine tar. It's not like a Vaseline ball or anything like that. It just helps you get a little better grip on it."

Then again, it comes back to discretion: in 2014, when the Yankees' Michael Pineda brazenly smeared pine tar on his neck on a chilly night at Fenway Park, it was so overt that the Red Sox felt compelled to object. Pineda got a 10-game suspension and widespread ridicule. But generally, as long as a pitcher is discreet, the other side has no problem with pine tar.

This was even true in perhaps the most famous case of pine tar on a pitcher. On a damp and windy day at the 1988 NLCS in New York, Mets manager Davey Johnson asked umpires to inspect the glove of Dodgers closer Jay Howell. Joe West, the plate umpire who took the glove, said Johnson was a reluctant whistleblower.

"Somebody saw it on TV, called the Mets, and the Mets' owners got together and sent a message down to Davey and said, 'Go check him,'" West says. "Davey didn't want to check him. I said, 'This is the playoffs, David.' He says, 'I know, but my boss is telling me I've got to check him, and I've gotta do what they say.'"

The Mets had been tipped off to Howell by Tucker Ashford, a minor league manager in their system who had played with Howell on the Yankees, and with Perry on the Padres. Perry often pitched with a smudge on his cap, and while watching Game 1, Ashford noticed that Howell did, too.

Howell was ejected from Game 3 and suspended for the next two games, but the Mets almost felt bad about it. Wally Backman, their second baseman, told reporters he felt Howell's infraction was less serious than the scuffing the Mets suspected Scott of two years earlier.

"Pine tar doesn't make you throw the ball harder," Backman said. "It doesn't make his curve break more. It's different than a guy using Vaseline or sandpaper. It's not up to me to pass judgment on the suspension, but I think the rule has to be rewritten or clarified."

All these years later, it never has been. In the 2006 World Series, at least, the penalty was less severe. When the Cardinals spotted a pine-tar-like smudge on the pitching palm of the Tigers' Kenny Rogers, La Russa asked the umpires to check. Rogers cleaned off his hand—he claimed it was dirt—and kept pitching, earning the Tigers' only victory of the series.

The next spring, I spent part of an exhibition game with Bob Feller as he signed autographs for fans in Winter Haven, Florida. One of them asked just what Rogers had been doing in that World Series game. Feller, as quick with opinions as he once was with fastballs, did not hesitate.

"He was trying to cheat," Feller said. "It's not the first time anyone's ever done it. They've been doing it from Day 1."

––––––––––

But how much do they really do it anymore? Pine tar is one thing—cheating by the letter of the law, yes, but not by the spirit. Whatever happened to the spitball, the Hall of Fame pitch of Chesbro and Walsh, Coveleski and Faber, Grimes and Perry? Richie Ashburn—he of the "crapping spitter" charge to Burdette—always thought of pitchers as shifty characters, never to be trusted. Where have all the scoundrels gone?

When I asked Perry in 2018 why more pitchers were not as, shall we say, *crafty* as they were in his day, he had a short but telling answer: "Well, maybe they don't need it." Dan Plesac, who pitched in more than 1,000 games, agreed.

"You're not looking for a Don Sutton now, a guy that can sink it and cut it and make the ball move," Plesac says. "If you don't have velocity, you can't pitch anymore. How many guys, how many real power pitchers, need to scuff the ball to be successful? Not many. You don't need to, if your stuff is that good."

Plesac works for MLB Network, founded in 2009, the hub of baseball's vast and ever-expanding visual empire. Every fan can watch games on the At Bat app. Every team has a bank of video screens, usually just off the dugout, showing every conceivable angle for replays and analysis. Good luck evading the most sophisticated alarm system in baseball history.

"When there's so many TV cameras, it's so hard to get away with it," says Jason Giambi, who played 20 seasons in the majors. "Obviously you're gonna get a few guys who've got pine tar in their glove and things like that to get a better grip on the ball. But the game has definitely evolved. You've got slow-motion, all these angles. Not only do you have players watching it, you've got the video guy down in the tunnel, and then your other video guys running the whole room upstairs.

"So you have so many sets of eyes on these guys, and especially if they see a pitch that looks really abnormal, the guy rewinds it 5,000 times: 'OK, what did he do different? Oh, he went to the side of his pants, he went to his belt, he went to the top of his hat.' Then they start to put together the timeline of every time he's pitched, does that ball do the same thing? What about his last start, his start before that? And before you know it, they've got it down—all right, go tell the umpire to check his hat, or check the side of his pants, or check inside his glove. You can't hide anymore."

But what if you could? What if maybe, just maybe, the next Preacher Roe was hiding in plain sight on a diamond near you, fiendishly fooling all the viewers and video technicians at the ballpark and beyond?

He could blacktop a lot of driveways by selling those secrets—and he'd probably keep the supplies after finishing the job. The sticky sealant just might come in handy.

THE
CUTTER

At the End, It Will Move

Roy Halladay threw the first no-hitter I ever saw, in Philadelphia for the opener of the 2010 playoffs. I was glad it was him. You never know if you'll see a no-hitter, and I felt honored to witness his moment. Halladay had enthralled me like nobody else when I covered the Yankees in the first decade of the 2000s, and he was the Blue Jays' ace. He made a lineup of seasoned stars look feeble, baiting them into check swings, weak pop-ups, and harmless ground balls.

"Toughest on me? Halladay, that sinker and cutter," said Derek Jeter, who batted .234 off Halladay. "I tried to just guess which way it's gonna go—and I always guessed wrong."

The playoff no-hitter, against the Cincinnati Reds, didn't feel random at all. All of us at Citizens Bank Park noticed something special going on, and even Halladay seemed to sense he might do it. After waiting 13 years to appear in the postseason, he looked like he could have kept going that way, forever.

"I was so ready for that opportunity, and I felt like I had prepared so long for it, it's just one of those where I felt like everything was on," he told me. "I was able to locate, I was able to work quick, I was able to do all the things I wanted to do. Those are few and far between."

Halladay and I spoke in March 2017 at a picnic table in Clearwater, Florida, in the shadow of the left field foul pole at the Phillies' spring training complex. He had just finished a morning session with the minor leaguers, coaching them on the mental side of pitching. He paused.

"But, you know, it's funny. When those actually happen it's so anti-climactic, because you're out there and it's simply just making pitches. And all of a sudden it's over, and it's kind of like, 'Well, now what?' You want to keep going. You feel like, 'Well, geez, there should be something more.'"

Eight months after our conversation, Halladay's family and friends gathered at that Clearwater ballpark to eulogize him. The son of a commercial pilot, he had learned to fly in retirement and reveled in the pursuit. Halladay was 40 years old and living his dream when he died, his small plane plunging upside down into shallow water in the Gulf of Mexico. He left behind a wife, two sons, and a legacy as a dedicated craftsman who strove constantly to improve.

Halladay always seemed very serious. You'd get to the ballpark four hours early and he'd be there, alone, running up the concrete steps like Rocky Balboa at the Art Museum. He never seemed much for conversation, but I had felt moved to shake his hand in the clubhouse before the 2008 All-Star Game in the Bronx, just to tell him I appreciated the way he went about it. He smiled and thanked me.

I didn't know it, but Halladay was in the process, right then, of reinventing himself for a brief but glorious final burst of success. He had already won a Cy Young Award and made five All-Star teams for Toronto. But he thought he could improve his cutter, which was not as consistent as he wanted. He suspected the problem was his thumb position, but he was not sure. Sharing a clubhouse with Mariano Rivera, he knew what to do.

Rivera was a legend by then, on his way to a record 652 career saves, five championships, and a 2.21 earned run average, the best of anyone born after 1889. He had become synonymous with the cutter, a pitch he found by accident but mastered like no other.

"Mariano really helped me," Halladay said. "When I got a chance to talk to him, sure enough, he told me that one of the keys for him was making sure he wrapped his thumb under and got it on the opposite side of the ball."

When Halladay was at his best, hitters had no time to tell which way his pitches would go. Would they bank this way for a sinker, or that way for a cutter?

To keep hitters honest, both pitches needed to be sharp. When he threw his sinker, with his index and middle fingers along the narrow seams, Halladay placed his thumb directly underneath his index finger on the bottom of the ball. When he threw his cutter, which he held with his index and middle fingers across the wide part of the seams, he had always put his thumb in the same spot.

Rivera showed Halladay his technique, bending his thumb at the knuckle and tucking it under the ball, so the nail was even with the middle finger, not the index finger. This kept the thumb pad from blocking the ball's spin as it left his hand, allowing the index and middle fingers to pull through, unimpeded, and send it on its path. I gave Halladay a ball and he wrapped it in Rivera's grip, holding his arm out straight.

"So now if you look at it from behind, you have all the ball sticking out on this side," he explained, and from the pitcher's perspective, you could see at least half the ball peeking out from the left side of the hand. The rest of the ball was covered up by Halladay's fingers.

"So now it's overloaded. It almost has to go that way. When I got my thumb underneath [the index finger], it was still centered. But as soon as I get it moved over, then all of a sudden, it overloads the ball on that side."

Did it feel natural right away?

"It took a little while," Halladay continued, "and it was so awkward at times that when it was really good, I traced my fingers on the ball with a pen. I just took a black ballpoint pen and traced it, right where my finger placement was, and I put it in my locker and just stored it and kept it with me. Well, the next spring, I was throwing it and it wasn't working, I wasn't getting results out of it. So I went back and picked up that ball and just grabbed it without looking at the marks. And sure enough, my thumb was back to here, where it felt comfortable.

"So I put it back on that mark where it was a little uncomfortable at first, but sure enough, it came right back. Then you get used to it, and you're like, 'OK.' But it was a pitch that you really had to monitor where you were, how you grip it, because you could get in bad habits just from long tossing. It's just an odd place to throw a ball."

Halladay beat the Yankees three times in the second half of the 2008 season; when Rivera's teammates learned of his generosity to a rival, they fined him in kangaroo court. For the next three seasons, one with Toronto and two with the Phillies, Halladay was never better. He went 57–26, won another Cy Young Award, threw a perfect game to go with the playoff no-hitter, and led all qualified pitchers in earned run average, at 2.53, while throwing the most innings.

A Phillies fan was so taken by Halladay that he started a blog called "I Want to Go to the Zoo with Roy Halladay"; when he retired, Halladay actually did go to the zoo with him. The site made "cutter" into a verb, and broke down Halladay's strikeouts into "cuttered" and "so cuttered." The pitch could not be ignored: in those first three seasons after the tip from Rivera, Halladay threw the cutter more often than he ever had before.

"I didn't get the Mariano cutter," Halladay insisted, but he never stopped trying to perfect it. He was never far from the baseball with Rivera's grip traced onto it.

"I'd keep it in my locker, and when we'd go on the road I put it in my travel bag," he said. "Stuck it in a shoe, wherever I went, and if I was struggling I'd just pick it up. I carried it the rest of my career."

Halladay retired after the 2013 season with three compressed discs in his back, a side effect of all that running he did between starts. He never reached the World Series, but found, to his surprise, that this did not really matter. In the end, all he wanted was a *chance* to win it, to prove to himself that he could be the same pitcher when the whole baseball world was watching. Maybe, he could be even better.

Halladay finished with a 203–105 record and a 3.38 ERA. In December 2018 he was scheduled to headline the Hall of Fame ballot, posthumously, with Mariano Rivera.

The first decade of baseball in the new century ended with a cutter. With two outs in the top of the ninth inning at Yankee Stadium, in Game 6 of the 2009 World Series, Rivera angled his tenth pitch to the Phillies' Shane Victorino just a bit lower than usual. It came in like a knee-high fastball, 91 miles an hour, and darted down and in—not much, but just enough for Victorino to pull a harmless grounder to second base for the final out. It was the fourth time Rivera had secured the last out of the World Series, more than anyone in baseball history.

The pitchers in that World Series highlighted the era's defining trick. Cliff Lee won Games 1 and 5. Rivera saved Games 2 and 4. Andy Pettitte won Games 3 and 6. All of them featured the cutter as their primary weapon. A month after their loss, the Phillies traded Lee and upgraded to Halladay. When they brought Lee back in 2011, they set a franchise record with 102 wins in the regular season.

Lee would pitch 13 years in the majors, with one Cy Young Award and a 7–3 postseason record. In his prime, nobody had better command. His fastball never averaged even 92 miles an hour, but it carried him through college and into the pros. It wouldn't have brought him much further without a cutter as a complement, in place of his ordinary slider.

"Cliff didn't throw hard, so what it did was it gave him another element of guys laying off his fastball," says Ace Adams, his pitching coach at Class A Jupiter in the Expos' farm system. "He threw 88 to 92, and when you have that late cutter instead of using a four-seamer in, that just jams 'em. They're looking for a fastball in a hitter's count and all of a sudden here comes a cutter and it's late, right on your hands. It blows their bat up. It gave him more leeway with his regular fastball. Now he could throw that thing right down the middle and let it run, and they couldn't sit on it because they knew he had this cutter. So that changed him."

Lee learned the cutter from Adams in 2001, and by the end of the next season, he was in the majors with Cleveland. Adams learned the pitch from Ray Fisher, a right-hander for the Yankees and the Reds from 1910 to 1920. When Fisher wasn't throwing the spitter—legal back then—he threw cutters. He started and lost Game 3 of the 1919 World Series, in Chicago's Comiskey Park against the infamous Black Sox, who had lost the first two games on their way to throwing the series.

After his pitching career, Fisher would spend decades as the head baseball coach at the University of Michigan, where the baseball field is named for him. He was retired by 1971, when Adams arrived at Michigan as a left-handed pitcher, but would help out the team almost every day, working with the pitchers at Yost Field House, where the hockey team now plays. Fisher was very thin and not quite six feet tall, but his hands were enormous; each one could hold five baseballs.

He was 84 then, too old to throw, but he could demonstrate technique, always emphasizing "wrist pop" to make the ball spin. Adams eagerly soaked up his tips and stories, and would walk to Fisher's house from his West Quad dorm in Ann Arbor to watch the World Series on TV. Fisher thought modern pitchers were soft, compared to those from his day, but he gladly analyzed their stuff for Adams, and shared memories of his time on that stage.

"They were blowing it on purpose and I still couldn't beat 'em," Fisher would say. "We all knew they were getting paid, and it actually made us a little nervous, because we knew they were trying to blow it and if we didn't beat 'em, it was embarrassing. So it wasn't fun. We knew it was going on, we heard everything. We didn't know everything behind the scenes, but we all knew. Damn right we knew."

Three of the White Sox who would be banned for life—Chick Gandil, Shoeless Joe Jackson, and Swede Risberg—had hits that led to runs off Fisher. Still, he did not pitch badly, allowing just two earned runs in seven and two-thirds World Series innings. There's no precise data on which pitches he threw, of course, but it's safe to say the cutter was among them, though Fisher always called it the cut fastball.

"He taught me to off-center it, hook my hand a quarter-turn, and let it rip," Adams says. "That's how I've always taught it. If you really throw it right, it goes across a little bit and then it goes down a little—just a little. And if you don't throw it right, if you get around it, it might break too early and it just goes across and might hang a little bit. But the ones that really have that lateness to it, it goes across and down and you really get a good rip down through your middle finger.

"Anyone can throw it—just off-center that son of a bitch, hook your hand, and let it fly, brother!"

The cutter lends itself to such excitement. It is meant to be thrown aggressively, and to act out the verb in its name. It aims to inflict damage, to take something whole and chop it up: the wood in the hitter's hands, yes, but also his confidence. A good inside cutter veers off course so late that the only way to hit it on the barrel is to pull it foul. The batter must guess where the pitch will end up; he does not have time to actually see its movement.

Pitchers, and not just Fisher, knew of this weapon long ago. Without video, we'll never know the exact movement on the extraordinary curveball of Hilton Smith, the Hall of Fame pitcher from the Negro

Leagues in the 1930s and '40s. But Smith could shape his breaking ball various ways; perhaps one moved like a cutter.

"We had to have two curveballs, a big one and a small one," Smith said in *Voices from the Great Black Baseball Leagues.* "Now they call it a slider, but those guys were throwing it years and years back."

Bob Shaw—who pitched for the White Sox in the 1959 World Series, their next after the Black Sox scandal—describes the cutter in his pitching manual as an offshoot of the slider, without using the term:

> When you don't have to throw a strike, break the ball flat and inside, belt-high. Percentages are that the batter will hit the ball foul if he makes contact. This is a good way to jam the hitter.

Billy Williams, the left-handed-hitting Hall of Famer who played most of his career for the Cubs in the 1960s, loved to drop his hands and attack the low slider. But just a slight adjustment, he said in 2015, turned that pitch into the toughest kind he faced: "It's a slider, but not down—coming in from a right-hander. It's belt-high, where you can't get extended. It's called a cutter now."

One of the most famous moments of baseball's black-and-white TV age—Bill Mazeroski's home run that won the 1960 World Series for the Pirates—came off a cutter.

"It was a high fastball; high cutter, really," says Ralph Terry, the Yankees pitcher who threw it. "It was moving a little."

The next Yankees pitcher to give up a World Series–ending hit also did it on a cutter. In Game 7 of the 2001 World Series, Luis Gonzalez floated a Rivera cutter into shallow left field for a single, winning the title for the Diamondbacks. By then, everyone knew what pitch Gonzalez had hit. Who knew they'd been throwing cutters so many decades before?

"Well," Terry says, smiling, "they just put a new name on it."

———

Chili Davis came to bat about 10,000 times in the majors. As a coach, he has studied countless more at-bats by his hitters. The cutter, he insists, has been around forever.

"Pitches have names now," he says. "They didn't have names back then. Back then it was fastball, breaking ball. You might have a curveball or a slider, some guys had better curveballs than others. You had the sinker guys, you knew the ball would sink and run away. And you had cutter guys—Dave Dravecky, Woodie Fryman, Jerry Reuss, Andy Pettitte, latter-day Mariano Rivera, even Jim Abbott threw a cutter.

"But you didn't walk out there and go, 'Hey, this guy, he's got a cutter, two-seamer, four-seamer, sinker. I mean, there's too many names for one pitch. It's a fastball—this guy can get into your kitchen if you let him, and he lives in there, because he's trying to break your bat. He's trying to crowd you, he's trying to jam you, and you knew that they could go out there, too. So basically you picked a side that you wanted to beat them on."

A fun example of the cutter's effectiveness was the pitch that ended the fourth game of the 2000 World Series. The Mets trailed the Yankees by one run, and with one more out they would fall behind three games to one. Matt Franco, a lefty, came up to pinch hit. He stood far from the plate, giving himself a little more room to clear his hands and connect with Rivera's best pitch.

The cutter would beat Franco, even though Rivera did not throw it. He and the catcher, Jorge Posada, recognized that with Franco standing way out there, he could never reach a four-seam fastball on the outside corner. So that is where Rivera put it, and Franco went down looking in his only World Series at-bat.

"I thought for sure he was going to come inside," Franco reflected the next spring. "He'd done it to me before, and I've seen it on TV a thousand times, just breaking bats with that cutter in. I wasn't going to get beat that way. He made two great pitches and there was basically no chance."

The cutter has that power. Nobody wants to face it, because it's so hard to square up no matter which way you hit. Mark Teixeira, a switch-hitter for 14 seasons, calls the cutter the pitch that equalizes everything. Deception is critical to every pitch, but the cutter changes its form so late that the hitter can feel helpless. It looks like a ball and zips into the strike zone, or it looks like a strike and bends in toward your belt.

"You almost have to commit and anticipate, but the problem with the cutter is you still have the velocity and it moves so late," Cal Ripken Jr. says. "If a ball spins, or a curveball starts at your front left shoulder and you know it breaks off, you can kind of gauge where it's gonna end up. But the cutter is more unpredictable in that it comes in like the fastball and sometimes it's just a little movement, sometimes it's bigger movement, sometimes it's a little later. And does it come in or go away? The sweet spot's only so wide, so you either hit on the end or you hit it in—but it hurts like hell either side."

For most pitchers, especially those who don't throw very hard, that kind of weak, uncomfortable contact is the whole point. Even for a pitcher who relies on other stuff, it can be essential. Marco Estrada was basically a league-average pitcher for parts of seven seasons, getting by with a changeup, a curveball, and a fastball with a high spin rate. He added a cutter in 2015, with Toronto, and led the AL in fewest hits per nine innings in each of his first two seasons with it.

"Back in the day when I'd fall behind, I'd have to go to a four-seam fastball that's about 88 miles an hour," Estrada said at the 2016 All-Star Game. "You're not gonna get away with much; you have to make sure you locate that pitch. Nowadays, if I fall behind and throw a cutter, I don't really have to be perfect with it, and I kind of want them to swing at it anyways. Maybe it'll cause weak contact, maybe a ground ball or a pop fly. It's just something with a little bit of movement that throws the hitters off."

Yet the hybrid nature of the pitch held back its spread for decades. It's not quite a fastball or a slider, so when a pitcher relies too heavily on his cutter, which requires pressure on one finger, he might lose velocity on his fastball, which requires pressure on two. This happened to Dan Haren, but Haren didn't mind; his fastballs at 90 and 91 were straight and hittable, and his cutters at 88 and 89 missed barrels. He loved the pitch, but for many, a slower, fastball-ish pitch is bound to be alarming.

Another problem, some coaches fear, is the umpire. When a startled hitter gives a theatrical response to the cutter's late action, the umpire might not call the pitch a strike. And because the cutter stays on or near the same plane as the fastball, without as much tilt as a slider, if it doesn't have much movement it's just an ordinary fastball begging to be crushed.

Then again, any pitch in the wrong location is dangerous for a pitcher. The advantage of the cutter is the timing of the action. Mark Melancon, a three-time All-Star closer, says he thinks about "literally cutting through the right half of the ball," and believes such conviction imparts the pitch with its ferocity. It's as if the pitch is just so determined to be a fastball that it won't give in and move until the very last moment.

"When you spin a bowling ball, it goes straight for three-quarters of the lane, and then that last quarter of the lane, it cuts—and that's when hitters' eyes can't actually catch up to the ball," Melancon says. "They can't see the last 13 to 15 feet. Hand-eye coordination isn't that good when a ball's coming in at that speed. They're literally guessing where it's going to end up, and not seeing where. They're anticipating but they can't physically see it."

Many pitchers find that their hand naturally finishes one way or the other, producing a cut or sink on their fastballs. Ron Darling, a righty, had no problem getting his fastball to run in on righties, but no matter what he tried, he could not get the opposite movement. Pitchers who mastered the sinker and cutter, like Halladay and Greg Maddux, conjured a delta effect in hitters' minds: the pitch would look the same for a while, but they never knew if it would take a left or right exit from the tunnel.

Before he learned to master the slider, perhaps as well as any pitcher ever, Steve Carlton threw a cutter. He thinks it's an ideal pitch to teach kids, because it generates the movement they want without the strain.

"All you do on the cutter is you load it up—say the top of the ball is 12 o'clock, you just load up your index finger and middle finger on the outside part of the ball, on the left or the right of what would be perceived as 12 o'clock—and throw it like your fastball, and it starts to cut on you," Carlton says. "That's fairly easy to do. That's how I teach kids, so that way you don't have to twist, because kids want to twist it to make it curve and dip and stuff like that."

When people ask Jon Lester about his cutter, they are often amazed by its simplicity. It is not what pitchers call a "feel pitch," one that requires precise, almost delicate, execution. Lester, one of the best big-game pitchers of recent times, says his hand naturally finishes inward and finger pressure takes care of the rest.

"I want to throw a fastball with my middle finger, basically; that's the feeling I want to feel," Lester says. "I don't want to say it's an easy pitch to learn—but it is."

———————

Jerry Reuss joined the Dodgers in a trade at the start of the 1979 season. The team had won the last two National League pennants, but stumbled to a losing record. Reuss went 7–14, turned 30, and lost his starting job.

Banished to the bullpen, where he would need just two pitches, Reuss focused on his fastball and curve. While throwing in the bullpen, his fastball started slicing in, late. Mark Cresse, the bullpen catcher, asked Reuss what he was doing. Quite by accident, Reuss said, he had been holding the ball a bit off-center and could feel it coming off the inside of his middle finger. He was putting it right where he wanted, too, and Cresse suggested he use it in games.

"I saw the reaction that the hitters gave," Reuss says. "They looked at the pitch and they looked out at me and I could see them squint their eyes as if to say, 'What was that?' And then I said, 'Whoa, we might have something here.'"

Hitters couldn't read the ball coming out of Reuss's hand; would it run, like the two-seamer he'd always thrown, or cut? Larry Bowa, the veteran Phillies shortstop, confronted Reuss one day: "I know you're cheating, and I'm gonna figure out how." Reuss humored him. He wasn't cheating, but he was glad to know he was in Bowa's head. With the cutter working, he could pitch more confidently with his other stuff. Never much of a strikeout guy anyway, Reuss embraced a pitch intended for weak contact, scribbling all the benefits on a legal pad as an unofficial contract with himself.

"It was one of those domino effect kinds of things," Reuss says. "You don't walk anybody if you get somebody out on three pitches. You're throwing strikes, and then it went into what happened defensively. I had a good defense behind me; there were some flaws, but each of them was made better because they played on their toes, they never got back on their heels. They would make plays for me that they weren't making for other pitchers that were going deeper into the count."

By shaving 10 or 20 pitches off each start, Reuss figured, he could be stronger later in the season and pitch a few more years. Both hunches were right. In 1980, Reuss would throw a no-hitter and win the *Sporting News'* comeback player of the year award. The next year he helped the Dodgers win a championship, shutting out Houston in the division series clincher and beating the Yankees' Ron Guidry, 2–1, with a five-hitter in Game 5 of the World Series. His first few seasons with the cutter were the best of a 22-year career that spanned four decades.

"I had a fabulous run, unlike anything else I had in my career," Reuss says. "And it was all due to the cutter."

Yet the cutter did not catch on. Surely others were throwing it, Reuss says, but he could not think of anyone. Many pitchers, it seems, developed cutters without knowing what they were really trying.

This is how it happened for a left-hander at the University of Michigan—what is it about that school and this pitch?—in the mid-1980s. The pitcher already had a natural cut to his fastball, and when he threw it with his index and middle fingers across the narrow seams, instead of with them, his middle finger caught the curve of a seam just as he finished, imparting more drastic inward movement.

Most people did not think of this pitch when they considered the pitcher, Jim Abbott, who was born without a right hand. He balanced his glove on his right arm as he delivered the pitch, then switched it to his left hand in case he needed to make a play. There has never been a pitcher like him, but it was not just courage and will that made Abbott an Olympian, a first-round draft pick by the Angels, and a 10-year major leaguer. It was the cutter.

"That little grip kind of became a pitch of its own," Abbott says. "And when I got up to professional baseball I heard people start referring to it as a cutter. It wasn't a slider, it wasn't a fastball, it was a cutter. And I said, 'Oh yeah, great—I have a cutter.'"

In 1989, his first pro season, Abbott went to spring training expecting an assignment to Double-A. But he made the Angels without a day in the minors, because his cutter was so explosive. Growing up in Flint, Michigan, Abbott had rooted for his catcher, the former Tiger Lance Parrish. Now he was hurting Parrish with a weapon that was ready for the majors.

"I rode one in on his thumb one day and he literally stood up and threw his glove on the ground, because his thumb hurt so much," Abbott says. "It was a striking experience, like: 'Man oh man, that's Lance!' And he started wearing this plastic thumb protector inside of his glove to stop it from running in on him. Definitely, some catchers didn't like it all that much."

Abbott won 40 games in his first three seasons with the Angels and peaked with a no-hitter for the Yankees in 1993. The final batter, the switch-hitting Carlos Baerga, chose to bat lefty against Abbott, to keep the cutter away instead of boring in. Abbott finessed him with a slider and Baerga grounded out to short.

The Yankees could have had another lefty with a cutter, Al Leiter, but by then they had traded him to Toronto. Leiter helped the Blue Jays win the World Series in relief that year, and two years later he began a decade-long run as a top-of-the-rotation starter, mostly for the Mets. With Toronto in 1995, he lost three times to the Rangers but still made a strong impression on their brawny lineup. After one of the games, Dean Palmer and others complimented him on his new pitch.

"When did you start throwing a cutter?" they said.

"A cutter?" replied Leiter, incredulous. "I throw a slider."

"Man, you can call it what you want," they said. "But that is a cutter."

For Leiter, it was a revelation. In his early years with the Yankees, Ron Guidry and Dave Righetti had emphasized the slider to complement his fastball and curve. In time, Leiter threw the pitch harder and harder—and when the Rangers called it something else, he realized it wasn't a slider anymore, but a fastball that cuts. To Leiter, that distinction is important.

"I've told minor league guys forever: 'When you're throwing your cutter, it's a *"fuck you"* pitch,'" says Leiter, whose enthusiasm for his craft is so endearing that you look right past the language. "You're off-set and you're throwing it with every bit the same effort as your fastball. Remember: a cutter is not a power breaking ball. It is a cut fastball, and that's a different mind-set. You've gotta understand: 'OK, I'm throwing a fastball and it's gonna cut, so I've got the same aggressiveness— and that's different than a slider.' A slider's a smaller, power breaking ball."

The pitch now called the cutter was widely dismissed as flat and useless—faster than a slider should be, without the sharp, downward angle, and slower than a pitcher's best fastball, without the precise location. Some pitchers knew how to use it; Leiter remembers Catfish Hunter describing how he baited pull-happy right-handed power hitters by cutting his fastball to get lazy flies to right center. But throwing cutters on purpose, with encouragement from coaches, was just starting to catch on in Leiter's prime.

In the 2000 World Series, Leiter matched cutters twice with Andy Pettitte of the Yankees. Pettitte started using it the same year as Leiter, in 1995, with encouragement from Billy Connors, a coach who had worked in Chicago with Maddux. In his early years, Pettitte said, he angled the pitch more like a slider, boring in on the back foot of a right-handed hitter. Toward the end, with a different pitching coach, Larry Rothschild, Pettitte made it a pure cutter again to compensate for his fading fastball.

"I was getting in on guys, but I was still giving up a lot of jam-shot hits," Pettitte says. "I was getting so frustrated, and Larry was like, 'Well, why don't we try to cut it like you used to?' So my last year and a half I broke out my cutter on the belt again, and that was a game-changer for me. By that time I had so much command of my mechanics and such an idea of pitching, of what I wanted to do."

In those final seasons, Pettitte had a winning record and a 3.49 ERA—better than expected for a pitcher over 40 who had retired for a year before his comeback. A few years later Pettitte suggested that C. C. Sabathia use the cutter, and Sabathia reversed three years of decline by throwing it almost 30 percent of the time.

But the cutter's best salesman was a man who used the pitch to take the final, triumphant leap for an athlete: from star to stratosphere.

———

Mariano Rivera comes to the World Series every year now, as a favor to Major League Baseball, to present a reliever of the year award named for him. The setting is quite familiar, since Rivera may be the greatest October pitcher ever. His ERA, across 96 postseason appearances, was 0.70. He earned 42 saves, matching his uniform number.

Before a game in the 2016 World Series, under the right field bleachers at Wrigley Field, Rivera reflected on the spread of the cutter.

Why was everyone throwing his pitch? Even a humble man had to state the obvious.

"Well, because they saw what I did for so many years, I believe," Rivera said. "There's no other explanation."

And what, exactly, makes that pitch so devastating?

"It's the rotation," Rivera said. "For me, it was the four-seam fastball rotation. You think it is something that will be straight, and it's not. At the end, it will move. That's a true cutter. Most of the guys using the cutter, they're kind of like sliders, because it has that slider spin; it doesn't have a fastball spin. A true cutter, it has four-seam fastball spin, and it moves. They think they're swinging at something that looks like a fastball, but it's not—and it comes with power."

Power was Rivera's specialty in 1996, his first full season, when he helped the Yankees win the World Series as a setup man and fanned nearly 11 batters per nine innings. He never matched that figure again, because he never pitched another season without the cutter.

It came to Rivera before a game at Tiger Stadium in June 1997, while playing catch with teammate Ramiro Mendoza. Just as Mendoza reached for Rivera's throw, the ball zinged about a foot to his right. Rivera could not explain the movement—he was simply throwing his regular fastball, he said—and after more of the same, Mendoza gave up. Rivera sought out the bullpen catcher, Mike Borzello, who would have equipment to protect himself from this sudden, violent action.

"He threw it at first and I'm like, 'OK, what was that?'" says Borzello, who joined the Cubs' coaching staff in 2011. "We took that ball out—maybe it was scuffed—and he did it again. I go, 'What are you doing?' He goes, 'I don't know.' This was a guy who used to have pinpoint four-seam command. It was an easy catch. He threw 95, 96, but it was straight—and now it was cutting."

Rivera got the save that night, but the next day he was still unsettled. He told Borzello they needed more work. The "cutter," as such, was not really a pitch; at that point, Rivera had never even heard of the term. He missed his precision four-seamer.

"He used to be able to throw the ball wherever he wanted," Borzello says. "So even though he pitched mostly with a four-seamer, he could use all quadrants of the strike zone. And now he didn't know where the ball was going."

After 20 pitches or so, Rivera still could not straighten the fastball. He kept trying to find it, for two or three weeks, but his old four-seamer was now a cutter. It was a gift so bountiful, Rivera would write in his book, that it might as well have been a million pounds of fish overwhelming his father's nets back home in Panama. But he did not know what he had.

"I didn't even try to do it," Rivera says. "I didn't try to make it. The Lord gave it to me. You ask me: 'Why me?' Well, I don't know. I don't know why me. You've got to ask the Lord that question."

In time, with subtle changes to his grip and finger pressure, Rivera could place the cutter wherever he wanted. But as soon as he unwrapped his new gift, the factory settings worked just fine: in to lefties, away from righties, the movement too late for hitters to detect.

It was enough to defeat a man before he even got to the batter's box. Facing Rivera with one out to go in the 1998 World Series, the Padres' Mark Sweeney lugged his bat to the plate with an unshakable thought rattling around his brain: *Don't strike out to end this.* It was the only time in his career, Sweeney said, that such a pessimistic vision entered his mind as he prepared to hit. Sweeney succeeded—kind of—by punching a ground out to third and bringing Rivera to his knees in joy.

The Padres' closer that fall, Trevor Hoffman, had 601 career saves to rank second on the career list. He stands in awe of Rivera.

"When you talk about pitching, you want to simplify things," Hoffman says. "I would have loved to be able to go: OK, here's ol' number one, little cut on it, mid-90s forever. I'm gonna get inside your kitchen and break your bat for a left-hander, and I'm gonna get it on the edge of your bat for a right-hander. It was pretty amazing."

Even those who could hit Rivera, like Ichiro Suzuki (6-for-15 life-time) routinely call his cutter the single toughest pitch they ever faced.

"If you say one pitch, then it's definitely Mariano Rivera's cutter, because you know it's coming and you still can't hit it," Suzuki says. "I think even if you take all the great pitchers that I've faced—besides the knuckleball, we'll put that aside—but even if they have a 100-mile-an-hour fastball and a split, if you knew the split was coming, you could do something with it. But in Mariano's case, you knew the cutter was coming, *you knew it was coming,* but it was still so tough."

The reason, to Lester, was that Rivera's cutter moved about two feet and did so later than anyone else's.

"Other guys' are back at 17, 18 feet from home plate, so there's longer to see the cut," he says. "Even though it's a smaller cut, there's longer to see it. That's what made Mariano's so unhittable: it was a four-seamer until it got to 12 feet. You have 12 feet to figure out how far that ball's gonna move."

Josh Donaldson ended the 2015 ALCS by bouncing a cutter from the Royals' Wade Davis to third base for the final out. It was a bitter ending for Donaldson, who would be named MVP of the American League, but the next spring he was convinced he'd been beaten by the best. Davis's cutter, he proclaimed, was the toughest pitch in baseball.

Maybe so—in that moment, anyway. But even Davis thinks Rivera's pitch was a cutter above his own.

"He's on a different planet," Davis says. "People have said he's the best because he mastered one pitch. It's like: no, he didn't master one pitch, he just threw a pitch that nobody else can throw. He had something that nobody sees. Hitters don't see that. You don't see a ball that moves like that, especially as accurate as it is. There'd be guys stepping in the box just waving at it, even later in his career, just waving at it. It's just a different pitch. That's why he's in a whole different category."

Rivera threw more than one pitch, and not just because of his extraordinary cutter command. He used a two-seamer effectively, especially near the end of his career, and always had the four-seamer to straighten a right-handed hitter who might be leaning over the plate. At the 2013 All-Star Game, he reminded the Giants' Sergio Romo—famous for his sweeping slider—to always protect his best pitch. Romo already knew this; he had ended the previous World Series with a tailing fastball down the middle to the Tigers' Miguel Cabrera, who was looking for the slider and never swung. Yet it thrilled Romo to hear the lesson reinforced from a master like Rivera.

"He protected that cutter the whole time," Romo says, "and nobody knew it."

The first two closers to eclipse Rivera's highest annual salary—$15 million—were Mark Melancon and Kenley Jansen, who both thrive with cutters. Neither learned the pitch from Rivera—Melancon, a former Yankee, got the most help from Brandon Lyon, a teammate with Houston—but Jansen's has a similar origin. He was throwing fastballs to Borzello, by then the Dodgers' bullpen catcher, without recognizing the natural weapon he held.

"Borzy caught Mariano, and he's the one who told me: 'You know your ball's cutting,'" says Jansen, a converted catcher. "That's when I started paying attention, and from there I realized the pitch was gonna become good for me. Because when I began, I always threw fastballs and I was like, 'Geez, why do they not hit that fastball?' I still didn't learn how to throw a secondary pitch, and they already put me in the big leagues without a secondary pitch. And then I find out my ball cuts."

Jansen's home mound, at Dodger Stadium, is right where Oakland's Dennis Eckersley stood as he faced a hobbled Kirk Gibson in the opener of the 1988 World Series. The right-handed Eckersley tried a backdoor slider to the left-handed Gibson, who famously swung on one leg to launch an indelible game-ending homer.

Somewhere in the stands that night was a 17-year-old from West Covina named Jason Giambi. In seven years he would be teammates with Eckersley, and later spend many years with Rivera on the Yankees. Before Rivera, Giambi says, the backdoor slider from Eckersley was about the only inward-moving pitch that a righty would throw to a lefty.

"Mariano really revolutionized the cutter inside, because that was always taboo for a right-handed pitcher, like, 'Oh, don't throw lefties in,'" Giambi says. "You could bank on it: it was sinkers down and away, changeups down and away, an occasional fastball inside to push you off the plate and then maybe like a runner—a running fastball at your hip to come back—but never was anybody talking about cutters in to lefties. Then Mariano took that fear away. Because he was so dominating, everybody was like, 'Shit, this guy's got one pitch and he's fucking dominating every lefty. I better learn it!'

"Because the advantage lefties had was, you would lean over the plate. If you really think about every pitch: changeup from a righty sinks down and away, a sinker sinks down and away, most guys' overhand breaking ball doesn't really break into you. There was Eck with the backdoor slider, but if you start to look, everything else is out over the plate—and Mo changed that. Everything started to be: *pound you in, pound you in* and then go away. So he really was a game-changer."

And if all that weren't enough, Giambi says, teams began to use more and more infield shifts toward the end of his career, which stretched through 2014. If lefties managed to pull the cutter fair on the ground, there was often another infielder stationed there to gobble it up.

Lots of cutters, lots of shifts, lots of misery for hitters.

"Now you're screwed," says Giambi, who was the oldest player in the league when he retired, a year after Rivera and apparently not a moment too soon.

Stephen Strasburg pitches for a living, and only hits because National League rules require it. The first cutter he ever saw from a batter's box came in a major league game, from the All-Star left-hander Cole Hamels. It terrified him.

"It looked so good," says Strasburg, who hits right-handed. "I was squared out there for the bunt and that thing comes right in on your hand. Your heart stops a little bit. You see it, you see it, you see it—and then all of a sudden you're like that."

Strasburg mimicked himself in a panic, reeling back his bat as the ball screams in and plunks it for a foul. Even if he had faced cutters as an amateur, the feeling then would have been much different, because of what he held in his hand. A hitter with an aluminum bat can still get jammed and make solid contact, because the whole bat is a sweet spot. A hitter with a wood bat knows how vulnerable it is; Rivera was so famously destructive that the Twins gave him a rocking chair made from lumber shards as a retirement gift.

"In college, with aluminum bats, the effects of a cutter weren't as apparent," Abbott says. "It wasn't until I started facing wood bats in spring training of my rookie year—when I broke a lot of bats, and a lot of balls got in on right-handed hitters—that the talk started coming: 'Oh, wow, what a cutter!' The wood bats really showed it more dramatically, the effectiveness of the pitch."

Even if pitchers resist the cutter as amateurs, they are wise to learn it quickly in the pros. The pitch is so easy to pick up and makes young hitters so uncomfortable that it can help achieve instant results. In the first decade of the 2000s, veteran hitters say, the cutter was not even mentioned on most advance scouting reports. Now it is essential for many pitchers to advance.

"Because it's so hard to handle opposite-sided hitters, the remedy by most pitching coaches in most organizations is, 'OK, we'll teach him a cutter,'" Astros manager A. J. Hinch said. "And as matchup-oriented as we've become as an industry, in order for guys to stay in the game and not be replaced by a specialist, most pitchers have resorted to the cutter."

As the cutter evolves, pitchers have become increasingly bold in where they throw it. The Angels' Mike Trout, the best player of his generation, calls the cutter the toughest pitch he faces—but not the kind from a left-hander.

"The front-door cutter," says Trout, a right-handed hitter. "If they have a two-seamer in and then they run a cutter front-hip, it's tough."

That's a risky pitch, designed to start on the hitter's body and then clip the front edge of the plate for a strike. If it catches too much of the plate, without the full force of a fastball, it can go a long way, which partially explains the surge in home runs in the middle of the 2010s. A lot of experiments blow up.

"Guys are getting killed with cutters, because hitters are adjusting to them," said Dave Duncan, the retired pitching coach, in late 2017. "They've been thrown enough of them now that they're reading them, number one, and they're not swinging at the ones that are off the plate inside. They're waiting for that pitcher to make a mistake with it, and when he does, it's like a batting practice fastball. More and more pitchers are getting beat on cutters and going, 'Goddamn, that was a good cutter!' Well, it wasn't a good cutter, because it was a strike.

"Cutters are purpose pitches now more than anything else, unless you have that really freaky guy that has a cutter like Mariano Rivera. That's different. That's a different pitch."

In 2017, Jon Lester threw the highest percentage of cutters among qualified major league starters: 27.6 percent, according to FanGraphs. At his peak, after Rivera's tutorial, Halladay threw it more than 40 percent of the time. On that March afternoon in 2017, Halladay could tell that patterns were changing.

"You'd hear hitters say that was the one pitch that really changed the game for a long time—but for some reason it's rare now to see many more guys that are still throwing cutters," Halladay said. "I see a couple here and there, but talking to a lot of guys it's just something that's not done a lot."

FanGraphs data shows that cutter usage had indeed dipped, but only a bit; it peaked at 6.2 percent usage by all pitchers in 2014, and was down to 5.5 percent in 2017. Those rates could be influenced by the tracking technology, though, and the fact that the cutter is a hybrid. Computers and scouts won't identify it precisely every time, but hitters know it's there.

The decline has been so slight that Leiter, now a broadcaster, says he hasn't even noticed it. Pitchers do throw more curveballs now, to complement the trend of high fastballs. But the best cutters still shatter hitters' bats, soften their contact, and scramble their senses.

"There's an embarrassment factor," Leiter says. "It's not just an end-of-the-bat roller to shortstop or fly ball to right. It's a jam-shot, my finger stings, my hands are sore, and I'm pissed off because I just broke my favorite bat. The effectiveness of this pitch goes beyond actually having a result from it. I used to do it a lot of times—bust a guy in and just miss. Let him be conscious of smelling that 88- to 91-mile-an-hour cut. It's an 'Oh shit!' pitch."

It's not a fastball. It's not a slider. But thankfully, for hitters, the best one has already come and gone. There will never be another Mariano Rivera. Roy Halladay knew that, and so does Rivera's own son, a minor league pitcher who cannot imitate his father's famous pitch.

Mariano Rivera Jr., drafted by the Nationals in the fourth round in 2015, throws a fastball, a slider, and a changeup. He has tried to throw a cutter, without much luck. He might find it someday, but he is realistic. The pitch already had its prophet.

"If it comes, it comes," Rivera Jr. says. "But only he can do it like that."

Acknowledgments

Some authors told me it was torture to write a book. I'm very lucky, then, because I loved it. I had three full years to write and report on a lifelong passion. But the biggest reason for all the fun was the deep roster of people who helped and inspired me.

Many years ago, Tony Gwynn told me he learned something new at the ballpark every day. At that moment, I knew I would need many lifetimes to understand even a small fraction of what really goes on in the game. Thank you to every person interviewed here for being my teachers, and giving so generously of your time and insights.

Brad Lidge was my first interview for this book, and, with his candor, set the template for all the other conversations to follow. Some of the people I was privileged to cover as a beat writer—especially Mike Mussina, Gil Patterson, Jamie Moyer, Bryan Price, Jason Giambi, Mark Teixeira, Al Leiter, and Bobby Valentine—were especially helpful. Others who took a keen interest included A. J. Ellis, R. A. Dickey, Ron Darling, Mike Montgomery, Dan Haren, Brian Bannister, and John D'Acquisto. I am grateful to you all.

I was there for C. J. Nitkowski's first major league win, when he beat Curt Schilling at the Vet, and he was there for me throughout this process, a one-batter specialist turned one-line-at-a-time pitching consultant.

Other friends in baseball helped more than they probably realize, with words of encouragement and acts of kindness. Thank you to Mark Attanasio, Jerry Dipoto, Derek Falvey, Mike Ferrin, Sam

Mondry-Cohen, J. P. Martinez, Dayton Moore, Rob Neyer, and Gus Quattlebaum. And I owe a lifetime of thank-yous to Dave Montgomery.

After nearly every interview, as soon as I shut off my recorder, I would text Derrick Goold and Ben Shpigel to share my excitement. Every time, wherever they were in the world, they responded immediately, and genuinely, as true friends do. Not once did they send me the "Are you for real?" Bitmoji in return.

Alex Ellenthal entered the game around the eighth inning, and gets the save for his cheerful, prompt, and accurate work transcribing hours of interviews. Thanks to Gaku Tashiro, a true pro, for tracking down and interviewing the God of Forkballs, Shigeru Sugishita.

Some of my favorite days in the last few years were the ones spent at the Giamatti Research Center at the Baseball Hall of Fame. It sounds almost too good to be true—*a library with everything ever written about baseball!*—but it's even better than I could have imagined. Thank you to all my friends in Cooperstown for their help and hospitality, including Jeff Idelson, Brad Horn, Jon Shestakofsky, Craig Muder, Cassidy Lent, John Odell, Matt Rothenberg, John Horne, Jim Gates, Jeff Katz, and Chris, Jen, Rick, and Christine Hulse. Thanks to Bob Kendrick of the Negro Leagues Baseball Museum in Kansas City, and also to Jon Wertheim and Emma Span for letting me peruse the incredible trove of archives at the *Sports Illustrated* library—and to Jeff Pearlman for encouraging me to do so.

Besides the books listed in the Bibliography, I used information from other books and articles found at those libraries, and at the library in Wilton, Connecticut, where much of this book was written (at least when I wasn't writing at the Coffee Barn). I copied hundreds of pages of news clippings at the Hall of Fame, some from as far back as the 1800s, on dozens of pitchers and topics. I also consulted my own articles and articles on many websites (the SABR biographies at Baseball-Reference.com were especially helpful), viewed footage of old games and highlights online, and watched the video documentaries *Lefty: The Life & Times of Steve Carlton* (1994), *Knuckleball* (2012), and *Fastball* (2016). Most statistics come from Baseball-Reference.com and FanGraphs.

Thank you to the many folks who connected me to the voices you read in these pages, or provided help with photos. All of these people, and more, helped set up interviews or photo rights: Harvey Araton, Scott Boras, Rob Butcher, Greg Casterioto, Peter Chase, Gene Dias, Shelley Duncan, Lorraine Fisher, Steve Grande, Brad Hainje, Dan Hart, Tim Hevly, Jay Horwitz, Craig Hughner, Nate Janoso, Brad Lefton, Paul Lukas, Tony Massarotti, Valerie McGuire, Tim Mead, Adrienne Midgley, Laurel Prieb, Josh Rawitch, Matt Roebuck, Mike Sheehan, Bill Stetka, Bart Swain, Mike Teevan, Jim Trdinich, Rick Vaughn, Shana Wilson, and Jason Zillo. The forever-friendly Larry Shenk, who gave me my very first press pass, pointed the way to Steve Carlton, my baseball hero and the man I most wanted to interview.

My real hero, though, has always been Jayson Stark, who is the reason I do this and my standard for both writing and integrity. "Gods don't answer letters," John Updike once wrote, but I know that's wrong because Jayson answered mine when I was 14 years old. "You can't wear No. 32 for the Phillies," he wrote, "but writing about baseball is the next best thing." Boy, was he right.

Not only do I get to learn more about baseball every day, I get to do it around so many dedicated and talented media members whose work and friendship constantly inspire me. I'll always be indebted to those who gave me such a solid foundation in how to be a professional: Steve Insler, Paul Hagen, Bill Lyon, Scott Graham, Tim Kurkjian, Buster Olney, Bob Costas, George F. Will, Zack McMillin, Lee Jenkins, John Lowe, Peter Gammons, Mike DiGiovanna, Kevin Acee, Jim Street, Art Thiel, Dave Sheinin, Jack Curry, Dave Anderson, and George and Laura Vecsey. And I would never have survived a decade on the Met and Yankee beats without the camaraderie of pals like Peter Abraham, Dom Amore, Sam Borden, Pete Caldera, Ken Davidoff, Mark Feinsand, Dan Graziano, Bryan Hoch, George King, Andrew Marchand, Anthony McCarron, Sweeny Murti, Jesus Ortiz, T. J. Quinn, and so many more. Thanks also to my buddy Gar Ryness; the world needs more people who can imitate Bo Diaz's batting stance anytime, anywhere.

My closest friends in the world—The Posse, as we called ourselves on the mean streets of Fort Washington, Pennsylvania—keep me laughing every day: Joe Benjamin, Mike Daly, Jeff Decker, Mike McCuen, John Pasquarella, Tim Pies, and Jamie Trueblood. John and I started a little baseball magazine together at Germantown Academy in 1988, with Jamie as the art director and Tim as a columnist. I guess I took our project to the extreme.

Tim Roberts (the best seventy-fifth-round draft pick in Seattle Mariners history) and Dave Cote coached Little League with me for years. I cherished every moment and learned a lot about baseball, too. Nothing but "good game," guys.

I am proud to have spent nearly two decades at *The New York Times*, striving daily to live up to its standard of excellence. From the moment I met Neil Amdur, I wanted to work for him and make him proud. Thank you for taking a chance on a beat writer who wasn't old enough to rent a car at his first spring training. The unwavering support of editors like Bill Brink, Tom Jolly, Patty LaDuca, Naila Meyers, Carl Nelson, Gwen Knapp, Jason Stallman, and the late, great Janet Elder has meant everything. Colleagues Dave Waldstein, James Wagner, and Billy Witz uphold our tradition of smart, incisive *Times* baseball writing, while Fern Turkowitz and Terri Ann Glynn have made the whole place go with patience and smiles. The incomparable Jay Schreiber and I worked together on more than 5,000 articles, and I've never met anyone whose judgment and commitment I trust more. Thank you all.

Dan Shaughnessy of *The Boston Globe* is more than my favorite columnist; he's also a matchmaker. Dan introduced me to David Black, my agent, who took the time to understand my goals and motivations. I never could have done this without David's vision, guidance, and belief. Thank you for all of that, and most of all for connecting me with Bill Thomas, my editor at Doubleday, who called all the right pitches with the calmness and wisdom of a veteran catcher helping a rookie through the biggest game of his life. Big thanks to Bill's assistant, Margo Shickmanter, for all her essential work behind the scenes.

From the very first moment I stepped on a major league field, I wanted to be part of that world. I got there, quite literally, by kicking and screaming until my parents gave in. It was fireworks night at Veterans Stadium in 1982, and we had perfect seats for the show, 20 rows behind the third base dugout. But I was seven, and all I noticed was that fans from the upper deck in center field were leaving their seats to watch from the field. *From. The. Field.* I yelled and cried until my mom lifted me over the fence in foul ground, and I stood on the red rubber warning track for a few seconds, gazing up at the lights that ringed the top of the ballpark. After that, there was no going back, and ever since, my parents—John and Mimi—have continued to lift me up, nurturing my dreams in every possible way. More important, they have set a shining example for how to live.

My brother Tim hid my lucky hat before Game 4 of the 1983 World Series, but I love him anyway. My wonderful sister-in-law, Colleen, probably has no idea she's married to a thief who cost the Phillies a championship, but now she does. My brother Dave wears his hair like a member of those '83 Phillies, and I love him for it. Tim and Dave go by Bonesaw and Hoag now, and they're rock stars in Austin, Texas. Yes, they got all the talent.

I did throw a shutout in the 2006 media game at Fenway Park, and the next year I invited my father-in-law, Mike Lockhart, to see me dazzle 'em again. Instead, I gave up 10 runs and didn't make it out of the third inning. Thankfully, Mike has been nice enough to keep me in the family. My mother-in-law, Sue McHugh, is endlessly warm, loving, and accepting. To Tina, Jessica, Kate, Lizzy, Matt, and all of my aunts, uncles, cousins, and in-laws, thanks for always being there for me.

Shortly after I met my wife, Jen, the Yankees played the Braves in the 1999 World Series. She chose Mariano Rivera as her favorite player because his job was to end the games, which meant I could come home. Covering this sport keeps you away from the people you love, and without a patient, selfless, and understanding wife, I could never do it. Jen is beautiful, smart, compassionate, and kind, a dreamer who brings out the best in everyone she meets. Asking her to marry me was the easiest decision of my life, and she is the best role model our children could ever have.

I've written many thousands of words here, but nothing could properly describe how lucky I feel to be the father of four such amazing children—Lily, Mack, Caroline, and Rory, who make me proud every day, in so many ways. I love them more than they could ever know, and I admire them as people who make the world a whole lot brighter every day.

Bibliography

Most of the information in this book comes from more than 300 interviews conducted in person and by phone and email between January 2015 and March 2018. I also purchased and read dozens of books, including the following:

Abbott, Jim, and Tim Brown. *Imperfect.* New York: Ballantine, 2013.

Adair, Robert K., PhD. *The Physics of Baseball.* New York: HarperCollins, 2002.

Angell, Roger. *Late Innings.* New York: Ballantine, 1984.

———. *Season Ticket.* Boston: Houghton Mifflin, 1988.

Barney, Rex, with Norman L. Macht. *Rex Barney's Thank Youuuu.* Centreville, Md.: Tidewater Publishers, 1993.

Bouton, Jim. *Ball Four: The Final Pitch.* Champaign, Ill.: Sports Publishing, 2000.

Cairns, Bob. *Pen Men.* New York: St. Martin's Press, 1992.

Craig, Roger, with Vern Plagenhoef. *Inside Pitch.* Grand Rapids, Mich.: Wm. B. Eerdmans, 1984.

Darling, Ron. *The Complete Game.* New York: Vintage, 2010.

Dickson, Paul. *Baseball's Greatest Quotations.* New York: HarperCollins, 1991.

Feller, Bob, with Bill Gilbert. *Now Pitching Bob Feller.* New York: HarperCollins, 1990.

Ford, Whitey, with Phil Pepe. *Slick.* New York: William Morrow, 1987.

Freedman, Lew. *Knuckleball.* New York: Sports Publishing, 2015.

Gibson, Bob, and Reggie Jackson, with Lonnie Wheeler. *Sixty Feet, Six Inches.* New York: Doubleday, 2009.

Gibson, Bob, and Lonnie Wheeler. *Pitch by Pitch.* New York: Flatiron Books, 2015.

Grant, Jim "Mudcat," with Tom Sabellico and Pat O'Brien. *The Black Aces.* Farmingdale, N.Y.: The Black Aces, 2006.

Gutman, Dan. *It Ain't Cheatin' If You Don't Get Caught.* New York: Penguin, 1990.

Hart, Stan. *Scouting Reports.* New York: Macmillan, 1995.

Hernandez, Keith, and Mike Bryan. *Pure Baseball.* New York: HarperCollins, 1994.

Hershiser, Orel, and Jerry B. Jenkins. *Out of the Blue.* Brentwood, Tenn.: Wolgemuth & Hyatt, 1989.

Hollander, Zander. *The Complete Handbook of Baseball 1976.* New York: Signet, 1976.

———. *The Complete Handbook of Baseball 1987.* New York: Signet, 1987.

James, Bill, and Rob Neyer. *The Neyer/James Guide to Pitchers.* New York: Fireside, 2004.

Kahn, Roger. *The Head Game.* New York: Harcourt, 2000.

Knight, Molly. *The Best Team Money Can Buy.* New York: Simon & Schuster, 2015.

Kurkjian, Tim. *Is This a Great Game or What?* New York: St. Martin's Press, 2007.

Leavy, Jane. *Sandy Koufax: A Lefty's Legacy.* New York: HarperCollins, 2002.

Marichal, Juan, with Lew Freedman. *Juan Marichal.* Minneapolis: MVP Books, 2011.

Martinez, Pedro, and Michael Silverman. *Pedro.* New York: Houghton Mifflin Harcourt, 2015.

Mathewson, Christy. *Pitching in a Pinch.* New York: Penguin, 2013.

McCaffrey, Eugene V., and Roger A. McCaffrey. *Players' Choice.* New York: Facts on File Publications, 1987.

McGraw, Tug, with Don Yeager. *Ya Gotta Believe!* New York: Penguin, 2004.

Monteleone, John J., ed. *Branch Rickey's Little Blue Book.* New York: Macmillan, 1995.

Morris, Peter. *A Game of Inches.* Chicago: Ivan R. Dee, 2006.

Moyer, Jamie, with Larry Platt. *Just Tell Me I Can't.* New York: Grand Central Publishing, 2013.

Niekro, Phil, and Tom Bird. *Knuckle Balls.* New York: Freundlich Books, 1986.

Niese, Joe. *Burleigh Grimes: Baseball's Last Legal Spitballer.* Jefferson, N.C.: McFarland, 2013.

Palmer, Jim, and Alan Maimon. *Nine Innings to Success*. Chicago: Triumph, 2016.

Passan, Jeff. *The Arm*. New York: HarperCollins, 2016.

Pearlman, Jeff. *The Bad Guys Won!* New York: HarperCollins, 2004.

Peary, Danny. *We Played the Game*. New York: Hyperion, 1994.

Perry, Gaylord, with Bob Sudyk. *Me and the Spitter*. New York: Signet, 1974.

Quigley, Martin. *The Crooked Pitch*. Chapel Hill, N.C.: Algonquin Books, 1984.

Reuss, Jerry. *Bring in the Right-Hander!* Lincoln: University of Nebraska Press, 2014.

Richard, J. R., and Lew Freedman. *J.R. Richard: Still Throwing Heat*. Chicago: Triumph, 2015.

Ritter, Lawrence S. *The Glory of Their Times*. New York: William Morrow, 1984.

Ryan, Nolan, and Harvey Frommer. *Throwing Heat*. New York: Avon, 1990.

Seaver, Tom, with Lee Lowenfish. *The Art of Pitching*. New York: Hearst Books, 1984.

Shaw, Bob. *Pitching*. Chicago: Contemporary, 1972.

Smith, Red. *To Absent Friends*. New York: Atheneum, 1982.

Sowell, Mike. *The Pitch That Killed*. New York: Collier, 1989.

Stark, Jayson. *Wild Pitches*. Chicago: Triumph, 2014.

Terry, Ralph, with John Wooley. *Right Down the Middle*. Tulsa, Okla.: Mullerhaus Legacy, 2016.

Thorn, John, and John B. Holway. *The Pitcher*. New York: Prentice Hall, 1987.

Vincent, Fay. *We Would Have Played for Nothing*. New York: Simon & Schuster, 2008.

Wendel, Tim. *High Heat*. Cambridge, Mass.: Da Capo, 2010.

Westcott, Rich. *Masters of the Diamond*. Jefferson, N.C.: McFarland, 1994.

———. *Splendor on the Diamond*. Gainesville: University of Florida Press, 2000.

Will, George F. *Met at Work*. New York: Macmillan, 1990.

Williams, Ted, with John Underwood. *My Turn at Bat*. New York: Fireside, 1988.

Wright, Craig R., and Tom House. *The Diamond Appraised*. New York: Simon & Schuster, 1989.

Index

Illustration Credits

ABOUT THE AUTHOR

Tyler Kepner started covering baseball as a teenager, interviewing players for a homemade magazine that was featured in *The New York Times* in 1989. He attended Vanderbilt University on the Grantland Rice/Fred Russell sportswriting scholarship, then covered the Angels for the *Riverside Press-Enterprise* and the Mariners for the *Seattle Post-Intelligencer*. He joined *The New York Times* in 2000 and covered the Mets for two seasons, then covered the Yankees from 2002 to 2009. Since 2010 he has been the *Times'* national baseball writer. He lives with his wife and four children in Wilton, Connecticut.

HOW to TALK
to a LIBERAL
(If You Must)

Also by Ann Coulter

HIGH CRIMES AND MISDEMEANORS
The Case Against Bill Clinton

SLANDER
Liberal Lies About the American Right

TREASON
Liberal Treachery from the Cold War to the War on Terror

HOW to TALK to a LIBERAL

(If You Must)

The World According to

ANN COULTER

CROWN FORUM
NEW YORK

Published by Crown Forum, New York, New York.
Member of the Crown Publishing Group, a division of Random House, Inc.
www.crownpublishing.com

CROWN FORUM and the Crown Forum colophon are trademarks of
Random House, Inc.

Portions previously published in slightly different form in *Human Events,*
the Universal Press Syndicate, and *George* magazine.

DESIGN BY BARBARA STURMAN

Library of Congress Cataloging-in-Publication Data
Coulter, Ann H.
How to talk to a liberal (if you must) : the world according
to Ann Coulter / Ann Coulter.
p. cm.
1. Liberalism—United States.   2. United States—Politics and government—
1989–   3. Mass media—Political aspects—United States.   I. Title.
JC574.2.U6C67   2004
320.51.'3'0973—dc22   2004014791

ISBN 1-4000-5418-4

2 4 6 8 10 9 7 5 3 1

First Edition

For my mother,

Nell Martin Coulter

Contents

HOW to TALK
to a LIBERAL

(If You Must)

1

How to Talk to
a Liberal

———————— ◼ ————————

Historically, the best way to convert liberals is to have them move out of their parents' home, get a job, and start paying taxes. But if this doesn't work, you might have to actually argue with a liberal. This is not for the faint of heart. It is important to remember that when arguing with liberals, you are always within inches of the "Arab street." Liberals traffic in shouting and demagogy. In a public setting, they will work themselves into a dervish-like trance and start incanting inanities: "BUSH LIED, KIDS DIED!" "RACIST!" "FASCIST!" "FIRE RUMSFELD!" "HALLIBURTON!" Fortunately, the street performers usually punch themselves out eventually and are taken back to their parents' house.

Also resembling the Arab street, liberals are chock-full of conspiracy theories. They invoke weird personal obsessions like a conversational deus ex machina to trump all facts. You think you're talking about the war in Iraq and suddenly you start getting a disquisition on Nixon, oil, the neoconservatives, Vietnam (Tom Hayden discusses gang violence in Los Angeles as it relates to Vietnam), or whether Bill O'Reilly's former show, *Inside Edition*, won the Peabody or the Peanuckle Award. This is because liberals, as opposed to sentient creatures, have a finite number of memorized talking points, which they periodically try to shoehorn into unrelated events, such as when Nancy Pelosi opposed the first Gulf war in 1991 on the grounds that it would cause environmental damage in Kuwait. Oddly enough, about half of liberal conspiracy theories involve the Jews. So be prepared for that.

A major impediment to arguing with liberals is: They refuse to argue. Liberals' idea of a battle of wits is to say "Bush lied!" in front of adoring college audiences and be wildly applauded for their courage. They're like hack road comics who coax a cheap round of applause out of audiences by declaring, "I just quit smoking!" or "My wife just had a baby!" Without a Roman Coliseum–style audience to give them standing ovations for every idiotic utterance, you get the liberal disappearing act.

At a loss whenever anyone argues back, liberals have a number of stratagems to prevent conservatives from talking. They shout conservatives down; unplug reporters' microphones; edit conservatives' answers in pretaped TV shows (*Hardball*) to make the conservative look like a monkey; burn student newspapers; and heckle conservative speakers. When John Stossel went to Brown University for a report on "date rape," he was mobbed by angry protesters chanting, "Rape is not TV hype!"—and then his microphone cord was unplugged by an angry student. College dropout Michael Moore put a microphone in Republican Congressman Mark Kennedy's face and asked for his help in getting more members of Congress to send their own family members to fight the war on terror. Kennedy replied that he would love to and that he already had two nephews in the military, one on his way to Afghanistan. Moore's documentary shows Kennedy's image—but cuts his answer from the film.

There is probably no conservative student newspaper in the country that has not been trashed or burned by liberals. Meanwhile, there is no known instance of College Republicans burning or trashing liberal student newspapers. To the contrary, conservatives get a kick out of watching liberals try to thrash their way to a coherent argument ("BUSH LIED, KIDS DIED!"). In fact, if it weren't for conservatives with a taste for schadenfreude, literally no one would be listening to Air America—assuming it's still on the air by the time this book hits the stores.

Life was much better for liberals when there were only three TV stations airing precious little news. Back in the pre–cable news days, public political debate consisted exclusively of liberal Democrats debating radical Democrats. Now that conservatives are physically present on cable news, liberals are terrified they might have to respond to a conservative point, so liberals filibuster and interrupt, hoping to never hear it. Turn on your TV right now and you'll see a liberal—probably Julian Epstein—trying to filibuster his way out of having to respond to a conservative.

If you can somehow force a liberal into a point-counterpoint argument, his retorts will bear no relation to what you said—unless you were, in fact, talking about your looks, your age, your weight, your personal obsessions, or whether you are a fascist. In the famous liberal two-step, they leap from one idiotic point to the next, so you can never nail them. It's like arguing with someone with Attention Deficit Disorder.

Inasmuch as liberals can only win arguments when no one is allowed to argue back, they enjoy creating fictional worlds in movies and on TV where liberals finally get to win. Remember the Andy Hardy movies? Mickey Rooney and Judy Garland would be headed for disaster—until Andy shouted out, "I tell you what! Let's put on a play!" With liberals, it's "We're losing on the facts! Let's make a movie!"

In movies, liberals are invariably morally and intellectually superior. They are also good-looking, witty, compassionate, and always right—basically Bob Byrd, Jerry Nadler, Al Franken, and Hillary Clinton rolled into one adorable bunch. Only in Hollywood is Robert Redford considered a dead ringer for Bob Woodward, Emma Thompson for Hillary Clinton, Dustin Hoffman for Carl Bernstein, and Andy Garcia for Al Franken. Typically, Republicans are played by hard-boiled B-list types whose only other roles are as cruel high school football coaches or rogue army drill instructors. Reflect on the fact that Anthony Hopkins played both Nixon and Hannibal Lecter.

The only policemen in the universe who are not aware that "cop-killer bullets" have never killed a cop are the ones on *Law & Order*. Only in liberal fantasy movies like *Coming Home* is a patriotic hawk the impotent klutz who shoots himself in the foot, and the liberal dove the sexually potent one. Only in Hollywood could a sitcom that parodies a U.S. president and is titled *There's My Bush* be about George Bush rather than Bill Clinton. (The show was unceremoniously and quietly canceled because of low ratings.) In movies, we always learn that there is NO REASON, EVER, to fight a war. Unless the Earth is invaded by aliens from outer space with huge scary spaceships and death rays and men of all races and nationalities can unite against a common enemy—like in *Independence Day*. So if the Earth is ever invaded by hostile aliens from outer space, you won't have to ask liberals twice to take up arms in defense of Planet Earth.

It was inevitable, given what liberals value, that on the popular sitcom *Friends* beautiful actresses would be depicted hyperventilating over

George Stephanopoulos's fictional manhood when he drops his fictional towel. Only in the bizarro world of Hollywood can such a harmless little chap as George exude massive sexual potency. On HGTV, the female host of *What Not to Wear* leeringly jokes about seeing Bill Clinton in a Speedo. In real life, Monica Lewinsky can be heard on tape describing Clinton's executive branch thus: "Think of a thumb." No wonder liberals prefer the world of make-believe.

In addition to all Oliver Stone movies and all Michael Moore documentaries (Oliver Stone Without the Talent!), an extremely abbreviated list of liberal fantasy movies includes:

The Day After Tomorrow (not to be confused with *Next Friday*, starring Ice Cube)—message: LIBERALS ARE RIGHT ABOUT GLOBAL WARMING! The hyper-silly disaster epic is based on a book coauthored by UFO/black-helicopter/the-CIA-is-beaming-microwaves-into-my-teeth-fillings guru and late-night AM radio maven Art Bell.

The Cider House Rules—message: LIBERALS ARE RIGHT ABOUT ABORTION! Kindly small-town abortionist (Michael Caine) just wants to help unwed pregnant girls. Disaster strikes when it turns out the young lad taking over Caine's practice (Tobey Maguire) is opposed to abortion because it's "wrong." The lad soon learns the error of his ways after a black teenaged girl from a family of apple pickers is raped and impregnated by her own father and needs an abortion. (You can't remind people too often that most women having abortions were raped by their own fathers.) This film was a veritable ode to moral relativism and the hideous notion that there are no rules save the ones we make up ourselves as we go along. Shockingly, it only won a single Oscar.

The American President—message: DEMOCRATS WILL VOTE THEIR CONSCIENCES EVEN IF IT HURTS THEM POLITICALLY AND ALL REPUBLICANS EVER DO IS CALL PEOPLE NAMES. In this movie, Michael Douglas plays Bill Clinton as Clinton would like to be—handsome, thin, courageous, liberal, and widowed. The president's top Republican adversary goes on national TV and calls the president's girlfriend a "whore." So it's a plausible story.

Dave—message: LIBERALS ARE RIGHT ABOUT FEDERAL SPENDING ON THE HOMELESS! Only the president can put an end to homelessness, and he's got to cut $500 million in pork from the discretionary budget to do so. He finds the money by poring over the entire federal budget (during an "all-nighter") with the help of his tax guy, played by Charles Grodin. (Of course, to do that, the president would need a line-item veto. Now which party, do you suppose, supports a line-item veto and which opposes it?)

Of the dozens and dozens of nonfiction books to come out about the Clinton presidency, only one was made into a movie: *The Hunting of the President,* by fanatical Clinton apologists Joe Conason and Gene Lyons. (Message: LIBERALS WERE RIGHT ABOUT CLINTON, EVEN IF THERE ARE ONLY TWO LIBERALS LEFT DEFENDING HIM!) The intriguing plotline is this: A lot of mean people tried to bring down a great president.

Leaving aside which account most closely resembles the truth, which one of these sounds like a better movie plot:

Movie Plot A: Through the freak accident of a third-party candidacy, a lying, horndog Jimmy Swaggart type somehow ends up as president of the United States. As his Eva Perón–style wife tries to socialize all industry, the president gallivants with Hollywood starlets, has repeated affairs, accepts illegal campaign donations from foreign enemies, and uses the vast powers of the federal government to frighten and intimidate the people who get in his way. Some end up dead, some have their secret FBI files pored over by a former bar bouncer, some are audited by the IRS. He is finally brought down when he ejaculates on an intern's dress and lies about it under oath—and it turns out the intern has kept the dress!

Movie Plot B: For no reason whatsoever, a few oddball private citizens develop a deep personal antipathy for a "Third Way," moderate Democratic president.

Amazingly, Hollywood actually made a movie, *Bob Roberts,* in which the slick, cosmetic tricks of the sophisticated right-wing political machine hoodwink the American people. (So that's why liberals are losing all the arguments in real life!)

Since cable news has begun forcing liberals to confront opposing points of view in real life rather than movie scripts where the Republicans' only argument is to call the president's girlfriend a "whore," liberals have been trying to drop emotionalism as their main argument. Their new posture is mock hardheaded realism. Now they begin sentences with phrases like, "The fact of the matter is," or "Experts say"—followed by comically false assertions. Liberals flex their spindly little muscles and announce that everything that used to make them cry—gun ownership, racial profiling, missile defense, school vouchers, torturing terror suspects—simply "doesn't work." *The fact is, it doesn't work, this is according to several studies, and no, you can't see them, why would you ask?*

After nineteen nearly identical-looking Muslim men hijacked four airplanes and murdered 3,000 Americans, people weren't in much of a mood for liberal preachiness about racial profiling. So instead of crying and trying to make Americans feel guilty, liberals pretended to be hardheaded realists. Asked if there was anything wrong with ethnic profiling at airports after 9/11, Harvard Law professor Alan Dershowitz said, "Yes, it doesn't work." Other, better ideas, he said, were face-recognition technology and national ID cards. These would work great—if only we knew who the terrorists were. But if we knew who the terrorists were, the only plane they'd be boarding would be headed to Guantánamo and we wouldn't need to search anyone at all.

On CNN, Juliette Kayyem, from the John F. Kennedy School of Government at Harvard, assured viewers that "no one is disagreeing" with extra scrutiny for potential terrorists. But profiling, she said, "won't work." It wouldn't work, allegedly, because al Qaeda "exists in places from Algeria to Zimbabwe." True, but since we're in America, wouldn't it be a big help if we could screen out most of the Americans? Liberals think "it doesn't work" has such a nice ring to it that the patent absurdity of what they're saying should not detract from their argument.

After Senator Teddy Kennedy tried to block federal funding for the government's program to fingerprint and photograph people entering the country from twenty-five Muslim nations, his sleazy back-door maneuver was defended on Fox News Channel's *O'Reilly Factor* by Sarah Eltantawi of the objective, nonpartisan, well-groomed Muslim Public Affairs Council. Eltantawi said it was a "huge mischaracterization" to think she was going to complain about racial profiling. "That's not the argument I'm here to make." To the contrary, her objection—and Kennedy's objection—was that fingerprinting immigrants from terrorist-producing countries is "completely inefficient." And we all know Teddy Kennedy cannot abide inefficiency!

Elizabeth Rindskopf Parker—former legal counsel to the CIA, the National Security Agency, and the State Department—has been quoted as saying, "We don't use torture because it doesn't work." (And it only took a little arm-twisting to get her to say that.) Torturing randomly chosen people on the off chance that they might be up to something—as was routinely done in liberals' favorite country, the USSR—clearly doesn't work. Torturing the guy you know for a fact is withholding information actually works quite well. There may be good and sufficient moral reasons for not torturing people for information, but efficacy is not among them.

After decades of womanly crying about guns, liberals finally admitted their earlier hysteria had been much ado about nothing. The real problem with guns was that they don't make people any safer. Fox News Channel's Alan Colmes said to Larry Pratt of Gun Owners of America, "Let's talk about some hard and cold facts, Larry. The fact of the matter is, Larry"—there's that "the fact of the matter is" qualifier I promised you—"that the odds that a home will be the scene of a homicide are much greater if there's a gun in the home." Soccer moms across America shot straight up and said, *I did not know that!* The study behind this flagrantly dishonest "cold hard fact" assumed that anyone killed by a gun in the vicinity of a home where anyone owned a gun was killed by "a gun in the home." The specious study merely attests to the fact that people who live in high-crime neighborhoods tend to own guns. As the inestimable economist John Lott says, on that theory of causation, hospitals must cause people to die, because lots of people die after being admitted to a hospital.

It's as if liberals held focus groups on how to best present their ridiculous ideas and were told, *Passion you've got. But what respondents say you lack is intellection, thinking things through, understanding elementary human nature, and a basic awareness of what people are like.* If conservatives have not yet persuaded liberals to give up on socialism and treason, we have at least gotten them to fake linear thinking.

Liberals' other new hobby is to call people "liars." After years of defending Clinton, they love the piquant irony of calling Bush a "liar." *Bush said he was a "reformer with results"*—LIAR! For fifty years liberals have called Republicans every name in the book—idiots, fascists, anti-Semites, racists, crooks, Constitution shredders, and masterminds of Salvadoran death squads. Only recently have they added the epithet "liar." Even noted ethicist Al Franken has switched from calling conservatives "big fat idiots" to calling them "liars." This is virgin territory for Democrats—they never before viewed lying as a negative. Their last president, Bill Clinton, was called "an unusually good liar" by a senator in his own party, and their last vice president, Al Gore, couldn't say "pass the salt" without claiming to have invented salt. Having only recently discovered the intriguing new concept of "lies," the Democrats are having a jolly old time calling Bush a liar. But they can't quite grasp the concept of a lie as connoting something that is intentionally untrue—or untrue at all.

About the time Baghdad was erupting in celebrations after receiving the news that Uday and Qusay were dead, liberals were still hopping mad that in January 2003 President Bush uttered the indisputably true fact that British intelligence believed Saddam Hussein had tried to acquire uranium from Africa. That was, and still is, believed by British intelligence. It also was, and still is, the conclusion in our own National Intelligence Estimate. The CIA, however, discounts this piece of intelligence. The CIA did such a bang-up job predicting 9/11, the Democrats have decided to put all their faith in it. They believe the nation must not act until absolutely every agency and every American is convinced we are about to be nuked. (Would that they had such strict standards for worrying about nuclear power plants at home!)

Sharing a chummy laugh about Republicans on *Meet the Press,* NBC's Tim Russert asked Senator Joe Biden what the Republicans would have done if a Democratic president had uttered sixteen mistaken words about national security in a State of the Union speech. Senator Biden said, "This is going to be counterintuitive for Biden to show his Irish instinct to restrain myself. You know the answer, I know the answer, the whole world knows the answer. They would have ripped his skin off." At least Bush put it in his *own* words—if you know what I mean. (Perhaps Biden is annoyed that Bush merely cited the head of the British Labor Party rather than plagiarized him.) Back to Russert's challenge, I shall dispense with Clinton's most renowned lies. (Every Democrat commits adultery and lies about it—fine, they've convinced me.) Clinton also lied every time he said "God bless America," and I don't recall any Republican ever ripping his skin off about that.

But how about a lie in a major national speech slandering your own country? In Clinton's acceptance speech at the 1996 Democratic National Convention, he said, "We still have too many Americans who give in to their fears of those who are different from them. Not so long ago, swastikas were painted on the doors of some African-American members of our Special Forces at Fort Bragg. Folks, for those of you who don't know what they do, the Special Forces are just what the name says; they are special forces. If I walk off this stage tonight and call them on the telephone and tell them to go halfway around the world and risk their lives for you and be there by tomorrow at noon, they will do it. They do not deserve to have swastikas on their doors."

Clinton was referring to an alleged act of racism in which the prime suspect was one of the alleged victims—a black soldier known for filing repeated complaints of racism. The fact that the leading suspect in an apparently racist incident was himself black had already been widely reported in the press. The soldier, not a member of the Special Forces, by the way, was later discharged. And yet Clinton lied about the swastika episode in speech after speech—including his speech at the Democratic National Convention—publicly citing a phony hate crime in order to accuse white Special Forces members of racism. (And he used a lot more than sixteen words to do it.)

Democrats didn't mind a president telling lies in order to defame his own country. They reserve their outrage for a president who defames the name of an honorable statesman like Saddam Hussein. (Note to the Democrats: Just because you defended Bill Clinton doesn't mean you have to defend every government official credibly accused of rape.) How dare Bush suggest Saddam was seeking uranium from Africa on the flimsy evidence of: the findings of British intelligence, the findings of our own NIE, the fact that Israel blew up Saddam's last nuclear reactor in 1981, and the fact that we learned about Saddam's reconstitution of his nuke program only in 1996, when his son-in-law briefly defected to Jordan. The Mr. Magoos from the UN Weapons Inspection Team had missed this fact while scouring the country for five years after Gulf War I. Apparently it's okay to get the facts wrong, but only in the service of slandering America—the country we're supposed to believe liberals love.

Most of this book will explain how to argue with liberals by example, not exegesis. But there are some useful pointers. Here are ten simple rules to keep in mind.

First, don't surrender out of the gate. This is a highly controversial approach among Republican politicians, obviously—otherwise we wouldn't already have a bipartisan consensus for the proposition that you should send half of what you earn to the government. Liberals always want to shame Republicans into making core concessions before the debate begins. *You raise taxes and then we'll discuss cutting spending. You admit the war in Iraq was a failure and then we'll argue about how to get out of it. You give us abortion on demand, then we'll discuss parental notification.* Never has any good come out of surrendering before negotiations begin.

Second, unless you were in the Ku Klux Klan like *Vanity Fair*'s "Profiles in Courage" winner Senator Bob Byrd, or you killed a woman like Senator Ted Kennedy, or you are credibly accused of rape by Juanita Broaddrick on NBC News within weeks of being impeached like You-Know-Who—you don't need to be defensive. Come to think of it, since our side does not accept Klansmen, murderers, or rapists, this rule may be simplified to: Don't be defensive.

Third, you must outrage the enemy. If the liberal you're arguing with doesn't become speechless with sputtering, impotent rage, you're not doing it right. People don't get angry when lies are told about them; they get angry when the truth is told about them. If you are not being called outrageous by liberals, you're not being outrageous enough. Start with the maximum assertion about liberals and then push the envelope, because, as we know, their evil is incalculable. They stand for the godless rule of dictators. They apologize for abortion, adultery, and everything bestial in society. They support al Qaeda and the Taliban as they once supported Stalin and Mao. They put Stalin apologist Paul Robeson on a stamp. Robeson is David Duke in blackface: This Stalin Peace Prize winner turned his back on Jewish refuseniks in the Soviet Union; after Joseph Stalin's death, he wrote a tribute to the dictator titled "To You Beloved Comrade." Most unforgivable of all, liberals have extended the public career of Martin Sheen by at least a full decade. The latest fashions dictated from European capitals ensure that Hating America is haute couture. Gwynnie Paltrow and Madonna—with their European homes, European husbands, and European accents—are demonstrating the same unblinking devotion to America's enemies that we have seen in the past. (Interestingly, the fake British accent Madonna uses in real life is better than the one Paltrow uses in her movies.) This crowd is always in search of approval from people who want to harm America. Nothing too extreme can be said about liberals, because it's all true. (That's why I almost called this book "You Don't Know the Half of It.")

Fourth, never apologize, at least not for what liberals want you to apologize for. These are the people who think Linda Tripp should apologize to the nation, but Bill Clinton was a hapless victim. After Dick "I Broke the

News About al Qaeda to Condi" Clarke had the audacity to apologize to the McWidows on behalf of the U.S. government, liberals started demanding President Bush apologize for 9/11, too. Suddenly public apologies had become trendy; the thing to do, like getting drunk and having unprotected public sex with Colin Farrell. Instead of fighting the war on terrorism, liberals would prefer a Cabinet-level Department of Closure to handle issues like "presidential apologies," with headquarters in a building shaped like a giant hug and Dr. Phil as Secretary of Closure.

Fifth, never compliment a Democrat. Unfortunately, when dealing with liberals, you have to set aside everything your mother told you about giving compliments. Mother is wise about many things, and when you go over to Mrs. Jaworski's house, you should still compliment her on her rosebushes. But that doesn't mean you should ever say anything nice about a Democrat. For one thing, it's such a colossal waste of time racking your brain trying to think up nice things to say to a liberal. "Gee, your head doesn't seem quite as large and misshapen as usual today, Senator Kennedy!" But, more important, compliments to Democrats are always returned with insults.

On any television political roundtable you will see Republican politicians droning on about what a fine human being some heinous Democrat is and what a pleasure it was to work with him, only to have the heinous Democrat turn around and accuse the Republicans of near-complicity in genocide.

Consider the first statements out of the mouths of three senators on *Larry King Live* on May 7, 2004:

Senator John Warner (Republican of Virginia): "First, if I may say of my colleagues on the committee, and twenty-four senators out of the twenty-five were present at that hearing, I think we comported ourselves individually and collectively as best I've ever seen it in the Senate. . . ."

Senator Jon Kyl (Republican of Arizona): "I agree with Senator Warner that the senators comported themselves well for the most part. . . ."

Senator Tom Harkin (Democrat of Iowa): "Well, [Rumsfeld should resign] for a couple of reasons."

A few days later, Republican senator Lindsey Graham used about half his allotted time on *Meet the Press* to make clear he had absolutely no criticisms of the Democrats:

"I didn't come here to beat on Senator Kerry or to defend any political position. This is not about Republican and Democratic politics. . . . [Let's] show the world that Republicans and Democrats may disagree on the policy and the war in Iraq, but we have the ability to make sure those accountable are going to be held accountable. . . . Republicans and Democrats need to come together to prove to the world that our system works."

The Democrats on the panel returned the love by accusing President Bush of responsibility for the Abu Ghraib prison abuse (Senator Carl Levin [Democrat of Michigan]: "I think he helped to create the atmosphere") and saying the mission in Iraq would probably fail (General Wesley Clark: "I think there's a greater than 50/50 chance, let's say a 2:1 chance, of a catastrophic early end to this mission").

Sixth, never show graciousness toward a Democrat. (Rules Nos. 5, 6, and 7 may seem similar, but I want to be sure I've covered all the bases.) Not only will any kindness not be returned, but it will be used against you. President Bush has repeatedly learned the hard way what happens when you are nice to Democrats. After it leaked that the dignified staff of the dignified former president had trashed the White House on its way out, Bush downplayed the property damage, saying, "There might have been a prank or two. Maybe somebody put a cartoon on the wall, but that's okay." If you happened to know anyone moving into the Bush White House who had seen the damage firsthand, you knew it was a lot more than a "prank or two." But instead of stopping while they were ahead, pocketing Bush's graciousness and moving on, the Democrats aggressively attacked other Republicans for having falsely impugned the honor of the Clinton White House staff—citing Bush's magnanimity as proof that Republicans had lied about the damage. *USA Today* ran a snippy article titled "Ex-Clinton Staffers on Vandalism: Got Proof?" Former Clinton press secretary Jake Siewert insinuatingly asked why there were no records of the alleged damage—creating the uniquely ironic scenario of a Clinton spokesman demanding proof of a statement's veracity. *Washington Post* columnist William Raspberry noted that the damage was never catalogued and asked, "Can it be because the alleged vandalism never happened either?" And then a year later, the full GAO report came back: The Party of the People had done $15,000 worth of property damage to the People's House. And that didn't even include the cost of cleaning and sterilizing the rugs from Clinton's office.

Seventh, never flatter a Democrat. When Bush was first elected, he invited Senator Teddy Kennedy to the White House for movie night—to watch the hagiographic Kennedy snoozefest *Thirteen Days*. He named a federal building after one of Kennedy's brothers and gushingly praised the other. He brought Kennedy over to discuss education several times. Hell, he did everything but split a bottle of Chivas Regal with the guy—which, come to think of it, might have actually won Kennedy over. Asked about Bush's overtures, the Fredo of the Kennedy family said, "It takes more than good intentions to make a difference." When specifically asked whether he thought Bush was smart—a meaningless concept in the case of college admissions, but a hard fact in the case of Republican presidents—Kennedy pointedly said he found Bush only "engaging and personable." Yes, there's that trademark Kennedy wit and boyish charm.

After Bush named the Department of Justice building after Robert Kennedy, Kerry Kennedy Cuomo displayed the celebrated Kennedy graciousness by viciously attacking the Bush administration at the prededication ceremony. Speaking from the podium to her daughter in the audience, Kennedy Cuomo said, "Kara, if anyone tries to tell you this is the type of justice system your grandpa embraced, you just don't believe it." (Oddly enough, she didn't add, "Actually, Kara, Grandpa's justice was more like the justice system your great uncle Teddy turned to after he drowned that girl.") This is as we have come to expect from a family of heroin addicts, statutory rapists, convicted and unconvicted female-killers, cheaters, bootleggers, and dissolute drunks known as "Camelot." Extend an olive branch to Democrats and they'll smack the living daylights out of you with it—while hugging the tree itself, naturally.

Eighth, do not succumb to liberal bribery. Faustian bargains are still not a good deal. Liberals are a seductive group of minxes. They recruit conservatives the way colleges recruit star athletes, deploying celebrity starlets as comfort women. Become a liberal and you will be lavished with great wealth and adulation. Nationally renowned liberal female journalists have been known to offer oral sex to elected officials just for keeping abortion on demand legal. Liberals have scores of money-laundering schemes to pay off anyone who attacks a conservative—foundation jobs, radio stations, websites, movie "options," university professorships, and jobs writing for the *New York Times*. Lots of goodies are available to any conservative willing to give up all his principles. Imagine Satan's temptation of Daniel Webster if the old beastmaster had been able to dangle "a development deal with Tristar," "one of those phony Harvard Ph.D.s," or even "a power lunch with Harvey Weinstein" in front of Mr. Webster. Go with liberals and they will give you a lifetime of wine, women, and song.

The more public and respected a conservative you are, the more goodies will be offered to you, starting with the cover of the *New York Times Magazine.* Even a halfwit can get a pretty good life out of liberal enticements, rather like a bureaucrat in the old Soviet Union. If a conservative giant like Rush Limbaugh or Sean Hannity ever became liberal, there would be parades down Fifth Avenue. At the freshman-liberal induction ceremony, Bill Moyers would MC, Bono would sing an original song, Maya Angelou would recite a poem, and Sean Penn would throw out the first punch.

Apparently it's difficult for some people to resist that kind of bribery. Weak and frightened conservatives crave liberal approval and will do anything to get it. The telltale sign is how quickly a conservative will publicly attack another conservative. These masters of the featherweight insight especially enjoy deploring evangelical Christians. (To do it right, every time you denounce a devout Christian or Jew for being a superstitious, intolerant ignoramus, you must praise radical Islam as "a religion of peace.")

It should have set off warning bells when David Brock, professional re-formed conservative, was committed to the psychiatric ward of Sibley Memorial Hospital in Washington, D.C. It's never a good sign when you have to wipe the spittle from your champion's mouth before he goes on TV—as Ed Asner's handlers are discovering even as we speak. But Brock was a former conservative attacking conservatives, so before long, liberals were dragging him out of "The Quiet Room" at Sibley so they could give him $2 million to start a liberal website. You cannot starve in America as a liberal. For $2 million, liberals now have a website exposing the shocking fact that conservative opinion columnists have opinions that are ... *conservative!* I could have told them that for, say, a hundred grand.

Ninth, prepare for your deepest, darkest secrets to become liberal talking points. Liberals' idea of a good retort to a conservative argument is to investigate your personal life and find out if you're into S&M. So if you have anything to hide—say, if you were married to a gay guy, but he was really, really rich and you knew you could talk him into running for the Senate—you'd best become a liberal. All will be forgiven. In fact, "something to hide" is often considered a résumé enhancer if you're a Democrat—just ask Bill Clinton, Barney Frank, Marion Barry ...

But if you're a conservative, prepare to have your every foible unveiled as if you were caught raping kittens. Even if you've led a blameless life, liberals invent absurd stories about you. They will say you're afraid of Cheshire cats and ordered nude statues at the Department of Justice covered with drapery. You'll be sneered at for your former line of work, such as Tom DeLay, who is derisively called "the exterminator" because he used to run a massive pesticide company. (This is apparently not nearly as classy as having been an ambulance-chasing lawyer.) You will simultaneously be described as ugly—and accused of being on TV only because you're pretty. You will be called an anti-Semite—and a shill for the Jews. You will be called a homophobe—and a fag hag. (As with their political positions, logical consistency is not liberals' métier.) If it gets really ugly they may even call you a "neoconservative," by which liberals mean "dirty Jew." Not only will you not be lavished with jobs, money, and celebrity starlets—you will be unemployable, unpublished, and embarrassed. For good measure, magazines will never, ever run an attractive picture of you. Finally, after liberals have done everything they can to destroy your career, you will be accused of being a conservative only for career advancement.

On the bright side, you know you've arrived when liberals start calling you a fag. Curiously, these proponents of tolerance always choose "gay" as their most searing epithet. Joe McCarthy, J. Edgar Hoover, Matt Drudge, Starr's prosecutors, Linda Tripp's lawyer, Christopher Hitchens, Mel Gibson—all these have been denounced as homosexuals at some point by liberals. The *New York Times*'s Frank Rich (now there's someone who would never be called a homo) outed David Brock when he was still on the right. Rich favorably cited Christopher Hitchens—who himself was called a fag by liberals when he crossed them—for calling Gibson's movie *The Passion of the Christ* an exercise in "sadomasochistic male narcissism." Arguing with liberals instantly becomes a game of gay-baiting musical chairs. We just don't think they should get married. Liberals actually hate homosexuals.

Tenth, always be open to liberals in transition. Go all out—be at least as hospitable to them as Saddam was to al Zarqawi. As with al Qaeda, if you can create second thoughts in just a couple of them, it will be a lot less trouble for the rest of us down the road. Liberals in transition will tend to approach you in hushed tones, repeatedly looking over their shoulders, and explaining they have a family to feed. You might not want these guys watching your back in a bar fight, but at least they are trying to be good. People "coming out" as conservatives for the first time face being ostracized by friends, neighbors, coworkers, even family members. Refer them to a local support network such as "Parents and Friends of Conservatives and Their Partners." Nurture them—and make sure they aren't killed before they can move to the other side. That's when it's most dangerous.

When Christopher Hitchens decided not to lie to a congressional aide to protect his friend, Clinton consigliere Sidney Blumenthal, Hitchens was quickly denounced by his former friends as a drunk and a sexual pervert. (Imagine the indignity of having a Clinton defender call you a sexual pervert!) According to sworn statements from Hitchens and Hitchens's wife, early in the Monica Lewinsky scandal—before Monica produced the dress—Blumenthal told them that Clinton said Monica Lewinsky was a "stalker." But later, when asked by congressional investigators whether he had told anyone that Clinton called Lewinsky a stalker, Blumenthal had said, "I didn't mention it to my friends. . . . I certainly never mentioned it to a reporter." Hitchens told the investigators otherwise.

For the treachery of declining to perjure himself, Hitchens's erstwhile close friend Alexander Cockburn wrote that Hitchens "gets a frisson we'd guess to be quasi-sexual in psychological orientation out of the act of tattling or betrayal. . . . The booze has finally got to him. . . . His behavior exhibits all the symptoms of chronic alcoholism." He said Hitchens's statement was probably uttered "while [a] pint of alcohol and gallons of wine . . . [were] coursing through his bloodstream." Oddest of all, Cockburn called Hitchens "a terrific fibber." All this for the "despicable" act of telling the truth. (Yes, Cockburn and Blumenthal are two of those liberal "friends" I warned you about earlier.)

To end on an optimistic note, remember there is some good in everyone. Hitler didn't smoke, for example. British traitor and spy Kim Philby had a pet fox. Even among the staunchest members of the Communist Party, there turned out to be a few good ones. Similarly, the vast majority of liberals are not intentionally sabotaging the nation. In fact, I don't think as many as 20 percent give a damn about the nation. That 20 percent, of course, deeply hates America. But the majority of liberals are just trying to sell books, get a TV show, be called "brave" in the *New York Times,* sound hip, or get a woman's phone number at an afternoon reception at the Westchester Kabbalah center. Intentions, of course, do not mitigate disastrous outcomes. If your doctor removes the wrong kidney because he was jet-lagged from a Doctors Without Borders flight with actor Noah Wyle, it makes precious little difference to you. This is why my philosophy on arguing with liberals is: Tough love, except I don't love them. In most cases I don't even like them. In other words, my "tough love" approach is much like the Democrats' "middle-class tax cuts"—everything but the last word.

I decided to write this book because I have liberals to thank for my career and I wanted something substantial to throw in their faces—oops, I mean I wanted to give something back. The majority of this book will be new to even my most devoted readers (who are able to locate the rare brave newspapers that carry my column). I've included columns too hot to be published until now—along with the editors' rejections. These columns, as well as any columns that caused more than the usual ruckus (like my 9/11 "kill their leaders" column), I preserved in their original form— so you can see what the fuss was about. Some columns I added a little to and some I added so much to that they grew from short columns to entire chapters (e.g., the Elián González and Confederate flag chapters). Even the unretouched columns are *my* unretouched columns, as they live on my computer—which was not always the same as the published version. I've occasionally run into editors with heavy hands, and I didn't necessarily care for their edits. These are bootlegs, never-released columns, NC-17 versions, lost classics, remixes, extended-play versions, and the director's cut.

There are many advantages to plumbing my old columns for a Coulterpalooza. For one thing, I am one of the most unpublished writers in America—except for my books, which sell pretty well. But unless you are on the Internet or a subscriber to *Human Events*—which everyone should read—all but a few intrepid newspaper editors have withheld these columns from you. Also, I have an ad hoc group of fanatical researchers doing fact-checking for me immediately after my columns go up on the Internet. If I get someone's middle initial wrong, it will be widely publicized on hundreds of reasonable, calm, objective, nonpartisan websites with names like www.I-hate-anncoulter.with.a.hot.hot.hate.com. (This is in addition to my fabulous official editor, Greg Melvin at Universal Press Syndicate, who does not consider it a "lie" to opine that taxes are too high.) Also, when you write for a small-circulation newspaper like *Human Events,* your columns are apparently considered community property by other journalists, who shamelessly poach your work without the briefest little credit. (At least I know who's been reading my stuff!) Now you can read the originals. Finally, I like my columns. Unlike liberals, who would rather have their old columns defending Ho Chi Minh just go away, I would prefer that my columns be more widely read. This includes columns from over a decade ago and columns deemed unpublishable—in fact *especially* the columns deemed unpublishable.

2

This Is War

---■---

Want to make liberals angry? Defend the United States. Below are my columns on the war on terrorism. It's interesting to review how the carping from the Treason Lobby has evolved during the course of the war. My position hasn't changed since the column I wrote the night of 9/11. For reasons I cannot understand, I am often asked if I still think we should invade their countries, kill their leaders, and convert them to Christianity. The answer is: Now more than ever!

☞ How 9/11 Happened

We don't need a "commission" to find out how 9/11 happened. The truth is in the time line:

President Carter, Democrat

In 1979, President Jimmy Carter allowed the Shah of Iran to be deposed by a mob of Islamic fanatics. A few months later, Muslims stormed the U.S. Embassy in Iran and took American Embassy staff hostage.

Carter retaliated by canceling Iranian visas. He eventually ordered a disastrous and humiliating rescue attempt, crashing helicopters in the desert.

President Reagan, Republican

The day of Reagan's inauguration, the hostages were released.

In 1982, the U.S. Embassy in Beirut was bombed by Muslim extremists.

President Reagan sent U.S. Marines to Beirut.

In 1983, the U.S. Marine barracks in Beirut were blown up by Muslim extremists.

Reagan said the United States would not surrender, but Democrats in Congress threw a hissy fit, drafting a resolution demanding that our troops be withdrawn. All seven Democratic presidential candidates called for our troops to be withdrawn. Reagan caved in to Democrat caterwauling in an election year and withdrew our troops—bombing Syrian-controlled areas on the way out. Democrats complained about that, too.

In 1985, an Italian cruise ship, the *Achille Lauro,* was seized and a sixty-nine-year-old American was shot and thrown overboard by Muslim extremists.

Reagan ordered a heart-stopping mission to capture the hijackers after the "allies" promise them safe passage. The daring plan to intercept the hijackers' flight was conceived by Oliver North—later crucified by Democrats over Iran-Contra—and executed by Admiral Frank Kelso, later savaged by Representative Patricia Schroeder for saying hello to his boys at Tailhook. Kelso's boys captured the hijackers and turned them over to the Italians, who then released them to safe harbor in Iraq.

On April 5, 1986, a West Berlin discotheque frequented by U.S. servicemen was bombed by Muslim extremists from the Libyan Embassy in East Berlin, killing an American.

Ten days later, Reagan bombed Libya, despite our dear ally France refusing the use of their airspace. Americans bombed Qaddafi's residence, killing his daughter, and dropped a bomb on the French Embassy "by mistake."

Reagan also stoked a long, bloody war between heinous regimes in Iran and Iraq. All this was while winning a final victory over Soviet totalitarianism.

President Bush I, Moderate Republican

In December 1988, a passenger jet, Pan Am Flight 103, was bombed over Lockerbie, Scotland, by Muslim extremists.

President-elect George Bush claimed he would continue Reagan's policy of retaliating against terrorism, but did not. Without Reagan to gin her up, even Prime Minister Margaret Thatcher went wobbly, saying there would be no revenge for the bombing.

In 1990, Saddam Hussein invaded Kuwait.

In early 1991, Bush went to war with Iraq the way liberals like—with approval from the UN and "the allies." Still, a majority of Democrats opposed the war. Democrats demanded that our troops stop at Baghdad, but then after 9/11, absurdly complained that Bush didn't "finish off the job" with Saddam.

President Bill Clinton, Democrat

In February 1993, the World Trade Center was bombed by Muslim fanatics, killing five people and injuring hundreds.

Clinton did nothing.

In October 1993, eighteen American troops were killed in a savage firefight in Somalia. The corpse of one American was dragged through the streets of Mogadishu as the Somalian hordes cheered.

Clinton responded by ordering our troops home. Osama bin Laden later told ABC News, "The youth . . . realized more than before that the American soldier was a paper tiger and after a few blows ran in defeat."

In November 1995, five Americans were killed and thirty wounded by a car bomb in Saudi Arabia set by Muslim extremists.

Clinton did nothing.

In June 1996, a U.S. Air Force housing complex in Saudi Arabia was bombed by Muslim extremists.

Clinton did nothing.

Months later, Saddam attacked the Kurdish-controlled city of Erbil.

Clinton lobbed some bombs into Iraq, hundreds of miles from Saddam's forces.

In November 1997, Iraq refused to allow UN weapons inspectors to do their jobs and threatened to shoot down a U.S. U-2 spy plane.

Clinton did nothing.

In February 1998, Clinton threatened to bomb Iraq, but called it off when the United Nations said no.

On August 7, 1998, U.S. embassies in Kenya and Tanzania were bombed by Muslim extremists.

Clinton did nothing.

On August 20, Monica Lewinsky appeared for the second time to testify before the grand jury.

Clinton responded by bombing Afghanistan and Sudan, severely damaging a camel and an aspirin factory.

On December 16, the House of Representatives prepared to impeach Clinton the next day.

Clinton retaliated by ordering major air strikes against Iraq, described by the *New York Times* as "by far the largest military action in Iraq since the end of the Gulf War in 1991."

The only time Clinton decided to go to war with anyone in the vicinity of Muslim fanatics was in 1999—when Clinton attacked Serbians who were fighting Muslim fanatics.

In October 2000, our warship the USS *Cole* was attacked by Muslim extremists.

Clinton did nothing.

President George Bush, Republican

Bush came into office telling his national security adviser, Condoleezza Rice, he was "tired of swatting flies"—he wanted to eliminate al Qaeda.

On September 11, 2001, after Bush had been in office for seven months, three thousand Americans were murdered in a savage terrorist attack on U.S. soil by Muslim extremists.

Since then, Bush has won wars in Afghanistan and Iraq, captured Saddam Hussein, probably killed and certainly immobilized Osama bin Laden, destroyed al Qaeda's base, and begun to create the only functioning democracy in the Middle East other than Israel. Democrats opposed it all—except their phony support for war with Afghanistan, which they immediately complained about and said would be a Vietnam quagmire. Now they claim to be outraged that in the months before 9/11, Bush did not do everything Democrats opposed doing after 9/11.

What a surprise. ■

☞ This Is War

SEPTEMBER 12, 2001

Barbara Olson kept her cool. In the hysteria and terror of hijackers herding passengers to the rear of the plane, she retrieved her cell phone and called her husband, Ted, the solicitor general of the United States. She informed him that he had better call the FBI—the plane had been hijacked.

According to reports, Barbara was still on the phone with Ted when her plane plunged in a fiery explosion directly into the Pentagon.

Barbara risked having her neck slit to warn the country of a terrorist attack. She was a patriot to the very end. This is not to engage in the media's typical hallucinatory overstatement about anyone who is the victim of a horrible tragedy. The furtive cell phone call was an act of incredible daring and panache. If it were not, we'd be hearing reports of hundreds more cell phone calls. (Even people who swear to hate cell phones carry them for commercial air travel.)

The last time I saw Barbara in person was about three weeks ago. She generously praised one of my recent columns and told me I had really found my niche. Ted, she said, had taken to reading my columns aloud to her over breakfast. I mention that to say three things about Barbara. First, she was really nice. A lot of people on TV seem nice but aren't. (And some who don't seem nice are.) But Barbara was always her charming, graceful, ebullient self. "Nice" is an amazingly rare quality among writers. In the opinion business, bitter, jealous hatred is the norm. Barbara had reason to be secure.

Second, it was actually easy to imagine Ted reading political columns aloud to Barbara at the breakfast table. Theirs was a relationship that could only be cheaply imitated by Bill and Hillary—the latter being a subject of Barbara's appropriately biting best-seller *Hell to Pay*. Hillary claimed preposterously in a *Talk* magazine interview that she discussed policy with Bill while cutting his grapefruit in the morning. But when asked about Monica Lewinsky, Hillary kept insisting she was waiting for the facts to come out. Couldn't she have asked her husband about the facts while cutting his grapefruit? Ted and Barbara really did talk politics—and really did have breakfast together. It's "Ted and Barbara" just like it's Fred and Ginger, and George and Gracie. They were so perfect together, so obvious, that their friends were as happy as they were on their wedding day. This is more than the death of a great person and patriotic American. It's a human amputation.

Third, since Barbara's compliment, I'd been writing my columns for Ted and Barbara. I'm always writing to someone in my head. Now I don't know who to write to. Ted and Barbara were a good muse.

Apart from hearing that this beautiful light has been extinguished from the world, only one other news flash broke beyond the numbingly omnipresent horror of the entire day. That evening, CNN reported that bombs were dropping in Afghanistan—and then updated the report to say they weren't our bombs. They should have been ours. I wanted them to be ours.

This is no time to be precious about locating the exact individuals directly involved in this particular terrorist attack. Those responsible include anyone anywhere in the world who smiled in response to the annihilation of patriots like Barbara Olson. We don't need long investigations of the forensic evidence to determine with scientific accuracy the person or persons who ordered this specific attack. We don't need an "international coalition." We don't need a study on "terrorism." We certainly didn't need a congressional resolution condemning the attack this week.

The nation has been invaded by a fanatical, murderous cult. And we welcome them. We are so good and so pure we would never engage in discriminatory racial or "religious" profiling. People who want our country destroyed live here, work for our airlines, and are submitted to the exact same airport shakedown as a lumberman from Idaho. This would be like having the Wehrmacht immigrate to America and work for our airlines during World War II. Except the Wehrmacht was not so bloodthirsty.

"All of our lives" don't need to change, as they keep prattling on TV. Every single time there is a terrorist attack—or a plane crashes because of pilot error—Americans allow their rights to be contracted for no purpose whatsoever. The airport kabuki theater of magnetometers, asinine questions about whether passengers "packed their own bags," and the hostile, lumpen mesomorphs ripping open our luggage somehow allowed over a dozen armed hijackers to board four American planes almost simultaneously on Bloody Tuesday. (Did those fabulous security procedures stop a single hijacker anywhere in America that day?)

Airports scrupulously apply the same laughably ineffective airport harassment to Suzy Chapstick as to Muslim hijackers. It is preposterous to assume every passenger is a potential crazed homicidal maniac. We know who the homicidal maniacs are. They are the ones cheering and dancing right now. We should invade their countries, kill their leaders, and convert them to Christianity. We weren't punctilious about locating and punishing only Hitler and his top officers. We carpet-bombed German cities; we killed civilians. That's war. And this is war. ∎

☞ The Hun Is at the Gate

NOVEMBER 29, 2001

This week's winner for best comedy line about the war is New York Democratic senator Charles Schumer. Referring to—well, it doesn't really matter what he was referring to, but it was military tribunals—Schumer said, "To come up with the best way to do this, Congress ought to be involved." Congress came up with the Internal Revenue code, right? And the Department of Education? Midnight basketball? The now-bankrupt Social Security "trust fund"? The entire welfare state? Yes, that's just what we need: Congress involved in emergency national security measures!

Democrats are channeling their frustration with America's imminent military victory in Afghanistan into hysterical opposition to reasonable national security measures at home. (Incidentally, the war in Afghanistan ought to prove once and for all what a bunch of paper tigers the Russians were. What were they doing over there for ten years? It hasn't taken us ten weeks.)

Under the strange delusion that their input is necessary during wartime, various congressmen are trying to haul Attorney General Ashcroft before them to answer questions about the detentions of suspected terrorists. Fortunately, Congress has no role in prosecuting this war either abroad or domestically. They are relieved of duty, free to "get back to normal," as the president has recommended—which in their case means enacting massive spending bills to fund comically useless government programs. That should make them happy.

Senator Patrick Leahy (Democrat of Vermont), chairman of the Senate Judiciary Committee, has blustered that there "has been no formal declaration of war and, in the meantime, our civilian courts remain open and available to try suspected terrorists." He said it was questionable "whether the president can lawfully authorize the use of military commissions to try persons arrested here." Though I am sublimely confident that the public will recognize Leahy for the sputtering fool that he is, I note that: We are at war. We have been at war since 8:48 A.M. Tuesday, September 11, 2001. After a massive attack on our nation, we do not need to wait for some precise talismanic formulation by Congress to inform us of the fact that we are at war.

Wars can exist even if Congress does not declare them—if, for example, thousands of American civilians are slaughtered in a surprise attack on U.S soil. On the off chance anyone didn't know that we were at war when we were attacked, Bush said so in his address to a joint session of Congress the week after the attack: "On September the 11th, enemies of freedom committed an act of war against our country." A formal declaration of war has certain consequences only under international law, which is not relevant to domestic security measures taken under the president's war powers.

And that's making the rather large assumption that it is ever relevant at all. International law is like Santa Claus. The only difference is that Santa Claus exists only in the imaginations of small children, whereas international law exists in the imaginations of law school professors. In the real world, international law is whatever the United States and Great Britain say it is.

Because we are at war, Bush, the commander in chief, had authority on September 11 to give orders to shoot down a civilian plane and he had authority to bomb Afghanistan. He didn't need congressional approval for those actions any more than he needs congressional approval right now to try suspected belligerents on U.S. soil in military tribunals. If Congress doesn't like it, the Constitution gives it two choices: It can cut off funding or it can impeach the president. Knock yourselves out, fellas. (Has anyone else noticed there have been no polls taken on the issue of military tribunals for terrorists? This is the most heavily polled populace in the history of the universe; whenever certain polls are not being taken, you should smell a big fat commie rat.)

In 1942, six months after Pearl Harbor, the Supreme Court upheld the use of military tribunals for eight German spies captured on U.S. soil, two of whom were U.S. citizens. In that case, *Ex Parte Quirin,* the court found that military tribunals were appropriate for suspected enemies who have "entered or after entry remained in our territory without uniform," intending to engage in an act of belligerency against the United States. And consider that the Huns were accused only of planning attacks on war materials—not on U.S. citizens. The Supreme Court decided *Quirin* in less than twenty-four hours. Three days later, the military tribunal found the saboteurs guilty. Five days after that, six of the eight were executed, including Herbert Hans Haupt, a U.S. citizen. Only the two who ratted out the plot were given prison sentences instead of death.

The fact that the "courts are open"—the phrase absurdly invoked by Senator Leahy—refers to the Supreme Court's decision in *Ex Parte Milligan,* a Civil War–era case. The *Milligan* court said a citizen could not be tried in a military tribunal "where the courts are open and their process unobstructed"—i.e., in the absence of martial law. But the crucial part of the Court's decision was its determination that Milligan was a nonbelligerent. As the Supreme Court would explain nearly a century later in *Quirin,* the court in *Milligan* "concluded that Milligan, not being a part of or associated with the armed forces of the enemy, was a nonbelligerent, not subject to the law of war." Milligan had not committed any act of war—he was being tried in a military tribunal only because of Abraham Lincoln's suspension of habeas corpus during the Civil War.

It was irrelevant to the Court's decision that Milligan was also a citizen: We know citizens can be tried in military tribunals, otherwise Haupt—Nazi spy-cum–American citizen—would not have been tried and executed by the military. The difference in the two cases is based on the law to be applied, not on the citizenship status of the defendants. Quirin and company were enemy belligerents and thus tried under military law; Milligan was not an enemy belligerent, and thus was to be tried under civilian law—as long as "the courts are open." Michael Moore may wish for Americans to die every bit as much as Jose Padilla does, but he has not conspired, plotted, or committed acts of war sufficient to make him an "enemy belligerent." Mere treason is tried in civilian courts.

Though Bush has ordered military tribunals only for noncitizens thus far, the *Quirin* court did not exempt citizens from military tribunals—far from it. If "unlawful belligerency" is the offense, the Court held, then U.S. citizenship provides no shelter. Citizens who associate with the enemy—taking its aid, guidance, or direction—are "enemy belligerents." When Ashcroft is forced to waste his time in Senate hearings this week taking him away from protecting the nation from more terrorist attacks, he should remind the committee that there's no exemption for senators either. ∎

☞ Attack France!

DECEMBER 20, 2001

As pundits mull whether America's next target in the war on terrorism should be Iraq or a smaller quarry first—such as Sudan or Somalia—it's time to consider another petri dish of ferocious anti-American hatred and terrorist activity. The Bush doctrine is: We are at war not only with the terrorists but also with those who harbor them. We've got to attack France.

Having exhausted itself in a spirited fight with the Nazis in the last war, France cannot work up the energy to oppose terrorism. For decades now, France has nurtured, coddled, and funded Islamic terrorists. (Moreover, the Great Satan is getting a little sick of our McDonald's franchises being attacked on behalf of notoriously inefficient French dairy farmers.) At the 1972 Olympics, Muslim terrorists assassinated eleven Israeli athletes and one German policeman. Five years later, acting on intelligence from Israeli secret police, French counterespionage agents arrested the reputed mastermind of the massacre, Abu Daoud. Both Israel and West Germany sought the extradition of Daoud. Afraid of upsetting Muslim terrorists, France refused on technical grounds and set him free.

In 1986, Libyan agents of Muammar Qaddafi planted a bomb in a West Berlin discotheque, killing an American serviceman and a Turkish woman. Hundreds more were injured. President Reagan ordered air strikes against Libyan military targets—including Qaddafi's living quarters. Quaking in the face of this show of manly force, France denied America the use of its airspace. As a consequence, American pilots were required to begin their missions from air bases in Britain. When the pilots finally made it to Tripoli, tired from the long flights and showing a puckish sense of humor, they bombed the French Embassy by mistake. Oops! Butterfingers!

France has repeatedly decried economic sanctions against Iraq and has accused the United Nations of manufacturing evidence against Saddam Hussein. The UN—not even the Great Satan! The French UN ambassador dismissed aerial photographs of Iraqi military trucks fleeing inspections sites just before UN weapons inspectors arrived as—I quote—"perhaps a truckers' picnic."

Along with the rest of the European Union, France sends millions of dollars to the Palestinian Authority every year. Sucking up to the P.A. has really paid dividends to the craven butterbellies. While visiting Arafat in Gaza last year to announce several million more dollars in aid, Prime Minister Lionel Jospin was attacked by angry, stone-throwing Palestinian students.

Earlier this year, France connived with human-rights champions China and Cuba to toss the United States off the UN Human Rights Commission. Sudan took America's place, and if its diplomats are not too bogged down with human torture and slave trading, they are very much looking forward to attending the meetings.

This summer, Paris made Mumia Abu-Jamal an honorary citizen of Paris. In America's cowboy, blood lust, rush-to-judgment approach to the death penalty, this convicted Philadelphia cop-killer has been sitting on death row—giving radio interviews and college commencement addresses—for twenty years. Luckily "Mumia" sounds like a Muslim name, so Parisians can keep using the same bumper stickers for the war on terrorism.

Two weeks into America's war in Afghanistan, *Le Figaro* began calling for "American restraint." In polls, 47 percent of the French said they believed the U.S. military action was failing and only 17 percent thought it was working (which was, admittedly, 17 percent more than on the *New York Times* editorial page). Flaunting France's well-established reputation as a fearsome fighting machine, the French foreign minister, Hubert Vedrine, immediately called on the United States to stop bombing Afghanistan.

The first indictment to come out of the September 11 attacks was of a French national, Zacarias Moussaoui. He is believed to be the intended twentieth hijacker on Bloody Tuesday. France quickly moved to extend consular protection for Moussaoui. Intriguingly, French justice minister Marylise Lebranchu has demanded that Moussaoui not be executed. Mlle. Lebranchu seems to have forgotten, but . . . WE ARE THE GREAT SATAN! We also have Moussaoui. It's annoying enough when these celebrated Nazi slayers refuse to extradite terrorists on the grounds that America does not observe the pristine judicial formalities of their pals, China, Cuba, and Sudan. But under what zany theory of international law does France think it can tell us what to do with a terrorist we caught right here on U.S. soil?

The Great Satan is wearying of this reverse hegemony, in which little pipsqueak nations try to impose their little pipsqueak values on us. Aren't we the ones who should be arrogantly oppressing countries that unaccountably do not have the death penalty? And now, as America goes about building support for an attack on Iraq—guess who's complaining again?

The turtlenecked chickens are terrified of offending fanatical Muslims. Meanwhile we are asking Arab leaders to face down the vastly larger populations of crazies living in their countries. While France whines, predominantly Muslim Turkey is preparing its airstrips for a possible U.S. attack on Iraq. If this is a war against terrorism and not a Eurocentric war against Islam, the conclusion is ineluctable: We must attack France. What are they going to do? Fight us? ■

☞ May I Turn Down Your Bed, Mohammad?

FEBRUARY 1, 2002

In the event of a surprise attack by North Korea, Secretary of State Colin Powell urged President Bush to ensure that the Office of Homeland Security have full resources and authority to respond to any anti-Korean hate crimes at home. Since you can't tell these days: That's a joke. Powell's real beef concerns the technical procedure by which the United States concludes that the terrorists held at Guantánamo are not "prisoners of war." (Also, Korean-Americans are great Americans and would be the last people to whine about ethnic profiling.)

What Powell really says is that we should apply the Geneva Convention to the Guantánamo detainees. As he admits, under the convention, the detainees are not prisoners of war, inasmuch as they masquerade as civilians, stage sneak attacks, slaughter innocent civilians, pretend they are surrendering before they come out shooting, take hostages, hide arms in mosques, and generally do not abide by the laws or customs of war. Other administration officials have concluded that the Geneva Convention doesn't apply in the first place—because the detainees masquerade as civilians, stage sneak attacks, slaughter innocent civilians, pretend they are surrendering . . . etc. etc.

The subtle distinction is this: If I showed up at the Super Bowl this Sunday demanding to play for the Patriots, I would be turned away on the grounds that I am not within the definition of people known as "the Patriots." Powell's argument is that we should appease our completely useless "allies" by playing a make-believe game that I am a Patriot. Then the Patriots would make a painstaking finding of fact that I am scrawny

99-pound weakling and, on the basis of that finding alone, conclude that I cannot play in the Super Bowl. Either the Taliban and al Qaeda fighters are not covered by the Geneva Convention or they are but still do not qualify for prisoner-of-war status. So the main problem with Powell's position is that it lacks what we used to call "a point."

What determines whether the Geneva Convention applies in the first place is whether we are at war with a signatory nation to the convention. To be sure, some decades ago, a different government of Afghanistan played for the Patriots—that is, was a signatory to the Geneva Convention. But we are not at war with Afghanistan. To the contrary! We are Afghanistan's biggest best buddy in the whole world right now. (Though they seem to think the name of our country is "The Pentagon.") We are at war with al Qaeda. The 158 Guantánamo detainees come from at least twenty-five different countries. To pretend that the Taliban is bound by a convention signed by an earlier Afghan government because the al Qaeda fighters happened to have been captured in Afghanistan would be like trying to collect a bill from a family that bought your debtor's house, razed it, and happened to occupy the same property twenty years later.

The most popular argument for the Powell view is that we have to be nice to the detainees because otherwise people won't be nice to captured American soldiers. Who are we trying to impress by this largesse exactly? I promise you, any Americans captured by al Qaeda will be tortured, disemboweled, and beheaded right before the traditional dancing on the American corpse begins. Indeed, it is difficult to conceive of the United States actually going to war against any country that would honor the Geneva Convention. Despite the enormous groundswell of support for an attack on France, for example, we probably won't invade France. The only people America ever goes to war against are utter savages.

In World War II, the Japanese tortured American prisoners of war. In the Vietnam War, the North Vietnamese tortured American prisoners of war. In the Gulf War, Iraq tortured U.S. prisoners of war—including a female officer who was sexually assaulted by her captors. So this Geneva Convention thing isn't really working out for us. The argument boils down to the claim that we have to treat the detainees the way humanrightsniks say we should in order to secure the approval of humanrightsniks. Even the late Justice William J. Brennan had more imaginative arguments than that.

Thus far in the war on terrorism, human-rights organizations have complained about: the detention of terrorism suspects, military tribunals for terrorists, a trial for John Walker, and (nonexistent) ethnic profiling at airports. No one in America cares. It must be galling to the UN human-rights commissioner. But for some reason, the human-rights organizations imagined that we would be impressed with their complaining about Guantánamo. The country is just shrugging that off, too. Afraid of seeming impotent and irrelevant, even Tony Blair immediately backed down from his criticisms of Guantánamo. Whether Muslim terrorists in Guantánamo are getting enough Froot Loops is not where the country is right now. We're too busy worrying about averting any potential hate crimes against Muslims. ∎

☞ Build Them Back

JUNE 7, 2002

Since September 11, we have been authoritatively informed that skyscrapers as tall as the World Trade Center will never be built again. A "consensus" quickly emerged among city officials to replace the soaring Twin Towers with some potty little buildings and a park. But then at a meeting to discuss the future of the site last week, hundreds of New Yorkers showed up and shocked the experts by demanding that the towers be rebuilt. One man, who had worked on the 77th floor of 1 World Trade Center, said, "Please do not diminish the memory of all of the people who died there by building fifty-, sixty-, or seventy-story mediocre buildings on the site." A little grassy park where people go to weep does lack something in the way of defiance. Instead of us crying, evidently many Americans feel, there should be a lot of Arabs crying.

The reason liberals prefer a park to luminous skyscrapers is that they are not angry. Liberals express sympathy for the victims, but they're not angry. Instead of longing to crush and humiliate the enemy, they believe true patriotism consists of redoubled efforts to expand the welfare state. Senator Hillary Clinton proposed a school for the World Trade Center site and Senator Charles Schumer, a park. Yeah, that'll show 'em! Meanwhile, the construction workers clearing away the rubble vowed they would work without pay to rebuild the World Trade Center. Of course, now that we have fourteen cows, that shouldn't be necessary. (In a genuinely touching story, a tiny cowherding village in Kenya only recently got word of the attack on America and this week made a special present of fourteen cows to the United States.)

The attack on the World Trade Center ripped America's soul not only for the thousands of lives it snuffed out. Even if the towers had been empty, the destruction of those buildings would have been heart-wrenching. Skyscrapers are the hallmark of civilization, monuments to human brilliance and creativity. I'm sure there are some nice trees, but I note that no one ever talks about the "heavenly suburb." Philosopher Jacques Ellul said cities exhibit "all the hopes of man for divinity." St. Augustine said the "house of God is itself a city."

It has become common wisdom that no one would rent property in a rebuilt World Trade Center. This is absurd. September 11 was a sucker punch. That trick doesn't work twice. We have the technology to make the buildings safe from incoming missiles. Moreover, by the time a new World Trade Center is built, Muslim fanatics will be about as threatening as Japanese kamikazi pilots. Who would have imagined after Pearl Harbor that the Japanese were governable? Yet Japan hasn't shown a disposition to fight in sixty years. Muslims feel humiliated now? We'll show them humiliated.

Aesthetes complain that the buildings were ugly. Perhaps. But the important thing is, they were really big. Whatever goes up on that site ought to be even bigger than the buildings the savages destroyed. Erecting enormous skyscrapers to replace the Twin Towers limns the distinction between us and the barbarians. We can ride elevators a quarter-mile into the sky and have a chocolate mousse. What can they do? Multimillionaire Osama bin Laden lived in a cave (and is now D-E-D dead under a Daisy Cutter in Tora Bora). Here in America, ordinary Americans consider seventy-story buildings "mediocre." As Donald Rumsfeld said of al Qaeda, their specialty is "destroying things they could never have built themselves using technologies they never could have developed themselves."

The urge to destroy may not come from Islam, but creation is not Islam's strong suit either. In his seminal book *The Creators*, historian Daniel Boorstin explains the Islamic approach to innovation. While Judaism and Christianity begin with the Creation, Islam reveres a God who creates nothing. It is a central tenet of Islam that God did not even create the Koran. According to Boorstin, mullahs teach that since "the speech of God is uncreate, the words must be eternal uncreate." The world comes into being not by God's energy and initiative, but by fiat—much like Supreme Court rulings. As Boorstin says, "For a believing Muslim, to create is a rash and dangerous act." I guess that would explain why they don't have chairs.

Mohammed Atta loathed skyscrapers. *Newsweek* reported that he viewed the emergence of tall buildings in Egypt as an odious surrender to Western values. The most fitting memorial to the victims of the World Trade Center attack is to build the world's most breathtaking skyscraper in the world on top of Mohammed Atta's corpse. ■

☛ This Whistle-Blower They Like

JUNE 13, 2002

In their enthusiasm to bash the Bush administration for its handling of the war—which Democrats consider an annoying distraction from the real business of government, which is redistributing income—the left has embraced FBI agent Coleen Rowley as a modern Joan of Arc. From liberal headquarters at the *New York Times,* Maureen Dowd fawns over Rowley, calling her "the blunt Midwesterner" who painted a "stunning and gruesome portrait of just how far gone the bureau is." Frank Rich calls her "a forthright American woman."

At least liberals seem to have gotten over their disdain for government whistle-blowers. Back when the world's most famous whistle-blower produced tapes proving the president of the United States had committed a slew of felonies, the Left was somewhat muted in its enthusiasm for female truth-tellers. Dowd called Linda Tripp a "witch" with a "boiling cauldron." Rich said Americans "despise" a "snitch." Fortunately for Rowley, she is only a snitch against the FBI. One shudders to think what names liberals would be calling the unglamorous agent if she were testifying against Bill Clinton.

Also fortunately for Rowley, liberals aren't listening to her. It is striking how the media have studiously ignored Rowley's specific indictment of the FBI, preferring to prattle on about her raw courage in the abstract. Dowd exclaimed that Rowley painted "a stunning and gruesome portrait of just how far gone the bureau is." Okay—but what did she say exactly? Bewildering news accounts leave the impression that Rowley's act of dauntless valor was to fly to Washington to tell the Senate that the FBI has really old computers.

In fact, the gravamen of Rowley's 13-page memo is essentially that FBI headquarters botched the Zacarias Moussaoui case by refusing to racially profile Muslims. Boiled to its essentials, Rowley's theory is that being a Muslim should constitute probable cause. Rowley condemned FBI brass for refusing to authorize a search warrant for Moussaoui based on the following information: (1) he refused to consent to a search of his computer; (2) he was in flight school; (3) he had overstayed his visa; and (4) he was a Muslim.

Let's see, which of these factors constitutes probable cause?

- Refusal to consent to a search? It is your right to refuse. Any other rule would allow cops to bootstrap their way into a warrant. "Hi, Zacarias, may we search your computer? No? That's suspicious! Grounds for a warrant!" I don't think so.
- In flight school? NO.
- Overstayed visa? NO.
- Is a Muslim? NOT ALLOWED.

As Rowley admits, "reasonable minds may differ as to whether probable cause existed" on the basis of the above facts. But, she says, once French Intelligence confirmed Moussaoui's affiliations with "radical fundamentalist Islamic groups," probable cause was "certainly established." Not under the law it wasn't. Being in league with known terrorists may be suspicious, but it is not probable cause to believe that a particular crime has been committed by a specific individual. (Were the law otherwise, cops could get a warrant to search anyone who associates with the Clintons.)

Moreover, any Muslim who has attended a mosque in Europe—certainly in England, where Moussaoui lived—has affiliated with "radical fundamentalist Islamic groups." A few months after the September 11 attack, 80 percent of British Muslims said they opposed the war in Afghanistan. The Muslim Council of Britain called for an immediate end to the war. A poll by the *Daily Telegraph* found that 98 percent of Muslims between the ages of twenty and forty-five said they would not fight for Britain, but almost half said they would fight for Osama bin Laden. A Gallup poll taken in nine Muslim nations last year found that only 18 percent of the people believed the yarn about Arabs flying planes into buildings on September 11. (Many subscribed to the Zionist plot theory.) This was based on almost ten thousand face-to-face interviews in Saudi Arabia, Iran, Pakistan, Indonesia, Turkey, Lebanon, Kuwait, Jordan, and Morocco. Seventy-seven percent said America's military action in Afghanistan was "morally unjustified." (Just to give you some idea how extreme that is, even liberals pretended to support war with Afghanistan!) In other words, if you associate with Muslims abroad, you are associating with Muslim fanatics. Rowley's position is that "probable cause" existed to search Moussaoui's computer because he was a Muslim who had lived abroad.

I happen to agree with her, but liberals don't. So how did Rowley become the Left's new Norma Rae? Given their nutty ideas, liberals should be applauding FBI headquarters for refusing to consider the fact that Moussaoui was a Muslim, and condemning this incipient Mark Fuhrman. Rowley is my hero, not theirs. FBI headquarters rebuffed Rowley's callous insensitivity to Muslims and denied a warrant request to search Moussaoui's computer—and thus failed to uncover the September 11 plot. The FBI allowed thousands of Americans to be slaughtered on the altar of political correctness. What more could liberals ask for? ■

☞ My Name Is Adolf

SEPTEMBER 12, 2002

Among the patriotic lesson plans for 9/11 was one proposed by the National Council for Social Studies, which recommends a short story titled "My Name Is Osama." Calculatedly inciting hatred toward white American boys, the story is about a nasty little boy, "Todd," who taunts an Iraqi immigrant named "Osama":

"Your mom is a rag head."

He doesn't know my mother has a Ph.D. in pharmacology. She taught my pediatrician at Baghdad University.

Todd says, "Your father forces your mother to wear a bag on her head. Your father must be a bully."

My mother wears a hijab because she likes to. (http://www.ncss. org/resources/moments/nameisosama.shtml)

This is the lesson to commemorate the biggest hate crime in history—committed by someone named "Osama" against people with names like "Todd." Liberals are incapable of embarrassment—they're like Arabs without the fighting spirit. How about a 1942 lesson plan titled "My Name Is Adolf"? And while we're on the subject, might the 9/11 lesson plan inquire into what little "Osama" thinks about the terrorist attack? May we ask? (Question from the actual lesson plan: "Why, do you think, did Osama's family leave Iraq?" Incorrect answer: Because his father wanted to attend flight school in America.)

To be sure, there have been a number of hate crimes committed since 9/11. But they were committed by Muslims. Hesham Mohamed Hadayet murdered two and wounded many more at Los Angeles International Airport. Suleyman al-Faris, aka "John Walker Lindh," joined an attack in Afghanistan that left Michael Spann dead. Abdel Rahim, aka "Richard Reid," tried but failed to murder a planeload of people on an American Airlines jet headed to Miami. Meanwhile, there has been precisely one confirmed hate crime committed in retaliation for the monstrous 9/11 attack. Some nut in Arizona murdered a Sikh thinking he was a Muslim. Current hate crime tally: Muslims: over 3,000 (and counting); White Guys: 1.

In the spirit of specifically targeting only the worrisome Muslims, I note that the media have inadvertently identified several of them with blinding clarity. In case you missed these stories, I bring them to your attention so you will be forewarned: Do not fly with any of these kids. Soon after the terrorist attack, the *New York Times* chatted with students at the Al Noor School, a private Islamic academy in Brooklyn—evidently the Arab equivalent of the Horace Mann High School (Anthony Lewis, '44). None of the students said they had experienced any harassment since September 11. To the contrary, their school had been deluged with support from local Catholic schools, hospitals, state education officials, and political leaders.

But the love was entirely one-sided. The students stated point-blank that they would not fight for America against a fellow Muslim. They denied that Osama bin Laden was behind the attacks. They criticized the United States for its cruel treatment of Muslims. "Isn't it ironic," one Islamic student sneered, "that the interests of America are always against what Muslims want?" That's why the last several major American interventions—in Kuwait, Somalia, and the Balkans—were all in defense of Muslims. Of course, there was the attack on Osama bin Laden, but according to them, he wasn't practicing "true Islam." I wish they'd get their stories straight: Do most Muslims support bin Laden or not? Though uniformly refusing to believe bin Laden was behind the terrorist attack, the students showed a remarkable lack of curiosity about who was behind it.

Students from the Al Noor School were interviewed again a few weeks later, this time by CBS's *60 Minutes*. The students instantly and enthusiastically agreed with the proposition that a "Muslim who becomes a suicide bomber goes to Paradise for that action." One student answered, "Definitely" and called a female suicide bomber "very brave." Others said they earnestly hoped the suicide bombers went to Paradise. "I mean, they're doing it for a good cause," one boy explained. "I pray that they go to Paradise," another said. Most comforting, one student said, "I think we'd all probably do the same."

Weeks later, at the urging of the principal, the students modified their answers. But according to CBS, "None of them changed their view that suicide bombers in Israel would go to Paradise." The Islamic studies teacher at Al Noor claimed the students misunderstood true Islam: "If you go to chapter 4, verse 29, it says so clear, 'Do not kill yourself.'" It's always so comforting when Muslims cite the precise verse from the Koran that tells them killing is wrong. Don't all empathic human beings understand instinctively that suicide and murder are wrong? What if they lost their Koran that day and couldn't remember the specific verse condemning murder?

In any event, and more to the point, the Koran does not strictly inveigh against killing *someone else* for Allah. In the eye-opening book *Unveiling Islam,* Christian-convert authors Ergun Mehmet Caner and Emir Fethi Caner say the Koran "promises Paradise to those who die in battle for Islam more certainly than it promises salvation to anyone else." Muhammad says, "Fighting is prescribed upon you. . . . Tumult and oppression are worse than slaughter." The Koran instructs, "Fight those who believe not in Allah nor the Last Day . . . until they pay compensation with willing submission, and feel themselves subdued." It promises, "If you are slain or die in the way of Allah, forgiveness and mercy from Allah are far better than all they could amass."

Among the most famous victims of Islam's will to slaughter as practiced on 9/11 was a man named "Todd"—just like the nasty little boy in the social studies lesson. When Todd Beamer and the other passengers on United Airlines Flight 93 realized the Muslim hijackers were on a mission of death, they fought back. The real Todd did not shout "God is great!" before ripping out an innocent man's entrails. Todd Beamer prayed, "The Lord is my shepherd; I shall not want. He maketh me to lie down in green pastures: He leadeth me beside the still waters. He restoreth my soul: He leadeth me in the paths of righteousness for His name's sake. Yea, though I walk through the valley of the shadow of death, I will fear no evil: for Thou art with me." ■

☞ Beauty Pageants Can Be Murder

NOVEMBER 28, 2002

The Religion of Peace suffered another PR setback this week when Muslims in Nigeria welcomed the Miss World beauty pageant by slaughtering Christians in the street and burning churches to the ground. At last count, more than two hundred people were dead, hundreds more were injured, and thousands were left without homes. Also, the Nigerian contestant's chances of winning "Miss Congeniality" were cruelly dashed.

Leaping at the one chance they had to attract positive press to their pissant country and begin the process of dragging themselves out of the thirteenth century, Nigerian Muslims instead chose to hack innocent people to death in the name of Allah. Pageant officials pulled up stakes and immediately took the show to London. One assumes the director of the Nigerian Department of Tourism isn't pleased. Winning the pageant site had been an uphill battle from the beginning. Some of the more closed-minded Miss World participants were already carping about the upcoming stoning of a Nigerian woman, in accordance with Islamic Sharia law.

The president of Nigeria, Olusegun Obasanjo, tried to downplay the Muslims' murderous rampage by cheerfully explaining, "The beauty queens should not feel that they are the cause of the violence. It could happen at any time irresponsible journalism is committed against Islam." Well, that's a relief. It seems an article in a Nigerian newspaper had mused that the Prophet Muhammad "would probably have chosen a wife" from among the Miss World contestants. This upset the practitioners of the Religion of Peace. (And for good reason. Their polygamous prophet actually preferred his wives a little younger—one of Muhammad's wives was six years old.) Muslims reacted to the article by bludgeoning, stabbing, and burning Christians to death. Some enforcers of the Religion of Peace in Nigeria ordered Muslims to kill the author of this blasphemy. (Overheard at the Miss World contest: "Does this make me look fatwa?")

As long as liberals are going to keep demanding that Americans refer to Islam as a "religion of peace," it would be a big help if Muslims would stop killing people. The *New York Times* simply refuses to admit that their little darlings—angry, violent Muslims—could ever be at fault for killing people. That makes no sense because Islam is a Religion of Peace. The *Times* reviewed the facts of the slaughter during the Miss World contest, processed them through a PC prism, and came to the conclusion that Islam is peaceful but religion causes violence. Thus, according to the *Times* headline, "Religious Violence in Nigeria Drives Out Miss World Event." It wasn't Muslims killing people; it was nonspecific "religious violence." The article explained that Muslims pouring out of mosques to kill Christians and torch churches in Nigeria resulted from "the tinderbox of religious passions in the country." The police step in to try to quell rioting Muslims, and the *Times* reports this as "fighting between Christians and Muslims." Ah, the cycle of violence.

Religion causes violence and never mind that the most bloodthirsty cult in the twentieth century was an atheistic sect known as "communism." It was not "true communism"! And Muslim terrorists are not practicing "true Islam." Ironically, liberals would hate Muslims who practiced "true Islam." Without the terrorism, Muslims are just another group of "antichoice" fanatics.

Winning "Best in Show" was the *Times*'s headline on an article about the Christian missionary shot dead in Lebanon by a Muslim: "Killing Underscores Enmity of Evangelists and Muslims." This is like referring to the enmity between a woman and her rapist. She hates him, he hates her. It's a cycle of violence! Except the funny thing about the Christians is, they still love the Muslims. The Muslims' main beef with the Christians was—I quote—Christians "destroy the fighting spirit of the children, especially of the Palestinian youth, by teaching them not to fight the Jews, [teaching] the Palestinians to forgive the Jews and leave them Jerusalem."

The *Times* seemed to agree the Muslims had a point with the evangelical. Just as no new data can shake the *Times's* belief that Islam is a religion of peace, nothing can disabuse them of the idea that Christians, as a general matter, deserve to be shot. In a news analysis, the *Times* said the missionaries *claimed* they were merely exposing people to Jesus Christ. "But," the *Times* said in a *j'accuse* tone, "a somewhat more direct goal emerges amid the Web site postings." The *Times* had caught the Christians red-handed committing irresponsible web postings against Islam! They were asking for it. (On the bright side, at least this means the *Times* is holding the gun innocent in this one instance.) Luckily for the *Times*, Christians do not rip out people's entrails in response to "irresponsible journalism" committed against Christianity. ■

☞ War-Torn Democrats

JANUARY 29, 2003

Last week Senator John Kerry gave a speech saying: "Mr. President, do not rush to war!" Rush to war? We've been talking about this war for a year. It's been three months since Kerry duly recorded his vote in favor of a war resolution to forcibly remove Saddam Hussein from power.

In 1991, Kerry voted against the Gulf War, saying the country was "not yet ready for what it will witness and bear if we go to war." Having been taunted for that vote and that prediction ever since, this time Kerry made sure to vote in favor of war with Iraq. This will allow the *New York Times* to describe him as a "moderate Democrat" forevermore. Indeed, a surprisingly large number of Democrats voted for the war resolution last October. But as soon as the November elections were over, Democrats like Kerry began aggressively attacking the very war they had just voted for.

These Democrats want to have it both ways. If the war goes well—a lot of them voted for war with Iraq, didn't they? But if the war does not go well, many of the very Democrats who voted for the war resolution will have emerged as leading spokesmen for the antiwar position. A vote for the war, surrounded by Neville Chamberlain foot-dragging, is a fraud.

The Neville Chamberlain Democrats are now claiming they didn't realize what they were voting for. John Kerry says he thought a resolution authorizing the president to use force against Iraq meant that the United Nations would have to approve. Dianne Feinstein said she voted for the resolution assuming it meant we would invade only if "our allies" approved. Joe Biden made the terrific argument that if we don't wait for UN approval, it would "make a mockery of the efficacy of the UN." The Democrats appear to be the only people who still believe there is any "efficacy" to the UN. In any event, I believe the United Nations should be more worried about that consequence than we should.

Kerry claims he is still foursquare behind disarming Saddam Hussein, but not "until we have exhausted the remedies available, built legitimacy, and earned the consent of the American people, absent, of course, an imminent threat requiring urgent action." As George Bush pointed out in his State of the Union address, dictators are not in the habit of "politely putting us on notice before they strike." By the time a threat is "imminent," the Capitol will be gone.

That's the short version. The long version of Kerry's position is this: "[I]f you have a breach that, by everybody's standard, at least in the United States, those of us in the House and Senate, and the president, join together and make a judgment, this is indeed a material breach, and then others—some of them can't be persuaded—if we have evidence, sufficient to show the materiality of the breach, we should be able to do what Adlai Stevenson did on behalf of the administration, Kennedy administration, and sit in front of the Security Council and say, 'Here is the evidence. It's time for all of you to put up. We need to all do this together.' And that's what I think the resolution that was passed suggests."

There's a call to arms to unite the Democrats! If there has been a material breach "by everybody's standard," then and only then, we can boldly go . . . to the United Nations! This is the fundamental problem of the antiwar movement. They can't bring themselves to say it's a mistake to depose Saddam Hussein, and "don't hurry" is not much of a rallying cry.

Why not hurry? Democrats claim they haven't seen proof yet that Saddam is a direct threat to the United States. For laughs, let's suppose they're right. In the naysayers' worst-case scenario, the United States would be acting precipitously to remove a ruthless dictator who tortures his own people, gassed the Kurds, and allows his sons to operate rape rooms. As

Bush said, after detailing some of Saddam Hussein's charming practices: "If this is not evil, then evil has no meaning." It's not as if anyone is worried that through some horrible miscalculation we could be removing the Iraqi Abraham Lincoln by mistake.

Either we're removing a dictator who currently has plans to fund terrorism against American citizens or—if Bush is completely wrong and Eleanor Clift is completely right—we're just removing a dictator who plans to terrorize a lot of people in the region, but not Americans specifically. Even for someone like me, who doesn't want America to be the world's policeman, the risk of precipitous action against Saddam Hussein doesn't keep me up at night.

The Democrats' jejune claim that Saddam Hussein is not a threat to our security presupposes they would care if he were. Who are they kidding? Democrats adore threats to the United States. Bush got a raucous standing ovation at his State of the Union address when he announced that "this year, for the first time, we are beginning to field a defense to protect this nation against ballistic missiles." The excitement was noticeably muted on the Democrats' side of the aisle. The vast majority of Democrats remained firmly in their seats, sullen at the thought that America would be protected from incoming ballistic missiles. To paraphrase George Bush: If this is not treason, then treason has no meaning. ■

☞ "Will of Allah" Preempts Iraq Invasion
FEBRUARY 6, 2003

I knew the media were up to something with their wall-to-wall coverage of the Columbia space shuttle explosion. The full story is: Shuttle disintegrated during reentry; all astronauts killed, including some very remarkable people; very sad; NASA picking up the debris to figure out what happened. It was a plane crash story, only a lot more expensive. So why was the shuttle explosion being covered like the 9/11 attack?

A quick review of the *Treason Times* laid bare the seditious objective. The shuttle presented a new argument for appeasement. *Warning, Great Satan: Your money and technology and little gadgets cannot insulate you from disaster!* The *New York Times* proclaimed, "As Iraq War Looms, a New Sense of Vulnerability." American hubris blunted again! Breathless news accounts of the shuttle blast were merely a more demure version of Islamic terrorists cheering in the street in reaction to the explosion. If the *Times* weren't afraid of violating the "wall of separation," it would have run an editorial titled "It was the will of Allah!"

The *Times* quoted a series of random Americans saying things like "Now I'm hearing a lot of people say if we go to war, we're going to endanger a lot more than seven lives." Another classic *Times* Man on the Street said that it reinforced his belief "that we should find diplomatic solutions instead of threatening other countries with war." For one year, in a nation ablaze with war fever, I don't believe the *Times* has managed to interview a single person who supports war with Iraq. Their Man on the Street always seems to be standing on a street suspiciously close to Central Park West.

The Gettysburg Address of liberal idiocy was a letter to the editor from a Jim Forbes of San Francisco two days after the crash. The *Times* titled his contribution to Liberalthink "A Time of Mourning for Shattered Dreams: A Period of Healing." In full-dress sanctimony, Forbes wrote, "The loss of the space shuttle Columbia and its crew of seven is a national tragedy. Time is needed for Americans to mourn. I hope that President Bush will do the right thing by slowing down his march to war and focusing instead on the healing that such a blow to national pride requires."

Here was a pithy concentration of the multiple idiotic things liberals were saying about the space shuttle, the insincerity, the audacity, the smarminess—he even worked in "the healing process." How Jim Forbes of San Francisco must have polished that little gem! The idea that liberals feel the shuttle explosion was a tragedy is patent nonsense. They were ecstatic at this new excuse to condemn the "march to war." The nation is marching to war at such breakneck speed, it will be two years from 9/11 before we finally attack Iraq.

Morose that their relentless nay-saying is having no effect on the president's war plans, *New York Times* columnists are now positing imaginary scenarios in which war with Iraq leads to a stock market crash and brings the nation to the brink of nuclear war. Nicholas Kristof has gone the Maureen Dowd route of using the op-ed page of the *Times* for a dream-sequence column. But instead of dreaming about Bush being retarded, as Dowd does, Kristof dreams of catastrophe for America. In Kristof's fantasy, Bush eventually apologizes to Secretary of State Colin

Powell for invading Iraq. The strain of not having a Democrat in the Oval Office to lose wars for America is driving liberals to fevered fantasies of America's defeat somewhere in the world.

In other appeasement news, former UN arms inspector Scott Ritter has completely vanished from the antiwar scene since news of his sex arrest broke. Three weeks ago, it was revealed that Ritter was nabbed soliciting sex from underage girls on the Internet in 2001. He was charged with attempted endangerment of a child and the case was adjourned in contemplation of dismissal, with directions for him to stay out of trouble for six months. Until news of his sex arrest became public, the *New York Times* had been treating Ritter's reincarnation as a peacenik as the greatest act of patriotism since Nathan Hale told the British he regretted only that he had but one life to give for his country. It's now Day 17 and counting of the *Times*'s refusal to mention Ritter's arrest. (As we go to press on the book, it's Day 562 of the *Times*'s refusal to mention Ritter's arrest.) Though the peace movement lost Ritter, it seems to have picked up Jerry Springer. Perhaps Springer is hoping he can get Scott Ritter's wife on the show to confront Ritter and the underage girl.

But Ritter was a freelance peacenik. At least the *Times* could count on stability and permanence from John Hartpence Kerry. Poor Kerry was just on the verge of figuring out whether he was for war with Iraq or against it when he was told he hadn't figured out his own last name. Kerry was shocked to be told that, despite years of allowing himself to be passed off as an Irish Brahmin, both his paternal grandparents were Jewish and his real name is Kohn. When confronted with the news, Kerry said there were signs he missed, such as his longtime, twice-requited desire to marry a rich shiksa. Now Kerry will need time for the healing process. We must halt the march to war. ■

☞ Kissing Cousins: New York Literati and Nazis

MARCH 20, 2003

It became clear the nation was finally going to war with Iraq this week when the *New York Times* pulled two dozen reporters off the Augusta National Golf Club story. On Monday, President Bush gave Saddam Hussein forty-eight hours to get out of Baghdad or the U.S. military would remove him forcibly. Many still held out hope that Saddam would abandon power without a fight—primarily so we could listen to liberals explain how a peaceful resolution was brought about by their urgent demands that we work through the United Nations, and had nothing to do with the fact that Saddam was surrounded by 200,000 American troops.

In response to Bush's ultimatum, Saddam's son, Uday Hussein, said Bush was stupid. He said Bush wanted to attack Iraq because of his family. And he said American boys would die. At least someone is finding the *New York Times* helpful these days!

In angry harangues largely indistinguishable from the one by Uday Hussein, the Democrats were outraged at Bush. Senator Joe Lieberman (Democrat of Connecticut) spent forty minutes detailing Saddam Hussein's manifest cruelties and violations of all human norms. Without breaking a sweat, Lieberman then said he could understand why the French were not bothered by these indisputable barbarisms: It was Bush's failure of "diplomacy." Bush, the clod, had failed to convince the inconvincible.

Senator Tom Daschle (Democrat of South Dakota) said, "I'm saddened, saddened that this president failed so miserably at diplomacy that we're now forced to war. Saddened that we have to give up one life because this president couldn't create the kind of diplomatic effort that was so critical for our country." Mostly, the Democrats were saddened that America was about to win a war.

With the nation on the verge of a glorious military triumph, liberals have had to put their predictions of a Vietnam "quagmire" on the back burner for a few weeks. Instead, they have turned with a vengeance to attacking "American arrogance." The day after President Bush's speech, *Washington Post* columnist David Ignatius spoke of self-defeating "American arrogance." The *Post* quoted "a senior U.S. official" (that's newspaper jargon for: "a janitor at the Pentagon who picked up the phone") warning of "a degree of hubris unprecedented in American history." The *New York Times*'s lead editorial the day after Bush's speech also bemoaned American "hubris." One front-page article called Bush trigger-happy and another bitterly accused him of breaking a campaign pledge to preside over a "humble" America. In the nineteen months since the 9/11 attack, the *Times* has used the phrase "American arrogance" nearly as many times (seventeen) as in the entire 96 months of the Clinton presidency (twenty-four). Instead of American arrogance, the *Times* yearns to return to Clintonian flatulence.

There was no more eloquent testimony to what liberals mean by "American arrogance" than an article in the March 10 *New Yorker,* which nonchalantly quoted a Nazi in support of the proposition that Americans are jingoistic, imperialist rednecks. Amid page after gleeful page of European venom toward Americans, Columbia University professor Simon Schama quoted the anti-American bile of Norwegian writer and renowned Nazi-sympathizer Knut Hamsun.

Schama admiringly cited Hamsun's contempt for American patriotism, neglecting to mention that Hamsun went for Nazi patriotism in a big way. Beginning in the early thirties and until his death in 1952, Hamsun was absolutely smitten with Adolf Hitler. When the Nazis invaded Norway, Hamsun wrote a newspaper column saying, "NORWEGIANS! Throw down your rifles and go home again. The Germans are fighting for us all." He exchanged gifts and telegrams with Goebbels and Hitler. Indeed, so enamored of Joseph Goebbels was Hamsun that he gave Goebbels his Nobel Prize medal. Inconsolable upon news of the Führer's death, Hamsun was quoted in an obituary on Hitler saying, "I am not worthy to speak his name." He never equivocated and he never apologized.

Between issuing tributes to Hitler, Hamsun wrote the ironically titled book *The Cultural Life of Modern America,* which, as professor Schama sniggeringly writes, was "largely devoted to asserting its nonexistence." Hamsun called America "a strapping child-monster whose runaway physical growth would never be matched by moral or cultural maturity." For "cultural maturity," Hamsun turned to Nazi Germany.

Hamsun hated America for all the same reasons liberals hate America. To the delight of New York sophisticates, Hamsun sneered at Americans who march in veterans' parades, "with tiny flags in their hats and brass medals on their chests marching in step to the hundreds of penny whistles they are blowing." America's little patriotic parades apparently compared unfavorably to a stirring Nazi war rally. This is the essence of liberal admiration for Europeans and their pompous cultural snobbery: For proof that Americans are jingoistic hicks, they cite a Nazi. ∎

☞ The Enemy Within

MARCH 28, 2003

Just five days into the war in Iraq, the *New York Times* was optimistically reporting that despite a strong start, American troops had gotten bogged down. This came as a surprise to regular readers of the *Times* who remembered that the *Times* thought we were bogged down from the moment the war began. The day after the first bombs were dropped on Baghdad, the *New York Times* ran a front-page article describing the mood of the nation thus: "Some faced it with tears, others with contempt, none with gladness."

Apparently some people were gladdened: The stock market had its best week in twenty years. What people do with their money is a rather more profound barometer of public sentiment than any stupid poll— much less bald assertions by *New York Times* reporters. *Times* news stories are beginning to have the ring of Arab-style proclamations in defiance of the facts. As with Saddam Hussein, the truth for them has no meaning. They say whatever honor commands them to say.

Five days after the *Treason Times* was morosely reporting that no one viewed the war with gladness . . . things had gotten even worse! In a single editorial, the *Times* said our troops were "faced with battlefield death, human error and other tragedies." The task "looks increasingly formidable." There were "disturbing events," and American forces were engaged in a "fierce firefight—an early glimpse of urban warfare." There were "downsides," "disheartening events," and "grievous blows." *We're losing this war! The Elite Republican Guard is assembling outside New York City! Head for the hills!* In fact, the "fierce firefight" referred to in the editorial concerned a battle in Nasiriyah in which American troops took an entire city with nine casualties. That's what most people call a "triumphal a**-kicking."

CNN's favorite general, Wesley Clark, has also been heard to opine that our troops are getting bogged down in Iraq. His competence to judge American generals is questionable, inasmuch as his command was limited to NATO. We prefer to hear from American generals, thanks. When Clark was NATO commander in the Balkans, his contribution to international peace consisted of mistakenly bombing the Chinese embassy in

Belgrade and ordering U.S. pilots to fly at such high altitudes that even the pilots complained they were being forced to incur unnecessary civilian casualties. On MSNBC, Forrest Sawyer compared Iraqi forces killing our troops to American revolutionaries and said the war was likely to turn into a "nightmare."

Liberals never quit. American forces have taken two-thirds of Iraq and are fast advancing on Baghdad. Saddam's lieutenants are so demoralized that they have turned to lashing out at the Jews. Saddam's vice despot Tariq Aziz says the war is being fought only to "create something called greater Israel." (If the dictator business doesn't work out for him, at least Aziz is well positioned to run for Congress as a Democrat.) Thousands of Iraqi soldiers have surrendered or disbanded, thousands more have been captured, and still thousands more have been killed. Meanwhile, American forces have suffered fewer than two dozen deaths. And if that's not enough to convince you the war is going splendidly, just look at the increasingly gloomy expression on Dan Rather's face.

Most auspiciously, the Arab League has appealed to the United Nations Security Council to stop the war. One can only hope the Security Council will agree to intervene. I'd like to see them try to stop us. Would France threaten us with war? Young men across America would have to enlist as a matter of honor. The army could use it as a recruiting slogan: "Are you too chicken to fight the French?" Even liberals would enlist as a way to pick up credit for military service with no risk of injury.

Not surprisingly, the *New York Times* gave Saddam's recent speech more exultant coverage than they did Bush's State of the Union address. Since the first bomb hit Baghdad, everyone at the *Times* had been itching to use the word "quagmire." Somewhat surprisingly, Saddam beat even Maureen Dowd to the punch. According to Saddam, the invading forces are "in real trouble." The *Times* agrees. Liberals aren't afraid we'll do badly in Baghdad. They're afraid we'll do well.

After the Arab television network al-Jazeera repeatedly ran footage of U.S. prisoners of war over the weekend, the New York Stock Exchange threw al-Jazeera reporters off the trading floor. This raises the question: When are they going to remove the *Times* reporters? ■

☞ At Least Saddam Wasn't at Tailhook!

APRIL 17, 2003

Despite liberals' calm assurance that Iraq wasn't harboring terrorists, this week Abul Abbas, mastermind of the 1985 *Achille Lauro* hijacking, was captured in Baghdad. This is the second time the United States has caught Abbas. The last time, the Europeans let him go. (Which may explain why liberals are so eager to have Europeans "help" with the war on terrorism—they've done such a bang-up job in the past.)

In 1985, Muslim terrorists hijacked the Italian cruise ship *Achille Lauro* and threatened to kill the passengers and crew unless fifty imprisoned Palestinians were released by Israel. The terrorists doused American and British women with gasoline and taunted them with matches. They forced passengers to hold live grenades. When their demands were not met, the terrorists shot a wheelchair-bound American, Leon Klinghoffer, and forced other passengers at gunpoint to throw him overboard in his wheelchair.

Even as the Americans were preparing a rescue mission, the Italian and Egyptian governments made a deal with the terrorists, offering the release of the Palestinians and safe passage to Tunisia to end the ordeal. The Europeans were delighted with this masterful act of diplomacy. The Americans were not so pleased.

So Oliver North conceived of an operation to get the terrorists back. Contrary to Egyptian president Mubarak's assurances that the terrorists had already left Egypt, North found out the terrorists were still there. Working with Israeli intelligence, North ascertained the precise EgyptAir flight that would carry the terrorists out of Egypt, right down to the flight number. He devised a plan to intercept the plane, modeled on the military's interception of Yamamoto, mastermind of Pearl Harbor during World War II.

President Reagan was briefed on the daring plan—along with copious warnings from timorous State Department officials that the Europeans might have their feelings bruised, America would look like a cowboy, and it would only strengthen the hard-liners in Egypt. Asked if the operation should proceed, Reagan said, "Good God! They've murdered an American here. Let's get on with it."

Admiral Frank Kelso, the officer in charge of America's Sixth Fleet in the Mediterranean, ordered his men to carry out the mission. In no time flat, Tomcat fighters had taken off from the U.S. aircraft carrier *Saratoga*. Guided by Hawkeyes, the Tomcats caught up with the EgyptAir flight. The fighters stealthily trailed their target in total darkness, their lights off, even in the cockpit. The American pilots flew so close to the EgyptAir flight, they used flashlights to read the plane's tail number. Then the Tomcats swooped in, surrounded the EgyptAir flight, and forced it to fly to a NATO base on Sicily controlled by the United States. The *New York Post* headline the next day was "GOT 'EM." And then Abul Abbas was released by the Europeans and given safe haven in Iraq under Saddam Hussein—whom liberals have assured us was not harboring terrorists. Republicans keep catching terrorists and liberals keep sending them back.

If there is a parable of how liberals support the enemy, this is it. Admiral Kelso, whose men carried out the dauntless EgyptAir interception, was cashiered out of the navy because of Tailhook. Feminists don't care about Saddam Hussein and his rape rooms. But they were hopping mad at Admiral Kelso for strolling through the Tailhook convention to say hello to his boys—among them, the ones who captured Leon Klinghoffer's murderers.

To jog the memory of the horror that was Tailhook, Lieutenant Paula Coughlin, the officer who made the most lurid allegations, accused a black Marine of molesting her. But then she kept identifying different black males as the perpetrator. Liberals managed to put their concern for racist accusations against blacks on the back burner in this case. (When liberals get going, the ironies never end.) Though Admiral Kelso was cleared of any wrongdoing after an official navy investigation, liberals still wanted him punished. Former Representative Patricia Schroeder (Democrat from Colorado) engaged in a hysterical witchhunt of Kelso, marching with her fellow termagants to the Senate to demand that their colleagues deny Kelso retirement with four stars. The *New York Times* editorialized against Kelso.

After a lifetime of honorable service to his country, Admiral Kelso barely managed to retire with four stars, in a 54–43 Senate vote. A majority of Democrats opposed Kelso, along with all the Republican women in the Senate—Kay Bailey Hutchison, Nancy Landon Kassebaum, and Arlen Specter. Had the Senate denied Kelso his retirement with four stars, this American hero would have received a pension of $67,000 per year, rather than the princely sum of $84,000 per year accorded a four-star admiral.

The Left's relentless attacks on Oliver North hardly require elaboration. He was investigated, charged with crimes, indicted by Lawrence Walsh, and his Senate campaign was destroyed. Al Gore compared North's supporters to Down syndrome children. Now Democrats are demanding that the Europeans be let into Iraq so they can release some more terrorists, while liberals do their part at home, carving up the colonels and admirals who capture the people who murder Americans. ∎

☞ Liberals Meet Unexpected Resistance

MAY 1, 2003

Though many had anticipated a cakewalk for the media in undermining the war on terrorism, instead liberals are caught in a quagmire of good news about the war. Predictions that liberals would have an easy time embarrassing President Bush have met unexpected resistance. They're still looking for the bad news they said was there. Experts believe the media's quagmire results from severely reduced troops. The Left's current force is less than half the size of the coalition media that lost the Vietnam War.

It's been a tough few weeks all around for the antiwar crowd. On Sunday, the London *Telegraph* reported that documents had been discovered in Baghdad linking Saddam Hussein to Osama bin Laden. Hussein and bin Laden had a working relationship as far back as 1998, based on their mutual hatred of America and Saudi Arabia. The Osama files showed that the Iraqis were working feverishly to establish a "future relationship" with bin Laden and to "achieve a direct meeting with him." The meeting with Osama's envoy took place a few months before al Qaeda bombed two American embassies in East Africa.

As we go to print, it's Day 4 of the *New York Times*'s refusal to mention these documents. (And as we go to print on the book, it's Day 492 of the *New York Times*'s refusal to mention these documents.) Government documents have also been found in Iraq showing that a leading antiwar spokesman in Britain, Member of Parliament George Galloway, was in Saddam Hussein's pay. Galloway says the documents are "forgeries" and the Iraqis set him up. Scott Ritter, former UN arms inspector turned peacenik, erstwhile suspected pederast, immediately defended Galloway in a column in the London *Guardian*. With any luck, Tariq Aziz will now step in to defend Ritter.

At least Tariq Aziz knows he lost the war. American liberals are still hoping for a late-inning rally. But the war was so successful, they don't have any arguments left. Liberals can't even sound busy. In their usual parody of patriotism, liberals are masters of the long-winded statement that amounts to nothing. They can't go on TV and say nothing, but all they can find to complain about are some broken figurines.

Liberals said chemical weapons would be used against our troops. That didn't happen. They predicted huge civilian casualties. That didn't happen. They said Americans would turn against the war as our troops came home in body bags. That didn't happen. They warned of a mammoth terrorist attack in America if we invaded Iraq. That didn't happen. Just two weeks ago, they claimed American troops were caught in another Vietnam quagmire. That didn't happen. The only mishap liberals can carp about is that some figurines from an Iraqi museum were broken—a relief to college students everywhere who have ever been forced to gaze upon Mesopotamian pottery. We're not talking about Rodins here. So the Iraqis looted. Oh well. Wars are messy. Liberalism is part of a religious disorder that demands a belief that life is controllable.

At least we finally got liberals on the record against looting. It seems the looting in Iraq compared unfavorably with the "rebellion" in Los Angeles after the Rodney King verdict. When "rebels" in Los Angeles began looting, liberals said it was a sign of frustration—they were poor and hungry. (As someone noted at the time, apparently they were thirsty, too, since they hit a lot of liquor stores.) At least the Iraqis were careful to target the precise source of their oppression: They looted Saddam's palace, official government buildings—and the French cultural center.

However many precious pots were stolen, it has to be said: The Iraqi people behaved considerably better than the French. After Americans liberated Paris, thousands of Frenchmen were killed by other Frenchmen on allegations of collaboration with the Nazis. Subsequent scholarship has shown that charges of "collaboration" were often nothing more than a settling of personal grudges and family feuds—which was made easy by the fact that so many Frenchmen really did collaborate with the Nazis. The

French didn't seem to resent the Nazi occupation very much. Nazi occupation is their default position. They began squirming only after Americans came in and imposed democracy on them.

Despondent over the success of the war in Iraq, liberals tried to cheer themselves up with the politics of personal destruction—their second favorite hobby after defending Saddam Hussein. Responding to the question of whether the Supreme Court should hold sodomy to be a fundamental constitutional right, Republican senator Rick Santorum made the indisputably true point that a general right to engage in consensual sex would logically include adultery, polygamy, and any number of sex acts prohibited by the states.

For the limited purpose of attacking Santorum, liberals agreed to stipulate that adultery is bad. After spending all of 1998 ferociously defending adultery as something "everyone" does and "everyone" lies about, liberals claimed to be shocked to the core that anyone would compare homosexuality to such a morally black sin as adultery. (While we're in a sensitive mood, how about the name "the DIXIE Chicks"? Isn't that name provocative to African-Americans?)

When you get liberals to come out against both looting and adultery in the same week, you know the Left is in a state of total disarray. They shouldn't feel so bad. Their boys put up a good fight in Iraq for seventeen days. ■

☞ We Don't Care

JUNE 4, 2003

Liberals have started in with their female taunting about weapons of mass destruction. The way they carry on, you would think they had caught the Bush administration in some shocking mendacity. (You know how the Left can't stand a liar.) For the sake of their tiresome argument, let's stipulate that we will find no weapons of mass destruction—or, to be accurate, no more weapons of mass destruction. Perhaps Hussein was using the three trucks capable of assembling poison gases to sell ice cream under some heretofore undisclosed UN "Oil for Popsicles" program.

Should we apologize and return the country to Saddam Hussein and his winsome sons? Should we have him on *Designer's Challenge* to put his palaces back in all their eighties Vegas splendor? Or maybe Uday and Qusay could spruce up each other's rape rooms on a very special episode of *Trading Spaces*? What is liberals' point?

No one cares. The question was never whether Saddam Hussein had weapons of mass destruction. We know he had weapons of mass destruction, because he used weapons of mass destruction against the Kurds, against the Iranians, and against his own people. The United Nations weapons inspectors repeatedly found Saddam's weapons of mass destruction in Iraq after the 1991 Gulf War, right up until Saddam threw them out in 1998. Justifying his impeachment-day bombing, Clinton cited the Iraqi regime's "nuclear, chemical and biological weapons programs." (Indeed, to date this constitutes the only evidence that Saddam didn't have weapons of mass destruction: Bill Clinton said he did.)

Liberals are now pretending that their position all along was that Saddam had secretly disarmed in the last few years without telling anyone. But that wasn't liberals' position—though it would finally explain the devilish question of why Saddam thwarted inspectors every inch of the way for twelve years, issued phony reports to the UN, and wouldn't allow flyovers or unannounced inspections: It was because he had nothing to hide!

Liberals also have to pretend that the only justification for war given by the Bush administration was that Iraq was knee-deep in nukes, anthrax, biological weapons, and chemical weapons—so much so that even Hans Blix couldn't help but notice them. But that wasn't the Bush administration's position.

Rather, it was that there were lots of reasons to get rid of Saddam Hussein and none to keep him. When President Bush gave the Hussein regime forty-eight hours' notice to quit Iraq, he said, "All the decades of deceit and cruelty have now reached an end." He told the Iraqi people there would be "no more wars of aggression against your neighbors, no more poison factories, no more executions of dissidents, no more torture chambers and rape rooms. The tyrant will soon be gone. The day of your liberation is near."

Liberals kept saying that's too many reasons. The *New York Times*'s leading hysteric, Frank Rich, complained, "We know Saddam Hussein is a thug and we want him gone. But the administration has never stuck to a single story in arguing the case for urgent pre-emptive action now." Since liberals never print retractions, they can say anything. What they said in the past is always deemed inadmissible and unfair to quote.

Contrary to their current self-advertisements, it was liberals who were citing Saddam's weapons of mass destruction—and with gusto—in order to argue *against* war with Iraq. They said America would suffer retaliatory strikes, there would be mass casualties, Israel would be nuked, our troops would be hit with Saddam's chemical weapons, it would be a Vietnam quagmire. Their position was "all" we needed to do was disarm him—which would have required a military occupation of Iraq and a systematic inspection of a thousand or so known Iraqi weapons sites without interference from the Hussein regime. In other words, pretty much what we're doing right now.

That's why liberals were so smitten with the idea of relying on UN weapons inspectors. As their title indicates, "weapons inspectors" inspect weapons. They don't stop torture, abolish rape rooms, feed the people, topple Saddam's statues, or impose democracy.

In January this year, the *New York Times*'s Nicholas Kristof cited the sort of dismal CIA report that always turns up in the hands of *New York Times* reporters, warning that Saddam might order attacks with weapons of mass destruction as "his last chance to exact vengeance by taking a large number of victims with him." Kristof said he opposed invading Iraq simply as a matter of the "costs and benefits" of an invasion, concluding we should not invade because there was "clearly a significant risk" that it would make America less safe.

In his native tongue, weaselese, Kristof claimed he would be gung-ho for war if only he were convinced we could "oust Saddam with minimal casualties and quickly establish a democratic Iraq." We've done that, and now he's angry that his predictions of calamity didn't come true. That's Bush's fault, too. Kristof says Bush manipulated evidence of weapons of mass destruction—an act of duplicity he calls "just as alarming" as a brutal dictator who has weapons of mass destruction.

If Americans were lied to, they were lied to by liberals who warned we would be annihilated if we attacked Iraq. The Left's leading intellectual light, Janeane Garofalo, was featured in an antiwar commercial before thewar, saying, "If we invade Iraq, there's a United Nations estimate that says, 'There will be up to half a million people killed or wounded.'" Now they're testy because they realize Saddam may never have had even a sporting chance to kill hundreds of thousands of Americans. ■

☞ Taking Liberties

JULY 16, 2003

After Pearl Harbor, President Roosevelt rounded up more than one hundred thousand Japanese residents and citizens and threw them into internment camps. Indeed, both liberal deities of the twentieth century, FDR and Earl Warren, supported the internment of Japanese-Americans. In the twenties, responding to the bombing of eight government officials' homes, a Democrat-appointed attorney general arrested about six thousand people. The raids were conducted by A. Mitchell Palmer, appointed by still-revered segregationist Democrat Woodrow Wilson, who won the 1916 election based on lies about intelligence and war plans.

In response to the worst terrorist attack in the history of the world right here on U.S. soil, Attorney General John Ashcroft has detained fewer than a thousand Middle Eastern immigrants. Ashcroft faces a far more difficult task than FDR did: Pearl Harbor was launched by the imperial government of Japan, not by Japanese-Americans living in California. The 9/11 Muslim terrorists, by contrast, were not only in the United States but, until the attack, had not broken any laws (aside from a few immigration laws, which liberals don't care about anyway). And yet, without internment camps or mass arrests, Ashcroft's carefully tailored policies have prevented another terrorist attack for almost two years since the 9/11 attack.

Naturally, therefore, the Democrats have focused like a laser beam on the perfidy of John Ashcroft. Representative Dick Gephardt recently said, "In my first five seconds as president, I would fire John Ashcroft as attorney general." (In his first four seconds, he would establish the AFL-CIO wing of the White House.)

Senator John Kerry has vowed, "When I am president of the United States, there will be no John Ashcroft trampling on the Bill of Rights." Experts are still trying to figure out why Kerry didn't mention his service in Vietnam during that last statement.

Senator John Edwards said that "we must not allow people like John Ashcroft to take away our rights and our freedoms." Apparently, we must, however, allow Janet Reno to run over our rights and our freedoms with a tank.

As usual, the Democrats have come up with a lot of bloody adjectives, but are a bit short in the way of particulars as to how Ashcroft is trampling on anyone's rights. Their case-in-chief seems to be Tarek Albasti. Albasti's story has now run in more than seventy overwrought news reports. His tale of torment led a *New York Times* report on terrorism suspects whose lives have been uprooted. He was the featured story on a PBS special about the civil-liberties crisis sweeping America.

Tarek Albasti is an Egyptian immigrant who married an American woman, brought seven of his Egyptian friends to America, and was enrolled in flight school when America was hit on 9/11. Based on a tip from the ex-wife of one of the men that they were plotting a suicide mission, the eight Egyptian immigrants were held for one week in October 2001— one week. The men were questioned and released. Since then, the government has issued copious apologies to the men and has expunged their records.

What are liberals claiming law enforcement was supposed to do with information like that? We're sorry for any Arabs whose dearest dream was to go into crop dusting, but this really isn't a good time. (Perhaps we could institute a five-day waiting period for Muslims who apply to U.S. flight schools for a background check.) Albasti told PBS—that's right, PBS, the television network owned, operated, and funded by the very same federal government Albasti now claims is oppressing him—that during his one-week confinement he was worried he would be hanged without anyone ever knowing what happened to him. For that remark alone, he should be deported. Is that what he thinks of America? But at least detained Arabs—and more to the point, their lawyers—have a monetary incentive to make absurd claims of persecution. What is the Democrats' excuse?

Based on the wails from our stellar crop of Democratic presidential candidates, you would think every Muslim in the country is cowering in fear of John Ashcroft. But their case-in-chief proving the existence of a civil-rights crisis in America is that eight Egyptian immigrants—one in flight school, no less—were detained for one week after the ex-wife of one of the men tipped off the FBI to a possible terrorist plot in the making.

Apparently, a lot of the false tips to law enforcement are coming from ex-wives. (Maybe Muslim men should have thought of that before introducing the burka.) Esshassah Fouad, a Moroccan student, was detained in Texas after his former wife accused him of being a terrorist. She is now serving a one-year prison sentence for making a false charge.

But someday, small children will be reading somber historical accounts about the dark night of fascism under John Ashcroft. Of course, thanks to Ashcroft, at least they'll be reading them in English rather than Arabic. If liberals applied half as much energy to some business endeavor as they do to creating the Big Lie, they would all be multimillionaires. What are we to make of people who promote the idea that America is in the grip of a civil-liberties emergency based on a hundred hazy stories of scowls and bumps and one-week detentions? Manifestly, there is no civil-liberties crisis in this country. People who claim there is must have a different goal in mind. ■

☞ How to Lose a War

SEPTEMBER 10, 2003

Vermont governor Howard Dean has been issuing diatribes against the Bush administration that would beat Tariq Aziz with severe menstrual cramps. This strategy has made him the runaway favorite of the Democratic Party. Even Mr. War Hero, John Kerry, is getting shellacked by Dean. At times Kerry seems almost ready to surrender, making him look even more French. (If only Kerry had a war record or an enormously rich spouse to fall back on!) In the wake of Dean's success, the entire Democratic Dream Team is beginning to talk like Dr. Demento. On the basis of their recent pronouncements, the position of the Democratic Party seems to be that Saddam Hussein did not hit us on 9/11, Halliburton did.

Explaining his vote for a war that he then immediately denounced, Kerry recently said his vote was just a head-fake, leading some to wonder how many of Kerry's other votes in the U.S. Senate this would explain. He voted for war only to bluff Saddam Hussein into letting in the UN weapons inspectors. "It was right to have a threat of force," Kerry said, "because it's only the threat of force that got Hans Blix and the inspectors back in the country." But he never imagined that Bush would interpret the open-ended war resolution as grounds to start an actual war! "The difference is," Kerry said, "I would have worked with the United Nations."

None of the Democrats has the guts to come out and demand that the United States turn tail and run when the going gets tough. If only one of them had the courage to demand cowardice like a real Democrat! Instead, they stamp their feet and demand that Bush go to the United Nations. Apparently it is urgent that we replace the best fighting force in the world with an "international peacekeeping force"—a task force both feared and respected worldwide for its ability to distribute powdered cheese to poor children. Inconsolable that their pleas to "work through" the UN did not stop Bush from invading Iraq and deposing Saddam Hussein, now the Democrats are eager for the UN to get involved. Since we didn't let the UN lose the war for us, the least we can do is let them screw up the peace. The idea that we would involve those swine in the postwar occupation of Iraq is so preposterous that it's under serious consideration as next week's slogan for the Howard Dean campaign.

I hesitate to raise it to the level of a serious argument by offering a rebuttal, but as luck would have it, we have two models for how to occupy a country after a war. At the risk of giving away the ending, getting "the allies" involved is not the successful model. After World War II, the United States ran the Japanese occupation unilaterally. Without the meddling of other nations, the Japanese occupation went off without a hitch. Within five years, General Douglas MacArthur had imposed a constitutional democracy on Japan with a bicameral legislature, a bill of rights, and an independent judiciary. Now the only trouble Japan causes us is its insistence on selling cars and small trucks to Americans at good prices.

By contrast, the German occupation was run as liberals would like to run postwar Iraq: a joint affair among "the Allies"—the United States, Britain, France, and the Soviet Union. It took forty-five years to clean up the mess they created. The Soviets bickered with the French, refusing to treat them as "allies" (on the admittedly sensible grounds that they didn't fight). While plundering their zone, the Soviets refused to relinquish any territory to France. Trying to be gallant, the Americans and the British carved a French zone out of their own sectors. The Soviets then blockaded Berlin and built the Berlin Wall, and Germany was split for the next half century. The British made Germany's war-torn economy worse by trying to impose socialism in their zone (as well as in their country). Predictably, economic disaster ensued. Over the next five years, the United States was required to spend the equivalent of about $200 billion annually in today's dollars to bail out Western Europe under the Marshall Plan. I note that there was no need for a Marshall Plan in Japan.

And the disastrous German occupation is the best-case scenario for "international peacekeeping." The less successful version includes our "international peacekeeping" in Somalia in 1993, leading to the corpses of American servicemen being defaced and one corpse being dragged through the streets by dancing, cheering savages. Showing that America is not a country to be toyed with, our draft-dodging, pot-smoking commander in chief responded by withdrawing our troops.

So naturally the Democrats are rooting for an international force in Iraq. The Democratic logic on national defense is: As soon as anyone in the military gets his hair mussed, we must pull out and bring in "international peacekeeping" forces. Our boys are in harm's way! People are dying! Bush lied when he said major combat operations were over! Let's run. That'll show 'em. It was not lost on Osama bin Laden that it only took eighteen dead in Somalia for the Great Satan to pull out. It should not be lost on Americans that this is what the Democrats are again demanding we do in Iraq. ∎

☞ "The Plan"

NOVEMBER 5, 2003

The Democrats' new method of opposing the war on terrorism while pretending not to oppose the war on terrorism is to keep demanding that Bush produce a "plan." Senator John Kerry said the difference in how he would have prosecuted the war in Iraq is: "I would have planned." Yes, the invasion of Iraq was the usual unplanned, spur-of-the-minute thing that took eighteen months of discussion.

Wesley Clark recently complained that Bush had put American troops in harm's way, "without a plan." Of course, Clark's "plan" would have been to create a quagmire, just like he did in Bosnia.

Senator John Edwards noted for the record that when he voted for war with Iraq, "I said at the time that it was critical for us to have a plan. . . . This president has no plan of any kind that I can see." Maybe it's that Beatlemania mop-top that's blocking Edwards's view.

Senator Joe Lieberman—the one Democratic presidential candidate too conservative for Barbra Streisand—said that President Bush gave the American people "a price tag, not a plan." He said, "We in Congress must demand a plan." You know, like that incredibly detailed plan the Democrats have in place to spend $400 billion buying prescription drugs for elderly millionaires.

Senator Edward Kennedy said, "The administration had a plan to fight the war, but it had no plan to win the peace." Kennedy's idea of "a plan" consists of choosing a designated driver before heading out for the evening. The Democrats' urgent need for an "exit strategy" apparently first arose sometime after 1993, when Bill Clinton sent all those U.S. soldiers to Bosnia—who are still there.

Interviewing Vice President Dick Cheney on *Meet the Press* about a month ago, Tim Russert echoed the theme, asking, "What is our plan for Iraq? How long will the 140,000 American soldiers be there? How many international troops will join them? And how much is this going to cost?" *Are we there yet, Daddy? Can I go to the bathroom? Are we there yet? How much longer?*

The same questions were asked of FDR over and over again by the American people after the Japanese attacked Pearl Harbor. *"How much will this cost?" "My husband's a sailor—how long will he be gone?" "What's your exit strategy, you warmonger?"* Wait—no. My mistake. That didn't happen.

The Democrats' incessant demand for a "plan" tends to suggest there is something called "The Plan," which would magically prevent bad things from ever happening—especially something as totally unexpected as violence in the Middle East. Violence in the Middle East constantly comes as a bolt out of the blue to liberals. We're at war with Islamic lunatics. They enjoy blowing things up and killing people. What further insights do liberals have to impart about this war? Bush said deposing Saddam Hussein and building a democracy in Iraq was an essential part of the war on terrorism. He did not say that invading Iraq would instantly end all Muslim violence and rainy days that make liberals blue.

A war is not as predictable as, say, a George Clooney movie (although generally more entertaining). Historian Stephen Ambrose described General Dwight Eisenhower's genius as a soldier, noting that "he often said that in preparing for battle, plans were essential, but that once the battle was joined, plans were useless." Transforming a blood-soaked police state dotted with mass graves into a self-governing republic might take slightly longer than this week's makeover on *Queer Eye for the Straight Guy.*

This is not the first time an evil tyrant was deposed only to have bloody elements of his regime remain. For example, it's been nearly five months since Howell Raines was removed as editor of the *New York Times*. What is Bill Keller's "plan" to turn the *New York Times* around, and how long will it take? And when will liberals give us an "exit" strategy for their utterly failed forty-year "War on Poverty"? The U.S. military has had considerably more success in turning Iraq around than liberals have had in turning the ghettos around with their "War on Poverty." Indeed, so far, fewer troops have been killed by hostile fire since the end of major combat in Iraq than civilians were murdered in Washington, D.C., last year (239 deaths in Iraq compared with 262 murders in the U.S. capital). How many years has it been since we declared the end of major U.S. combat operations against Marion Barry's regime? How long before we just give up and pull out of that hellish quagmire known as Washington, D.C.?

The Democrats' conception of a "plan" is like the liberal fantasy that there's a room somewhere full of unlimited amounts of "free" money that we could just give to teachers and hospitals and poor people and AIDS sufferers and the homeless if only the bad, greedy Republicans would give us the key to that wonderful room. Republicans should claim the "plan" is in that room, in a lockbox.

It's interesting that after we've finally gotten liberals to give up on seven decades of trying to plan an economy, now they want to plan a war. Extra-credit question for the class: Comparing a peacetime economy with a war, which do you think is more likely to shoot back at the planners and require subsequent readjustments? No, no, not the usual hands from the eager YAFers in the front row. Are there any liberals in the back rows who want to take a stab at answering this one? Paul Krugman?

Needless to say, the Democrats have no actual plan of their own, unless "surrender" counts as a plan. They just enjoy complaining about every bombing, every attack from Muslim terrorists, every mishap. Back in the 1870s, General William Tecumseh Sherman told a group of graduating cadets, "There are many of you here who think that war is all glory. Well, war is all hell." We didn't start it, but we're going to win it. ∎

DECEMBER 14, 2003: Saddam Hussein is captured.

☞ It's Like Christmas in December!

DECEMBER 17, 2003

Say, has anyone asked Dick Gephardt if this falls under "miserable failure"? Obviously we'll have to wait for all the politics to play out, but at this stage it's hard to say which was worse for Howard Dean this week: the capture of Saddam Hussein or Al Gore's endorsement. Until Sunday, Governor Mean's big applause line in speeches has been to sneer about the Bush administration's failure to catch Saddam Hussein. It seems the governor is better at prescribing bitter pills than at swallowing them. In a speech to the Pacific Council the day after Saddam was captured, Dean nearly choked on the words, "The capture of Saddam is a good thing," before quickly adding, "but the capture of Saddam has not made America safer." (Possible headline: "Dean Says Saddam's Capture Good Thing, Just Not Really Good Thing.") If George W. Bush announced that a cure for cancer had been discovered, Democrats would complain about unemployed laboratory rats.

On Fox News Sunday, Senator John F. Kerry said of Saddam's capture, "This is a great opportunity for this president to get it right for the long term. And I hope he will be magnanimous, reach out to the UN, to allies who've stood away from us." It's as if he were reading my mind! After listening to all the bellyaching from European leftists for the past eight months, I think I speak for all Americans when I say I've been waiting for just the right opportunity to grovel to the French. And now we have it—a major win is the perfect opportunity! That Kerry, he has an uncanny sense for what the average American is thinking.

Actually, to tell the truth, he lost me with that one. Maybe it's a good opportunity for the French and the United Nations to reach out to us, but by what logic is this an opportunity for us to reach out to them? As I understand it, the situation is: We caught Saddam. So the obvious next move is . . .

     (a) Put him on trial.
     (b) Get information from him.
     (c) Torture him.
     (d) Turn him over to the Iraqis.
     (e) Appeal to the French.

What was interesting about Kerry's suggestion was that it was the exact same suggestion liberals were making when they claimed the war was going badly. The day before Saddam's capture, the *New York Times* editorialized, "The way to deal with all that is going wrong in Iraq remains as clear as it was on the day that Mr. Bush declared an end to major combat operations. . . . Instead of driving away France, Germany, Russia and Canada with financial sanctions, the president should be creating the room for compromise." Damn that Bush. He squandered the good will of a bunch of people who hate our guts.

I guess, this is what liberals mean by "a plan":

Military setback:	Appeal to the French.
Military victory:	Appeal to the French.
Saddam captured:	Appeal to the French.
Osama captured:	Appeal to the French.
Osama catches Saddam:	Appeal to the French.

In twenty-four months, Bush has perceptibly degraded terrorist operations throughout the world. The rebuilding in Iraq is going better than could possibly have been expected. Liberals don't care. They just want to turn everything over to the French. (And apparently, the recent capture of Saddam presents us with a golden opportunity to do so!) The Birchers were right about these people. They believe in world government more than they believe in the United States.

One strongly suspects that the White House sat on the story of Saddam's capture for a day so the *Times* could put out its regular Sunday bad news: "A Baghdad Neighborhood, Once Hopeful, Now Reels as Iraq's Turmoil Persists," "Saboteurs, Looters and Old Equipment Work Against Efforts to Restart Iraqi Oil Fields," "It's Going to Be a Bloody Christmas." The *New York Times* hasn't looked this foolish . . . well, I guess since the day before. Liberals should perk up. It's not all bad news. True, Saddam Hussein has been captured. But Norman Mineta is still at large. ■

☞ Al Qaeda Barks, the Spanish Fly

MARCH 17, 2004

After a terrorist attack by al Qaeda that left hundreds of their fellow countrymen dead, Spanish voters immediately voted to give the terrorists what they want—a socialist government that opposes America's war on terrorism. Al Qaeda has changed a government.

Until the bombings last week, the center-right Popular Party of outgoing Prime Minister José Maria Aznar had been sailing to victory. But then the al Qaeda bombs went off and Spaniards turned out in droves to vote against the government that had been a staunch Bush ally in the war on terrorism. (I guess it's okay for a Spanish socialist to "politicize" a terrorist attack just to get elected.)

In a videotaped message, the al Qaeda "military commander" for Europe claimed credit for the bombings, saying that the terrorist attack was meant to punish Spain for supporting the war in Iraq. The message came as a total shock to liberals, who have been furiously insisting that Iraq had absolutely nothing to do with al Qaeda. Apparently al Qaeda didn't think so. After the Madrid bombings, it looks like liberals and terrorists will have to powwow on whether there was an Iraq/al Qaeda link. Two hundred dead Spaniards say there was.

The *New York Times* called the Spanish election "an exercise in healthy democracy." And an ATM withdrawal with a gun to your head is a "routine banking transaction." Instead of vowing to fight the people who killed their fellow citizens, the Spanish decided to vote with al Qaeda on the war. A murdering terrorist organization said, "Jump!" and an entire country answered, "How high?" One Spaniard who decided to switch his vote in reaction to the bombings told the *Times:* "Maybe the Socialists will get our troops out of Iraq and al Qaeda will forget about Spain so we will be less frightened." That's the fighting spirit! If the violent Basque separatist group only killed more people, Spain would surely give them what they want, too.

After his stunning upset victory, Socialist Party leader José Luis Rodríguez Zapatero said he would withdraw Spanish troops from Iraq if the United States does not turn over Iraq to the United Nations. He also vowed that all of Spain's remaining trains will run on time. Zapatero said the war with Iraq had "only caused violence" and "there were no reasons for it." One reason for the war, which would be a sufficient reason for a more manly country, is that the people who just slaughtered two hundred Spaniards didn't like it. But like the Democrats, the Spanish hate George Bush more than they hate the terrorists. Zapatero said the war in Iraq was based on "lies" and called on President Bush and Tony Blair to "do some reflection and self-criticism." So don't think of the Spanish election as a setback for freedom—think of it as a preview of life under President John Kerry!

What kind of lunatic would blame Bush for two hundred Spaniards killed by al Qaeda bombs? Oh wait—Howard Dean just did. Summarizing the views of socialists everywhere, Dean said, "The president was the one who dragged our troops to Iraq, which apparently has been a factor in the death of two hundred Spaniards over the weekend." Yes, with 1,700 dead or injured Spaniards, George Bush certainly has some explaining to do. What have the terrorists ever done besides kill and maim thousands of innocent civilians? Bush isn't fully funding No Child Left Behind, for God's sake!

Before he was put into office because he supported policies favored by al Qaeda terrorists, appeasement candidate Zapatero said, "I want Kerry to win." Kerry is also supported by North Korean dictator Kim Jong II, who broadcasts Kerry speeches over Radio Pyongyang with favorable commentary. So now Kerry really does have two foreign leaders on record supporting him: a socialist terrorist-appeaser and a Marxist mass murderer who dresses like Bea Arthur.

Zapatero predicted that his own victory would help the antiwar party "in the duel between Bush and Kerry." *Would you mind repeating that, sir? I was distracted by that large white flag you're waving.* However Spain's election affects Americans, we can be sure that Spain's surrender to terrorism hasn't been lost on the terrorists. It's difficult to imagine the American people responding to a new terrorist attack by deciding to placate the terrorists, as the Spanish did. A mollusk wouldn't react that way to an attack. Only a liberal could be so perverse.

No matter how many of our European allies may surrender to the terrorists, America will never be alone. This is a country founded in a covenant with God by people who had to flee Europe to do it. Sailing to the New World in 1630 on the ship *Arabella*, the Puritans' leader and governor, John Winthrop, said Americans were entering a covenant with God to create a "city upon a hill." He said we would be judged by all the world if we ever broke that covenant. But if we walked with God, "We shall find that the God of Israel is among us, when 10 of us shall be able to resist a thousand of our enemies." He has intervened in our affairs before, such as in 1776, 1861, and 1980. With the Spanish election, we are witnessing a capitulation to savagery that makes full-scale war inevitable. The Democratic candidate wants to represent godless Europeans. The Republican candidate wants to represent Americans. As Winthrop said, "The eyes of all people are upon us." ■

☞ Tit for Tet

MAY 25, 2004

Abu Ghraib is the new Tet offensive. By lying about the Tet offensive during the Vietnam War, the media managed to persuade Americans we were losing the war, which demoralized the nation and caused us to lose the war. And people say reporters are lazy.

The immediate consequence of the media's lies about the Tet offensive was a 25 percent drop in support for the war. The long-term consequence for America was twelve years in the desert until Ronald Reagan came in and saved the country.

Now liberals are using their control of the media to persuade the public that we are losing the war in Iraq. Communist dictators may have been ruthless murderers bent on world domination, but they displayed a certain degree of rationality. America may not be able to wait out twelve years of Democrat pusillanimity now that we're dealing with Islamic lunatics who slaughter civilians in suicide missions while chanting "Allah Akbar!"

And yet the constant drumbeat of failure, quagmire, Abu Ghraib, Bush-lied-kids-died has been so successful that merely to say the war in Iraq is going well provokes laughter. The distortions have become so pervasive that Michael Moore teeters on the brink of being considered a reliable source.

If President Bush mentions our many successes in Iraq, it is evidence that he is being "unrealistically sunny and optimistic," as Michael O'Hanlon, of the liberal Brookings Institution, put it.

O'Hanlon's searing indictment of the operation in Iraq is that we need to "make sure they have some budget resources that they themselves decide how to spend that are not already pre-allocated." So that's the crux of our challenge in Iraq: Make sure their "accounts receivable" columns all add up. Whenever great matters are at stake, you can always count on liberals to have some pointless, womanly complaint.

We have liberated the Iraqi people from a brutal dictator who gassed his own people, had weapons of mass destruction, invaded his neighbors, harbored terrorists, funded terrorists, and had reached out to Osama bin Laden. Liberals may see Saddam's mass graves in Iraq as half-full, but I prefer to see them as half-empty.

So far, we have found chemical and biological weapons—brucella and Congo-Crimean hemorrhagic fever, ricin, sarin, aflatoxin—and long-range missiles in Iraq.

The terrorist "stronghold" of Karbala was abandoned last week by Islamic crazies loyal to cleric Moqtada al-Sadr who slunk away when it became clear that no one supported them. Iraqis living in Karbala had recently distributed fliers asking the rebels to please leave, further underscoring one of the principal remaining problems in Iraq—the desperate need for more Kinko's outlets. Last weekend, our troops patrolled this rebel "stronghold" without a shot being fired.

The entire Kurdish region—one-third of the country—is patrolled by about three hundred American troops, which is fewer than it takes to patrol the Kennedy compound in Palm Beach on Easter weekends.

But the media tell us this means we're losing. The goalpost of success keeps shifting as we stack up a string of victories. Before the war, *New York Times* columnist Nicholas Kristof warned that war with Iraq would be a nightmare: "We won't kill Saddam, trigger a coup or wipe out his Republican Guard forces." (Unless, he weaseled his way out, "we're incredibly lucky.")

We've done all that! How incredibly lucky.

Kristof continued, "We'll have to hunt out Saddam on the ground—which may be just as hard as finding Osama in Afghanistan, and much bloodier."

We've captured Saddam! And it wasn't bloody! Indeed, the most harrowing aspect of Saddam's capture was that he hadn't bathed or been deliced for two months.

Kristof also said, "Our last experience with street-to-street fighting was confronting untrained thugs in Mogadishu, Somalia. This time we're taking on an army with possible bio- and chemical weapons, 400,000 regular army troops and supposedly seven million more in Al Quds militia."

And yet, somehow, our boys defeated them in just a few weeks! Incredibly lucky again! And just think: all of this accomplished without even having a "plan."

Now we're fighting directly with Islamic loonies crawling out of their ratholes from around the entire region—which liberals also said wouldn't happen. Remember how liberals said the Islamic loonies hated Saddam Hussein—hated him!—because he was a "secularist"? As geopolitical strategist Paul Begala put it, Saddam would never share his weapons with terrorists because "those Islamic terrorists would use them against Saddam Hussein because he's secular."

Well, apparently the crazies have put aside their scruples about Saddam's secularism to come out in the open where they can be shot by American troops rather than fighting on the streets of Manhattan. (Where the natives would immediately surrender.)

The beauty of being a liberal is that history always begins this morning. Every day liberals can create a new narrative that destroys the past as it occurred. *We have always been at war with Eastasia.*

To be sure, Iraq is not a bed of roses. As the Brookings Institution scholar said, we have yet to give the Iraqis "budget resources" that "are not already pre-allocated." I take it back: It is a quagmire. ■

☞ This Is History Calling—
Quick, Get Me Rewrite!

JUNE 3, 2004

The invasion of Iraq has gone fabulously well, exceeding everyone's expectations—certainly exceeding the doomsday scenarios of liberals. The Bush-haters' prewar predictions—hundreds of thousands dead, chemical attacks on our troops, retaliatory terrorist attacks in the United States, an invasion by Turkey, oil facilities in flames, and apocalyptic environmental consequences—have proven to be about as accurate as Bill Clinton's "legally accurate" statements about Monica Lewinsky.

Inasmuch as they can't cite any actual failures in Iraq, liberals busy themselves by claiming the administration somehow "misled" them about the war.

As I understand it, there would be no lunatics shouting "Bush lied, kids died!" if Paul Wolfowitz had admitted before the war that Saddam "probably hadn't rebuilt his nuclear program"—the one that was unilaterally blown up by the Israelis in 1981, thank God. What Wolfowitz should have said is that "proof beyond a reasonable doubt is the way you think about law enforcement, and I think we're much closer to being in a state of war than being in a judicial proceeding."

Liberals would be all sugar and sweetness if only—instead of blathering about nukes, nukes, nukes—Wolfowitz had forthrightly conceded back in 2002 that "there's an awful lot we don't know, an awful lot that we may never know, and we've got to think differently about standards of proof here."

Also, I assume we wouldn't be hearing that the administration is frustrated by its failure to instantly create a Jeffersonian democracy in Iraq if Wolfowitz had said something like "Well, Japan isn't Jeffersonian democracy, either." If only Wolfowitz had lowered expectations by saying that "even if [Iraq] makes it only Romanian style, that's still such an advance over anywhere else in the Arab world."

Also, the media would have no grounds for complaint if Wolfowitz had said Iraqi democracy "is not the president's declared purpose of 'regime change' in Iraq, which is to get rid of a very bad man." If only he had mentioned that Saddam Hussein "has been known to have children tortured in front of their parents."

But guess what? That is exactly what Wolfowitz did say! All these quotes are from a September 22, 2002, article in the *New York Times Magazine* written by Bill Keller, now editor-in-chief at the seditious rag. The last paragraph, about Saddam's torture of children, is Keller paraphrasing Wolfowitz; the rest are direct quotes from the wily neoconservative himself.

But you'd have to put liberals in Abu Ghraib to get them to tell the truth about what people were saying before the war—and then the problem would be that most liberals would enjoy those activities. No torture has yet been devised that could get a liberal to mention the poor, beleaguered Kurds dancing in the streets because Saddam is gone.

To refresh everyone's recollection, before the war began, the Democrats' argument was that Iraq was not an "imminent" threat to the United States. The Republicans' argument was: By the time the threat is imminent, Chicago will be gone. Bush's January 2003 State of the Union address specifically responded to the Democrats' demand that we wait for nuclear and biological threats to be "imminent" before we act, saying that if we waited for this threat to "fully and suddenly emerge, all actions and words, and all recriminations would come too late." But now liberals want to have their Nigerian yellow cake and eat it, too.

In January 2003—or three months after Senator Tom Daschle voted for the Iraq war resolution hoping to fool the voters of South Dakota this November—he was horrified that Bush seemed to be actually contemplating war with Iraq! According to Daschle, Bush should have waited for Iraq to grow into a problem of crisis proportions before deciding to do anything—citing the Cuban Missile Crisis as a model to be emulated. "If we have proof of nuclear and biological weapons," Daschle asked, "why doesn't [Bush] show that proof to the world as President Kennedy did forty years ago when he sent Adlai Stevenson to show the world U.S. photographs of offensive missiles in Cuba?"

The answer is: Because by the time Saddam had nuclear weapons, we wouldn't be able to do anything. That's why it's known as the "Cuban Missile Crisis," not the "Cuban Missile Triumph."

Before the war, Democrats were carping about the Bush administration's inability to predict the future and tell us everything that would happen in Iraq after the war. On MSNBC in September 2002, for example, Robert Menendez (Democrat of New Jersey) was complaining that Secretary of Defense Donald Rumsfeld "didn't have an answer for what happens in a post-Saddam Iraq." But now liberals are acting as if the Bush administration said they knew exactly what would happen after liberating a country from a thirty-year barbaric dictatorship—and got it wrong.

The good news is: Liberals' antiwar hysteria seems to have run its course. I base this conclusion on Al Gore's lunatic antiwar speech last week. Gore always comes out swinging just as an issue is about to go south. He's the stereotypical white guy always clapping on the wrong beat. Gore switched from being a pro-defense Democrat to a lefty peacenik— just before the 9/11 attack. He grew a beard—just in time for an attack on the nation by fundamentalist Muslims. He endorsed Howard Dean—just as the orange-capped Deaniacs were imploding. Gore even went out and got really fat—just before America officially gave up carbs. This guy is always leaping into the mosh pit at the precise moment the crowd parts. Mark my words: Now that good old Al has come lunging in, the antiwar movement is dead. ∎

3

A Muslim by Any Other Name Blows Up Just the Same

———◼———

☞ John Davis: American Hero

JULY 29, 1999

My life is almost complete. Tonight I was on a TV show on "extreme catfighting"—the closest I'll ever get to Jerry Springer—*and* I shook hands with John Davis, hero to frequent flyers everywhere. Now if I can just manage to rear-end Kate Michelman of NARAL I can call it a day.

Mild-mannered Davis was attempting to fly Continental Airlines to Florida with his wife and toddler child a couple of weeks ago. (For frequent flyers, your stomach is already in a knot.) After the standard two-hour delay, Davis's child broke from his parents and ran onto the jetway leading to the aircraft, presumably hoping to start a trend. The accounts of the resulting altercation begin to differ at this point, so, to be fair, I'll go with the version that reflects most poorly on my hero.

As John Davis and his wife were running for their pre-preboarding toddler on the jetway, the Continental Airlines ticket-taker blocked Mr. Davis's way, stood between father and child, and informed Mr. Davis that he could not enter the jetway without a boarding pass.

Remember, all this Continental Airlines readily admits.

The father responded the way fathers are wont to do in such situations, which is violently. Davis is a slight man; the damage he did to the ticket-taker reminds one of biology class lessons on adrenaline that involve mothers lifting Volkswagens to release pinned children.

The lesson of this and many other happy travel stories is that humans are fascists by nature. Give some humans control over other humans and they will seamlessly transform into brownshirts, patting you down, ripping apart your belongings, breaking your valuables, and telling you where to stand, to drink, and to smoke and when to go to the bathroom. And if you complain they will arrest you. Worse, they will bump you or your luggage or take away your nice aisle seat and give you a center seat.

But the head of Continental Airlines reacted as if his faithful employee had brilliantly averted another toddler-down-the-jetway scam. He called for a federal law, not banning hairless simians from total control over other people's lives at airports, but banning "violent" passengers from the air-ways. Interestingly, he said "air rage" cannot be tolerated—no matter what the reason.

No matter what the reason? Even in case of rape or incest, or if the mother's life is in danger? A No-Matter-What-the-Reason standard could come only from a person who flashes a "Chief Executive, Continen-tal Airlines" card when he flies.

Admittedly, I have seen plenty of dumb and nasty passengers—some Hollywood celebrities don't even have the common courtesy to wait their turn to defecate on a beverage cart—and also plenty of patient, saintly air-line employees, who have completely suppressed the human instinct to fascism. And that's not just the Stockholm syndrome talking.

But if we're passing federal laws, a really useful federal law would be one that prohibits pilots from talking. There is nothing that makes you feel like you are in Orwell's *1984* so much as being trapped on an airplane with a pilot who thinks he's Shecky Greene. You can't leave the plane, ob-viously. You generally can't even leave your seat or turn on your Walkman. The only other places in this country where you can be forced to listen to someone talk are prison and grade school. And prison guards and teachers have more interesting information than "If you look out your right win-dow, you can see Cleveland."

Several years ago, one of my father's business colleagues was trapped on a plane when the pilot began to play out his fantasy of being a tour guide. The colleague called a flight attendant over, handed her a section of his paper, and asked her to give it to the pilot so he'd stop with his incessant jabbering. When the plane landed, the businessman was arrested. That's a true story.

Americans may vote for creeping socialism, but deep in their beings they sense that they are still free, that this is not yet Orwell's *1984*. As long as there are some people who are not willing to roll over for the airline fascists and be docile sheep—*Stand in line, open your bag, walk through the metal detector again, take off your belt, take off your coat, take off your jewelry, stand in line, turn on your computer, present your ID, has anyone given you anything?, no drinking, no smoking, you'll have to check that, stand here, sit down, don't get up, put your seatback up, turn off your computer, we're at 30,000 feet and if you look to your left you can see Pittsburgh . . . whoops!* and another plane down not because of the Waterford crystal the X-ray goon just broke in your carry-on luggage, but because of pilot error—there will be John Davises.

Most of the fascistically controlling airline regulations are the result of—surprise!—government regulations. I would risk terrorist sabotage not to have to be mauled by the X-ray crew, who see their sole life's work as trying to cause passengers to miss planes. That would be a completely rational trade-off, by the way, but the government won't allow consumers to make it.

On average, there is one fatality for every 3 million people who fly on a commercial aircraft. You are more likely to drown in your bathtub than die in an airplane. Ten times more likely. In any six-month period, more people will die in car accidents than have ever died in airplanes—in the history of flight.

But the government doesn't require anyone to shake you down before you take a bath. You don't get the third degree every time you get behind the wheel of a car. So why are the consumers of airline travel patted down and interrogated like denizens of a crack house?

Most of those rare air flight fatalities are the result of accidents, not terrorists, anyway. Accidents are caused by pilots, government bureaucrats, and airline personnel—not passengers. But every time there's an airline crash due to pilot error the government immediately springs into action by piling on yet more intrusive passenger interrogations.

Moreover, if the airlines weren't required by the government to engage in moronic exercises like asking every passenger if he packed his own bags (what are the odds that a terrorist would answer, "Why no, the bomb squad back at terrorist headquarters did"?), they would undoubtedly come up with actually plausible methods to keep their planes accident- and terrorist-free. In-flight bombings are terrible PR.

Airlines could, for example, put undercover armed guards on all their flights. They could allow passengers to fly armed. This would not only make air travel safer, it would prove once and for all the most compelling argument for gun rights by posing the rhetorical question, "Would you ever try to hijack a plane if you knew that every passenger aboard might be armed?" Imagine how much more pleasant airline travel would be if the airport security moron were required to ask every passenger, "And did you load your concealed weapon yourself today, sir?" The government already carves out a little exception for itself on the no-guns rule. FBI agents are allowed to pack heat on commercial airlines, and let me hasten to add, it wasn't armed civilians who mistakenly shot down Randy Weaver's wife, child, and dog.

Alternatively, airlines could allow frequent flyers to submit to personal investigations in return for a special airline passport allowing them to skip the Make-Them-Miss-Their-Flights X-ray crew. (These would be just like the ones flight attendants and pilots already have.)

But creative, consumer-friendly solutions are not possible, because the government has given itself monopoly control of air safety.

Let's just hope they don't find out about bathtub drownings. ■

☞ Where's Janet Reno When We Need Her?

SEPTEMBER 20, 2001

Just as I predicted, the new "security procedures" adopted by the U.S. Department of Transportation in response to the most deadly hijackings in history will be incredibly burdensome for millions of American travelers but, at the same time, will do absolutely nothing to deter hijackers. The single most effective thing we could do in this country to protect travelers from terrorist attacks would be to abolish the Department of Transportation.

The government's logical calculus on flight security has long been: Really Annoying = Safe Plane. (Does anyone not know how to use a seat belt? Say you were an alien from a distant galaxy and had never in your entire life seen a seat belt before—couldn't you figure it out?) The FAA's new hijacker repellant is this: Passengers will now have to show boarding passes to get to the gates. This wily stratagem will stop cold any hijackers on suicide missions who forgot to buy airline tickets! It's times like this that I get down on my knees and thank God we have a federal Department of Transportation.

The genius security procedures laboriously implemented by the government over the past decade certainly served this country well on Bloody Tuesday. The real puzzler is how the hijackers managed to evade the "Did you pack your own bags?" trap. Only further investigation will solve that mystery. If only we'd implemented the tough new "Cross your heart and hope to die?" follow-up question in time!

Last week a CNN anchor raised the "Did you pack your own bags?" dragnet and somberly remarked—this is a quote—"No one will answer those questions so cavalierly again." We certainly won't. We will all remember that if those asinine questions hadn't been asked of millions of travelers day in day out year after year, enragingly stupid every time, nineteen murderous hijackers might have boarded four separate commercial jets in America almost simultaneously one morning. Oh—no, wait. The hijackers weren't foiled. But somehow the manifest irrelevance of the "Did you pack your own bags?" question has become its principal selling point.

We are also grateful for the magnetometers. The McDonald's rejects who man the machines are so efficient and courteous, you hardly notice them anymore. That's sarcasm. Despite addled TV commentators claiming that, heretofore, travelers had breezed right through the metal detectors, these are obviously people who haven't flown since the fifties.

Back on Earth, the sullen, dictatorial security personnel invariably stop all passengers who are not likely to punch them (girls), rifle through their belongings, slowly wipe some wand over their computers (a procedure that takes just long enough for you to almost miss your plane), carefully examine their persons—down to the tiny metallic bra-strap hook—and then methodically break any crystal vases the passenger is carrying. So don't tell me they're lazy.

It may be annoying, but the rash of hijackings by Connecticut WASP girls surely explains the time-consuming—but still somehow completely useless—examination of my personal effects. We all have to make sacrifices for airline safety.

Even with the shakedowns, I personally have carried a deadly plastic shiv and FBI Mace through metal detectors dozens of times. Dozens. I wasn't even trying. I just forgot I was carrying them. Unless the government is going to require passengers, crew, and pilots to travel naked and with no luggage, there is no spot search devisable that can keep the skies safe—no matter how irritating.

Consequently, I propose an all-new standard for airline safety procedures. Bear with me here, but my idea is this: We should be looking for procedures that make the airplane safer. With this new standard as my guide, I have a five-point plan.

1. Pilots should be the first to board the plane and the cockpit door should be locked like Fort Knox behind them, impenetrable by anyone until the plane lands. The cabin crew should be able to communicate with the pilots only to request an emergency landing. But nothing that needs to be spoken over an intercom, such as "Fly to Kabul or every passenger gets his throat slit."

2. Every flight should carry at least two undercover agents capable of discharging hollow-point bullets, poison darts, and electric shocks. The armed guards have to be incognito so that hijackers can't knock them off—and also to improve in-flight courtesy.

3. We should require passports to fly domestically. Passports can be forged, but they can also be checked with the home country in case of any suspicious-looking swarthy males. It will be a minor hassle, but it's better than national ID cards. It's also far less annoying than being told how to use a seat belt.

4. All nineteen hijackers in last week's attack appear to have been noncitizens. As far as the Constitution is concerned, visitors to this country are here at the nation's pleasure. Congress could pass a law tomorrow requiring that all aliens from Arabic countries leave. Congress could certainly pass a law requiring that all aliens get approval from the INS before boarding an airplane in the United States.

5. Of course, any security procedure imaginable can be breached by well-financed fanatics willing to commit suicide for their cause. The main deterrent to terrorists is to create despair and hopelessness by destroying their home sponsors. Donald Rumsfeld is just the man for the job. But on the off chance that he is insufficiently ruthless, someone should tell Janet Reno that Islamic fundamentalism is an offshoot of the Branch Davidians. ■

☞ HillaryCare for the Airports

NOVEMBER 8, 2001

The main sticking point between the Senate and House versions of the aviation security bill now headed for conference is whether airport magnetometers will be run with private-sector values or the smooth efficiency of the Department of Motor Vehicles. In the event that Congress chooses the latter, anyone planning to travel by air during this calendar year is hereby advised to leave for the airport now.

This is lesson #1,475,607,033 on the point that the free market is a counterintuitive concept. Only liberals still associate the words "government employee" with "efficiency" and "competence." Without constant reminders of the material bounty produced by the glorious Soviet Union, people, by which I mean "liberals," will list toward socialist solutions time and again.

Even the lily-livered Europeans, usually cited warmly by the Left for their progressive views on adultery, have abandoned the idea of government bureaucrats running security at airports. If there's one thing the Europeans know it's how efficient a government employee who can't be fired can be. But the *New York Times* has been editorializing daily against private security firms in deference to—and I quote—"a highly trained federal force." The only rhetorical flourish the *Times* avoided was to call private sector workers "shiftless." When was the last time you heard someone say, "The help here is way too slow and incompetent. Why don't they hire some civil service people"?

Far be it from me to defend airport security personnel, but making them government employees, I assure you, will not improve matters. We're not going to call out the Marines to rifle through little old ladies' handbags before they board flights to Cleveland. This is HillaryCare for the airports.

The reason airports already resemble the torture chambers in Orwell's *1984* is that they are natural monopolies. If you live in Chicago, you can't decide you really prefer to fly out of Dallas because you like the airport better. You're stuck in Chicago, and O'Hare knows you're stuck with Chicago airports. (There is no other explanation for why there even is an airport in Chicago. Planes are only allowed to fly in or out of O'Hare for approximately twenty minutes every week.) The absence of competition among airports leads to phenomenally stupid inconveniences that would be unfathomable in a competitive environment.

Only a monopoly would ban the world's most popular soft drink, Coca-Cola, from being sold on its premises or sell a tasteless tuna salad sandwich for about what you'd pay for a kobe beef steak dinner in Tokyo. Only a monopoly would have bathrooms that still employ those ridiculous Potemkin hand dryers in lieu of something that might possibly dry your hands . . . like, say, paper towels. Only a monopoly could force people to stand in two-hour lines in order to answer phenomenally stupid questions with a straight face or risk being denied service. Natural monopolies everywhere adopt a philosophy on customer service best summed up with the words, "Take it or leave it."

The liberal's solution to a monopoly is invariably to create an even bigger monopoly by turning it over to the federal government. Not surprisingly, the only experiences nearly as unpleasant as commercial air travel are those enterprises run by the government. If you had to get up tomorrow morning and get a driver's license or a lamp, which would you dread more? At least natural monopolies only lead to bathrooms with no paper towels. Government monopolies have been known to lead to the Khmer Rouge.

The only effective solution to a natural monopoly is for the government to create artificial competition by setting standards (off the top of my head, for example: no box cutters on airplanes) and fining airports that fail random spot checks. In other words, conform to these national standards or we'll penalize you monetarily. We could call it the No Airport Left Behind Act. Even for major criminal offenses like cigarette-smoking in Los Angeles bars, the government doesn't send in a government workforce to tend bar. It fines bars that fail to comply with the law. Moreover, I wish the security guards luck, but keeping weapons off planes is not the linchpin to safe skies anyway. It better not be: We can't keep weapons out of prisons; we certainly can't keep them off airplanes.

The airport shakedowns do, however, comply with the government's primary criterion for airport safety, which is that all travelers be inconvenienced with absolutely no increase in airline safety. Thus, one of the FAA's recent safety innovations is to demand photo IDs from passengers at various checkpoints throughout the airport. For maximum annoyance, this includes the moment at which you are about to board the plane, when you are balancing carry-on luggage, a newspaper, and a Starbucks coffee, and clenching a boarding pass between your teeth. Studies have shown that demanding photo ID is a highly effective method of keeping vampires off airplanes.

There's only one small flaw in the photo ID requirement: There is absolutely no reason to imagine terrorists don't have photo IDs. Indeed, the 9/11 terrorists not only had ID cards but blessed their ID cards. Instruction #12 of the terrorists' pre-attack manual was "bless your ID, your passport, and all of your papers." The instructions give another clue to the hijackers' state of mind that, in the hands of creative safety professionals, might lead to a practical safety check: Instruction #1 was to put on cologne; Instruction #2 was to shower. See—it doesn't work if you put on cologne and *then* take the shower. (Instruction #3: "For a definition of the word 'shower,' consult the glossary.")

If the government demanded results, airports wouldn't have time to engage in man's truly oldest profession, oppressing his fellow man. Instead, this natural monopoly would finally be forced to stop harassing passengers for the fun of it and to adopt safety procedures that would have the novel attribute of making planes safe. ■

☞ The New Roman Arena: Airports

NOVEMBER 22, 2001

If the airlines had hired the most expensive consultants in the country to help them figure out a way to make the flying experience even more unpleasant than it was before September 11, the consultants would have given up in despair. But chalk one up to American ingenuity: The airlines have done it on their own!

Getting a head start on the holiday season, airport security guards have already begun their Christmas shopping by stealing travelers' belongings.

Unless they pilfer possessions worth more to you than making your plane and getting to wherever you are going, there's nothing you can do. And the guards know there's nothing you can do, which adds to the innate charm of airport security personnel. A security guard took a piece of my jewelry at the Spokane Airport last Saturday with approval from his Olympic Security supervisor. The alert supervisor called airport police when I asked for her name.

I want it back. It was a silver charm from Aspen in the shape of a bullet with a great deal of sentimental value. But in a strange coincidence, a few hours later it was missing from the Olympic Security box of confiscated loot. It's probably already wrapped. I'm now carrying gift certificates from Zales in my carry-on bag just to save the guards time during the busy holiday season.

If you are not a halfwit—and not Christmas shopping from other people's stuff—you will instantly recognize that a silver charm is a silver charm, and it doesn't matter if it's in the shape of the anthrax virus. Even a real bullet can't cause any harm without a gun. A silver charm soldered to a key chain is less threatening than a tube of lipstick. Of course, my lipstick would undoubtedly also have been deemed a grave security risk by Olympic Security if it had been in the supervisor's color. Since September 11 alone, that silver-charm key chain has been through airport security dozens of times. But security guards are on high alert. There are only twenty-nine more shopping days till Christmas!

There has been more caterwauling about the Bureau of Prisons listening to the conversations of prison inmates suspected of plotting terrorist attacks on America than to the universal physical inspections of Americans trying to board airplanes. If law-enforcement officers ever dared paw through the belongings of an Egyptian immigrant named Mustafa with the fascistic intensity of airport security patting down little old ladies suspected of flying to Iowa, liberals would explode in righteous indignation.

As long as the airlines insist on going through the manifestly absurd exercise of treating all passengers alike in some obscure desire to impress the *New York Times* editorial page, they ought to abandon the personal inspections altogether. It's absurd to imagine that personal inspections are going to keep weapons off airplanes—even by turning airports into the pleasant and welcoming environment of a federal penitentiary. You'd keep more weapons off planes just by banning Christian Slater from commercial air travel.

After airport security confiscates any jewelry that might make a nice Christmas gift, the airlines hand out weapons on the planes. They still serve wine in glass goblets that can be smashed to create jagged glass daggers. They serve soda in cans that can be twisted apart to create razor-sharp knives. Not to worry, though. If you think about it for up to three seconds, it will occur to you that terrorists don't want to knife a few passengers. If terrorists just wanted to kill a bunch of people in one place, they could go to shopping malls, restaurants, movie theaters—anywhere, really. So why aren't there security guards at the Cineplex pawing through our purses and stealing our jewelry?

Airports are attractive to terrorists for one reason: There are airplanes at airports! And what is alluring about airplanes is that they can be turned into cruise missiles or blown up in the air. The only safety precaution that will make the planes safer would be impenetrable cockpit doors and bomb checks for all cargo—two security measures airlines doggedly refuse to implement.

While still completely vulnerable to another terrorist attack, Americans submit like good Germans to these purposeless airport shakedowns—which are about as useful as those national guardsmen hanging around in airports right after 9/11 carrying unloaded rifles. Most sickening is the relish other Americans are taking in their new roles as fascist storm troopers. In a famous study conducted at Yale in the sixties by professor Stanley Milgram, members of the public willingly administered what they thought were fatal electric shocks to another human being—simply because they were told to do so by an authority figure.

Believing they were participating in a study on memory, the volunteers watched a "pupil" being strapped to a chair and wired with electrodes. The volunteers were then taken to an adjacent room, where they were told to read questions to the pupil and to administer increasingly powerful electric shocks for every incorrect answer. The electric-shock buttons seemed to go up to one administering a jolt of 450 volts on a button labeled "Danger: Severe Shock."

As the shocks were administered, the mock pupils acted as if they were being subjected to increasingly greater pain. Even as the pupils writhed and screamed in pain, the volunteers readily administered the shocks. Finally, the pupil would emit a bloodcurdling scream and then suddenly fall totally silent, apparently dead. Two-thirds of the volunteers continued to administer the shocks. The study was scandalous: If asked to do so by an authority figure, a majority of people will kill another human being completely unknown to them. It would be interesting to know if professor Milgram advised the airlines on their security procedures. ■

☞ Would Mohammed Atta Object to Armed Pilots?

MAY 30, 2002

In a new safety initiative, the Department of Transportation has instituted an affirmative-action program for Arabs interested in pursuing careers in aviation. Transportation Secretary Norman Mineta explained the security advantages of the program, saying, "Surrendering to discrimination makes us no different than the terrorists." Since you can't tell these days: This is not, in the strict sense, true.

It is true that the department has prohibited pilots from carrying guns and has rejected the idea of a "trusted traveler" program. In fact, it's not doing anything to make the airlines any safer. This should come as no surprise, inasmuch as Mineta recently said he was unaware of any specific threat against aviation. They hate us. They're trying to kill us. They use airplanes as weapons. If Mineta doesn't read intelligence reports, can't he at least read the newspapers?

In congressional testimony last week, Mineta mercifully spared the senators a recap of his experience in a Japanese internment camp and allowed his assistant, longtime Bush crony and ATF apologist John Magaw, to explain the department's key security improvements. The reason Magaw decided to prohibit pilots from having guns is—I quote—"they really need to be in control of that aircraft."

This is literally the stupidest thing I've heard in my entire life. It is like saying women walking home late at night in dangerous neighborhoods shouldn't carry guns (or Mace, for my liberal friends) because they "really need to be walking home." If the undersecretary for transportation security thinks we have to debate whether pilots "really need to be in control of that aircraft," someone other than him really needs to be in control of airline security.

The scenario under which a pilot might need a gun is this: Islamic crazies have penetrated the locked cockpit, thwarting air marshals, passengers, and crew. It's going to be a little difficult for the pilot to "be in control of that aircraft" when he's fighting off an angry mob of sweaty Arabs. There is nothing that could go wrong at that point—a wounded passenger, a hole in the side of the plane, terrorists wresting control of the gun—that would be worse than the alternative.

Ah, but Magaw is worried that the terrorists will now be in possession of a firearm. Think of the havoc they could wreak with a gun! Of course, they'll also be in possession of a Boeing 767 careering at 480 miles per hour toward the nearest landmark building. Magaw seems to think the real danger is that terrorists will shoot at the White House from the cockpit window, not that they'll fly the plane into it.

Magaw is the worst kind of government bureaucrat. He defends fascistic government abuses, but the citizenry is no safer as a consequence. Fascism has its bad points, but at least trains are supposed to run on time. As the head of the Bureau of Alcohol, Tobacco and Firearms, Magaw famously defended an unprovoked government assault against Randy Weaver and his family, culminating in the murder of Weaver's wife. In testimony before a Senate committee investigating the raid at Ruby Ridge, Magaw stubbornly refused to admit the ATF had done anything wrong. Indeed, he even refused to acknowledge a jury verdict finding that the government had entrapped Weaver. Of the jury's verdict, Magaw said, "Do you believe Randy Weaver—or do you believe the federal agents who have sworn to tell the truth and are carrying out a career in this government?"

If only airline pilots worked for the ATF. Then Magaw would not only allow them to carry guns, he would also allow them to shoot law-abiding passengers at random. (The Senate report found Magaw's testimony not credible and recommended abolition of his entire agency.)

Magaw's other airline safety improvement was to reject the idea of a "trusted-traveler" program, which would allow passengers to avoid three-hour airport security lines in return for submitting to an intrusive background check. As reported by the *New York Times*, Magaw spurned the trusted-traveler idea on the ground that "he is not sure who could safely be given the card." I don't know, how about . . . NO ARABS? (Religion-of-Peace Update: As Pakistanis prepare to stone a rape victim to death, the latest suicide bombing in Israel claimed the lives of a grandmother and her eighteen-month-old granddaughter.)

Amazingly, President Bush has actually found someone even dumber than Norman Mineta to be Mineta's assistant. The secretary of transportation is the only person on the face of the globe who thinks the airlines face no terrorist threat, and his deputy—by his own admission—hasn't the first idea how to figure out which airline passengers can be "trusted."

If these guys were doing their jobs right, civil libertarians would be screaming bloody murder, Congress would be reining them in, and professional ethnic victims would be holding candlelight vigils and singing "We Shall Overcome." Instead, Congress is forced to pass laws overruling Mineta and Magaw, civil libertarians are scratching their heads wondering why profiling is prohibited, and professional complainers are sending these guys flowers. Maybe somebody else should be doing this job.

———

POSTSCRIPT: On July 18, 2002, the Bush administration fired Magaw. On November 25, 2002, Bush signed legislation that would allow pilots to carry guns. ■

☞ Thank You for Choosing United, Mr. Bin Laden

APRIL 14, 2004

Last week, 9/11 commissioner John Lehman revealed that "it was the policy [before 9/11] and I believe remains the policy today to fine airlines if they have more than two young Arab males in secondary questioning because that's discriminatory." Hmmm . . . Is nineteen more than two? Why, yes, I believe it is. So if two Jordanian cabdrivers are searched before boarding a flight out of Newark, Osama bin Laden could then board that plane without being questioned. I'm no security expert, but I'm pretty sure this gives terrorists an opening for an attack.

In a sane world, Lehman's statement would have made headlines across the country the next day. But not one newspaper, magazine, or TV show has mentioned that it is official government policy to prohibit searching more than two Arabs per flight.

Meanwhile, another 9/11 commissioner, the greasy Richard Ben-Veniste, claimed to be outraged that the CIA did not immediately give intelligence on 9/11 hijackers Nawaf Alhazmi and Khalid Almihdhar to the

FBI. As we now know—or rather, I alone know because I'm the only person in America watching the 9/11 hearings—Ben-Veniste should have asked his fellow commissioner Jamie Gorelick about that.

In his testimony this week, John Ashcroft explained that the FBI wasn't even told Almihdhar and Alhazmi were in the country until weeks before the 9/11 attack—because of Justice Department guidelines put into place in 1995. The famous 1995 guidelines were set forth in a classified memorandum written by the the deputy attorney general at the time—Jamie Gorelick. The memo was titled "Instructions for Separation of Certain Foreign Counterintelligence and Criminal Investigations" and it imposed a "draconian" wall between counterintelligence and criminal investigations.

What Ashcroft said next was breathtaking. Prohibited from mounting a serious search for Almihdhar and Alhazmi, an irritated FBI investigator wrote to FBI headquarters, warning that someone would die because of these policies—"since the biggest threat to us, OBL [Osama bin Laden], is getting the most protection." FBI headquarters responded, "We're all frustrated with this issue. These are the rules. NSLU [National Security Law Unit] does not make them up. But somebody did make these rules. Somebody built this wall."

The person who built that wall, Ashcroft said, "is a member of the commission." If this had been an episode of *Matlock*, the camera would have slowly panned away from Ashcroft's face at this point and then quickly jumped to an extreme close-up of Jamie Gorelick's horrified expression. Armed marshals would then escort the kicking, screaming Gorelick away in leg irons as the closing credits rolled. The 9/11 Commission has finally uncovered the proverbial "smoking gun"! But it was fired by one of the 9/11 commissioners. Maybe between happy reminiscences about the good old days of Ruby Ridge, Waco, and the Elián Gonzáles raid, Ben-Veniste could ask Gorelick about those guidelines. Democrats think it's a conflict of interest for Justice Scalia to have his name in the same phonebook as Dick Cheney. But there is no conflict of interest having Gorelick sit on a commission that should be investigating her.

Bill O'Reilly's entire summary of Ashcroft's testimony was to accuse Ashcroft of throwing sheets over naked statues rather than fighting terrorism. No mention of the damning Gorelick memo. No one knows about the FAA's No-Searching-Arabs counterterrorism policy. Predictions that conservatives have finally broken through the wall of sound coming from the mainstream media may have been premature.

When Democrats make an accusation against Republicans, newspaper headlines repeat the accusation as a fact: "U.S. Law Chief 'Failed to Heed Terror Warnings,'" "Bush Was Told of Qaida Steps Pre-9/11; Secret Memo Released," "Bush White House Said to Have Failed to Make al-Qaida an Early Priority." But when Republicans make accusations against Democrats—even accusations backed up by the hard fact of a declassified Jamie Gorelick memo—the headlines note only that Republicans are making accusations: "Ashcroft Lays Blame at Clinton's Feet," "Ashcroft: Blame Bubba for 9/11," "Ashcroft Faults Clinton in 9/11 Failures."

It's amazing how consistent it is. A classic of the genre was the *Chicago Tribune* headline that managed to use both constructs in a single headline: "Ashcroft Ignored Terrorism, Panel Told; Attorney General Denies Charges, Blames Clinton." Why not: "Reno Ignored Terrorism, Panel Told; Gorelick Denies Charges, Blames Bush"?

Democrats actively created policies that were designed to hamstring terrorism investigations. The only rap against the Bush administration is that it failed to unravel the entire 9/11 terrorism plot based on a memo titled "Bin Laden Determined to Attack Inside the United States." I have news for liberals: Bin Laden is *still* determined to attack inside the United States! Could they please tell us when and where the next attack will be? Because unless we know that, it's going to be difficult to stop it if we can't search Arabs. ∎

☞ Arab Hijackers Now Eligible for Preboarding

APRIL 25, 2004

In June 2001, as Mohammed Atta completed his final "to do" list before the 9/11 attacks (". . . amend will to ban women from my funeral . . . leave extra little Friskies out for Mr. Buttons . . . set TiVo for Streisand on *Inside the Actors Studio* . . ."), Secretary of Transportation Norman Mineta was conducting a major study on whether airport security was improperly screening passengers based on ethnicity. As Mineta explained, "We must protect the civil rights of airline passengers." Protecting airline passengers from sudden death has never made it onto Mineta's radar screen.

A few months later, nineteen Muslim men hijacked U.S. airplanes and turned them into weapons of mass destruction on American soil; suddenly, Mineta was a whirlwind of activity. On September 21, as the remains of thousands of Americans lay smoldering at Ground Zero, Mineta fired off a letter to all U.S. airlines forbidding them from implementing the one security measure that would have prevented 9/11: subjecting Middle Eastern passengers to an added degree of preflight scrutiny. He sternly reminded the airlines that it was illegal to discriminate against passengers based on their race, color, national or ethnic origin, or religion. Mineta would have sent the letter even sooner, but he wanted to give the airlines enough time to count the number of their employees and customers who had just been murdered by Arab passengers.

On September 27, 2001, the ACLU sent out a press release titled "ACLU Applauds Sensible Scope of Bush Airport Security Plan," which narrowly won out over the headline "Fox Approves Henhouse Security Plan." As a rule of thumb, any security plan approved by the ACLU puts American lives at risk. Former ACLU Associate Director Barry Steinhardt praised Bush's Transportation Department for showing "an admirable degree of restraint by not suggesting airport security procedures that would deny civil liberties as a condition of air travel." As usual the ACLU had zeroed in on the true meaning of 9/11: Americans needed to be more tolerant of and sensitive toward ethnic minorities.

Flush with praise from the ACLU, Mineta set to work suing airlines for removing passengers perceived to be of Arab, Middle Eastern, or Southeast Asian descent and/or Muslim. If we're going to start shifting money around based on who's rude to whom, my guess is Muslims are going to end up in the red. But that's not how Mineta's Department of Transportation sees it.

Despite Mineta's clearly worded letter immediately after the 9/11 terrorist attacks and another follow-up letter in October, the Department of Transportation found that in the weeks after the 9/11 terrorist attacks carried out by Middle Eastern men, the airlines were targeting passengers who appeared to be Middle Eastern. To his horror, Mineta discovered that the airlines were using logic and deductive reasoning to safeguard their passengers—in direct violation of his just-issued guidelines on racial profiling!

The Department of Transportation filed a complaint against United Airlines, claiming United removed passengers from flights in "a few instances" based on their race, color, national origin, religion, or ancestry.

Mineta gave United no credit for so scrupulously ignoring ethnicity on September 11 that it lost 4 pilots, 12 flight attendants, and 84 passengers (not including the 9 Arab hijackers). In November 2003, United settled the case for $1.5 million.

In another crucial antiterrorism investigation undertaken by Norman Mineta, the Department of Transportation claimed that between September 11, 2001, and December 31, 2001, American Airlines—which lost 4 pilots, 13 flight attendants, and 129 passengers (not including 10 Arab hijackers) on September 11 by ignoring the ethnicity of its passengers— removed 10 individuals who appeared to be Middle Eastern from American Airline flights as alleged security risks. On March 1, 2004, American Airlines settled the case for $1.5 million.

The Department of Transportation also charged Continental Airlines with discriminating against passengers who appeared to be Middle Eastern after the September 11 terrorist attacks. In April 2004, Continental Airlines settled the complaint for $500,000.

Like many of you, I carefully reviewed the lawsuits against the airlines in order to determine which airlines had engaged in the most egregious discrimination, so I could fly only those airlines. But oddly, rather than bragging about the charges, the airlines heatedly denied discriminating against Middle Eastern passengers. What a wasted marketing opportunity! Imagine the great slogans the airlines could use:

"Now Frisking All Arabs—Twice!"

"More Civil-Rights Lawsuits Brought by Arabs Than Any Other Airline!"

"The Friendly Skies—Unless You're an Arab!"

"You Are Now Free to Move About the Cabin—Not So Fast, Mohammed!"

Worst of all, the Department of Transportation ordered the settlement money to be spent on civil-rights programs to train airline staff to stop looking for terrorists, a practice known as "digging your own grave and paying for the shovel." Airlines that have been the most vigilant against terrorism are forced by the government into reeducation seminars to learn to suppress common sense. Airlines are being forced, at their own expense, to make commercial air travel more dangerous.

Despite the deployment of fifty thousand government-paid screeners since 9/11, it's still fairly easy to sneak knives, box cutters, and even guns onto most commercial flights. But there's good news, too. It's now virtually impossible to hijack a plane using an oversized carry-on bag or a set of nail clippers.

Americans lull themselves into a sense of security by simply assuming the government is secretly screening airline passengers who look like the last two dozen terrorists. No, it isn't. To the contrary, the government aggressively punishes airlines that have not abandoned rationality. The government fines airlines that give a secondary security check to more than two Arabs per flight, and Norman Mineta is busy suing airlines for millions of dollars if the airline removes passengers who share any physical characteristics with the people who recently killed three thousand Americans using airplanes as their weapon. (Also, Mineta is pushing to broaden the definition of "on-time arrival" to include planes that crash into buildings ahead of schedule.) If any airline hijackings in the United States have been averted since 9/11, it is only because Attorney General John Ashcroft already has the terrorists in lockup. They're certainly not being stopped at the airport.

Mineta doggedly insists that aviation security does not justify "discrimination" against passengers. Why not? The entire concept of "security" consists of a rational, experience-based process of discriminating between likely attackers and unlikely ones. If you could bring someone back in a time machine from pre–Politically Correct America, he would survey the situation after September 11 and say, "Well, you've got one advantage in this war with al Qaeda—at least you know what the enemy looks like. They're all Muslim men, so just work over those guys. . . . Why is no one saying anything? Hello? Norman? Wow, you could hear a pin drop in this room."

Not coincidentally, the only airline terrorist stopped since 9/11 was stopped by passengers. Fortunately, the passengers on an American Airlines flight 63 from Paris were unburdened by Department of Transportation guidelines forbidding them to take Richard Reid's appearance into account. Not having been warned not to make judgments based on appearance because that might send a message of inferiority to Muslims, the passengers were able to take one look at Reid and know he was trouble. They wrestled Reid to the ground just before he detonated a shoe bomb that would have blown up a plane with 185 passengers.

An Australian newspaper titled its article on Reid "Would You Let This Man Board a Plane?" Norman Mineta responded by ordering airport security to start checking all passengers' shoes. ∎

☞ Even with Hindsight Liberals
Can't See Straight

MAY 5, 2004

Over in the alternative universe of the 9/11 Commission hearings watched only by me, Richard Ben-Veniste recently proposed an amazing new standard for investigating Arabs in this country. In the middle of haranguing Condoleezza Rice, Ben-Veniste demanded to know why the suspected twentieth hijacker, Zacarias Moussaoui, had not been more aggressively investigated, despite the fact that—I quote—he had "no explanation for the funds in his bank account, and no explanation for why he was in the United States."

So let me get this straight: Airport security can't acknowledge that a person is an Arab, but they should be allowed to audit his bank records? (Come to think of it, "Can't Explain His Bank Account or Why He's Here" is also a pretty good description of John Kerry.)

Can we use that as a standard going forward? The government prohibits airlines from searching more than two Arabs per flight, so it would be terrific if liberals would let us examine their financial statements. If Democratic Party shills like Ben-Veniste—who himself looks like someone who ought to be searched at airports—are going to make ludicrous, macho statements like that in order to win applause from weeping widows in the peanut gallery, can't we hold them to that policy when it matters?

Ben-Veniste thinks the key to stopping the 9/11 attack was for the FBI to have drawn the obvious conclusions from an Arab in-flight school. If only the FBI had searched Moussaoui's computer, they would have found a flight-simulator computer program, information about the Boeing 747, and extensive files on crop dusters. From this, apparently, Ben-Veniste imagines the FBI would have concluded that on September 11, nineteen Muslims were going to hijack airplanes out of Logan, Newark, and Dulles airports and fly them into buildings.

A somewhat more direct chain of causation traces its way back to the aviation-security commission chaired by Vice President Al Gore in 1997. If that commission had done its job, you wouldn't have to wait for one of my columns to find out that there was a commission on airline safety years before the 9/11 attacks. Isn't it curious that Democrats aren't bragging about Gore inventing air safety? The reason Al Gore hasn't added "anti-terrorism" to the list of things he invented is that Gore's commission concluded that passenger profiling must ignore ethnicity and nationality. Or as Gore himself might have put it, "I took the initiative in making it easier for Muslims to use airplanes to slaughter innocent American citizens."

The Gore commission on air safety decided that profiling should be based on "reasonable predictors of risk, not stereotypes or generalizations." Amazingly, all those "reasonable predictors of risk" failed to stop a single Muslim terrorist on 9/11. One wonders whether a profiling system that included ethnicity and nationality would have been more helpful in stopping nineteen Muslim men, fifteen of whom were from Saudi Arabia, all speaking Arabic to one another, from boarding planes on September 11.

Recently—that is, about the time Ben-Veniste was shocked that the FBI hadn't uncovered the 9/11 plot based on the fact that Moussaoui had overstayed his visa—Senator Hillary Clinton and Senator Chuck Schumer were clamoring for the release of Ansar Mahmood, a twenty-six-year-old Pakistani immigrant detained in October 2001 after he was observed taking photographs at a water-treatment plant in upstate New York. Mahmood later pleaded guilty to committing a felony by giving financial aid to illegal immigrants from Pakistan. Schumer says Mahmood should be permitted to stay in the United States because he "was cleared of terrorist links," and he has already served his time for "a non-violent felony." Hillary simply calls Mahmood's detention "disturbing."

Where is Ben-Veniste when we need him? What happened to the "We Don't Know Why He's Here or His Sources of Money" standard for harassing Muslim immigrants? In contrast to Mahmood, Zacarias Moussaoui had committed no felonies; his only apparent offense was to have overstayed his visa. But Ben-Veniste is appalled that the FBI didn't beat Moussaoui for information. The French had linked Moussaoui to al Qaeda—based largely on the information that he took frequent trips to Afghanistan and Pakistan, Mahmood's home country. When FBI agents in Minneapolis requested a warrant to search Moussaoui's computer, FBI headquarters wrote back, "We don't know he's a terrorist"—the same argument Schumer is making for Mahmood's release right now.

Liberals always claim to know exactly what to do as soon as it's too late. After Muslims attack with airplanes, they want to investigate flight schools. After Muslims attack with shoe bombs, they want to investigate shoes. After a Muslim introduces *E. coli* into New York's water supply, liberals will be enraged that Muslim immigrants taking pictures of New York water-treatment plants weren't investigated more aggressively—as soon as they are done blaming Bush for not stopping the attack. Liberals are the only known species whose powers of reasoning are not improved by the benefit of hindsight. Not only are they always fighting the last war, in most cases they're surrendering. ∎

4

At Least They Didn't Run Jimmy Carter This Time

———————■———————

Inasmuch as John Kerry's campaign strategy is to hide until election day, and let his many positions on every issue speak for themselves, there isn't a lot to say about the gigolo. Kerry wants to let people know what he stands for, but first he has to decide what he stands for. (Just the other day a reporter asked Kerry, "Are you for or against gay marriage?" As usual, his answer was, "Yes.") So I'm including a few columns on the Democratic presidential candidates who are already appearing on *Hollywood Squares*. The idea that there are any meaningful differences among the Democratic contenders is absurd anyway. They're all the same—except Dennis Kucinich: only Kucinich could have held up a pie chart during a Democratic debate that was broadcast *only on radio*. (Even more embarrassing: Al Sharpton asked the moderator what kind of pie it was.)

☞ American Women to Kerry: We Don't Think You're So Hot Either

MAY 7, 2003

Senator John F. Kerry has been citing his valorous Vietnam record more often than General George Patton cursed. It's a good theme for him. Liberals keep loudly proclaiming that they support "the troops"—while simultaneously running sneering articles that portray the troops as coarse, semiliterate cads. So a tax-and-spend Massachusetts liberal like Kerry could finally provide them with one "troop" they really do like. (By contrast, for the first time ever, I find myself in favor of the war but against the troop.)

Kerry has been aggressively brandishing his military service with the bristling connotation that if you didn't fight, you can't quarrel with him on war and peace. In a catfight with former Vermont governor Howard Dean during the Democrats' first presidential debate in South Carolina, Kerry snarled at Dean, "I don't need any lectures in courage from Howard Dean." If John Kerry had a dollar for every time he bragged about serving in Vietnam— Oh wait, he does.

Though Kerry makes liberal ladies' bosoms heave with his self-advertisements about his Vietnam experience, the Democrats might not want to let Kerry pursue this particular line of argument. According to Thomas Ricks's book *Making the Corps,* the vast majority of officers currently serving in the military are conservative Republicans—"largely comfortable with the views of Rush Limbaugh." Citing a series of studies expressing alarm at what they viewed as a disquieting trend, Ricks says that "open identification with the Republican Party is becoming the norm— even, suggests former army major Dana Isaacoff, part of the implicit definition of being a member of the officer corps." Why the officer corps would take a dim view of a party that has spent the last three decades systematically trying to emasculate the military in pursuit of every conceivable social cause is anybody's guess. Still, there it is. So, by Kerry's own logic, in a few years only right-wing Republicans will be eligible for the presidency.

But that's the Democrats' problem. For now, there are other, more urgent implications to Kerry's argument. As long as we're going to get uppity about our personal experiences, why is John Kerry allowed to have any opinion about taxes? He has spent his entire life marrying a succession of heiresses and living off the fortunes amassed by other men. (It must be the luck of the pseudo-Irish.) How can Kerry claim to understand the anguish of people who pay high taxes? What does this pompous, whining, morally superior, mincing habitué of Boston drawing rooms know about confiscatory taxes on hard-earned money? (Not that his nuptial path to wealth is not also hard-earned.) If Kerry doesn't need lectures on the military from Howard Dean, do the rest of us need lectures from this sponge on how much we should be willing to pay in taxes? What is this male Anna Nicole Smith's expertise in average people paying taxes? I don't have a rich wife supporting me. And I don't look French.

There was a firestorm of indignation when an unnamed Bush adviser recently remarked to the *New York Times* that Kerry "looks French." Up until five minutes ago, the entire Kerry family used adjectives like "European" as statements of the highest praise. Kerry's sister cited her brother's cultured refinement in a 1994 profile of Kerry in *Rhode Islander Magazine* by saying, "Our parents felt deeply that we needed to absorb the culture and know the Europeans as friends." In his 1996 Senate campaign, reporters were dazzled and awed when Kerry responded to a Canadian reporter in French, snootily noting that Kerry's French was much better than his opponent's.

In a profile of Kerry's current heiress wife, Teresa Heinz, in the June 2003 issue of *Elle* magazine, noted journalist Lisa DePaulo quotes Kerry oozing with admiration for his wife, saying she is "very earthy, sexy, European." "Earthy" and "European" sound like euphemisms for hairy armpits and body odor. But we get it. American girls aren't good enough for Frenchy. Well, we don't think he's so hot either. Even after Kerry was attacked for looking French, Heinz thought the best course would be to defend her husband by haughtily snipping that the Bush aides "probably don't even speak French." Take that, you boorish Americans! If the Democrats nominate Kerry, Bush should take the high road and pledge not to raise the issue of his opponent looking French. But the question of Kerry's fitness to discuss taxes while living off rich women is still on the table. ■

☞ General Democrat

OCTOBER 1, 2003

According to a new survey, six out of ten Americans can't name a single Democrat running for president. And that poll was actually taken among the ten current Democratic candidates. According to the survey answers, "the military guy" leads with 19 percent, followed by "that doctor—what's his name?" with 12 percent, and "the French-looking guy" with 9 percent. Since Wesley Clark entered the race, Democrats have been salivating over the prospect of a presidential candidate who is a four-star general—and has the politics of Susan Sarandon! Clark's entry into the race was seen as a setback for John Kerry, the only other Democratic contender with combat experience. (Although back in the 1970s, Dennis Kucinich served in the Kiss Army.)

Before Clark becomes the answer to a Trivial Pursuit question, consider that his main claim to fame is that he played a pivotal role in what most of his supporters passionately believe was an illegal, immoral war of American imperialism in Vietnam. How does that earn you points with Democrats?

Clark said he would have supported the war in Iraq if he had been in Congress last year, but now he opposes the way the war is being fought and he wants U.S. troops out of Iraq as soon as possible. This was very exciting for Senator Joe Biden, because for the first time ever he can now credibly accuse someone of plagiarizing him.

Clark's other credential to lead the free world was that he supervised the "liberation" of Kosovo by ordering our pilots to drop bombs from 15,000 feet at a tremendous cost in innocent civilian life in a 100 percent humanitarian war against a country that posed absolutely no threat to the United States—imminent or otherwise—and without the approval of the almighty United Nations. So you can see why Clark supported, then opposed, then supported, then opposed the current war in Iraq. (Say, is there a website where I can get up-to-the-minute updates on Wesley Clark's current position on the war in Iraq, kind of like a Nasdaq ticker?)

Possible Clark campaign slogans are already starting to emerge:

"I Was into Quagmires Before Quagmires Were Cool"

"Honk If You Got Bombed in Kosovo"

"Only Fired by the Pentagon Once!"

"The OTHER Bush-Bashing Rhodes Scholar From Arkansas"

"No, Really, Vice President Would Be Fine"

On *Meet the Press,* on June 15, 2003, Clark told Tim Russert that he got a lot of calls after 9/11 telling him to go on television and say, "This has to be connected to Saddam Hussein." Asked who had told him that, Clark said, "The White House; it came from people around the White House. It came from all over."

But under cross-examination by Sean Hannity on the Fox News Channel a few weeks later, Clark would say only that he had gotten a call from "a fellow in Canada who is part of a Middle Eastern think tank who gets inside intelligence information." So in two weeks' time, Clark had gone from "the White House" to "people close to the White House" to "some guy in Canada." Clark is for abortion, tax hikes, affirmative action, and he is against the war in Iraq. But he served in Vietnam. So he's basically Howard Dean with scarier flashbacks.

Howard Dean is not a general, but he is a doctor. Democrats are enthusiastic about Dean, since they figure that if this Democrat was ever caught with a naked intern, he could just say it was her annual physical. Dean has leapt beyond criticizing Bush and is now embracing terrorists. He has called Hamas terrorists "soldiers in a war" and said the United States should not take sides between Israel and Palestinian suicide bombers. This has won him a spot in the hearts of the Democratic Party base—middle-class white kids from Ben-and-Jerryville who smash Starbucks windows whenever bankers come to town for a meeting. If Dean doesn't get the Democratic nomination, perhaps he could throw his hat into the ring to replace Arafat.

The also-rans are trying to distinguish themselves by competing to see who can denounce George Bush with greater zeal. Senator John Kerry has said we need to "de-Americanize" the war—I guess on the theory that the "de-Americanizing" process has worked so well for the Democratic Party. He is furious at Bush for prosecuting a war Kerry voted for, saying the difference is "I would have been patient." He would have had to be extremely patient in the case of Germany, inasmuch as Gerhard Schroeder announced before the war began that he would never authorize war in Iraq under any circumstances.

Florida senator Bob Graham recently told the Council on Foreign Relations that in "answer to any questions about the Bush administration on the war on terror," the answer is "No, they are not doing a good job." This would explain Graham's commanding lead among members of his own household, although his maid is still "Undecided."

Dick Gephardt has taken to calling President Bush a "miserable failure"—as opposed to Gephardt, who is a "happy failure." Things have gotten pretty bad when you're being called a "failure" by a guy who spent thirty years sucking up to labor but still can't get the AFL-CIO's endorsement.

Dennis Kucinich recently proposed a new U.S. policy for Iraq, known in military circles as "unconditional surrender." He wants all U.S. troops to leave immediately and be replaced by UN troops. The head of the UN Human Rights Commission—Syria—would surely have things back to normal in no time. Kucinich has also offered his services as a consultant to any city in Iraq that's thinking about filing for bankruptcy. According to most polls, the Democrat who stands the best chance to beat Bush is a guy named "Generic." ∎

☞ The Party of Ideas

NOVEMBER 20, 2003

With economic growth and name recognition of the average Democratic presidential candidate both running at about 7 percent, the Democrats are in trouble. It turns out that given a choice between "shock and awe" and "run and hide," the American people prefer the former. Unable to rouse more than the Saddam-supporting left with their kooky foreign-policy ideas, the Democrats had been counting on a lousy economy. Now that the Bush tax cuts have already started to kick in and boost the economy, it was beginning to look as if the Treason Lobby would have nothing to run on.

But the Democrats have discovered a surprise campaign issue: It turns out that several of them have had a death in the family. Not only that, but many Democrats have cracker-barrel humble-origins stories and a Jew or lesbian in the family. Dick Gephardt's campaign platform is that his father was a milkman, his son almost died, and his daughter is a lesbian. Vote for me!

So don't say the Democrats aren't the party of ideas. As they keep reminding us, their ideas are just too darn complex to fit on a bumper sticker. Consequently, the Democrats can't tell us their ideas until after the election. Instead, their version of a political campaign is to stage a "Queen for a Day" extravaganza—which has special resonance in the case of the Democrats.

Al Gore famously inaugurated the family tragedy routine at the 1992 Democratic National Convention, where his idea of an inspiring political speech was to recount the story of his son being hit by a car. At the 1996 convention, Gore told a tearjerker about his sister's long, painful death from lung cancer. It got to the point that Gore's family members had to fear any more runs for higher office.

In the current campaign, Gephardt has taken to spinning out a long, pitiful tale of his son's near-death three decades ago. At dozens of campaign stops, Mrs. Gephardt weeps anew as her husband tells the same gut-wrenching story over and over again. The relevance of their son's illness to Gephardt's run for the presidency is this: It inspired Gephardt's call for national health insurance. With his wife softly weeping in the background, he intones, "I get it."

At least when Gephardt exploits a family tragedy, he doesn't expect praise for not exploiting a family tragedy. John Edwards injects his son's fatal car accident into his campaign by demanding that everyone notice how he refuses to inject his son's fatal car accident into his campaign. Edwards has talked about his son's death in a 1996 car accident on *Good Morning America,* in dozens of profiles, and in his new book—"It was and is the most important fact of my life." His 1998 Senate campaign ads featured film footage of Edwards at a learning lab he founded in honor of his son, titled the Wade Edwards Learning Lab. He wears his son's Outward Bound pin on his suit lapel. He was going to wear it on his sleeve, until someone suggested that might be a little too "on the nose."

If you want points for not using your son's death politically, don't you have to take down all those "Ask me about my son's death in a horrific car accident" bumper stickers? Edwards is like a politician who keeps announcing that he will not use his opponent's criminal record for partisan political advantage. *I absolutely refuse to mention the name of my dearly beloved and recently departed son killed horribly in a car accident, which affected me deeply, to score cheap political points.* I wouldn't want John Edwards to be president, but I think even Karl Rove would be willing to stipulate that the death of a son is a terrible thing.

Howard Dean talks about his brother Charlie's murder at the hands of North Vietnamese Communists. If a death in the familly is the main qualification for becoming a Democratic presidential candidate, what's Scott Peterson waiting for? Bizarrely, after working on the failed George McGovern campaign, Charlie Dean went to Indochina in 1974 to witness the ravages of the war he had opposed. Not long after he arrived, the apparently ungrateful Communists captured and killed him. *Hey fellas! I'm on your si—CLUNK!* Howard Dean wears his brother's battered 1960s belt every day. (By contrast, Ted Kennedy honors the memory of his deceased family members with several belts every day.) Dean told Dan Rather about his brother's death at some length on CBS News: "It gave me a sense that you ought to live for the moment with people; that you really—you really need to tell people you love them if you love them. It was certainly the most awful thing that ever happened to our family. It was terrible for my parents; it was even worse for them than it was for us."

Dammit, if a man wants to be my president, I have a right to know where he stands on the issue of when to tell the people you love that you love them! Couldn't the Democratic Party go back to plagiarizing British Labour Party leader Neil Kinnock the way Senator Joe Biden did, rather than plagiarizing *Lifetime: TV for Women*? Do any men at all vote for the Democrats anymore?

Carol Moseley Braun's personal tragedy is that she's being forced to run for president even though it turns out the Democrats won't need her to split the black vote anyway. *Please, can I drop out now? Al Sharpton is only polling at 2 percent. I hate this!*

Sharpton is the counterpoint to his sob sisters in the Democratic Party. Sharpton libeled innocent men in the Tawana Brawley case. He inflamed angry mobs in Brooklyn's Crown Heights, leading to the murder of Yankel Rosenbaum. He incited an anti-Semitic pogrom against a Jewish-owned clothing store in Harlem, Freddy's, ending in a blaze of bullets and a fire that left several employees dead. So while the other Democrats talk about their personal tragedies, Sharpton goes around creating personal tragedies.

In addition to having a number of family deaths among them, the Democrats' other big idea—too nuanced for a bumper sticker—is that many of them have Jewish ancestry. There's Joe Lieberman: Always Jewish. Wesley Clark: Found Out His Father Was Jewish in College. John Kerry: Jewish Since He Began Presidential Fundraising. Howard Dean: Married to a Jew. Al Sharpton: Circumcised. Even Hillary Clinton claimed to have unearthed some evidence that she was a Jew—along with the long-lost evidence that she was a Yankees fan. And that, boys and girls, is how the Jews survived thousands of years of persecution: by being susceptible to pandering.

Clark said that when he discovered he was half-Jewish, he remembered growing up in Arkansas and feeling "a certain kinship" with Jewish families in the dry-goods business. (I, too, have always felt a certain kinship with Calvin Trillin.)

The Democrats' urge to assert a Jewish heritage is designed to disguise the fact that the Democrats would allow the state of Israel to perish as Palestinian suicide bombers slaughter Jewish women and children. Their humble-origins claptrap is designed to disguise the fact that liberals think ordinary Americans are racist scum. Their perverse desire to discuss the deaths and near-deaths of their children is designed to disguise the fact that they support the killing of more than a million unborn children every year. (Oh, by the way, what did their milkman and millworker fathers think about abortion?) Be forewarned: If the Democrats start extolling you—get a gun. ■

☞ The Jesus Thing

JANUARY 7, 2004

When they were fundraising, the Democratic candidates for president all claimed to be Jewish. Now that they are headed for Super Tuesday down South, they've become Jesus freaks. Listening to Democrats talk about Jesus is a little like listening to them on national security: They don't seem terribly comfortable with either subject.

To ease Democrats into the Jesus thing, the Democratic Leadership Council is actually holding briefings for Democratic candidates teaching them how to talk about religion. As has been widely reported, the DLC gingerly suggests that Democrats start referring to "God's green earth." The participants were also warned that millions of Americans worship a supreme being whose name is not Bill Clinton. Democrats never talk about believing in something; they talk about simulating belief in something. *Americans believe in this crazy God crap that we don't, so how do we hoodwink them into thinking we believe in God?* It's part of the casual contempt Democrats have for the views of normal people.

What is arresting is the Democrats' fantastic habit of openly talking about how they plan to fake out the American people. The Democrats candidly say, *How do we make sure the Americans don't know what we're really thinking? Let's get a Southerner, let's talk about Jesus, let's talk about NASCAR—white Southern guys seem to like that. Let's see . . . if we could get a general on the ticket, Americans will forget how much we hate the military and long to see America humiliated.* Never has a major political party talked so openly about their plans to fool the voters. It's the damnedest thing I've ever seen. They seem not to realize the people they are talking about are listening.

In the current *New Republic* magazine, Peter Beinart points out that the capture of Saddam has hurt the antiwar cause and left the Democrats with nothing to say. He proposes that Democrats pretend to support the war on terrorism by calling for a massive campaign to catch Osama. Yeah, let's try that. That'll fool 'em. In the debate this week, John Kerry responded to a question about how he would appeal to Southerners by saying he could put a Southerner on his ticket. As Howard Dean has explained, they're stupid enough: It's just a bunch of white guys in pickup trucks with Confederate flags.

Dean himself has recently made the fascinating discovery that a lot of Americans believe in God. Hold the phones—the Democrats have a soothsayer in their midst! Next, Dean will be announcing that he's just discovered how important this sex thing is. Before the poll numbers came out on religious belief in America, Dean said, "We have got to stop having our elections in the South based on race, guns, God and gays." Higher taxes, gay marriage, abortion on demand, and surrender in Iraq—that'll do the trick in Mississippi!

Then about a month ago, the Pew Research Center for the People and the Press released a poll showing that people who regularly attend religious services supported Bush 63 percent to 37 percent, and those who never attend religious services opposed him 62 percent to 38 percent. When you exclude blacks (as they do in Vermont), who are overwhelmingly Baptist and overwhelmingly Democratic, and rerun the numbers, basically any white person who believes in God is a Republican. The only Democrats who go to church regularly are the ones who plan to run for president someday and are preparing in advance to fake a belief in God.

Though Dean is pursuing the Jesus thing with a vengeance, the results so far have been mixed. In Iowa last week, Dean said, "Let's get into a little religion here," and then began denouncing Christian minister Jerry Falwell. "Don't you think Jerry Falwell reminds you a lot more of the Pharisees than he does of the teachings of Jesus?" I don't even know what Dean means by that. I am sure his audience doesn't.

Rapping with reporters about God on the campaign plane, Dean said, "If you know much about the Bible, which I do"—and then proceeded to confuse the Old Testament with the New Testament.

Dean illiterately claimed his favorite book of the New Testament was the Book of Job. (He said his least favorite was the Book of Numbers and then explained how he planned to balance the budget.) Having already complained to DNC chairman Terry McAuliffe about other Democrats attacking him, Dean recently said, "I'm feeling a little more Job-like recently." That's comforting. A few snippy remarks from the likes of Dick Gephardt and Dean thinks it's the wrath of the God of Abraham. Yeah, that's definitely the guy we want leading the nation in perilous times.

Dean's epiphanic religious awakening occurred over a bike path—and that's his version of what happened. He was baptized Catholic and raised an Episcopalian, but left the Episcopal Church in a huff when he finally found his true religion: environmentally friendly exercise. The Episcopalians don't demand much in the way of actual religious belief. They have girl priests, gay priests, gay bishops, gay marriages—it's much like the *New York Times* editorial board. They acknowledge the Ten Commandments—or "Moses' talking points"—but hasten to add that they're not exactly "carved in stone." After Bush said that the most important philosopher to him was Jesus Christ, the Episcopal bishop in Des Moines, Iowa, C. Christopher Epting, said the answer was "a turnoff." So there isn't a lot of hair-shirt-wearing and sacrifice for the Episcopalians.

But the bike-path incident was too much for Dean. A key tenet of the Druidical religion of liberals is non–fossil-fuel travel. So Dean left the Church of the Proper Fork because the Episcopal Church in Montpelier hesitated before ceding some of its land for a bike path.

On CNN, Judy Woodruff asked Dean in amazement, "Was it just over a bike path that you left the Episcopal Church?"

Dean: "Yes, as a matter of fact it was."

Dean waxed expansive on the theological implications of bike paths, saying, "I didn't think that was very public-spirited."

But recently, Dean has leapt even beyond the DLC-recommended "God's green earth" and begun talking about Jesus, saying, "He was a person who set an extraordinary example that has lasted 2,000 years, which is pretty inspiring when you think about it." Gosh, to hear Dean tell it, Jesus is even giving Oprah a run for her money! Also, Christ died for our sins, but let's not get into the hocus-pocus part of Christianity. The gist of the New Testament is about bike paths. Dean's relationship with Jesus is a little like David Lloyd George's relationship with the Slovaks. At the Treaty of Versailles conference, the British prime minister was heard to whisper, "Who are the Slovaks again? I can never place them." ■

☞ What Happened to Your Queer
Party-Friends?

JANUARY 21, 2004

The endless receding nightmare of the Iowa caucuses has finally produced something interesting: The Democrats have one hellacious catfight on their hands. After all the hoopla about Howard Dean's new mass movement of "Deaniacs," it appears that blanketing Iowa with self-righteous twenty-year-olds in orange wool caps may not have been the ideal campaign strategy. Dean's distant third-place finish makes you want to ask him the question Jack Nicholson put to his down-and-out gay neighbor in *As Good as It Gets*: "What happened to your queer party-friends?"

At the behest of the Democratic Party establishment, the media dutifully destroyed Howard Dean, the legitimate leader of the opposition. Democratic voters are such lemmings. The *New York Times* told them to switch from Dean to John Kerry, so they all obediently switched from Dean to Kerry. But Dean still has the money and foot soldiers and endorsements to stay in the fight for the foreseeable future. And being from Vermont, Dean should do well in New Hampshire. I went to a public school, but if I remember my high school geography correctly, New Hampshire and Vermont are the same state.

Until Kerry won Iowa, Wesley Clark was viewed as the preeminent electable Democrat, principally because he's a Republican. Dean said he thinks Clark is a fine fellow but truly a Republican. In response, General Clark immediately put on a third sweater. Sadly, it may turn out that Clark's whole raison d'être is now gone. Never was so much money, media, chicanery, Gwyneth Paltrow, Madonna, conniving, and Kabbalah deployed to promote a quote-unquote "electable" Democrat. Clark was supposed to be the phony American to stop Dean, but Kerry is the even better phony American! And he's already stopped Dean in Iowa. Kerry and Clark now represent the two major wings of the Democratic Party—the Kennedy wing and the Clinton wing. One drowns you after the extramarital affair; the other one calls you a stalker.

Other than that, there isn't a hair's difference between any of the Democrats on any substantive issues. All the Democrats are for higher taxes. All of them favor Hillary's socialist health-care plan. All of them are for higher pay for teachers and nurses—and no pay at all for anyone in the pharmaceutical or oil industries, especially Halliburton executives, who should be sent to Guantánamo. All the Democrats believe the way to strike fear in the hearts of the terrorists is for the federal government to invest heavily in windmills.

All the Democrats oppose the war. And all the Democrats who took a position on the war before it began were for it, but now believe that everything Bush did from that moment forward has been bad! bad! bad! This is with the exception of Joe Lieberman who, as an observant Jew, is forbidden to backpedal after sundown on Fridays. Representing a large flabby chunk of the Kennedy wing, Ted Kennedy gave a speech last week in which he called the liberation of Iraq a "political product." Then again, Ted Kennedy calls Chivas Regal "that life-sustaining liquid." Finally, all the candidates are willing to sell out any of these other issues in service of the one burning desire of all Democrats: abortion on demand. If they could just figure out a way to abort babies using solar power, that's all we'd ever hear about.

For all his talk, even Dick Gephardt was willing to abandon blue-collar workers in a heartbeat. The Teamsters haven't asked for much, only two big votes in the past decade: (1) Oppose NAFTA, and (2) support drilling on a small, godforsaken patch of the Alaskan wilderness, as the people who actually live there have been begging us to do for decades. Like all the other Democrats, Gephardt voted against the Teamsters—but with Barbra Streisand—to oppose drilling in the godforsaken Alaskan wilderness. When Gephardt entered politics he was pro-life. But then— like Al Gore, Jesse Jackson, Dennis Kucinich, and scores of other Democrats with national ambitions—he quickly figured out that position wasn't, well . . . viable. In short order he had adopted the whole NARAL party line. That's how you woo old-time union Democrats.

On Monday night in Iowa, Gephardt was shocked to discover that blue-collar Democrats have gone the way of all patriotic Democrats: They're all Republicans now. (But thanks for that NAFTA vote a decade ago!) You knew Gephardt was toast when even responsible journalists started using words like "decent" and "solid" to describe the two-faced weasel from Missouri. Though I suppose "decent" has a pretty broad meaning in a party that still admires Bill Clinton.

The Iowa caucus was just another one of the Democrats' ongoing public debates about how to fake out the American people. Fifty percent of Iowa Democrats participating in the caucus said they "strongly disapprove" of the war with Iraq and another 25 percent "somewhat disapprove." But more important to Democrats than their pacifism was "electability." The entire Iowa electorate was committed to the proposition: How do we fool the neighbors? In the end, the caucus-goers chose a decorated war hero who voted in favor of the very war that 75 percent of them oppose. So much for the antiwar fever sweeping the country. The Democrats aren't even man enough to run a genuine coward for president. ■

☞ Just a Gigolo

JANUARY 28, 2004

After the New Hampshire primary, Dennis Kucinich's new slogan is ".001 Percent of America Can't Be Wrong!" John Edwards's new slogan is "Vote for Me or We'll See You in Court." Joe Lieberman's new slogan is "Sixth Place Is Not an Option" (bumper sticker version: "Ask Me About My Delegate") Wesley Clark's new slogan is "Leading America's War on Fetuses." Howard Dean's new slogan is "I Want to Be Your President . . . And So Do I!" Al Sharpton's new slogan is "Hello, Room Service?"

That leaves John Kerry (new slogan: "Nous Sommes Nombre Un!"), who is winning Democratic voters in droves on the basis of his superior ability to taunt George Bush for his lack of combat experience. Like every war hero I've ever met, John Kerry seems content to spend his days bragging about his battlefield exploits. Wait, wait . . . let me correct that last sentence: Like *no* war hero I've ever met . . .

As everyone has heard approximately one billion times by now, Kerry boasts that he has REAL experience with aircraft carriers, and if Bush wants to run on national security, then . . . BRING IT ON! I note that when George Bush directed that precise phrase at Islamic terrorists who yearn to slaughter American women and children, liberals were enraged at the macho posturing of it. But they feel "Bring it on!" is a perfectly appropriate expression when directed at a dangerous warmonger like George Bush. ("Bring it on!" won out over Kerry's first impulse, "Let's get busy, sister!")

Kerry was indisputably brave in Vietnam, and it's kind of cute to see Democrats pretend to admire military service. Physical courage, like chastity, is something liberals usually deride but are tickled about when it accidentally manifests itself in one of their own. One has to stand in awe of Kerry's military service thirty-three years ago. Of course, that's where it ends, including with Kerry—inasmuch as, upon his return from war in 1970, he promptly began trashing his fellow Vietnam vets by calling them genocidal murderers.

But if Bush can't talk to Kerry about the horrors of war, then Kerry sure as hell can't talk to anyone about the plight of the middle class. Kerry's life experience consists of living off other men's money by marrying their wives and daughters. For over thirty years, Kerry's primary occupation has been stalking lonely heiresses. Not to get back to his combat experience, but Kerry sees a room full of wealthy widows as "a target-rich environment." This is a guy whose experience dealing with tax problems is based on spending his entire adult life being supported by rich women. What does a kept man know about taxes?

In 1970, Kerry married into the family of Julia Thorne—a family estimated to be worth about $300 million. She got depressed, they separated, and soon he was seen catting around with Hollywood starlets, mostly while he was still married. (Apparently, JFK really was his mentor.) Thorne is well bred enough to say nothing ill of her Lothario ex-husband. He is, after all, the father of her children—a fact that never seemed to constrain him.

When Kerry was about to become the latest Heinz family charity, he sought to have his marriage to Thorne annulled, despite the fact that it had produced two children. It seems his second meal ticket, Teresa Heinz, wanted the first marriage annulled—and she's worth more than $700 million. Kerry claims he will stand up to powerful interests, but he can't even stand up to his wife. Heinz made Kerry sign a prenuptial agreement, presumably aware of how careless he is with other people's property, such as other people's Vietnam War medals, which Kerry threw on the ground during a 1971 antiwar demonstration.

At pains to make Kerry sound like a normal American, his campaign has described how Kerry risked everything, mortgaging his home in Boston to help pay for his presidential campaign. Technically, Kerry took out a $6 million mortgage for "his share" of "the family's home"—which was bought with the Heinz family fortune. (Why should he spend his own money? He didn't throw away his own medals.) I'm sure the average working stiff in Massachusetts can relate to a guy who borrows $6 million against his house to pay for TV ads. Kerry's campaign has stoutly insisted that he will pay off the mortgage himself, with no help from his rich wife. Let's see: According to tax returns released by his campaign, in 2002, Kerry's income was $144,091. But as the *Washington Post* recently reported, even a $5 million mortgage paid back over thirty years at favorable interest rates would cost $30,389 a month—or $364,668 a year. Paying it off "himself," is he?

The Democrats' joy at nominating Kerry is perplexing. To be sure, liberals take a peculiar, wrathful pleasure in supporting pacifist military types. And Kerry's life story is not without a certain feral aggression. But if we're going to determine fitness for office based on life experience, Kerry clearly has no experience dealing with problems of typical Americans, since he is a cad and a gigolo living in the lap of other men's money. Kerry is like some character in a Balzac novel, an adventurer twirling the end of his mustache and preying on rich women. This lowborn poseur with his threadbare pseudo-Brahmin family bought a political career with one rich woman's money, dumped her, and made off with another heiress to enable him to run for president. If Democrats want to talk about middle-class tax cuts, couldn't they nominate someone who hasn't been a poodle to rich women for the past thirty-three years? ■

☞ Boobs in the News

FEBRUARY 4, 2004

Just to give you a snapshot of the current Democratic Party, in the North Dakota primary, Dennis Kucinich got three times as many votes as Joe Lieberman did. After that, Lieberman quit the race. In sympathy with Lieberman and facing similar odds—I quit the race too. To my supporters: Hey, we didn't go all the way, but just look how much we accomplished! In his concession speech, Lieberman thanked each one of the Democratic presidential candidates for contributing to the race and thanked Al Sharpton in particular for inciting no additional violence against the Jews.

Former front-runner Howard Dean managed to make news by ridiculing the FCC's plan to investigate MTV's halftime show at the Super Bowl. Dean pronounced the proposed investigation "silly." He explained that since he's a doctor, a naked breast is "not exactly an unusual phenomenon" for him. That's an interesting standard. Presumably a prime-time exhibition of Janet Jackson having a full pelvic exam and pap smear would not be "exactly an unusual phenomenon" for Dean either. Let's just be grateful Dean's not a proctologist.

Meanwhile, the rest of the country was not so copacetic about being flashed with what the *New York Times* called Janet Jackson's "middle-aged woman's breast." Janet Jackson said she decided to add "the reveal" following the final rehearsal, which I found pretty shocking. Not the reveal—the fact that the number in question was actually rehearsed. Even CBS executives were enraged by MTV's halftime show, saying they could have gotten the identical show from *National Geographic* for a fraction of the price.

Speaking of boobs, after sustaining his first losses in two primaries Tuesday night, senator and trophy husband John Kerry has said he's going to concentrate on solidifying the support of his base. People like David Gest, Claus von Bulow, and Tom Arnold. Liberals laughed at George Bush for citing Jesus Christ as his favorite philosopher, but are impressed that John Kerry's favorite philosopher is Louis Prima ("Just a Gigolo"). Kerry thinks people are dying to hear his economic plan. In fact, the only economic plan most male voters want to hear about is how Kerry snookered two babes worth hundreds of millions of dollars into marrying him.

Kerry might as well start giving out dating tips. He's running out of other ideas. A few weeks ago, the *Washington Post* reported that Kerry has taken more money from paid lobbyists than any other senator over the past fifteen years. In a face-saving move, Senator Botox has quietly dropped the part of his stump speech where he inveighs against Washington special interests: "We're coming, you're going, and don't let the door hit you on the way out." (Interestingly, these were also Senator Kerry's words to his first wife after he hooked up with Teresa Heinz.)

Not only that, but according to Kerry's principal cheerleaders—Teddy Kennedy and the *New York Times*—Kerry absolutely refuses to talk about his Vietnam service. Kennedy insists that Kerry "just won't talk about" Vietnam. Apparently Vietnam was a brief, death-defying interlude that Kerry would simply prefer not to discuss. You might say it's his

Chappaquiddick. In the objective part of a factual news story, the *New York Times* reported that Kerry "has been careful to avoid being seen as exploiting his service politically." He simply will not do it. This came as a shock to most Americans, who were discovering for the very first time that Kerry had served in Vietnam.

While there is indisputably nothing cooler than having fought for your country, John Kerry's status as a Vietnam veteran is unlikely to change a single vote. Military guys will support Bush, and liberals don't admire bravery. After starting the Vietnam war, the Democratic Party suddenly decided it was an illegal, immoral, undeclared war, and soldiers like John Kerry were baby-killers. Today, vast majorities of Democratic primary voters tell pollsters they opposed the war in Iraq—which their boy Kerry voted for. Kerry's sole appeal is that he gives pacifist cowards cover to fume about Bush.

Just a few years ago, the Democrats thought a pot-smoking draft-dodger would make a splendid president. But now they act as if they are inflamed at the thought that Bush didn't fight in Vietnam. In other words, it's honorable to march in anti-American protests in Europe when America is at war, but not to be a fighter pilot in the Texas Air National Guard.

Democrats know they can't beat Bush, but they intend to enjoy being hysterical about him throughout the campaign. Calling Bush a draft-dodger, which he is not, will join the Democrats' list of other cogent, reasoned arguments, such as "You're stupid" and "Halliburton!" Democrats think they invented war heroes, but being a war hero didn't help Bob Dole. It didn't help George Herbert Walker Bush. It didn't help John McCain. The Democrats didn't invent war heroes. What they invented is the scam of deploying war heroes to argue for surrender. ■

☞ In Desperate Move, Kerry Adopts Puppy

JULY 7, 2004

I guess with John Kerry's choice of John Edwards as his running mate, he really does want to stand up for all Americans, from those worth only $60 million to those worth in excess of $800 million.

In one of the many stratagems Democrats have developed to avoid telling people what they believe, all Edwards wants to talk about is his cracker-barrel humble origins story. We're supposed to swoon over his "life story," as the flacks say, which apparently consists of the amazing fact that . . . his father was a millworker!

That's right up there with "Clinton's stepdad was a drunk" and "Ted Kennedy's dad was a womanizing bootlegger" on my inspirational-life-stories meter. In fact, I'm immediately renouncing my university degrees and going to work for the post office just to give my future children a shot at having a "life story," should they decide to run for president someday.

What is so amazing about Edwards's father being a millworker? That's at least an honorable occupation—as opposed to being a trial lawyer. True, Edwards made more money than his father did. I assume strippers make more money than their alcoholic fathers who abandoned them did, too. This isn't a story of progress; it's a story of devolution.

Despite the overwrought claims of Edwards's dazzling legal skills, winning jury verdicts in personal injury cases has nothing to do with legal talent and everything to do with getting the right cases—unless "talent" is taken to mean "having absolutely no shame." Edwards specialized in babies with cerebral palsy who he claimed would have been spared the affliction if only the doctors had immediately performed Caesarean sections.

As a result of such lawsuits, there are now more than four times as many Caesarean sections as there were in 1970. But curiously, there has been no change in the rate of babies born with cerebral palsy. As the *New York Times* reported, "Studies indicate that in most cases, the disorder is caused by fetal brain injury long before labor begins." All those Caesareans have, however, increased the mother's risk of death, hemorrhage, infection, pulmonary embolism, and Mendelson's syndrome.

In addition, the "little guys" Edwards claims to represent are having a lot more trouble finding doctors to deliver their babies these days as obstetricians leave the practice rather than pay malpractice insurance in excess of $100,000 a year.

In one of Edwards's silver-tongued arguments to the jury on behalf of a girl born with cerebral palsy, he claimed he was channeling the unborn baby girl, Jennifer Campbell, who was speaking to the jurors through him:

"She said at 3, 'I'm fine.' She said at 4, 'I'm having a little trouble, but I'm doing OK.' Five, she said, 'I'm having problems.' At 5:30, she said, 'I need out.'"

She's saying, "My lawyer needs a new Jaguar. . . ."

"She speaks to you through me and I have to tell you right now—I didn't plan to talk about this—right now I feel her. I feel her presence. She's inside me, and she's talking to you."

Well, tell her to pipe down, would you? I'm trying to hear the evidence in a malpractice lawsuit.

To paraphrase Oscar Wilde on the death of Little Nell, one must have a heart of stone to read this without laughing. What is this guy, a tent-show preacher? An off-the-strip Las Vegas lounge psychic couldn't get away with this routine.

Is Edwards able to channel any children right before an abortionist's fork is plunged into their tiny skulls? Why can't he hear those babies saying, "Let me live! Stop spraying this saline solution all over me!" Edwards must experience interference in channeling the voices of babies about to be aborted. Their liberal mothers' hands seem to muffle those voices.

And may we ask what the pre-born Jennifer Campbell thinks about war with Iraq? North Korea? Marginal tax rates? If Miss Cleo here is going to be a heartbeat away from the presidency, I think the voters are entitled to know that.

While making himself fabulously rich by taking a one-third cut of his multimillion-dollar verdicts coaxed out of juries with junk science and maudlin performances, Edwards has the audacity to claim, "I was more than just their lawyer; I cared about them. Their cause was my cause."

If he cared so deeply, how about keeping just 10 percent of the multi-million-dollar jury awards, rather than a third? In fact, as long as these Democrats are so eager to raise the taxes of "the rich," how about a 90 percent tax on contingency fees?

For someone who didn't care about the money, it's interesting that Edwards avoided cases in which the baby died during delivery. Evidently, jury awards average only about $500,000 when the babies die, and there is no disabled child to parade before the jury.

Edwards was one of the leading opponents of a bill in the North Carolina legislature that would have established a fund for all babies born with cerebral palsy. So instead of all disabled babies in North Carolina being compensated equitably, only a few will win the jury lottery—one-third of which will go to trial lawyers like Edwards, who insists he doesn't care about the money.

Despite the now-disproved junk science theory about C-sections preventing cerebral palsy that Edwards peddled in the channeling case, the jury awarded Edwards's client a record-breaking $6.5 million. This is the essence of the modern Democratic Party, polished to perfection by Bill Clinton: They are willing to insult the intelligence of 49 percent of the people if they think they can fool 51 percent of the people.

So while Michael Moore, Al Franken, George Soros, Crazy Al Gore, and the rest of the characters from the climactic devil-worshipping scene in *Rosemary's Baby* provide the muscle for the Kerry campaign, Kerry picks a pretty-boy milquetoast as his running mate, narrowly edging out a puppy for the spot. Just don't ask the Democrats what they believe. Edwards's father was a millworker, and that's all you need to know.

5

Barbra Streisand Feels Your Pain (According to Her Publicist)

———————◼———————

☞ I Like Black People Too, Julia!

MARCH 28, 2002

I tuned in late and consequently can speak only to the last three hours of Halle Berry's acceptance speech at the Academy Awards last Sunday. But inasmuch as she engaged in wild race-baiting to get her Oscar, Berry's expressions of shock were not very believable. She had spent weeks complaining about one time she did not get a role because of her color. It was the part of a forest ranger. Arnold Schwarzenegger probably has trouble getting roles as a ballet dancer, too. And yet still, somehow, white guilt worked on Hollywood liberals! Berry had successfully mau-maued her way to a Best Actress award—and then acted surprised.

It's interesting that Berry makes such a big deal about being black. She was raised by her white mother who was beaten and abandoned by her black father. But clearly, Berry has calculated that it is more advantageous for her acting career to identify with the man who abandoned her rather than the woman who raised her.

Demanding that everyone marvel at her accomplishment, Berry gushed, "This moment is so much bigger than me." Whenever people say something is not about them, it's always just about them. This is a turn of phrase meant to remind the audience of the importance and beauty of them. Berry said her triumph was a victory "for every nameless, faceless woman of color who now has a chance because this door tonight has been opened." Yes, at long last, the "glass ceiling" had been broken. Large-breasted, slightly cocoa women with idealized Caucasian features will finally have a chance in Hollywood! They will, however, still be required to display their large breasts for the camera and to discuss their large breasts at some length with reporters.

Thus, Berry has explained her philosophy on nude scenes, saying, "If it's what the character would do, then I'd use my body in any way that would best serve that character." This, she said, is her "strong belief." But what does it mean, exactly? Don't all people undress sometimes? All people pick their noses, but vapid Hollywood actresses don't insist on showing us that in every movie on the grounds that it is "what the charac-ter would do." In fact, Berry's unseemly enthusiasm for displaying "these babies," as she genteelly refers to her breasts, reduces the number of roles for any women who lack Berry's beauty-queen features.

If movies must include soft-porn scenes, the audience is entitled to de-mand performers with sexual characteristics they would like to see in a soft-porn movie. Somehow, characters played by Whoopi Goldberg are never the sort of characters who would do things in real life like undress or have sex. (And by the way, Billy Bob Thornton isn't cutting it for the fe-male audience.) When they are young, nubile Hollywood actresses all utter the same idiotic clichés about the artistic value of nudity in movies. Then they expect us to feel sorry for them when parts dry up after they be-come old and start to sag. Live by the breast, die by the breast.

But Berry's self-aggrandizing pap was merely a footnote to the main event of the awards ceremony, which was: Julia Roberts loves all the black brothers! It was a point Roberts felt could not be made too often or with too much condescension. Her presentation of the Best Actor award began with the exciting revelation that she had just kissed Sidney Poitier! Hav-ing once dramatically proclaimed she did not want to live in a world in which Denzel Washington had not won an Oscar for Best Actor, Roberts preceded her announcement of Washington's award saying, "I love my life!" This was about her, not him. It was Julia Roberts's personal triumph over racism. The only patronizing remark Roberts skipped was to note that Washington and Poitier were "articulate."

After Washington accepted his award, Roberts leapt on him and would not let go. It was as if he had grown some sort of exotic Julia Roberts wart. Washington—and, more urgently, his wife—deserve great credit for their forbearance. Whatever indignities Hollywood has visited on blacks in the past, it would be hard to top Roberts's performance.

Apparently, Oscar night was Hollywood's shot at patronizing blacks to generate good will—perhaps as wartime penance for its long-standing hatred of America. Like clockwork, whenever white liberals are in trouble, they run to the blacks. After his abomination of a presidency, Jimmy Carter built housing in Harlem. Immediately after the Monica Lewinsky scandal broke, Monica went to a Washington Wizards game, where she hoisted some poor unsuspecting black girl onto her lap in full view of the TV cameras. Bill Clinton dropped the subtlety and dashed off to Africa. It's too bad Denzel Washington's Oscar was tainted by Hollywood's self-serving night of condescension. He deserved that award. And he deserves a special award for not punching Julia Roberts in the mouth. ∎

☞ Dumb Hires Dumber

NOVEMBER 9, 1999

Just when you thought Al Gore could get no more comical, it turns out he's been taking masculinity lessons from a feminist. Since January, the Gore campaign had been covertly funneling $15,000 a month to "controversial feminist author Naomi Wolf"—as she is invariably described. The payments were funneled through other consulting firms, thus eliminating the embarrassing prospect of having to mention her name in the campaign's reports to the FEC. As has been widely reported, Wolf advised the vice president to shed his beta-male characteristics and become an alpha male like Bill Clinton—who is virile in the sense that a filthy, rabid stray dog humping your ankle is virile. The insight that first caught Al's attention was Wolf's article in the June 1998 *George* magazine titled "Al's Inner Alien." ("Gore should let his defenses down and allow his inner oddness out.") While it's true the citizens of this nation don't want a pervert and crook in the Oval Office, I don't know that we're clamoring for an idiot either.

There would have been enough guffaws to go around if Bill Bradley had been caught paying exorbitant fees to some bimbo babbling about alpha males and earth tones. But it was nearly perfect that it was Gore. This was Dumb hiring Dumber. Gore already gives off a strong impression

of being mentally deficient. It has something to do with his habit of enun-
ciating basic points as if he's talking to an extremely slow four-year-olds—
to say nothing of his lunatic claims to having invented the Internet and
been the inspiration for *Love Story*. But then he was caught paying a ludicrous salary to a mind-bogglingly stupid girl. To be sure, stupid isn't the
worst thing in the world. The worst thing in the world is: Stupid trying to
pass itself off as smart. Like Gore, Wolf insists on posing as a great intellect
instead of just working at Hooters. (One wonders if, like Gore, Naomi's
friends also claim she's much smarter and uproariously funny "in person.")

In her latest book, *Promiscuities,* Wolf argued—if that is the appropriate verb—that schools should teach teenagers masturbation and oral sex.
If we don't act now, onanism could become a lost art! "Teaching sexual
gradualism is as sensible as teaching kids to drive," Wolf says. Adding sexual "gradualism" to the high school curriculum: now that's what I call a
workable "Stay in School" program. I'm all for the government teaching
our kids how to have sex, provided they also have to be licensed by the
DMV before they go at each other.

In fact, I don't know why we couldn't combine sex ed with driver's ed
just for the sake of efficiency. Why not require an operator's license, issued
by the DMV, for any kid who wants to have sex? I'm picturing millions of
kids who think they're finally going to have sex, only to be told, "You don't
have the right form. Go to the back of the line."

It is that kind of "out-of-the-box thinking"—as Gore press secretary
Chris Lehane described Wolf's talent—that gets you paid $180,000 per
year by the Gore campaign. Except teaching kids to masturbate really isn't
that new an idea. Indeed, for quite some time liberals have been not only
discussing but sometimes actually *teaching* small children things I can't
discuss in a family newspaper. That's what got New York City schools
chancellor Joseph Fernandez removed from office as long ago as February
1993 and Clinton's surgeon general Joycelyn Elders fired in 1995—to
mention a few times this "out-of-the-box thinking" has been thought of
before. Shhhhhhh. No one tell the Gore campaign. Now, I don't know
much about that fancy "out-of-the-box thinking," but it seems to me such
thinking must, at a minimum, consist of ideas that forty-seven people
haven't thought of before.

Wolf's only serious advice to Gore was: Distance yourself from Clinton.
Not to brag, but I've been giving the whole country that advice totally free
for quite some time now. Fifteen thousand a month. The money was good,

especially for the "breadwinner for a growing family," as Wolf claimed to be. (Her husband must have enjoyed hearing that.) Still, Wolf resented her anonymity in the Gore campaign. Indeed, *Time* magazine says Wolf's claims that she had been trying to disguise her role in the campaign came as "news to some Gore campaign officials." To the contrary, campaign officials said, Wolf had been "agitating for a more public profile." She made an "ostentatious appearance" at Gore's New Hampshire debate and "ignored suggestions to stay away from reporters." After her cunning plan of talking to reporters somehow failed to keep her role a secret, Wolf ignored the Gore campaign's request that she not go on TV and discuss her role any further. This was her "out-of-the-box thinking" for which I am most grateful.

On ABC's *This Week*, George Will asked Wolf what she meant about Gore being "a Blakeian deep inside" as she had said in her article "Al's Inner Alien." She may as well have been asked to do long division. While clearly having no idea, Wolf proclaimed delight that they were "talking about nineteenth-century romantic and mystical poets." No, they weren't actually, and not only because Blake was mostly an eighteenth-century poet. They were talking about *talking about* a nineteenth-century poet—who was actually an eighteenth-century poet. Whenever really stupid people try to sound intellectual, this is as far as they get: nonsubstantive recitations of important-sounding names. They love to exclaim that they are "talking about" poets, world leaders, or God, when all they're doing is saying the names. "I can't believe—I'm pleased, but I can't believe, at this early in the morning," she said, we are "talking about" poets.

When the seemingly interminable subject of the subject had at last been exhausted, Wolf "explained" how Gore was a "Blakeian" by unleashing a series of meaningless clichés: "What I'm talking about is a vision that incorporates many disparate parts for a whole that's more than the sum of its parts." The clichés ultimately led, somehow, to the stirring conclusion that Gore was a Blakeian because of his yearning to resolve this critical federal crisis: "How do you get working parents home in time so that they have a chance to read a bedtime story to their kids?" Another of Wolf's other self-described "wacky" and "larger picture" ideas were things like . . . school uniforms! George Will dryly asked the "larger picture" gal, "Who ever said school uniforms are wacky, by the way?"

In her tawdry book *Promiscuities*, Wolf unloads a tanker of "out-of-the-box" thoughts. She writes, for example, "If thirteen-year-old Juliet were to fall in love with Romeo today, she could get a condom in the ladies' room of the train station and instructions from *Cosmo* ('Your Sexual Style'), and Shakespeare would have to look elsewhere for his plot." Um. No. The problem fair Juliet had with Romeo was *not* that she could not find suitable birth control. But then Naomi and I went to different schools. Different planets, if you credit her account. It may explain a lot that she's the one teaching Al Gore to be a man. ∎

☞ Checks and Balances, but Mostly Checks

JULY 31, 2002

Having dragged a group of Manhattan elites back from the Hamptons in the summer of 2002 to attend a fundraiser at a tony Chelsea nightclub, Al Gore criticized the Bush administration for "working on behalf of the powerful, and letting the people of this country get the short end of the stick."

Back when he was exhibiting the Democrats' renowned good sportsmanship after he lost the presidential election, Gore managed to fund his tantrum with donations sent in from such ordinary Americans such as dot-com multimillionaire Steven Kirsch ($500,000), former Slim-Fast Foods chief S. Daniel Abraham ($100,000), and Minneapolis multimillionaire Vance Opperman ($100,000). He got help from the Manhattan "working poor," such as Loews Hotels scion and tobacco company beneficiary Jon Tisch ($50,000); ex-wife of pardoned financier Marc Rich, Denise Rich ($25,000); and investment banker Jon Corzine ($25,000), who is now representing working families against "the powerful" in the U.S. Senate. Also moved by Gore's pledge to fight for "working families" were some of Hollywood's typical "working families." Notorious inseminator and Hollywood "producer" Stephen Bing ponied up $200,000. (In Democratic Party parlance, "producer" evidently means "a do-nothing who inherited a lot of money.") Actress and traitor Jane Fonda gave the Gore-Lieberman fund $100,000.

By contrast, George W. Bush limited donations to his Election Recount Fund to $5,000 or less. But normal Americans saw what the Democrats were up to, and thousands upon thousands of small contributions poured in to Bush from across the country. Bush raised four times as much money as Gore did. Even with individual donations of half a million dollars, Gore raised only $3.2 million. Small individual donors, none contributing more than $5,000, gave $13.8 million to Bush.

Two-thirds of Gore's Tantrum Fund came from just 38 rich liberals, who contributed $2.1 million. Eighty-four individuals donated $2.8 million of Gore's $3.2 million recount fund. This, in a country of 280 million people. Without Malibu, there would be no Democratic Party. Of the 84 rich liberals who nearly single-handedly bankrolled Gore's Tantrum Fund, 30 were from California and 23 from New York—and that doesn't include rich liberals who ought to be in Malibu but whose legal residence is Georgia, like Jane Fonda. Only $56,216 of the entire Gore-Lieberman fund came from donations of $200 or less—that is, about half the size of the check cut by Jane Fonda to Gore's fund. Bush raised more than the entire amount of Gore's fund in individual donations of $200 or less.

The tale of the two recount funds once again proved the division between the two parties as: Those Who Make Their Own Beds and Those Who Do Not. But that's not the story the media told. Amazingly, the media turned the facts upside down, absurdly implying that Bush had been bankrolled by billionaires while Gore made do with small donations from the working poor. The genuine and spontaneous outrage of ordinary Americans against a small band of Democratic royalists became another story about mythical Rich Republicans beating down the working class with their polo mallets.

Newspaper headlines simply ignored the size of the individual donations, and instead broadcast only the raw totals of the two funds—amid copious reminders that Republicans are the Party of the Rich. In an article titled "Bush Far Outspent Gore on Recount," the *Washington Post* referred to "the powerful fund-raising abilities of the Republican Party." The *Chicago Tribune*'s headline was "Bush Spent 4 Times as Much as Gore in Florida Recount" and the AP headline was "IRS: Bush Spent Four Times as Much as Gore on Florida Recount." How about: "Gore Bankrolled by 84," "Small Donors Flock to Bush, Billionaires to Gore," or "Malibu Pool Party Finances 7/8ths of Gore Recount Fund"?

A year later, the Democratic National Committee took in its largest single donation ever: $5 million from "producer" Stephen Bing—our featured Democrat this week. In the current *Vanity Fair,* Bing is described by other Hollywood billionaires as a self-effacing, modest man. As evidence, they note that he has only one maid. "Name anyone else with his wealth who has only one maid," Man of the People Rob Reiner says. "You'd be hard-pressed." I'd be hard-pressed to think of one of my friends who *has* a maid. Marie Antoinette did not flaunt her wealth the way "progressive" liberals in America do.

Other Hollywood progressives commented on how Bing helps strippers when they're down on their luck. (And, one may surmise, also down on their knees.) "I've helped so many," Bing says, "you'd have to get me the names." That's "self-effacing" for a liberal. Bing's admiration for the under-class is mainly shown by his predilection for siring children out of wedlock. This seems to be the new status symbol among liberals, with Bing currently leading Jesse Jackson 2-to-1 in disclosed illegitimate children. (Q: How do you empty a room full of rich liberals? A: Ask for a paternity test.) In a romance born of progressivism, the mother of one of Bing's illegitimate children, Elizabeth Hurley, crossed a Screen Actors Guild picket line—and Bing gallantly paid her fine to the union. So much for the little people. Also, he plays the blues on the piano. I take it back: He is a man of the people.

Interestingly, Bing doesn't make a fuss about the estate tax. His profes-sional accomplishments amount to having dropped out of Stanford—which we can assume he did not enter on the basis of his SAT scores—and then spending a decade writing a single episode of *Married . . . with Chil-dren*. Bing's credentials as a producer are as credible as his belief that women are not attracted to him for his money. The current Democratic Party is a crowd of idle, rich degenerates, the likes of which hasn't existed since the czar's court. When not occupied with abortions or strippers, they busy themselves denouncing the cossacks as "the powerful." ■

☞ The Robert C. Byrd Bridge to Poverty

FEBRUARY 14, 2002

The poor's sense of class superiority over the rich is getting out of hand. At a Senate Budget Committee hearing last week, Senator Robert Byrd (who was named after a bridge in West Virginia) viciously attacked Treasury Secretary Paul O'Neill for having made a success of himself. Claiming to speak for worthless layabouts, Byrd snippily informed O'Neill, "They're not CEOs of multibillion-dollar corporations. . . . In time of need, they come to us, the people come to us." And evidently, what the people-in-need are crying out for are a lot of federal projects named after Senator Byrd.

Some items paid for by taxpayers—but inexplicably named after

"Robert C. Byrd"—are: the Robert C. Byrd Highway; the Robert C. Byrd Locks and Dam; the Robert C. Byrd Institute; the Robert C. Byrd Life Long Learning Center; the Robert C. Byrd Honors Scholarship Program; the Robert C. Byrd Green Bank Telescope; the Robert C. Byrd Institute for Advanced Flexible Manufacturing; the Robert C. Byrd Federal Courthouse; the Robert C. Byrd Health Sciences Center; the Robert C. Byrd Academic and Technology Center; the Robert C. Byrd United Technical Center; the Robert C. Byrd Federal Building; the Robert C. Byrd Drive; the Robert C. Byrd Hilltop Office Complex; the Robert C. Byrd Library; the Robert C. Byrd Learning Resource Center; the Robert C. Byrd Rural Health Center.

And then it got late, and I had to stop searching Google. But it appears that every slab of concrete in West Virginia is named after Bob Byrd.

Really warming to his class-envy tirade, the King Tut of the Senate further informed O'Neill, "I haven't walked in any corporate boardrooms. I haven't had to turn any millions of dollars into trust accounts. I wish I had those millions of dollars." Instead, Byrd had to scrape by with billions of dollars forcibly extracted from the taxpayers to build grotesque banana-republic tributes to himself. At least the money O'Neill "turn[ed] into trust accounts" came from his own pocket. Coincidentally, the money Byrd turned into eponymous monuments also came from O'Neill's pocket. A humble display of gratitude to O'Neill might have been more appropriate.

An astonished O'Neill responded to the harangue: "I started my life in a house without water or electricity. So I don't cede to you the high moral ground of not knowing what life is like in a ditch." And then the hearing spun totally out of control as Senator Tut redoubled his own sob story: "Well, Mr. Secretary, I lived in a house without electricity, too, no running water, no telephone, a little wooden outhouse." (Though Byrd was manifestly enamored of all the tiny particulars of his life story, he unaccountably skipped the part about his youthful membership in the Ku Klux Klan.)

When did a lack of money and accomplishment become a mark of virtue? Some rich people may be swine, but so are some poor people. A lot of rich people work harder, are more creative, and are a lot nicer than the poor—especially rich people who earned it themselves, unlike Democratic senators. Paul O'Neill was never in the Klan and Paul O'Neill never filched taxpayers' hard-earned money to build a vast complex of shrines to himself. More perplexingly, when did a scoundrel whose only source of capital comes from other people's paychecks assume the "high ground" over a rich man who gave people paychecks? Paul O'Neill is rich, I'm not. Oh well. At least he didn't steal half my paycheck.

Every society must have concentrations of wealth in order to build and create. Even the Soviet Union of beloved memory had concentrations of wealth—but it was in the government rather than in corporations. It's called capital. Capital is needed to launch society's most important projects—factories, bridges, skyscrapers, inventions, and telescopes named after Bob Byrd. O'Neill's concentration of money came to him through the voluntary decisions of investors and consumers. Byrd's far larger concentration of money came to him by force. Send half your paycheck to the government or go to jail.

The lie at the heart of liberals' mantra on tax cuts—"tax cuts for the rich"—is the ineluctable fact that unless taxes are cut across the board, nobody's taxes ever get cut. As loaded Hollywood liberals are always reminding us, they don't "need" a tax cut. Alas, the rich we shall always have with us, kind of like the poor. At least conservatives defend the right of middle-class people to keep their money, too.

The only rich people deserving of malice are rich liberals who express bemusement at the nonrich's desire for a tax cut. In their campaign to make the middle class pay more in taxes, liberals use the lumpen poor as a battering ram against these hated, acquisitive coupon-clippers. Despite his maudlin self-flattery, Robert Byrd and the rest of his party don't resent the rich on behalf of the poor. They resent the rich on behalf of the government. Poor Senator Byrd can't rest knowing there may still be a toilet in West Virginia that is not named for Bob Byrd. ■

☞ Chair-Warmer on the Hot Seat

MARCH 24, 2004

Are you sitting down? Another ex–government official who was fired or demoted by Bush has written a book that . . . is critical of Bush! Eureka! The latest offering is Richard Clarke's new CBS-Viacom book, *Against All Enemies,* which gets only a 35 on "rate a record" because the words don't make sense and you can't dance to it. For those of you who haven't heard of Dick Clarke—that is to say, all of you—he's a career back-bencher who was passed over as National Security Adviser in favor of Condoleezza Rice, who later demoted him (speaking of hidden agendas).

As long as we're investigating everything, how about investigating why some loser no one has ever heard of is getting so much press coverage for yet another "tell-all" book attacking the Bush administration? Kiss-and-tell books about the Bush administration by disgruntled ex-employees looking to make a quick buck are coming out as fast as "Elvis and Me" books by distant relatives of the King after his death. This is not to compare the two: At least the authors of the Elvis books had more than "facial expressions" to report.

When an FBI agent with close, regular contact with President Clinton wrote his book, he was virtually blacklisted from the mainstream media. Upon the release of Gary Aldrich's book *Unlimited Access* in 1996, White House adviser George Stephanopoulos immediately called TV producers demanding that they give Aldrich no airtime. *Larry King Live* and NBC's *Dateline* abruptly canceled their scheduled interviews with Aldrich. Aldrich was mentioned on fewer than a dozen TV shows during the entire year of his book's release—many with headlines like this one on CNN: "Even Conservatives Back Away from Aldrich's Book." That's almost as much TV as Lewinsky mouthpiece William Ginsburg did before breakfast on an average day. (Let's take a moment here to imagine the indignity of being known as "Monica Lewinsky's mouthpiece.") In terms of TV exposure, Aldrich's book might well have been titled "No Access Whatsoever."

But a "tell-all" book that attacks the Bush administration gets the author interviewed on CBS's *60 Minutes* (two segments), CNN's *American Morning*, and ABC's *Good Morning America*—with an "analysis" by George Stephanopoulos, no less. In the first few days of its release, Clarke's book was hyped on more than two hundred TV shows.

In contrast to Aldrich's book, which was vindicated with a whoop just a few years later when the Monica Lewinsky scandal broke, many of Clarke's allegations were disproven within days of the book's release. Clarke claims, for example, that in early 2001, when he told Condoleezza Rice about al Qaeda, her "facial expression gave me the impression that she had never heard the term before." (If only she used Botox like Senator Kerry!) Sean Hannity has been playing a radio interview that Dr. Rice gave to David Newman on WJR in Detroit back in October 2000, in which she discusses al Qaeda in some detail. This was months before chair-warmer Clarke claims her "facial expression" indicated she had never heard of the terrorist organization.

But in deference to our liberal friends, let's leave aside the facts for now. A few months before Clarke was interpreting Dr. Rice's "facial expression," al Qaeda had bombed the USS *Cole*. Two years before that, al Qaeda bombed U.S. embassies in Kenya and Tanzania. In fact, al Qaeda or their allies had been responsible for a half dozen attacks on U.S. interests since Clinton had become president. (Paper-pusher Clarke was doing one heck of a job, wasn't he?) In the year 2000 alone, LexisNexis lists 280 items mentioning al Qaeda. By the end of 2000, anyone who read the paper had heard of al Qaeda. It is literally insane to imagine that Condoleezza Rice had not. For Pete's sake, even the *New York Times* knew about al Qaeda.

Rice had been a political science professor at Stanford University, a member of the Center for International Security and Arms Control, and a senior fellow of the Stanford Institute for International Studies. She had written three books and numerous articles on foreign policy. She worked for the first Bush administration in a variety of national security positions. All this was while Clarke was presiding over six unanswered al Qaeda attacks on American interests and fretting about the looming Y2K emergency. Of course, Madeleine Albright also had some fancy degrees and important positions, so let me add: Anyone who has listened to Rice for sixty seconds knows that she is very smart. But chair-warmer Clarke claims that on the basis of Rice's "facial expression" he could tell she was not familiar with the term "al Qaeda."

Isn't that just like a liberal? The chair-warmer describes Bush as a cowboy and Rumsfeld as his gunslinger—but the black chick is a dummy. Maybe even as dumb as Clarence Thomas! Perhaps someday liberals could map out the relative intelligence of various black government officials for us.

Did Clarke have the vaguest notion of Rice's background and education? Or did he think Dr. Rice was cleaning the Old Executive Office Building at night before the president chose her—not him—to be national security adviser? If a Republican ever claimed the "facial expression" on Maxine Waters—a woman whose face is no stranger to confusion or befuddlement—left the "impression" that she didn't understand quantum physics, he'd be in prison for committing a hate crime.

As we know from Dr. Rice's radio interview describing the threat of al Qaeda back in October 2000, she certainly didn't need to be told about al Qaeda by a government time-server. No doubt Dr. Rice was staring at Clarke in astonishment as he imparted this great insight: *Keep an eye on al Qaeda! We've done nothing, but you should do something about it. Tag—you're it.* That look of perplexity Clarke saw was Condi thinking to herself, "Hmmm, did I demote this guy far enough?" ■

6

When Bad Ideas
(Liberalism) Happen to
Good People (You)

◼

☞ The *New York Times*'s Crusade
Against Capitalism

JANUARY 24, 2002

Before the *New York Times* starts running "Portraits in Grief" of former Enron employees, it's worth remembering that even after the collapse, Enron stock is still worth more than the entire Social Security "trust fund." Liberals have suspended their typical class-envy paradigm long enough to weep huge crocodile tears for the almost-rich. Weren't these the precise people we were trained to hate in the nineties as they high-fived one another amid extravagant claims of retirement by age forty? In record time, we've gone from schadenfreude to lachrymose liberal pity. Poor ghetto blacks must be transfixed by the turn of events that supplanted them with erstwhile "yuppie scum" as the new class-war victims.

When this much bathos is expended on middle-class white people with stock portfolios, liberals are up to no good. The only coherence to the *Times*'s wildly contradictory feelings toward rich yuppies is that they want to scare people away from the stock market. The *Times* is openly rooting for a prolonged recession, if not a depression. They are desperately trying to destroy people's faith in the market, in 401(k)s—in capitalism. When President Bush merely acknowledged that the economy was in a recession soon after he took office, liberals screamed that he was "talking down the economy." But now liberals are willing to wreck the whole country to help the Democratic Party. A continuing weak stock market would serve the Democrats' short-term interest of bashing Bush as well as their long-term interest of keeping Americans dependent on the government.

Thus, the *Times* cites Enron in order to sneer about the "view" that investing in the market would provide Americans with robust retirement funds amid snippy references to the "now dormant" idea of privatizing Social Security. Even the *Times*'s pet cause of campaign-finance reform is somehow more urgently needed in the wake of Enron's collapse. The morality play being showcased in the *Times* concerns "the plight of loyal workers who lost retirement savings while company officials cashed in $1.1 billion in stock." This puts a human face on the *Times*'s vicious attacks on "the integrity of markets."

Not so fast. Even if Enron executives had sold no stock whatsoever in 2001, Enron shares would still be worthless. Enron executives may well be guilty of criminal misconduct: That is a separate, discrete matter to be determined by the criminal laws. But just because your boss is a criminal doesn't make you a victim. Contrary to lugubrious news stories, there is no causal relationship between the boss selling his stock and the employees' losses.

The reason the employees lost money is that Enron had a faulty business model and the company went bankrupt. Whenever a company collapses, the people who own it (stockholders) lose money. That's why people always tell you not to put all your money in a single company's stock. Enron employees had eighteen investment options, but many decided to invest heavily in the high-flying company stock.

The only beef Enron employees have with top management is that management did not inform employees of the coming collapse in time to allow them to get in on the swindle, too. If Enron executives had shouted, "Head for the hills!," the employees might have been able to sucker other Americans into buying their wildly overinflated Enron stock, as their bosses apparently did. The employees were victims only in the sense that they were not able to get in on the rip-off, too.

Moreover, the billions of dollars Enron employees "lost" in paper profits they had gained only in the last few years. Between 1997 and 2000, Enron stock quadrupled in price, while the Standard & Poor's 500 index edged up only a few percentage points. In 2000, Enron stock was trading at an astronomical 66 times recent earnings. Until ten minutes ago, people who made a quick buck in the stock market were dot-com millionaire yuppie scum. Now when the market collapses before they cash out, they are, as the *Times* puts it, "the tale's most sympathetic characters, its victims." Compared with what the stock was worth in 1997, Enron employees lost an average of about $20,000 per employee in the largest company failure in U.S. history. I've lost more money on Social Security in that time, and no one's weeping for me.

Liberals have leapt on Enron's collapse to try to persuade Americans to avoid the market altogether. They would prefer that the middle class put all its money under the mattress. The stock market, the *Times* instructs, is not for the little people because—as the headline of the Week in Review proclaimed—"The Rich Are Different. They Know When to Get Out." Manifestly, the rich do not know when to get out. Otherwise, we wouldn't be hearing about the ripple effect of Enron's collapse hitting the likes of Citicorp—despite the lobbying efforts of billionaire Democrat Robert Rubin. The rich do, however, have more money, a point that is endlessly intriguing to liberals. The lesson liberals want the middle class to glean from this is: Do not invest in the market! End hope! Trust Big Brother. ■

☛ It's Just About Money

JULY 25, 2002

Liberals' comprehension of corporate scandals is like the Woody Allen joke about reading Tolstoy's *War and Peace* in twenty minutes after taking a speed-reading course. *Q: What's it about? A: It involves Russia.*

George Bush and Dick Cheney's connection to corporate corruption consists primarily of the media's capacity to mention their names in the same sentence as "corporate corruption" one million times a day. Liberals think their saying someone's name in an accusatory tone of voice is sufficient to impute criminality to Republicans. Since Republicans are intrinsically evil, merely mentioning their names suffices to make any point liberals want to make. Bush and Cheney have bought and sold stock! The swine!

Whenever the media start intoning darkly about "perceptions," "the full details," "unanswered questions," and—most pathetic—"the shadow of Enron"—that rustling you hear is the sound of wool being pulled over your eyes. In fact, there are no "unanswered questions" about Bush and Cheney. There are only insipid insinuations.

The facts are: Bush sold his stock in Harken Energy to purchase the Texas Rangers. The price of the stock later went down. (And then it went up to more than what he sold it for.) Amid hectoring from liberals that he do so, Cheney sold his interest in Halliburton before he assumed the vice presidency to eliminate the possibility of a conflict of interest. Later, the price of that stock went down—in large part because trial lawyers were filing asbestos suits against Halliburton. It's not illegal to sell or buy stock. It's illegal to sell stock based on insider information that the price is about to tank or to buy stock based on the insider information that the price is about to soar.

Thus, the Democrats' theory is that Bush bought the Texas Rangers and Cheney became vice president only as part of wily scams to conceal their real reason for selling stock: insider information! Of this, there is no evidence. Literally no evidence, in contradistinction to when liberals say there is "no evidence," meaning there hasn't been a conviction in a court of law but there is lots of evidence. The imputation of criminality to Bush and Cheney is so ludicrous that even in the girly-girl, eye-poking attacks on the *New York Times* op-ed page it has been roundly admitted that there is no question of "any criminality" (Frank Rich) and that "Mr. Bush broke no laws" (Nicholas Kristof). Representative Barney Frank, the only honest Democrat in the House, has repeatedly said that it is "not a case of Dick Cheney violating the law." Rather, the media explain their baseless sneering about the president and vice president as attempts to "add to our knowledge of the ethics, policies and personnel of a secretive administration," as Rich put it.

It's a little late for liberals to pretend they care about ethics. These are the people who angrily defended a president who perjured himself, hid evidence, suborned perjury, was held in contempt by a federal court, was disbarred by the Supreme Court, and lied to his party, his staff, his wife, and the nation. The ethics of that president included having staff perform oral sex on him in the Oval Office as he chatted on the phone with a congressman about sending American troops into battle. The secular saints of liberalism indignantly defended all this on the grounds that it's fine to lie and commit crimes if it's "just about sex."

Well, evidently some corporate chieftains took that lesson to heart and concluded that it's also fine to commit crimes if it's "just about money." Just as Ronald Reagan gave American culture a renewed patriotism and self-confidence that outlasted his presidency, Clinton has bequeathed America a culture of criminality and rationalization by the powerful. But still, somehow, Republicans are said to be more vulnerable whenever a businessman becomes a crook on the basis of their general support of capitalism. But if criminality and not capitalism is to blame, then Democrats are to blame for their general support of crooks. As part of the Left's long-standing fanatical defense of their favorite criminal, Bill Clinton, it will be screeched that conservatives want to blame everything on Clinton, including the wacky idea that a direct assault on honor and honesty led some people to behave dishonorably and dishonestly.

Not everything. But some of us called this ball and this pocket years ago:

"If Congress doesn't have the will to throw him out, Clinton will have set a new standard for the entire country. The new standard will be a total absence of standards. . . . If you get caught and don't have a good enough legal team to escape, you might have to pay a fine or go to prison. But there's no shame in it. The country doesn't really condemn this. We adore a lovable rogue. . . . It is fine to lie and cheat and manipulate because honor is just a word, just hot air and the country doesn't believe in it" (*High Crimes and Misdemeanors: The Case Against Bill Clinton*, 1998).

It took a bear market to inexorably repeal the Clintonian national motto of "Just Do It!" ■

☞ This Just In: Price Controls Cause Shortages

FEBRUARY 2 , 2001

Another "Dog Bites Man" story has once again taken the American press corps by storm. California's electricity crisis is treated in the media as if it were some sort of natural disaster, like a hurricane. But the only fact of nature operating here is the hard-and-fast rule that whenever you come across a screw-up this big, you know the government is behind it. The California legislature created this problem about five years ago when it deregulated the wholesale market for electricity but fixed prices at the retail level, based on economic principles that have made Cuba the happy, prosperous country that it is today.

Needless to say, eventually wholesale prices soared, but the utilities were prohibited from passing their increased costs on to consumers. Buy high, sell low! (Isn't that what they teach you in business school?) Since the California utilities are about to go bankrupt on the governmentally imposed "Buy high, sell low" strategy, no one will sell them electricity. So now there's no electricity in California—but at least it's cheap!

You are probably wondering how it is that multibillion-dollar corporations with highly paid business school graduates populating their corporate risk-management departments could have failed to anticipate price fluctuations in the electricity market and entered into long-term contracts. The answer is: Remember what I said about screw-ups this big. California actually prohibited utilities from entering into long-term contracts. (The California legislature came up with many other idiotic ways to mess up the electricity market; this is just the highlight reel.) If California utilities had relied on evil, bloodsucking hedge-fund managers rather than the California Centralized Committee to Fix Prices and Plan Markets, they'd have plenty of electricity now.

To repeat: The California Legislature fixed prices at which electricity could be sold to consumers and prohibited utilities from entering into long-term contracts to hedge the electricity market, leading like night into day to wild fluctuations in the price of electricity, but the utilities couldn't recoup their costs because the government had fixed prices in the retail market. In the mainstream media, this is known as "deregulation."

In point of fact, the California electricity crisis resulted from government policies that are the opposite of deregulation, the antimatter of deregulation, as antithetical to deregulation as class and decorum are to Courtney Love. If the California legislature had helped the Soviet Union with its transition from Communism to a market economy, the farmers would be experiencing their eighty-fourth year of "bad weather" again this year. Instead, only California utilities had "bad weather." The utilities signed on to what was a politically attractive package at the time, and now it turns out they stepped on a rake and the rake hit them in the face.

Why is it so difficult for people to grasp the advantages of a free market? It's never going to get any easier than this. Only a little over a decade ago, the centralized planning of the Eastern bloc was exposed as having created a squalid, poverty-stricken abyss. Meanwhile, corrupt running-dog lackeys of the capitalist system here in America managed to produce a society in which the poorest citizens have televisions, refrigerators, telephones, and the opportunity to appear on the *Jerry Springer Show*.

But no matter how often capitalism manages to produce good products at low prices, and no matter how spectacular the failures of government intervention are, some segment of the population continually lists toward the old Soviet bread-distribution model. Evidently, the free market is a counterintuitive concept. People have to be constantly reminded how excellent the market is at distributing goods and services.

The basic idea of a free market is that the consumer and seller enter directly into mutually beneficial transactions. The consumer has the best information about what he wants and how much he is willing to pay; the seller has the best information about what he can provide and what it will cost him. That's how we end up with great products like reasonably priced Chia pets in the shape of Jerry Garcia's head.

The government bureaucrats' rallying cry is "Insert a middleman!" They simply cannot shake the conviction that they are in possession of the millions of constantly changing pieces of information that the market processes continually and effortlessly. If we ever let these bureaucrats run free, stores everywhere would run with the smooth Austrian precision of the Department of Motor Vehicles. Naturally, the California legislature's solution to a problem created by the government is: more government! California voters ought to say what the Democratic Party is now gently trying to convey to Bill Clinton—thanks, but you've already done enough. ∎

☞ The Democrats' Laboratory: The Host Organism Dies

AUGUST 13, 2003

In June 2002, the liberal *American Prospect* magazine was hailing California as a "laboratory" for Democratic policies. With "its Democratic governor, U.S. senators, state legislature and congressional delegation," author

Harold Meyerson gushed, "California is the only one of the nation's 10 largest states that is uniformly under Democratic control." In the Golden State, Meyerson said, "the next New Deal is in tryouts." (Can't you just feel the tension building?)

Just a few years before that, the impresario of this adventure in Democratic governance, Governor Gray Davis, was being touted as presidential material—which wasn't nearly as insulting a thing to say to a politician back then as it is now that we've seen the current crop of Democrats running for president. Analyst Charles Cook said Davis was "a major player in the Democratic Party." Around the time of the 2000 Democratic National Convention in Los Angeles, Davis was forced to announce that he would decline offers to be Al Gore's running mate. Gore advisers cooed that "Gray would certainly be one of those names that would have to be in the mix." Perhaps their campaign slogan could have been "bland and blander." Both were said to be "cautious, moderate 'New Democrats.'" Both were veterans, after a fashion, of Vietnam, which would make a Gore-Davis presidential ticket the only compelling argument yet in favor of friendly fire.

California is, in fact, a perfect petri dish of Democratic policies. This is what happens when you let Democrats govern: You get a state—or as it's now known, a "job-free zone"—with a $38 billion deficit, which is larger than the budgets of forty-eight states. There are reports that Argentina and the Congo are sending their fiscal policy experts to Sacramento to help stabilize the situation. California's credit rating has been slashed to junk-bond status, and citizens are advised to stock up for the not-too-far-off day when cigarettes and Botox become the hard currency of choice. At this stage, we couldn't give California back to Mexico.

Democrats governed their petri dish as they always govern. They buy the votes of government workers with taxpayer-funded jobs, salaries, and benefits—and then turn around and accuse the productive class of "greed" for wanting their taxes cut. This has worked so well nationally that more people in America now work for the government than work in any sort of manufacturing job.

Strictly adhering to formula in California, as the private sector was bleeding jobs and money, Governor Davis signed off on comically generous pensions for government workers. Government employees in the Golden State earn more than the private-sector workers who pay their salaries—and that's excluding the job security, health benefits, and 90 percent pension plans that come with "Irish welfare," as government jobs used to be called.

Economists refer to this backward ratio between public and private-sector salaries as "France." (Inasmuch as they are paid more and work less than private-sector employees, perhaps we could ease up on treating public school teachers like Mother Teresa washing the feet of the poor in Calcutta.) The public-sector unions repaid Davis with massive contributions to his reelection campaign. Davis bought himself reelection and is now the most hated officeholder in America. The people of California are willing to plunge their state into humiliation and chaos just to get rid of him in a recall election. The fact that Arianna Huffington hasn't been laughed off a stage yet is a pretty good gauge of the public's frustration with Governor Davis.

And yet Bill and Hillary Clinton and the rest of the Democratic Party think Gray Davis is doing a super job. Democrats have denounced the California recall—a genuine citizens' revolt—as a "circus." According to recent polls, two out of three people in this overwhelmingly Democratic state want Davis out, and still the recall is being called a "Republican power grab." Most touchingly, Democrats claim to be shocked at the exorbitant cost of a recall election. They were not such penny-pinchers when contemplating Enron-style pensions for school crossing guards. Nor did their fiscal conservatism kick in when Davis announced this week that he would sign legislation providing "intolerance and hatred control training" for all California schoolteachers. Yeah, this guy definitely deserves another crack at straightening out the budget.

National Republicans are reluctant to let Davis go. They had been enjoying watching the Democrats' petri dish disintegrate into a parasite's paradise. So there were long faces all around when the Terminator threw his hat into the ring. No longer content to play an evil robot, actor Arnold Schwarzenegger will now be running against one. Far be it from me to tell Republicans to stop enjoying the Democrats' pain, but California is about to fall into the ocean. Either Schwarzenegger will come and dismantle the government employees' Versailles Palace, or California will continue to be a laboratory for failed liberal policies and we won't be able to give it back to Mexico. ■

☞ Nine Out of Ten Caribou Support Drilling

APRIL 18, 2002

Having wearied of opposing the war on terrorism, Democrats are now trying to sabotage the country's energy policy. George Bush has proposed drilling in a tiny, desolate portion of Alaska's Arctic National Wildlife Refuge, or ANWR. A better idea, Democrats think, is to keep sending large amounts of money to countries that nurture homicidal Muslims intent on destroying America.

ABC-NBC-CBS have been accompanying discussions of ANWR with picturesque footage of caribou frolicking in lush, fertile fields—all of which happens to be nowhere near the site of the proposed drilling. ANWR is 19 million acres—larger than Massachusetts, New Jersey, Hawaii, Connecticut, and Delaware combined. If oil is found, less than 2,000 acres would be directly affected. The area targeted for drilling looks a little like the moon, but less inviting.

Consequently, Gale Norton, the secretary of the interior, responded to the campaign of lies by unveiling actual film footage of the area at issue. She sent a true and accurate film of the proposed drilling site to the networks and also posted the footage on the department's website. Representative Ed Markey of Massachusetts (Democrat, needless to say) claims this underhanded dissemination of the truth is illegal. Telling the truth is not merely contrary to the principles of the Democratic Party, now they claim it's against the law. As Markey explains, the law prohibits agencies from promoting any "film presentation designed to support or defeat legislation pending before the Congress." At least we have Markey on the record admitting that a truthful presentation of the proposed drilling site would persuade Congress to support drilling. According to a leading Democratic opponent of the plan, lying is the key to defeating ANWR.

It was bad enough when Democrats just lied a lot themselves, purported not to know what "is" means, and claimed that "everybody" lied, perjured themselves, and suborned the perjury of others. Markey has staked out a more aggressive position by announcing that Republicans who tell the truth are breaking the law.

ANWR exploration is overwhelmingly supported by Alaskans, Eskimos, Teamsters, and caribou. It is opposed by Northeastern liberals who would never set foot anywhere near ANWR and haven't the first idea what it looks like. The word "wildlife" in ANWR's title is somewhat misleading. The coastal plain—where the drilling would occur—is in total darkness half the year and reaches temperatures of 50 below zero. Most of the time it is uninhabited and uninhabitable by wildlife. The only living things in the vicinity of the coastal plain—Eskimos and caribou—enthusiastically support drilling.

When oil exploration began in Alaska's Prudhoe Bay thirty years ago, environmentalists claimed it would yield only a "few months' supply" of oil and would wreck the ecosystem. We started drilling and Prudhoe Bay turned out to be the largest deposit of oil ever found in North America. Not only that, but the caribou of the famous "ecosystem" loved the pipeline. They frolic and play by it, leaping to and fro near the warmth. Apparently, the pipeline makes them frisky, too: In twenty years, the caribou population has skyrocketed, from 3,000 to almost 27,100.

The Teamsters have been huge supporters of drilling in ANWR, but Democrats treat union members the way they treat blacks: Vote for us and we'll give you nothing. Ed "The Truth Is Illegal" Markey responded to Teamster support for ANWR by dismissively sniffing that it was only "one issue." Democrats expect union money and endorsements, but when the prospect of half a million high-paying jobs comes along, the Democrats tell workers it's only "one issue." Luckily, the Democrats have all those other issues dear to the heart of the average blue-collar worker: abortion on demand, gay marriage, and taxpayer-funded crucifixes-submerged-in-urine.

So much for "everyone" sacrificing for the war on terrorism. Little old ladies get strip-searched at airports, but the environmentalists won't budge on an uninhabitable wasteland at the continent's edge. The Democrats' idea of sacrifice after 9/11 is for Senator Teddy Kennedy to stop getting drunk on airplanes and goosing stewardesses.

When not jetting around the country on his private plane, paid for by the deceased husband of his second wife, Senator John Kerry has emerged as a leading opponent of ANWR. Developing new sources of energy, Kerry says, is "old thinking." The Democrats' innovative new thinking is for the little people to wear sweaters and drive smaller cars.

That's a bold stroke: We'll delay starvation by eating a little less each day. The illogic of it confounds reason. Everyone is against waste—except

Democrats telling the rest of us to conserve from their Gulfstream private jets. (How about they set an example by conserving our money?) We need more energy. Postponing death is not an energy policy.

Markey has similarly "innovative" ideas. He proposes that we "bring OPEC to its knees" by "our technological superiority." What he means by "technological superiority" is this: "Let's make SUVs get 30 miles a gallon"! How about we make cars and airplanes that run on dirt? Or hot air, and run a pipeline from the Capitol? There is not a thinking man's Democrat in the country. If only caribou voted instead of Democrats, the country would finally have a serious energy policy. ■

☞ All the News We Heard from a Guy at Handgun Control, Inc.

MAY 16, 2002

Having been assured by "Handgun Control, Inc." (aka the Brady Campaign) that the Constitution protects only kiddie porn and says absolutely nothing about guns, the *New York Times* has been viciously denouncing Attorney General John Ashcroft for having the temerity to suggest that the Second Amendment protects the "right of the people to keep and bear arms." This, the *Times* proclaims, is "radical," "ominous," and a "betrayal of [Ashcroft's] public duty." In an eerie coincidence, the Second Amendment actually says, "the right of the people to keep and bear arms shall not be infringed."

In its inimitable Stalinist style, the *Times* claims Ashcroft's position is "contrary to longstanding and bipartisan interpretation of the Second Amendment." This is always how liberals engage in obvious jabberwocky: They smugly announce a "broad consensus" among "respected academics"—meaning one of their interns went to the trouble of calling "Handgun Control, Inc."

First of all, any journalist who is completely unaware that there is debate about the Second Amendment ought to be fired. But more preposterously, though a "bipartisan consensus" has begun to develop, it has gone heavily against the *Times*'s position. For over a decade now, liberal law professors keep setting out to disprove the "pro-gun extremists"—as the *Times* calls people who disagree with the *Times*. Gleefully intending to establish that the Second Amendment refers only to the right of state militias to have guns, the professors invariably conclude, with great lugubriousness, that the gun nuts are right.

By now, the growing roster of law professors who support the "radical," "ominous" Ashcroft position includes Larry Tribe of Harvard, Akhil Amar of Yale, and Sanford Levinson of the University of Texas. (In happier circumstances, these professors are known as "respected" at the *Times*.) Among sitting Supreme Court justices, five have raised the Second Amendment in opinions just since 1990. The Second Amendment even made a cameo appearance in the very opinion that constitutes definition of constitutional law at the *Times: Roe v. Wade*. Every single one of those citations assumes that the right to bear arms belongs to "the people," not only militia members.

Indeed, the one guy the *Times* dredged out of the left-wing toilet willing to provide tepid endorsement to their bunkum was Stanford history professor Jack Rakove. Even Rakove—the only academic still defending Michael Belleszies's fraudulent antigun book *Arming America*—wouldn't stoop to supporting the *Times*'s preposterous claims. Far from asserting a "bipartisan consensus" for the *Times*'s view, Rakove said it is "no secret" that controversy over the Second Amendment "has escalated in recent years." (Except at the *Times*, where it remains a huge secret.) Moreover, Rakove's big rebuke to Ashcroft consisted of his meek observation that "it is far from clear that the Justice Department's new position would prevail." For taking a position that an antigun zealot says might not prevail, the *Times* says Ashcroft is betraying "his public duty."

But for bald-faced lies, nothing beats the *Times*'s preposterous characterization of Supreme Court precedent. The most recent case directly raising the Second Amendment was *United States v. Miller*, decided in 1939. (Any conservative who demanded deference to a case from 1939 would be accused of trying to lynch blacks and brutalize women.) The *Miller* case simply defined the types of guns protected by the Second Amendment, not who was entitled to have guns. Reviewing the case of two bootleggers charged with failing to pay federal taxes on a sawed-off shotgun, the Court concluded that the "instrument" was not covered by the Second Amendment. Since the *Times* lies about the relevant language, I will quote it in full:

> In the absence of any evidence tending to show that possession or use of a "shotgun having a barrel of less than 18 inches in length" at this

time has some reasonable relationship to the preservation or efficiency of a well-regulated militia, we cannot say that the Second Amendment guarantees the right to keep and bear such an instrument. Certainly it is not within judicial notice that this weapon is any part of the ordinary military equipment or that its use could contribute to the common defense.

The vigilant observer will note that the Court did not find that since the defendants were bootleggers—and not members of a militia—they had no Second Amendment rights. Rather, the Court's conclusion turned solely on the fact that a sawed-off shotgun was not "ordinary military equipment." As Professor Levinson (card-carrying member of the ACLU) said of the decision, "Ironically, *Miller* can be read to support some of the most extreme anti–gun control arguments, e.g., that the individual citizen has a right to keep and bear bazookas, rocket launchers and . . . assault weapons."

Now observe how the *Times* mischaracterizes the *Miller* decision. In a ham-handed deception, the *Times* substitutes the word "rights" for "guns," and claims that the Court found that "the Second Amendment protects only those rights that have 'some reasonable relationship to the preservation of efficiency of a well-regulated militia.'" If the *Times* is going to dismiss the views of Harvard and Yale law professors, Supreme Court justices, and constitutional scholars Joseph Story and Thomas Cooley in deference to the press releases of a fanatical antigun lobbying group, they might want to find one with smarter lawyers than Handgun Control, Inc. ■

7

More Liberal Ideas!
Sex, Segregation,
Gay Marriage, and Banning
the G-Word (God!)

———————————■———————————

☞ Chicks with D****

JANUARY 2000

(or about one year before *Vanity Fair* noticed *Sex and the City* was
about gay men even though everyone yelled at me for saying it
in *George* magazine)

It's getting so you can't turn on the TV or open a newspaper without hearing some girl boasting about her latest sexual conquest. From Hollywood starlets embarrassing the adorable Conan O'Brien with their inane prattle about "phallic" symbols, masturbation, and breast augmentation, to every tabloid in the country publishing preposterous female "sex columnists," it seems as if the country has been inhabited by an alien breed of women. The first thing that strikes you about the slutty-girls phenomenon is: This is not how women talk. This is how some men might talk—if women would let them. We have some idea what that sounds like. Some men, oddly enough, aren't willing to curb their instinctive promiscuity and embrace monogamy in order to get a girl. They're known as gay men.

See if you can spot the cultural clues here: In HBO's *Sex and the City*, a classic in the slutty-girl genre, the fictional characters blather endlessly about anal sex, oral sex, casual sex, wrinkled buttocks, spanking, boy toys, sex toys, and the ennui of marriage. This is not girls talking like girls, it's not even girls talking like guys exactly, but girls talking like gay men. (Another hint is that the only appealing male character is a gay man.)

The odd thing is, this campy joke of women playing gay men is apparently lost on everyone outside of Manhattan—at least if you credit the hayseeds who have been eagerly furnishing miss-the-point quotes to various news outlets. Girls living out in America steadfastly insist they find *Sex and the City* totally realistic. "I feel like they really are saying the things we're all thinking," Alana Peters told the *New York Times*. Are sweet Southern belles in Atlanta really all thinking about sex in "coarse euphemisms for body parts"—as the *Times* delicately describes the dialogue on *Sex and the City*? And is Alana's boyfriend having sex with *his* dog? (That was one recent episode.) Please. They're lying. But why?

Curiously, claims about the amazing realism of *Sex and the City* are often accompanied by defensive statements about how cosmopolitan Atlanta or Milwaukee is. "We are a mini–New York here," proclaimed Atlanta resident Lara Preister, explaining her enthusiasm for the show to a *Times* reporter. "It's not like we're Scarlett O'Hara and we get all upset when people swear." Oh dear. These girls seem to imagine *Sex and the City* is real.

In the "Cheese State," Pam Schlesner was quoted in the *Milwaukee Journal Sentinel* saying she, too, sees herself in the fictional characters. Really? The ones encouraging one another to have anal sex? That episode drove a reviewer from the *Village Voice* to remark that the character's "enthusiasm was the tipoff that a man wrote the scene." And yet, Ms. Schlesner praised the dead-on accuracy of *Sex and the City*, saying the show's "writing crew must follow her around for script fodder." More probably, Pam is following the show for life fodder. Pam said she and her friends recently took it upon themselves to spend a weekend "having sex like a man"—a hobby of the *Sex and the City* characters—picking up strangers for sex and then plotting to get the studs out of their homes as early in the morning as possible.

This is taking New York envy to dangerous extremes. A few years ago, I realized that my friends in the Midwest, avid Seinfeld devotees, had no idea that Jerry Seinfeld was Jewish. But that was merely droll: It did not lead them to invite Ted Bundy back to their apartments for sex. Okay Miss Cheese State, we won't call you a backwater hick, but think hard: Do you actually know girls who talk about sex using the d-word and c-word to describe specific body parts? No you don't. You know gay men who do. See, e.g., the *Village Voice*. Indeed, even the show's perky star, Sarah Jessica Parker, reportedly uses language no coarser than "Oh God!" or "geeze Louise" off the set. Girls talking the way they do on *Sex and the City* is about as realistic as George Bush playing a gangsta rapper, talking about "ho's" and "bitches."

Instead of wiping away years of humorless feminist tyranny, this new breed of smutty girls have taken the error of the feminists and raised it. There are differences between boys and girls. One of the big ones is: Girls do not relentlessly pursue casual sex. In one famous study conducted at the University of Hawaii—and one that drives the sexual egalitarians crazy—male and female "researchers" approached single college students of the opposite sex in bars to propose only one of three options: (1) a date, (2) going back to the questioner's apartment, or (3) immediate sex. Fifty percent of men accepted the date; 69 percent agreed to go back to the apartment; and 75 percent agreed to immediate sex. Half the women agreed to a date; 6 percent consented to go to the apartment, and none—zero—agreed to sex.

Not to belabor the obvious, but the only girls who actively seek casual sex seem to be girls in Milwaukee who think *Sex and the City* is how the cool New York City chicks really behave. (Or girls in New York City who think *Sex and the City* is how the cool New York City chicks really behave.)

Meanwhile, gay men totally get it. Hell, a gay man writes it. The TV show *Sex and the City* is the creation of wunderkind Darren Star. Star was also the creator of *Melrose Place* and *Central Park West*, described in the press as "almost cultishly gay faves." The openly gay Star sardonically remarked of his *Sex and the City* creation, "I guess I just have a strong feminine side." Not long after the original *Sex and the City* column debuted in the *New York Observer*, the *New York Times* reported that "'The boys at World Gym' said in a fan letter that they were convinced [the authoress] was a gay man in a woman's body." That's the irony. While being celebrated for being so very outré, even Hollywood is not ready to let gay men out of the closet but has to disguise them in women's bodies. ■

DECEMBER 5, 2003: Trent Lott Toasts Strom Thurmond at
Thurmond's 100th Birthday Party

☞ Democrats: A Lott of Trouble

DECEMBER 18, 2002

I'm just glad Strom Thurmond isn't around to see this. Statisticians believe Trent Lott is now on track to break Bill Clinton's single-season record for public apologies. During his recent *B.E.T.* appearance, Lott said he supported affirmative action and regretted voting against the Martin Luther King Jr. holiday, and that he'd give *The Bernie Mac Show* another try.

What the Lott incident shows is that Republicans have to be careful about letting Democrats into our party. Back when they supported segregation, Lott and Thurmond were Democrats. This is something the media are intentionally hiding to make it look like the Republican Party is the party of segregation and race discrimination, which it never has been.

In 1948, Thurmond did not run as a "Dixiecan," he ran as a "Dixiecrat"—his party was an offshoot of the Democratic Party. And when he lost, he went right back to being a Democrat. This whole brouhaha is about a former Democrat praising another former Democrat for what was once a Democrat policy.

Republicans made Southern Democrats drop the race nonsense when they entered the Republican Party. Democrats supported race discrimination, then for about three years they didn't, now they do again. They've just changed which race they think should be discriminated against. In the 1920s, the Democratic platforms didn't even call for antilynching legislation as the Republican platforms did.

Thurmond's Dixiecrat Party was not the only extremist spin-off from the Democratic Party in 1948. Henry Wallace, formerly FDR's vice president and agriculture secretary, left the Democratic Party that year to form the Communist-dominated and Soviet-backed "Progressive Party." Much as Thurmond's Dixiecrat Party was expressly prosegregation, Wallace's Progressive Party was expressly pro-Soviet. Indeed, this was the apex of Moscow-directed subversion of U.S. politics. The Progressive Party platform excluded even the mildest criticism of Soviet aggression. It will come as no surprise that many American celebrities supported Wallace. The Progressives received one million votes nationwide, about the same as Thurmond's Dixiecrat Party.

Thurmond went on to reject segregation, become a Republican, and serve his country well as a U.S. senator. By contrast, running a Communist-dominated presidential campaign was Wallace's last hurrah. Yet only an off-the-cuff remark at a birthday party praising Thurmond's presidential campaign is the career-destroyer. Not so fawning references to Wallace's Soviet-backed presidential campaign.

Just two years before Lott's remarks, a hagiographic book on Wallace's life was released, *American Dreamer*. How about a book about a segregationist titled "American Dreamer"? Wallace's version of the American "dream" was Communism every bit as much as Strom Thurmond's dream was segregation. Aren't dreams of murderous dictators, gulags, and death camps at least comparable in evil to segregated lunch counters?

The dust jacket on *American Dreamer* featured a nauseating statement of praise by Senator Edward Kennedy. Kennedy said that the book deserved "to be read by all who care about the American dream." The American dream: Communist totalitarianism. Why wasn't the lecherous liberal asked to retire for his flattering remarks about a proven Soviet fifth-columnist?

In 1999, the Clinton administration dedicated a room at the Agriculture Department to Wallace. At the dedication, former Democratic presidential candidate George McGovern gave a speech explicitly praising Wallace's pro-Soviet positions, such as the idea that the Cold War was "overdone" and that "problems" between the nations "could not be resolved by military means."

McGovern fondly recalled that he himself had voted for Wallace. He chipperly reminded the audience that he had run for president in 1972 "on a similar platform"—with the help of a young Yale law school graduate named Bill Clinton. Inasmuch as Trent Lott was in kindergarten in 1948, he did not vote for Thurmond. He did not run on a "similar" platform to the Dixiecrats. He did not write a jacket-flap endorsement calling a segregationist an "American Dreamer."

The idea that Lott took the occasion of an old-timer's birthday to introduce a new policy initiative to bring back segregation—a Democrat policy—is ludicrous. Lott is a fine fellow; he just has some sort of liberal-Tourette's syndrome that makes him spout Democrat ideas at random. A few years ago, Lott practically wanted to give the adulterous Air Force pilot Kelly Flinn a silver star for her service. Remember that?

Up until two weeks ago, conservatives were clamoring for Lott's removal precisely because of his annoying habit of saying dumb things.

(Showing their inferior intellect, liberals have only recently figured that out.) Republicans should ask Lott to step down as leader, but only for all the nice things he's said about Teddy Kennedy. ∎

☞ Ashcroft and the Blowhard Discuss Desegregation

JANUARY 18, 2001

Republican presidents need to start sending at least one Potemkin nominee to the Senate for confirmation hearings. If there were just one cabinet nominee willing to sacrifice his appointment for the opportunity to yell back at that adulterous drunk, Senator Teddy Kennedy might not be so cavalier before launching his premeditated vituperations.

Whatever else the "Stop (fill in name here)! Task Force" can say about John Ashcroft, they cannot say that he drunkenly plunged a woman to a horrifying watery death and then fled the scene of the accident, relying on his family's connections to paper over the woman's drowning. Indeed, Ashcroft has never done anything drunkenly, making him an object of fascination for Mr. Kennedy.

They cannot say that John Ashcroft, like Senator Kennedy, was thrown out of college for cheating on a Spanish test—or that he got into college on the basis of his family pedigree. (Inasmuch as Ashcroft attended an Ivy League college, it was not much help having a father who was a Pentecostal minister, rather than, say, a bootlegger.) And a pants-less, drunken John Ashcroft has never been wandering nearby while his nephew was having sex with a woman whom he had just met and who subsequently accused him of rape at the family compound in Florida on Good Friday. The Ashcroft family doesn't even have a compound in Florida.

Poor John Ashcroft couldn't say any of that when Senator Kennedy erupted in gin-soaked venom at Ashcroft's nomination hearings. He has higher aspirations than talking back to a dissolute slob for laughs. But surely there is someone out there who would go for laughs. Bush should find that guy. Heck, I'll volunteer for this mission myself—if only for the once-in-a-lifetime opportunity to say, on C-SPAN, "We'll drive off the side of that bridge when we come to it, Senator Kennedy."

On the first day of the Ashcroft hearings, Senator Kennedy waxed nostalgic over a court-ordered "voluntary desegregation" plan imposed by an unelected judge on the good people of Kansas City back in the 1980s. Kennedy issued bloodcurdling screams about "the kids": "How costly was this going to be, Senator Ashcroft, before you were going to say that those kids going in lousy schools, that you were going to do something about it?"

You remember what a fabulous success court-ordered "desegregation" plans have been. Few failures have been more spectacular. Illiterate students knifing one another between acts of sodomy in the stairwell is just one of the many eggs that had to be broken to make the Left's omelet of transferring power from cities to the federal courts. In the case of the Kansas City schools, a judge issued an edict doubling the property taxes of the school district's residents. Twelve years and $2 billion later the district is more racially segregated than it was before. Test scores are lower for black students than in the rest of the state. This is the remedy Senator Drunkennedy was so passionately defending.

It's one thing for the federal courts to inform the states and localities that they cannot discriminate on the basis of race—that was duly accomplished back in 1954. It's really quite another for unelected judges to be imposing $2 billion property taxes and ordering school districts to build opulent school campuses replete with Olympic-sized pools, 25-acre wildlife sanctuaries, and a model United Nations with simultaneous translation facilities. The only way this plan could have been more absurd would be if school board members had begun actually, literally throwing bundles of cash at the students. But that's what a federal judge did to Kansas City, under the Olympic-Sized-Pool and Tax-Them-Till-They-Scream clauses of the U.S. Constitution. As a matter of technical constitutional law, the Constitution does not strictly require states to provide public school students with petting farms.

What happened was that over the past several decades, federal judges got it into their heads that black students had to sit next to white students in order to learn. It was all the rage at the elite universities—Harvard in particular. Justice Clarence Thomas responded to the theory by saying, "It never ceases to amaze me that the courts are so willing to assume that anything that is predominantly black must be inferior." The idea was that if the federal courts ordered the states to spend gobs of money building "model schools" with petting farms (and highly paid teachers' unions) in the mostly black city schools, the all-important white students would come. Surrounded by white people, black students' education would improve. The popular appeal of this charming notion gives you some idea why the most frequent modifier to "federal judge" is "unelected." Needless to say, having federal judges and Harvard professors run local school districts on the basis of a preposterous racist theory wrecked school system after school system.

Federal judges managed to wrest control of the school systems in the first place through scam lawsuits between nonadverse parties. It worked like this: A few parents would sue the school board, and the school board would quickly admit guilt. Then the nonadverse adversaries would giddily enter "voluntary" settlements requiring "the school boards" to make lavish improvements, including generous salary increases for school administrators. The court would enter an order confirming the "voluntary" settlement—and the taxpayers would be stuck with the bill. It was nothing but a scam dreamed up by parents and school boards to bilk taxpayers for more money. The educational community refers to this as a "court-ordered remedy." In the real world, such arrangements are known as "organized crime."

These "voluntary" desegregation plans were voluntary in the same way you "volunteer" your wallet to a couple of con men who have just staged a phony confrontation to abet picking your pocket. As Ashcroft explained it to Senator Kopechne, parents and schools would enter into agreements, but "the state was going to have to pay for everything." The plans had as much to do with desegregation as, well, a pickpocket does. It's time for Bush to send in Alan Keyes. He could probably explain all this to the Massachusetts drunk with some trenchancy. ∎

☞ Bizarre Political Sect Ousted from Judicial Nomination Process

MARCH 28, 2001

A few years ago I was bitterly disappointed to discover that appellate court judge Pasco Bowman, the otherwise impeccable federal judge I clerked for after law school, had gotten a "Qualified" rating from the ABA. Maybe even—God forbid—"Well Qualified." I don't remember, it was a dark day. For those of you not familiar with the ABA, this would be the equivalent of a would-be ethicist getting a "two thumbs up!" rating from Bill and Hillary. Upon discovering this contretemps I called him to complain. Almost all the cool guys had gotten "Qualified/Not Qualified" ratings. Why not him? Oh, the humiliation!

Among the judicial nominees who won the ABA's coveted "Qualified/ Not Qualified" rating is Judge Richard Posner—once described by archliberal Supreme Court Justice William Brennan Jr. as one of the two geniuses he had met in his life. Others were Judges Frank Easterbrook, Stephen Williams, James Buckley, Jerry Smith, and Laurence Silberman. If jurisprudence were an Olympic sport, these guys would be the "dream team." (As would Judge Bowman, but for nagging questions about that ABA endorsement.) Clarence Thomas got an impressive "Qualified/Not Qualified" rating from the ABA—the lowest score ever given to a Supreme Court nominee. Meanwhile, David Souter—that jurisprudential giant, plucked from a state court where he had been deciding pig-trespassing cases—was unanimously voted "Highly Qualified."

Finally and most acclaimed, the ABA ratings committee couldn't decide whether Judge Robert Bork, one of the twentieth century's foremost constitutional and legal authorities, was qualified. Four members voted him "Not Qualified," thus clearly defining "qualified" as "favoring unrestricted abortion on demand." The head of the ABA's selection committee then perjured himself by telling a Senate committee reasonable minds could differ about Bork's qualifications. Oh, okay. How about we compare LSAT scores? There was no possibility the ABA could ever be a nonlaughable organization after that.

Demonstrating its eagle eye for ferreting out unfit judges, the ABA gave "Qualified" or "Well Qualified" ratings to all three federal judges impeached in the last half century. These were Harry E. Claiborne (appointed by Lyndon Johnson), Alcee L. Hastings (appointed by Jimmy Carter), and Walter L. Nixon (appointed by Jimmy Carter). Perhaps this is all a big misunderstanding and what the ABA's rating system really means is "well qualified for future impeachment." This does not include other stellar Carter appointees who served prison terms without ever being impeached, like U.S. District Judge Robert F. Collins of New Orleans. While serving a six-year sentence for taking part of a $100,000 bribe to fix a drug-smuggling case, Collins continued to receive his federal salary from prison—he even got a raise. Only when the House brought impeachment proceedings against him did Collins finally resign. The ABA had ruled Collins "Qualified."

In my judge's defense: (1) Justice Antonin Scalia also got "Qualified"/ "Well Qualified" ratings (keep your eye on that guy), and (2) despite the ABA adjudging him "Qualified," Judge Bowman has never been impeached.

Magazines like the *Economist* and *Time* actually cited the impeachments of Democratic-appointed, ABA-approved judges in order to denounce Reagan's judicial nominees for getting low marks from the ABA. The *Economist* mentioned Judge Hastings (ABA rating: QUALIFIED!) and Judge Claiborne (ABA rating: HIGHLY QUALIFIED!) before asserting that criminal indictments of judges were "rare largely because screening of candidates for federal judgeships is so much more rigorous." *Time* magazine repeatedly pondered the irony of the Senate voting on Reagan's nomination of Daniel Manion—whom forty law school deans had opposed—just a month after "Highly Qualified" Claiborne began serving a two-year criminal sentence. (Judge Manion has served with distinction since his appointment in 1986.)

On the basis of the ABA's record, one could certainly understand why Senate Democrats like Chuck Schumer and Patrick Leahy were upset when President George Bush decided to scrap the ABA's review. You wouldn't want to tinker with a fine-tuned system like that. Schumer said eliminating the ABA's role in judicial nominations showed that "instead of quality, they are looking for ideology." Schumer then voted against Bush nominee Miguel Estrada—who had graduated from Harvard Law School magna cum laude, where he had been an editor of the law review; had clerked for the Supreme Court; had been a federal prosecutor; had served for almost five years in the solicitor general's office; had argued more than a dozen cases before the Supreme Court; and was then a partner in one of the most prestigious law firms in the country—because Estrada had not given the Democrats a blood oath that he would uphold abortion on demand. The *New York Times* also attacked Bush for removing the ABA from the process, editorializing that the ABA's ratings were crucial because its "stamp of approval . . . gave people confidence that federal judges were highly regarded members of the profession." If so, only among people who weren't paying attention.

I've been going to ABA annual conventions every few years since my parents took me as a little kid. It used to be that you couldn't get on an elevator at the hotel without stepping on a Supreme Court justice, an appellate court judge, or a U.S. senator. Big important people gave big important speeches. Now it's all nobodies. Every single panel discussion is on women and minorities. Once a convocation of esteemed legal minds, the ABA convention has morphed into a weird sort of twelve-step meeting for the disbarred. That's not entirely fair. The ABA still has marquee speakers, but instead of prominent attorneys, now they're prominent criminals. After he was impeached and held in contempt by a federal court—but before he had his license to practice law suspended and was banned from ever appearing before the U.S. Supreme Court—the ABA invited Bill Clinton to speak. Also joining the list of celebrated felons speaking at the ABA was ex-con Webster Hubbell. Apparently Hubbell was a last-minute stand-in after Mumia Abul-Jamal dropped out because of a scheduling conflict.

Maybe they could get O.J. for one of the minority panels next year. There's no one left to complain—everyone serious has resigned. The first wave of resignations came in 1987, when the ABA couldn't decide on Judge Bork's qualifications. The next major exodus came in 1992, when, on a break from Ya-Ya Sisterhood meetings, the ABA's House of Delegates declared the ABA in favor of abortion on demand. For the next several months, thousands of members exercised their freedom to choose by terminating their ABA memberships. After that, the ABA got loopier and loopier. One distinguished federal judge claims to join every few years just so he can resign in protest. Another said he was compelled to resign because the "impartiality of any judge who continues to belong to the ABA is subject to serious question."

For years now, the ABA has been issuing wild proclamations more appropriate to Janeane Garofalo than a professional association of lawyers. One former ABA president, George Bushnell, called the Republican leadership in Congress "reptilian bastards," paraphrasing the noted constitutional scholar and dictionary buff Julia Roberts. (Why couldn't my judge have gotten that appellation?) The esteemed ABA president also called the Contract with America "an attack on the Constitution comparable to that of the invasion of our shores by foreign forces." You remember the Contract with America? It included pernicious ideas like a balanced-budget amendment and tax incentives for adoption. If I had a nickel for every time I've confused an armed invasion of the U.S. mainland with a balanced-budget amendment, John Kerry would be trying to raise my taxes right now.

Two ABA presidents viciously denounced a proposed flag-burning amendment to the Constitution and—most shockingly—didn't even wait for the results of a study on how flag-burning might contribute to global warming. One former president, Roberta Ramo, said the flag-burning amendment proved Congress had "lost sight of the United States Constitution and Bill of Rights as our nation's lodestar and our soul." Instead of saluting the American flag, the ABA is considering a special seminar on how to burn it. Bushnell said Senator Bob Dole's support for the flag-burning amendment had compromised his "decency as an individual"— proving that it's still okay to vilify a disabled American combat veteran who actually did sustain his injuries on the field of battle.

The decency police at the ABA were offended by Bob Dole, but they didn't have a problem with Bernardine Dohrn, the Charles Manson–admiring former Weatherman and erstwhile member of the FBI's "Ten Most Wanted." The ABA made Dohrn head of their Litigation Task Force on Children. As Bushnell said, "We are tremendously fortunate to have her." That is true in the sense that it is somewhat miraculous that Dohrn didn't blow herself up making pipe bombs as a member of the Weathermen back in the 1970s.

But my judge is "Qualified"? Coming from this gang of leftist-fringe kooks, them's fightin' words. I demand a recount. ∎

☛ Liberals Shocked— Rush Not Jesus Christ

OCTOBER 15, 2003

So liberals have finally found a drug addict they don't like. And unlike the Lackawanna Six—those high-spirited young lads innocently seeking adventure in an al Qaeda training camp in Afghanistan—liberals could find no excuses for Rush Limbaugh.

After years of the mainstream media assuring us that Rush was a has-been, a nobody, yesterday's news, the Rush painkiller story was front-page news last week. (Would anyone care if Howell Raines committed murder?) The airwaves and print media were on red alert with Rush's admission that after an unsuccessful spinal operation a few years ago, he became addicted to powerful prescription painkillers.

Rush Limbaugh's misfortune is apparently a bigger story than his nearly $300 million radio contract signed two years ago. That was the biggest radio contract in broadcasting history. Yet there are only twelve documents on LexisNexis that reported it. The *New York Times* didn't take notice of Rush's $300 million radio contract, but a few weeks later, it put Bill Clinton's comparatively measly $10 million book contract on its front page. Meanwhile, in the past week alone, LexisNexis has accumulated more than fifty documents with the words "Rush Limbaugh and hypocrisy." That should make up for the twelve documents on his $300 million radio contract.

The reason any conservative's failing is always major news is that it allows liberals to engage in their very favorite taunt: Hypocrisy! Hypocrisy is the only sin that really inflames them. Inasmuch as liberals have no morals, they can sit back and criticize other people for failing to meet the standards that liberals simply renounce. It's an intriguing strategy. By openly admitting to being philanderers, draft dodgers, liars, weasels, and cowards, liberals avoid ever being hypocrites.

At least Rush wasn't walking into church carrying a ten-pound Bible before rushing back to the Oval Office for sodomy with Monica Lewinsky. He wasn't enforcing absurd sexual harassment guidelines while dropping his pants in front of a half-dozen subordinates. (Evidently, Clinton wasn't a hypocrite because no one was supposed to take seriously the notion that he respected women or believed in God.)

Rush has hardly been the antidrug crusader liberals suggest. Indeed, Rush hasn't had much to say about drugs at all since that spinal operation. The Rush Limbaugh quote that has been endlessly recited in the last week to prove Rush's rank "hypocrisy" is this, made eight years ago: "Drug use, some might say, is destroying this country. And we have laws against selling drugs, pushing drugs, using drugs, importing drugs. . . . And so if people are violating the law by doing drugs, they ought to be accused and they ought to be convicted and they ought to be sent up."

What precisely are liberals proposing that Rush should have said to avoid their indignant squeals of "hypocrisy"? Announce his support for the wide and legal availability of a prescription painkiller that might have caused him to go deaf and nearly ruined his career and wrecked his life? I believe that would have been both evil and hypocritical.

Or is it simply that Rush should not have become addicted to pain-killers in the first place? Well, no, I suppose not. You've caught us: Rush has a flaw. And yet, the wily hypocrite does not support flaws!

When a conservative can be the biggest thing in talk radio, earning $30 million a year and attracting 20 million devoted listeners every week—all while addicted to drugs—I'll admit liberals have reason to believe that con-servatives are some sort of superrace, incorruptible by original sin. But the only perfect man hasn't walked the Earth for two thousand years. In liber-als' worldview, any conservative who is not Jesus Christ is ipso facto a "hyp-ocrite" for not publicly embracing dissolute behavior the way liberals do.

In fact, Rush's behavior was not all that dissolute. There is a funda-mental difference between taking any drug for kicks—legal, illegal, pre-scription, protected by the Twenty-first Amendment, or banned by Michael Bloomberg—and taking a painkiller for pain.

There is a difference morally and a difference legally. While slamming Rush, Harvard Law professor Alan Dershowitz recently told Wolf Blitzer, "Generally, people who illegally buy prescription drugs are not prosecuted, whereas people who illegally buy cocaine and heroin are prosecuted." What would the point be? Just say no to back surgery?

I haven't checked with any Harvard Law professors, but I'm pretty sure that, generally, adulterous drunks who drive off bridges and kill girls are prosecuted. Ah, but Teddy Kennedy supports adultery and public drunk-enness—so at least you can't call him a hypocrite! That must provide great consolation to Mary Jo Kopechne's parents.

I have a rule about not feeling sorry for people worth $300 million, but I'm feeling sentimental. Evan Thomas wrote a cover story on Rush for *Newsweek* this week that was so vicious it read like conservative satire. Thomas called Rush a "schlub," "socially ill at ease," an Elmer Gantry, an actor whose "act has won over, or fooled, a lot of people." He compared Rush to the phony TV evangelist Jim Bakker and recommended that Rush start to "make a virtue out of honesty." (Liberals can lie under oath in legal proceedings and it's a "personal matter." Conservatives must scream their every failing from the rooftops or they are "liars.")

As is standard procedure for profiles of conservatives, *Newsweek* gath-ered quotes on Rush from liberals, ex-wives, and dumped dates. Covering himself, Thomas ruefully remarked that "it's hard to find many people who really know him." Well, there was me, Evan! But I guess *Newsweek* didn't have room for the quotes I promptly sent back to the *Newsweek* researchers. I could have even corrected *Newsweek*'s absurd account of how Rush met his wife. (It's kind of cute, too: She was a fan who began arguing with him about something he said on air.)

Thomas also made the astute observation that "Rush Limbaugh has always had far more followers than friends." Needless to say, this floored those of us who were shocked to discover that Rush does not have 20 million friends.

So the guy I really feel sorry for is Evan Thomas. How would little Evan fare in any competitive media? Any followers? Any fans? Any readers at all? And he's not even addicted to painkillers! This week, Rush proved his motto: He really can beat liberals with half his brain tied behind his back. ∎

☞ It's the Winter Solstice, Charlie Brown!

SEPTEMBER 24, 2003

David Limbaugh's book *Persecution: How Liberals Are Waging War Against Christianity* will make you cry for your country. (But don't pray for your country if you're anywhere near a public school!) Released this week, Limbaugh's copiously researched book documents how the courts, the universities, the media, Hollywood, and government institutions react to any mention of Christianity like Superman recoiling from kryptonite, Dracula from sunlight, or Madonna from soap and water. His straight, factual narrative of what is happening in our public schools makes you wonder how much longer America can survive liberalism.

In a public school in St. Louis, a teacher spotted the suspect, fourth-grader Raymond Raines, bowing his head in prayer before lunch. The teacher stormed to Raymond's table, ordered him to stop immediately, and sent him to the principal's office. The principal informed the young malefactor that praying was not allowed in school. When Raymond was again caught praying before meals on three separate occasions, he was segregated from other students, ridiculed in front of his classmates, and finally sentenced to a week's detention.

Before snack time in her kindergarten class in Saratoga Springs, New York, little Kayla Broadus held hands with two of her classmates and recited this prayer: "God is good, God is great, thank you, God, for my food." The alert teacher pounced on Kayla, severely reprimanded her, and reported her to the school administration. In short order, the principal sent a sternly worded letter to Kayla's parents advising them that Kayla was not allowed to pray in school, aloud or with others.

The school board then issued a triumphant press release crowing about its victory over a kindergartner praying before snack time. Thus was creeping theocracy in Saratoga Springs stopped dead in its tracks! Kayla's mother brought a lawsuit, winning Kayla the right to pray out loud. But she was still prohibited from holding hands with others while she prayed. Hearing the G-word in kindergarten might interfere with the school's efforts to teach proper sexual techniques in the first grade.

Thanks to the vigilance of a teacher at Lynn Lucas Middle School outside of Houston, two sisters carrying Bibles were prevented from bringing their vile material into a classroom. The teacher stopped the students at the classroom door and marched them to the principal's office. (Maybe it was just the sight of public school students carrying a book of any kind that set off alarm bells.) The sisters' mother was called and warned that the school intended to report her to Child Protective Services. When the mother arrived, the teacher threw the Bibles in the wastebasket, shouting, "This is garbage!"

In another display of tolerance at Lynn Lucas Middle School, school administrators snatched three students' books with covers displaying the Ten Commandments, ripped the covers off, threw them in the garbage, and told the students that the Ten Commandments constituted "hate speech." (Also, it would be insensitive to expose the Ten Commandments to students who had never been taught to count to ten.)

After the massacre at Columbine High School, students and families were invited to paint tiles above student lockers. The school district had taken all reasonable precautions, immediately deploying an army of secular "grief counselors" with teddy bears to descend on the school after the attack. Nonetheless, some students painted their tiles with "objectionable" messages, such as "4/20/99: Jesus Wept" and "God Is Love." This would not stand: The school removed ninety tiles with offending religious messages. They might have offended the sensibilities of students as they listened to the latest Ludacris or 50 Cent CDs.

A federal court upheld the school's censorship of the religious tiles. Of course, Columbine school officials had earned a measure of deference after having inculcated such a fine sense of morality in their students that two boys could walk into school one day and stage a bloody massacre. You don't argue with a track record like that.

Not all mentions of religion constitute "hate speech." In State College, Pennsylvania, school administrators methodically purged all Christmas carols of any religious content—and then led the children in a chant of "Celebrate Kwanzaa!" At Pattison Elementary School in Katy, Texas, Christmas songs are banned, but students are threatened with grade reductions for refusing to sing songs celebrating other religious faiths.

In New York City, the chancellor of the Department of Education prohibited the display of Nativity scenes in public schools, while expressly allowing the Jewish menorah and the Islamic star and crescent to be displayed. Some would say that was overkill, inasmuch as New York City is already the home of the world's largest public display built in commemoration of Islam: Ground Zero.

Between issuing laws prohibiting discrimination against transgendered individuals and running up a $38 billion deficit, the California legislature mandated a three-week immersion course in Islam for all seventh-graders. A "crash course" in Islam, you might call it, if that weren't so ironic. Students are required to adopt Muslim names, plan a trip to Mecca, play a jihad game, pray to "Allah, the Compassionate," and chant "Praise to Allah! Lord of Creation!" They are encouraged to dress in Muslim garb. Students are discouraged, however, from stoning girls at the school dances, abusing their "Jew" math teachers, or blowing up their classmates.

A popular student textbook, *Across the Centuries,* treats the Inquisition and Salem witch hunts as typical of Christianity, but never gets around to mentioning the Muslims' conquest of Spain, the Battle of Tours, or the execution of Jews in Qurayza. Or 9/11.

There is no surer proof of Christ's divinity than that he is still so hated some two thousand years after his death. Limbaugh's *Persecution* covers it all in staggering, heartbreaking detail. His methodical description of what is happening in our public schools alone will call to mind the hate speech banned in Columbine: "Jesus Wept." ∎

☞ Massachusetts Supreme Court Abolishes Capitalism!

NOVEMBER 27, 2003

Last week, the Massachusetts Supreme Judicial Court discovered that the state constitution—written in 1780—requires the state to allow gay marriages. The court gave the legislature six months to rewrite the law to comply with the heretofore unnoticed gay-marriage provision in a 223-year-old constitution, leaving countless gay couples a scant six months to select a silverware pattern. Out of respect for my gay male readers, I'll resist the temptation to characterize this ruling as "shoving gay marriage down our throats."

The Massachusetts Constitution was written by John Adams, who was quite religious. It is the most explicitly Christian document since the New Testament, with lots of references to "the great Legislator of the universe." Adams certainly would have been astonished to discover that the constitution he wrote provided for gay marriage—though one can see how a reference to two men marrying might get lost among the minutiae about the "duty of all men in society, publicly and at stated seasons, to worship the Supreme Being, the great Creator and Preserver of the universe."

The main lesson from the court's discovery of the hidden gay-marriage clause is that these judges are in the wrong job. If they can find a right to gay marriage in the Massachusetts Constitution—never before detected by any human being—we need to get them looking for Osama bin Laden. These guys can find anything!

And if we don't get Massachusetts judges out of the country soon, we could start reading headlines like "Mass. Supreme Court Abolishes Capitalism; Gives Legislature 6 Months to Nationalize All Industry."

The Democratic presidential candidates reacted with glee to the court's gay-marriage ruling, relieved that they could talk about gay marriage instead of their insane ideas on national defense. But then they realized this meant they would have to talk about gay marriage. Except for the nut candidates who always forget to lie about their positions, all the Democratic presidential candidates earnestly insist that they oppose gay marriage. They are for "civil unions" with all the legal rights of marriage. But not marriage! No sir.

As governor of Vermont, Howard Dean actually signed a bill providing for these magical "civil unions." Having already been forgiven for his remarks about the Confederate flag by both of the black people currently living in Vermont, now Dean wants to be the candidate for guys with Confederate flags in their flower shops. But even Dean emphasized that Vermont's civil-union law does not legalize gay "marriage."

And even in Ben-and-Jerryville, incidentally, it took a court to force the state to recognize civil unions by discovering that right in the Vermont Constitution. (WHERE'S OSAMA?)

The big argument for "civil unions"—but not marriage!—is that gays are denied ordinary civil rights here in the American Taliban. This is where gays usually bring up the argument about all the straight couples living in "sham" marriages, but I see no point in dragging the Clintons into this.

The classic formulation was given by John Kerry in the Democratic debate earlier this week: "What we're talking about is somebody's right to be able to visit a loved one in a hospital, somebody's right to be able to pass on property, somebody's right to live equally under the state laws as other people in the country." You would think there were "Straights Only" water fountains the way Democrats carry on so (as if any gay man would drink nonbottled water).

Apparently, health care in this country is better than we've been led to believe if so few Americans have ever been to a hospital that they think there's a guest list. In case you don't know: Gays already can visit loved ones in hospitals. They can also visit neighbors, random acquaintances, and total strangers in hospitals—just like everyone else.

Gays can also pass on property to whomever they would like, including their cats. Every few years you read about some daft rich widow leaving her entire estate to a cat. It's perfectly legal. You just need to write a will. Liberals have figured out how to get abortions for thirteen-year-old girls without their parents' permission to cross state lines. But we're supposed to believe that they just can't get their heads around how a gay guy could leave property to his partner.

As for "living equally under the state laws as other people in the country," unless Kerry is referring to the precise thing he claims to oppose— gay marriage—gays do live equally under the state laws as other people in the country. There are no special speed-limit laws or trespassing laws for gays. (There is, however, some evidence of gay profiling with regard to the enforcement of fashion "don'ts.")

What gays can't do is get married—something all Democrats swear up and down to oppose. Instead, the Democrats demand "civil unions" and then throw out a series of red herrings to explain why. In fact, the only difference between what the Democrats claim to support (civil unions) and what they claim to oppose (gay marriage) is the word "marriage." As John Kerry explained, "I think the term 'marriage' gets in the way of what is really being talked about here."

Republicans ought to try that: We don't support "guns"—the term "gun" gets in the way of what is really being talked about here—we want choice in personal security devices. We don't want a "ban" on partial-birth abortions; we just don't want there to be any of them. We don't support "tax cuts"; we support a "union" between people and 70 percent of their money. We don't support "war" with Iraq; we are talking about somebody's right to be able to visit a loved one in a hospital. (Huh?)

Except the difference is: All those positions are popular with voters, so Republicans don't have to lie. The Democrats' purported opposition to gay marriage is like all their other phony policy statements that are the opposite of what they really believe.

When they're running for office, all Democrats claim to support tax cuts (for the middle class), to support gun rights (for hunters), and to "personally oppose" abortion. And then they get into office and vote to raise taxes, ban guns, and allow abortions if a girl can't fit into her prom dress.

The common wisdom holds that "both parties" have to appeal to the extremes during the primary and then move to the center for the general election. To the contrary, both parties run for office as conservatives. Once they have fooled the voters and are safely in office, Republicans sometimes double-cross the voters. Democrats always do. ■

☞ The Passion of the Liberal

MARCH 3, 2004

In the dozens and dozens of panic-stricken articles the *New York Times* has run on Mel Gibson's movie *The Passion of the Christ,* the unavoidable conclusion is that liberals haven't the vaguest idea what Christianity is.

The *Times* may have loopy ideas about a lot of things, but at least when they write about gay bathhouses and abortion clinics, you get the sense they know what they're talking about.

But Christianity just doesn't ring a bell. The religion that has transformed Western civilization for two millennia is a blank slate for liberals. Their closest reference point is "conservative Christians," meaning people you're not supposed to hire. And these are the people who carp about George Bush's alleged lack of "intellectual curiosity."

The most amazing complaint, championed by the *Times* and repeated by all the know-nothing secularists on television, is that Gibson insisted on "rubbing our faces in the grisly reality of Jesus' death." The *Times* was irked that Gibson "relentlessly focused on the savagery of Jesus' final hours"—at the expense of showing us the Happy Jesus. Yes, Gibson's movie is crying out for a car chase, a sex scene, or maybe a wisecracking orangutan.

The *Times* ought to send one of its crack investigative reporters to St. Patrick's Cathedral at 3 P.M. on Good Friday before leaping to the conclusion that *The Passion* is Gibson's idiosyncratic take on Christianity. In a standard Sunday ritual, Christians routinely eat the flesh and drink the blood of Jesus Christ, aka "the Lamb of God." The really serious Catholics do that blood- and flesh-eating thing every day, the sickos. The *Times* has just discovered the tip of a 2,000-year-old iceberg.

But the loony left is testy with Gibson for spending so much time on Jesus' suffering and death while giving "short shrift to Jesus' ministry and ideas"—as another *Times* reviewer put it. According to liberals, the message of Jesus, which somehow Gibson missed, is something along the lines of "be nice to people" (which to them means "raise taxes on the productive").

You don't need a religion like Christianity, which is a rather large and complex endeavor, in order to flag that message. All you need is a moron driving around in a Volvo with a bumper sticker that says "be nice to people." Being nice to people is, in fact, one of the incidental tenets of Christianity (as opposed to other religions whose tenets are more along the lines of "kill everyone who doesn't smell bad or answer to the name Mohammed"). But to call it the "message" of Jesus requires . . . well, the brain of Maureen Dowd.

In fact, Jesus' distinctive message was: People are sinful and need to be redeemed, and this is your lucky day because I'm here to redeem you even though you don't deserve it, and I have to get the crap kicked out of me to do it. That is the reason He is called "Christ the Redeemer" rather than "Christ the Moron Driving Around in a Volvo With a 'Be Nice to People' Bumper Sticker on It."

The other complaint from the know-nothing crowd is that *The Passion* will inspire anti-Semitic violence. If nothing else comes out of this movie, at least we finally have liberals on record opposing anti-Semitic violence. Perhaps they should broach that topic with their Muslim friends.

One *Times* review of *The Passion* said, "To be a Christian is to face the responsibility for one's own most treasured sacred texts being used to justify the deaths of innocents." At best, this is like blaming Jodie Foster for the shooting of Ronald Reagan. But the reviewer somberly warned that a Christian should "not take the risk that one's life or work might contribute to the continuation of a horror." So the only thing Christians can do is shut up about their religion. (And no more Jodie Foster movies!)

By contrast, in the weeks after 9/11, the *Times* was rushing to assure its readers that "prominent Islamic scholars and theologians in the West say unequivocally that nothing in Islam countenances the Sept. 11 actions." (That's if you set aside Muhammad's many specific instructions to kill nonbelievers whenever possible.) *Times* columnists repeatedly extolled "the great majority of peaceful Muslims." Only a religion with millions of practitioners trying to kill Americans and Jews is axiomatically described as "peaceful" by liberals.

As I understand it, the dangerous religion is the one whose messiah instructs, "If one strikes thee on thy right cheek, turn to him the other also" and "Love your enemies . . . do good to them that hate you, and pray for them that persecute and calumniate you." By contrast, the peaceful religion instructs, "Slay the enemy where you find him" (Surah 9:92).

Imitating the ostrich-like posture of certain German Jews who ignored the growing danger during Hitler's rise to power, today's liberals are deliberately blind to the real threats of violence that surround us. Their narcissistic self-image requires absolute solicitude toward angry savages plotting acts of terrorism. The only people who scare them are the ones who worship a Jew. ■

☞ W.W.J.K.?: Who Would Jesus Kill?

MARCH 10, 2004

The *New York Times*'s Frank Rich described Mel Gibson's movie *The Passion of the Christ* thus: "With its laborious build-up to its orgasmic spurtings of blood and other bodily fluids, Mr. Gibson's film is constructed like nothing so much as a porn movie, replete with slo-mo climaxes and pounding music for the money shots." (I'll leave it to your imagination as to how the *Times*'s film and theater critic knows gay porn well enough to be tossing industry lingo around.) Yes, Christ's followers take pleasure at the thought of his torture. The people sobbing throughout *The Passion* all around the country were clearly having the time of their lives.

Six months ago, Rich was predicting that *The Passion* would be a box office disaster. In the August 3, 2003, *New York Times,* he wrote, "Indeed, it's hard to imagine the movie being anything other than a flop in America." Now that *The Passion* is breaking box office records, Rich sneers that Gibson was just in it for the money. On *Hardball* last week, he condescended to Tony Blankley, "I hate to break it to you, Tony, but this was a movie made to make money." So Rich is obviously someone whose opinion is to be respected.

I guess calling Gibson a fag is all liberals have left now that the pogroms have failed to materialize. The fact that Frank Rich is still alive would seem to be proof positive that Americans are incapable of being roused to anti-Semitic violence.

But William Safire wasn't so sure. Safire, the *New York Times*'s in-house "conservative"—who endorsed Bill Clinton in 1992, like so many conservatives—was sure Mel Gibson's movie *The Passion of the Christ* would incite anti-Semitic violence. With all the subtlety of a Mack truck, Safire called Gibson's movie a version of "the medieval 'passion play,' preserved in pre-Hitler Germany at Oberammergau, a source of the hatred of all Jews as 'Christ killers.'" (Certainly every Aryan Nation skinhead murderer I've ever met was also a devoted theater buff and "passion play" aficionado.)

The "passion play" has been put on in Germany since at least 1633. I guess 1633 would be "pre-Hitler." In addition, Moses walked the Earth "pre-Hitler." The wheel was invented "pre-Hitler." People ate soup "pre-

Hitler." Referring to the passion play as "pre-Hitler" is a slightly fancier version of every adolescent's favorite argument: You're like Hitler!

Despite repeated suggestions from liberals—including the in-house "conservative" and Clinton-supporter at the *Times*—Hitler is not what happens when you gin up Christians. Like Timothy McVeigh, the Columbine killers, and the editorial board of the *New York Times*, Hitler detested Christians. Indeed, Hitler denounced Christianity as an "invention of the Jew" and vowed that the "organized lie [of Christianity] must be smashed" so that the state would "remain the absolute master." Interestingly, this was the approach of all the great mass murderers of the last century—all of whom were atheists: Hitler, Stalin, Mao, and Pol Pot.

In the United States, more than 30 million babies have been killed by abortion since *Roe v. Wade,* versus seven abortion providers killed. Yeah—keep your eye on those Christians!

But according to liberals, it's Christianity that causes murder. (And don't get them started on Zionism.) Like their Muslim friends still harping about the Crusades, liberals won't "move on" from the Spanish Inquisition. In the entire 350 years of the Spanish Inquisition, about 30,000 people were killed. That's an average of less than 100 a year. Stalin knocked off that many kulaks before breakfast.

But Safire argues that viewers of *The Passion* will see the Jewish mob and think, "Who was responsible for this cruel humiliation? What villain deserves to be punished?" Let's see: It was a Roman who ordered Christ's execution, and Romans who did all the flaying, taunting, and crucifying. Perhaps Safire is indulging in his own negative stereotyping about Jews by assuming they simply viewed Romans as "the help."

But again I ask: Does anyone at the *Times* have the vaguest notion what Christianity is? (Besides people who go around putting up Nativity scenes that have to be taken down by court order?) The religion that toppled the Roman Empire—anyone?

Jesus' suffering and death is not a Hatfields-and-McCoys story demanding retaliation. The gist of the religion that transformed the world is: God's only son came to Earth to take the punishment we deserved. If the Jews had somehow managed to block Jesus' crucifixion and He had died in old age of natural causes, there would be no salvation through Christ and no Christianity. Whatever possible responses there may be to that story, this is not one of them: Damn those Jews for being a part of God's plan to save my eternal soul!

Gibson didn't insert Jews into the story for some Machiavellian, racist reason. Christ was a Jew crucified by Romans at the request of other Jews in Jerusalem. I suppose if Gibson had moved the story to suburban Cleveland and portrayed Republican logging executives crucifying Christ, the Left would calm down. But it simply didn't happen that way.

Of course, the original text is no excuse in Hollywood. The villains of Tom Clancy's book *The Sum of All Fears* were recently transformed from Muslim terrorists to neo-Nazis for the movie version. You wouldn't want to upset the little darlings. They might do something crazy. The only religion that can be constantly defamed and insulted is the one liberals pretend to be terrified of. ■

JUNE 5, 2004: President Ronald Reagan passes away
at the age of ninety-three.

☞ Let's Rewrite One for the Gipper!

JUNE 16, 2004

I read the *New York Times* last week and apparently a fellow named "Iran-Contra" died recently. But that's all I'll say about the people who have consistently been on the wrong side of history and whose publisher is a little weenie who can't read because he has "dyslexia." The three key ingredients to Ronald Reagan's sunny personality were: (1) his unalterable faith in God; (2) for nearly thirty years, he didn't fly; and (3) he read *Human Events* religiously but never read the *New York Times*.

Even in his death, liberals are still trying to turn our champion into a moderate Republican—unlike the religious-right nut currently occupying the White House! The world's living testament to the limits of genetics, Ron Jr., put it this way at Reagan's funeral: "Dad was also a deeply, unabashedly religious man. But he never made the fatal mistake of so many politicians of wearing his faith on his sleeve to gain political advantage."

Wow. He's probably up in heaven—something Ron Jr. doesn't believe in—having a chuckle about that right now. To hear liberals tell it, you'd think Reagan talked about God the way Democrats do, in the stilted, uncomfortable manner of people pretending to believe something they manifestly do not. (In a recent *Time* magazine poll, only 7 percent of respondents say they believe Kerry is a man of "strong" religious faith, compared to 46 percent who believe Bush is.) Or, for that matter, the way Democrats talk about free-market capitalism.

The chattering classes weren't so copacetic about Reagan's religious beliefs when he was in office. In 1984, *Newsweek* breathlessly reported that "Reagan is known to have read and discussed with fundamentalist friends like [Jerry] Falwell and singer Pat Boone such pulp versions of biblical prophecies as Hal Lindsey's best-selling *The Late Great Planet Earth*, which strongly hints of a nuclear Armageddon." One hundred Christian and Jewish "leaders" signed a letter warning that Reagan's nuclear policy had been unduly influenced by a "theology of nuclear Armageddon." In the second presidential debate that year, President Reagan was actually asked to clarify his position on "nuclear Armageddon."

Most confusing to Democrats, at the time Reagan was doing all of this Bible reading and consorting with preachers, he hadn't even been accused of cheating on his wife. *What kind of angle is he playing?* liberals asked themselves.

Meanwhile, President Bush says he appeals to "a higher father" and liberals act like they've never heard such crazy talk from a president.

Newsweek's Eleanor Clift says Bush is unlike Reagan because Reagan "reached out, and he was always seeking converts." That's true, actually. I think Reagan would have favored converting Third World people to Christianity. (Now why does that idea ring a bell?) Clift continued: "That is the big difference between Ronald Reagan and the president we have today. The president today would like to consign his political opponents to oblivion."

Here is how Reagan "reached out" to Democrats:

Reagan on abortion: "We cannot survive as a free nation when some men decide that others are not fit to live and should be abandoned to abortion or infanticide."

Reagan on gay rights: "Society has always regarded marital love as a sacred expression of the bond between a man and a woman. It is the means by which families are created and society itself is extended into the future. In the Judeo-Christian tradition it is the means by which husband and wife participate with God in the creation of a new human life. It is for these reasons, among others, that our society has always sought to protect this unique relationship. In part the erosion of these values has given way to a celebration of forms of expression most reject. We will resist the efforts of some to obtain government endorsement of homosexuality."

Reagan on government programs to feed the "hungry": "We were told four years ago that 17 million people went to bed hungry each night. Well, that was probably true. They were all on a diet."

Would that more Republicans would "reach out" to Democrats the way Reagan did!

Most peculiar, the passing of America's most pro-life president is supposed to be a clarion call for conservatives to support the disemboweling of human embryos—in contrast to that heartless brute President Bush always prattling on about the value of human life. Someone persuaded poor, dear Nancy Reagan that research on human embryos might have saved her Ronnie from Alzheimer's. Now the rest of us are supposed to shut up because the wife of America's greatest president (oh, save your breath, girls!) supports stem-cell research.

Ironically, the always market-oriented Ronald Reagan would probably have asked his wife, "Honey, if embryonic stem-cell therapy is such a treasure trove of medical advances, why isn't private research and development funding flocking to it?"

President Bush has never said that fetal stem cells cannot be used for research. He said "federal money" cannot be used to fund such research. If leading scientists believed fetal stem-cell research would prove to be so fruitful in curing Alzheimer's, why is the private money not pouring in hand over fist? Do you realize how many billions a cure for Alzheimer's would be worth, let alone all the other cures some are claiming fetal stem-cell research would lead to? Forget Alzheimer's—do you know how much middle-aged men would pay for a *genuine* baldness cure? Then again, if we ever cured baldness Porsche sales would probably fall off quite a bit.

But you can't blame Nancy. As everyone saw once again last week, she's still madly in love with the guy. She'd probably support harvesting full-grown, living humans if it would bring back Ronnie. Of course, I thought it was cute and not creepy that she consulted an astrologer about Reagan's schedule after he was shot. That didn't make astrology a hard science. But liberals who once lambasted Nancy for having too much influence on Reagan's schedule now want to anoint her Seer of Technology.

The lesson to draw from what liberals said about Reagan then and what they are forced to say about him now is that the electable Republican is always the one liberals are calling an extremist, Armageddon-believing religious zealot. That certainly bodes well for President George W. Bush this November, thank—you should pardon the expression—God. ∎

8

The Battle Flag

■

During the Democratic primaries for the 2004 presidential election, Howard Dean set off a tsunami of indignation when he said he wanted to be "the candidate for guys with Confederate flags in their pickup trucks" (just like Bill Clinton was the candidate for the guy with the Astro-turf in the bed of his pickup truck). Like clockwork, every presidential election year the Confederate flag becomes a major campaign issue. This always thrills the Democrats, because it finally gives them an issue to run on: Their support for the Union side in the Civil War.

After Dean's contretemps, Al Sharpton denounced the Confederate flag as an "American swastika," saying, "Imagine if I said that I wanted to be the candidate of people with helmets and swastikas." After briefly considering a personal-injury lawsuit, Senator John Edwards lectured Dean, saying, "Let me tell you, the last thing we need in the South is somebody like you coming down and telling us what we need to do." John Kerry said he wanted to be "the candidate of the guy whose limo driver keeps a Confederate flag in the back window of his Towne Car" and Dennis Kucinich said he wanted to be "the candidate for the guys in the low-emission hybrid vehicles with the Confederate flags in them."

At first, Dean refused to apologize, prolonging the Democrats' joyous self-righteousness. Dean defended himself saying, "I think the Confederate flag is a racist symbol"—apparently under the impression that it would help matters to explain that, yes, in fact, he did want to be the candidate of racists. But eventually Dean buckled and said it was Republicans' fault: "I think there are a lot of poor people who fly that flag because the Republicans have been dividing us by race since 1968 with their Southern race strategy." Carol Moseley Braun backed him up, saying the Democrats needed to "get past that racist strategy that the Republicans have foisted upon this country." Okay, so just for the record, this was Carol Moseley Braun urging someone *not* to play a race card.

In fact and needless to say, it is the Democrats who have turned the Confederate flag into a federal issue, because they relish nothing more than being morally indignant. Not about abortion, adultery, illegitimacy, the divorce rate, or a president molesting an intern and lying to federal investigators. Indeed, not about anything of any practical consequence. Democrats stake out a clear moral position only on the issue of slavery. Of course, when it mattered, they were on the wrong side of that issue, too.

In addition to expressing outrage over a nonissue, Democrats take sadistic pleasure in telling blacks that everyone hates them. Demonstrating their famous appreciation of "nuance," liberals believe the Confederate flag is pure evil and anyone who flies the flag is pure evil—and George Bush is a moron who sees the world in simplistic black-and-white terms of good and evil. I guess that's what liberals mean by "nuance."

Despite recent revisionist history written by liberal know-nothings— the "nuance" devotees—the Civil War did not pit pure-of-heart Yankees against a mob of vicious racist Southerners. If it had, the North might not have fought so hard to keep Southerners as their fellow countrymen. President Lincoln—the Great Emancipator himself—wrote to the editor of the *New York Tribune* in August 1862, "If I could save the Union without freeing any slave, I would do it; if I could save it by freeing all the slaves, I would do it; and if I could save it by freeing some and leaving others alone, I would also do that." Indeed, Lincoln did not even issue the Emancipation Proclamation until well into the Civil War, and then largely as a war tactic. Yes, the South had slaves. Martin Luther King was an adulterer. Life is messy.

In his second inaugural address, Lincoln said the Civil War was God's retribution to both the North and the South for the institution of slavery. By allowing slavery to continue past God's appointed time, Lincoln said, all of us had sinned: God "gives to both North and South this terrible war as the woe due to those by whom the offense came." *Jerry Falwell, please pick up the white courtesy phone. Jerry Falwell . . .* If only Falwell had said the

9/11 terrorist attack was God's retribution for abortion, sodomy, and *slavery*, maybe liberals wouldn't have been so snippy. Six hundred thousand white men died to end the offense to God of slavery. Never have so many died to prove what "all men are created equal" means. God have mercy on us when the country is called to account for abortion.

What is commonly known as the "Confederate flag"—by Vermonters, for example—is the Southern Cross, the battle flag Confederate troops carried into the field. It was not the official flag of the Confederacy and never flew over any Confederate buildings. It was the flag of the Confederate army.

The great Confederate general Robert E. Lee opposed slavery and freed his slaves. Lee fought on the Confederate side because Virginia was his home and he thought Virginia had the right to be wrong. Lee was an honorable man as well as a great general. His men followed him, many of them hungry and barefoot, because of his personal qualities and because they lived in the South—not because they held a brief for slavery. Shelby Foote describes perplexed Union soldiers asking a captured Confederate, poor and shoeless, why he was fighting when he clearly didn't own any slaves. The soldier answered, "Because you're down here." Indeed, a small number of blacks served in the Confederate army, presumably for reasons other than their vigorous support of slavery. At an abstract level, of course, the war was about slavery, but that's not why the soldiers fought. They didn't own slaves—their honor is really inviolate.

And they were good soldiers. The Confederate battle flag is a symbol of military valor, a separation from the "Do as I say, not as I do" North. It symbolizes what F. Scott Fitzgerald called a romantic lost cause fought by charming people. Ask any male who ever played Civil War games as a boy if there was a marked preference for one side or the other. Invariably, little boys fight bitterly over who gets to play the Confederates. This obviously has nothing whatsoever to do with slavery: The preference for the South is based purely on the military criteria of little boys. Soldiers in the Confederate army were simply cooler than those in the Union army. They had better uniforms, better songs, and better generals. And they had the rebel yell. Who would you rather be—J.E.B. Stuart in the dashing gray uniform and a plume in his hat or some clodhopper from Maine?

The Civil War was hideous as only civil wars can be. But the victors allowed the vanquished to go home knowing they had done their duty with unsurpassed courage and devotion. Because the South was treated with honor and respect, the war did not degenerate into an unending guerrilla war, as has happened with other nations' civil wars. Confederate soldiers became a romantic army of legend, not sullen losers.

When Confederate soldiers surrendered their arms, the Union general accepting the surrender, Joshua Chamberlain, ordered his men to salute the defeated army. In response, Confederate general John Gordon reared his horse and—as Chamberlain described it—"horse and rider made one motion, the horse's head swung down with a graceful bow and General Gordon dropped his sword point to his toe in salutation." General Ulysses S. Grant drew up generous surrender papers for Lee to sign, precluding trials for treason. After Lee had signed, General Grant ordered Union troops to turn over a portion of their food rations to hungry Confederate troops. Years later, Lee would allow his students to say no unkind words about Grant, calling him a great man who had honored the dignity of the South. When the news came to Washington that Robert E. Lee had surrendered, President Lincoln came out on the White House lawn to announce the South's defeat. He asked the band to play "Dixie." This was an unbelievable way to end a war—and ensured that it really did end. Winston Churchill described the Civil War as the "last war fought between gentlemen." (Perhaps F. Scott Fitzgerald and Churchill should be banned along with the Confederate flag.)

It is the proud military heritage of the South that the Confederate flag represents—a heritage that belongs to all Southerners, both black and white. The whole country's military history is shot through with Southerners. Obviously boys from all over fought in this country's wars, and fought bravely, but it is simply a fact that Southerners are overrepresented in this country's heroic annals.

These are just some of the sons of the South:

- Sergeant Alvin York, who received the Medal of Honor in World War I for leading seven men to capture 128 Germans, including four officers, was from Tennessee.
- The most decorated soldier of World War II, Audie Murphy, was from Texas.
- The first Marine awarded the Medal of Honor in World War II, Hank Elrod, was from Georgia.
- General Lucius Clay, commander of the Berlin Airlift, was from Georgia.

- General Dwight Eisenhower was born in Texas.
- Admiral Chester W. Nimitz, the Pacific commander in chief of the Navy during World War II, was from Texas.
- General Douglas MacArthur, who commanded Allied forces in World War II in the Southwest Pacific, was from Arkansas.
- General William Westmoreland, commander of U.S. troops in Vietnam, was from South Carolina.
- Lieutenant General Lewis Burwell "Chesty" Puller, considered by many to be the greatest Marine ever and the only Marine to be awarded the Navy Cross five times for heroism and gallantry in combat, was from Virginia.
- Tommy Franks, the army general who led the attack on the Taliban in Afghanistan after the attack of 9/11, grew up in Texas.
- Famous draft-dodger Bill Clinton was from Arkansas—showing once again that the exception proves the rule.

Phil Caputo, author of the anti-Vietnam book *Rumor of War,* was one of the first Marines in Vietnam. He says all his best soldiers were Southerners: They could walk for hours and hit anything—as he puts it—just like their Confederate grandfathers.

In his book about World War II, *Citizen Soldiers,* Stephen Ambrose tells of the amazing feats of Lieutenant Waverly Wray from Batesville, Mississippi: "A Baptist, each month he sent half his pay home to help build a new church. He never swore. . . . He didn't drink, smoke, or chase girls. Some troopers called him 'The Deacon,' but in an admiring rather than critical way." With his "Deep South religious convictions," Wray's worst curse was to exclaim "John Brown!"—referring to the abolitionist whose actions helped spark the Civil War. Wray single-handedly killed eight German officers by sneaking up on them "like the deer stalker he was," Ambrose writes. "You don't get more than one Wray to a division, or even to an army." There was only one like him in World War I, Ambrose reports—"also a Southern boy."

The love of home that motivated Confederate soldiers would be transmuted generations later into a virulent patriotism in the South. James Webb, former secretary of the navy, describes Southern soldiers in his military novels whispering "and for the South" under their breath when saying their duty to their country (as if Southerners need to be reminded not

to commit treason). They die at war not for Old Glory, "but for this ves-
tige of lost hope called the South." When General George Pickett rallied
his men before their history-making charge at Gettysburg, all he had to
say was "Don't forget today that you are from old Virginia."

The majority of military bases in the continental United States are
named after Confederate officers—Fort Bragg, Fort Benning, Fort Hood,
Fort Polk, Fort Rucker. Are you beginning to see the pattern? Or consider
this: When was the last time you heard a GI being interviewed on TV
who didn't have a Southern accent? These are the guys who are in the military when there isn't even a war. It is career military people—largely
Southerners—who are left with the job of drafting fresh-faced kids from
civilian life and whipping them into shape when it's time to go to war.
Southerners are truly America's warrior class.

This is a shared cultural ethic among all Southerners, not just the
"Sons of the Confederacy." And there are, incidentally, black members of
"Sons of the Confederacy." In February 2003, just a few months before the
Democrats were working themselves into a lather over Dean's remark
about the Confederate flag, a Confederate funeral was held for Richard Quarls, whose unmarked grave had recently been unearthed. The
memorial service was organized by the Sons of Confederate Veterans and
the United Daughters of the Confederacy. Though Quarls had died in
1925, the service was packed with about 150 people, including Quarls's
descendants, community leaders, Civil War reenactors, and Confederate
daughters. They sang "Dixie." Quarls's great-granddaughter told the
newspapers, "He was a proud man and would have been honored to
see this." The honored man was a former slave who had fought for the
Confederacy.

The disproportionate number of blacks in the military is a reflection of
the disproportionate number of Southerners in the military. Five black
Marines were posthumously awarded the Medal of Honor for their service in Vietnam. In mind-boggling acts of heroism, they actually dove on
exploding enemy grenades to protect their comrades. This is what they
were trained to do. Three of the five were from the South.

In 2001, about 30 percent of blacks in Mississippi voted to keep the
1894 state flag, which displays the Confederate flag in the upper left corner. As Larry Elder has noted, would 30 percent of Jews vote to keep a
swastika on a state flag? After touring the South, General Colin Powell

concluded that there was no impediment to a black being elected president in America, noting that he received his strongest support from white Southerners.

Slavery is among the ugliest chapters in this nation's history—the ugliest after abortion, which Democrats will get around to opposing in the year 3093. But it was not unique to this country and it was not unique to the South. The American flag could more plausibly be said to symbolize slavery than can the Confederate flag. Slavery was legal under the Stars and Stripes for more than seventy years—far longer than any Confederate flag ever flew. The Ku Klux Klan did not begin using the Confederate flag until the fifties. Before that, they flew the Stars and Stripes. White-supremacist nuts living in their mothers' basements don't have a copyright to the Confederate battle flag any more than they own the copyright for the Chevy pickup truck or the Christian cross—another symbol appropriated by the Klan.

And why does native African kinte cloth get a free pass? It is a historical fact that American slaves were purchased from their slave masters in Africa, where slavery exists in some parts to this day. Indeed, slavery is the only African institution America has ever adopted. But while some Americans express pride in their slave-trading ancestors by calling themselves "African-Americans" and donning African garb, pride in Confederate ancestors is deemed a hate crime. Perhaps, in a bid for the Catholic vote, Democrats could demand that those Masonic symbols be removed from the Great Seal of the United States. And how about the American eagle? The eagle is a bird of prey and hence offensive to rodents, a key Democrat constituency.

It is a vicious slander against the South to claim the Confederate battle flag represents admiration for slavery. It is pride in the South—having nothing to do with race—and its honorable military history that the Confederate battle flag represents, values that exist independently of the institution of slavery. Anyone who has ever met a Texan has an inkling of what Southern pride is about. Ever heard of a bar fight starting because somebody said something derogatory about the North? The battle flag symbolizes an ethic and honor that belongs to all the sons of the South.

Liberals love to cluck their tongues at such admiration for militaristic values. (The only time liberals pretend to like the military is when they claim to love soldiers so much they don't want them to get hurt fighting a war.) We do well to remember that it was disproportionately Southerners—some wearing Confederate battle flags under their uniforms—who formed the backbone of the military that threw back tyrants from Adolf Hitler to Saddam Hussein. Somebody had to engage in all those insane, mind-boggling acts of heroism, and it wasn't going to be graduates of Horace Mann High School (Anthony Lewis's alma mater). It was graduates of places like the Citadel and the Virginia Military Institute.

Every year after the war was over, Civil War veterans used to return to Gettysburg to reenact the famous battle. On the 50th anniversary, as the Confederate veterans began reenacting Pickett's charge, the Northerners burst into tears and ran down the hill to embrace the Rebels, overcome with emotion at how insanely brave Pickett's charge had been. That's how much Union soldiers respected Confederate soldiers. Man for man, the Confederate army was the greatest army the world had ever seen. It is outrageous for Northern liberals and race demagogues to try to turn the Confederate battle flag into a badge of shame, in the process spitting on America's gallant warrior class. ■

9

Give Us Twenty-two Minutes, We'll Give Up the Country

———————■———————

"[People should not] believe everything they read in the newspapers."
—JAYSON BLAIR, former *New York Times* reporter extraordinaire

Four days after the *New York Times* factually identified the Drudge Report as "notoriously unreliable," the *Times* misidentified Republican Senate candidate Pete Coors in a photo as a Ku Klux Klan member who murdered a black sharecropper. (Coors spokeswoman Cinamon Watson remarked of the notoriously unreliable *Times*'s screw-up, "It could have been worse, she joked. Pete could have been identified as John Kerry.")

Less than a decade ago, more people would have read the *Times*'s unsubstantiated assertion that the Drudge Report was "notoriously unreliable" than would ever have read how actually unreliable the *New York Times* is. In December 1995, only 14 percent of Americans were on the Internet. By December 2003, two-thirds of Americans were on the Internet, 66 million on a typical day. While the old, notoriously unreliable media still act as if they are the commissars of truth for the now-dead Soviet Union, imagine what they were like when only 14 percent of Americans could get the truth online.

In 1996, *Nightline* ran a vicious smear on Pat Buchanan, then running for president, accusing him of being a racist, an anti-Semite, and generally a very bad man. Apart from vague accusations from anonymous Buchanan-haters and Pat's professional

rivals, *Nightline*'s only evidence, such as it was, connecting
Buchanan to anything anti-Semitic was the claim that his father
listened to an anti-Semitic radio broadcaster from the thirties. In
Ted Koppel's words, Buchanan's father "listened to the bigoted
and isolationist radio orator Father Coughlin, who stirred populist
passions and controversy on the eve of World War II." So if your
dad is accused of being anti-Semitic, that automatically makes you
anti-Semitic, too. (Gee, I hope this doesn't cause Mel Gibson any
problems.)

Koppel then ran quotes from Father Coughlin as if Coughlin
were Buchanan's campaign manager: "Now we risk our American-
ism and our Christianity, therefore, for the blood profits to be
gained by the internationalists." Internationalists, Koppel explained,
meant "Jews." Here's Ted's line of reasoning: The patriarch
Buchanan listened to a Jew-hating priest on the radio almost seventy years ago, so Pat must hate Jews today. If only the prosecu-
tion's burden of proof had been that easy in the O.J. Simpson case.

Except the problem was, Buchanan's father had never even
heard of Father Coughlin, much less listened to him. *Nightline* just
made it up. In fact, the closest any member of the Buchanan family has ever come to listening to an anti-Semitic radio broadcast
was the time Pat accidentally tuned into NPR. Responding to a series of calumnies in the *Nightline* broadcast in a press conference
six days later, Bay Buchanan, Pat's sister, said, "Neither Pat nor I
have ever heard my father refer to the late Father Charles Coughlin, the so-called radio priest of the 1930s," and the first time Pat
"ever heard of this fellow was when he went to New York City to
do graduate work and studied about him at that time." She continued: "Somebody tells me that my father spoke about things in my
home, and no one called to ask one of us if it's ever been done in
our home, and puts it on his television as fact."

Even other members of the press—who know how menda-
cious they are—were stunned that no one from *Nightline* had even
called to ask about the Father Coughlin story.

> QUESTION: You're saying that no one from *Nightline* ever con-
> tacted you or anyone in your family prior to that airing?
> BAY BUCHANAN: Nobody. No one. No one. That is correct.

When told *Nightline* was "standing by" its report, Bay said, "Go
ahead and stand by it, but somebody maybe should have some
ethics here, some standards, some journalistic standards. Don't

they exist anymore for Ted Koppel? He could just put anything he wants on television without even making a phone call?"

This was evidently the first time Bay had ever seen *Nightline*. No one's been so unjustifiably shocked by a lie since the last time Jimmy Carter dealt with the Soviets. In a related story, the phrase "journalistic standards" recently set a new record for "world's biggest oxymoron."

Despite all the gobbledygook about the "profession" of journalism and the absurd conceit that "journalism" is a well-honed craft one has to master over time, the only standard journalists respect is: Will this story promote the left-wing agenda? Like all good propagandists, the major media mix truth with lies and then make a big show of correcting trivial errors while doggedly refusing to issue corrections for the real whoppers. They stare into a camera and claim that they are "professional enough to keep their reporting evenhanded" and then hide behind startled laughter when anyone calls them on it.

After the *New York Times* star reporter Jayson Blair was exposed as making up facts for his articles, the paper conducted an internal investigation to figure out how inaccurate reporting could have ended up in the august pages of the *Times*. (During his first job interview at the *Times* Blair said, "I still believe in a place called Hope," which should have been a huge red flag for somebody.) Apart from the catchall "a failure of communication" and a reminder that the black kid was sneaky, the *Times*'s main excuse for Blair's reporting was their claim that there had been "few complaints from the subjects" of Blair's articles. By "few complaints," apparently what the *Times* means is "There were lots of complaints about facially implausible facts reported in Blair's articles, but the editors decided not to issue any corrections."

In one of the *Times*'s major front-page articles on the Virginia/ D.C. sniper investigation in October 2002, Blair reported that sniper John Muhammad had been on the verge of confessing to local officials—when the U.S. Attorney's office broke off the interrogation. It was a stunning revelation, showing an appalling disregard for justice by overeager officials in the Bush administration. Curiously, no other news organization had anything on this major story. The Associated Press and others picked up the *Times*'s story and soon the botched "confession" was being repeated in news outlets across the country, based solely on the fact that it had appeared in the pages of the *New York Times*. *Slate* magazine referred to the "Abbott-and-Costello competition" between state and federal law enforcement, stating, "Already, investigators have complained that [the U.S. Attorney's] rush to file federal charges against Muhammad and Malvo cost them a possible confession." The *Rocky Mountain News* proclaimed, "Let the States Prosecute the Sniper," saying, "The overly eager actions of a U.S. attorney might have cost investigators a chance of obtaining a confession from John Muhammad."

Meanwhile, the subject of the story, U.S. Attorney Thomas M. DiBiagio, was screaming from the rooftops that the story was patent nonsense. He issued a statement saying, "The allegations in the *New York Times* article today are false." Muhammad had not been about to confess, and in fact, DiBiagio said, there was "no indication throughout the day that either of the individuals were yielding any useful information." FBI Agent Gary Bald denied the *Times*'s claim that federal officials were acting on orders from the White House and the Department of Justice. Numerous other unnamed government officials also contradicted the *Times*'s account.

Not only were the subjects of the article publicly denying Blair's article, legal commentators were remarking on the sheer implausibility of the *Times*'s account. On CNN, Joe DiGenova called the *Times*'s story "hokum," saying that "if there had been a confession about to occur, they never would have moved that suspect." Roy Black said, "I also don't believe anybody would interrupt in a confession going on."

So here was a case where there were lots of public complaints from the subject of Blair's article, scores of on- and off-the-record denials, in addition to widespread skepticism from legal commentators. In response, the *Times* concluded . . . Blair's account was accurate. A correction to the story of how federal officials botched sniper John Muhammad's confession would not run until May 2003—more than six months after the story had run and only when the *Times* was engulfed in the Jayson Blair scandal. Even then, the *Times* issued a halfhearted correction, claiming that Blair's story was "plainly accurate in its central point." Evidently, the "central point" was not the point considered "central" at the time and which was repeated in newspapers across the country, to wit: that federal officials had broken off John Muhammad's interrogation as he was about to confess. The "central point," according to the *Times*'s correction, was simply that "local and federal authorities were feuding over custody of the sniper suspects." That is not a story that, under ordinary circumstances, would make the front page.

The *Times* is caught lying, so they lie to explain why they were lying: There were "few complaints from the subjects" of Blair's articles. This is like recommending a surgeon by saying, "Why, he hasn't killed anyone in almost a week!" But even that wasn't true. It wasn't even plausible. The *Times* routinely ignores all complaints. The only reason Blair was exposed is that another member of the Fourth Estate, the *San Antonio Express-News,* caught Blair plagiarizing its stories. (On May 1, Jayson Blair submitted his letter of resignation, which began with the words "To be, or not to be" and ended with the words "You won't have Jayson Blair to kick around anymore.") Indeed, just a few months after the Jayson Blair scandal broke, the *Times* was again ignoring angry denials from the people quoted in articles. They're like cockroaches, these liberals. You stomp on them, they lie still for a few minutes, and then they start moving again.

A *Times* article by Charlie LeDuff quoted Lieutenant Commander Mike Beidler as he headed off to Iraq commenting on the antiwar protests: "It's war, Commander Beidler said, and the nation is fat. 'No one is screaming for battery-powered cars,' he added." The *Times* reporter then quoted Beidler's wife "as she patted down [her husband's] collar" saying, "'I'm just numb, I'll cry myself to sleep, I'm sure.'" Amazingly, LeDuff had gotten the perfect quote for an article titled "As an American Armada Leaves San Diego, Tears Are the Rule of the Day." This is what's known among purveyors of the craft of journalism as a "big whopper."

When Beidler saw the article—like U.S. Attorney DiBiagio—he immediately wrote to the *Times* strenuously denying virtually every aspect of LeDuff's account. His alleged comments about national fatness and battery-powered cars, he said, "were completely fabricated by Mr. LeDuff." According to Beidler, he simply said, "Protesters have a right to protest, and our job is to defend those rights. But in protesting, they shouldn't protest blindly; instead, they should provide reasonable solutions to the problem"—all of which sounds suspiciously unlike "the nation is fat." Beidler denied that his wife had said she would cry herself to sleep and even pointed out that his wife did not "pat down my collar either, which was impossible for her to accomplish with my civilian shirt hidden under my jacket and a duffel bag hanging on my shoulder closest to her."

After "thoroughly" looking into Beidler's complaint, senior editor Bill Borders wrote back to Beidler, saying Mr. LeDuff "thinks that he accurately represented his interview with you and your wife, and therefore so do I." Thus, a man in New York who had never met the Beidlers described for them a conversation they recently had with a reporter in San Diego. Borders then returned to his primary task of polishing up the new *Times* slogan, "All the News That's Fit to Print, and Then Some!" No correction ever ran. If not for the Internet, no one would know the *Times* simply invented the Beidlers' quotes.

The principal goal of *Times* reporters is to prevent an articulate opposition statement to escape into the world. As long as you can't get them to admit they're lying, they say you can't prove they're lying. They respond with such mystification to corrections of their lies, it is legitimate to ask: How intelligent are the people reporting the news, these constitutionally protected guardians of the truth?

☞ Great Gray Lady in Spat with Saloon Hussy

NOVEMBER 20, 2002

I did not realize how devastating the midterm elections were to liberals until seeing the Great Gray Lady reduced to starting a catfight with Fox News Channel. It has come to this. The *New York Times* was in high dudgeon this week upon discovering that Fox News chairman Roger Ailes sent a letter to the Bush White House nine days after September 11. As the corpses of thousands of his fellow Americans lay in smoldering heaps, Ailes evidently recommended getting rough with the terrorists. One imagines Karl Rove running down the hallway to the president's office waving Ailes's letter and shouting "Mr. President! Mr. President! I have the memo! We've got to fight back!"

I assume it's superfluous to mention that there is nothing illegal about Ailes giving advice to the president—though admittedly, I have not consulted the "living Constitution" in the past twenty-four hours to see if a new penumbra specifically about Fox News has sprouted. But the *Times* was a monument of self-righteous indignation, because hard-news men are supposed to stay neutral between America and terrorists.

Of course, the *Times* hasn't been reticent in giving the president advice on the war. (Surrender now!) Other great moments in journalistic neutrality include NPR's Nina Totenberg leaking information about Anita Hill that she got from Senator Howard Metzenbaum's staff, and the *Washington Post*'s Ben Bradlee yukking it up on the phone with President Kennedy and later cheering when President Nixon resigned. So it's interesting that the *Times* viewed Ailes's letter as an affront to objective journalism.

But this was more than the media's usual insane point that they—the least impartial industry in America—must maintain absolute neutrality between George Bush and the terrorists. The *Times* went further to imply that by supporting his own country in the war on terrorism, Ailes had unmistakably marked himself as a "partisan conservative."

If Ailes had written a letter recommending a tax hike, a new hate-crimes law, or going easy on the terrorists, I assume the *Times* would not have accused Ailes of showing a conservative bias. Instead, he had recommended the harshest measures possible against the terrorists. As far as the *Times* was concerned, this was the smoking gun of partisanship. The paper railed that Ailes purports to be an "unbiased journalist, not a conservative spokesman." Fox News is "the self-proclaimed fair and balanced news channel." But now the *Times* had caught him red-handed, pursuing "an undisguised ideological agenda." Ailes is secretly rooting for America!

At least we finally have it from the horse's own mouth. The *Times* openly admits that the "conservative" position—but not the liberal position—is to take America's side against the terrorists. Why do they get so snippy when I say that? The *Times* was a whirligig of pointless insinuations—"secretly gave advice to," "back-channel message," "shocking," "confirmed yesterday," and "revelations." (Eager *Times* readers will have to wait another day for any "revelations" about Pinch Sulzberger's SAT scores.) Belittling Fox News is so pleasurable for the *Times* that it didn't occur to them that they had given up the ghost on their faux patriotism. It is simply taken for granted that liberals root against their own country. As the *Times* said of Ailes's letter, it "was less shocking than it was liberating—a little like the moment in 1985 when an ailing Rock Hudson finally explained that he had AIDS." Same back at you! We always knew you were traitors, and now you've admitted it.

Fox News should agree to admit it is conservative if all other media outlets will admit they are liberal. Fox is manifestly closer to the center than the others. Referring here to the *Times's* definition of "conservative" (harsh with the terrorists) and "liberal" (soft on the terrorists), I believe the public is with Fox News. We took a pretty conclusive poll on that a couple of weeks ago. The people, in their infinite wisdom, have spoken. ■

☞ How a White Male from Alabama Learned the Craft of Journalism from a Young Reporter Named Jayson Blair

MAY 14, 2003

The *New York Times* is to be commended for ferreting out Jayson Blair, the reporter recently discovered to be making up facts, plagiarizing other news organizations, and lying about nonexistent trips and interviews. A newspaper that employs Maureen Dowd can't have had an easy time settling on Blair as the scapegoat. Blair's record of inaccuracies, lies, and distortions made him a candidate for either immediate dismissal or his own regular column on the op-ed page.

The editors have set up a special e-mail address for readers to report falsehoods they discover in Jayson Blair articles. Okay, but how about setting up one for Paul Krugman? The *Times* ought to seize the moment and claim all those front-page articles predicting a "quagmire" in Iraq were also written by Blair.

The *Times* has now willingly abandoned its mantle as the "newspaper of record." It was already up against the Internet and LexisNexis as a research tool. But with Jayson Blair it has managed to leapfrog beyond mere technological obsolescence. All the *Times* had left was its reputation for accuracy. As this episode shows, the *Times* is not even attempting to preserve a reliable record of events. Instead of being a record of history, the *Times* is merely a record of what liberals would like history to be: *The Pentagon in Crisis! A Quagmire in Iraq! Global Warming Is Melting the North Pole! Protests Roil the Augusta National Golf Club!* Publisher Arthur "Pinch" Sulzberger has turned the paper into a sort of bulletin board for Manhattan liberals.

In the Soviet-style reporting preferred at the *Times*, its self-investigation of the Blair scandal included copious denials that race had anything to do with it:

- "Mr. Boyd [managing editor] said last week that the decision to advance Mr. Blair had not been based on race."
- "Mr. Blair's *Times* supervisors . . . emphasize that he earned an internship at *The Times* because of glowing recommendations and a remarkable work history, not because he is black."

Did Jayson Blair write the article on the investigation of Jayson Blair?

The very next sentence notes that the *Times* offered Blair "a slot in an internship program that was then being used in large part to help the paper diversify its newsroom." If the *Times* "diversity" program did not consider Blair's race, then it wasn't much of a diversity program, now was it? This is like job advertisements that proclaim, "Equal Opportunity, Affirmative Action Employer." Well, which is it?

In one of several feverish editorials supporting the University of Michigan's race-based admissions program, the *Times* denounced the Bush administration for imagining "that diversity can be achieved without explicitly taking race into account." Any diversity program that failed to do so, the *Times* lectured, was "necessarily flawed." But then it gets caught publishing Jayson Blair and the *Times* demurely insists that its own affirmative-action program scrupulously ignored race. Oh, okay.

The *Times* not only expressly took race into account but also put Blair's race above everything—accuracy, credibility, and the paper's reputation. It hired a kid barely out of college. In fact, it turns out Blair was not yet out of college. He had no professional journalistic experience, except at the *Times*. He screwed up over and over again, and the paper had to print over fifty corrections to articles he'd written.

Despite all this, Blair was repeatedly published on the front page, promoted, and sent love notes from the editor in chief, Howell Raines. Ignoring the warnings of a few intrepid whistle-blowers, top management kept assigning Blair to bigger stories in new departments without alerting the editors to Blair's history, because—as Raines said—it would "stigmatize" him. (Speaking of stigmas, after this scandal, does the demand for black heart surgeons go up or down?) Raines jettisoned the *Times*'s famous slogan, preferring the slogan "The *New York Times*: Now With Even More Black People!"

Publisher Sulzberger summed up the episode with these words: "The person who did this is Jayson Blair. Let's not begin to demonize our exec-

utives." To put that in plain English: Even though we hired him, we promoted him, and we covered up for him, and even though it's our name on
the masthead, we assume absolutely no responsibility for any of this whatsoever. If mismanagement at Enron had been this clear-cut, the *Times*
would be demanding the death penalty for Ken Lay. Indeed, taking a page
from all corporate chieftans caught in scandals, the *Times* insists that the
organization is fine; it was just one bad apple. As I recall, the *Times* editorial page did not accept that explanation when Merrill Lynch said it about
Henry Blodget.

Raines's behavior is far worse than the corporate chieftains'. He clearly
bears the most responsibility for this fiasco, but when disaster strikes ... he
blames the black kid! So far, Raines's response has been basically to say,
"You try to help these people ..." (Raines's other great contribution to race
relations was his unintentionally comical magazine piece about his black
maid, "Grady's Gift.") It is absolutely Clintonian. Just as Clinton blamed
"THAT WOMAN" and said anyone who blamed him was probably a Christian fundamentalist and a menace to a woman's right to choose, Raines is
setting up the defense that his detractors must be bigots opposed to affirmative action. You posture, posture, champion this righteous cause and
that righteous cause, abuse your responsibility—and when you get in
trouble, you blame "THAT WOMAN." ("The b—— set me up.")

Put aside whether race should be used as a hiring criterion. Even
people who support affirmative action don't have to support Raines's approach of refusing to hold blacks responsible for anything, ever—including fake reporting. What Raines did to Blair was cruel. Think of it in a
nonracial context: Suppose the owner of a big company sends his kid to
learn the business and tells low-level managers to treat him just as they
would treat anyone else. The managers try to curry favor with the boss by
reporting that his son is doing great and is a natural genius for this business. So the kid keeps getting praised and promoted, until one day he is
actually put in charge of something he has no ability to run. That is cruel.
And it's the story of Pinch Sulzberger, isn't it? ■

☞ The Weather's Great, Wish I Were Here

MAY 21, 2003

RIO DE JANEIRO—Actually I'm in Brooklyn right now, but I'm counting on my employer to follow the strict fact-checking methods in operation at the *New York Times*. Under the *Times*'s scrupulous reporting procedures, reporter Jayson Blair kept turning in reports with datelines from places like West Virginia and Maryland—while submitting expense receipts for the same time period from Joe's Bar in Brooklyn. You can't really blame him. He couldn't very well turn in articles with the dateline "My Mom's House."

In the current *Newsweek* magazine, Seth Mnookin reports that Blair was forced to resign from the student newspaper at the University of Maryland, the *Diamondback,* for precisely the same misconduct he engaged in at the *Times*—phony reporting, plagiarism, irresponsibility, and fantastic lies. Once known as "the Newspaper of Record," the *Times* is now trying out the motto "Almost as Accurate as the Maryland *Diamondback*."

Editor Howell Raines ignored Blair's repeated, brazen mendacity. He ignored his editors' urgent demands that Blair be fired. He ignored press conferences in which public officials remarked that Blair's stories were full of lies. Raines ignored it all—until finally one day, another newspaper caught Blair plagiarizing one of its stories and blew the whistle on the *Times*. And then Raines claimed to be shocked to discover that Blair was engaging in "a pathological pattern of misrepresentation, fabricating and deceiving." After all, the *Times* had issued Blair a series of warnings. (One sternly worded memo urged Blair to be "more black.")

This episode is considered a low point in the paper's 152-year history. Not as low as when it endorsed Jimmy Carter, but still pretty low. As has now been widely reported, publisher Arthur Pinch Sulzberger responded to the meltdown at the *Times* by bringing a stuffed toy moose to an internal meeting with reporters to discuss the burgeoning scandal last week.

Also at the meeting, Raines finally admitted the blindingly obvious fact that he engaged in egregious mismanagement because Blair was black. Raines said, "Does that mean I personally favored Jayson? Not consciously, but you have a right to ask if I as a white man from Alabama with those convictions gave him one chance too many by not stopping his appointment to the sniper team. When I look into my heart for the truth of that, the answer is yes." So for being a warmhearted white liberal, he wants a pat on the head (much as his black maid, Grady, used to give him).

Raines said he would not resign, and Pinch said he would not accept Raines's resignation if offered. Which brings us to Pinch.

While we are having a debate about diversity and race-based policies, can't we all agree that no one should be defending nepotism? In one of 4 billion columns attacking President Bush this year, *Times* columnist Maureen Dowd accused him of getting into Yale only because he was a legacy. She sneered at the argument of White House aides that Bush also earned a degree from Harvard Business School, despite there being no Bush relatives who went to Harvard. Dowd responded, "They seemed genuinely surprised when told that Harvard would certainly have recognized the surname and wagered on the future success of the person with it."

I believe Sulzberger is a pretty well-known name, too. The Sulzberger-Ochs dynasty has controlled the most powerful newspaper in the world for the last century. A college admissions committee would not have to wager on young Pinch's future success. It was his birthright to run the *New York Times* someday. No messy elections could stand in his way. And yet it appears that Harvard managed to turn him down. He was a legacy at Columbia University, but they didn't want him either. Maureen might want to stay mum on the subject of dumb rich kids, at least as long as her boss is Pinch Sulzberger.

Like Raines, Pinch blithely washed his hands of the stunning mismanagement at the *Times*. Commenting through his spokesman, a small stuffed moose, Pinch made the Churchillian pronouncement "We didn't do this right. We regret that deeply. We feel it deeply. It sucks." Uday Hussein had more right to be in charge of Iraq's Olympic committee than Pinch Sulzberger does to be running a newspaper.

Under the race-based admissions at the University of Michigan, applicants are given four points for being a legacy and twenty points for being black. Does anyone think Pinch got only four points to be publisher of the *Times*? Couldn't the Sulzberger family just buy him a boat? ■

☞ Here's a Traitor!

SEPTEMBER 17, 2003

During my recent book tour, I resisted the persistent, illiterate request that I name traitors. With a great deal of charity—and suspension of disbelief—I was willing to concede that many liberals were merely fatuous idiots. (In addition, I was loath to name names for fear that liberals would start jumping out of windows.) But after the *Times*'s despicable editorial on the two-year anniversary of the 9/11 terrorist attack, I am prepared— just this once—to name a traitor: Pinch Sulzberger, publisher of the *New York Times*.

To be sure, if any liberal could legitimately use the stupid defense, it is the one Sulzberger who apparently couldn't get into Columbia University. At a minimum, Columbia has four hundred faculty members who start each day by thinking about how to get their kooky ideas onto the *Times*'s op-ed page. For an heir to the *Times* not to attend Columbia, those must have been some low SAT scores.

But the clincher was an editorial on the two-year anniversary of the September 11 attack in which the *Times* endorsed the principle of moral equivalence between the United States and the 9/11 terrorists. In the *Times*'s meandering, mind-numbing prose, it explained that the terrorists might have slaughtered thousands of Americans in a bloody attack on U.S. soil—but the United States has had imperialistic depredations of its own!

By not opposing a military coup by the great Augusto Pinochet against a Chilean Marxist, Salvador Allende, the *Times* implied, the United States was party to a terrorist act similar to the 9/11 attack on America. This is how the *Times* describes Pinochet's 1973 coup: "A building—a symbol of the nation—collapsed in flames in an act of terror that would lead to the deaths of 3,000 people. It was Sept. 11."

Allende was an avowed Marxist, who, like Clinton, got into office on a plurality vote. He instantly hosted a months-long visit from Castro, allowing Castro to distribute arms to Chilean leftists. He began destroying Chile's economy at a pace that makes California governor Gray Davis look like a piker. No less an authority than Chou En-lai warned Allende that he was pursuing a program that was too extreme for his region. When

General Pinochet staged his coup against a Marxist strongman, the United States did not stop him—as if Latin American generals were incapable of doing coups on their own. And—I quote—"It was Sept. 11." Parsed to its essentials, the *Times*'s position is: We deserved it.

This from a paper that has become America's leading spokesman for the deposed Baathist regime in Iraq. Interestingly, we started to lose this war only after the embedded reporters pulled out. Back when we got the news directly from Iraq, it was all victory and optimism. Now that the news is filtered through the mainstream media here in America, all we hear is death and destruction and quagmire. See if you can detect a pattern in two weeks of news at the *Treason Times:*

- "Since the beginning of the Iraq war, 292 soldiers have been killed in Iraq and Kuwait, including **152 SINCE PRESIDENT BUSH DECLARED ON MAY 1 THAT MAJOR AMERICAN COMBAT OPERATIONS HAD ENDED.**" (September 13, 2003)
- "So far, 290 American troops have died in Iraq or Kuwait since the beginning of the Iraq war, including **150 SINCE PRESIDENT BUSH DECLARED ON MAY 1 THAT MAJOR AMERICAN COMBAT OPERATIONS HAD ENDED.**" (September 12, 2003)
- "It was impossible to watch Mr. Bush's somber speech without remembering that **FOUR MONTHS AGO, WHEN THE PRESIDENT MADE HIS 'TOP GUN' LANDING ON AN AIRCRAFT CARRIER AND DECLARED AN END TO 'MAJOR COMBAT OPERATIONS,'** the White House was worried about giving the world the impression that Americans were gloating." (September 8, 2003)
- "The speech was Mr. Bush's first extended address about Iraq **SINCE HE DECLARED AN END TO MAJOR COMBAT OPERATIONS** in a May 1 speech." (September 8, 2003)
- "When President Bush **DECLARED AN OFFICIAL END TO MAJOR HOSTILITIES IN IRAQ** in May, Reuters moved Dana to Baghdad to give him a safer assignment." (September 7, 2003)
- "**SINCE PRESIDENT BUSH DECLARED THE END OF MAJOR COMBAT OPERATIONS IN IRAQ,** hundreds of violent and disruptive attacks have been waged by an array of forces." (September 7, 2003)
- "The address will come . . . four months after Mr. Bush's last nationally televised prime-time speech on Iraq, from the deck of

the carrier *Abraham Lincoln,* WHERE HE DECLARED THAT 'MAJOR COMBAT OPERATIONS' HAD ENDED." (September 6, 2003)

- "Eleven British soldiers have been killed SINCE PRESIDENT BUSH DECLARED AN END TO MAJOR COMBAT ON MAY 1." (September 5, 2003)
- "Not long AFTER PRESIDENT BUSH DECLARED AN END TO THE MAJOR FIGHTING IN IRAQ, Jessica Porter hatched an ambitious plan: She would make a quilt for every family of an American soldier who had died in the war." (September 3, 2003)
- "At least 64 American troops have now died from hostile attacks SINCE PRESIDENT BUSH DECLARED THE END TO MAJOR COMBAT OPERATIONS IN IRAQ ON MAY 1." (August 28, 2003)
- "More American troops have now died SINCE PRESIDENT BUSH DECLARED AN END TO MAJOR COMBAT ON MAY 1 THAN WERE KILLED FIGHTING THE WAR IN IRAQ." (August 27, 2003)

Hey—does anyone know when Bush declared major combat operations had ended? Because I think there may have been one article in the sports section of the *Times* last week that didn't mention it. The *Times* is even taking shots at the war in the Arts section, stating authoritatively in a recent movie review, "And with the war in Iraq threatening to turn into a Vietnam-like quagmire . . ." (How about getting some decent, impartial reporters embedded at the *Times*?)

Apparently, the *Times*'s stylebook now requires all reports of violence anywhere within a thousand miles of Iraq to be dated from Bush's speech declaring an end to "major combat" operations. How about dating everything from the day Pinch Sulzberger got his SAT scores back and realized he wasn't going to Columbia University?

I gather the *Times* is trying to convey something by the infernal references to Bush's speech declaring an end to major combat in Iraq—but what? That we haven't turned a savage fascist dictatorship into a peace-loving democracy overnight? Iraq is considerably better off than Chile was under Salvador Allende—the *Times*'s second-favorite world leader after Saddam Hussein. ∎

☞ CBS Could Show Augusta How to Really Discriminate

DECEMBER 11, 2002

The *New York Times* is in such a lather about the Augusta National Golf Club's ban on women members, it has briefly interrupted news coverage of *The Sopranos* to write about it. The outrage over Augusta is not a naturally occurring phenomenon that is simply being reported by the media. It's a synthetic scandal cooked up in the *New York Times*'s PC laboratory. One of the best female golfers in the world, Nancy Lopez of the World Golf Hall of Fame, has said she has no problem with Augusta's policy. But scribblers at the *Times* have flogged Augusta so relentlessly, it almost seems as if the nation is about to go to war over a golf club's "no girls" policy.

Anyone who compares the plight of women to the plight of blacks is a racist. Only the bizarre antisexual psychology of liberals could fail to grasp the insanity of treating gender like race. Men and women are ineluctably bound to one another. They are also utterly different. Phyllis Schlafly's point that no one wants to end the tradition of separate bathrooms for men and women is so fundamentally true that there is nothing else to be said. (Except in France, where the practice is common.)

But it is really more than the public should have to bear to listen to the last bulwark of legal discrimination in America harping about the membership policies of a private club. The media openly discriminate against half of America: Republicans. There is not a single person in any half-important job in the mainstream media who might have voted for Ronald Reagan. That can't be easy. There aren't that many people in the country who didn't vote for Reagan. In 1984, he won the largest electoral landslide in history.

Fittingly, the only member to resign in protest from Augusta so far is Thomas Wyman, the former chairman of CBS News—specializing in intolerance for half a century. Wyman was never disturbed by the blatant discrimination at CBS. He proudly presided over a club where membership ran the gamut from Walter Cronkite to Dan Rather. Indeed, CBS was so discriminatory and hateful toward Republicans there's even a book about it: *Bias*, by former CBS star reporter Bernard Goldberg.

While privileged enforcers of the ideological Jim Crow system like Wyman received million-dollar bonuses, talented young journalists were excluded from Wyman's elite media club. Aspiring newsmen who happened to be Republicans had to find work elsewhere or get used to peanut butter for dinner and fourth-floor walk-ups. Dreams were dashed and careers ended. Hearing Wyman complain about discrimination at a golf club would be like hearing Hugh Hefner complain about bawdy language on TV sitcoms.

Inasmuch as he hails from the most discriminatory industry in the nation, if Wyman hadn't resigned in a self-righteous snit, he probably could have taught Augusta a few tricks of the trade. Frankly, Augusta has been going about this in entirely the wrong way.

Point One: Simply deny that Augusta excludes women. Try something like: "Augusta is not exclusive. It's humanitarian." This is how CBS's Walter Cronkite explained the employment of only liberals in the mainstream media: It's not "liberal, it's humanitarian." Or how about "I have always believed that if you get women out of the way, then decent, reasonable golfers would figure out a way to run a golf club." Don Hewitt, executive producer of CBS's *60 Minutes* said, " I have always believed that if you get the NRA out of the way, decent, reasonable Americans would figure out a way to respect the Second Amendment."

Point Two: Claim that *both* men and women feel they are excluded from Augusta. Cite ludicrous "studies" proving it. As Lesley Stahl said of the liberal media, "Everybody complains about us, right wing, left wing, Democrats, Republicans. They all pound on us. They all think we're unfair to them." She said "this big huge study" had concluded that "the mainline media is sucked in by the right-wing conspiratorialists."

Point Three: While openly excluding women, make a big ruckus about any discrimination based on minor, inconsequential differences among men. Commission studies to determine if tall men are getting as much tee time as short men. The glossy magazines won't allow a single Republican to write for them. But they are consumed with grief that not enough models of color have appeared on their covers.

Point Four: Patronizingly instruct women to stop whining and go start their own golf club. Then if they do, attack it. This is what media elites told conservatives for years. We finally got Fox News, and now they savagely denounce it.

This is how an entire industry serving the public interest explains its own continuous and ongoing discrimination against half the country. Poor little Augusta just wants to exclude girls from a golf club. ∎

☞ Give Us Twenty-two Minutes, We'll Give Up the Country

FEBRUARY 19, 2003

Rich liberals are planning to fund a talk-radio network because they be-lieve—as the *New York Times* put it—they have been "overshadowed in the political propaganda wars by conservative radio and television person-alities." If liberals think they are losing elections because of conservative bias in the media, they might as well give up right now. Their first prob-lem is going to be finding liberals who can work on their little project, since they're all already employed at the networks.

But liberals insist they need a radio network "to counterbalance the conservative tenor of radio programs like *The Rush Limbaugh Show*." Rush has been driving them crazy for years. In 1994, CNN dedicated an entire program to figuring out how the "mainstream media" could combat Rush Limbaugh, asking the question "Does Rush Limbaugh deserve all this at-tention, and what should the mainstream media be doing about it?" In 1996, the Democratic National Committee went so far as to establish a speakers' bureau/talk-radio initiative to strike back at conservative talk radio by monitoring talk radio and teaching liberals "radio skills."

Among the "alternatives to Rush" that liberals have tried over the years are: former New York governor Mario Cuomo, Harvard law professor Alan Dershowitz, former Connecticut governor Lowell Weicker, former California governor Jerry Brown, former U.S. senator (and *Monkey Busi-ness* skipper) Gary Hart, and former Virginia governor Doug Wilder. Lib-erals keep serving up their own dreary radio hosts, and the public keeps turning the dial back to Rush Limbaugh.

To be sure, conservative radio talk-show hosts have a built-in audience unavailable to liberals: people driving cars to some sort of job. But it should not be surprising that when given a choice, people don't want lib-eral hectoring being piped into their homes and cars. It would be like being Winston Smith in George Orwell's *1984*, forced to listen to Big

Brother twenty-four hours a day. Indeed, it's difficult to imagine a world in which people voluntarily choose to listen to liberals. There is no evidence that it has ever happened.

For years, liberals would pass off mediocrities as broadcasting geniuses for surviving the brutal competition of . . . a monopoly. In the precable era, Phil Donahue was promiscuously called a "legend," a "star," the "daytime guru," "daytime television's biggest star"—even a "major star." In 1993, Donahue was inducted into the Academy of Television Arts & Sciences' Hall of Fame. His millions of viewers were touted as proof of his massive talent.

Of course, back when there were only three TV stations, it was a little difficult to tell whether "major stars" like Donahue had any talent to attract viewers. Did people actually enjoy watching a man with the IQ of a bright chimpanzee who passed himself off as Bertrand Russell, or did they just want to watch something on TV?

Now we have the answer!

In a controlled scientific experiment, Donahue was given his own TV show on MSNBC in the new competitive environment of cable TV. *That Boy's* ratings were the lowest in prime-time TV for any news program. In fact, his ratings were so low, Nielsen could barely detect them. If only MSNBC could go back and give shows to all the other pompous liberal blowhards once forced on the public, like Edward R. Murrow and Walter Cronkite, we could see how they would have fared with a little competition. My hunch is Nielsen would not have been able to *See It Now*.

Liberal speakers lose in all competitive environments; they win only by cheating or by force. One of many failed "alternatives" to Rush, Jim Hightower recommended that liberals make "stronger efforts to insist that their voices be heard." Conservatives, he said, "do this all the time." They "hammer the networks and the owners to be heard." And that's how we ousted Katie Couric and Dan Rather from the airwaves and ended up with a solid lineup of authentic Americans on ABC, NBC, and CBS. Oh, no wait. That didn't happen.

One thing about liberals is they're pesky devils. They'll never quit. And now they are back again looking for the next "liberal alternative" to Rush. They have the money, the business consultants, the radio talent. Now all they need are ideas! Ah, there's the rub.

The paradox of liberal talk radio is that if liberals cared about ideas or knew any facts, they would cease being liberals. Liberalism thrives on ignorance. Even the audience for the Left's government-supported radio network, National Public Radio, has more conservative listeners than liberal listeners. (As Mickey Kaus said, "No wonder conservatives are so pissed off.") According to a Pew Research Center study released in the summer of 2002, conservatives consume far more news than liberals—including listening to NPR and watching PBS more than liberals. Liberals get their news from Lifetime: TV for Women, NBC's *The West Wing,* and 4 billion *Law & Order* episodes in which the perp turns out to be a white, Christian male who recites the Second Amendment before disemboweling a poor minority child.

Liberal persuasion consists of the highbrow sneer from self-satisfied snobs ladled out for people with a 40 IQ. This is not an ideology that can withstand several hours a day of caller scrutiny where their goofball notions can be shot down by any truck driver with a cell phone. ■

☞ Journalism: Where Even the Men Are Women

JANUARY 2, 2003

I generally avoid mentioning even widely published lies about me, or I'd never have time to do the things that provoke liberals to lie about me. But inasmuch as one of the media's favorite pastimes is to invent inane quotes and attribute them to conservatives—and then refuse to run corrections—I thought we could use a few real-life examples to examine the ethics of the scribbling profession.

One apocryphal quote that has long perplexed me was the one falsely attributed to me in Salon.com by Christina Valhouli, renowned expert on "fat farms" and "squishy tummies." (See www.curve-film.com: "You don't need to be a size 2 to be a perfect 10.") What I never said, but fat-farm expert Valhouli thinks I *should* have said, is this: "Women like Pamela Harriman and Patricia Duff are basically Anna Nicole Smith from the waist down. Let's just call it for what it is. They're whores."

I don't even understand what that sentence means. Aren't all women basically the same "from the waist down"? (No wonder liberals are so insistent on sex education classes.) That quote has now been attributed to me in the *Washington Monthly,* the *Washington Post,* and hundreds of websites—all citing Salon.com. I have racked my brain to understand why a fat-farm expert and "plus size" historian would do me such a bad turn. Readers? Anyone?

One of my favorite fabricated statements was the one created for me by Andrew Grossman of the *Hollywood Reporter*. He was reporting an exchange on the *Today* show about my 9/11 column in which I said of the terrorists and their sympathizers, "We should invade their countries, kill their leaders, and convert them to Christianity." *Today* host Katie Couric asked me if I thought that was the best way to battle terrorism.

Here is my precise answer: "Well, point one and point two, by the end of the week, had become official government policy. As for converting them to Christianity, I think it might be a good idea to get them on some sort of hobby other than slaughtering infidels. I mean, perhaps that's the Peace Corps, perhaps it's working for Planned Parenthood, but I've never seen the transforming effect of anything like Christianity."

Grossman's full account of this exchange in the *Hollywood Reporter* was: "'Do you still believe that's the best way to fight terrorism?' Couric demanded. That quote was taken out of context, Coulter insisted." My parents are still waiting for the day that I formulate an argument as succinct and elegant as "That was taken out of context. Now I'll go back to eating my turkey." Even my worst enemies would not believe I was a nonparticipant in an argument about me. This is the form of stupidity I admire the most: *How should I know how to work LexisNexis?* Apart from being a college professor, there is no job in the universe easier than being a journalist. For 99.999 percent of writers, there is no heavy lifting, no physical danger, no honest day's work. Andrew Grossman has found a way to make it even easier. No research!

At the other end of the spectrum are energetic journalists who think all words spoken by Ann Coulter are one long ticker tape that can be cut up and strung together at random to produce any imaginable quote. On December 8, 1998, the topic on *Rivera Live* was how long an impeachment trial would take. Alan Dershowitz said it would take up to ten months. Geraldo Rivera said three months. Lawyer Roy Black offered the important and persuasive point that "people with a brain" wanted me to stop talking.

This is the relevant exchange about the length of the impeachment trial—which, I note, took about one week:

MS. COULTER: The idea that a Senate trial would go on and on and on is absurd. It would take about a week. . . .

PROF. DERSHOWITZ: Can you make a tape of that? Yeah, Geraldo, make a tape of that and replay that over and over again as we get into the sixth week, the tenth week, the twentieth week, the thirtieth week, the fortieth week. We'll have Ann Coulter saying, "It will take a week. It will take a week."

MS. COULTER: Well, I don't know. So far, I could be quoted back to myself many times, like on the Secret Service privilege, the attorney-client privilege, the dead man's privilege. Really, my track record is pretty good on predictions.

On another TV show the following March, about the time Hillary Clinton was first thinking about running for the Senate and her presumed opponent was Rudolph Giuliani, I said I thought Whitewater would prevent Hillary from challenging Giuliani. Giuliani got prostate cancer and decided not to run, so now we'll never know. The *Washington Monthly* reported my quotes as "I think [Whitewater]'s going to prevent the first lady from running for Senate. . . . My track record is pretty good on predictions."

They get an A for effort on that one. Little Andrew Grossman wouldn't even look up the show he was writing about. These people search the record for two different quotes, in two different places, on two different TV shows, on two different topics, months apart, reverse the order, and patch them together to try to make a monkey out of me.

I've also said "yes." How about stringing these sentences together to make me look brilliant:

Q: Will Jimmy Carter win the Nobel Peace Prize, Madonna make a movie that bombs, and North Korea develop nuclear weapons?

ANN COULTER: Yes.

I think I'm owed that.

Most journalists are so stupid, catty, lazy, and vengeful that the fact that they are also humorless is often overlooked. For an example of journalists' fine-tuned sense of humor, consider CBSNews.com's response to the first sentence of my column about the gnashing of teeth over Trent Lott's toast to Strom Thurmond on his hundredth birthday. I wrote, "I'm just glad Strom Thurmond isn't around to see this." CBSNews.com earnestly corrected me: "At last check by CBS News, the world's most famous 100-year-old was doing fine."

A *People* magazine reporter writing a profile on me in 2001 asked me if I had a boyfriend. My precise answer—typed out in an e-mail no less—was: "No. When I feel a need for intimacy, I go to an airport security checkpoint." As quoted by *People,* my answer was "No. I go to an airport security checkpoint."

But the winner of "best in show" for journalists' great sense of humor, sadly, does not involve one of my own quotes. Amid liberal squawking about William Safire's calling Hillary Clinton a "congenital liar" in his *New York Times* column, Safire claimed it was a typo and that he meant to say she was a "congenital *lawyer.*" That hotbed of liberal wit, the *Nation* magazine, indignantly responded, "Sure, Bill, we believe you. Say, that steno's name wasn't Rosemary Woods, was it?"

From their commitment to exactitude to their terrific sense of humor, all of the feminists' very best qualities now dominate the profession of journalism. Poor Jayson Blair just happened to be the one who got caught. ■

☞ I Guess You're Right: There Is No Liberal Media Bias

OCTOBER 8, 2003

Response to interview questions of Edward Nawotka of *Publishers Weekly:*

QUESTION: [Al] Franken claims that there are numerous falsehoods in your book, especially buried in the footnotes. . . . Who is ultimately responsible for the errors, you, the publisher, or both?

COULTER: I see we're off to a good start! In your interview with Al Franken, after suggesting that some readers may want Franken to run for president, you ask him hardball questions like:

- "It's got to be a little grating to see your book on the same *New York Times* best-seller list as the Ann Coulter book."
- "You fact-checked Ann Coulter's book and found a lot of inconsistencies, outright lies, and quotes that are taken out of context. Who is responsible for those kinds of errors, the author or the editors?"

- "How should booksellers deal with this?"

You ask me questions like these:

- "Who is ultimately responsible for the errors [in your book], you, the publisher, or both?"
- "What gives—was this an honest mistake or malfeasance as he suggests?"
- "Why all the name-calling?"

Apparently, Ed, it never occurred to you that Franken's allegations of errors in my book—or "outright lies" as you put it—are false.

It's interesting that the most devastating examples of my alleged "lies" keep changing. As soon as one is disproved, I'm asked to respond to another. This is behavior normally associated with tinfoil-hat conspiracy theorists. One crackpot argument after another is shot down—but the conspiracy theorists just move on to the next crackpot argument without pause or reconsideration. Certainly without apology.

So before responding to the two alleged "lies" you cite from Franken, the source of all wisdom, I shall run through a few of the alleged "lies" from Franken's book that I have already been asked to respond to—and which have now been dropped by the Coulter hysterics as they barrel ahead to the next inane charge.

Franken's very first charge against me is that I told a reporter from the Observer *that I was "friendly" with Franken, when in fact, we are not "friendly."*

Needless to say, I never claimed to be friendly with Al Franken. Inasmuch as I barely know Franken, a normal person might have looked at that and realized the reporter misunderstood me. But apparently Franken thinks he has a pretty cool name to drop—the oddest case of reverse name-dropping I've ever heard of.

I don't hear about this "lie" so much anymore.

Franken hysterically accuses me of "lying" for calling my endnotes "footnotes" in interviews on my book.

Yes, notes at the end of a book are technically "endnotes," not "footnotes." Franken will have to take his case up with the *New York Times,* the *Los Angeles Times,* and the *Washington Post* and the rest of the universe—all of which referred to my 780 endnotes as "FOOTNOTES." Also God, for inventing the concept of "colloquial speech."

I don't hear so much about this "lie" anymore.

Franken claims I complain that conservatives don't get on TV enough.

Inasmuch as I am on TV a lot, this would be a hilarious point. Too bad I never said it. My book *Slander*—which Franken seems to have gone over with a fine-tooth comb—would have been a good place to make that point if I wanted to make it. *Slander* contains an entire chapter on the media, and yet I never claim that conservatives are not on TV enough. What I say is: "Democrats in the media are editors, national correspondents, news anchors, and reporters. Republicans are 'from the right' polemicists grudgingly tolerated within the liberal behemoth."

By the way, I also say, "The distinction between opinion journalism and objective news coverage is seemingly impossible for liberals to grasp." Franken's absurd description of my point proves it.

I haven't heard so much about this "lie" anymore.

I claim Evan Thomas's father was the socialist party presidential candidate, Norman Thomas.

Franken drones on and on for a page and a half about how Norman Thomas was not Evan Thomas's father—without saying that he was Evan's grandfather. This was one of about five inconsequential errors quickly corrected in *Slander*—and cited one million times by liberals as a "LIE." Confusing "father" with "grandfather" is a mistake. Franken's deliberate implication that there was no relationship whatsoever between Norman and Evan Thomas is intentional dishonesty.

I haven't heard so much about this "lie" anymore.

I incorrectly claimed Dale Earnhardt's death was not mentioned on the front page of the New York Times the day after his death.

In my three best-selling books—making the case for a president's impeachment, accusing liberals of systematic lying and propagandizing, arguing that Joe McCarthy was a great American patriot, and detailing fifty years of treachery by the Democratic Party—this is the only vaguely substantive error the Ann Coulter hysterics have been able to produce, corrected soon after publication.

CONGRATULATIONS, LIBERALS!!!

The *Columbia Journalism Review* was crowing about this great victory over Ann Coulter a year ago. A search of "coulter" and "earnhardt" on Google turns up over a thousand hits. Now Franken dedicates another two pages in his book to it. I believe this triumph of theirs has been sufficiently revisited by now. At least I didn't miss the Ukrainian famine. See Pulitzer Prize–winning *New York Times* reporter Walter Duranty.

I don't heard so much about this "lie" anymore.

Frazier Moore, a fantasist for the Associated Press, wrote an article accusing me of using "routinely sloppy" research and "contrived" facts. Like you, the AP fantasist treats Franken as the source of all wisdom, citing one killer example from Franken:

"Here's one: On pages 265–266, Coulter blasts *New York Times* writer Thomas Friedman for opposing racial profiling in a December 2001 column. She quotes (and credits) several passages that seem to back up her complaint. But it turns out that Coulter misappropriated Friedman's words in a way that has nothing to do with racial profiling or anything else addressed in his column, as anyone who reads it will discover. His column actually drew the less-than-startling conclusion that a new age of terrorism threatens our personal safety and our free society."

This is what is known as "bicycle accident reporting." I defy anyone to explain what head-injury boy is trying to convey in his crucial, accusatory sentence: "Coulter misappropriated Friedman's words in a way that has nothing to do with racial profiling or anything else addressed in his column." Huh? The AP could throw a deck of cards out the window and wait to see who picks up the four of clubs to find someone who writes better than Frazier Moore.

But as long as I'm already breaking my rule about not responding to meritless, overwrought attacks, I'll go for broke and break my rule about not responding to gibberish. Apparently, head-injury boy here is very upset about how I characterize a Friedman column and it has something or other to do with racial profiling.

In the column at issue, titled "Fly Naked," Friedman spends six of ten paragraphs discussing airport security after 9/11 and concludes that flying naked is the only solution, because, inter alia, "It's much more civilized than racial profiling." I wrote, "*New York Times* columnist Thomas Friedman sniffed that racial profiling was not 'civilized.'" I'm really trying to grasp the lie in that statement, but I don't see it.

Incidentally, contrary to head-injury boy's characterization, only four paragraphs at the end of the Friedman column discuss "personal safety and our free society"—as anyone who reads it will discover. I salute the AP's unorthodox affirmative-action program, but they might want to assign reporters who are not developmentally disabled to write the articles accusing me of "sloppy" research and "contrived" facts.

I haven't heard much about this "lie" since the AP article came out and normal people took the trouble to look up Friedman's column and post it on the Internet.

Now you spring two all-new alleged "outright lies" on me. I shall respond to these two, and then I'm through. Henceforth, I shall rely on sensible people to see that I have answered the liberal hate groups' first seventeen rounds of indignant charges against me. If they had a better example out there, we would have heard it before the eighteenth round.

First, you say, "At one point [Franken] accuses you of having taken a quote from a book review quoting a book [page 14 of Franken's book] to argue your point. Do you feel this is an accurate representation of what you wrote? An accurate use of a quote? If not, then why? If yes, then who is ultimately responsible for the errors, you, the publisher, or both?"

I'm not sure I grasp the accusation here and I'm sure you do not. I wrote, "For decades, the *New York Times* had allowed loose associations between Nazis and Christians to be made in its pages." Among the quotes I cited, one came from a *New York Times* book review. The quote made a loose association between Nazis and Christians. *New York Times* book reviews are printed in the pages of the *New York Times*. The *Times* allowed that quote to run in its pages. How else, exactly, are you suggesting I should have phrased this, Ed?

Second, you say, "Likewise, [Franken] accuses you of sloppy research, in so far as you appear to have missed a number of *New York*

Times articles citing such things as speeches by Jesse Jackson. What gives—was this an honest mistake or malfeasance as he suggests?"

It was neither, but thanks for asking. I wrote, "In an upbeat message delivered on British TV on Christmas Day, 1994, Jesse Jackson compared conservatives in the U.S. and Great Britain to Nazis: 'In South Africa, the status quo was called racism. We rebelled against it. In Germany, it was called fascism. Now in Britain and the U.S. it is called conservatism.' The *New York Times* did not report the speech."

The *New York Times* did not, in fact, report the speech. Franken does not say otherwise. My guess is—and this is just a stab in the dark—Franken doesn't say otherwise because he can't say otherwise, inasmuch as . . . THE *NEW YORK TIMES* DID NOT REPORT THE SPEECH. What Franken says is that my search method was faulty—though, somehow, it still managed to produce the truth! (To wit: The *New York Times* did not report the speech.)

Among my searches, I searched the *New York Times* database for all of December 1994 and January 1995 for "Jesse Jackson and Germany and fascism and South Africa." (In my footnotes, I often give my readers clear descriptions of some of the LexisNexis searches I run—something, as far as I know, no other writer does.)

Franken does not mention the lines I had just quoted from Jackson's speech—you know, the one that was *not* reported in the *New York Times*—but refers to it only as a "controversial speech." He then acts incredulous that I would run a search for "Jesse Jackson and Germany and fascism and South Africa," as if I tossed in the terms "Germany" "fascism," and "South Africa" for no reason whatsoever. To my observation that this search turned up no documents, he says sarcastically, "Well, yeah."

To borrow a line from a trained journalist: What gives, Ed? Was this an honest mistake or malfeasance? ∎

10

Say, Does Anyone Know If Max Cleland Lost His Limbs in Combat?

———————■———————

☞ Cleland Drops a Political Grenade

FEBRUARY 11, 2004

Former Senator Max Cleland is the Democrats' designated hysteric about George Bush's National Guard service. A triple amputee and Vietnam veteran, Cleland is making the rounds on talk TV, basking in the affection of liberals who have suddenly become jock-sniffers for war veterans, and working himself into a lather about President Bush's military service. Citing such renowned military experts as Molly Ivins, Cleland indignantly demands further investigation into Bush's service with the Texas Air National Guard.

Bush's National Guard service is the most thoroughly investigated event since the Kennedy assassination. But the Democrats will accept only two possible conclusions to their baseless accusations: (1) Bush was "AWOL," or (2) the matter needs further investigation.

Thirty years ago, Bush was granted an honorable discharge from the National Guard—which would seem to put the matter to rest. But liberals want proof that Bush actually deserved his honorable discharge. (Since when did the party of Bill Clinton, Ted Kennedy, and Robert Byrd get so obsessed with honor?)

On *Hardball* Monday night, Cleland demanded to see Bush's pay stubs for the disputed period of time, May 1972 to May 1973. "If he was getting paid for his weekend warrior work," Cleland said, "he should have some pay stubs to show it."

The next day, the White House produced the pay stubs. This confirmed what has been confirmed a million times before: After taking the summer off, Bush reported for duty nine times between November 29, 1972, and May 24, 1973—more than enough times to fulfill his Guard duties. (And nine times more than Bill Clinton, Barney Frank, or Chuck Schumer did during the same period.)

All this has been reported—with documentation—many times by many news organizations. *George* magazine had Bush's National Guard records three and a half years ago. All available evidence keeps confirming Bush's honorable service with the Guard, which leads liberals to conclude . . . further investigation is needed! No evidence will ever be enough evidence. That Bush skipped out on his National Guard service is one of liberals' many nondisprovable beliefs, like global warming.

Cleland also expressed outrage that Bush left the National Guard nine months early in 1973 to go to Harvard Business School. On *Hardball,* Cleland testily remarked, "I just know a whole lot of veterans who would have loved to have worked things out with the military and adjusted their tour of duty." (Cleland already knows one who did—Al Gore!)

When Bush left the National Guard in 1973 to go to business school, the war was over. It might as well have been 1986. Presidents Kennedy and Johnson had already lost the war, and President Nixon had ended it with the Paris Peace Accords in January. If Bush had demanded active combat, there would have been no war to send him to.

To put this in perspective, by 1973 John Kerry had already accused American soldiers of committing war crimes in Vietnam, thrown someone else's medals to the ground in an antiwar demonstration, and married his first heiress. Bill Clinton had just finished three years of law school and was about to embark upon a political career—which would include campaign events with Max Cleland.

Moreover, if we're going to start delving into exactly who did what back then, maybe Max Cleland should stop allowing Democrats to portray him as a war hero who lost his limbs taking enemy fire on the battlefields of Vietnam.

Cleland lost three limbs in an accident during a routine noncombat mission where he was about to drink beer with friends. He saw a grenade on the ground and picked it up. He could have done that at Fort Dix. In fact, Cleland could have dropped a grenade on his foot as a National Guardsman—as one of what Cleland sneeringly calls "weekend warriors." Luckily for Cleland's political career and current pomposity about Bush, he happened to do it while in Vietnam.

There is more than a whiff of dishonesty in how Cleland is presented to the American people. Terry McAuliffe goes around saying, "Max Cleland, a triple amputee who left three limbs on the battlefield of Vietnam," was thrown out of office because Republicans "had the audacity to call Max Cleland unpatriotic." Mr. Cleland, a word of advice: When a slimy weasel like Terry McAuliffe is vouching for your combat record, it's time to sound "retreat" on that subject.

Needless to say, no one ever challenged Cleland's "patriotism." His performance in the Senate was the issue, which should not have come as a bolt out of the blue, inasmuch as he was running for reelection . . . to the Senate! Senator Cleland had refused to vote for the Homeland Security Bill unless it was chock-full of pro-union perks that would have jeopardized national security. ("OH MY GOD! A HIJACKED PLANE IS HEADED FOR THE WHITE HOUSE!" "Sorry, I'm on my break. Please call back in two hours.")

The good people of Georgia—who do not need lectures on admiring military service—gave Cleland one pass for being a Vietnam veteran. He didn't get a lifetime pass.

Indeed, if Cleland had dropped a grenade on himself at Fort Dix rather than in Vietnam, he would never have been a U.S. senator in the first place. Maybe he'd be the best pharmacist in Atlanta, but not a U.S. senator. He got into office on the basis of serving in Vietnam and was thrown out for his performance as a senator.

Cleland wore the uniform, he was in Vietnam, and he has shown courage by going on to lead a productive life. But he didn't "give his limbs for his country" or leave them "on the battlefield." There was no bravery involved in dropping a grenade on himself with no enemy troops in sight. That could have happened in the Texas National Guard—which Cleland denigrates while demanding his own sanctification. ∎

☞ My Readers Respond!

Dear Ms. Coulter:
I referenced your comment about Max Cleland losing his limbs in a non-combat accident to a local talk-show host. He told me I was wrong. I told him he was wrong because you said it in your column. He said you distort the truth regularly. Would you please tell me where to find your source for how Max lost his limbs?

Dan, Kansas City

A right-wing hit lady named Ann Coulter charged that Max Cleland, who won a Silver Star in Vietnam and is a prominent Kerry supporter, lost his three limbs while getting ready to drink beer with pals. She said it just as easily could have occurred in the Texas Air National Guard. That's irrelevant, that's vicious, and that's a lie. Captain Cleland lost his legs and an arm on a reconnaissance mission in Vietnam. They don't usually carry live grenades and M-16s in the Texas Air National Guard. This despicable venom was carried on the Heritage Foundation website.

Al Hunt, CNN's The Capital Gang, *February 14, 2004*

The reason why Democrats are doing this [being hysterical about Bush's National Guard service]—let me give you an example. Today in her column, Ann Coulter attacked Max Cleland, the Vietnam war hero. She said Cleland lost three limbs "in an accident during a routine noncombat mission, where he was about to drink beer with friends. He saw a grenade on the ground and picked it up. He could have done that at Fort Dix as a National Guardsman." Now, that's the sort of thing—I also have here— I also have here Cleland's citation for his Silver Star that he received four days before that at Khe Sanh in Vietnam in 1968.

Joe Klein, CNN's Paula Zahn Now, *February 12, 2004*

It doesn't take much imagination to guess how far into the gutter the presidential race will dip before it's all over [such as] the continuing, shameful treatment of former Georgia Senator Max Cleland by the likes of Ann Coulter, who in a recent Townhall.com column derided his loss of three limbs in Vietnam. . . .

Joy-Ann Reid, Miami Herald, *February 16, 2004*

Friday, it was the Democrats' turn for outrage. . . . The villain in this case is conservative pundit Ann Coulter, whose column on the Heritage Foundation website said that Cleland, who lost three limbs in a grenade accident in Vietnam during the war, "didn't 'give his limbs for his country.'"

Dana Milbank, Washington Post, *February 15, 2004*

But for sheer, vicious nastiness, no one can compete with Ann Coulter, whose latest error-riddled effusion is an attack on former Georgia Senator Max Cleland, who has been critical of the Bush administration. Apparently in an effort to make George W.'s incomplete in the National Guard look better, Coulter wrote a column distributed by the Heritage Foundation saying Cleland, a triple amputee, had showed "no bravery" in Vietnam, "didn't give his limbs for his country," is not a war hero. My favorite sentence is, "Luckily for Cleland . . . he happened [to lose his limbs] while in Vietnam," her point being that if he had been injured at Fort Dix, he wouldn't be a hero.

Molly Ivins, February 17, 2004 ■

☞ File Under: "Omission Accomplished"

FEBRUARY 19, 2004

Liberals are hopping mad about last week's column. Amid angry insinuations that I "lied" about Senator Max Cleland, I was attacked on the Senate floor by Senator Jack Reed, Molly Ivins called my column "error-ridden," and Al Hunt called it a "lie." Joe Klein said I was the reason liberals were being hysterical about George Bush's National Guard service. (No wonder liberals can't win politically if little scrawny me gets them so upset.)

I would have left it at one column, but apparently Democrats want to go another round. With their Clintonesque formulations, my detractors make it a little difficult to know what "lie" I'm supposed to be contesting, but they are clearly implying—without stating—that Cleland lost his limbs in combat.

It is simply a fact that Max Cleland was not injured by enemy fire in Vietnam. He was not in combat, he was not—as Al Hunt claimed—on a reconnaissance mission, and he was not in the battle of Khe Sanh, as many others have implied. He picked up an American grenade on a routine noncombat mission and the grenade exploded. In Cleland's own words: "I didn't see any heroism in all that. It wasn't an act of heroism. I didn't know the grenade was live. It was an act of fate." That is why Cleland didn't win a Purple Heart, which is given to those wounded in combat. Liberals aren't angry because I "lied"; they're angry because I told the truth.

I wouldn't press the point except that Democrats have deliberately "sexed up" the circumstances of Cleland's accident in the service of slandering the people of Georgia, the National Guard, and George Bush. Cleland has questioned Bush's fitness for office because he served in the National Guard and was not sent to Vietnam. And yet the poignant truth of Cleland's own accident demonstrates the commitment and bravery of all members of the military who come into contact with ordnance. Cleland's injury was of the routine variety that occurs whenever young men and weapons are put in close proximity—including in the National Guard.

But it is a vastly more glorious story to claim that Cleland was injured by enemy fire rather than in a freak accident. So after Saxby Chambliss beat Cleland in the 2002 Georgia Senate race, liberals set to work developing a carefully crafted myth about Cleland's accident. Among many other examples, last November, Eric Boehlert wrote in *Salon:* "During the siege of Khe Sanh, Cleland lost both his legs and his right hand to a Viet Cong grenade."

Sadly for them, dozens and dozens of newspapers had already printed the truth. Liberals simply can't grasp the problem LexisNexis poses to their incessant lying. They ought to stick to their specialty—hysterical overreaction. The truth is not their forte.

One of the most detailed accounts of Cleland's life was written by Jill Zuckman in a long piece for the *Boston Globe Magazine* on August 3, 1997:

"Finally, the battle at Khe Sanh was over. Cleland, 25 years old, and two members of his team were now ordered to set up a radio relay station at the division assembly area, 15 miles away. The three gathered antennas, radios and a generator and made the 15-minute helicopter trip east. After unloading the equipment, Cleland climbed back into the helicopter for the ride back. But at the last minute, he decided to stay and have a beer with some friends. As the helicopter was lifting off, he shouted to the pilot that he was staying behind and jumped several feet to the ground.

"Cleland hunched over to avoid the whirring blades and ran. Turning to face the helicopter, he caught sight of a grenade on the ground where the chopper had perched. It must be mine, he thought, moving toward it. He reached for it with his right arm just as it exploded, slamming him back and irreparably altering his plans for a bright, shining future."

Interestingly, all news accounts told the exact same story for thirty years—including that Cleland had stopped to have beer with friends when the accident occurred (a fact that particularly irked Al Hunt).

"He told the pilot he was going to stay awhile. Maybe have a few beers with friends. . . . Then Cleland looked down and saw a grenade. Where'd that come from? He walked toward it, bent down, and crossed the line between before and after" (*Milwaukee Journal Sentinel*, December 5, 1999).

"[Cleland] didn't step on a land mine. He wasn't wounded in a firefight. He couldn't blame the Viet Cong or friendly fire. The Silver Star and Bronze Star medals he received only embarrassed him. He was no hero. He blew himself up" (*Baltimore Sun*, October 24, 1999).

"Cleland was no war hero, but his sacrifice was great. . . . Democratic Senate candidate Max Cleland is a victim of war, not a casualty of combat. He lost three limbs on a long-forgotten hill near Khe Sanh because of some American's mistake" (*Atlanta Journal-Constitution*, September 29, 1996).

The story started to change only last year when the Democrats began citing Cleland's lost Senate seat as proof that Republicans hate war heroes. Indeed, until the myth of Republicans attacking Cleland for his lack of "patriotism" became central to the Democrats' narrative against George Bush, Cleland spoke only honorably and humbly about his accident. "How did I become a war hero?" he said to the *Boston Globe* reporter in 1997. "Simple. The grenade went off."

Cleland even admitted that but for his accident, he would have "probably been some frustrated history teacher, teaching American government at some junior college." (Okay, I got that wrong: in my column I said he'd probably be a pharmacist.)

Cleland's true heroism came after the war, when he went on to build a productive life for himself. That is a story of inspiration and courage. He shouldn't let the Democrats tarnish an admirable life by "sexing up" his record in order to better attack George Bush. ■

☞ My Readers Respond! (Part II)

E-MAIL EXCHANGE WITH *TIME* MAGAZINE

Friday, February 20, 2004
Ann:
I'm a correspondent in *Time*'s Washington bureau. I'm
interested in the back-and-forth over the military service of
President Bush and former Sen. Max Cleland.
—Eric Roston, *Time* magazine

QUESTION: *1. Why write a second column about Cleland?*
ANSWER: Liberals were lying—which isn't new—but the facts were indisputable, and it's always fun pointing out when liberals are lying.

QUESTION: *2. What role could the veteran vote play in November?*
ANSWER: I am sublimely confident that most military types will vote for
Bush.

QUESTION: *3. Traditionally, the Republicans have been popularly thought to
be the party for veterans, not Democrats. If Sen. Kerry becomes the Democratic nominee, could that confuse these traditional categories?*
ANSWER: No.

QUESTION: *4. What is a good definition of "combat mission" and "battlefield"?
Is it useful to draw a distinction between "combat" and "combat zone"? Four
days before then–Capt. Cleland's accident, four soldiers were killed near that
spot by enemy mortar. Would you characterize it then as occurring in a "combat zone"?*
ANSWER: The Purple Heart committee seems to have figured it out, you
may take up your quarrel with them.

QUESTION: *5. The validity of your arguments appear to hinge on how you
define these words. How do you explain the discrepancy of what appears to
be very technical usages of "combat" and "battlefield" and what appear to be
nontechnical uses of words such as "treason" and "slander"?*
ANSWER: a) Again, you may pursue your argument with the people who
award Purple Hearts, but whatever else it means, I believe the technical

definition of "combat" would include: "a time and place when you are not about to have beer with your friends."

b) I do use treason and slander "technically," I simply apply the terms to liberals as a group, not a single individual.

QUESTION: *6. You write: "Cleland could have dropped a grenade on his foot as a National Guardsman." The grenade was said to be dropped by the soldier behind Cleland. The problem, according to people on the scene, was that this soldier had been straightening the pins in his grenades, for easier access during enemy fire. Since that would not likely have been the case at Ft. Dix, do you still stand by that notion?*

ANSWER: Look up the meaning of "ordnance." As I said in my column, whenever young men and ordnance are put together, there are a staggering number of casualties, which is why military training and discipline are so important. I would hazard a guess that more pilots are killed in National Guard flight training than servicemen are killed by negligently picking up grenades. Perhaps you could put one of your crack investigators on this.

QUESTION: *7. People familiar with Cleland's experience say that he requested to be moved from a desk job in Saigon, to a place closer to the action. Then from there, he requested to become active in Khe Sanh. Do you believe this to be accurate? If so, does it affect your argument?*

ANSWER: It has absolutely nothing to do with my argument. I hear he's also nice to his mother. If I ever write about how Cleland treats his mother or write a review of his entire military career I'll be sure to mention both. I simply accused snivelers like you, who in the blink of an eye have gone from being Army-haters to jock-sniffers for war veterans, of sexing up Cleland's accident.

QUESTION: *8. Approximately one-third of US casualties in Vietnam were caused by some sort of "friendly fire" or accident. Following your logic, does that mean that none of these soldiers died or were wounded for their country?*

ANSWER: No, to the contrary, they all died for their country, but they did not die in combat. Dishonest reporters like you apparently think that's not good enough and have insisted on suggesting that Cleland lost his limbs in combat.

QUESTION: *9. You appear to belittle then-Capt. Cleland for being willing to drink a beer under noncombat conditions. Given an opportunity to drink a beer over a hill from the battle of Khe Sanh, would you do so?*

ANSWER: a) I'm not belittling it at all—but I'm glad you're finally willing to concede it was "noncombat."

b) It is so breathtakingly stupid to claim I was "belittling" Cleland for "being willing to drink a beer under noncombat conditions" that I question your ability to comprehend anything you read.

c) Yes, I might, but if I then stepped on a grenade, I would not accept canonization from the likes of you or believe that it entitled me to a job for life in the US Senate.

> *Tuesday, February 24, 2004*
> Ann:
> Thanks for your help last week. The story was held for
> space. Will advise. ER
> —Eric Roston, *Time* magazine ∎

NEW YORK TIMES

THE 2004 CAMPAIGN: THE FORMER SENATOR:
For Ex-Senator, Kerry Race Is Chance to Rejoin the Battle

February 26, 2004

BY SHERYL GAY STOLBERG

[Last big scoop: "Many Americans believe marriage is between a man and a woman."—Reporter Sheryl Gay Stolberg in her July 2, 2003, article, "White House Avoids Stands on Gay Marriage Measure," www.timeswatch.org]

Excerpt:

One exception is Ann Coulter, the conservative columnist, who has recently taken Mr. Cleland to task for "allowing Democrats to portray him as a war hero" when his injuries were the result of an accident, rather than enemy fire.

The accident occurred on April 8, 1968. Mr. Cleland, then a twenty-five-year-old army captain and communications officer, had taken a helicopter to a hill near Khe Sanh, to set up a radio relay site for battle. He unloaded his equipment and boarded the copter for the return trip, only to change his mind at the last minute, deciding to stay on the hill to finish the job and drink a beer with friends.

As he ducked under the helicopter blades, he spotted a grenade on the ground. Thinking it was his own—and that the pin was intact—he picked it up, and it exploded. "He could have done that at Fort Dix," Ms. Coulter wrote.

———

E-mail to *New York Times* ombudsman and letter to the editor, which the *Times* did not print:

> *Friday, February 27, 2004*
> To the editor:
> Sheryl Gay Stolberg lied about what I wrote. ("For Ex-
> Senator, Kerry Race Is Chance to Rejoin the Battle,"
> February 26, 2004).
>   I simply pointed out that the same people who are
> demanding George Bush's dental records from his Alabama
> National Guard service are routinely "sexing up" Max
> Cleland's record in order to smear Bush's service and the
> National Guard. Liberals falsely claim Cleland lost his
> limbs in combat rather than in an accident. Fantastically
> enough, Stolberg actually quotes an academic in her ar-
> ticle—Merle Black of Emory—who repeats the standard
> lie, claiming Cleland lost his limbs in "battle." My point
> was that the truth of Cleland's own accident demonstrates
> the bravery of all members of the military who routinely
> come into contact with ordnance.
> —Ann Coulter

> *Friday, February 27, 2004*
> Dear Ms. Coulter,
> Bill Borders, the senior editor in charge of following up on
> corrections, has asked me to have you clarify your complaint.
>   Where did Sheryl Stolberg lie about what you wrote in
> her article?

Ann Coulter's reply:

Friday, February 27, 2004
"One exception is Ann Coulter, the conservative columnist, who
has recently taken Mr. Cleland to task for 'allowing Democrats
to portray him as a war hero' when his injuries were the result
of an accident, rather than enemy fire."

It is a lie to say I complained that Cleland was being
portrayed as a "war hero." My complaint was that liberals
were portraying Cleland as having LOST HIS LIMBS IN
COMBAT. Stolberg intentionally edited out the rest of that
sentence in order to give a completely different meaning
to what I said. I wrote: "Cleland should stop allowing
Democrats to portray him as a war hero WHO LOST HIS
LIMBS TAKING ENEMY FIRE ON THE BATTLE-
FIELDS OF VIETNAM." The point was how Cleland lost
his limbs—on the battlefield or in an accident—NOT
whether he was a "war hero."

"As he ducked under the helicopter blades, he spotted a
grenade on the ground. Thinking it was his own—and that the
pin was intact—he picked it up, and it exploded. 'He could have
done that at Fort Dix,' Ms. Coulter wrote."

I did not lightly dismiss Cleland's injuries, which is precisely what this sentence suggests. The point of my saying
Cleland could have had an accident with ordnance at Fort
Dix was to defend the National Guard by pointing out that
all military training is dangerous, even far away from enemy
fire. By quoting nothing but my saying "that could have
happened at Fort Dix," Stolberg falsely suggests I was dis-
missing Cleland's accident as not such a big deal. You may
read both columns at www.anncoulter.com.

Monday, March 1, 2004
Dear Ms. Coulter,
Thank you for your message.

I include below a response from Bill Borders, senior editor in charge of following up on corrections.

I have studied Ann Coulter's letter about Stolberg, and so have responsible editors in the Washington bureau and on the national desk. We all agree that no correction is needed. Here are Ms. Coulter's two points:

On the "war hero" quote: Stolberg did indeed quote only part of what Coulter wrote. But the rest of Stolberg's sentence renders the rest of Coulter's thought accurately. Stolberg's paraphrase following the words "war hero" precisely defines the "war hero" concept in exactly the way Coulter did, making the point that there was nothing heroic about the way Cleland was wounded. Neither of them is addressing whether he might have been a "war hero" in some other way at some other time. In other words, Stolberg represents what Coulter said exactly right.

On the Fort Dix quote: Coulter says that the Stolberg quote "suggests" that Coulter made light of Cleland's injuries with the Fort Dix quote. But there is really no way that such an interpretation can be read into the Stolberg sentence. Stolberg's use of the Fort Dix quote precisely reflects Coulter's point—that it was in no way a battlefield injury. But nothing in the Stolberg piece says that Coulter or anyone else thinks that Cleland's injuries were not extremely serious. (I mean, how could they? That would be ridiculous.) There is simply no way that Stolberg's representation of what Coulter wrote could be interpreted as meaning that Coulter thinks his accident was "not such a big deal."

Sincerely,
Arthur Bovino
Office of the Public Editor
The *New York Times*

———

POSTSCRIPT: My column: Cleland didn't lose his limbs in combat.
New York Times version: Cleland isn't a war hero.
New York Times ombudsman: those are the same thing.

Once known as "the newspaper of record," the *Times* is now referred to as "one way of looking at things." ■

11

The Only Cop the *New York Times* Likes Is the One in the Village People

■

JUNE 19, 2000

Topping off the National Puerto Rican Day Parade in New York City last Sunday—making their strongest case yet for statehood—hordes of marauding Puerto Rican men entered Central Park and began stripping women and groping their breasts and buttocks. Some women were stripped naked. The attacks occurred in broad daylight in a well-traveled area near Central Park South.

Chanting, "Soak her! Soak her!," the mob sprayed water on a honeymooning French tourist, pulled off her skirt and underpants, and yanked two gold chains from her neck. The woman's husband clawed his way through the crowd and threw himself on top of her until the men moved to their next target. The couple ran from the park and reported the attack to law-enforcement officers, who called for reinforcements.

In another attack, the men besieged a kickboxing instructor on in-line skates, knocking her to the ground and trying to rip off her shorts. The kickboxing instructor later said, "I never felt in my entire life that I couldn't protect myself until then." At last count, there were thirty-seven victims of the sexual assaults. Police have arrested eight men in the attacks.

Naturally, the victims are suing the city for failing to protect them, and the *New York Times* is raising dark accusations that the police were negligent. Yes, you heard me right: The *New York Times* thinks the police weren't aggressive enough. And that's not just the malt liquor talking. Since reading that, I've been lost in a reverie imagining what the *Times*'s news story would be if the police had reacted with somewhat greater vigor.

I think it would go like this:

HEADLINE:
Police Shoot Unarmed Man in Central Park Melee

BODY: An unarmed Bronx man with no criminal record was killed late yesterday by a New York City police officer who fired four shots at him at close range in Central Park, the police said.

It was unclear yesterday why the police officer had opened fire on the man at 6:35 p.m. in the southeast section of the park near Central Park South and the Avenue of the Americas. The man, Jose Rivera, 23, of the Bronx, who had attended the Puerto Rican Day parade earlier in the day, died at the scene, the police said. Relatives and friends described Mr. Rivera as a hardworking entrepreneur with a ready smile.

In another public relations disaster for the crisis-wracked Giuliani administration, the shooting grew out of a violent confrontation between police officers and members of New York's Hispanic community. The melee began when five baton-wielding police officers entered the park and set upon a group of parade revelers.

Police officials said officers patrolling the area near Central Park South were approached at 6:15 p.m. by a French couple on their honeymoon. The 28-year-old woman told the officers—Continued on Page B14—she had been accosted moments earlier by a group of men in the park.

Mayor Rudolph W. Giuliani urged people to withhold judgment on the case and defended the police. "These courageous police officers were attempting to subdue a mob of hoodlums who had attacked a woman in Central Park," he said.

But it was not clear yesterday whether the French couple had been attacked by the men or had merely misunderstood the revelers' intentions. Some witnesses to the incident suggested that the woman's husband attacked her, and blamed the fracas on the police. "This was another overreaction by Giuliani's racist Gestapo," one woman said.

Jane Doe, a kickboxing instructor, who had been skating in the park at the time of the fray, said the police acted without provocation. "It was broad daylight in Central Park. I felt perfectly safe," Doe said. "To be a Hispanic man and go into Manhattan, you're walking around with a target on your back."

Ms. Doe said she planned to attend a rally organized by Rev. Jesse Jackson outside police headquarters at 1 p.m. on Tuesday.

In unusually harsh language, Hillary Rodham Clinton, who is running for the U.S. Senate, accused Mayor Giuliani last night of intentionally polarizing New York City by leading "a rush to judgment" over the disputed circumstances of Sunday's fatal police shooting of an unarmed Hispanic man. "Unfortunately," she said, "the mayor is willing to try, convict and execute a man simply for enjoying our great park after a parade."

The U.S. Attorney in Manhattan, Mary Jo White, said her office would open an inquiry into the shooting. The Rev. Al Sharpton, lawyers for Mr. Rivera's family, and Bruce Springsteen have requested a meeting with Deputy Attorney General Eric Holder, the Justice Department's second-ranking official. The officer involved in the shooting has been put on administrative leave.

All eight revelers attending the Puerto Rican Day Parade appear to have been Hispanic. An investigation into racial profiling charges is pending. The French couple avoided being charged with inciting a riot by agreeing to attend racial sensitivity training classes. ∎

☞ Murdering the Bell Curve

JUNE 27, 2002

Despite their hysteria a few years ago over Charles Murray and Richard Hernstein's book, *The Bell Curve*, liberals have finally embraced the concept of IQ—provided it is used only to spring vicious killers from death row. In 1996, Eric Nesbitt, a U.S. airman at Langley Air Force Base, was brutally murdered by Daryl Renard Atkins, a repeat violent criminal. It was a heinous and pointless murder: Atkins already had Nesbitt's money and car when he unloaded his gun into the defenseless airman. According to a cellmate, Atkins later laughed about the murder. After hearing the overwhelming evidence against him, a jury sentenced Atkins to death.

Last week, the Supreme Court overturned Atkins's death sentence. The Court ruled that Atkins cannot be executed if he can prove he is "retarded." In other words, Atkins avoids his capital sentence if he is at least smart enough to know how to fail an IQ test. The only silver lining is, at least we can start using the word "retarded" again.

Consider what "retarded" means in this context. It does not mean that Atkins could not understand the difference between right and wrong. The law already accounts for that possibility with the concept of legal insanity. It does not mean he could not assist in his own defense. The law already accounts for that possibility with the concept of legal incompetence. Nor, incidentally, does it mean that Atkins was so retarded that he could not plan a crime, murder a man, and then hide the gun. (The police never retrieved the murder weapon.) This may be why the jury heard the evidence that Atkins was retarded but still decided to impose the death penalty.

Atkins is just dumb—not an uncommon trait among violent criminals. As far back as 1914, criminologist H. H. Goddard concluded that "25 percent to 50 percent of the people in our prisons are mentally defective and incapable of managing their affairs with ordinary prudence." Crimes of violence in particular—murder, rape, and assault—are all correlated with low IQs. Thus, the Supreme Court has now prohibited the death penalty for precisely those people who are most likely to commit death-penalty-level crimes, which is a bit like excluding women from a program of maternity benefits.

As noted in the excellent new book *Slander: Liberal Lies About the American Right,* liberals acknowledge the concept of IQ only when attacking Republican presidents or trying to spring a criminal from death row. According to the Supreme Court, using an IQ test to hire employees is a civil-rights violation (*Griggs v. Duke Power Co.*), but now we have to give IQ tests before executing killers.

Back when *The Bell Curve* was released, liberals denounced the idea of intelligence as a sadistic, racist ploy. Yale University psychologist Robert Sternberg was widely quoted as saying that IQ accounts for less than 10 percent of the variation in human behavior—including the tendency to commit crimes. "Would you want to make your entire national policy around something that has less than a 10 percent effect?" No, it turns out—not unless we are talking about a national policy banning the death penalty.

The publication of *The Bell Curve* unleashed a frenzied campaign to discredit the idea of a standardized measure of intelligence, including the infamous "emotional intelligence" movement, which holds that intellectual capacity is really a measure of one's emotional well-being. Yes, being emotionally "centered" really comes in handy when solving quadratic equations.

The *New York Times* made the sophisticated argument that one of the authors of *The Bell Curve*—Murray—was "a political ideologue." (Is it ironic that the notion of measurable intelligence is attacked with such a stupid argument—or is that just funny?) While admitting that *The Bell Curve* had created "an aura of scientific certitude," the *Times* warned that other scholars would soon "subject its findings to withering criticism." Not yet—but soon! The *Times* was especially irritated that the book had "ignored the huge gaps in understanding the precise nature of intelligence" and implied that low test scores proved only "biased testing." (Those must have been some low SAT scores publisher Pinch Sulzberger had. I say Dan Quayle outscored Pinch on the SATs and I'll contribute to Emily's List if I'm wrong.)

But now liberals are overjoyed that such a biased test—of a human trait that we don't even vaguely understand—is going to be used to empty the nation's death rows. In an editorial titled "The Court Gets It Right," the *Times* gushed that "there are scores, perhaps even hundreds, of inmates whose low IQs will now qualify them for a sentence reduction to life in prison." Great, now we're even dumbing down murder and rape.

Now that the topic of *The Bell Curve* is a matter of constitutional law, rather than "pseudo-scientific racism," "indecent, philosophically shabby and politically ugly," "disingenuous," and "creepy"—all quotes from the liberal *New Republic* describing *The Bell Curve*—let's turn to the guys who were experts in the field before liberals admitted it was a field. According to *The Bell Curve*, the truly retarded are far underrepresented in the criminal population because those with very low IQs "have trouble mustering the competence to commit most crimes." As Justice Scalia put it in his dissent, the Court's portrayal of the retarded as "willfully cruel" does not comport with experience. To the contrary, he said, "being childlike generally suggests innocence rather than brutality."

But we've got liberals on the record: The *New York Times* claims that people with low IQs have "little understanding of their moral culpability"—

a notion that would also account for much of the content of the *Times*'s editorial page. If IQ is such a precise gauge of self-awareness, will liberals finally agree to consider it as a basis for admission to University of Michigan Law School? ■

☞ The *New York Times* Goes Wilding on the Central Park Jogger

OCTOBER 16, 2002

Probably feeling "humiliated," in 1989, a mob of feral beasts descended on Central Park to attack joggers and bicyclists. They brutalized a female jogger while incomprehensibly chanting "Wild Thing" in their ghetto patois. The jogger, a 110-pound, white female investment banker, was beaten so badly she was declared "dead on arrival" at the hospital. Her skull was crushed and she had lost two-thirds of her blood. Her attackers spent the night in jail joking about the attack, singing a rap song, and whistling at policewomen. In his written confession, Yusef Salaam said, "It was fun."

At the onset of the first Central Park rape trial, the *New American,* a black newspaper in New York City, ran a front-page headline about the jogger titled "The Truth About the Whore." (Or as the *New York Times* described the headline, it employed "a sexual epithet.") The article spun out the "theory" that her boyfriend had attacked her. The editor "acknowledged that the article was not based on any specific evidence. 'That's why it was called a theory,' he said. 'A theory means no evidence.'" Recently the media have been spinning out their own theories about the attack, using the precise same definition of "theory."

The newsflash being billboarded across every New York news outlet right now is that prison inmate Matias Reyes has confessed to being the jogger's sole attacker. Breathless news accounts claim that the police were shocked to discover that new DNA testing has now proved Reyes alone attacked the jogger and that the others did not.

This is a lie. Liberals so long to claim that every criminal is innocent, they forget that the Central Park rape case received a lot of media attention when it happened, so they can't lie and scream about another phony DNA "exoneration" this time. The facts are easily accessible on Lexis-Nexis. In fact, it was undisputed that the semen found on the jogger did not match any of the defendants. Headlines at the time proclaimed,

"Semen Tested in Jogger Case Was Not That of Defendants" (*New York Times*); "Semen, Suspects No Match, Says DNA Expert in Jog Case" (*Newsday*); "DNA Expert: No Semen Links to Defendants" (Associated Press); and "Expert Says Semen on Jogger Is Not Teens'" (*The Record*). Whatever evidence convinced two juries to convict the five animals, it was not DNA evidence. As usual, the media simply waited a decade, and then rushed to print with the same arguments used by the defense at the time claiming it was "new evidence." This is standard operating procedure in "exonerating" convicted criminals.

In a stunningly dishonest article, the *New York Times* states that "results from a battery of new DNA tests, which show that Mr. Reyes raped the jogger, have all been consistent with his version of events." The new DNA tests are consistent with precisely one part of Reyes's story: Matias Reyes raped the Central Park jogger. This is not new information. It was always known that a sixth rapist was out there; the police just didn't know who he was. In her summation to the jury, prosecutor Elizabeth Lederer told the jurors, "Others who were not caught raped her and got away."

Consequently, the new DNA tests are also consistent with the version of events presented in court, subjected to attack by defense counsel, and believed unanimously by two multiracial juries. The five primitives on trial were described as among those who attacked the jogger. No new evidence contradicts those five guilty verdicts. Knowing that a sixth rapist had gotten away, the jury still convicted the five who were caught.

The evidence that convinced two juries to convict the savages was primarily their videotaped confessions. There was other evidence—such as one defendant's undershorts full of semen, dirt, grass, and other debris. (According to accounts of their deliberations, one juror held up the undershorts and said, "How do you think they got this way?" What was the kid doing, fertilizing the lawn?) The ten videotaped statements were made in the presence of the suspects' parents, provided graphic details about the attack, were tested in court, and were believed by unanimous juries. Antron McCray's videotaped confession included this: "We charged her. We got her on the ground. Everybody started hitting her and stuff. She was on the ground, everybody stomping and everything. . . . I grabbed one arm, some other kid grabbed one arm and we grabbed her legs and stuff. Then we all took turns getting on top of her." Now these confessions are supposed to be trumped by the untested, unchallenged jailhouse confession of a murderer and serial rapist who claims he acted alone.

At trial, the defense was that the boys had lied in their confessions. The defendants' lawyers vigorously attacked the confessions, leaping in to highlight any inconsistencies or exculpatory facts now being treated as "new evidence" by the *New York Times*. Antron's father told the jury that he had instructed his son to lie to the police and tell them he raped the girl, so the police would let him go. This is often what happens when you tell the police in graphic and gruesome detail how you gang-raped a woman: The police let you go. With arguments like that, Antron's father could soon be giving legal commentary on *On the Record with Greta Van Susteren*.

The jurors evaluated the credibility of the stories and the witnesses. They observed the demeanor of the defendants, the police, and other witnesses. After carefully weighing all the evidence, the jurors decided the defendants were guilty. The public got a glimpse of what the jurors saw when Yusef Salaam was interviewed by Mike Wallace on *60 Minutes* in 1992. Salaam said he suspected the jogger—the one declared DOA at the hospital—was "faking." He also said that even though he lied in his confession, people should believe he was telling the truth about the confession being a lie because he was a Muslim. "That's all a Muslim has," he said— explaining why he lied—"his word." That may be good enough for the *New York Times*, but apparently it wasn't good enough for the jury.

Providentially, our criminal justice system presupposes that juries are better positioned to evaluate the truth than *New York Times* reporters looking for the next Scottsboro Boys case. Two juries already heard all the arguments now being reported as shocking "new evidence"—and unanimously disbelieved the defendants. This isn't the latest Scottsboro Boys case. It's the latest Tawana Brawley case. ∎

☞ DNA Evidence Exonerates Hitler!

OCTOBER 23, 2002

The anti–death penalty lobby never sleeps. Unable to convince the public that savage murderers should be given radio shows rather than lethal injections, anti–death penalty zealots lie about murderers being "exonerated." None of their rabid emotionalism on behalf of rapists and murderers ever had the slightest effect on public opinion. Support for the death penalty only started to decline when people were told that convicted felons were constantly being "proved innocent." The phony DNA "exoneration" project was the first attack on the death penalty that ever worked.

What the public doesn't realize is that years after juries have rendered their guilty verdicts and the police, prosecutors, and victims have all died, moved on, gotten new jobs, left the state—criminal defense lawyers are still hard at work. With no one to argue back, procriminal zealots are free to hatch new theories of innocence and dredge up synthetic "new" evidence. The defense bar can spin its lies to gullible reporters without contradiction. Evidently, it has never occurred to any journalist that criminal defense lawyers might be giving them only one side of the story. Sensational cases in which the defendants were manifestly guilty are particularly vulnerable to these one-sided attacks. Nothing undermines the public's faith in the criminal justice system so completely.

The current baby seals of the "exoneration" racket are the feral beasts who raped, brutalized, and nearly murdered a female jogger in Central Park. It was only a matter of time before the criminal defense lobby would turn to the widely publicized 1989 wilding attack. Strictly adhering to formula, the defense bar has produced a shocking confession from a criminal who—coincidentally—can no longer be prosecuted for the attack. Matias Reyes now claims he alone raped the jogger.

This barbaric crime is a good target for the phony "exoneration" project. The savages have served their time, the victim remembers nothing, and no one cares as much as the anti–death penalty fanatics. In fact, the Manhattan district attorney himself adamantly opposes the death penalty. With zero political cost, he can guarantee himself a favorable obituary in the *New York Times* by overturning the jury verdicts.

In addition to the media's lies about the DNA evidence covered in last week's column, credulous reporters are also retailing these lies about Reyes:

—Reyes's claim to have acted alone is supported by the fact that he does not know the five males already convicted of the crime.

This is preposterous. It is undisputed that about thirty savages were rampaging through Central Park the night of April 19, 1989, engaging in wolfpack attacks on joggers and bicyclists. The thirty savages didn't know one another any more than the mob of hoodlums molesting women after the 2000 Puerto Rican Day Parade knew one another. Two defendants, Antron McCray and Raymond Santana, had never met their codefendant,

Yusef Salaam, until the night of the attack and did not know his name. This did not cause the jury any consternation before voting to convict all three.

—Reyes is thirty-one, much older than the defendants, "all of whom were sixteen or younger at the time," as the Associated Press reported.

This is the sort of fallacy of construction that makes you wonder if reporters are as dumb as you suspect or if they just think their readers are that dumb. Reyes is thirty-one *now*. Thirteen years ago—when the gang-rape occurred—he was a teenager, too.

—In the words of the criminal defense bar's sock puppets at the *New York Times* (reporters Jim Dwyer and William K. Rashbaum), Reyes had committed a "nearly identical crime" nearby days earlier.

"Nearly identical" evidently refers to the fact that both crimes were: (1) rapes, (2) in Central Park. That's where the similarity ends. In the first rape, Reyes casually approached a woman doing tai chi in Central Park in broad daylight and began chatting her up. When she moved away from him, he pounced, beating her about the head and raping her. Her screams attracted a man, who broke off the attack.

The gang rape of the jogger two days later was an ambush in the dark of night. The victim was dragged 200 yards, rendered unconscious, and left in a coma. The crimes are so dissimilar that, under the rules of evidence, one rape could not have been admitted into evidence in a trial on the other rape—but the *New York Times* deems it sufficient to overturn two jury verdicts.

—Reyes's claim to have committed the rape by himself is supported by the fact that acting alone "was typical of [Reyes's] other crimes"—as the *New York Times* put it.

In addition to convictions for robbery and burglary, Reyes's "other crimes" include:

- raping and butchering a pregnant woman in the presence of her three children
- a sexual attack on his mother

- rape at night
- rape in broad daylight
- rape in a park
- rape in a home
- rape on a street
- rape of a woman doing tai chi

I believe the only "typical" characteristic of Reyes's crimes is their utter bestiality. But according to the *Times*, Reyes's "typical" crime is absolutely inconsistent with a gang rape.

—As the criminal lobby's sock puppet at the *Times* also excitedly reported, the rapes of the woman doing tai chi and the jogger "were the second and third of the year in the Central Park precinct."

The idea that rape is such a rare occurrence in New York that only one rapist could possibly be responsible for both rapes is insane. There were 3,254 reported rapes in New York in 1989. Prolific though he was, Reyes had some help from other rapists.

Every criminal "exoneration" you have ever read about was concocted by anti–death penalty zealots and pawned off on journalists who are either extraordinarily stupid or extraordinarily duplicitous. The only difference this time is that the truth about the original case is available on Lexis-Nexis. ■

☞ Media Support Citizenship Awards for Central Park Rapists

DECEMBER 4, 2002

Hoping for a different result, journalists are relitigating the Central Park rape case in their pages, skipping the fuss and bother of trial. The *New York Times* recently announced that "so far," there is "almost nothing to back the original findings of guilt." That's if you don't count ten videotaped confessions and five guilty verdicts rendered by two duly constituted juries. But don't fall for the cheap substitute of a trial by jury when there are one-sided accounts available in the pages of the *Times*! (Remember the good old days when being "tried by media" resulted in a guilty verdict?)

As part of the media's continuing series on how every criminal is innocent (except asbestos manufacturers and abortion clinic protesters), the *Los Angeles Times* said of the Central Park rapists, "Jurors were swayed by physical evidence during the trial, such as a blond hair apparently from the victim found on one teenager's clothes. New forensic testing has shown that the hair did not come from the jogger."

If reporters bothered to do research rather than accepting whatever the "Innocence Project" tells them, they would know that the lone hair evidence used against defendant Kevin Richardson could not possibly have "swayed" the jurors.

According to AP reports at the time, the most powerful testimony about the hairs found on Richardson's clothes came from a detective who boldly proclaimed that the hairs "could have" come from the jogger. On cross-examination, he admitted "he could not determine that a hair definitely came from a specific individual." He also said "that hair could end up on someone's clothing by casual contact or from being airborne."

On the other hand, evidence tending to implicate Richardson included this:

- He led prosecutors to the scene of the crime.
- There were grass stains and dirt in the crotch of his undershorts.
- He confessed on videotape to being at the scene of the attack.
- He gave a detailed description of the attack.
- He admitted that the deep scratch wound on his cheek was inflicted by the jogger.

So it's not quite accurate to say a single stray hair was the sole fact in favor of convicting him.

But wait! The "Innocence Project" has produced an eleventh-hour confession from a sixth rapist, Matias Reyes. Stunning no one but idiot reporters, Reyes claims he acted alone. As is always the case with surprise confessions allegedly exonerating convicted criminals, Reyes faces no penalty for this confession. The statute of limitations has run out on the rape and Reyes is already serving life in prison. To the contrary, Reyes is surely the toast of his cell block—where, by happenstance, he is serving time with one of the convicted Central Park rapists, Kharey Wise. (The only convicted criminal the *New York Times* has ever doubted was Pedro Hernandez, imprisoned with Reyes, who claimed Reyes had admitted to him that he raped the jogger along with the five other animals. You won't read much about Hernandez in the Criminal Defense broadsheets.)

Compare Reyes's new confession to the videotaped confessions of the five animals back in 1989. Their confessions were "statements against interest" in the strongest sense of the phrase. Knowing they would go to prison if they confessed, all five still confessed. Their confessions were tested in court, attacked by defense counsel, and believed by two unanimous juries.

But liberals treat these confessions as laughable frauds. Only Reyes's literally inconsequential confession is treated like Holy Scripture.

The odds of an innocent man being found guilty by a unanimous jury are close to nil. When the media assert a convict was "exonerated," what they mean is: "his conviction was thrown out on a legal technicality." Up and down the criminal justice system, guilty criminals are constantly being set free. Evidence of guilt is excluded at the drop of a hat. Not so, evidence of innocence. The criminal justice system is a one-way, prodefendant ratchet. So is the media, the only difference being that in court, evidence of guilt is not actually prohibited.

Consider only the odds of a false confession leading to a conviction. If the judge believes a confession is not an expression of free will, the confession will be thrown out. If the jury believes a confession is not an expression of free will, the confession will be thrown out. If an appeals court finds the confession was not voluntary, the confession will be thrown out. If the police fail to read the suspect his Miranda rights, the confession will be thrown out. If the defendant lyingly claims he was not read his Miranda rights and gets some appeals court to believe him, the confession will be thrown out. If the police question a juvenile outside the presence of his parents, the confession will be thrown out.

The videotaped confessions of the animals convicted in the Central Park attack were not thrown out. They were admitted into evidence and believed by two multiracial juries. In ten videotaped statements, members of the wolf pack implicated one another as well as themselves. They corroborated aspects of one another's stories.

The idea that the police randomly chose five black men to frame for the attack and then forced them to confess is absurd. Recall that when the savages confessed, it was still possible that the jogger would emerge from her coma, remember everything, and scream out "my boyfriend did it!" (Of course, if she had identified her attackers with eyewitness testimony we would now be reading copious articles in the *New York Times* about how head injuries can easily distort memory and render eyewitness testimony unreliable.) The police had obtained statements from dozens of teenagers who were in the park the night of the attack. In the end, only five of those who gave statements were prosecuted for the attack on the jogger.

It is more likely that the Central Park jogger was raped by space aliens than that Matias Reyes acted alone. But through their loudmouthed lobbying in the media, criminal defense lawyers are determined to turn these beasts into Rosa Parks.

———

POSTSCRIPT: The Manhattan district attorney, Robert M. Morgenthau, called for the convictions to be overturned, assuring himself a nice obituary in the *New York Times* someday. Justice Charles J. Tejada of State Supreme Court in Manhattan, who overturned the convictions, was quickly rewarded in the *Times* with an article that said he was "known as a fair, thorough judge" with a "reputation for understanding the problems of poor people" and had a "very good reputation for being thorough and patient and scholarly."

Three of the five animals later sued the city for $50 million apiece.

Michael Warren, the criminal defense attorney who produced Reyes's implausible "I acted alone!" confession—and who also represented charmers like Sheik Omar Abdel Rahman—was later involved in a major witness-intimidation scandal. Three eyewitnesses to a murder had picked his client out of a lineup as the murderer, but the witnesses later conveniently retracted their identifications on tape in Warren's office. Curiously, they had been brought to Warren's office by a member of the Bloods gang, who stayed in the room to hear the witnesses' retractions—something Warren neglected to mention on the tape. When a fourth witness who had refused to retract his statement was murdered, the first three renounced their retractions, saying the Bloods gang member who had escorted them to Warren's office had told them, "Lie or die."

The criminal lobby now has a bloody shirt to wave every time a guilty criminal confesses. In an April 4, 2004, article, the *New York Times* argued for the innocence of a man who had confessed to—and been convicted of—killing his parents, saying, "The concept of false confession was little known then, though modern DNA evidence has since proved it can happen, as in the Central Park jogger case" (Bruce Lambert, "Questions About a Son's Guilt, and a Cop's Methods"). ■

12

What the Clintons' Ghostwriters Should Have Written

■

☞ At Least with Monica He Only Bit His Own Lip

MARCH 6, 1999

Well, we got another "first" last week. In the Barbara Walters interview, Monica Lewinsky affirmed—happily, giddily—that Clinton did things "that made [her] feel, as a woman, happy and contented." Now, I can't remember back to the Nixon era, but I'm pretty sure Clinton just became the first president to have his capacity to induce orgasm described on national TV. He can add this to his growing list of firsts, including "first president accused of rape within two weeks after being acquitted in an impeachment trial."

Monica admitted that she was an emotional wreck over her affair with the president, whining to anyone who would listen, and throwing fits at the White House West Gate. She said she does not have the "self-worth a woman should have." During her ten-month banishment from the White House, she consoled herself with a sexual relationship with a man at the Pentagon, a certain "Thomas," which led to a pregnancy and an abortion. (I wondered how Thomas was enjoying the interview.) She described the thong-flashing incident as a "subtle flirtation." She admitted that she's had affairs with other married men before, that she was in therapy, that she's contemplated suicide, and that she was currently on antidepressants. Barbara Walters should have taken Monica's deposition for the Senate trial, especially if the lusty little tart promised to load up on the Prozac again.

At least Monica seems to have overcome that self-worth problem. Instead of wanting to crawl into a hole the way a normal person might, Monica seemed to think she was Gwynnie Paltrow promoting a new blockbuster movie.

Though Clinton didn't know Monica's name until the third time she showed up to earn her presidential kneepads—apparently having to swat away half the national press corps to get there—Monica earnestly told her interlocutor she thought Clinton "loved" her. He never actually *said* he loved her, though he did tell her, "You look skinny." In response to her profession of love he said, "That means a lot to me." Many people would have taken that as a hint. But Monica thought he loved her by "the way he looked at me."

What really sold Monica on the idea that Bill "These Allegations Are False" Clinton loved her was the now-famous gift: Walt Whitman's *Leaves of Grass*. That, she told Walters, is the "sort of gift that you wouldn't give someone that you didn't hold in a certain place in your heart." Except Clinton apparently had a closet full of them. The *Leaves of Grass* gift was reputedly the detail that finally sent Hillary over the edge: It was the first gift he gave her, too. There are probably a lot copies floating around out there.

The very first time Monica earned her presidential kneepads, Clinton was (1) on the telephone, and (2) didn't know her name. They had their first substantive discussion—defined loosely—after their sixth sexual encounter. Porno movies have more intriguing plotlines and a lot more dialogue than what she terms her "relationship" with the president. But Monica assured viewers that Clinton did not see her as his "sex object." Why? Because Bill "These Allegations Are False" / "Monica, You Look Skinny Today" / "I Was Never Alone in a Hotel with Paula Jones" / "I Promise a Middle-Class Tax Cut" / "I Will Pull American Troops Out of Bosnia in One Year" Clinton said so. He even "started to tear up" when the astute young Monica complained of feeling like his sex object. Monica began her description of the crying episode by saying, "You'll probably find it hard to believe." Not that hard, actually. At least with Monica, he only bit his own lip.

Everyone makes fun of Linda Tripp for saying "I am you," but far more disconcerting was Monica's smug assumption of what a sympathetic figure she cut. Whenever I hear about Monica's fabulous wit, intelligence, and personality, I wonder—who's *not* witty, intelligent, charming? I just want to know for purposes of comparison. Consider that Monica's answer to the question of whether she thought the president was genuinely remorseful or just sorry he got caught was a real cliff-hanger. (She did get it right.)

I'm not sure what I would have done if I had been in Linda Tripp's untenable position, though I think I would have air-dropped the tapes across America. The only person whose reaction was without precedent in the animal kingdom was Monica's father, Dr. Bernard Lewinsky. Upon discovering the married president had been using his halfwit daughter for sex games, Dr. Lewinsky decided to earn his own presidential kneepads.

Monica explained her father's psychotic reaction by saying it was hard for him to express his anger when the guy who "hurt [his] baby" is the president of the United States. Yes, Dr. Lewinsky did have a little trouble expressing that thought. Some might say he sent a mixed message when he gushed to Katie Couric on the *Today* show: "I respect President Clinton," and remarked that he and the president had something in common— "two young daughters that are intelligent." By contrast, Dr. Lewinsky venomously attacked Independent Counsel Ken Starr—who only asked Monica questions—for "persecuting my daughter with McCarthyism tactics, grip-torture technique." As Monica snippily said of Linda Tripp, "I pity her. I wouldn't want to be her." ■

☞ Hillary: Pro-Dung

OCTOBER 5, 1999

Hillary's presumed Senate campaign is off to a smashing start. She has now established herself four-square *pro*-dung. Dung on the Virgin Mary. Dung and graphic pornographic pictures on the Virgin Mary. Mayor Rudy Giuliani must have thought he'd died and gone to heaven when this feminist cornpone decided to throw her hat into the ring.

It took Giuliani about thirty seconds to flush out Hillary on the dung issue. About a week ago, New York Mayor Rudy Giuliani proposed that the Brooklyn Museum of Art stop using taxpayer money to fund attacks on religion. As he put it, "Hard-earned public tax dollars should not be used for what I consider to be, and I think many people in the city, a desecration of religion and then, also, some other very, very sick things. The animals. The pedophiles. So don't use public tax dollars." The exhibit, titled "Sensation," includes, among other works, animals submerged in formaldehyde, maggots eating an ox's head, and—most notoriously—a picture of the Virgin Mary with elephant dung and pornographic pictures affixed thereto.

Hillary attacked the mayor, saying, "Our feelings of being offended should not lead to the penalizing and shutting down of an entire museum." Well, for one thing, she's not all that offended. Liberals are only offended by religious symbols that are displayed respectfully, caterwauling about the nonexistent "separation of church and state" they claim is in the Constitution. But publicly funded *attacks* on religion, they like. You can't "tolerate" the things you like. As Joe Sobran has remarked, this is like saying the Pope "tolerates" Catholics. Free speech that liberals don't like is labeled "hate speech" and banned.

But moreover, the mayor was not trying to "shut down" any museum. On Hillary's theory, the government is guilty of "censoring" anything it doesn't subsidize. Based on this conception of free speech, I feel the cruel lash of government censorship when the government doesn't pay me to write this column. As Giuliani said, "Just use your own money."

One only has to read the press's straight-faced descriptions of the exhibit to see what a political home run the pro-dung stance was for Hillary. On Friday, October 1, the *New York Times* ran a front-page photo of one of the exhibits, dryly reporting, "A shark in a tank of formaldehyde drew positive responses, but some thought a cut-up cow did not work as well."

The Associated Press reported that at a chichi private showing of the exhibit several attendees "said they enjoyed the show, particularly a controversial dung-decorated Madonna." Commenting on *The Holy Virgin Mary*, a painting of a black Madonna with elephant dung on one breast and cutouts of genitalia from pornographic magazines in the background, one art lover explained, "Dung is considered a respectful symbol."

Museum director Arnold Lehman—no stranger to dung himself—said of the dung-covered Madonna and other charming exhibits, "What they tell us is not a statement of blasphemy, but of reverence, but in a language that may be foreign to many of us. . . . If people do not make the effort to understand, if people do not exercise tolerance and mutual respect, then we all suffer." That statement itself is a work of art.

I paid a little field trip to the Brooklyn Museum to see "Sensation" and this is what it made me think. I'd say the Elephant Man's oeuvre is a piece of s***, but that would be a really bad pun. I wouldn't have even noticed it if I hadn't been guided by the audio tour—which, by the way, was the single most creative part of the exhibit. Until going to the "Sensation" exhibit, I did not know it was possible to use the words "ironic" and "whimsical" five thousand times in thirty minutes. I just couldn't figure out why the audio tour guide sounded like a very pompous Michael Caine. I was in *Brooklyn*. Why not Brooklyn accents? That would have been much more appropriate, to say nothing of ironic and whimsical.

The famous Madonna is barely recognizable as a depiction of a woman. If the Elephant Man hadn't managed to get the nose between the eyes, I wouldn't have known it was a human. The female genitalia pasted on the picture were, however, very true to life, which is not surprising inasmuch as they were actual cutouts from pornographic magazines. Very deep—even "ironic" and "whimsical," I would say. The artist has said that his use of elephant dung, which he gets from the zoo, is intended to reflect African culture. Haven't the poor people of Africa suffered enough without some phony artiste using elephant dung to symbolize Africa? One collector defended the Elephant Man's use of dung, saying it took "some work" to air out the rancid odor, but it was worth it because the artist was simply trying "to make you think."

The exhibit did not provoke "shock, vomiting, confusion, panic, euphoria, and anxiety" as the much ballyhooed signs at the exhibit entry had warned. Or let's just say, not nearly as much as the subway ride to the exhibit did. There was a lot of gross pornographic stuff, centering mainly on the pedophilic. If *Hustler* magazine editor–cum–Clinton aide Larry Flynt could make a buck appealing to the prurient interests of pedophiles, this would be the official *Hustler* museum. One artist, or combination of artists, had the "ironic" and "whimsical" idea of taking department store dummies of little girls and redesigning them (this is where the artistic talent comes in) so that some of their noses were penises, mouths were anuses or vaginas, and their little bodies were fused together in various bizarre Siamese twin fashions. In one of several such exhibits, the little girls' bodies were fused in ways that looked as though they were engaged in various forms of non-Euclidian sex. It was a statement about society.

I'll grant them that it did make me think. I kept thinking, What commonplace couldn't be touted as a "statement about our society"? I am chewing gummy bears. In masticating the diminutive and brightly colored creature constructs—imagine Michael Caine saying this on the audio— and transforming them into new paradigms, resembling wads of chewed-up gum, I am making a statement about the kind of society that would eat cute little bears.

The pretentious audio tour described a refrigerated bust made out of the artist's own blood—which was not even sculpted, just poured into a cast—as a statement about life itself. When the blood is inside us, you see, we think of it as part of us, but when the blood is outside our bodies, it's something outside of us. Just like toenail clippings. I didn't take notes, but I swear that is an accurate rendering of the meaning of the blood bust. (Except the toenail clippings point, which was my own artistic addition.)

Also "ironic" and "whimsical" is the fact that if the refrigeration is turned off, the blood bust would melt to liquid. This shows the transitory nature of our essential beings. Or that solids can melt to liquid if you turn off the refrigerator. I think it may have also said something about society. Or maybe it was life. Or death. Or sex.

On a few occasions, the audio tour indicated that such-and-such an artist had been rejected from various art schools before having the grand vision to put a bunch of poor dumb animals in formaldehyde. The audio guide seemed unaware that this sort of datum is interesting only if the art school reject turns out to be a brilliant artist. But it wasn't really that ironic here. I think the art schools were on to something. The director of the Metropolitan Museum of Art, Philippe de Montebello, no slouch in these matters, wrote an op-ed for the *New York Times* about the "Sensation" exhibit, remarking that these artists "deserve to remain obscure or be forgotten."

The only actual art in the exhibit consisted of four large paintings of horses. Oddly enough, they were identifiable as horses, which is so unlike modern art. After having come up with words to describe a 6-by-6-foot painting that was entirely red (titled *Raspberry*), the audio tour guide was absolutely garrulous in describing paintings that actually looked like something. But the horse paintings would have felt neglected if the guide didn't say something idiotic about them, too. The horses, it seems, belonged to the artist, who lives in England . . . and in England there is a lot of racism and sexism. The taped tour really did say that.

Back in New York City, where there's a lot of asinine-ism, the media are in high dudgeon about Mayor Giuliani's decision not to bilk the taxpayers for this preposterous exhibit. In a phony poll taken by the New York *Daily News*, respondents were asked this completely ridiculous question:

"The Brooklyn Museum of Art is planning a show that includes a controversial portrait of the Virgin Mary *that Mayor Giuliani finds offensive.* The mayor wants to withdraw city funding for the museum if it goes through with the show. The museum says withdrawing city funds would violate the museum's First Amendment right to exhibit works of art it finds appropriate. Whose position do you agree with more?"

Needless to say, only 30 percent agreed that the mayor ought to be able to distribute public funds on the basis of his personal reaction to an art exhibit. Sixty percent agreed "more with" the museum. Not to belabor the obvious, but the issue is not whether Mayor Giuliani personally finds the art offensive—it's that the taxpayers are being forced to subsidize alleged art that consists of, for example, the Holy Virgin Mary covered in vaginas and cow dung.

But in Manhattan's elite salons, it is received wisdom that Giuliani's decision to cut the Brooklyn Museum's public funds is going to kill him politically. Indeed, when Giuliani showed up for opening night at the Metropolitan Opera House recently, he was greeted with a round of boos from the society crowd.

At least when I'm out of touch with the average American, I know it. Not to put too fine a point on it, but opera fans aren't numerous enough to sustain the opera. They're not going to make or break a Senate campaign. Indeed, opera buffs are so expendable that they are regularly dismissed with derision by populist politicians in debates over government-sponsored art. (In case you were wondering, Congress got into the business of sheering taxpayers for "art" pursuant to the "provide-funds-for-chocolate-covered-women" provision of Article 1 section 8 of the Constitution.)

During a Senate hearing on the National Endowment of the Arts back when I was working in the Senate, one of the Republican senators actually began denouncing the NEA for subsidizing "opera tickets for the rich"—rather than bringing art to the poor and disadvantaged, or some such cant. (When did our guys start getting weepy about the poor? Republicans should go back to being crusty old men complaining about *high* taxes.) For a brief fleeting moment, I supported the NEA. I figured at least the rich are getting some of their tax money back. But my reverie is unimportant. The point is: No politician has ever been hurt by ticking off opera lovers.

Still, the *New York Times* quoted a couple of experts confidently asserting that Giuliani's battle with the Museum would hurt him with voters. Mitchell L. Moss, director of the Taub Urban Research Center at New York University, said, Giuliani is "going to lose some of the Democrats who otherwise might have voted for him." Lee M. Miringoff, director of the Marist College Institute for Public Opinion, concurred, saying that Giuliani's position "is going to turn off the people who were neutral on Rudy, who were kind of the moderate types."

Admittedly, New York is a liberal state: It is not an accident that of all the states Hillary has never lived in, she chose New York as the place to run for public office. But there is one profession in which a capacity to accurately discern voter sentiment is a job requirement—unlike university professorships, one need hardly add. However talentless they are at everything else, the one hundred members of the United States Senate know what sells politically. About the time experts were claiming Giuliani had shot himself in the foot and opera fans were booing him, the United States Senate voted unanimously—unanimously—in favor of a resolution supporting the withholding of federal funds from the Brooklyn Museum unless the Museum canceled the "Sensation" exhibit. Giuliani is anti-dung. Hillary is pro-dung. And I am now taking bets on the New York Senate race. I'm not gambling, I'm making an ironic and whimsical statement about society. ∎

☞ We're Number Two!

NOVEMBER 19, 1999

We almost won the title. In the *New York Post* poll of the "Top 25 Most Evil People of the Millennium," only Hitler edged out our own Bill Clinton, by 39 votes. The president's impressive second-place showing handily beat Joseph Stalin ("One death is a tragedy but a million is only a statistic"), who came in at number 3. Our boy also beat Pol Pot and Dr. Joseph Mengele—numbers 4 and 5, respectively. Hillary took a respectable 6th place, ahead of Saddam Hussein, Adolf Eichmann, and Charles Manson.

Moreover, when their scores are combined, Bill and Hillary slaughtered Hitler. Together, the Power Couple—"Buy one, get one free"—got 2,390 votes. That's 726 more than Hitler's paltry 1,664. Of course, Bill and Hillary were severely handicapped *by not appearing on the ballot.* The president and his lovely wife, Hillary, were the only entries on the entire "Most Evil" list who made it on write-in votes alone. Hillary was the only woman on the list. Finally: A poll I can believe. The poll was conducted over the entire month of October on the *New York Post*'s Internet site and received over 19,000 responses. Where were all those Americans who opposed impeachment of the lovable rogue and allegedly despise Linda Tripp? Don't they know how to use the Internet?

One of the most interesting aspects of the poll is that 16 of the 25 "Most Evil" made their mark working for the government. This is not surprising. In his book *Death by Government* political scientist R. J. Rummel estimates that in the twentieth century alone governments have killed almost 170 million people. As Rummel notes, "governments—particularly nondemocratic governments—clearly should come with a warning label: 'This power may be a danger to your life and limb.'" So keep voting to send more power to Washington.

Of all the grisly government bureaucrats on the list, from Vlad the Impaler to Muammar Qaddafi, only two were from America: Bill and Hillary! On write-in votes! The six other American winners were all murderers—Charles Manson, Jeffrey Dahmer, Ted Bundy, John Wayne Gacy, Jim Jones, and Timothy McVeigh. Their combined score was lower than the First Couple (2,169 votes for six of America's worst multiple murderers, and 2,390 votes for Mr. and Mrs. Clinton). The only nongovernment workers on the list were the American mass murderers, plus the Marquis de Sade (number 23) and Jack the Ripper (number 25).

Fascists took places number 1, 5, 8, 13, and 17 for a combined total of 3,779 votes (Adolf Hitler, Dr. Joseph Mengele, Adolf Eichmann, Benito Mussolini, and Ivan the Terrible). Excluding the Clintons, Communists took numbers 3, 4, and 18 for a combined total of 2,486 votes (Joseph Stalin, Pol Pot, and Fidel Castro). This is odd when you consider that the Nazis killed a mere 12 million people, while the Soviet regime slaughtered almost 62 million. Chairman Mao ("A revolution is not a dinner party") didn't even make the list and he murdered about 35 million people in the "Great Leap Forward" alone. (It is believed that Mao may have lost points in the "Most Evil" poll for killing so many intellectuals.)

But this is no time for nitpicking. Back to number 2. Bill Clinton scored higher than Charles Manson, Jeffrey Dahmer, Ted Bundy, and John Wayne Gacy together (1,625 to 1,615). He did better than the combined score of Joseph Stalin and Ivan the Terrible (1,625 to 1,589). Our number 2 received almost 6 times the number of votes as Timothy McVeigh and more than 7 times the number of votes as the Marquis de Sade. Clinton got almost 1,000 more votes than Saddam Hussein. Apparently, Saddam's score took a hit when he became SCUD missile target practice for some lunatic trying to distract from his personal problems last December. So, for now, Bill Clinton will have to settle for being second. This is probably good because, like Avis, being number 2 will only make him try harder. ■

☞ These Charges Are False—
Reel No. 857

JULY 18, 2000

At least you could print what John Rocker said. The latest in a long list of "false" (subject to later revision) stories circulated about the Clintons comes from Jerry Oppenheimer's page-turner *State of a Union,* in which he reports that Hillary called one of the people working for Bill Clinton a "f–ing Jew bastard." The Clinton era was once again charting new ground in television standards!

The World's Smartest Woman did *not* respond to the charges by saying, *I might well have said that, but those obviously aren't my feelings, people sometimes use ugly words when they're angry, I'm sorry if I used those, but please judge me by my record and not some childish tantrum I threw twenty-six years ago.*

No, what Hillary said was that it was a lie put out by her political opponents:

"You know, there's a history of these kinds of charges coming from the people in question [author's note: the other charges were all eventually proved true, even if it took a full federal investigation], and they've been false in the past [author's note: only the denials, the excuses, and the defamatory charges against the Clintons' accusers have turned out to be "false"]. They're false now [author's note: that's what she said the last time]. And I don't know what the reason behind it is, but it didn't happen."

For the record, I personally did not go ballistic over some baseball player's (printable) remarks to *Sports Illustrated*. I personally thought that O.J. cutting off Nicole Brown Simpson's head was worse than Mark Fuhrman using the N-word. But even stipulating that the charges aren't career-ending—Hillary is the one who has now put the veracity of the charge at issue. Did she say it or didn't she?

The most persuasive evidence that Hillary said it, of course, is that she denies having said it. And if that's not enough for you, America's most famous perjurer, President William Jefferson Clinton, denies it too.

The *New York Times* ran a lead editorial on Hillary's "current complication"—as the paper called her anti-Semitic slur—titling it "Mrs. Clinton's Credible Response." The *Times's* evidence that Hillary was telling the truth is that she opposed the Vietnam War and tried to get President Nixon impeached. This is normal *New York Times* logic. But even weirder, the editorial sportingly stressed that Ms. Vast Right-Wing Conspiracy gave "a passionate, almost teary response to the allegation of anti-Semitic language." Huh? A Clinton denial is supposed to mean something now?

When did we make the transition from treating a Clinton denial—subsequently discredited or retracted—as just so much necessary political filler because "anyone would have lied in those circumstances" to suddenly treating it as truth because the Clintons said it? Wouldn't anyone have lied about using the phrase "f–ing Jew bastard," too—particularly if that anyone was running for a Senate seat from New York? Why do we have to keep considering each successive denial by the Clintons as if it occurred in a vacuum? It's as if we're living in an eerie *Twilight Zone* episode in which no one can remember what happened yesterday.

It's not as if Tipper Gore stands accused of saying "f–ing Jew bastard." We're talking about Hillary. Hillary the lamp-throwing harpie whose warm Southern charm was widely credited with costing her husband his second race for the Arkansas governorship and whose concern for the little guy resulted in the Travel Office bloodbath. Curiously, neither Hillary nor her husband disputed that she had used the phrase "f–ing bastard." But they insist Hillary would not have alluded to the religion of the f–ing bastard. Even when cursing like a sailor, she's ethnically sensitive.

And just by the way, there are three witnesses to this particular charming utterance of Hillary's: Paul Fray, the campaign manager of Clinton's failed 1974 congressional bid and target of the slur; Fray's wife, Mary Lee, who was in the room at the time; and a third campaign worker, Neil Mc-Donald, who was standing outside the room. Fray's wife said Hillary shouted so loud "it rattled the walls."

Other witnesses, from Dick Morris to the Arkansas state troopers, corroborate similar statements from the Dragon Lady. Their track records on truth-telling are somewhat more impressive than those of America's Most Famous Perjurer and his wife. By now, the troopers have been completely vindicated on even their most bizarre charges against the Clintons. Trooper Larry Patterson has said he heard Hillary use the phrases "Jew bastard" or "Jew boy" or "Jew MF" on numerous occasions—"four, five, six times." Instead of a War Room to put out "bimbo eruptions," Hillary may need a War Room to put out Hebraic-slur eruptions.

Conforming to pattern, Hillary's accusers came under a swift attack. Clinton flacks Lanny Davis and Gail Collins showed up for work with long research packets on Hillary's accusers. This was especially striking in Collins's case, since, generally, she avoids including facts in her columns. But even Collins was bursting with information about the little-known Frays. As with the Clintonian denials themselves, we're supposed to pretend this is the first time we've seen a rapid-response team smear witnesses against the Clintons. The rapid-response team's denunciations of the Frays are starting to blend with earlier denunciations of Gennifer Flowers, Paula Jones, Monica Lewinsky, Linda Tripp, Kathleen Willey, Juanita Broaddrick, the Travel Office employees, and Elián's "Miami relatives." All witnesses against the Clintons are: trashy people looking for publicity, have a minor criminal offense in their past (such as drunk driving or shoplifting), once sent nice letters to the Clintons, have a bitter relative somewhere who doesn't much care for them and will say so on the record, and are part of a right-wing conspiracy to bring false charges against the long-suffering, completely innocent Clintons.

I must say, I've been looking forward to this moment for years. You may have forgotten this, but back in the pre-Clinton era, sexual harassment was bad. It was bad even if it was just smutty remarks and there was only a single spurned woman who claimed it had happened. But then Clinton was caught doing it, and it turned out sexual harassment really isn't such a big deal. Women lie about these things all the time, everybody does it, and a real woman would have slapped the lovable rogue and walked away. Groping your female employees also used to be bad. But then Clinton did it, and Gloria Steinem announced on the *New York*

Times op-ed page that the new standard is: The boss gets one free grope. Rape also used to be bad. But then Clinton was accused of rape by a credible woman with four corroborating witnesses. Clinton didn't deny it, and only 18 percent of Americans polled said they thought the accusation was probably not true. But no one cared, the country wanted to "move on," so I guess rape isn't such a bad thing now either.

The single accusation that remained a career-killer was to be accused of using an ethnic slur. Even cutting off a white woman's head wasn't so bad if the cop who found the evidence against you was accused of having used the N-word almost ten years earlier. That's why I've been waiting and waiting for one of the Clintons to be caught using an ethnic slur. Now there's nothing you can't do.

———

POSTSCRIPT: In 2004, Hillary Clinton had to apologize for joking that Mahatma Gandhi once worked as a gas station attendant in St. Louis. Mrs. Clinton later admitted that the gas station owner in question was probably not from India, since he once tried to "Jew her down" on a set of new tires. ∎

☞ Liberals Shocked: Impeached Felon Took Ottoman

FEBRUARY 11, 2001

I always thought it would be thrilling to be a liberal. Because I'm a cranky conservative, the world simply reinforces my prejudices on a daily basis. But for liberals, everything is always an exciting surprise. They seem to live in a state of perpetual shock. I used to keep a file of *New York Times* headlines expressing breathless astonishment at the achingly obvious. There would be bold proclamations along the lines of: "Parole Officers Shocked Child-Murderer Kills Again"; "Experts Baffled: Crime Rates Decline While Prison Populations Surge"; "Mental Illness Surprisingly High Among Homeless"; and "New Study: Rent Control Reduces Available Housing."

Most recently, liberals have made this exciting new discovery: Bill Clinton is a crook! I hate to sound indifferent to this development, but it wasn't too long ago that liberals were defending this guy on charges of perjury and obstruction of justice. They had no problem with the president killing foreigners to distract from his personal problems. They were willing to overlook credible charges of rape against a sitting president. They didn't mind that the president chatted with congressmen about going to war while Monica was earning her "presidential kneepads." (Speaking of which, they didn't mind that Clinton introduced the phrase "presidential kneepads" into the national dialogue.) But the Clintons take an ottoman when they leave the White House and the entire liberal establishment goes apoplectic.

I guess you find out who your real friends are when you lose the ability to save *Roe v. Wade*. It's nice that the whole country is finally on the same page about Bill Clinton, but frankly the Vast Right-Wing Conspiracy is getting a little bit bored with the Born-Again Clinton-haters. Back when Clinton could choose Supreme Court justices, the *New York Times* sneered about those yahoo Republicans thinking perjury, obstruction of justice, and numerous other felonies committed by the president constituted impeachable conduct. Now that he's out of office, the *Times* has finally developed the capacity for outrage. How is it, the *Times* recently demanded to know, that "a departing president and his wife come to put sofas and flatware ahead of the acute sense of propriety that ought to go with high office"? Bill Clinton—a lack of propriety? Wait a minute. Are we talking about the same Bill Clinton? Chubby fellow? Used to be president?

The *Washington Post* has run two editorials denouncing Clinton's most recent felonies. The first, titled "Count the Spoons," said the Clintons' decision to create a gift registry for people who wanted to give the First Couple farewell gifts "demonstrates again the Clintons' defining characteristic: They have no capacity for embarrassment." The editorial continued, "Words like 'shabby' and 'tawdry' . . . don't begin to do it justice." How about this for a word that does Bill Clinton justice: "Impeached"! (And no thanks to you and your petulant editorials opposing impeachment, *Washington Post*!) In a follow-up editorial titled "And Count the Couches," the *Post* called the Clintons' sticky fingers with the White House furniture "ultimately the Clintons' worst offense." If this is the worst, I'm just wondering where the *Post* ranks rape. How about that thing with the cigar? How about bombing an aspirin factory in Sudan on the day Monica Lewinsky returned to the Grand Jury?

Two years ago, the *Economist* magazine denounced Clinton's impeachment as a "partisan witch-hunt." Recently, the *Economist* ran an item titled "Beyond Shame," informing its readers that with Clinton, "the sleaze keeps coming in." Yeah, see, that was the thinking of the partisan witch hunters, which is why we wanted to get him out of office a long time ago. The *Economist*'s groundbreaking news was that a guy who perjured himself repeatedly in front of a federal judge and grand jury, bought off witnesses, bombed innocent foreigners to distract from a sex scandal, and sodomized an intern hours after a Bible-toting stroll from church on Easter Sunday *also* did this: "On February 5th the *Washington Post* revealed that the 'personal' gifts that the Clintons carted off with them included $28,000 worth of furnishings that were given not to the Clintons but to the National Parks Service."

At this very moment, you could knock me over with a feather.

Former Clinton Kool-Aid drinker Margaret Carlson dedicated her entire *Time* magazine column to the Clintons' "tacky" farewell-gift registry. It "just smells bad," Carlson was compelled to say. Oral sex from a White House intern was evidently a more ambiguous case. Carlson said the Clintons' friends "insisted Hillary simply wouldn't do" such a thing, but now— now!—"we have proof they would"! Wondering why the Clintons would "troll for freebies they can surely afford," Carlson sadly concluded, "only Freud could sort it out."

Not to brag, but that's what the Vast Right-Wing Conspiracy has been trying to tell you. But do we get thanks, maybe even a little apology, or at least a polite nod in our direction for having grasped the obvious years before Carlson? Oh no. To the contrary, Carlson takes a shot at the "vast right-wing conspiracy," incoherently claiming that since only conservatives complained about the felonies, but now liberals are upset about the ottoman, the Clintons had better take note. "The Clintons have long dismissed the criticism of those in the vast right-wing conspiracy whom they don't respect," Carlson says. "But how do you dismiss the views of those you do respect—who insist you would never sink so low, until they are silenced by proof of your grasping?" I'm not sure I grasp Carlson's point here, but I think she's trying to appeal to the consciences of felons by citing the opinions of idiots.

Another loony-left columnist, Mary McGrory, spent the seventies demanding President Nixon's impeachment and spent the eighties demanding President Reagan's impeachment, and then when the nineties finally produced an actual presidential impeachment, McGrory was grumpy about it. "The Republicans are beyond reason," she screeched a few years ago, and Clinton's impeachment "will disgrace them as much as Bill Clinton has disgraced himself." But that was before the Clintons had sunk so low as to take the ottoman. Recently, McGrory wrote of the Clintons' classy departure, "If the Bushes had called in an exorcist it would not have been excessive." Gee. We just wanted to impeach him.

And all this liberal hysteria was just about the furniture. I haven't even mentioned the pardons. The heretofore unshockable Left was truly shocked—shocked—about Clinton selling a presidential pardon to fugitive financier Marc Rich.

Representative Major Owens (Democrat of New York), member of the Clinton-loving Black Caucus, said of the impeachment of a known felon and probable rapist, "Our posterity will spit upon us for allowing this madness to reach this level. This is a political crucifixion." But this past week, referring to the Marc Rich pardon, Owens said of his constituents, "They think, 'I may have done one-millionth of what they did, but I'm sitting in jail.'" (His constituents must have been thrilled with that description.) I wonder what happens to Owens's "constituents" when they tamper with just one witness? What happens to them when they get caught telling just a few lies under oath? How many employees are they able to grope and flash before losing their jobs?

Senator Patrick Leahy of Vermont, who had criticized the Clinton impeachment as the result of "extreme partisanship and prosecutorial zealotry," sputtered that the Rich pardon was "inexcusable . . . outrageous." It was also made possible by the decision of senators such as Leahy not to remove Clinton from office when they had the chance. Senator Paul Wellstone (Democrat of Minnesota) voted to acquit Clinton, saying anyone with "a sense of fairness and proportionality" knows that "the House overreached" when it voted to impeach the felon. But the Rich pardon, Wellstone said, raised "all the questions about values and ethics in relation to the Clinton administration." What were those questions again? Clinton lied to the country, lied to his staff, lied to his wife, lied to his party, lied in private, lied in public, and lied under oath. The Senate Democrats voted to keep him in office anyway. But now they profess shock that the man can't be trusted.

Barney Frank called Clinton's impeachment an "extraordinary triumph of ideology." If it's the Republicans who elevate ideology over reality, how come it's always the Democrats who are being floored by reality? These days Frank can be found wandering around wailing about "a real betrayal by Bill Clinton of all who had been strongly supportive of him." Senator

Joseph Biden (Democrat of Delaware) accused Clinton of being "brain-dead" when he granted the Rich pardon. Yeah, what kind of idiot would have failed to anticipate that the same Democrats who warmly embraced perjury, obstruction of justice, and sexual perversion would draw the line at a presidential pardon?

Senator Arlen "Not-Impeachable-Under-Scottish-Law" Specter responded indignantly to the pardon, saying, "President Clinton technically could still be impeached." Maybe under Scottish law, but not under the U.S. Constitution. In his passion for truth, Specter once again stopped short of reading the Constitution. Representative Christopher "Rape-Isn't-Impeachable" Shays (Republican of Connecticut) has announced that Clinton's pardon of Rich is "sleazy." A rapist sleazy? Who woulda thunk? When you're sending half your bank account to the IRS this April, remember it's because the government thinks geniuses like Chris Shays can spend your money better than you can.

During the impeachment proceedings, *Washington Post* columnist David Broder described the evidence against Clinton on obstruction of justice as "very shaky." The evidence included: testimony from Clinton's secretary that Clinton coached her to lie in her testimony; Monica Lewinsky's testimony that Clinton told her how to hide the gifts he had given her from Paula Jones's lawyers; and Vernon Jordan's testimony that, at Clinton's behest, he had frantically called corporate magnates to line up a job for Monica, a crucial witness against the president. That, according to Broder, was a shaky case. But now Broder has written that of all the scandals, felonies, lies, and general slime to come out of the Clinton White House, "nothing came close to matching Clinton's exercise of the pardon authority." The Rich pardon finally demonstrated Clinton's "sheer arrogance of power." These people are literally insane.

Most beautifully, the *New York Times*—the same *New York Times* that haughtily instructed the Senate on its "duty to restrain the zealous House prosecutors" from removing Clinton from office—is now demanding that both the House and Senate investigate the Rich pardon. "A thorough investigation and a reconstruction of the events leading to the pardon are required. . . . It may be appropriate for the Justice Department and the Federal Bureau of Investigation to examine whether any laws were violated."

Well, well, well. Kind of a Johnny-come-lately on the need for an investigation, aren't we? In a breaking development, Ken Starr already performed an investigation. And surprisingly enough, it turned out laws *were* broken by the president. Lots of 'em, too. But for all his diligence and hard work, the *New York Times* got snippy with Ken Starr. So why exactly do we need another investigation now? If the idea is to find out whether Clinton sold presidential pardons, I think I can save the country the trouble of an investigation. The answer is: Yes, Virginia, Clinton did sell presidential pardons. In case you missed the Clinton presidency, he also sold the Lincoln bedroom, plots in Arlington Cemetery, government jobs, access to the president, a naval facility in Long Beach, California, and anything else the Park Service couldn't physically nail down.

Without embarrassment, the *Times* lauded Republican Dan Burton for investigating the pardons, reminding its readers that "this page has had scant praise" for Burton. Yeah, I remember that. "This page" was really annoyed with Burton for trying to point out that Clinton was a crook. Now the *Times* is hopping mad at having just discovered that Clinton is a crook. Who's been hiding that from the *Times*? Either the entire liberal establishment has been guzzling truth serum or they don't need Clinton to save *Roe v. Wade* anymore. ■

☞ Tell Him There's a Stopover in Bangkok

APRIL 10, 2001

On April 1, Chinese pilots harassing our surveillance planes over international waters got too close and caused a crash and both planes went down. The Chinese pilot died and the Chinese government seized our crew, refusing to release them until President Jiang Zemin received a fulsome apology from the United States for not preventing a Chinese plane from ramming an American plane. President Bush was in a pickle. On one hand, it is totally humiliating for an American president to have to apologize to a three-foot-tall dictator for his plane crashing into our plane. But on the other hand, short of all-out thermonuclear war, there was no other choice if we can't bear the idea of Americans being treated the way the Chinese government treats its own people.

So this was my idea: Have President Clinton apologize. He'd get all weepy, bite his lower lip, ramble on and on and on—the full Jimmy Swaggart routine. But at the same time, everyone would know he didn't mean it. We could even have two separate tape reels, one short action shot for

Jiang's "constituencies" and one with the outtakes for American viewers. Remember the footage of Clinton at Ron Brown's funeral? The full tape showed Clinton happily strolling along, smiling and laughing—until he catches sight of a camera. Then he quickly hangs his head and pretends to wipe away a tear. It's a beautiful moment.

And now his country needs him. No other human so thoroughly lacks a capacity for embarrassment. (He's probably headed in China's direction right now on that Thai sex tour anyway.) Actually, we don't even need Clinton. Darrell Hammond from *Saturday Night Live* could do it. Americans can barely tell the difference; the Chinese surely can't.

In lieu of the Jimmy Swaggart solution, I have Backup Auxiliary Plan Number 2. This one I call the "win-win solution." But it requires some background information. In the last election, Bush won: the election, two recounts in Florida permitted by law, a third recount not permitted by law, and a count of all Florida absentee ballots—before the U.S. Supreme Court finally said enough. (It seems like I'm getting off-topic, but bear with me.) Now it turns out Bush also won *every conceivable method of counting the Florida ballots concocted by the *Miami Herald* (which endorsed Gore) and *USA Today* (which did not endorse a presidential candidate)—but one. Pursuant to this one single counting method—which was not among the seventeen methods requested by Al Gore or ordered by the Democratic Florida Supreme Court—Gore might be three votes ahead of Bush. Literally, five months after the election, they think they've finally found a method of counting ballots that puts Gore three votes ahead. Commenting on the media recounts that produced the exact same result as all the official tabulations, the *New York Times* said the postelection vote counts "provide stark evidence of how imprecise our voting system is."

More important background information: In a classic Tax-Cuts-for-the-Rich exposé, the *New York Times* began a story last week, "Carrie Villa of Heiena, Mont. has a dream—a house of her own on a nearby mountain." She thought she might achieve her dream when President Bush came through Montana recently, promoting his tax cut. She'd "heard the president talk about a 'typical family' making $40,000 a year" and that "the Bush plan would return $1,600 to that family." Excitedly, she rushed home, "took out a calculator and a tax form and did some numbers." Sadly, Villa's hopes were dashed. After working with the calculator for a while, "Ms. Villa discovered that the president's tax cut would not put a single extra dime in her pocket"—no doubt because the *entire tax cut* was going to Halliburton. All that information was on the front page, above the fold. You had to persevere to page A-18 to find out that Ms. Villa *doesn't pay any federal income tax.* What the hell was she doing with the calculator? *Hmmm, I pay zero dollars in federal income tax now, so if my entire tax burden were reduced to zero under the Bush plan, I'd be up . . . zero dollars! Let's run those numbers again.*

So this is my plan. Don't we have journalists in China? Next time let's make a trade. They give us the Americans and we'll let them keep any *New York Times* reporters. ■

☞ True Grit

JUNE 11, 2003

I could hardly breathe. Gulping for air, I started crying and yelling, "What do you mean? What are you saying? Why are the Clintons back again?"

Interviewing Hillary Clinton last Sunday night about her book *Living History*, ABC's Barbara Walters began with such hardball questions as:

- "Are you a saint?"
- "[Is it] tougher than being first lady, being a senator?"
- "You know, you have been working on so many bills with Republicans. . . . How do you turn old enemies into allies? . . . I mean, no hard feelings?"
- "How do you get on with this?"
- "There were the accusations that [your husband] was a womanizer." (I believe a DNA test revealed that they were more than accusations.) "How'd you deal with it?"

Hillary dealt with it. Hillary is a survivor. As Walters said, Hillary's book *Living History* is a "wife's deeply personal account of being betrayed in front of the entire world." In fact, it was so deeply personal, it took several ghostwriters to get it right.

Walters brazenly probed the question on everyone's mind: How could Hillary be so brave, so strong, so downright wonderful? As Walters recounted, once our plucky heroine even lived in Arkansas! Summarizing Hillary's sacrifice, Walters said, "You were young. You were smart. You had a future in Washington. But you gave it up to be with Bill Clinton, to move to Arkansas. . . . Why on earth would you throw away your future?" Admittedly, even Bill Clinton couldn't wait to get out of Arkansas. Manhattanites cannot conceive of a greater hardship.

Walters also astutely observed that "in addition to being first lady, you're a mother." Will Hillary's mind-boggling feats never end?

Describing interviews like these, *New York Times* television reviewer Alessandra Stanley said Hillary was finally able to show her "grit, an outsize will and discipline that has nothing to do with gender." This, Ms. Stanley said, was a welcome change from Hillary's more recognized role as "an emblem of the modern female condition." So on one hand, Hillary has grit and determination. But on the other hand, she is a living, breathing icon. It's good to see the *New York Times* really going the extra mile to give both sides these days.

In "her" book, Hillary explains that the story of how Nelson Mandela forgave his jailers inspired her to forgive Bill for his infidelity. Okay, but they locked up Mandela only once. Revealingly, Ms. Stanley claims that "millions of women have forgiven far worse of philandering husbands." Far worse? Really? No wonder liberal women hate men so much.

If you credit news reports, the public can't get enough of Hillary. The crush of ordinary people buying Hillary's book seems baffling in light of recent polls. According to an ABC poll, 48 percent of Americans have an unfavorable impression of Hillary, 53 percent of Americans don't want Hillary to ever run for president, and 7 percent of Americans have been date-raped by Bill Clinton.

First in line for Hillary's book at Barnes & Noble at Lincoln Center on Sunday night was Charles Greinsky, who told the New York *Daily News* he rushed out at midnight to get one of the first books because he supported Hillary's health-care plan. A few years ago, the Associated Press identified Greinsky more fully. It turns out he is "a longtime Clinton campaigner" from Staten Island, who has been the Clintons' guest several times both at the White House and at their home in Chappaqua, New York. Lining up at midnight to buy Hillary's book is street theater for liberals. I suppose shelling out $30 to support the concept of Hillary is less dangerous than the pernicious nonsense liberals usually fund. Hillary has already gotten a record $8 million advance from Simon & Schuster for the book—reportedly the most anyone has ever received for rewriting history.

Another average individual eager to get Hillary's book was Greg

Packer, who was the centerpiece of the *New York Times*'s "man on the street" interview about Hillary-mania. After being first in line for an autographed book at the Fifth Avenue Barnes & Noble, Packer gushed to the *Times*, "I'm a big fan of Hillary and Bill's. I want to change her mind about running for president. I want to be part of her campaign."

It was easy for the *Times* to spell Packer's name right because he is apparently the entire media's designated "man on the street" for all articles ever written. He has appeared in news stories more than a hundred times as a random member of the public. Packer was quoted on his reaction to military strikes against Iraq; he was quoted at the St. Patrick's Day Parade, the Thanksgiving Day Parade, and the Veterans' Day Parade. He was quoted at not one—but two—New Year's Eve celebrations in New York's Times Square. He was quoted at the opening of a new "Star Wars" movie, at the opening of an H&M clothing store on Fifth Avenue, and at the opening of the viewing stand at Ground Zero. He has been quoted at Yankees games, Mets games, Jets games—even getting tickets for the Brooklyn Cyclones. He was quoted at a Clinton fundraiser at Alec Baldwin's house in the Hamptons and the pope's visit to Giants Stadium.

Are all reporters writing their stories from Jayson Blair's house? Whether or not it will help her presidential ambitions, it occurs to me, *Living History* definitely positions Hillary nicely for a job as a reporter. ∎

☞ Moby's Dick

JUNE 23, 2004

According to the front page of the *New York Times*—so it must be true!— the release of Bill Clinton's latest round of lies, *My Life*, has "many of his old antagonists . . . gearing up again." Among many others, MSNBC's Bill Press said the book was "bringing all the Clinton haters out from under their rocks. I mean, they're salivating because they get another chance to get into all of these issues."

We're not salivating with anticipation—that's drool as we fall into a coma.

Since Clinton was impeached, liberals have been trapped in a time warp. They just can't seem to "move on." Books retelling Clinton's side of impeachment—only since the decadent buffoon left office—include: Joe

Conason's and Gene Lyons's *The Hunting of the President: The Ten-Year Campaign to Destroy Bill and Hillary Clinton* (endorsed by America's most famous liar!), David Brock's *Blinded by the Right: The Conscience of an Ex-Conservative*, Sidney Blumenthal's *The Clinton Wars*, Joe Eszterhas's *American Rhapsody*, Joe Klein's *The Natural: The Misunderstood Presidency of Bill Clinton*, Hillary Rodham Clinton's *Living History*, and now, the master himself weighs in with *My Life*.

As far as I know, conservatives have produced one book touching on Bill Clinton's impeachment in this time: In 2003, *National Review*'s Rich Lowry decided it was finally safe to attack Clinton and thereupon produced the only Regnery book with Bill Clinton's mug on the cover that did *not* make the *New York Times*'s best-seller list. That's how obsessed the Clinton-haters are.

Now there's even a documentary version of liberals' Vast Right-Wing Conspiracy fantasy *The Hunting of the President*. If we're so obsessed with it, why do they keep bringing it up? O.J. had more dignity.

Okay, uncle. You win, Mr. President. If I buy a copy of your book, will you just shut up once and for all, go away, and never come back? It will cost me $35, but, judging strictly by weight, that isn't a bad price for so much cow manure. At 957 pages, this is the first book ever published that contains a twenty-minute intermission. Readers are advised to put it down and read a passage from Clinton's 1988 DNC speech nominating Dukakis just to stay awake. This thing is so long, he almost called it *War and Peace*. Or, I suppose, more properly, *War and a Piece*.

Considering how obsessed liberals are with turning their version of Clinton's impeachment into the historical record, it's interesting how these books spend very little time talking about Clinton's impeachment. In lieu of discussing the facts of his impeachment, Clinton simply makes analogies to grand historical events—events notable for bearing not the remotest relationship to his own sordid story.

Clinton claims, for example, that conservatives decided to target him in lieu of the Soviet Union after the Cold War ended and conservatives needed a new villain. In other words, Clinton is equating himself, in scale and importance, to the Soviet Union, the global Communist conspiracy, and the Marxist-Leninist Revolution. Nope, no ego problem there. (*My Life* was Clinton's second-choice title, after the publisher balked at naming the book *I Am God, and You Are All My Subjects*.)

Alternatively, Clinton claims conservatives hated him because he represented "the '60s." As is now well known, four lawyers, toiling away after-hours and on weekends, worked quietly behind the scenes to propel the Paula Jones case to the Supreme Court and bring Monica Lewinsky to the attention of the independent counsel. All four of us were five to eight years old when Bill Clinton graduated from Georgetown in 1968.

So I'm pretty sure it wasn't our anger about "the '60s" that inspired feelings of contempt for Bill Clinton. (Actually, it was the seventies that I really hated, but that's another column for another day.) It must have been something else—some ineffable quality. Let's see, what was it again? Ah yes! I remember now! It was that Clinton is a pathological liar and sociopath.

If Clinton wasn't the Soviet Empire or "the '60s," then he was Rosa Parks! Clinton actually compares his battle against impeachment to civil rights struggles in the South. Haven't blacks been insulted enough by the constant comparison between gay marriage and black civil rights without this horny hick comparing his impeachment to Selma?

And that's when Clinton is even talking about his presidency. From what I've heard, roughly half of Clinton's memoir—hundreds and hundreds of pages—is about every picayune detail of his life before becoming president. Through sheer force of will I shall resist the urge to refer to this book as a "blow-by-blow" account of Clinton's entire miserable existence.

Most presidential memoirs start right away with the president part, on the assumption that people would not be interested in, for example, Harry Truman's deal-making as Jackson County executive or Jimmy Carter's initiatives as a state senator in Georgia—let alone who they took to their junior high school proms. When Ulysses S. Grant wrote his memoirs, he skipped his presidency altogether and just wrote about what would be most interesting to people—his service as a Civil War commander.

But Clinton thinks people are dying to read nine hundred pages about his very ordinary life. He views being president as just one more episode in a life that is fascinating in all its stages because he is just so fascinating as a person—at least to himself. In a perverse way, it's utterly appropriate. What actually happened during the Clinton presidency? No one can remember anything about it except the bimbos, the lies, and the felonies. Fittingly, in the final analysis, Clinton will not be remembered for what he did as president, but for who he did. ■

13

Elián González: The Only Immigrant Liberals Ever Wanted to Deport

———————— ■ ————————

"I think that it is important for everyone now to move on."
—JANET RENO, the day after ordering a SWAT team raid on
Elián González's residence in Florida

I'm not quite ready to move on. After all the nonsense that was reported about the Elián González case, the truth is breathtaking. When it came to Elián, liberals abandoned every seditious cause they had once held dear—dysfunctional families, judicial activism, illegal immigrants, their opposition to the use of military force, their fear and hatred of "assault-type weapons," the Constitution as a living document, Fourth Amendment rights, and a weak executive branch. As with abortion, the rules kept changing in order to achieve liberals' driving objective—in this case, sending a small boy back to Cuba.

Now that the nation is embroiled in the war on terrorism, liberals are enraged about the dangerous new powers given to the attorney general by the Patriot Act. But look at all Janet Reno managed to accomplish in Miami—and Waco—without a Patriot Act. Would that liberals directed a little of that venomous anger they had for a Cuban immigrant toward foreign enemies on U.S. soil.

I wasn't paying much attention to the Elián González story for the first seventeen weeks of nonstop, front-page coverage in the *New York Times*, beginning in the fall of 1999. Cuba is a lousy country, if you go for things like freedom, but so are a lot of countries. I figured Reagan won the Cold War, and Fidel Castro was going to have to get around to dying someday. Living in a nice free country, I didn't have to bother myself about what to do with little Elián. But I did have to bother myself about little Elián because I occasionally picked up a newspaper or turned on the TV, and it was "All Elián! All the Time!" Liberals were obsessed with Elián González from the moment he arrived on our shores. They forced me into paying attention and, as usual, it turned out liberals were up to no good. As far as liberals were concerned, the Cold War was very definitely not over. Sending Elián back to Cuba had become a cause célèbre bigger than defending Alger Hiss. Liberals lost 300 million people when their beloved Soviet Union was defeated by Ronald Reagan, but Elián gave them a chance to grab one back! The Elián González case became the Left's last stand for Communism.

Until Elián arrived, liberals were constantly wailing about the senseless cruelty of deporting illegal immigrants, criminal aliens, and immigrants with AIDS. If only Elián had knocked over a liquor store and maybe pistol-whipped an old lady in the process, we could have kept him, by golly! At the Oscars in 1993, Tim Robbins and Susan Sarandon used their presentation of an award to make a plea for the hundreds of AIDS-infected Haitians who had been captured trying to enter America illegally. Alas, Elián was not infected with a dread disease, or perhaps they would have spoken up for him, too.

After Congress passed a law requiring the deportation of aliens con-victed of committing felonies in this country, New York Times columnist Anthony Lewis wailed about the "human realities" of deporting a "person who made a mistake long ago." But when Elián's Miami relatives fought to keep him from being returned to a totalitarian dictatorship, Lewis com-pared the relatives to "howling mobs confronting federal marshals" trying to enforce school desegregation in Little Rock, Arkansas. "Are we going to be governed in this country by law or by mob?" Let an AIDS-infected drug dealer dash across the border and liberals get teary-eyed about the American dream. But if the immigrant is a little boy who lands on our shores only because his mother wanted him to grow up in freedom so badly that she was willing to risk her life bringing him here, liberals can't get him deported fast enough. At least liberals are consistent with regard to the rights of the innocent and the guilty: They also believe it's perfectly acceptable to kill an innocent unborn baby, but morally unthinkable to execute a serial rapist/murderer.

More jarring than liberals' sudden urge to deport an illegal alien was their newfound respect for "family values." At the outset of the Elián ordeal, liberals mentioned Elián's father only as an afterthought. The main point was: Cuba was a glorious socialist paradise and Elián was goddamn lucky to live there! As *Newsweek*'s Eleanor Clift said, "To be a poor child in Cuba may, in many instances, be better than being a poor child in Miami." Without laughter or even skepticism, CBS news ran a clip of a Cuban citizen in December 1999 saying, "I think that the children in the U.S. cannot have a life similar to the one they have in Cuba, because we have been seeing on television, for example, that there have been many shootings in the schools even. So I think that the education here in Cuba is good." On another episode of *CBS News,* Dan Rather said, "There is no question that Castro feels a very deep and abiding connection to those Cubans who are still in Cuba. And, I recognize this might be controversial, but there's little doubt in my mind that Fidel Castro was sincere when he said, 'listen, we really want this child back here.'"

But most liberals realized it wasn't helping to say such things out loud, so they concentrated on the biological father's right to take his son into his custody. Liberals had never been particularly enamored of the family unit before this. Hillary Clinton, for example, famously compared the family to slavery (prompting Pat Buchanan to remark, even more famously, "Speak for yourself, Hillary"). Inasmuch as liberals deny what Hillary said, I shall quote her in full. In the 1973 *Harvard Education Review,* Hillary wrote:

"The basic rationale for depriving people of their rights in a dependency relationship, is that certain individuals are incapable of or undeserving of the right to take care of themselves and consequently need social institutions specifically designed to safeguard their position. . . . Along with the family, past and present examples of such arrangements include marriage, slavery and the Indian reservation system." (Quick reminder: This woman wants to be your president someday.)

Hillary was not alone. Liberals have long directed a bewildering barrage of abuse at television shows like *Father Knows Best* and *Leave It to Beaver*—apparently for failing to portray the family as the den of incest and dysfunction they believe it to be. The Clinton administration wasted little time in signing the completely preposterous United Nations Convention on the Rights of the Child, which had been repeatedly rejected by Presidents Ronald Reagan and George Bush. The Rights of the Child treaty would have bound the United States to a panoply of children's "rights" against their parents. (Fortunately, the treaty went straight from the White House to Senator Jesse Helm's in-box, where it sat gathering dust for the next several years.) Liberals think parents shouldn't be allowed to force their children to wash the dishes but should be allowed to force them to live in a Communist dictatorship.

If liberals take a dim view of the family, fathers they deem positively malignant. The National Organization for Women has worked tirelessly to defeat fathers'-rights laws in legislatures across the country. They despise anything paternal—except the state. Parents are not important enough to deserve notification of their minor daughter's abortions, and fathers are so irrelevant under the law that they have no say about whether their own children will be aborted. Dan Quayle was savaged for criticizing the glamorization of single motherhood on the TV show *Murphy Brown*. Elián González was the only child liberals ever believed needed a father. Liberals believe that Elián's mother should have been able to abort Elián without input from the father but that she could not give him freedom without the father's consent.

At least the Elián case finally gave liberals a cause they were willing to go to war for. On April 22, 2000, at 5:10 in the morning, Attorney General Janet Reno ordered about two dozen INS agents to stage a commando raid on the home of Elián González's Miami relatives in a preemptive attack without approval from France or Germany. Masked, machine-gun-toting federal agents doused protesters outside the house with pepper spray and tear gas before smashing through the gate, bursting into the house, and seizing the terrified little boy, who was hiding in a closet. As the SWAT team carried Elián away, he cried out in Spanish, "What's happening? What's happening? Help me! Help me!" If only he had been a Muslim terrorist, we might have heard from Amnesty International. (At least the INS agents did not demand a list of books Elián had checked out of the local library!)

According to Janet Reno's Press Office at CNN, a member of the Miami SWAT team later said he had "never encountered this much resistance." If a seven-year-old boy in the home of law-abiding, unarmed citi-

zens presented the most resistance a border patrol officer has ever encountered, I suppose we shouldn't be shocked that Mohammed Atta slipped
through their net a few years later.

Before Reno was aware that there was a photo clearly showing a federal agent pointing a machine gun at Elián's head, she informed reporters,
"The gun was pointed to the side." (The gun wasn't pointed at Elián; the
gun was pointed *with* Elián.) If not for that photograph, Reno would have
announced that the agents' guns were never out of their holsters. You always need documentary proof with these Democrats—photos, DNA-
stained dresses, roll-call Senate votes. Naturally, the media spent more time
chastising themselves for showing the photo than actually showing it.

The *New York Times* reported that "some officials had urged Ms. Reno
to allow the agents to take steps to prevent photographs from being taken.
But Ms. Reno had rejected the idea, along with a proposal to park a large
vehicle in front of the house to block television crews from filming the
event." Reno's much-heralded rejection of the idea was apparently not
communicated to the SWAT team. "We got Maced, we got kicked, we got
roughed up," said Tony Zumbado, the NBC cameraman on duty to provide the pool coverage shared by all the networks and cable channels.
When Zumbado got inside the door of the house, he was kicked in the
stomach by a federal agent and knocked to the floor. Mr. Zumbado's only
weapon was a camera.

Shortly after the raid, Reno said, "one of the beauties of television" is
that it can show "exactly what the facts are." That's interesting. Then why
did the SWAT team incapacitate the only television cameraman at the
house? What possible law-enforcement objective could this serve? And
what law-enforcement objective was served by the federal commandos
wearing ski masks? Reno gamely noted that the photo proved that the
agent pointing a machine gun at Elián did not have his finger on the trigger. As any halfwit knows, the only time your finger is on the trigger is
when you are about to shoot. The fact that the federal agent did not have
his finger on the trigger proves nothing more than that he didn't actually
shoot Elián. Good for him!

Relying on the media's complete, abject ignorance of firearms, the administration and its lackeys insisted on calling the MP-5 submachine
guns carried by the Delta Force Gang "automatic rifles." That sounds so
much more gentle than "machine gun"—which is what an "automatic

rifle" is. (By contrast, those "assault weapons" liberals are so terrified of are semi-automatic rifles, considerably less lethal than the gun pointed at Elián's head.) The ACLU was "troubled" by the government instituting a SWAT team raid to seize a child, the only legal justification for which was an invalid warrant, but believe the Patriot Act is going to "turn our country into a police state"—in the words of Howard Simon, executive director of the Florida ACLU.

We were repeatedly told that Reno was merely enforcing "the law." But upon examination it turned out—just as with impeachment—everything liberals said about "the law" was a lie. One "law" those wily Cuban-American scofflaws were allegedly violating was the legal presumption that a father be given custody of his son. The *Economist*, for example, authoritatively stated, "American and international law are both clear—the boy should go back to his father." This was in an item that used such legally precise phrases as "frenzied Castro-hater[s]" and "the bloody-mindedness of Miami's Cuban-Americans."

As long as we're going to be sticklers about "the law," the laws that grant a father custodial rights to his children refer only to legitimate children. Though the media tried to hide it, a close reading of their bilge revealed that Elián was Juan Miguel González's illegitimate son. González was not married to Elián's mother when Elián was born. He wasn't even married to Elián's mother when Elián was conceived. According to the *New York Times*, Elián's parents were divorced in May 1991; Elián was born on December 6, 1993. I know Cuba is in the advanced stages of HillaryCare, but I don't think even Cuban health care could screw up the length of a pregnancy. Nor did Juan Miguel ever rectify Elián's bastardy. Elián's true father was his stepfather who drowned at sea along with Elián's mother trying to bring him to America. By contrast, the woman with whom Elián was forcibly "reunited" was not—as the media called her—his "stepmother." She was the woman married to the man who knocked up his mother.

At common law, biological fathers had absolutely no rights to their illegitimate children. This quaint legal notion preceded the Magna Carta by a considerable stretch. Indeed, that was the law roughly from the beginning of history until the early seventies. Of course, we've come a long way since marriage was considered a consequential institution. But even in swinging, post–sexual revolution America, a father's legal right to an illegitimate child is highly contentious—and prodigiously litigated. The U.S. Supreme Court last weighed in on the legal rights of unwed fathers in 1989, when it cut off all of the biological father's rights to his child, including visitation rights. Visitation!

Florida law takes an especially dim view of the legal prerogatives of fathers toward their illegitimate children. In the early nineties, white-trash sperm donors kept appearing out of nowhere to demand that their biological children be ripped from the arms of loving, adoptive parents. In the wake of the "Baby Jessica" and "Baby Richard" cases, Florida, like many other states, enacted a "pre-birth abandonment" law. The law provides that, in the absence of a marriage contract, the biological father's rights to a child hinge on whether he had provided "emotional support" to the mother during her pregnancy. In a 1995 case, *In re: The Adoption of Baby E.A.W.*, the Florida supreme court found that the father had "abandoned" his illegitimate child during gestation and therefore had no legal right to object to an adoption, relying on such evidence as the mother's testimony that the father was an "ice cube" during a visit to the doctor. In 1999, a Florida appellate court described the rights of an unwed father to his biological child as "a mere inchoate right to establish legal fatherhood." In other words, if Elián's biological father had lived in Ohio rather than Cuba, he would probably have been denied custody of Elián. Unfortunately for Elián, his father lived in Cuba, a place liberals admire, in contradistinction to a tacky state like Ohio.

But forget that Juan Miguel was not married to Elián's mother when Elián was born (or anytime thereafter). Let's assume Cuba's own José Buttafuoco had made Elián's mother an honest woman. Child custody laws always make an exception for parents who are deemed "unfit." This is obviously a high hurdle, but Juan Miguel didn't become Castro's toady for lack of effort. Before allowing Juan Miguel to leave Cuba in April 2000, Castro gave a speech about Elián. In splendid dictatorial style, he claimed to be reading from a letter written by Juan Miguel. Oddly enough, Juan Miguel's demands were identical to Castro's! (Another clue that Castro might have helped draft Juan Miguel's letter: It took over eight hours to read it out loud.) In the alleged letter, Juan Miguel demanded that U.S. officials allow him to "travel from the airport to wherever I am told the child is"—the "child" being his son—"pick him up, return to the airport, and return, immediately, to Cuba." What with thousands of Americans

hopping on rickety rafts every year to escape this hellhole and flee to
Cuba, this was only a necessary precaution. In another extremely realistic
touch, just four months earlier, Juan Miguel told *Nightline* that he could
tell Elián was "being made to do things against his will because if he were
able to say or to defend Fidel, he would do it." If there's one thing six-
year-old boys really go for, it's murderous Stalinist dictators who look like
Bigfoot in fatigues. The burden of being a dictator is that no one will dare
tell you that it is completely preposterous to imagine that six-year-old
boys are constantly bubbling over with fulsome praise regarding your leadership qualities.

But let's leave aside the fact that Juan Miguel was a Communist tool—
a bounder, a bum. What is absolutely uncontested is this: Instead of going
to Miami to retrieve Elián himself, Juan Miguel allowed a federal SWAT
team armed with submachine guns to stage a military-style assault on his
son in Miami. The *New York Times* reported that even Janet Reno—who
had no trouble gassing all those kids at Waco—was reluctant to use force
to retrieve Elián. But Elián's father insisted on it. To be fair, according to
Newsweek, the horror experienced by the last pro-Castro relatives to visit
Elián's Miami home was that they were "rudely rebuffed." So one can certainly understand why Elián's father would order a machine-gun raid on
his son to avoid that sort of unpleasantness.

Whatever else "unfit" means, I believe it would include: someone who
demands that his son be subjected to a machine-gun, predawn raid in
order to gain custody. What kind of father would knowingly put his son in
harm's way simply to avoid a minor inconvenience to himself? The kind,
evidently, that Janet Reno gave custody to. (One wonders what might have
happened if Reno, in her Solomonic wisdom, had decreed that Elián be
cut in two so one half could be returned to Cuba and the other half remain
here.)

Ah, but, we were told, Reno was just enforcing "the law" and the
Miami relatives kept "moving the goalposts." One would think, the way
we kept hearing paeans to the "rule of law," that every court to have looked
at Elián's case had ruled that he had to go back to Cuba, pronto. In point
of fact, the courts largely ruled in favor of keeping Elián here in the
United States. But the Clinton administration kept changing its mind
about which tribunal it would listen to—depending on the results. When
liberals first discovered that one of Castro's subjects had escaped, they

were adamant that Florida state courts decide Elián's fate as a simple custody dispute. Liberals assumed that if the case was treated as a child custody matter, the Florida courts would order Elián sent back to Cuba to be with his biological father. This way, Elián could be sent back to Cuba without the Clinton administration expressly ordering it.

Under the headline, "Courts, Not Feds, to Decide Custody," one typical news story dated November 30, 1999, reported, "U.S. government officials said yesterday they will not intervene in deciding whether 5-year-old Elián González . . . should rejoin his father in Cuba or remain with relatives in Florida—a question they said can be answered only in state courts. . . . State Department and immigration officials concluded in a late-afternoon meeting that they simply have no legal say in the matter. 'It is our understanding this is an issue for the courts,' said a State Department official."

In early December, the *New York Times* reported that Elián's case "was referred to the Florida state courts because they take precedence in custody disputes." The *Times* explained that "American officials said a Florida state court should decide whether Elián should be raised in the United States or returned to his father and grandparents in Cuba." NBC reported, "Tonight the U.S. State Department and the Department of Justice once again reiterated that they do not believe this is an issue for them to deal with. They say this belongs in family court in Florida's court system."

But then, to liberals' shock and dismay, the Florida courts ruled that Elián should stay in the United States. In what the *Washington Post* called "a surprising legal victory" for Elián's relatives, a Florida state court ruled on January 11, 2000, that Elián was to stay with his uncle. Returning Elián to Cuba, the court found, could cause him "imminent harm."

In an act some might compare to "moving the goalposts," the administration promptly denounced the Florida state court, saying it had no jurisdiction in the matter. Janet Reno fired off a letter to the Miami relatives' lawyer the next day, announcing that any ruling from a Florida state court "has no force or effect" on the administration's decision to return Elián to Cuba. The question of what to do with Elián, Reno said, "is a matter of federal immigration law." Forget moving the goalposts—this was more like tearing them down altogether. And yet, suddenly, "legal analysts" consulted by the *New York Times* said Reno was right: federal immigration law takes precedence over a child custody ruling by a Florida court. This left unexplained why the INS didn't just deport Elián to begin with, instead of allowing the Florida state courts to spend weeks deciding the matter, amid the administration's loud proclamations that Elián's fate would be decided in the Florida courts.

Liberals were a little vague about what other "laws" the Miami relatives might be violating, but there were a lot of nasty insinuations. On March 28, Peter Jennings opened ABC's *World News Tonight* saying, "In Miami today, immigration officials met with the Miami relatives of Elián González again and once again the government has failed to get the kind of cooperation from the relatives that might allow the case of this young boy to end in a civilized manner that is best for him." In fact, Elián's Miami relatives consistently abided by the law even insofar as "the law" consisted of Janet Reno's personal feelings. From the moment the very first court ruled, there was never a time when the Miami relatives did not have either a state or federal court ruling in their favor.

The crucial point to understand is that when the administration talked about "the law," they were referring to Janet Reno's feelings—no court order, no official ruling, no agency proceeding. As an illegal alien, Elián was always technically in the "custody" of the INS, over which the attorney general presides. Fortunately, even the Clinton administration didn't think it was a good idea to send small children to live with Janet Reno. Consequently, after Elián's rescue, the INS paroled him to the care of his great-uncle, Lázaro González, in Miami. Under "the law," the attorney general could theoretically revoke an illegal alien's parole at any time, without a court order, and reparole the alien to anyone else—Jeffrey Dahmer, a guest on the *Jerry Springer Show*, or his Commie stooge father. But the INS did not revoke Elián's parole to his great-uncle until April 12, 2000. So lo those many months we kept hearing about the Miami relatives defying the law—"moving the goalposts," blah blah blah—they were doing no such thing. The INS itself had granted Uncle Lázaro legal custody of Elián.

Most important, even after the INS finally did revoke Elián's parole on April 12, the uncle was still not violating any law. He had no legal responsibility to do anything but wait for the INS to come get Elián. Though Janet Reno acted as if she had the powers of a Communist dictator, she was not technically authorized to order Uncle Lázaro to travel to Washington, D.C. The INS's revocation of Elián's parole did not mean the uncle had to bring Elián anywhere. It meant only that the uncle would have to hand Elián over if the INS showed up and asked for him. This the INS never did.

Indeed, though there were plenty of recriminations from Elián's Miami relatives about Reno's plan to send Elián back to Cuba, their lawyers consistently said they would release Elián if the INS ever came to get him. On April 1, for example, Manny Diaz, attorney for the Miami relatives, said, "If INS says, 'The father is here, and we hereby revoke the parole, and we're coming to pick up Elián because we're sending him to his father tomorrow morning,' the family would not interfere." A few days later on ABC's *This Week*, Sam Donaldson asked Diaz point-blank if the relatives would release the child to federal officials. "Yes," he said. "If the INS shows up tomorrow morning to their house and says, 'We are here, we have revoked the parole, we are here to take Elián with us,' they will of course comply with that mandate."

In a *Washington Post* op-ed piece dated April 9, 2000, two former INS general counsels eager to return Elián to a Communist dictatorship said that the INS's unwillingness to revoke the relatives' custody and go pick Elián up could only be based on "the fear that the family might not comply." In other words, when a Muslim who has trained in al Qaeda training camps is loose in the United States, government officials aren't allowed to act until he actually blows something up. But when the government anticipates that law-abiding Cuban-Americans might not comply with them, it's appropriate for the government to act both "preemptively" and "unilaterally" by sending in a federal SWAT team. Even the former INS lawyers had to admit, "To date the relatives have obeyed every order of the federal government, and they have repeatedly stated that they will continue to do so." They were right, of course—the Miami relatives did continue to obey the law.

By contrast, the Department of Justice did not. In applying for a search warrant from a federal judge, INS Senior Special Agent Mary Rodriguez signed an affidavit stating that Lázaro González had "concealed" Elián. Concealed? The entire time Elián was at his uncle's home, Elián was the only person in the entire universe whose whereabouts could be established twenty-four hours a day by the simple expedient of turning on the television. The only way Elián could have gotten any more media coverage would be if he had been living at the Neverland Ranch. Rodriguez also said Elián was being, I quote, "unlawfully restrained"—perhaps by a child car seat. On behalf of U.S. Attorney Thomas E. Scott, Assistant U.S. Attorney Dexter A. Lee signed an application for the search warrant, reiterating the absurdity that Elián was being "unlawfully restrained" by his great-uncle. The application cited the government's need "to protect the life and well-being of the kidnap victim"—making Elián the first kidnap victim in history to be delivered into the hands of his abductors by his own mother.

The claim that Uncle Lázaro was unlawfully restraining Elián—much less that the boy was a "kidnap victim"—was an outrageous lie. Elián was at Uncle Lázaro's home only because no one from the INS ever showed up and asked for him. And yet the allegation that Uncle Lázaro was "unlawfully restraining" Elián was the judge's sole basis for issuing the search warrant justifying the SWAT team's raid. You don't need to believe in a "living Constitution" to grasp that the Fourth Amendment prohibits federal agents from storming a private home on the basis of an invalid warrant. But liberals want us to believe that John Ashcroft is a menace to our constitutional rights. Unfortunately, even a legal finding that the search warrant for Uncle Lázaro's home was obtained by deceit—as it manifestly was—would not prevent Elián from being returned to liberals' favorite Communist paradise after North Korea. The government always had the right to do what it could have done in the first place: Knock on Uncle Lázaro's door and say, "Hi! We're here for Elián" and then send him back to Cuba.

To summarize: The Miami relatives were never, not once, in violation of any law. In June, long after Elián had been snatched from his Miami relatives, a federal court of appeals pointedly said, "It has been suggested that the precise policy adopted by the INS in this case was required by 'law.' That characterization of this case, however, is inaccurate." The only time the relatives had any legal obligation to do anything other than care for Elián in their home came on April 12, 2000, when the INS revoked Elián's parole. At that point, they had the additional legal obligation of not interfering if someone from the INS—on a break from sending out green cards to terrorists—came to retrieve Elián. The predawn, machine-gun raid was an outrageous, unfathomable violation of law-abiding citizens' constitutional right to be secure in their homes. (But apart from these few details, Reno's handling of the Elián González case was beyond reproach.)

A few weeks after the raid, Elián and his father spent a Saturday night at a dinner party at the Georgetown home of Smith and Elizabeth Bagley, major Democratic fundraisers. Must have been a barrel of laughs for a six-year-old. (It is unclear whether father and son were free to mingle during the party or were kept in a glass cage in the center of the dining room for the amusement of the other guests.) This was an important engagement: Time was running out on reacclimating Elián to life under a Communist dictator, and a Georgetown dinner party with a bunch of Democrats was just the place to start! Soon there were leaks from Reno's reeducation camp, claiming Elián had expressed a desire to go back to Cuba. It's possible. At least he'd be safe from Janet Reno there.

We were told so repeatedly that the administration was merely enforcing "the law" by sending Elián back to Cuba, it started to ring true, albeit irrelevant. It was "the law," after all, that the slave Dred Scott be returned to his master in Missouri. The Supreme Court's refusal to look beyond "the law" to a higher moral authority in *Dred Scott* has not gone down in history as one of the Court's nobler moments. Under scrutiny, however, it turned out that resort to higher law was not even necessary in Elián's case. This time, the law was on the slave's side. The Clinton administration was simply hell-bent on returning Elián to Cuba. When the Florida courts didn't order Elián back to Cuba, administration officials invoked immigration law and denied Elián asylum.

The law on asylum states that "any alien . . . irrespective of such alien's status, may apply for asylum." The Clinton administration first rejected Elián's application, claiming that the words "any alien" excludes six-year-olds. A federal appeals court rejected this absurd interpretation, saying, "The I.N.S. has not pointed to (nor have we found) statutory, regulatory or guideline provisions which place an age-based restriction on an alien's ability to apply for asylum. And we have found no pre-existing requirement that a minor, in submitting an asylum application, must act through the representative selected by the I.N.S." Inasmuch as Elián was an "alien," he came within the meaning of "any alien." (The law isn't as complicated as liberals would like you to believe.)

But a grant of asylum also requires a finding that the alien would face political persecution from his home government. That is a question committed to the discretion of the executive branch—which was then occupied by one William Jefferson Clinton. Cuba has no freedom of speech and no freedom of the press and it jails journalists and homosexuals—but that's not persecution. "Persecution" is John Ashcroft detaining Muslim illegal immigrants after 9/11. Clinton concluded that Elián would not face persecution in Cuba. No court could overrule him.

In June 2000, the Eleventh Circuit Court of Appeals upheld the Clinton administration's decision to deny Elián González asylum, explaining that a federal court had no authority to overrule the president's foreign policy. You can't build a restaurant in this country without fifteen years of litigation. But the courts were very efficient when clearing the way for the government to send Elián back. While noting that many people "might regard things like involuntary and forcible 're-education' as persecution," the court said that was not for the judiciary to decide—apparently unlike abortion, contraception, gay marriage, and the religious content of high school convocations. A judicial decree stating that a person would face persecution in his home country "would have significant consequences for the President's conduct of our Nation's international affairs," the court said, because such a rule concerned "the qualities of the government." And in "no context," the court said, "is the executive branch entitled to more deference than in the context of foreign affairs." Why is it that whenever the federal courts see the merits of judicial restraint, it's in a case where we could really use a little judicial activism, like whether to send a little six-year-old boy back to a Communist dictatorship?

Essentially, the court ruled that it was not for the courts to overturn the president's Commie-loving foreign policy. The determination that a Communist country is a fine place to live was President Clinton's call alone. Naturally, therefore, Elián was sent back to Cuba. Elián was always going to be sent back to Cuba. Liberals like Cuba more than they like the U.S.A.—which admittedly isn't saying much. But they really like Cuba. *Newsweek* reporters Brook Larmer and John Leland sentimentally described Elián's transition from America to Cuba, saying, "The boy will nestle again in a more peaceable society that treasures its children." They even threw in the old chestnut about Cuba's "education and health-care systems" being "among the best in the Americas." Yes, and apparently the concentration camps where Cuban AIDS patients are kept against their will are particularly nice. On the April 3, 2000, *Today* show, NBC's Katie Couric said, "Some suggested it's wrong to expect Elián González to live in a place that tolerates no dissent or freedom of political expression. They were talking about Miami." You'd be arrested for committing a "hate crime" if you talked about Muslim Americans the way liberals talk about Cuban-Americans.

The lesson of Elián González is: If you put a Democrat in the White House, be prepared to live with his foreign policy, which in the Democrats' case consists of warm admiration for Fidel Castro. Unfortunately, Democrats can't grasp that the reverse is also true: A Republican president gets to effect his foreign policy, too. When the Bush administration announced plans for military tribunals in the war on terrorism, Democratic senator Patrick Leahy accused the Bush administration of thinking it had a "monopoly on authority." In fact, when it comes to waging war, the man the Constitution calls the "Commander in Chief" actually does have a "monopoly on authority." But the Democrats were testy with Bush for not treating the Senate as his "partner" in being commander in chief. The *New York Times* editorialized that Bush's plan for military tribunals was "an insult to the exquisite balancing of executive, legislative and judicial powers that the framers incorporated into the Constitution." The *Times* thinks the president's foreign affairs powers are absolute only when being used to send a child back to a Communist dictatorship. Perhaps we could get liberal support for detaining terrorists if instead of placing them in military tribunals, we sent them to North Korea.

Elián González was sent back to Cuba not because of any law but simply because President Clinton was partial to Communist dictatorships. This is among the many reasons that Democrats should be kept away from foreign policy. I know what you're thinking, but, nope, not even to keep them away from domestic policy.

Fortunately, Cuban-Americans in Florida figured that out just in the nick of time. After giving nearly 40 percent of their vote to Clinton in 1996, they turned out in force in 2000, giving an estimated 77 percent of their votes to George Bush.

Elián's arrival in America had always seemed like a miracle. There were thirteen people in Elián's escape party, including Elián's mother. All of them but Elián drowned at sea. Alone in the world, this little six-year-old boy held on to his inner tube for two days, tossed and turned by the sea under a hot tropical sun. On Thanksgiving Day, 1999, fishermen found him a few miles off of Fort Lauderdale. Some Cuban-Americans compared Elián to Moses and some compared him to Jesus. In April 2000,

Maria Elena Quesada told the *Washington Post*, "Elián is a sign from God saying to the exile community: 'I haven't forgotten you.'" Whatever happened next, she said, was "in the hands of God."

The presidential election that year was decided by less than 500 votes in Florida. If Elián González had never landed in America, Al Gore would have been in the White House on September 11, 2001. Thank you, Elián González, for doing more for freedom in this country than Chuck Schumer, Nancy Pelosi, Tom Daschle, and the rest of that party combined has ever done. ■

14

The Democrats'
New Symbol:
Two Sets of Standards

—————■—————

Whenever you hear that "both Republicans and Democrats" are guilty of something, it's a lie. That's the sound of Republicans surrendering. Democrats savagely attack Republicans, and then Republicans think they've scored a magnificent comeback if they can persuade people that "both Republicans and Democrats" are at fault. (The Republican negotiating motto should be "I'll meet you nine-tenths of the way.") It's never true. Democrats are always worse.

Trent Lott's allegedly racially insensitive toast to Strom Thurmond in late 2002 was nothing compared with Senator Chris Dodd's ostentatiously racially offensive tribute to Senator Robert Byrd less than a year and a half later. Lott's remark was an impromptu toast at an old-timer's hundredth birthday party; Dodd's remark was made before C-SPAN cameras in a speech on the Senate floor. The subject of Lott's toast, Strom Thurmond, had once been a segregationist presidential candidate; the subject of Dodd's tribute, Byrd, had once been a member of the Ku Klux Klan. And not just a member—Byrd had been a recruiter for the Klan, known as a "Kleagle," signing up Klan members for $10 a head.

Most important, Lott didn't mention anything about race at all; Dodd did. In his toast, Lott said if Thurmond had been elected president, "we wouldn't have had all these problems over all these years." That could have been a reference to anything from Jimmy Carter's Iran policy to Bill Clinton's intern policy to *Hee-Haw* reruns. But liberals rushed to fill in the blanks, claiming Lott obviously meant "blacks" when he said "all these problems." By contrast, Dodd left nothing to the imagination in his speech on the Senate floor, saying loud and clear that former Klanner Byrd "would have been right during the great conflict of Civil War in this Nation." A former Kleagle would have been "right" during the *Civil War*?

The difference was so stark it was as if Dodd were taunting Republicans: *Now let me show you what Democrats can get away with.* For months after Lott made his toast, it was headline news across the country. The *New York Times* alone mentioned Lott's toast in 99 articles over a six-month period, including 18 major, front-page stories, totaling about 30,000 words. Indeed, the *Times* did everything short of renaming him Trent "Segregation Defender" Lott. Eventually Lott was forced to step down as Senate majority leader.

But a little over a year later, when a Democratic senator said a former Ku Klux Klan Kleagle "would have been right" during the Civil War, the *Times* ran only one small item on page B-6, titled "Dodd Says He Regrets 'Poor Choice of Words.'" Even that article again flogged Lott's toast—and misidentified Thurmond as a "Republican" during his prosegregation period. Someone at the *Times* might have noticed that the official name of the segregationist party was "The States' Rights *Democratic* Party." Someday, the *Times* will be identifying Byrd's organization, the Ku Klux Klan—an organization that was originally formed to engage in terrorism against Republicans—as "the Republican Party."

Even Democrats complained about a double standard—but they meant against the Democrats. When Lott made his toast to Thurmond, Dodd had gone on CNN's *Late Edition* and said, "If Tom Daschle or another Democratic leader were to have made similar statements, the reaction would have been very swift. I don't think several hours would have gone by without there being an almost unanimous call for the leader to step aside." But about a year later, when Dodd said something indisputably worse, no senator—Republican or Democrat—called for any sanction against Dodd, and the media largely ignored his gaffe.

Moreover, Tom Daschle *did* make a similar statement. The Democratic Senate leader expressly reiterated Dodd's racist point, agreeing that Senator "Kleagle" Byrd "would have been a great senator at any moment," apparently including—as Dodd said—

during the Civil War. Democrats seem to have decided blacks are safely on the plantation and Democrats can say or do anything. Not one Republican senator—not even Lott—commented on the Democrats' unseemly tributes to a former recruiter for the KKK. Daschle had the audacity to say Lott's comment was worse than Dodd's. Conservative pundits said the comments were either equally bad or equally innocent—despite the fact that on every score Dodd's comment was worse. Like America's approach to al Qaeda before 9/11, the Democrats have declared war on Republicans and Republicans aren't even aware there's a war going on.

Democrats repeatedly start World War III over Republican Supreme Court nominations, and conservatives respond by saying— as Peter Berkowitz wrote in National Review Online in April 2002—that "both parties must bear responsibility" for the "crude politicization" of judicial nominations. Let's look at that.

After Senate hearings on Clarence Thomas's nomination to the Supreme Court had concluded uneventfully, with even the abortion-on-demand crowd admitting that Thomas's nomination seemed viable and his confirmation all but certain, Democrats suddenly produced a woman who claimed she had been sexually harassed by Thomas years earlier. The harassment was so severe that his accuser, Anita Hill, continued working for Thomas for years, followed him to other jobs, exchanged friendly correspondence with him, and kept the story of her brutal victimization a secret for the next, oh, decade or so. Thomas passionately denied the accusations, as did a dozen witnesses who had worked with both Thomas and Hill. Indeed, every single person who knew both Thomas and Hill believed Thomas. In polls after the hearings, two-thirds of Americans said they believed Thomas. Democratic senator Joe Biden believed Thomas. Even Senator Arlen Specter believed Thomas. Not surprisingly, Republicans believed Thomas, too. Not only that, but they had the audacity to defend him from the Democrats' scurrilous eleventh-hour attack.

On ABC's October 15, 1991, Nightline, after Thomas had been confirmed, Ted Koppel described the entire imbroglio as "a battle in which both Republicans and Democrats found themselves covered, not with glory, but with mud." Indeed, Koppel suggested that Thomas had been confirmed because victory had gone "to the side that was better at gutter politics"—a point subtly alluded to in the title of the program: "Did Gutter Politics Get Thomas Confirmed?" You mean like checking the video stores in Thomas's neighborhood to see if he had rented any porno tapes? That kind of gutter politics, Ted? Just think: The same Democratic Party hacks and leg-breakers who looked up Thomas's video rental records from the 1970s are now complaining about the Patriot Act being too intrusive.

Democrats attack, and if Republicans do not immediately acquiesce they are being vicious brutes. It is conservatives' obligation to surrender whenever liberals bully them. Otherwise liberal lips quiver and they start crying and claim you've injured them cruelly. How about: Democrats stop lying about Republicans and then Republicans won't have to defend themselves thereby hurting Democrats' feelings? Why does the armistice begin only after they've taken the first punch?

The confirmation hearings on Democratic nominees to the Supreme Court go somewhat more smoothly. This is because Republicans would apparently confirm a doorknob. During Ruth Bader Ginsburg's confirmation hearings, the nominee said laws against abortion violated the Equal Protection Clause because only women can get pregnant. It's quite a challenge, but this is a legal premise even nuttier than the "penumbra" rationale actually used by the Court in *Roe v. Wade*. On Ginsburg's theory, topless beaches are mandated under the Equal Protection Clause of the Constitution, at least if men are allowed to go topless at a beach. (But the Equal Protection Clause says absolutely nothing about "recounting" some ballots in Florida three times more than other votes.) Some ninety minutes later, when most of the Judiciary Committee members had stopped giggling, Ginsburg said the death penalty for rape was unconstitutional because rape laws were intended to avenge a man's property right: "If [a woman] was raped before marriage, she was damaged goods. It was a theft of something that belonged first to the father, and then to the husband"—whereupon the Judiciary Committee declared a fifteen-minute recess so that Ginsburg's Thorazine could kick in.

Despite the fact that Ginsburg was obviously crazier than a bedbug, Republicans didn't even oppose her on the merits. They certainly did not produce some long-ago coworker to level outrageous sexual harassment charges against her. Then–Senate Republican leader Bob Dole of Kansas said of Ginsburg's nomination to the highest court in the land, "It looks like a good choice." Republican Senator Charles Grassley said, "She's a Democrat nominee that even conservatives can like and respect." Former

Grassley aide Samuel Gerdano said the Senate hearing on Ginsburg was like "Barney the dinosaur for adults: 'I love you. You love me.'"

In other words, *both Republicans and Democrats* engage in mudthrowing, gutter politics over Supreme Court nominations.

It is also not true that both Republicans and Democrats failed to do enough to prevent the 9/11 terrorist attack. We wouldn't have mentioned it if Democrats hadn't started blaming the Bush administration for failing to stop 9/11, but gee, I kind of remembered it was the Democrats who imposed absurd restrictions on law enforcement and spent the last three decades trying to bulldoze the CIA and FBI. But I must be wrong. Otherwise how could Democrats have the effrontery to complain about the FBI and CIA not having done enough to stop 9/11?

In the early 1970s, when Democrats had dominant majorities in both houses of Congress, the Church Committee—so named for its chairman, Democratic senator Frank Church—went after the CIA like it was going after the Nazis. The agency was gutted, hampered, and hamstrung with endless bureaucratic regulations. In 1980, Congressman Ron Dellums (California Democrat)—who believed that Fidel Castro "would have been right" during the great conflict known as the Cold War—vowed to "totally dismantle every intelligence agency in this country, piece by piece, nail by nail, brick by brick." In 1993, the Democratic caucus voted Dellums chairman of the House Armed Services Committee in a 198–10 vote. The *New York Times* took the occasion to shower Dellums with praise. Throughout the 1990s, Senator John Kerry repeatedly voted to cut billions of dollars from intelligence services, so money spent fighting terrorism could be spent on something more important, like reducing class size. In a 1997 speech on the Senate floor, Kerry bleated, "Why is it that our vast intelligence apparatus continues to grow even as government resources for new and essential priorities fall far short of what is necessary?" There were half a dozen terrorist attacks on Clinton's watch; all of them went unanswered. Ronald Reagan responded more forcefully to Islamic terrorism when he was busy toppling a fifty-year-old Evil Empire. Clinton was in office for eight years preceding the 9/11 attack; Bush had been in office for less than eight months. Most enragingly, everything liberals complain Bush was not doing before the 9/11 attack is what they are furious at him for doing *after* the 9/11 attack.

So let's review: Which party was constantly trying to strip intelligence agencies of money? Which party made it impossible for the CIA and the FBI to talk to each other? Which party demands proof that crime was committed before allowing law enforcement to look for evidence? Which party was responsible for preventing the government from opening Moussaoui's laptop? I think we're talking about the Democrats and their pals. Rules that Republicans disagreed with were put in place over their objections, which prevented them from doing a better job in ferreting out a terrorist plot before it was executed on 9/11—and then the Democrats have the chutzpah to blame Republicans for not breaking the laws Democrats wrote. In response to this, Republicans think it's a great comeback to say "both parties" were equally responsible for the flaws in law enforcement that failed to prevent 9/11.

Finally, it is not true that George Bush would have behaved like Al Gore after the 2000 election had the situation been reversed. This is patently absurd, but it is an absurdity that has gained credibility with the Left's usual mind-numbing repetition. As luck would have it, I know how conservatives would have responded if Bush had lost the election while winning the popular vote. The day before the 2000 election, I was at the editorial meeting of *Human Events*—Ronald Reagan's favorite newspaper, and the most influential conservative publication in America. Editor Terry Jeffrey began the meeting by raising the prospect of Gore's winning the electoral college and losing the popular vote. (Everyone forgot this later, but before the election, that was considered the more likely prospect. No one seems to have ever imagined that the reverse would occur.) Jeffrey said if Gore won the electoral college and lost the popular vote, *Human Events* would run a front-page article vehemently defending the electoral college. No one at the meeting disagreed.

Of course, you don't have to take my word for it. The entire world knows how a Republican presidential candidate would react to winning the popular vote, but losing the electoral college because . . . that's exactly what happened in 1960. Despite the myth of John F. Kennedy's popular vote victory in 1960, more popular votes were cast for Richard Nixon that year. As Pulitzer Prize–winning historian Walter A. McDougall explained in an op-ed in the *New York Times,* in the 1960 election Kennedy did not win all the Democratic ballots in Alabama. Five Democratic independent electors cast their votes for Senator Harry Byrd's segre-

gationist States' Rights Democratic Party that year. Thus, Mc-
Dougall notes, "at least 173,620 Alabama Democrats were not voting for Kennedy on Election Day." Democrat voters and States'
Rights Democratic Party voters together won the national popular vote in 1960 by only 113,000 votes, so that means Kennedy actually lost the popular vote by about 60,000 votes—and this isn't
including the massive vote fraud in Illinois and Texas. The myth
of Kennedy's popular vote victory in 1960, McDougall says, was
started by "Kennedy admirers in journalism and the academy"
who at some point began counting the popular votes for Byrd in
Alabama as popular votes for Kennedy. Nixon's response to losing
the electoral college while winning the popular vote was to concede the election. Al Gore showed the world how a Democrat re-
sponds. (So which man goes down in history as "shredding the
Constitution"?)

After the 2000 election the media simply assumed that conservatives would have thrown a tantrum had the shoe been on the
other foot. One much trumpeted article by *Daily News* reporter
Michael Kramer had quoted an anonymous "Bush aide" before the
election saying Bush planned to stage a major assault on the election if he lost the electoral college but won the popular vote.
Adding credibility to Kramer's account, the anonymous "Bush
aide" predicted that if Bush challenged the election . . . the media
would back him! Yep, Republicans can often be found whiling
away the days boasting about how pro-Republican the media is.
(And if all else fails, we can always count on NPR!) But according
to Kramer, Mr. Anonymous said, "I think you can count on the
media to fuel the thing big-time. Even papers that supported Gore
might turn against him because the will of the people will have
been thwarted." Mr. Anonymous also confided to Kramer, "You
think 'Democrats for Democracy' would be a catchy term for
them?" (In fairness, it sure beats "The People, Not the Powerful.") I
gather by "Bush aide," Kramer meant "some guy I met on a bus."
Inasmuch as the chairman of the Democratic National Committee
has gone on CBS's *Face the Nation* and called me—an opinion
columnist with no connection whatsoever to the Republican Party
or George Bush—"a top Republican operative," what liberals mean
by terms like "Republican operative" and "Republican aide" is
rather broad, including "anyone to the right of Barbra Streisand."

While *Human Events* was prepared to back Gore if he was the
electoral college winner, liberals' affection for the electoral college

seems to depend on how the election comes out, revealing the essence of being a liberal: the absolute conviction that there is one set of rules for you, and another, completely different set of rules for everyone else. Before the election—when Gore was the one who was supposed to win the electoral college but lose the popular vote—University of Southern California law professor Erwin Chemerinsky stated categorically, "The Constitution says that it is the electoral college that determines who is the president. It leaves no doubt." But after Gore lost the electoral college, Chemerinsky found room for doubt! This apparently follows from Chemerinsky's notion that the Constitution is a "living document"—as in Dr. Frankenstein screeching, "It's alive! It's alive!" In the *Los Angeles Times,* Chemerinsky demanded that Florida's 25 electoral votes be split evenly between Bush and Gore in order "to effectuate the will of the people." Florida voters had divided their votes evenly, giving about 3 million votes apiece to Bush and Gore; thus, Chemerinsky said, their "will" was to split their electoral college votes. But that's not how the electoral college works. It was the "will" of 42 percent of California voters that Bush get their electoral college votes, and yet every single one of California's 54 electoral votes went to Gore. Chemerinsky was not so troubled about ignoring the will of 4.6 million Bush voters in California.

As we know from the media consortium that examined Florida ballots after Gore finally conceded, Bush would have won under every recount requested by any party or ordered by any court. But it took the media consortium eleven months of playing "Carnac" with Florida ballots to tell us that. Had the Democrats gotten their way, Florida election officials still would have been holding ballots to the light by the fairly important date of September 11, 2001. ■

NOVEMBER 7, 2000: The networks incorrectly call a Gore victory in Florida while the polls are still open in the Florida Panhandle, suppressing the vote for Bush, who still wins. The networks switch their call to Bush. Gore concedes the election and then retracts his concession, beginning our long election nightmare.

HOW TO TALK TO A LIBERAL (If You Must)   281

☞ Elections in Clintonville

NOVEMBER 10, 2000

I have a sick, sinking feeling: It's impeachment all over again. But this time it's about the results of a presidential election. Like his mentor Bill Clinton, Al Gore is willing to precipitate a constitutional crisis in order to hold on to power. Democrats are going to turn the world's most successful method of transferring power into another O.J. slow-speed car chase. I no longer care about taxes, abortion, affirmative action—I just want to be rid of these people.

Gore's endgame is to delay confirmation of the Florida vote for as long as possible—just the way his role model of a boss would in these circumstances. (Maybe Hillary can find some extra Gore votes in the White House living quarters where she found those missing Whitewater files that had been under subpoena for two years.) Under the Twelfth Amendment, the president is to be chosen by "a majority of the whole number of Electors appointed." If Gore can prevent Florida from appointing its electors by December 18, when the electors meet, Florida's electors will be excluded. Gore will win with 260 electoral votes. In football this is known as "running out the clock." In politics it's called "cheating."

Gore has a number of stratagems for throwing roadblocks in the way of Florida's appointing electors, mostly featuring time-consuming legal challenges. Nostalgic Stalinists from Brooklyn, now transplanted to Florida in their dotage, have already trotted out lawsuits demanding a second chance to vote because they were confused by the ballot. I've been to law school and I've still never heard of the "Stupidity Clause." It doesn't matter that Gore's legal machinations are precisely as meritorious as President Clinton's "Secret Service privilege" claim. If enough lawsuits are filed, maybe Gore will win the lottery. But in any event, pointless litigation buys him more time.

The law schools are chock-full of droning professors who will attest to the legitimacy of the Democrats' phony legal claims. Having rested up from impeachment and the O.J. trial, they're ready to tackle a presidential election. Liberals have even dusted off the old impeachment catchphrases, condescendingly instructing the public not to make a "rush to judgment" and to "take a deep breath."

As with impeachment, the spin is having its effect: We've gone from a Bush win—subject to a single state's recount—to "the next president, whoever that may be." We've gone from *this will be resolved by 5 P.M. to-morrow* to *this could take weeks.* We've gone from rolling our eyes at hapless old people claiming they slipped and voted for the wrong guy to Morton Kondracke saying of the ballot, "Well, yeah, sure, *now* it looks easy." We've gone from stark horror at the idea of a hostile takeover deter-mining the next leader of the free world to *New York Times* lawyer Floyd Abrams saying that lawsuits are "part of the process." Perhaps strangest of all, the networks have taken the Chinese curse "may you live in interesting times" and begun referring to it as merely a "saying," a "proverb"—even a "blessing"!

We are being inured to the proposition that Bush has not won. Inured to the idea that any states and districts that Gore lost should be subject to a do-over. Inured to the idea that meaningless expressions of popular ap-proval should prevail over constitutional mechanisms for selecting the president. Inured to the notion that the presidential election is not decided on election day, or even the next day, but can sometimes be a months-long process. Once we were shocked by the suggestion that the president could be shown to have committed felonies and still continue in office. But after a while, we got used to that, too.

This isn't a two-out-of-three match. If it were, Bush would have won already. If Gore loses the third recount (which may have been mercifully curtailed by the time we go to press), there will be a fourth. Even if we pretend there is no such thing as a "deadline," it is simply not the case that each recount increases the accuracy of the vote count. Each recount in-creases the number of scores we have—it does not increase their accuracy. As statisticians quoted in the *New York Times* have said, "Every time you count [large numbers], you're going to get a different answer." Democrats will not accept a recount as true and accurate until they finally concoct one that makes Gore the winner.

When and if that happens, righteous prigs in the Republican Party will somberly call on Bush to concede, to show how honorable "we" are—for-getting the little detail about Bush having already won. Even when they've won, Republicans instinctively lunge toward defeat. In response to the in-sanely partisan recount of three Democratic districts in Florida, many Re-publican flacks simply demanded that Republican counties be included in the hand recount, too. How about this for a Republican bargaining position: Bush won. Let's move on (as they used to say about a certain felon in the White House).

John O'Sullivan, editor-at-large of *National Review,* has counseled losing, saying a Gore presidency could be a "blessing in disguise" in light of the fact that the economy is likely to tank during the next president's term. That certainly is a good disguise—it bears not the slightest resemblance to a "blessing." Republicans have gotten good at losing and they want to stick with what they're good at. I'm not convinced you ever really hit pay dirt by losing, but I am positive it's not a good idea right now. It's bad enough for Americans to have witnessed a known lawbreaker sitting in the Oval Office. Criminal methods—perjury, obstruction of justice, witness tampering, using the instruments of federal government to intimidate witnesses—all these have been shown to work. On the heels of a Clinton presidency, it cannot be good for the country to watch a presidential election being openly stolen by the horny hick's vice president. To put it in liberal terms, letting Gore steal this election might "send the wrong signal."

On Day 2 of America Held Hostage, former president George Bush—father of President-elect Bush—was on television commending his son for the dignity he had shown during this national emergency. Yes, we're all very proud. Al Gore, the rube, has demanded a recount in Florida, while Bush has decorously refrained from requesting recounts in Iowa, Wisconsin, and New Mexico—not to mention Missouri, where anti-Bush vote fraud was credibly charged. Bush's brother, the Florida governor, graciously removed himself from involvement in the Florida recount, but Florida's attorney general—who happens to be Al Gore's campaign chairman in that state—boorishly did not. Al Gore goes around loutishly declaring himself the popular-vote champion, while Bush genteelly refrains from any such boasts. The symbol for the Democratic Party shouldn't be a donkey, it should be two sets of standards.

This is no time for Republicans to be putting their good breeding on display. The Democrats have declared war. Jesse Jackson is presiding over rioting in the streets. There is a movement afoot to call in Janet Reno. (Maybe she could send federal troopers to Midland, Texas, to gas George Bush.) All we need now are chickens in the street and beggars with leprosy to complete the picture. This is no time for dignity. President Bush had dignity. Senator Bob Dole had dignity. They lost. In particular, they lost to the two blackguards in the White House now dragging the country into yet another constitutional crisis. It will never end until these people are gone. It's time for Bush to stop acting like a lockjaw Connecticut WASP and start acting like a Texan. ■

NOVEMBER 11, 2000: Bush files suit in federal district court, arguing that the selective recounts violate the Constitution's Equal Protection Clause.

NOVEMBER 13, 2000: U.S. District Court Judge Donald M. Middlebrooks, appointed by Clinton, finds that the selective recounts do not violate the Constitution and orders the partial hand recount to continue.

☞ New Equal Protection Clause: One Man, Several Votes

NOVEMBER 13, 2000

As Soviet dictator Joseph Stalin said, "It doesn't matter who votes. It only matters who counts the ballots." That's just what Al Gore is betting on as he demands his third recount in Florida, this one conducted exclusively in Democratic bastions such as Palm Beach County. A selective hand recount is calculated to ensure that Gore's margin will increase, even if an equal number of Bush votes were missed by voting machines statewide. Any hand recount will increase the total number of votes cast by resuscitating formerly invalid ballots—even ballots that would never be accepted by any voting machine—and the revived ballots will tend to reflect the voting preferences of the district. So hand recounts conducted only in counties Gore won will undoubtedly swell his votes. This is like having mothers judge their own babies in a beauty contest. No one even remotely familiar with the principles of free and fair elections would allow such a procedure to take place, which may explain why we haven't heard from Jimmy Carter.

The media have been portraying the Bush legal team's argument as a general attack on all hand recounts. That's part of it certainly, which

should not come as a surprise to anyone who has seen the nudnicks counting ballots on TV—holding punch cards to the light, interpreting smudge
marks on the ballots, and consulting tarot cards to divine the voters' elusive intent. This could be the first time in U.S. history the results of a presidential election are determined by TV psychic Miss Cleo. The room for
error, manipulation, and general mayhem is gargantuan. Punch card ballots are not like wine; they do not improve with age. Not only do different
counties have different rules about how to read the animal entrails, but
whenever humans are introduced into any process, there will be errors.
Ask NASA about that Mars landing.

But Bush has a separate equal-protection argument that does not in-
dict hand counts across the board but only hand counts conducted exclusively in three lucky Florida Democratic counties. Voters in only certain
select counties get to have their ballots given an extra visual inspection,
while voters in other counties are denied the right to a visual inspection of
their ballots. Allowing the voters of only certain Democratic counties two
chances to have their ballots read (first by machine, then by hand) while
allowing voters in the rest of the state only one chance to have their ballots
read (by machine only) is as unconstitutional as a state's giving Democratic counties two days to vote and Republican counties only one day.
Only an insane, rogue judge would allow such a selective recount to take
place. (Let's just hope this doesn't end up in the Florida Supreme Court!)

It is true—as Gore's combatants never tire of pointing out—that the
scam they've pulled off is permitted under Florida law, which allows candidates to request hand recounts in particular counties within a specified
time period after an election. But we have a tradition in this country of
striking down state laws that violate the U.S. Constitution. It is hardly
"ironic"—the Democrats' attack du jour—for *Republicans* to argue that
the Florida law is unconstitutional. Respecting states' rights does not
mean respecting a state's right to enforce unconstitutional laws. Even assuming Bush was ambushed and it's his own fault for not demanding a
hand recount in Republican-leaning districts, neither Bush nor any candidate has the right to waive someone else's constitutional rights. If Florida
citizens have an equal-protection right to have their votes count as much
as those of citizens who live in other parts of the state, this is not a right
that can be taken away by state law—or the happenstance of one candidate not asking for a recount because he already won the election.

There isn't a lot of relevant precedent—it's not often someone tries to steal a presidential election—but in a case called *O'Brien v. Skinner*, 414 U.S. 524 (1974), the Supreme Court struck down a New York election law less insane than the three-county hand count in Florida. The law at issue in *O'Brien* permitted pretrial detainees to obtain absentee ballots only if they were jailed in a county other than the county of their residence, while inhabitants of jails in the counties of their residence were denied absentee ballots. Because the law distinguished voting rights on the basis of one's residence, the court held, it placed "an unconstitutionally onerous burden on the . . . exercise of the franchise."

But now a federal judge appointed by Clinton found that a state's decision to give the ballots of only some lucky (Democratic) counties an extra visual inspection—based solely on the county of their residence—doesn't violate the Equal Protection Clause. (How odd that a Bill Clinton appointee could have so little regard for the Constitution.) If nothing else, at least it can now be said: The U.S. Supreme Court is more solicitous of the voting rights of the criminally accused than a Clinton-appointed judge is solicitous of the voting rights of Republicans. ∎

☞ The Liar Next Time

NOVEMBER 14, 2000

In a fast-breaking story like the Democrats' attempt to steal a presidential election, it can be hard to keep up with the barrage of lies. Before today's lies become "old news," I thought it would be useful to begin a running tabulation. A recount shall be ordered in Democratic counties only.

Lie No. 1: We don't know who won the election yet.

Yes we do. George W. Bush won, albeit extremely narrowly in one state, with a total of 271 electoral votes. Al Gore demanded a recount in one of the states he lost narrowly. After the Gore Loser got his recount, it turned out the winner was . . . Bush again! (Subject only to a final count of the overseas ballots, which have historically gone Republican in Florida and elsewhere.)

Consequently, Gore insisted upon yet a third count, this time with a highly manipulable and probably unconstitutional hand recount in

Democratic counties only. By his fourth try Gore will be insisting on counting only the ballots of Gore campaign staff.

Lie No. 2: Gore has nothing to do with the Florida recount, which is mandated by law.

This is false. Gore is completely responsible for dragging the country through this nightmare. The recount is not like some unstoppable Star Chamber death warrant. Gore set the recount in motion when he retracted his concession to Bush on election night. The "shall order a recount" language means only that the loser doesn't have to pay for a recount in close elections. This is not an insignificant point: Recounts are extremely expensive. But it does not mean that in a national election to determine the next leader of the free world the loser is absolutely required to drag the country though seventeen recounts and endless litigation before finally conceding. The Florida recount provision explicitly states, "A recount need not be ordered with respect to the returns for any office, however, if the candidate or candidates defeated . . . request in writing that a recount not be made."

The current crisis is all Gore's fault. He could put an end to this madness at any time by conceding like a man. Bush can't stop it, because he's not the loser. Gore is.

Lie No. 3: The butterfly ballot is illegal under Florida law.

In the November 10 *Washington Post*, Philip Heymann, former Harvard Law School professor and Clinton deputy attorney general, claimed that the now infamous butterfly ballot was "a plain violation of the law." (What a pity that so many Florida precinct chiefs, almost all of them Democrats, approved of the butterfly ballot before the election.) Heymann said the law requires voters to "vote for a candidate whose name is printed on the ballot—place a cross [x] mark in the blank space at the right of the name of the candidate" (Section 101.151). The "critical point" he said, is that the butterfly ballot sometimes required voters to "mark on the right, as the law required, and sometimes on the left."

It might have struck a lot of readers that in addition to stating that the mark must be on the right, the law requires a "cross [x] mark" to be put on the ballot. The butterfly ballot does not permit cross marks anyplace. Stay with me here because this can get pretty confusing if you've never completed the "think and do" section in a *Highlights* magazine. Apparently what voters are required to do with a butterfly ballot is: Find the name of their preferred candidate, follow the arrow from his name to a circle, and punch a hole in the circle. It's all quite baffling, and thank heaven we have fancy, high-priced lawyers to explain complicated legal issues like this.

The reason the circles were not "at the right" of candidate names on the butterfly ballot is that the "at the right" requirement has nothing to do with butterfly ballots. That phrase comes from a chapter tellingly titled "Voting by paper ballot"—you know, the kind of ballot on which it is possible to "place a cross [x] mark in the blank space"—not to be confused with a butterfly ballot. If you read down just a little bit, down past the section on "paper ballots," there is a completely different chapter titled "Voting machine ballots"—which would include butterfly ballots. This section clearly states that the location of the "push knob, key, lever, or other device" must simply "indicate to the elector" which candidate the "push knob, key, lever, or other device" refers to. Remember this episode the next time you hear a Harvard Law professor rambling on about what "the law" requires.

Lie No. 4: Pat Buchanan could not *possibly* have received three thousand-odd votes in Palm Beach County.

Just four years ago Pat Buchanan received three times that many votes in a primary in Palm Beach. A primary! So we know there are at least 9,000 potential Buchanan voters in Palm Beach—and they're the kind of dedicated voters who come out for primaries. This year, the Reform Party candidate for the House of Representatives received over seven thousand votes from Palm Beach.

Lie No. 5: I believe President Clinton.

Whoops! That's "old news." ■

☞ This Is What the Electoral College Is Supposed to Prevent

NOVEMBER 16, 2000

Like many of you, I've been on tenterhooks waiting for New York's junior senator to weigh in on the electoral college. Just days after her election, Hillary finally ended the suspense. She vowed to combat the electoral college so that "the popular vote, the will of the people" will reign triumphant. Where was all this concern for the will of the people when she was trying to shove HillaryCare down our throats?

It should come as no surprise that Hillary opposes the electoral college. Alexander Hamilton explained that the whole point of the electoral college was to interpose "every practicable obstacle" to "cabal, intrigue, and corruption," which, interestingly enough, are the three virtues embossed on the Clinton family coat of arms. The Constitution's roundabout method of choosing a president was intended to frustrate "the adversaries of republican government" and prevent them from gaining "an improper ascendant in our councils."

The framers opposed a pure popular vote for president, believing it would reward oily candidates practiced, as Hamilton put it in *Federalist* No. 68, at the "little arts of popularity"—such as feeling our pain. Instead of relying upon "existing bodies of men who might be tampered with beforehand to prostitute their votes," the people would vote for electors, and the electors would have the "temporary and sole purpose" of choosing the president. The system obviously isn't foolproof: Bill Clinton slipped through the net. But the electoral college has largely been free of the corrupting influences that worried the framers. Electors have occasionally wandered off the reservation, as in 1988 when a lone Dukakis elector cast his vote for Lloyd Bentsen, but as a group they've been pretty incorruptible.

No elector has ever been convicted of taking bribes—as judges and members of Congress have been. The profoundly senile are generally not chosen to be electors, but they can and often do attempt to vote in Palm Beach County. The *New York Times* has never run an op-ed piece proposing that electors trade their votes—as it did recently with regard to Nader and Gore voters trading popular votes across state lines. Electors have never been stolen outright by a Chicago mayor or Texas precinct captain—as popular votes have been. If you try to dump ten thousand electors into Lake Michigan, somebody's bound to notice.

The electoral college is supposed to be enigmatic and complex—the better to foil "foreign powers," "cabals," and other "enemies of republican government," as Hamilton put it. It remains to be seen if the electoral college can frustrate the Clintonized Democratic Party. The current crisis foisted on the nation by Al Gore illustrates with some clarity the sort of mischief the electoral college is intended to prevent. By tallying presidential votes state by state, the electoral college isolates the effect of voter fraud in any one state. If the national total were up for grabs, the whole country would quickly be initiated into the Chicago vote-stealing customs now taking place in Florida. Mysterious ballot boxes would be turning up in every black church in America. Hapless old people nationwide would be taking to the airwaves to claim they were really trying to order a Whopper but somehow ended up voting for Pat Buchanan. Homeless people in Milwaukee would be bribed with cartons of cigarettes to vote for Al Gore—wait, that one actually happened.

Even assuming Gore's popular vote advantage holds (and Bush's numbers would surely be higher if the media hadn't incorrectly projected a Gore win in Florida before the polls closed), the candidates' nationwide tallies are separated by a sneeze. At some point you have to cut off debate or there will be chaos and warfare. People can't live like liberals, endlessly jawboning hypothetical possibilities and refusing to submit to rules. This is America, not the UN. If a lawyer is one day late filing the complaint, Granny loses her slip-and-fall case. That's how rules work. There have to be institutional boundaries to curtail endless navel-gazing. Legitimate claims—which Gore's is not—are sometimes devalued for a stable social order. More horrifying than the curious prospect of a popular-vote "winner" losing the electoral vote is the fact that Hillary "Cattle Futures" Clinton is going to be a United States senator, but those are the rules, and we've learned to live with that.

The electoral college establishes a set of rules and those rules make Bush the winner. Bush has already won more popular votes than Bill Clinton got in either of his elections. You remember Clinton—he was the guy liberals said we couldn't impeach because that would overturn "the results of an election." ■

☞ The Law, Not the Court, Has the Last Word

NOVEMBER 20, 2000—
the day before Florida's Kangaroo Court issued its
first opinion on Gore's tantrum

It ought to be apparent from the way the media have been carrying on about the "highly respected" Florida Supreme Court that the court is on the verge of openly violating the law. By the time this early Thanksgiving issue arrives in your mailbox, the court's willful disregard of the law will probably have attained the status of hard fact.

The portion of Florida election law the court intends to violate is this, Section 102.111: "If the county returns are not received by the Department of State by 5 P.M. of the seventh day following an election, all missing counties *shall be ignored,* and the results shown by the returns on file shall be certified" (part to be flagrantly violated by the Florida Supreme Court in italics). Note that the law, duly enacted by the other two branches of Florida government, does *not* say that results submitted past the deadline "may be ignored." It says "shall be ignored." Note that it also does not say "shall be ignored, unless the Florida Supreme Court disagrees because Al Gore needs more time to steal votes." There's also no reference here to confused, elderly Jews.

That's not the only provision in Florida law that makes the seven-day deadline for submitting election returns mandatory. Section 102.112 (helpfully titled "Deadline for submission of county returns to the Department of State; penalties") states—again unequivocally—"Returns *must be* filed by 5 P.M. on the seventh day following the . . . general election" (part to be flagrantly violated by the Florida Supreme Court in italics).

Under the law, the only person who has discretion to waive the mandatory seven-day deadline is Florida's secretary of state: "If the returns are not received by the Department [of State] by the time specified, such returns *may* be ignored and the results on file at that time may be certified by the department" (part to be flagrantly violated by the Florida Supreme Court in italics).

Whether or not the secretary of state—in her discretion—accepts any late-filed election returns, she is commanded to fine "each board member" of the country election board "$200 for each day such returns are late, the fine to be paid only from the board member's personal funds."

So the seven-day deadline imposed by law is pretty unambiguous. Two sections of Florida law make the deadline mandatory ("shall be ignored" and "must be filed"); another gives the secretary of state discretion to ignore any late-filed returns ("may be ignored")—in which case, the delinquent board members are to be fined personally. There are a lot of murky, complex issues in the law. This isn't one of them.

Naturally, therefore, the Democrats argue that the seven-day deadline imposed by Florida law is optional—just a suggestion, nonbinding thoughts tossed out by the legislature, something akin to Democrats' view of the Commandments against lying and adultery: you're free to take it or leave it. The *New York Times* has referred to "the Republicans' contention that state law allowed no leeway in the deadline." Unambiguous statements of the law are now called mere "contentions" of Republicans.

Al Gore lost the election, lost the recount, and also lost the third manual recount to the point permitted by law. Now he wants a bunch of corrupt judges to change the law two weeks after the election has taken place, to give him yet a *fourth* opportunity to steal enough votes to win.

And the "highly respected" Florida Supreme Court will probably let him. Leave it to Democrats to turn a presidential election into the sequel to "The Night the Lights Went Out in Georgia." Not to worry, though. The Florida Supreme Court justices may think they have the powers of Pol Pot, but there are other branches of government capable of following the law, despite the rulings of this Kangaroo Court.

One surmises that Secretary of State Katherine Harris will have some crucial role to play. The giveaway is that Harris hasn't done anything yet, but she is already being viciously attacked by the Democrats' Election-Stealing Task Force. Harris has been called a "crook" by O.J.-and-Clinton defender Alan Dershowitz. She has been called a "hack" and "Soviet commissar" by Gore spokesman Chris Lehane. (Liberals take a principled stand against the death penalty in all circumstances except in cases of killing the messenger.)

The *Washington Post* devoted an entire article to sneering about Harris's makeup: "they were the [eye] lashes of Tammy Faye . . . cartoon lashes," "she looked as if she were wearing a mask," "to be honest, [she] seems to have applied her makeup with a trowel." Would that the evil Katherine Harris were a ravishing sexpot like Janet Reno or Ruth Bader

Ginsburg! This is the same crowd that will tell you with a straight face that Bill Clinton is "handsome"—exhibit A of people being literally blinded by their ideology. Harris is getting the Linda Tripp treatment from liberals because she seems like the sort of person inclined to follow the law. Democrats hate that. The Florida Supreme Court they can work with; obsessive rule-followers are the bane of Democrats' existence.

Suppose the Florida Supreme Court directs the secretary of state to violate the law—as they surely will—by ordering Harris not to ignore election returns submitted after the mandatory statutory deadline she is required by law to follow. Should Harris obey the written law, enacted by the legislature and signed by the governor prior to knowing whom the law would benefit? Or should Harris follow the results-oriented, lawless ruling of seven judges—all appointed during Democratic administrations—intended to give a Democratic presidential candidate yet a fourth shot at stealing an election he's already lost? Hmmm . . . that's a tough one. The rule of law, or a partisan scam—which should prevail? Either way, Harris will be violating some official decree.

Harris ought to follow the real law. That's not going to be easy. The *Washington Post*'s attacks on Harris's mascara are just a sample of what is to come if Harris fails to obey a dishonest ruling from the Kangaroo Court. The *Washington Post* has a rapid-response team fully assembling even now, prepared to attack Harris's hair, her wardrobe, even her accessorizing if it will help Al Gore. If Harris follows the written law, the Florida attorney general, Bob Butterworth—also known as "Gore's Florida Campaign Chairman"—may well try to prosecute Harris for violating a court order.

In the end, it might dawn on the members of the Florida Supreme Court that other government officials will be reviewing their handiwork. The U.S. Supreme Court might do loopy things from time to time, but it's hard to imagine that the justices could miss the unmistakable language of Florida's seven-day deadline on election returns. It's also hard to imagine that they would overlook the rank corruption inherent in a court altering the rules for judging a presidential election after the election has already been held. If the Florida Supreme Court judges are not as stupid as they are partisan, the court might well follow the law to avoid being overruled by the U.S. Supreme Court and shut down this nightmare once and for all. But I wouldn't count on it. The "most ethical administration in history" can't seem to leave without giving the country one last kick in the pants. ■

NOVEMBER 21, 2000: The Florida Supreme Court orders manual recounts to continue until November 26, or early November 27.

☞ Certify the Electors, Then the Judges

NOVEMBER 22, 2000

After having denounced the Florida Supreme Court as a corrupt and dishonest Kangaroo Court long before its lawless ruling earlier this week, I'm kind of relieved that they didn't prove me wrong. Still, it's breathtaking how totally detached from any sort of legal reasoning the court's decision is. While taking a sledgehammer to the law, this Warren Court with a thyroid condition insisted it was engaging in a delicate and serious balancing analysis, affording due concern to competing interests. Except the problem is: That's not their job. The Florida legislature had already engaged in a balancing of competing interests. And it came to a different conclusion.

Taking into account many and various factors—finality, accuracy, sore losers demanding interminable recounts, and so on—the Florida legislature decided that counties would be permitted to indulge in all the recounting they desired, but then they had to turn in their election returns seven days after the election. The decision of where to strike the balance has already been made and enacted in law—written by the legislature, signed by the governor, put on the Florida statute books. But Al Gore lost the election, lost the recount, lost the absentee ballot returns, and lost all the manual recounts that could be completed within seven days. So he asked the Florida Supreme Court to give him more time to keep recounting, relying on Bill Daley's genetic vote-counting skills to eventually make him the winner.

The problem was that pesky seven-day deadline (aka "the law"). The Florida Supreme Court was not interpreting an ambiguous statute, resolving a conflict, or filling in a blank space in the law. What Gore requested, and what the Kangaroo Court granted, was a judicial coup overturning the unambiguous seven-day deadline put on the books by the other two branches of government and replacing it with a nineteen-day deadline.

The court papered over its lawless ruling with this inane sophistry: If the law permits recounts, it must permit recounts to go on and on and on, until the loser can finally steal enough votes to win or the whole country dies of exhaustion. It is true that manual recounts are permitted by Florida law. But that doesn't mean there's no deadline. Gore may as well have argued that because there's Christmas shopping, there's no such thing as Christmas. You can shop and shop and shop—but Christmas imposes a deadline. Florida counties can indulge in recounts to their hearts' desire, but seven days after the election is the deadline. If Florida election law had a motto, it would be "When it absolutely, positively has to be filed within seven days."

To put the law in terms understandable to Democrats: You can give homeless people cigarettes in exchange for votes, you can register felons and illegal immigrants, you can count "dimpled chads," animal entrails, ballots pulled out of disappearing Vote-o-Matics. But you have to steal all the votes you're going to steal by 5 P.M. seven days after the election. If Gore still hasn't won, you have to stop bothering everyone and go home.

But Gore's idiotic demand found a receptive audience with the Florida Supreme Court. It appears that the justices' mental acuity has been impaired from the fumes of all those ambulances they spent their careers chasing. (The chief justice of that court gave $500 to Clinton-Gore in 1992, but did not recuse himself from a case in which Gore is a party—which at least reversed the usual flow of funds one expects in such a court.) The justices claimed to be stumped by blindingly clear statements of the law. It's as if the justices of the Florida Supreme Court read Oliver Wendell Holmes's stirring words about judges having "jurisdiction only to declare the law" and not "authority to make it"—and said, "Huh? Does anybody know what that means?" Now the whole country isn't sure whether to wait out the process or call 911.

The Florida court's ruling is even more insane than the typical judicial imperialism. Usually, when judges are hankering to legislate, they choose territory where there is no written law at all. Where the law is silent, they concoct "penumbras" and "emanations" and discover hitherto unnoticed, invisible provisions. At least with *Roe v. Wade*, the U.S. Supreme Court invented clauses where the Constitution was silent. The Florida decision is even more lawless than *Roe*. Florida law isn't silent on the question of when the election is over. In no uncertain terms, the law imposes a mandatory seven-day deadline on the submission of election returns. The Kangaroo Court simply took the seven-day statutory deadline and replaced it with a nineteen-day deadline.

Poor Secretary of State Katherine Harris is subject to directly opposed legal commands. She is, of course, required to follow Florida law, as are all Florida residents (except, evidently, judges). And Florida law explicitly directs her to "ignore" any election returns submitted after the seven-day deadline and to certify the electors. This is, quite literally, the job she swore an oath before God she would faithfully execute. But at the same time, the order of the Florida Supreme Court commands Harris to defy the law—the one duly enacted by proper legislative channels long before anyone knew precisely how much time Al Gore would need to steal votes (which is apparently nineteen days). In order to follow the real law, she will have to violate the court's lunatic order.

It's as if state law set a 60-mile-an-hour speed limit and the Florida Supreme Court came along and ordered Katherine Harris to drive her car at 120 miles per hour and to disregard traffic signals (provided George W. Bush were in front of her car). Sane state officials in Florida still have to do their jobs. As Ken Starr can attest, Democrats make it extremely difficult for people to do their jobs when that consists of enforcing the law. But it's Katherine Harris's job to certify the electors as provided in the real law (seven-day deadline) and not the Junta's manifesto (nineteen-day deadline—until we sober up long enough to start issuing more orders).

The legislature has a responsibility to protect its authority to write laws and have them given effect. It should act promptly to confirm the electoral slate certified by Harris. And Governor Jeb Bush has a duty to enforce the law. We're sorry he's the president-elect's brother, but it was the networks that created this fiasco in Florida—rather than in a state where the president's brother is not the governor—by incorrectly calling the election for Gore while the polls were still open in Florida. Instead of being a gentleman to thieving Democrats, it's time for Jeb to exhibit a little of that famous Bush gallantry toward a beleaguered state official trying to obey the law. ■

NOVEMBER 22, 2000: Gore says both he and Bush should start planning their White House transitions.

NOVEMBER 24, 2000: After legal experts have assured us that the U.S. Supreme Court won't hear Bush's appeal of the Florida Supreme Court's decision, the Court agrees to hear the case.

NOVEMBER 26, 2000: Florida Secretary of State Katherine Harris certifies the election results on the date set by the Florida Supreme Court. Bush wins a 537-vote victory over Gore.

☞ Things Only a Democrat Will Say with a Straight Face

NOVEMBER 29, 2000

If you have any doubt that Al Gore's selfless pleas for "democracy" are part of his scheme to steal the election, consider this: In one of Gore's many pending lawsuits against the Florida election results, he asked the court to declare him the winner on the grounds that there are still thousands of votes to be counted. That's funny. If the ballots haven't been "counted" yet, how does he know he's the winner? In order to make sense of this, you have to presume that Gore won the election (as Gore clearly has done) and work backwards from there.

In the category of "Things Only a Democrat Would Say with a Straight Face," Florida State Representative Debra Danburg told Chris Matthews on CNBC's *Hardball* that some voters meant to vote but didn't actually punch the ballot (for Gore, no doubt) because—I quote—they were "afraid to hurt the machine."

Unpunched ballots are a gold mine for Democrats. As we know from the chads littering the floors of the "counting" areas, these late-breaking votes are not being "counted" three weeks after the election—they are being cast. Through pure brazenness Democrats are turning uncast votes into votes for Gore. We've entered the *Alice in Wonderland* realm of polls, spin, and counting earwax on punch card ballots. This is the liberals' playing field. Truth doesn't matter, honor doesn't matter, fairness doesn't matter. Once Democrats are freed from the tyranny of objectivity, they are liberated to lie and cheat and steal.

Liberals always prefer spin to hard facts. They promote the concept of a "living" Constitution unbounded by the objective and determinant words in the document. They want phony polls to determine constitutional questions like impeachment. They want the census to be determined by "sampling" rather than an "actual enumeration," as the Constitution specifies. They want criminals punished not merely for the act of, say, committing murder, but also on the basis of a subjective determination of whether the murder was committed out of "hate"—in contradistinction to all those crimes being committed out of love. They want SAT scores dropped as a criterion for college admissions, preferring purely subjective evaluations of the applicant's "diversity." It's probably just a matter of time before someone in the Gore camp declares the recounts irrelevant because "people have different ways of voting."

After suffering through months and months of polls purporting to demonstrate that 20 million "swing voters" were wildly rushing back and forth each week from Bush to Gore, Gore to Bush, and on and on, finally—finally!—we took the only poll that counts. A focus group of 100 million Americans chose a president by casting secret ballots. Gore lost but refused to concede . . . and now we're right back to hearing who the polls say should be president.

Gore's lawyer David Boies—fast becoming the William Ginsberg of the 2000 election—argued that the unambiguous seven-day deadline for election returns imposed by Florida law is optional. In short order the media took up the cudgel—*Who's to say? There are arguments on both sides. Democrats and Republicans are both just playing politics.* . . . And giving the final patina of legitimacy to a crackpot argument, the Florida Kangaroo Court "interpreted" "seven days," as written in the law, to mean "nineteen days." That really happened.

Only a Democrat could come up with such brazenly illogical arguments. Gore insists on manual recounts. But he wants manual recounts in only three heavily Democratic counties in a single state—so that "every vote" will count! Democrats denounce the "butterfly" ballot as racist and borderline sadistic. But the ballot was designed by, and its use approved of by, Democrats. Democrats claim a manual recount will remedy the dastardly "butterfly" ballot which caused confused old people to vote for someone other than Gore by mistake. But they have not explained how a manual recount is going to help people who claim they voted for the wrong candidate. Democrats claim Gore voters were intimidated from approaching the polls—which I suppose is possible if Gore voters follow traffic laws as well as they follow voting laws. But they have not explained how a manual recount will rectify alleged voter intimidation. It is all utterly incoherent, but coherence is irrelevant. Only spin matters. Al Gore and the Democrats will say anything, do anything to win. ∎

NOVEMBER 30, 2000: A Florida legislative committee recommends a special session to name the state's 25 representatives to the electoral college.

DECEMBER 1, 2000: The U.S. Supreme Court hears arguments on the Florida Supreme Court's extension of the election deadline.

DECEMBER 4, 2000: The U.S. Supreme Court vacates the Florida Supreme Court's decision and remands to the court with instructions to please read the Constitution and federal law next time.

☞ *National Lampoon*'s Florida Supreme Court Vacation

DECEMBER 6, 2000

Despite morale-boosting claims in the mainstream media that the U.S. Supreme Court's unanimous ruling didn't really do anything—or as Al Gore put it (*Twilight Zone* theme music here), was "neutral," perhaps even "favorable"—the U.S. Supreme Court's opinion just knocked the air out of the Supreme Court of Florida (SCOFLA).

For openers, the Supreme Court vacated SCOFLA's silly ruling. It didn't have to do that. The Court could have remanded with instructions without vacating the decision. The Court could have declined to review the decision altogether—as scores of legal "experts" swore up and down it would. Not least of all, the Court could have affirmed the opinion as a proper exercise of SCOFLA's judicial powers. As Florida's learned state senator Debbie Wasserman explained on CNN's *Crossfire*, "There is something called the separation of powers, and the system of checks and balances. And the judicial branch—unfortunately, Governor Bush doesn't realize this—but the judicial branch interprets the laws." Apparently, the United States Supreme Court didn't "realize" it either. After getting a gander at how SCOFLA exercised the "separation of powers," a unanimous U.S. Supreme Court said: VACATED. The Court referred SCOFLA to the Constitution and federal law as helpful little guideposts the Florida court might want to consult before issuing any more opinions. (The Court also ordered state senator Wasserman to retake ninth-grade U.S. history.)

The Supreme Court repeatedly invoked the deference normally accorded state courts, but said there are exceptions. After one such tribute to the nobility of state courts, the Supreme Court said, "But in the case of a law enacted by a state legislature applicable not only to elections to state offices, but also to the selection of presidential electors, the legislature is not acting solely under the authority given it by the people of the state, but by virtue of a direct grant of authority made under Article II, Section 1, Clause 2 of the United States Constitution."

State courts may deserve deference, but if a state court orders federal troops to attack Canada, for example, the order is going to be reversed. And if a state court "interprets" a seven-day deadline in the state's law on presidential elections to mean a nineteen-day deadline, the court's decision will be reversed. The real Supreme Court reminded SCOFLA that a presidential election is a federal issue, a matter committed to the state *legislatures* by the U.S. Constitution—and if you try to usurp the role of the legislature, the real Supreme Court is ready to reverse you.

It's going to be an adjustment for SCOFLA. Back during the halcyon days when SCOFLA thought it was immune from review, the court's hearings resembled nothing so much as a Soviet show trial. During oral argument, one Florida justice impertinently demanded of Bush's attorney, "What are the laws in Texas, Mr. Carvin?" What does one say to something like that? The justice may as well have asked him if he didn't think "nineteen" was a prettier word than "seven." For the benefit of the justices on the Florida Supreme Court, as well as anyone else without a working knowledge of the law, the election laws of other states have no bearing on the election laws of Florida. None whatsoever. The election laws of Uganda have as much binding authority in Florida as the laws of Texas. Raising the election laws of Texas is the sort of glib political jab the six viewers of CNN's *Crossfire* expect to hear from Paul Begala right before he cuts to a commercial. It is astonishing that a judge would make it.

While claiming total befuddlement at SCOFLA's decision, the Supreme Court said it sure hoped the court hadn't ignored the Constitution and federal law! This is how parents discipline small children: *I sure hope no one's reading under her covers after bedtime!* The Court's face-saving directive was clear to all but the willfully blind. Of course, SCOFLA found the meaning of the word "seven" to be an impenetrable mystery, so there's no assurance that subtlety will work with these guys. But there is one entity for whom we can be pretty sure the Supreme Court's ruling will not be a devilish puzzle—the Florida legislature. As the Supreme Court reminded the world, the Constitution provides that states shall appoint presidential electors "in such manner as the legislature thereof may direct." So knock yourself out, Seminole County! Exclude military ballots! Exclude ballots from all registered Republicans! The Florida legislature has the last word. ■

DECEMBER 8, 2000: The Florida Supreme Court orders manual recounts for 43,000 ballots that registered no vote. The court adds 383 votes to Gore's total.

DECEMBER 9, 2000: The U.S. Supreme Court orders the manual recounts stopped.

DECEMBER 11, 2000: The U.S. Supreme Court hears oral arguments on the Florida Supreme Court's decision.

DECEMBER 12, 2000: The Florida House of Representatives votes to certify a slate of electors for George W. Bush.

DECEMBER 12, 2000: The U.S. Supreme Court finds that the half-assed recount ordered by the Florida Supreme Court is unconstitutional. Seven justices find it violates the Equal Protection Clause; three of the seven find it also violates Article II of the Constitution, which grants state legislatures authority to determine the manner of choosing presidential electors (the correct grounds). Only two justices, Ruth Bader Ginsburg and John Paul Stevens, find that a partial recount of only some ballots in some Florida counties does not violate the Equal Protection Clause. According to Justice Ginsburg, the Equal Protection Clause refers only to abortion, it has nothing to do with voting rights.

☞ My Court Is Bigger Than Your Court

DECEMBER 12, 2000

Apparently, there are few better methods of becoming a trusted TV legal "expert" than being consistently wrong in your legal analysis. Smugness while issuing idiotic opinions is especially valued. There was a lot of both the week before the real Supreme Court vacated the Florida Kangaroo Court's crackpot interpretation of "seven days" in Florida election law to mean "nineteen days." Now that the U.S. Supreme Court has overruled everything the Florida Supreme Court did and ordered the recounts to stop, let's look at how the professors fared in their predictions over the last few weeks.

On CNBC's *Rivera Live,* Harvard Law professor Alan Dershowitz, finally emerging from his shell, explained the Supreme Court's original decision to hear the case this way: "Let me give you a theory of why I think the Supreme Court took the case. I think the Supreme Court took the case because of Jim Baker. The Supreme Court saw Jim Baker trashing a state Supreme Court, saying, in effect, that it's okay to defy the law of the highest court of the state, and I think there's some justices who said, 'We have to protect the judiciary here.'"

"Reversed!"

On Fox News's *O'Reilly Factor,* another Harvard Law professor, Martha Field, predicted that the "main principle" of the Supreme Court's ruling would be that "the U.S. Supreme Court will not interpret the meaning of state law." The learned professor sniffed, "I don't think the U.S. Supreme Court has a lot to say about this."

So there you have it. Except—oops—"Reversed!"

Professor Field was not only completely wrong, but irritated that Florida legislators had the audacity to disagree with her uniformly incorrect statements of the law. She scoffed at the little people in the Florida legislature for "suggesting that their decision would trump a decision of the Florida Supreme Court." If they believed that, Professor Field said, "they're pretty far out of line."

In fact, what the U.S. Supreme Court found "pretty far out of line" was the Florida Supreme Court's delusion (shared by Professor Field) that it could trump the Florida legislature in determining the manner in which presidential electors are appointed. So out of line that it reversed SCOFLA's ruling, explaining that "the State legislature's power to select the manner for appointing electors is plenary; it may, if it so chooses, select the electors itself." Students at Harvard Law School intent on learning the law, as opposed to learning to be arrogant while incorrectly stating the law, would be well advised to take some sort of legal correspondence course.

And not just Harvard students are in trouble. Nat Stern, a law professor at Florida State University, was quoted in the *St. Petersburg Times* saying that the election case was "a fairly ordinary matter" of a state court doing its job and that of course Bush would lose. Constitutional law professor Martin Redish of Northwestern University said, "I'd be flabbergasted if the Supreme Court actually accepted the Bush argument." (This was in contradistinction to the watertight argument of the Florida Supreme Court, which is: "It depends on what the meaning of 'seven' is.") In an article for *American Lawyer Media*, Vikram David Amar, constitutional law professor at Hastings College, referred to the "creative—and dare I say extraordinary"—argument of the Bush lawyers that the Florida Supreme Court ruling was invalid because it extended election deadlines that were set before the election.

A unanimous U.S. Supreme Court didn't find the Bush argument so "extraordinary." To the contrary, the Court agreed with Bush's lawyers, saying, "A legislative wish to take advantage of the 'safe harbor' [by enacting a seven-day deadline for election returns] would counsel against any construction of the Election Code that Congress might deem to be a change in the law." Seven justices agreed that what the Florida Supreme Court had done violated the Constitution's Equal Protection Clause. Five justices found that the only remedy was to stop the recount and allow the legislature to certify the electors.

Blowhard liberal law professors can never stick to just being wrong. They are compelled by some invisible force to be both wrong and supercilious. Law professor Lis Wiehl of the University of Washington repeated the Dershowitz theory that the Supreme Court had agreed to hear the case in order to express its deep and profound respect for SCOFLA. On CNBC's *Rivera Live,* Professor Wiehl said, "And I think that's why the Supreme Court decided to take this, not because they thought there was something wrong with the decision, but that they're going to uphold the [Florida] Supreme Court decision."

Professor Wiehl got testy with fellow *Rivera Live* panelist Joe DiGenova for questioning the great and inscrutable wisdom of the SCOFLA: "When he—when he talked about the Florida courts' actions being questionable, I'm so tired of that." The tired Professor Wiehl continued, "If you look at the Florida Supreme Court opinion, what you'll see is that they took two conflicting statutes and they did what courts all over the country do every day. They interpreted two statutes, and they chose to go with the statute that was the more recent statute and the one that is more particularized. That is just common, everyday judicial interpretation."

And now it's also: "Reversed!" ■

15

Hello, Room Service?
Send Up a Bottle,
a Blonde, and a Gun

———————◼———————

☞ Ruger Is a Girl's Best Friend

JULY 1999

About a year ago a mugger just waltzed right up to me on a bridge here in Washington, D.C. It was early evening and I was a stone's throw from my apartment in what is considered a nice neighborhood, as neighborhoods go in "Murder Capital"—the richly deserved nickname for the nation's capital. I won't belabor my cunning and completely fortuitous escape, except to say that for the few minutes I was standing there waiting to be mugged, I was fuming. I knew he knew I didn't have a gun.

It's illegal here in Murder Capital. Not merely illegal, but a felony carrying up to a five-year prison sentence. Just as I could look at my prospective mugger and see that he was not the kind of fellow who would be a fanatic about property rights, he could see from fifty yards that I was not the type to be casually committing felonies.

I wanted a gun, but more than that, I wanted him to think I might possibly have a gun. I wanted him to at least accord me the respect I get from criminals in other cities, where they have to exercise a little creativity, lying in wait, sneaking up from behind, hiding in bushes and dark alleyways, that sort of thing. No, in Washington, they just walk right up to you on a brightly lit street. As an apparently law-abiding citizen, I am ostentatiously defenseless.

But let's forget about completely defenseless little me on the bridge for a moment.

The framers' primary reason for including the right to bear arms in the Bill of Rights was so that the people could defend their liberties against a tyrannical government, just as they do by virtue of the vastly overrated First Amendment. As Alexander Hamilton observed in *Federalist*, No. 29, if the government were to "form an army of any magnitude, that army can never be formidable to the liberties of the people while there is a large body of citizens, little if at all inferior to them in discipline and the use of arms, who stand ready to defend their rights and those of their fellow citizens." Some may be willing to rely on withering editorials in the *New York Times* to preserve their liberty. I'd prefer a tasteful Sigsauer.

If the courts ever interpreted the Second Amendment the way they interpret the First Amendment, we'd have a right to bear nuclear arms by now. Interestingly, the Supreme Court is constantly having to remind Americans of their First Amendment rights, issuing over a hundred decisions in the past half century alone. The Court has only ruled on the Second Amendment in a handful of cases ever—the last time in 1939. But still, about half the citizenry deeply, passionately believe that they have a right to bear arms. Give the First Amendment no support from the courts for over half a century and see if anyone remembers why we're supposed to let Nazis march in Skokie.

But the half of the country that intuitively assumes a right to bear arms don't live in my neighborhood. That's why I'm getting exasperated with the constitutional argument. Too few people—girl people in particular—appreciate the central point: Guns are our friends.

When it comes to the First Amendment, everyone gets warm patriotic feelings, tearing up over John Stuart Mill's "marketplace of ideas." They think immediately of our right to engage in political speech, scientific research, and avant-garde art and to burn politicians in effigy (or maybe that's just me). Speech on the fringe, like Aryan Nation propaganda or *Screw* magazine, is understood to be an unpleasant if inevitable by-product of a freedom we cherish.

But with the Second Amendment, all we hear about is the downside.

It's all *Screw* magazine. No upside, just school shootings and the apocryphal danger of "gun accidents." In 1945, for every million Americans, there were 350,000 firearms and 18 fatal gun accidents. By 1995 the supply of guns had more than doubled to 850,000 per million, but fatal gun accidents had plummeted by two-thirds to only 6 per million.

Guns are our friends because in a world without guns, I'm what's known as "prey." All females are. Any male—the most sickly 98-pound weakling—could overpower me in a contest of brute force against brute force. For some reason, I'm always asked: Wouldn't I prefer a world without guns? No. I'd prefer a world in which everyone is armed, even the criminals who mean to cause me harm. Then I'd at least have a fighting chance.

What the arms-control faithful really want is a world without violence—not a world without weapons. These are the ideological descendants of the authors of the Kellogg-Briand Pact, which purported to outlaw war. But we can't have a world without violence, because the world is half male and testosterone causes homicide. A world with violence— that is to say, with men—but without weapons is the worst of all possible worlds for women. As the saying goes, God made man and woman; Colonel Colt made them equal.

Prey like me use guns against predators about a million times a year. Fifteen different studies (including studies sponsored by gun-control groups) estimate that guns are used to stop a crime several hundred thousand times per year at the low end and several million times at the high end.

I especially want criminals to have to worry that I might be armed. In numerous surveys, criminals have confirmed the blindingly obvious point that they are disinclined to attack a victim who might be armed. Countries with those fabulously low crime rates and fabulously fascistic gun-control laws—like Canada, the Netherlands, and Britain—have more burglaries of occupied homes than we do in the armed-to-the-teeth United States. Canada's burglary rate of occupied homes is over three times that of the United States. Although murder is lower in Britain, rape, robbery, burglary, and assault are all substantially higher than in the United States.

It must be said, the framers were not unaware of the crime-prevention qualities of firearms. Standing armies in this country and in France had become nothing more than roving bands of criminals. The Second Amendment was, in part, a response to these earliest cases of police brutality.

(Why is it that the same people who have the least confidence in the police and military are the most willing to allow only the police and the military to have guns?)

Democratic darling Thomas Jefferson, for example, wrote, "Laws that forbid the carrying of arms . . . disarm only those who are neither inclined nor determined to commit crimes. . . . Such laws make things worse for the assaulted and better for the assailants; they serve rather to encourage than to prevent homicides, for an unarmed man may be attacked with greater confidence than an armed man."

That night in Washington, by the way, I was rescued by a man. I'm all for men, I like to have them around all the time. But they can't be. Sometimes they have to go buy things for us. More pertinently, sometimes they're ex-husbands coming after us with machetes. We live in a world in which men are supposed to freeze when we say "no," our bodily integrity is sacrosanct, we are autonomous beings, I am woman hear me roar, but we're not allowed to defend ourselves from a physical attack with the only effective means possible. Just stand waiting on the bridge, and hope for a nice man to come along. ■

☞ I'd Burn My Neighbor's House Down

SEPTEMBER 15, 2000

I did everything I could and it's not my fault. As a legal resident of the noble 4th District of Connecticut—once represented by glamorous, brilliant, smart-aleck Clare Boothe Luce, and currently represented by a hand-wringing pantywaist—I tried to take out the pantywaist.

For those of you who don't have Irish Alzheimer's (we forget everything but our grudges), Representative Chris Shays was one of only five Republicans to vote against the impeachment of a lying, felonious, contemptible president; one of only two Republicans to go on a whirlwind, grandstanding campaign against the impeachment of the lying, felonious, contemptible president; and the only Republican called on by Representative John Conyers (Democrat of Michigan) on the day of the vote to argue against impeachment of a lying, felonious, contemptible president.

I didn't run in the primary against Shays, because, as a writer, I'd have to give up my livelihood to do so. If I were a dentist, I could continue to remove molars while campaigning against Shays. As a writer, I'd have to abandon my career the moment I announce. I'll give up a month or two for a grudge match, but not six, seven, or eight.

Moreover, an excellent Connecticut Republican, Jim Campbell, did step to the plate to primary the pantywaist, offering Nutmeggers the enticing prospect of voting for someone who not only would represent Republicans but also would represent the district, rather than representing the *New York Times*. No one had ever heard of Campbell. He emerged out of nowhere, and the principleless Connecticut Republican Party establishment was dead-set against him. (If Joseph Stalin called himself a Republican and was an incumbent in Connecticut, he'd have the full backing of the state party apparatchiks.) Still, Campbell took about 40 percent of the vote from Shays.

Though I wasn't willing to sacrifice my profession (and life) for the absolute minimum six months it would have required to run in a primary, I was willing to forsake my profession (and life) for about six weeks simply to achieve the greater glory of causing Shays to lose. My idea was that I'd run a total sham, media-intensive, third-party, Jesse Ventura campaign for one month before the election, and hope for enough votes to cause the (official) Democrat to win.

I just needed to find a third party that would have me. Since I hate the government, and the Libertarians hate the government, I figured: That's my party. Except the thing is, the local Libertarians' opposition to government is totally focused on one small aspect of government: the drug laws. Until going through several weeks of negotiations with the Connecticut Libertarian Party over their pro–drug legalization stance, my position on drugs was to refuse to discuss drug legalization until I don't have to pay for the food, housing, transportation, and medical care of people who want to shoot up heroin all day.

It's not like we live in the perfect Libertarian state of nature with the tiny exception of those pesky drug laws. We live in a Nanny State that takes care of us from cradle to grave and steals half our income. I kept suggesting to the local Libertarians that we might want to keep our eye on the ball. (One of the Libertarians' other big issues is privatizing Yosemite. Seriously.)

In theory, our areas of agreement should have included, among other things: eliminating the Department of Health and Human Services; eliminating the Department of Education; eliminating the Department of Commerce; eliminating the National Endowment for the Arts; eliminating the National Endowment for the Humanities; eliminating the Department of Agriculture; eliminating the Department of Housing and Urban Development; eliminating the Department of Transportation; and eliminating the progressive income tax and instituting a flat tax.

Our sole area of disagreement was whether to abolish the drug laws before or after completing the above tasks. But that wasn't good enough for them. I was deemed not a "true Libertarian" by the CT-LP because my idea was to defer the drug-legalization issue until we had made a little more headway in dismantling the Nanny State.

(The National Office of the Libertarian Party grasped this point, and was only concerned about what I would say about their presidential candidate. I believe we could have worked something out, but that was at least a practical problem. While I'm sure someone who loathes the government would make a splendid president, I couldn't credibly pretend I thought either that Harry Browne had a real shot at winning or that a Gore presidency wouldn't wreck the country.)

The other "evidence" these Sherlocks found contradicting my claim that I do too hate the government was that in a computer search of my name plus "conservative," versus my name plus "libertarian," there were only 400 hits with "libertarian" and over a thousand with "conservative."

But, of course, unless I throw a tantrum and demand a particular designation, I have no control over how I am identified on television or anywhere else. For example, TV producers have an annoying predilection of calling anyone who is not a socialist a "GOP adviser." I finally blew up at this uninvited designation, saying I only wished the "GOP" would take my @#%&* advice. That ended the "GOP adviser" title.

Once I was on a program with Angela Davis, who has run for president on the Communist Party ticket several times. I worked for a Republican senator one time for two years and that's the extent of my involvement in partisan politics. Davis was identified as a "community activist" and I was called a "Republican lawyer." To be completely accurate, I don't call myself anything. As far as I'm concerned, I'm a middle-of-the road moderate and the rest of you are crazy.

The final nail in my coffin was that I hadn't been attending the CT-LP's meetings, which seemed rather incongruous to the concept of libertarianism. These people oppose organized government, but demand an organized CT-Libertarian Party that will enforce party discipline like a Soviet commissar. In any event, I've changed my position on the drug-legalization issue after conferring (interminably) with the Libertarians on the matter. There's a joke about a Frenchman, an Englishman, and a Russian who are told they have only one day until the end of the world. The Frenchman says he will spend his last day with a bottle of Bordeaux and a beautiful woman. The Englishman says he will take his favorite sheepdog for a walk across the moors. The Russian says he will burn his neighbor's house down. I'm with the Russian.

Consequently, since the CT-LP has denied me my sole remaining goal of defeating Chris Shays, I have moved from being completely uninterested in drug legalization to being virulently, passionately opposed to it. See this space next week for why drug legalization is an incredibly dumb idea—the second in my new Irish Alzheimer's series. ■

☞ Drug Shills

SEPTEMBER 14, 2000

Like everyone else in America, I had never really listened to the arguments of the drug-legalization crowd since: It's not going to happen. These are like people whose area of expertise is pottery in ancient Tibet. Their ideas could be completely spurious, but no one cares enough to bother arguing with them.

Stupid Argument No. 1: The first argument one always hears about drug legalization is: Alcohol and cigarettes are at least as bad and probably worse than marijuana.

Gary Johnson, governor of New Mexico, only the most recent Republican to discover that the path to fawning media coverage is to adopt liberal positions, is quoted in just such a fawning article in the *New York Times*, saying, "Last year 450,000 people died from smoking cigarettes. Alcohol killed 150,000, and another 100,000 died from legal prescription drugs. How many people died last year from the use of marijuana? Few, if any. From cocaine and heroin? Five thousand."

I'll accept all the drug legalizers' lying statistics and demonstrate that their arguments are still stupid, but you have to say, someone who lies in formulating an argument is not to be trusted. And that figure on cigarette deaths is a bald-faced lie.

The 450,000 figure refers to all "smoking-related" deaths. A "smoking-related" death is any death that, theoretically, could be connected to smoking—even if the person who died never came within a mile of a lit cigarette. "Smoking-related deaths" include emphysema, any respiratory disease, heart attacks, and a plethora of cancers. If an obese ninety-nine-year-old man dies of a heart attack while shoveling snow, his death would be listed as a "smoking-related" death.

Under the methodology used by the American Cancer Society to come up with the statistics on "smoking-related" deaths, 504,000 people die each year from insufficient exercise, and 649,000 die from improper diets. Indeed, the books are so cooked on the "smoking-related deaths" that a 1993 article in the *American Journal of Epidemiology* was able to show that by using the exact same methodology, smoking *saves* 277,621 lives each year.

There are no serious studies of the long-term effects of daily marijuana use, but we know marijuana smoke is much worse for the respiratory system than cigarette smoke. The only reason you never hear about people dying from marijuana is that—well, for one, like the old-timer shoveling snow, a pot smoker who dies of emphysema is listed as a "smoking-related" death. But also people don't smoke pot the way they smoke cigarettes. One reason for that is: Marijuana is illegal. If people smoked pot as much as they drink and smoke, we undoubtedly would have a much better sense of the health consequences of sustained marijuana use, but by then it would be too late. Once people have spent a few decades smoking pot at restaurants, family gatherings, and football games, it's going to be hard to create a taboo around marijuana use. See, for example, Prohibition.

But even stipulating to the drug legalizers' phony statistics, let's assume alcohol and cigarettes induce dependency; ruin lives; cause disease, depression, countless traffic injuries, and fatalities; and increase the incidence of homicide and suicide. This is supposed to be an argument for legalizing another drug like them?

Stupid Argument No. 2: Prohibition failed.

No it didn't. Prohibition resulted in startling reductions in alcohol consumption (over 50 percent), cirrhosis of the liver (63 percent), admissions to mental health institutions for alcohol psychosis (60 percent), and arrests for drunk and disorderly conduct (50 percent).

That doesn't mean Prohibition was a good thing. Christ's first miracle wasn't turning wine into water. But Prohibition is one of the strongest arguments *against* legalizing marijuana. The reason Prohibition failed was that alcohol had become a respectable libation, it was part of the social fabric in high society and low. Once the genie is out of the bottle (so to speak), it's hard to put it back.

Stupid Argument No. 3: One of the leading Libertarian arguments made for legalization is that drug use would decrease if drugs were legal, because, I quote, the government just "messes everything up." While it's hard to argue with that premise, one thing governments are really good at is criminalizing stuff. People like me hate the government because of the things it prohibits—earning money, flushing toilets, owning and developing property, and engaging in political speech—not because the government isn't good at it. The idea that making an activity legal would reduce its incidence is preposterous. This is exactly like the Clintonian statement about wanting to make abortion "safe, legal and rare." The most effective way to make something "rare" is to make it illegal.

It ought to stop you in your tracks that politicians like Gary Johnson want to legalize drugs so the government can tax drugs. Whenever politicians say they want to restrict something by taxing it, you know they're lying: The very fact that they are taxing it means they need people to keep doing it. Otherwise they'd run out of revenue. Just as they are doing with gambling, the government is trying to horn in on a criminal enterprise. It never occurs to politicians to make government more like Microsoft. Successful capitalist enterprises they want to destroy. It's the Crips and Bloods they see as a useful organizational model.

Stupid Argument No. 4: We've "lost" the drug war.

We've "lost" the murder war too—if winning is defined as total abolition. People persist in taking drugs because they want to. We don't have laws prohibiting what no one wants to do. Laws against drugs have surely reduced drug use, just as laws against murder and robbery reduce the incidence of murder and robbery.

Stupid Argument No. 5: As aspiring pothead Governor Johnson puts it, "Half of what we spend on law enforcement, half of what we spend on the courts and half of what we spend on the prisons is drug related. Our current policies on drugs are perhaps the biggest problem that this country has."

I won't dispute the governor's presumably apocryphal facts. We spend a lot of money enforcing murder and robbery laws, too. So what? It's supposed to be a disaster for the country that the drug laws keep a lot of people gainfully employed working for law enforcement and prisons? That doesn't mean we should randomly criminalize things to create jobs for prosecutors and prison guards, but the horrifying consequence of providing people with good jobs at good wages is not a strong argument for repealing drug laws. As an added benefit, the drug laws help rid the streets of people who are, by definition, the sort of people who are willing to break laws.

Stupid Argument No. 6: The quintessential Libertarian argument for drug legalization is that people should be allowed to do what they want with their own bodies even if it ruins their lives. But that's not true. Back on earth, we live in a country that will not allow people to live with their own stupid decisions. Ann has to pay for their stupid decisions.

We have to "invest" in our future by supporting people who freely choose to inject drugs in their own bodies and then become incapable of holding jobs, obtaining housing, and taking care of their children. So it's not really quite accurate to say drugs hurt no one but the user, at least until we've repealed the welfare state. And don't give me the now-we'll-have-to-regulate-fatty-foods slippery-slope argument. Precisely because you can see a difference in eating a hamburger and smoking crack means there is a difference between the top of the slope and the bottom. That, in a nutshell, is why pure slippery-slope arguments are always fatuous.

Even John Stuart Mill said there were some things people could not be permitted to choose to do with their own bodies in a free society: "The principle of freedom cannot require that he should be free not to be free. It is not freedom to be allowed to alienate his freedom." Drugs enslave people. Maybe cigarettes and alcohol do too, but that just brings us back to Stupid Argument No. 1. ■

☞ Capitol Punishment

APRIL 1999

The really, totally appropriate setting for writing an article about dating in the nation's capital would be in my D.C. apartment home, alone on a

Saturday night. By chance, however, I'll be in New York this weekend. By chance, I've been in New York every weekend for approximately the previous 147 weeks, give or take a few shuttle mishaps.

But since all my stuff is in D.C., I do have to drop in occasionally. Consequently, I've become a minor authority on dating in Washington. Maybe not dating exactly but one crucial element of any date: "the Ask." Boys in Washington don't know how to ask for a date. What they do is try to trick you into asking them for a date. They say, "I know you're really busy, so call me when you'd like to go out to dinner" or "Call me when you're back in Washington" or, my favorite, "Are we ever going to get together?"

What are you supposed to say to completely insane things like that? I've never figured that out, which is why these conversations tend to end in hostile silences. "Call me when you'd like to go out to dinner" isn't asking for a date; it's asking me to ask you for a date.

For my male readers in Washington, asking for a date entails these indispensable components: an express request for a female's company on a particular date for a specific activity. Oh yes, and the request has to be made to the female herself. Roughly once every two weeks, I get a female on my answering machine asking me if I'd like to go out with some dumbass male friend of hers who's too afraid to call me himself. (For those outside Washington, I'm not kidding.)

This isn't a screeching, hate-filled, anti-male screed. It is a screeching, hate-filled anti-D.C. screed. There's no large sociological point about relations between the sexes here. It's Washington.

I know this, because while D.C. males are on my answering machine with vague announcements that they've called, I still get messages from boys in New York saying, for example, "I have tickets for the opera next Friday. Would you like to go?" (If you're having trouble following the plotlines here, I never actually answer my phone; I sit at my computer listening to people leave messages and respond, if necessary, by typing out an e-mail.)

Males in every other city know how to ask for dates. So it's not me, it's not feminism, it's not the millennium.

I've begun aggressively inquiring of every female I come across, "Pardon, but have you noticed that boys in Washington don't know how to ask for dates?" The consistent response has been a raft of stinging denunciations too numerous to catalogue here. If I were asking something preposterous, like "Say, have you noticed all the alligator carcasses in the street lately?," I wouldn't be getting such emphatic affirmations every time.

Recently, I asked a female on Capitol Hill about the phenomenon and she said right off, as if I were a psychic, "We were just talking about that on Saturday night!" She had been talking about it in a mixed crowd and reported that the boys began hectoring the girls—*C'mon, this is the twentieth century. You're modern women, you can ask for dates.*

I asked her if waiting for women to ask them for dates had worked for these guys. No, they just sit around with friends, year after year, waiting for their theory to play out. This is also how government programs are conceived and tested, so it makes perfect sense that only in Washington are males still waiting for action on the no-ask dating plan.

In fact, the incapacity of the D.C. male to ask for a date is the perfect synecdoche for this whole pathetic city. First, there is a total absence of normal civilized conventions in Washington. The customer is always wrong, the cabs don't have meters, and complete strangers ask for the sports section of your paper on the subway. In every real job I've ever had, it was standard for the boss to give a Christmas gift to the people who work for him. In Washington, minimum-wage staffers take up a collection to buy Christmas gifts for the senator and chief of staff.

There's a reason boys asking for dates is a convention of civilized society. Someone's going to have to face rejection. It may as well be the aggressive, testosterone-pumping, hunter male. Speaking for myself, I'll take 69 cents on the dollar (or whatever the current feminist myth is) never to have to ask for a date. But the whole point of this convention is to reduce, if not eliminate, the need for rejection anyway.

The entire dating system runs on implicit understandings. If the hunter male doesn't like a girl, he doesn't call. That's the end of it. If the hunted female doesn't like the boy, she's unavailable without a good excuse three times in a row. No explanations, no hurt feelings. When you start fiddling with a centuries-old system like this, you're just asking for trouble. If you can't operate by covert signals, you're going to get horrifying, misery-inducing explanations. (And if you ask a stranger for her sports section on the subway, you're going to get Maced.)

Second, no one makes any money in D.C. From this, I deduce that it's important for young men to make loads of money. There may be grating aspects to twenty- and thirty-somethings earning kazillion-dollar bonuses, but at least it gives them the self-confidence to ask for a date.

Third, TV is reality in Washington. Restaurants close at 8 P.M. There are a few really, really late-night places that stay open until nine or ten, but even these sometimes close unexpectedly at eight. (In addition to being always wrong, the customer is an impediment to the serious business of Washington, which is watching TV.) So everyone is home watching TV all the time.

Like most New Yorkers, I never had a TV, but I got one when I moved to Washington. The peculiar thing about watching TV after a long lapse is that you are actually aware of TV changing your perception of reality. I've started subconsciously associating men of the cloth with murderous, Nazi conspiracies, for example. I've got a million more television-induced perception shifts, but the relevant one here is that females are invariably the sexual aggressors on TV. The typical romantic overture on the small screen is: Boy meets girl, girl drops dress.

TV hasn't ruined me yet, though. My romantic fantasy is still this: Girl meets moving-company guy, girl moves back to New York. ■

☞ A Republican Tribute to John

JULY 22, 1999

If you grew up when the most prominent living Kennedy was Teddy, a lot of the Camelot imagery is probably lost on you. So it was a little disconcerting, for this Republican at least, to be bombarded with the usual Camelot cant in connection with the death of John F. Kennedy Jr. John was no run-of-the-mill Kennedy. The media's Kennedy fever demonstrates nothing but journalists' own insularity and narrow-minded parochialisms. I knew John F. Kennedy Jr. I worked with John F. Kennedy Jr. John F. Kennedy Jr. was a friend of mine. And you, Senator Kennedy, are no John F. Kennedy Jr.

So before the public memory of John is overtaken by the deluge of nauseating news coverage reminiscent of the bulimic princess Lady Di, I'd like to pay a Republican tribute to John. You don't have to believe in abortion on demand to see that John Kennedy Jr. actually did have the looks, charm, intelligence, humility, kindness, and class the mainstream media mysteriously discern in all Kennedys.

The first time I met John was at a *George* magazine luncheon at Le Cirque a few years ago to honor the magazine's "Twenty Most Intriguing Women in Politics." First of all, consider that I was named one of them. I've been reading those women's magazines' special power-woman editions for years and have yet to see a right-winger in the lineup. Gloria Steinem and Patricia Schroeder—yes. Phyllis Schlafly and Bay Buchanan—not a chance. But the magazine founded and edited by the scion of the country's most famous Democratic family was truly a political magazine, not a Democratic magazine (as *Vogue, Cosmopolitan, GQ, Esquire, Time,* and *Newsweek* are).

After the lunch, John asked me what the reaction had been at MSNBC to a blurb *George* magazine had run on some unflattering remarks I had made on air about Pamela Harriman earlier in the year. It was nothing worse than what the *New York Times* had said about Harriman in its formal obituary, and considerably less harsh than what Maureen Dowd had written about Harriman's funeral, but unflattering nonetheless. I told John MSNBC had fired me for it—but rushed to assure him, not to worry, they fired me a lot and had always hired me back. I still felt kind of bad about all the firings. The network had hired me because I was a conservative and then would fire me every time they discovered I was a conservative. But I might as well have told John I had won the Nobel Peace Prize. He perked right up, his face brightened, and he asked me what other comments I had been fired for.

Now, my Democrat friends in Washington had seen the tapes and they thought MSNBC was nuts, but this was the first time anyone had treated the firings as if they were a notch in my belt. And not just anyone, but Über-Democrat, definition-of-cool John Kennedy Jr. He thought it was tremendous that MSNBC kept firing me—he told me I was like Howard Stern—and a few months later *George* ran a bemused item on my repeated firings. That was the first time I stopped feeling lousy about my tenuous work relationship with MSNBC. (And the first time I stopped feeling lousy about John's death was when someone sent me an e-mail saying only "maybe he's waving at you." I keep waving out my window back at him now.)

About a year and a half after the luncheon, John hired me as a regular *George* columnist. Wow! This really was a new kind of Democrat. John wasn't a part of the older generation of Stalinist liberals who try to censor differing viewpoints and engage in the "politics of personal destruction" to harm those who disagree with them. As his magazine's motto says, this was "not just politics as usual." The importance of what John was doing to political discourse in this country cannot be overstated. If you've ever been on the receiving end of the "politics of personal destruction," it's not always fun being called a racist, sexist, homophobe, etc. etc. One can see why a lot of people might decide to opt out of the whole political enterprise altogether. Through his magazine, and his very being, John had begun to take the bitter acrimony out of political dialogue. While political neophytes out of Hollywood yammer about getting the younger generation involved in politics, John actually did it.

Precisely because he was a both Democrat and a celebrity, John was able to begin altering the political dialogue in a way that no one else ever could. Not only was he making politics fun and interesting, but he was fair and kind to his presumed political opponents. This, truly, was "not just politics as usual." That is why it is so painful to hear the media talk of John in terms of the Kennedy mystique of liberal mythology or to hear him compared to a dysfunctional, airhead princess. Despite the liberal media's praise, John was a great man. Perhaps more important, he was a good man.

I was often asked—and not just by Republicans—if John was a mere figurehead at *George* and an intellectual lightweight. Neither could be farther from the truth. John would call me directly to propose article ideas. When I accepted and then tried to reject his idea that I write a column about dating in Washington, he refused to let me change my mind. He was right: For a while, that piece was my most-read column. He read all my columns during editing, and would sometimes call to comment on them full of the sort of enthusiastic praise that makes a writer want to write an even better one next time. And let me mention again: I'm a *Republican*. My most recent article for *George* was a paean to the virtues of guns. John was particularly fond of a piece I wrote for *George* attacking a certain congressman (representing the fourth district of Connecticut)—for being a rotten liberal. In one of our last conversations, he made fun of one of the magazine's liberal columnists for being a predictable bore.

Despite the massive publicity John had received for flunking the New York bar examination, he was quite bright—contrary to all my preconceptions about a Kennedy. During my book tour for *High Crimes and Misdemeanors,* I spoke at a *George* magazine breakfast about my book. John came to the meeting, and after my presentation he was the first to start asking questions. He had clearly read the book—unlike so many interviewers—and his questions, though from an opposing view, were good ones. In fact, John's questions raised some of the exact same points renowned intellectual William F. Buckley would be raising with me on *Firing Line* a few weeks later. I was so surprised by what clever questions John was asking that I realized even I had been subconsciously assuming that someone so good-looking could not possibly be intelligent, too.

It's not particularly meaningful that he failed the bar exam, if you think about it. I've taken the New York bar exam, and I can tell you it's not an IQ test. It's an exam about facts you have to learn. I would imagine that a celebrity stud living in New York City in his twenties might well be tempted away from the grindstone.

That is part of what was so impressive about John. Though on some level it sounds preposterous, it probably isn't a day at the beach to be remarkably wealthy, famous, and good-looking. Why bother getting up in the morning? Why not go the way of Howard Hughes or Elvis? It has always impressed me about Steve Forbes, for example, that he was born fabulously rich and still manages to be productive and civic-minded and have a normal, happy family life. John, too, could have become a degenerate rich kid. But he didn't. Rather, he was making it safe to talk about politics again. For that, this Republican is deeply grateful and mourns his loss. ∎

16

What You Could Have Read If You Lived in a Free Country

———————— ■ ————————

Take heart, young right-wingers. Just a few short years ago, I was nearly living in a box under the Brooklyn Bridge. For more than a decade, virtually no one would publish me. Even after actively soliciting articles from me, magazine editors always decided they were more interested in publishing conservatives in the abstract than in reality. (Maybe a sensible conservative like David Gergen, who worked for Clinton, but not that nut Ann Coulter.) I was the polar opposite of Maureen Dowd, who has apparently never written anything that was rejected. For the first few years my literary agent had me as a client, all she did was negotiate "kill fees," which magazines pay writers for articles they've commissioned but don't publish, like a consolation prize. It's like a parting gift that a game show loser gets after they say, "Thanks for playing our game!" and hustle you off the set. Turning lemons into lemonade, conservative writer George Gilder has managed to get kill fees from magazine after magazine for the exact same article.

Interestingly, other than scholarly journals, the only two magazines that would publish me were Ronald Reagan's favorite publication, *Human Events*—even though it had to break a half-century "no girls" rule to hire me—and John Kennedy Jr.'s *George* magazine. Even after I wrote my first *New York Times* best-seller, *High Crimes and Misdemeanors,* no newspaper in America big enough to be on LexisNexis would carry my syndicated column. In fact, so few papers carried it, I only earned a few hundred dollars a month from that column (for tax mavens, that works out to about $6 after taxes). I would have made more money by delivering newspapers than by writing for them.

Even my books got killed. After my second book, *Slander*, was killed by the publisher, I went months and months without a possibility of publication, even as prepublication orders were pouring in. I not only had no publisher, I had to pay back the book advance I had originally gotten from HarperCollins (owned by right-wing media magnate Rupert Murdoch, pretty much proving Al Franken's theory of a *conservative media bias*—italics added to indicate sarcasm, Al!). In other words, I had a somewhat different experience from that of Jayson Blair, who was writing front-page articles for the *New York Times* before he had, in the strict sense, graduated from college.

But then Crown Publishers came along and published *Slander* and it was another hit. And then they published *Treason* and it was my third hit. Now everything has changed. I live in a nice house. It is still the case, however, that, except for *Human Events*, no national publication will print my columns. And it is still true that no newspaper in America big enough to be on LexisNexis will carry my syndicated column. Apparently the only people who want to read me are actual Americans. Liberals defend every manner of pornography and filth on the grounds that it's "what the people want." Editors, we are constantly lectured, only "want to sell newspapers." The only material too prurient to let the public read is anything written by a conservative.

And I'm a conservative success story! If editors believe the general public has no interest whatsoever in hearing from a conservative whose three books were best-sellers, how many right-wing writers out there have we never heard from at all? How many never had a Crown Publishers come along and publish them after a decade of rejection? How many switched careers—or switched their politics? How many boxes can fit under the Brooklyn Bridge? Alas, we will never be among *Cosmopolitan* magazine's "fun fearless females" like Kate Harrington (February 2000) "because as costume designer for last summer's smash hit *The Thomas Crown Affair*, she made the fearless move to dress Rene Russo in Celine and Halston." With no rich liberals to give us MacArthur Foundation "genius" grants or to buy up radio stations for us (after throwing minorities off the air in Los Angeles, New York, Chicago, and San Francisco), conservative writers merely face starvation. On second thought, young right-wingers, abandon hope of ever being a writer. Become an editor.

The few conservative publications that exist aren't much help. Among the stupidest theories liberals have about conservatives is the idea that we are a well-oiled political machine. Hillary Clinton somberly warns of a Vast Right-Wing Conspiracy. The *New York Times* has actually published a flowchart of the "neoconservative" cabal. Conservatives couldn't put together a three-car funeral without producing six books denouncing one another. It is doubtful that two neoconservatives could agree on where to have lunch— which is going to complicate their secret plans to trick the nation into perpetual war. Even apart from the pathetic efforts of craven conservatives to win admiring glances from editors of the *New York Times* by attacking fellow conservatives, right-wingers get into death-match struggles about who said what at a dinner party ten years ago when no one is watching. And those are the good times. With precious few column inches to fight over in conservative publications, conservative writers typically detest one another.

By contrast, liberals are good Leninists: They care only about power. Teddy Kennedy crawls out of Boston Harbor with a quart of Scotch in one pocket and a pair of pantyhose in the other, and Democrats hail him as their party's spiritual leader. President John F. Kennedy would actually edit news articles written about him by his flunkies in the press. Consequently, only recently have we discovered that for the last eight years of his life, JFK was a stupefied drug addict basically being carried around on a gurney with a needle hanging out of his arm. (The *New York Times* noted that "even a partial list" of Kennedy's medications as president is "a daunting one, including hydrocortisone, testosterone, codeine, methadone, Ritalin, antihistamines, antianxiety drugs, barbiturates to help him sleep, and regular injections of Procaine to ease his back.") Ah, the charm and athleticism of "Camelot." Al Franken is fawned over in a *New York Times Magazine* cover story written by Russell Shorto, who is fawned over in a *New York Times* book review written by Kevin Baker, who is fawned over in a *New York Times* "New and Noteworthy" list. But leave the reservation and the liberal admiration ends. Myrna Blyth, who was editor of *Ladies' Home Journal* for two decades, wrote a book saying women's magazines are run by liberals and the *Times* gave it a snippy review—written by the daughter of Clinton's White House counsel.

Liberals never argue with one another over substance; their only dispute is how to prevent the public from figuring out what they really believe. Meanwhile, it is a source of constant alarm to conservatives that the public will *not* understand what they really believe. After the spectacular success of Ronald Reagan's presidency, white-shoe WASPs took a look at Reagan's legacy and said, "That's enough of that. Now we're going to make liberals love us." Vice President George Bush promised conservatism with a smiley face. To show how nice he was, Bush even raised taxes. Unfortunately, that made the rest of the country hate him and liberals weren't voting for him. That's our well-oiled political machine!

Until a few years ago, there was no alternative media that allowed conservatives to make themselves clear. This generated terrific defensiveness. As an upstart insurgency fighting all organs of elite opinion, a lot of conservatives talk in the stilted, paranoid manner of people who believe they will be shot by the Nazi SS if their words are somehow misconstrued.

> *Don't mention the blacks!*
> But I just said Lincoln freed the slaves.
> *People will misunderstand.*

> *Don't mention the Jews!*
> I just said I supported Israel.
> *Shhhh! Liberals will say that's anti-Semitic.*

I never got the hang of being scared of liberals. The technical term for conservatives who are not afraid of liberals is: "unpublished." But my columns won't be put in a lockbox! The following columns are what editors didn't want you to see. Perhaps these columns are not as good as I thought they were. But on rereading them, I still think they're better than they are! So here it is—a right-wing Lollapalooza, Ann Coulter's Private Stock.

NATIONAL REVIEW

Far from a right-wing cabal greasing the wheels for young conservatives, *National Review* would not even publish my article on "Feminist Legal Theory" in 1991 after soliciting the piece. I was a year out of law school and had about as much interest in "Feminist Legal Theory" as I did in handicrafts or gardening, but that's what editor John O'Sullivan wanted. He gave me a 1988 symposium on "Women in Legal Education—Pedagogy, Law,

Theory, and Practice" in the *Journal of Legal Education* and asked
me to write about it. (I didn't grasp the concept of "word limit"
yet, so this is basically the first half.)

☞ Call Me Ms.

1991

At a party on the Lower East Side last night I happened to glance up
at the video screen as it was showing a man slitting the throat of a beautiful naked woman lying face-up on a table. I was in a cab headed back up-
town approximately sixty seconds later, and it occurred to me: I'm pretty
sure that, even in her wild youth, Mother never attended parties that included video displays of women's throats being erotically slit. This naturally led me to wonder: Just why is it that my generation is constantly
being harangued into paying obeisance to the dazzling triumphs of the
feminists?

We are now more frequently raped, pimped, divorced, cheated on,
and—if one's dating proclivities run toward Democrats—expected to
spring for dinner. But at least no sane man would dare speak the word
"Miss." Freedom at last! It's not just because bras burned while men
fiddled that I hate the feminists. The real reason I loathe and detest feminists is that real feminists, the core group, the Great Thinkers of the
movement, which I had until now dismissed as the invention of a frat boy
on a dare, have been at the forefront in tearing down the very institutions
that protect women: monogamy, marriage, chastity, and chivalry. And sur-
veying the wreckage, the best they have to offer is: "Call me Ms."

No, wait, that's not entirely fair. They can also credibly lay claim to an
entire complex of idiot rules that can only be explained as a pathetic effort
to recapture the power women once had. But frankly, chastity, virtue, and
the affectation of weakness were nuclear weapons in the area of social control. "Nonsexist" phraseology doesn't rise to the level of a peashooter.
Where we once had chivalry and protectiveness, feminists now promote a
"duty to rescue." Where the crime of seduction once protected our reputa-
tions, feminists offer only "date rape." And where the concept of virtue
once prevented "unwanted" pregnancies, they give us our precious legal
right to knock off the fetus.

I'd like to mention at the outset that roughly 90 percent of women who call themselves feminists haven't a clue what the Grand Wizards of the movement are up to, nor do they particularly behave like good feminists. Many do, of course, presume deep primal malevolence on the part of the male of the species, quickly take offense at courteous gestures from men, and call themselves "Ms." But I have yet to meet a female who could respect any man who tries to split the check with her. We pretty much emerge from the womb with an instinctive understanding that all research and development costs fall to the male.

I definitely sympathize with the impulse to ignore feminist source material. Of all the ludicrous victim groups debuting every five minutes in this country, Rich White Women From Scarsdale is responsible for more rolled eyeballs than the rest combined. Having delved into the Womyn's white papers, I'm here to report that it's what I imagine alternating between Quaaludes and nitrous oxide would be like—and for the record, I have no actual experience with this little experiment. On one hand, you get absolutely ox-sedating sentences like these: "People are decontextualized from the analysis, yet no one really lives an acontextural life." But then you get real howlers like "We especially attach ourselves to such categories as male/female because of our own psychological development in a culture that has made gender matter." (Boy, think of all the neato articles *Cosmopolitan* magazine would run but for the importance our "culture" has placed on gender: "How to Weld Sprockets with a Socket Wrench." Let me just say, I am on tenterhooks awaiting the coming of this revolution!) Having read the stellar compendium of feminist writings about the "law," I present the following not as an account of substance abuse but as a report on feminist "legal" "theory."

One scholarly piece on "Women in Legal Education" begins cheerfully with this long self-description: "Feminism is a dirty word. I never fail to be amazed at the strength of the hostility the word generates. . . . Feminists are portrayed as bra-burners, man haters, sexists . . . castrators, [lesbians] . . . bitchy, demanding, aggressive, confrontational and uncooperative, as well as overly sensitive and humorless."

I would add to this that feminists are also marauding, bloodthirsty vipers—but more on that later. Considering the number of otherwise sane and apparently heterosexual men who openly call themselves "feminist men," regularly employ the convoluted "he or she" phraseology, and will endure tongue-lashings for such high crimes as opening doors for distaff ingrates, I would say this description tends toward the self-indulgent.

Be that as it may, what, really, is the most open of possible minds to make of this: "There is substantial ferment within the feminist community . . . over whether a reasonably clear line can be drawn between forced sexual encounters, which should be criminalized as rape, and all mutually chosen heterosexual encounters." Of course, it would be narrow-minded stereotyping to leap to the conclusion that these girls, as it used to be phrased, "wear comfortable shoes." They could just be really dumb.

But even brains with improperly firing neurons could be expected to occasionally hit upon some positive aspect of heterosexuality. Not the feminist "legal theorists." Heterosexuality for these gals is just another form of oppression—the "heterosexist assumption" is right in there with racism and sexism as an oppression that must be eradicated. Thus, one feminist law professor provides examples of classroom exercises to "help us guard against the presumption of race, the presumption of class, and that one presumption that seemed to occur more than all the others: the heterosexist assumption."

She delightedly describes the effect these exercises worked upon her students: By the end of the course, students were able to call each other on their own biases.

Consider the following student dialogue:

FIRST STUDENT: It isn't fair, men never worry about birth control. I mean don't they even care? Finally I asked one of them, "Why don't you ever ask?" And he said it was because he knew I wouldn't risk it. Really, how could he know? . . . That leaves women with only two choices: take full responsibility or claim celibacy!
[Slight pause, second student looks at professor before speaking.]
SECOND STUDENT: Only two choices? Don't you want to reconsider that statement?
FIRST STUDENT *[in a defeated whisper]*: The heterosexist assumption again. [38 *Journal of Legal Education,* March/June 1988, 169–70.]

One wonders if extra credit was offered to students who went whole-hog and proclaimed themselves lesbians by the end of the semester.

While men generically are termed "patriarchs" and "oppressors," and feminism is described as an attempt "to have access to everything men have always kept for themselves" and "to get this foot off our necks," gay men are described as, I quote, "friend of women." Now, I have no dispute with gay men, but I consider an evening out sorely incomplete if it does not include at least one heterosexual member of the opposite sex.

And when I start thinking about these evenings out with heterosexual members of the opposite sex, I realize that the feminist "legal theorists" do not have my interests in mind. Dating, if not my life, is at least my hobby. So when feminists start yammering about "exposing patriarchy" and the "ambiguous phenomenon of male domination and hierarchy," I feel I am in an authoritative position to say: Huh? Are the patriarchs the ones who pay for our food and entertainment, send flowers and chocolate, and enable us to go through our entire lives without the tiresome exertion of opening a door?

I hate to give the game away, but men were essentially put on earth to serve women. It was much better when everyone pretended all their little projects—philosophy, math, science, world government, and so on—were much more important than carrying on the human race. Back in the prelapsarian fifties, women worked if they happened to fall into the .01 percent of the population who are able to have interesting jobs or they retired in their twenties to raise children and, incidentally, do what all serious people would like to do anyway—be a dilettante in many subjects. As far as I'm concerned this was a division of labor nothing short of perfect. Men worked, women didn't. So when our benefactors come under attack as "patriarchs" and "oppressors," I realize, someone has to put in a kind word for the oppressors. For cocktails alone, I figure I owe the male population several thousand dollars. So I will be the one to step forward and say: To the extent one gender is oppressing the other, it's not women who should be complaining.

The one solid defense feminists have to the man-hating accusation is that compared with what they think of women, their description of men is a bowl of cherries, a picnic in the sun, a day at the beach. Feminist "legal" "theory" places women somewhere around lawnmowers in the free-will/ individual-responsibility department. Not only can women not be expected to voice an objection to having sex with a man—the man is apparently expected to sort of intuit that his companion is not in the mood—but neither can she be expected to intervene should her boyfriend decide to beat her children to death. It is yet another unfortunate example of white male patriarchy to hold women responsible for the murder of their children, at least during the first year of the child's life. Legal doctrine that holds otherwise—that is to say, that treats women as rational beings—"reveal[s] that the doctrinal law ignores the realities of women's lives."

The "realities of women's lives" mantra is used to excuse women from responsibility for little things, like not being able to say, "Not tonight dear, I've got a headache," as well as bigger things, like crimes against man and God. One legal theorist writes that "[a]nother example of lack of knowledge of women's lives occurs with the failure of act cases," and goes on to describe a woman who was convicted of assault for allowing her boyfriend to beat up her child. "It may never have crossed counsel's mind to try to construct a duress or diminished capacity defense for Walden based on her fear" (Id at 110–11).

A sewer rat does better than this to protect her offspring. So why is it that the Hedda Nussbaums of the world are considered feminist heroes rather than the pitiable creatures that they are?

Even if I were to concede, which I don't, that the role of the criminal defense attorney is to offer up any half-baked arguments that are beamed into his head and which he is capable of making without giggling—including the Twinkie defense, insanity pleas, and bedwetting theories—it is not clear why legal arguments in defense of women who allow their children to be beaten should be categorized as "pro-woman" rather than "pro-criminal." Am I to consider this a great triumph for womankind because the defendant in such cases is a woman as am I? It seems to me that by the same logic, men would be within their rights to root for rapists, all of whom are men. (Feminists have become so crazed in demanding equal representation in all walks of life that this fact inevitably distresses them to the point that they will proudly cite the efforts of two or three noble equality-seeking females who *assisted* rapes and thus are technically brought up on rape charges. But the idea that it would take a threat of violence to get a man to have sex is so ludicrous, I refuse to acknowledge the concept of a female rapist.) In fact, maybe I should be pro-rapist because rapists and I are all part of the personhood family. The urge to have sex is at least a normal human impulse. I know of no mother not on crack, who would not exert herself just a little bit—say, throwing herself in front of an oncoming train—to protect her child.

In the feminist worldview, women are more likely to be throwing their children in front of trains. Not to worry though—it's just one of those "realities of women's lives" most women have never heard of until reading feminist legal theory, in this case, "postpartum depression." Inasmuch as many women suffer depression after giving birth, feminist legal theorettes would give them pretty much a free shot at their child's life for one year, because "the doctrinal law ignores the realities of women's lives." The author described a case of a woman who was convicted of killing her three-month-old child, explaining, "The mother, however, stated that she was depressed. Is it possible that she was suffering from postpartum depression?" (Id at 109). For a more humane approach, the Legal Theoress cites British law, "where a woman cannot be charged with the murder of her infant in the first twelve months after she gives birth . . . [but only] manslaughter, on the theory of diminished responsibility because "the balance of the mother's mind was disturbed by reason of her not having fully recovered from the effect of giving birth" (Id at 109–10).

If women are so gaga insane as to be very likely to murder their offspring for one full year after giving birth, is it really wise to allow them to cast votes in important national elections in which the leader of the free world is chosen? Or for that matter, in stupid irrelevant local dogcatcher elections? If they manage to resist murdering their children during that first year, maybe we could just send them a lifetime supply of Tupperware or handsome designer luggage or something.

Where did this fixation on what is a fairly unusual phenomenon come from anyway? Really, you would think the principal female hobbies were shopping, dieting, and murdering their children. Moreover, the victims aren't even our white male patriarchal oppressor friends. They're children, babies, and at the risk of pointing out the obvious, some of them are even going to be female children. Don't at least the girl babies figure into an allegedly pro-female legal movement? Have the feminists no faith that some of these pink-cheeked, cooing baby girls could blossom into dour, hateful lesbians someday? Finally, it's bad enough to think about any person reaching a point at which he is capable of viciously beating or killing a child. That there are mothers who would do that to their own flesh and blood is really disturbing. Feminist legal theorists may credit themselves with this much: They have demonstrated that there is something still worse than that. And that is privileged academics sitting in their comfortable offices thinking up Twinkie defense theories to exculpate infanticidal mothers as part of an ideological cause.

———

O'Sullivan wrote back, in part:

> Greatly simplifying, I would like to suggest that the structure of the article (which would include most of what you have but this time ON VALIUM) would be as follows:
>
> a) What is the purpose of the law? (To create an orderly society in which people can pursue their own interests without coercion, interference, etc.)
>
> b) How in particular, does the law achieve this for women?
>
> c) From what general social and political theories to these criticisms spring? What view of men, women, children and the relationships between the sexes do they imply?
>
> d) What legal proposals flow from such theories? What obligations would be placed on women, what lifted, etc.?

There was obviously nothing to be done. Confusing "feminist legal theory" with an article about "the law" is like confusing *Plessy v. Ferguson* with Sarah Ferguson, former Duchess of York and current Weight Watchers spokesman. ∎

CIGAR AFICIONADO

———

On the basis of a recommendation from George Will, *Cigar Aficionado* (popularly known as *Cigar, Fishing, and Auto*) asked me to write a column on campaign-finance reform a few years ago. This is what I submitted.

☞ This Congressman Bought for You by the *New York Times*

MAY 27, 2000

I'm toying with the idea of becoming an outlaw. You would too, if your representative in Congress were Chris Shays (Republican, of the *New York*

Times). I won't bore you with his entire tedious and pathetic career, but just for starters, Shays was one of only five Republicans to vote against the impeachment of a lying, felonious president.

I'm hopping mad about it, to the point that I want to commit an act of free speech against him.

In a country that enshrined the right of free speech—political speech in particular (also known among constitutional cognoscenti as "core First Amendment speech")—this would be easy. I could take out television, radio, and newspaper ads detailing Mr. Shays's perfidy, or—if, say, I had a life—I could pay his political opponents to do it for me.

But in this country it's impossible for me to do that without becoming a lawbreaker or, at the very least, a suspect. Even if I hire a band of lawyers to advise me on navigating the narrow legal path to engaging in core First Amendment speech, I will undoubtedly be investigated, audited, and publicly accused of being a scofflaw. In the end, I might even be found to have broken a campaign-finance law or two.

The catch is that the whole point of my free speech would be, in a sense, to help Mr. Shays's opponent get elected. If Mr. Shays were pumping gas somewhere, I wouldn't feel compelled to run radio ads denouncing him for his political views. I want him to lose his job as my representative. The only way for that to happen is for his opponent to win. If his opponent is Mickey Mouse, I'm for Mickey Mouse.

If I were to run ads attacking Shays, those ads would inevitably help Mickey Mouse, and my free speech would be portrayed as a "thinly disguised campaign contribution" to the Mouse campaign. Campaign contributions, you see, are strictly limited to $2,000 per person. (Otherwise we might end up with idiots in Congress, like Chris Shays.)

This is what happened when Texas businessman Sam Wyly ran television ads attacking John McCain just before the New York primary earlier this year. The *New York Times* immediately demanded an investigation by the Federal Election Commission of Mr. Wyly's "subterfuge" and "secret sponsorship" of the ads. (Political speech should be left in the hands of responsible *New York Times* editorial writers.)

The *Times* identified such wanton free speech by a private citizen as a menace to the "integrity of politics" and "a serious threat to the integrity of future elections." There was evidence, you see, that Mr. Wyly actually wanted McCain's opponent, George Bush, to win (!)—and "equally intriguing news that the ads were placed through an advertising agency with ties to Gov. George Pataki." (Also believed by law-enforcement officials to be a Bush supporter.)

So if you're tempted to engage in political speech, the only safe course is to run a wholly ineffective ad campaign that could not possibly persuade anyone to vote one way or another. Any indication, for example, that I actually want Chris Shays to lose, or any communication with his political opponents, no matter how indirect, will constitute evidence of "coordination"—a secret campaign contribution to his opponent!

Meanwhile, let's say I don't care about my country, politics, or civic affairs. All I want to do is make porno movies. Without limitation or consultations with fancy lawyers, I could spend a million dollars producing speech of the *Debbie Does Dallas* variety. But if I want to engage in speech of the "Vote Against Chris Shays" variety, I can only spend $2,000. It is easier to pander obscenity in this country than it is to engage in core First Amendment speech.

Advocates for campaign-finance reform claim they have no problem with political speech, it's just the "horrifying" amounts of money being spent on campaign speech that bother them. ("Horrifying" was the technical term used by one "specialist" quoted in a recent *Washington Post* article on campaign-finance reform.) But saying you have a right to do something, and the government is merely placing limits on how much money you can spend doing it, isn't even a clever ruse.

How about this: You have a right to engage in the free exercise of your religion but can only spend $2,000 a year on it. (Otherwise, rabbis, priests, and ministers might be bought!) We'll call it "religion-finance reform."

Yes, you're saying to yourself, but no one wants to bribe a man of the cloth. What are you going to get out of it? A quick path to salvation? Pah! Congress can screw your competitors, grant you a cartel, subsidize your business, create little welfare programs ("for the children") that will send federal booty your way, or create legal bars to people suing you.

Far be it from me to quarrel with the proposition that politicians are corrupt, but first of all, no law has ever been written that could stop the citizenry from trying to get at the $1.7 trillion of taxpayer money Congress doles out every year. Indeed, the only serious and workable solution to political corruption is for politicians to be worth substantially less. Until that time, though, even stipulating that politicians are corrupt, it still does not follow that suppressing free speech will make them any less so.

The theory of "campaign-finance reform" devotees is that if Congress would further limit speech by non–news-media-owning citizens, any taxpayers who want to get some of that $1.7 trillion would at least not be able to do it by engaging in speech. That's really the theory.

Citizens can bribe politicians by arranging favorable cattle futures trades, selling them stocks and bonds at a loss, buying their houses above market price and selling them houses below market price, building million-dollar pantheons in their names, hiring their wives and mistresses, sending them on exotic vacations—er, "fact-finding missions"—and giving to their favorite charities. But the one way you can't bribe a politician is by engaging in free speech (at a cost of more than $2,000) saying "Reelect [or Defeat] Senator Blowhard."

Of course, for bribing politicians, nothing beats owning a newspaper. Newspapers like the *New York Times* have absolutely no limitations on running editorials exhorting, "Vote for Chris Shays"—as that paper did in violation of an almost uninterrupted, century-long tradition of endorsing only Democrats. Nor are there any restrictions on how often the *Times* can run "news" articles describing Chris Shays as a "moderate."

Indeed, assuming a favorable editorial in the *New York Times* were worth only as much as a half-page paid political ad in that paper, the *New York Times* gave Shays about a million dollars in campaign donations in 1999 alone. (To put this in perspective, Shays typically spends about $500,000 on his entire reelection campaign.)

It was a wise investment. Shays voted against almost every member of his party—but with the *Times*—on the not insignificant issue of a president's impeachment. Most strikingly, he repeatedly introduces "campaign-finance reform" bills that would grant special rights to the *Times* and other newspapers to engage in political speech without contradiction by upstarts like Sam Wyly.

I'm not saying free speech can't function as a bribe. I just think private citizens ought to be able to bribe politicians as easily as the *New York Times* does.

––––––

POSTSCRIPT: My *Cigar, Fishing, and Auto* editor responded with a long e-mail suggesting that instead of making the strong argument against campaign-finance restrictions, I make the weak argument. To wit: I should complain that rich people can spend whatever they like on their own campaigns. (It is a source of endless fascination to liberals that the rich can do things poor people can't.) In retrospect, maybe it was a mistake to try to attack Bill Clinton in the pages of *Cigar Aficionado*. As I recall from the Starr Report, Mr. Clinton has been known to enjoy a good cigar.

For simplicity, e-mail exchanges of approximately one million messages are distilled to a point-by-point exchange, edited only for spelling.

> CIGAR AFICIONADO: Here are a few of my thoughts. "Felonious" implies some degree of conviction. Whatever your political leanings or mine, or the implied injustice of the impeachment proceedings, he was not convicted . . . therefore, felonious becomes potentially libelous, but the jury, as they say, is still out on the lying issue. In other words, you can call a public official a liar, but to suggest he is a felon is a bit more problematic. (This may be entirely a semantic issue based on the Webster's definition, but nonetheless, I'm suggesting another modifier, or just leave it at liar.)
>
> COULTER: Just for the record, I do disagree that speech conventions have to follow legal conventions (innocent until proven guilty), especially in egregious and obvious cases. O.J. is innocent before the law, but he's not innocent. I know a lot of newspapers won't call him a "murderer" unless he's a "convicted murderer," but I'm against that policy. By the way, several prominent federal judges—whose names I will give you in something other than an e-mail— are known to refer to the president exclusively as "that felon." But anyway, I'll change that.
>
> CIGAR AFICIONADO: Secondly, you rail against the rules & regs but without neatly defining what they are, or what alternative you propose. While that may be implicit, I think you need to be more explicit, probably in one paragraph about exactly what the rules are, whether or not you're talking about "soft money" issue, and what exactly you mean by letting the first amendment dictate the rules here: i.e., I can spend as much money as I have to get the candidate elected that I want without any restrictions. The piece needs a graf that concisely outlines the exact issue you are tackling here. . . . It may fit after the graf, "*The Times* identified . . ." with some additional transitional work in the following graf.

COULTER: I'll put in a graf on the rules. (I just didn't want to go over my word limit.)

[Coulter off-camera: zzzzzzzzzzzzzzzzzzzzzzzzzzzzzzzzzzzzzz]

CIGAR AFICIONADO: Finally, I find your basic argument weakened somewhat by the *New York Times* angle in the second half of the story; for better or worse, from William Randolph Hearst to Arthur Sulzberger, the Fourth Estate has been granted the territory of political endorsement on its editorial pages. You can quibble with me over the use in the news pages of the word "moderate" to describe Shays, but in his constituency I wouldn't be surprised to find the *New York Post* calling him every name under the sun on the opposing side of the ledger. Pitting individual restrictions against the established precedent of newspapers doesn't build your case. I'd find it more compelling to explore some of the inherent contradictions in the campaign financing law that, for instance, allows Jon Corzine and Steve Forbes to spend their millions on their own elections but not on others, thus building on the whole Wyly case in Texas.

I just end up feeling that the reader shouldn't be distracted by your partisan bias against the *New York Times* (which is a whole other column sometime) when what you really want them to focus on is the campaign finance issue. Full disclosure here; I used to freelance for the *New York Times*, but I would say [BLAH, BLAH, BLAH]. . . . Your comments are awaited.

COULTER: The *NYT* angle is the only edit that really goes to the heart of my argument, which is a constitutional argument, *not* a pragmatic argument. It's not just that the rules are inconsistent and have perverse consequences (e.g., Forbes and Perot examples), though that's certainly true. But that would be true even if we didn't have a First Amendment.

My argument is that the First Amendment doesn't just apply to working journalists. The First Amendment protects speech that is robust, wide open, etc. etc., and not just speech that is robust, wide open, etc. as between competing newspapers (like the *Post* and the *Times*). The First Amendment refers to "the people," not to "the newspaper editors."

Moreover, the *NYT* is my focus *not* because I hate them and their speech is contrary to mine, but because they are the ones demanding campaign-finance "reforms" that would further reduce the free-speech rights of non-media citizens. It's outrageous and hypocritical for the *NYT* to be incessantly promoting their own special interest in denying First Amendment rights to normal citizens while pretending to be the great protector of the First Amendment.

I can make that point more clearly in a couple sentences, so that it's clear that this IS my argument, but I'll have to go over my word limit.

CIGAR AFICIONADO: Ann, don't worry too much about the word limit.

I see your point about the *NYT*, but you do need to make that part of the argument more explicit, otherwise it just sounds like an anti-*NYT* attack. In fact, the next to last graf of the e-mail puts it pretty concisely. . . .

I guess my overall point, and the way I'm justifying putting in a column that I disagree with on some basic points, is that we have been hearing way too much about the evils of campaign finance and not enough about the opposing point of "let the people speak" that you espouse. I want that point to come through loud and clear.

After not "worry[ing] too much about the word limit" through several more drafts, pointless e-mails, and wasted weekends, I was informed that the editors at *Cigar Aficionado* decided that they definitely wanted my point "to come through loud and clear"—just not in their magazine.

In conclusion, here are some comments on my original column from two Yale Law grads:

Yale Law grad 1: "I think it's great."

Yale Law grad 2: "My one piece of advice: Make the same point in another article from a different direction. Point out that a company that wants to make a campaign contribution can make whatever contribution it wants—as long as you substitute 'labor union' for 'company.'"

And no, not *those* two Yale Law School graduates. We haven't been on speaking terms since I called him a lying felon. ∎

WALL STREET JOURNAL

This was the only one of the rejected columns that was not so-licited by the publication. A professor read my draft and in-sisted I submit it to the *Wall Street Journal.* I said the *Wall Street Journal* would sooner publish Jane Mayer—hate-mongering au-thor of the Clarence Thomas hatchet job *Strange Justice*—than publish me. Then I remembered that the *Journal* did publish Mayer. I sent the column, and the *Journal* turned it down, explain-ing they just weren't interested in the topic. A few weeks later, they asked someone else to write about the exact same topic. It was a good article, except for one tiny detail: It overlooked the fact that the central charge against Thomas Jefferson was actually disproved by DNA evidence.

☞ Sally Does Monticello

JUNE 21, 2001

In a terrifically humiliating episode, Pulitzer Prize–winning historian Joseph Ellis was recently exposed by the *Boston Globe* as an exotic Walter Mitty of the Ivory Tower. For years, he claimed he had gone to Vietnam in the 101st Airborne, had served under General William Westmoreland in Saigon, had been a rider on the Freedom Trail in Mississippi (beaten up by racist cops), and had been a high school football hero, once scoring the winning touchdown, among his other fanciful claims. None of it was true. Faced with the evidence, Ellis was forced to apologize for having "let stand" the "assumption" that he had been telling the truth.

You might say Ellis had fancied himself the Thomas Jefferson of the twentieth century, except that Jefferson's reputation is shot, thanks in part to Joseph Ellis. Between 'Nam flashbacks and Freedom Rider reunions, Ellis coauthored the ground-breaking 1998 report "Jefferson Fathered Slave's Last Child." You might remember this report if you weren't on the moon when it was released—it was the Clinton defenders' giddiest "Gotcha!" moment. It was unveiled to instant acclaim—just weeks before the House impeachment vote on William "You Know Who" Clinton's impeachment stemming from his sexual affair with an intern. As Ellis put it, "It is as if Clinton had called one of the most respected character witnesses in all of U.S. history to testify that the primal urge has a most distinguished presidential pedigree." Ellis said the new testing proved "beyond any reasonable doubt that Jefferson had a long-term sexual relationship with his mulatto slave." As author of the award-winning *American Sphinx: The Character of Thomas Jefferson*—and a Vietnam veteran—Ellis spoke with some authority on the matter. (We're still waiting for the publication of *American Liar: The Joseph Ellis Story.*)

An editorial in the *Washington Post* promptly denounced Jefferson for carrying on "a private sexual relationship with an inherited young slave girl" and proclaimed that having sex with slaves smacked of racism—separate and apart, evidently, from merely holding them as property. It was as if Jefferson was morally obligated to carry on exploitative relationships with Latina, Asian, snd Caucasian chattel as well, just for the sake of appearances. *USA Today* reported, "Thomas Jefferson owned lots of slaves and had lots of sex with at least one of them, Sally Hemings. . . . According to new DNA tests, Jefferson sired at least one child, Eston, through that union and probably six others."

Unfortunately for the gang of harpies defending Clinton, proof of a Jefferson-Hemings liaison was as fanciful as Professor Ellis's military service. Two months after the report's "findings" had been published in every news outlet where English is spoken, a correction had to be issued. Ellis's coauthor pathologist Eugene Foster—the actual scientist—admitted to the British science journal *Nature* that they had not proved Thomas Jefferson fathered any children by Sally Hemings. "We never proved it," Foster told the *Washington Times*. "We never can. We never will." What they meant to say was "Jefferson *could have* fathered slave's last child." (And it was also *not* true that Jefferson met Hemings while serving in the 101st Airborne during the Vietnam War.) The press was not as interested in the "we lied" correction as it had been in the original inflammatory (and false) charge. Less than a half dozen newspapers admitted that the report had traced the paternity of Hemings's last child to any one of several Jefferson males.

Besides Jefferson, there were twenty-five Jefferson adult males alive when Hemings conceived her last son, seven of them at Monticello. Many scholars consider Jefferson's younger brother, Randolph, a more likely suspect, on account of his frequent socializing with the slaves. While Jefferson was busy entertaining prominent international visitors in the main house, Randolph would generally retire to the slave quarters. As Randolph was described by one slave, "Old Master's brother, Mass Randall, was a mighty simple man: used to come out among black people, play the fiddle and dance half the night; hadn't much more sense than Isaac" (Isaac was one of the slaves evidently not known for his intellectual prowess. Today we would say, "He hadn't much more sense than Justice Souter.")

Stunningly, the Ellis study actually exonerated Jefferson on the principal charge against him. The Hemings rumor was based on two sources: The contemporaneous attacks of a political enemy and the "oral history" passed down through Hemings's descendants—and lovingly promoted by twentieth-century Clinton-defenders. In 1802, muckraking, alcoholic journalist James Callender, who had earlier served prison time for his particular brand of journalism, tried to blackmail Jefferson into appointing him postmaster at Richmond. When blackmail failed, Callender publically accused Jefferson of miscegenation with Sally Hemings—or as Callender put it, "a slut as common as pavement." He wrote of Jefferson, "It is well known that the man . . . keeps and for many years has kept, as his concubine, one of his slaves. Her name is Sally. The name of her eldest son is Tom. His features are said to bear a striking, though sable resemblance to those of the president himself." Thus began the rumor of "President Tom," as Callender called Jefferson's putative illegitimate son. The "oral history," passed down through Hemings's children, also pointed to Tom as Jefferson's child. From there, it was simply assumed that if Tom was Jefferson's son, the rest of Hemings's children were his, too.

Now here's the crescendo: The preimpeachment, get-Jefferson study specifically proved that Tom, at least, was *not* fathered by Jefferson. After testing six different genetic lines from "President Tom," the DNA tests ruled out *any* Jefferson as the father. The study that allegedly proved "JEF-FERSON FATHERED CHILD WITH SLAVE" had scientifically disproved the centerpiece of the accusation! But that wasn't the title of Professor Ellis's report. Nor was it mentioned in the blanket news coverage of the report's false accusation against Jefferson. In fact, there was no news coverage—not a single article—on the amazing fact that the DNA study had actually exonerated Jefferson of fathering Tom. To repeat: The famous Tom, the Tom who got the whole reputation-blackening ball rolling, was proved by DNA tests not to be fathered by any Jefferson.

The preimpeachment report had to fall back on an entirely new suspect in order to smear Jefferson: Hemings's last-born son, Eston, whose claims to paternity are far more incredible. Eston, the only Hemings child who could be tied by DNA to some Jefferson, was born in 1808, when Thomas Jefferson was sixty-four years old. Randolph—the Jefferson fiddling and dancing with the slaves—was twelve years younger. But more significant, Eston was conceived five years *after* Callender made his scurrilous accusation against Jefferson! In order to implicate President Jefferson, the theory must be that he waited five years to start engaging in the depraved conduct Callender accused him of back in 1802.

Amazingly, a few years after the principal charge against Jefferson was disproved, the Thomas Jefferson Memorial Foundation issued a "report" purporting to acknowledge that Jefferson fathered all six of Hemings's illegitimate children. (Katie Couric is one of the renowned historians on the board of the Monticello Foundation.) Guided tours of Monticello today include the provably false information that Jefferson fathered all of Hemings's children. The Monticello Association, a group of Jefferson descendants, invited the Hemings descendants to join Jefferson family reunions at Monticello.

Apparently there are limits to "oral history." For example, most people would prefer to be descendants of a former president, rather than, say, descendants of his halfwit brother. If anyone ought to have recognized the possibility of self-aggrandizement in such "oral histories," you'd think it would have been Professor Ellis. ∎

GOOD HOUSEKEEPING

For about a year after each one of these happy experiences in publishing, I would refuse to waste one second writing anything for any publication without an ironclad promise that whatever I submitted would be published, even if it was twenty pages of "All work and no play makes Ann a dull girl." But time would pass, a new opportunity would arise, and I'd tell myself, *This time it will be different!* And then the same thing would happen all over again. To put it in terms comprehensible to a women's magazine editor, I was like a battered wife, clinging to a series of abusive publications.

The last time was in the fall of 2003, when *Good Housekeeping* asked me to write about a proverb. Inasmuch as their proverbs were the kinds of sayings that make you want to kill yourself—"A friend in need is a friend indeed" and "The early bird catches the worm"—this assignment was not exactly my cup of tea. But it was no less heinous than writing about "feminist legal theory," and at least this column would be published. Or so I thought. Now that I had three best-sellers under my belt, I figured magazine editors were finally willing to throw caution to the wind and publish Ann Coulter! Not only that, but at about the same time I was writing my proverb column, British *Good Housekeeping* ran a consumer review of vibrators. Could I say anything racier than that?

Why yes I could! Here's the column that was too hot for *Good Housekeeping*.

☞ If You Sup with the Devil, Use a Long Spoon

FALL 2003

A few years ago, when I was on radio promoting my book about the Clinton scandals, *High Crimes and Misdemeanors*, a woman called in with the standard DNC talking point informing me that "everybody does it"—to wit, all men cheat on their wives. People who say "everybody does it" are announcing nothing more than the implacable fact that *they* do it. As Edmund Burke said, "He who accuses all of mankind convicts only one." But this caller didn't have the glib, vaguely contemptuous tone of the typical Clinton defender. She was on the verge of tears. The pain in this woman's voice made clear that the "everybody" was not her, but her spouse.

I'm not clinically trained to deal with despair, but I did tell the caller that she was wrong and she needed to start hanging with a new crowd. In fact, according to the only serious, long-term scientific study of the sexual behavior of Americans ever performed, 75 percent of married men and 85 percent of married women have never been unfaithful. (John Gagnon, Robert Michael, and Stuart Michaels, *The Social Organization of Sexuality* [Chicago: University of Chicago Press, 1994]). *Never.* And consider that that figure includes couples who are separated or headed toward divorce court. (And further consider that residents of Manhattan and Malibu were included in the category "Americans.")

But you can be sure that in any town, the 20 percent of adulterers will know one another. Alcoholics hang around alcoholics, drug addicts hang around drug addicts, liars hang around liars. Vices of a feather flock together. This is a great tip for figuring out which of your friends are liars and cheats: They are the ones who seem to know a curiously large number of people who lie and cheat. But it's also a warning to keep those friends at a distance.

It's hard enough to resist temptation—the one thing Oscar Wilde said he could not resist—without also feeling like you are the only person on earth being asked to engage in the Herculean task of not committing a mortal sin. When every fiber of your being wants to do something and the only thing stopping you is the knowledge that it would be wrong, it's not going to make it easier to know that a lot of your friends apparently do not care that it is wrong. It's especially not going to be easy if the ones who do not care seem no worse for the wear.

This is part of what is so corrupting about television shows and Hollywood movies that show gorgeous people with an endless supply of witty lines and fabulous clothes engaging in wildly promiscuous behavior. Americans' friends are NBC's *Friends*. If you think people can distinguish between TV characters and real-life friends and neighbors, consider the firestorm of indignation Dan Quayle ignited when he made the incontrovertibly true point that the scriptwriters for the fictional television character Murphy Brown were not performing a public service by portraying the heroine as having a child out of wedlock. Apparently a lot of people believed Murphy Brown was a real person and Dan Quayle had just cruelly insulted her. A decade later, when the writers for *Friends* wrote in an out-of-wedlock pregnancy for a popular character, no one made a peep.

Perhaps the greater disservice of Hollywood movies is their cartoonish villains. In real life, I promise you, the devil will look more like Julia Roberts than Snidely Whiplash. Evil does not arrive with a flashing neon sign: MEPHISTOPHELES! LUCIFER! SATAN! FOR ETERNAL DAMNATION, APPLY HERE. Evil arrives packaged as a winsome movie about a long-legged brunette who manages to marry a rich, handsome bachelor and live happily ever after—all by turning tricks on Hollywood Boulevard! There's a reason Beelzebub is known as the prince of lies.

Evil presents itself like a beautiful banquet. That's why Adam and Eve were tempted with a delicious-looking apple instead of a spoonful of castor oil. Satan takes the form of gorgeous actresses, successful politicians, and pop icons cavorting across the gossip columns, subliminally exhorting the reader: *Be like me! Don't be a prude! This is how the glamorous people live!* But as in Wilde's *Picture of Dorian Gray,* the sinner's beauty conceals a soul growing uglier by the minute.

People don't commit acts of great evil or great courage out of thin air. Character is developed out of a lifetime of choices. Almost every decision you make, however small, will be a step closer to God or a step closer to the devil. When you are unkind to a clumsy shop clerk, you are taking a step closer to the devil. When you snap at your mother, you are taking a step closer to the devil. When you gossip enviously about a friend, you are taking a step closer to the devil. When you go along with the in crowd and don't speak out against liars, against promiscuity, against abortion, you are taking a step closer to the devil. But it's never too late to stop and begin taking steps toward God. It's a lot easier to make that journey with companions who know the way.

POSTSCRIPT: *Good Housekeeping* kept telling me to make it more "personal," which was like telling a dog to make a soufflé. I'm a Republican. That column is as personal as it gets. Moreover, I consider a person's view of God, right, wrong, and eternity as eminently "personal." What could be more personal than that? In *Good Housekeeping*-ese, "personal" seems to mean "something involving victimhood and tragedy" or "something having more to do with bodily functions." How about: "My Secret Shame: Why I Became a Conservative" or "How Inappropriate Touching Led Me to Believe in Elimination of the Capital Gains Tax."

Alas, I can't write magazine essays about being abused or neglected, because I never had those opportunities. (By contrast, Naomi Wolf has them all indexed: *Sexual harassment? I got that. The curse and tragedy of being beautiful? I wrote a book about it. How awful men are? Got it right here. The trauma of motherhood? Hold on to your hats!*) My father wasn't a racist, my mother was never arrested, and my brother wasn't a cross-dresser. In other words, I come from a disadvantaged, minority background: I am the product of an intact and loving family. My parents are Caucasian, native-born, English-speaking, happily married, monogamous, and self-supporting. The best word to describe my early family life would be "functional." Thus, I had no one to blame but myself when I didn't succeed at something, which in turn led me to the dreaded, upward spiral known as "achievement." Having no one to blame, I had nothing to fall back on my whole life but my native talents. Then again, nobody ever said that life was supposed to be fair. I'm a survivor.

Several months after my proverb column was rejected, I came across a *Good Housekeeping* magazine in a waiting room and immediately looked up the proverb column to see exactly what the editors meant by "personal." The proverb was "You can lead a horse to water, but you can't make him drink." The story illustrating this proverb was as follows: The author's son refused to practice his piano lessons, so the author told him he didn't have to take piano lessons anymore, and now he takes harpsichord lessons. Truth be told, that story did create a deep, emotional reaction in me: *Who do I sue to get that five minutes of my life back?* At least now I know what "personal" means: really, really boring. That may work for *Good Housekeeping,* but I'm afraid such columns would not make "Ann Coulter: The Director's Cut." ∎

Acknowledgments

I have a lot of careers to jeopardize here.

Luckily for me, I have a posse of smart friends who are absurdly generous with their time. Two must be singled out for special mention. First, the funniest man I know, Ned Rice, is a joke-writing machine who has given me more lines than I care to admit and breaks it to me gently when my jokes are "hacky." Second, Merrill Kinstler is my main talking partner and general consigliere. He probably would be a professional joke writer, too, except he doesn't have time because he's on the phone with me.

As for the rest, I have been blessed with so many brilliant friends, I will not attempt to describe their individual contributions, but will simply thank them: Hans Bader, Jon Caldera, Robert Caplain, George Conway, Jim Downey, Miguel Estrada, Steve Gilbert, Melanie Graham, John Harrison, James Higgins, Jim Hughes, Gary Lawson, David Limbaugh, Jay Mann, Jim Moody, Jeremy Rabkin, and Younis Zubchevich. Also, Gene Meyer performs an invaluable service by regularly placing nervous phone calls to me pleading with me not to use a certain line, which is how I know what the most popular line of the column is going to be. So I want to thank him for that. (And please don't let my mentioning it deter you, Gene!)

The original editor for much of the material in this book was Greg Melvin at Universal Press Syndicate—who is also a friend from his days singing in a rock band. *Human Events* has been my longtime home and, inasmuch as it is run by men like Tom Winter and Terry Jeffrey, published me when no one else would. In addition, I was lucky enough to have two Crown editors on this book, which would normally constitute sarcasm coming from me, but not in the case of Jed Donahue and Doug Pepper. Jed was called in to pinch-hit for my longstanding editor, Doug—who was so good, now he's running a publishing house in Canada. I am indebted to all my editors, and that's coming from someone who, as a rule, detests editors.

I remain eternally grateful to my publisher, Steve Ross, and my sainted agent, Joni Evans, who together unleashed me on liberal America. Also thanks to my publicist, Diana Banister, who works tirelessly on each new book. Most of all, I thank my family for their unwavering support: my parents, Jack and Nell; my brothers, John and Jim; my sisters-in-law, Pam and Diane; and my nieces, Kimberly and Christina.

Index

About the Author

ANN COULTER is the author of three *New York Times* best-sellers: *Treason, Slander,* and *High Crimes and Misdemeanors.* She is the legal correspondent for *Human Events* and a syndicated columnist for Universal Press Syndicate. A frequent guest on many TV shows, she was named one of the top 100 public intellectuals by federal judge Richard Posner in 2001. Coulter is a Connecticut native and a graduate of Cornell University and University of Michigan Law School.

DATE DUE

WITHDRAWN